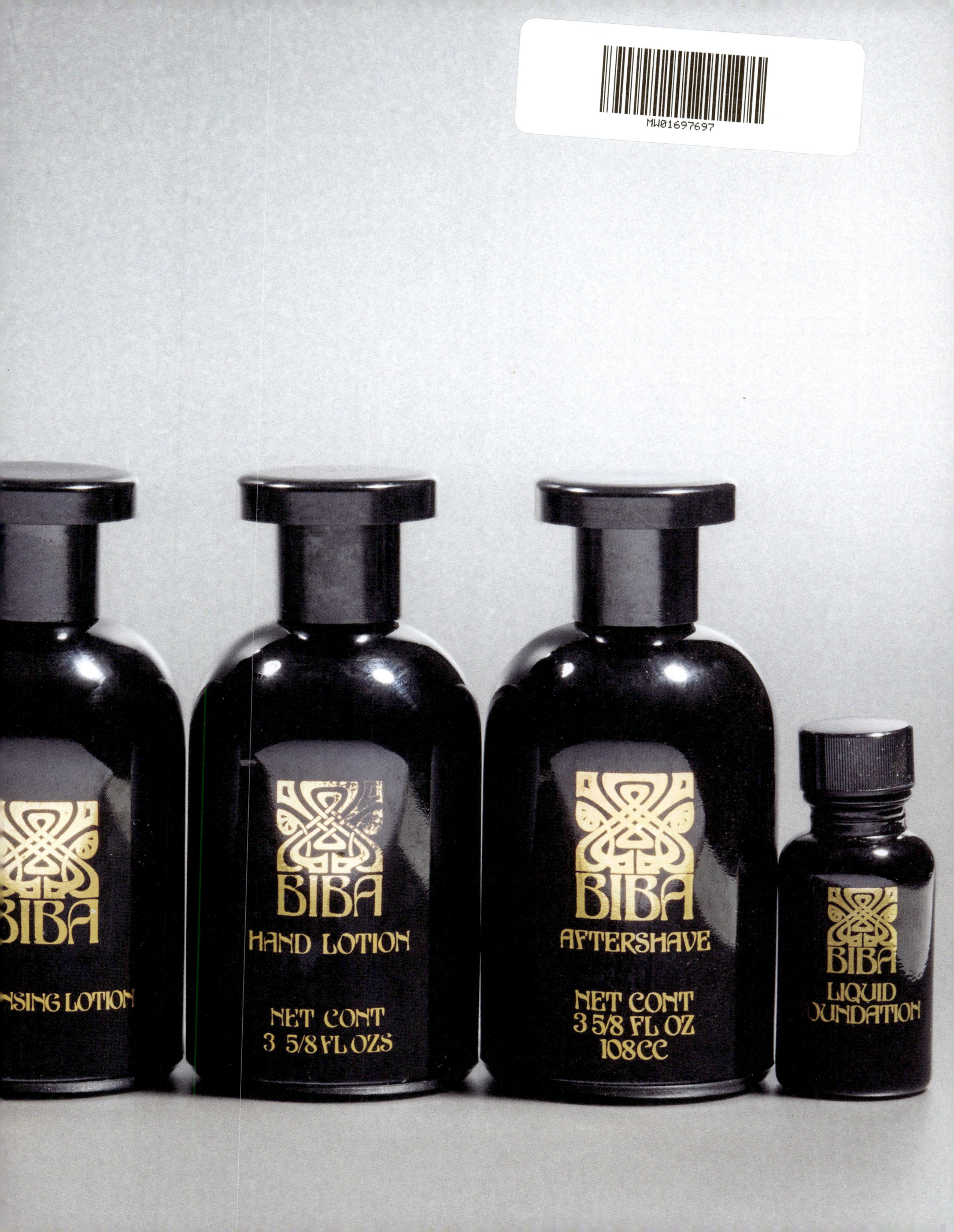
BIBA
BIBA
HAND LOTION
NET CONT
3 5/8 FL OZS
BIBA
AFTERSHAVE
NET CONT
3 5/8 FL OZ
108CC
BIBA
LIQUID

BIBA

BIBA

THE FASHION BRAND THAT DEFINED A GENERATION

BARBARA HULANICKI
AND MARTIN PEL

YALE UNIVERSITY PRESS
NEW HAVEN AND LONDON

"I DIDN'T WANT
MY NAME UP FRONT.
I DIDN'T WANT IT
TO DISTRACT
FROM BIBA.
I JUST WANTED
BIBA, BIBA, BIBA"

BARBARA HULANICKI

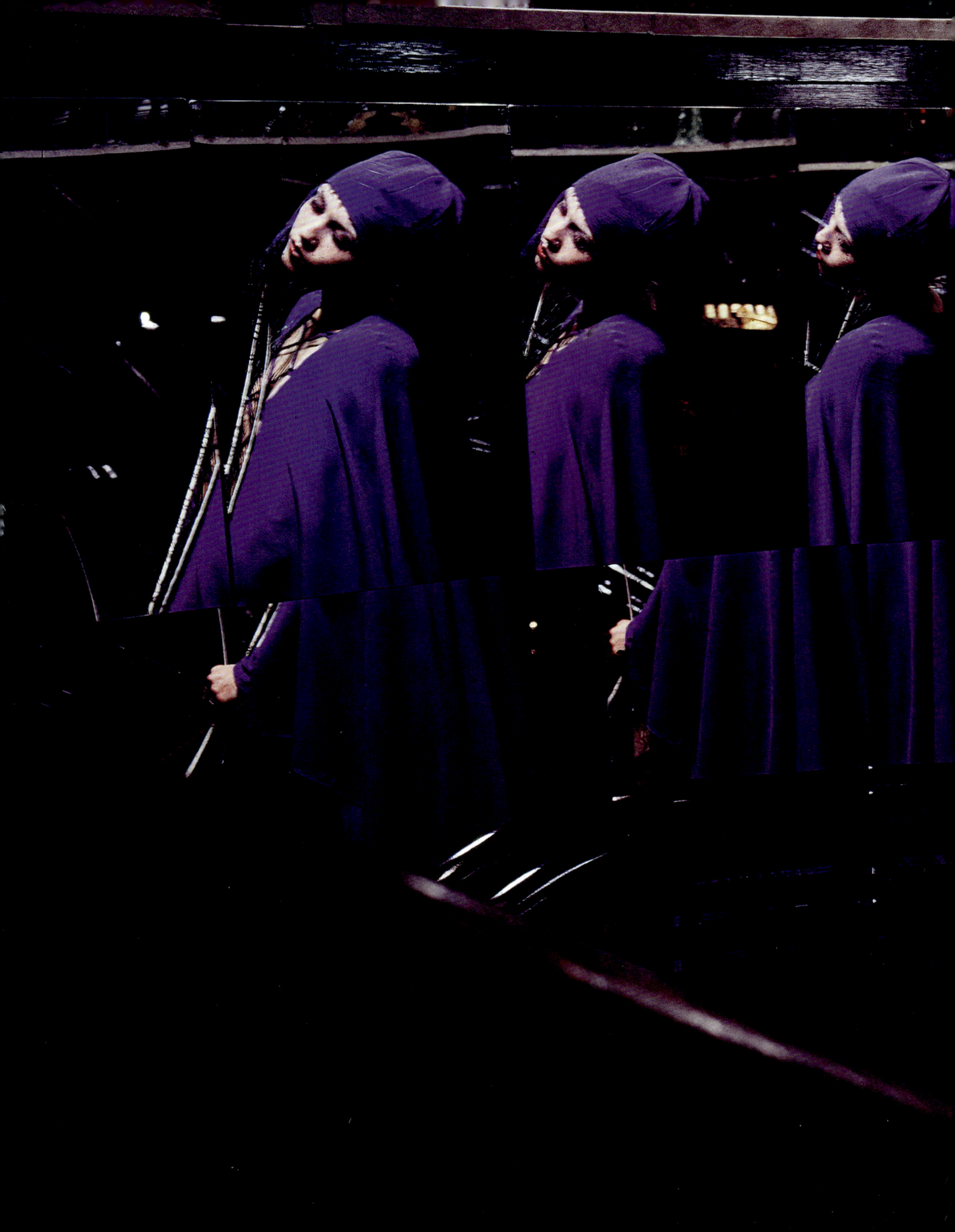

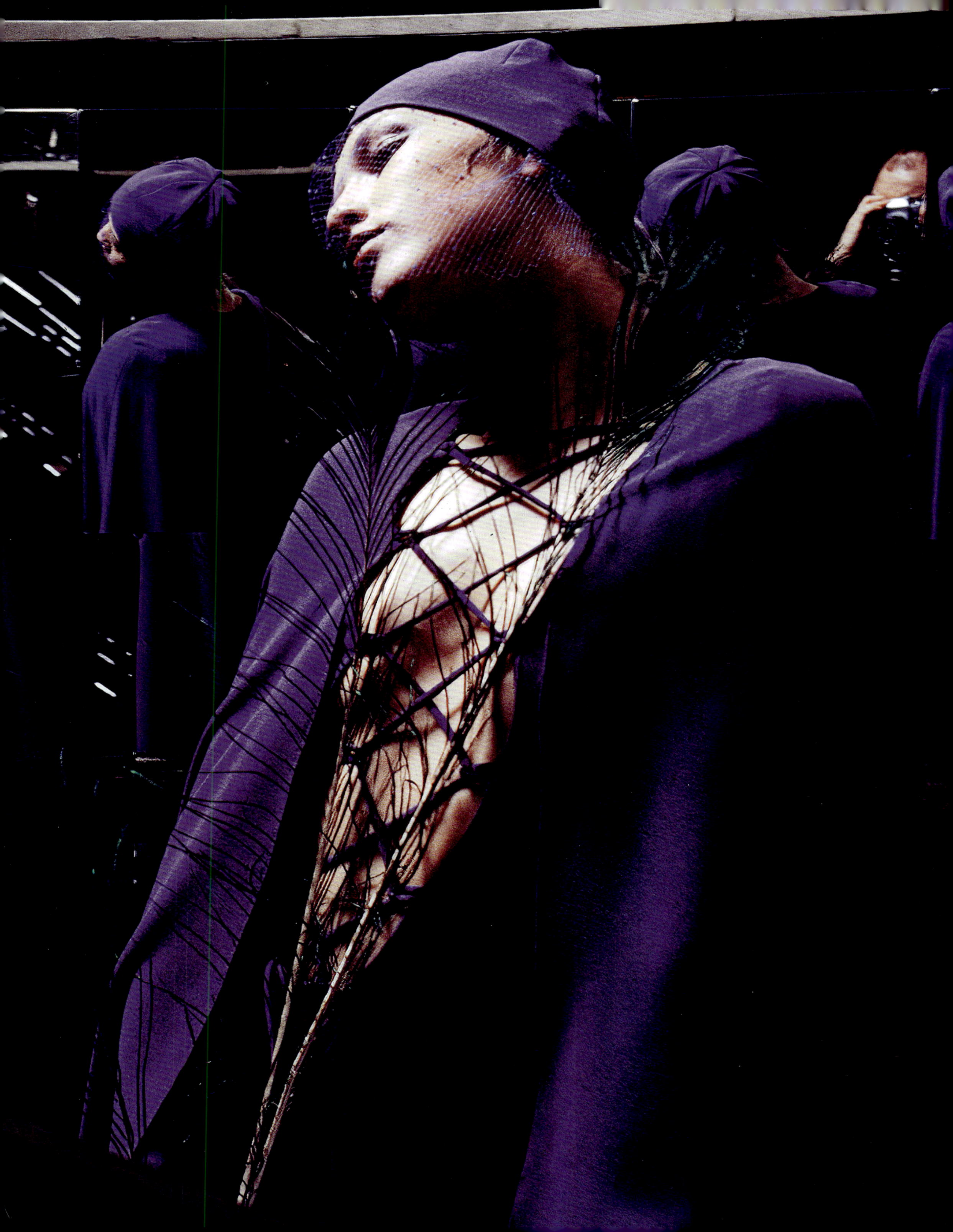

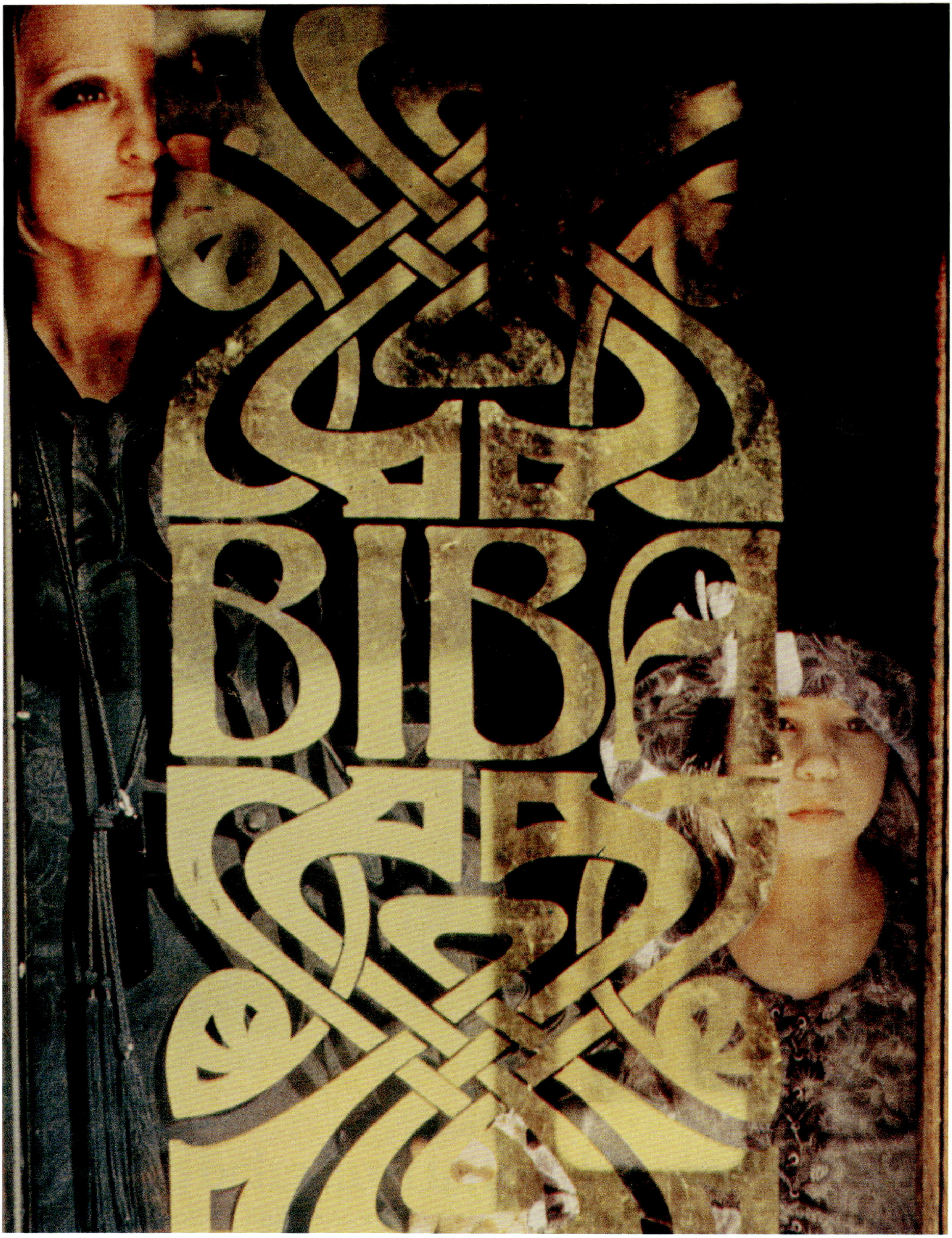
BIBA

CONTENTS

FOREWORD

At the beginning of the 1960s, when I was in my early teens, it was very hard to find affordable, fashionable clothes for my age group in London. Department stores tended to sell clothes for women and clothes for children, but very little in the way of teenage clothing. In 1964, when I was 14 years old, I was a mod. It was very important to me to wear the right clothes, but, because I was unable to buy them, I used to make most of them myself. At this time I was a schoolgirl and had a Saturday job in a hairdresser's shop. I became very friendly with another teenage girl who was the junior stylist, and also a mod. I think she was the one who told me about a new boutique that had opened in Kensington. One Saturday lunchtime we jumped on the tube to go the two stops to Kensington High Street. We then discovered the most wonderful shop I had ever been to. It was called Biba. It was like walking into a magical kingdom full of the most wonderful clothes and accessories that I had ever seen. It was also decorated in the most beautiful way: amazing colours, Victoriana furnishings, Art Deco lamps, feather boas and velvet drapes, and the latest pop songs would drift out of loudspeakers. The sales staff were all beautiful young girls dressed in the latest Biba fashions. My friend and I became completely obsessed with this shop and its contents and would save up our pocket money so we could visit every few weeks and buy these inspirational, fantastic clothes, which were also very affordable. I distinctly remember the first dress I ever bought in Biba: it was yellow with a bright pink zigzag pattern diagonally across it, with puffed sleeves and little pearl buttons on one shoulder. I was instantly in love.

Biba became part of my life, and, as it moved to bigger and better premises, I moved with it. Each new store was more fantastic and more beautiful than the last. Then, in 1966, I was discovered and became a model. It was during this time that I first met the remarkable Barbara Hulanicki, who was the owner and designer of Biba, and I thought she was the most beautiful and stylish woman I had ever met. I was so in awe of her talent, and she was so lovely to me; we very swiftly became the best of friends. Her clothes and accessories were always my favourites at that point, and I would get very excited every time a new collection came out. When Barbara and Fitz, her husband/business partner, took over the old department store on Kensington High Street, they transformed it into the most beautiful store I had ever encountered. With her amazing talent as an interior designer, as well as a fashion designer, they turned this rather tired 1930s department store back into an Art Deco dream store. Every floor was breathtaking, from the Rainbow Room to the rooftop gardens, which actually had live flamingos among the luscious greenery and ponds. And, of course, Barbara continued to design the most wonderful collection of clothes, accessories and make-up. It was *the* place to go and shop for the fashionable and famous.

Over the years, Barbara and I have worked together on various projects. When I played Cinderella in London's West End, she designed and made me the most beautiful costumes. When I see her interior design work in places like Miami Beach and the Bahamas, her talent never ceases to amaze me. Barbara is not only one of the most talented designers to come along in my lifetime, but she is also an exceptional woman and a wonderful friend. I love her very much. I feel privileged to have her in my life.

DAME TWIGGY LAWSON

OPENING IMAGE Elizabeth Bjorn Neilson modelling on the staircase of Biba, Kensington High Street, 1970

PREVIOUS PAGE Barbara Hulanicki, with her friend's daughter, behind the windows of Biba, 1970

OPPOSITE Twiggy in Big Biba, shoot for British *Vogue*, photographed by Justine de Villeneuve, 1973

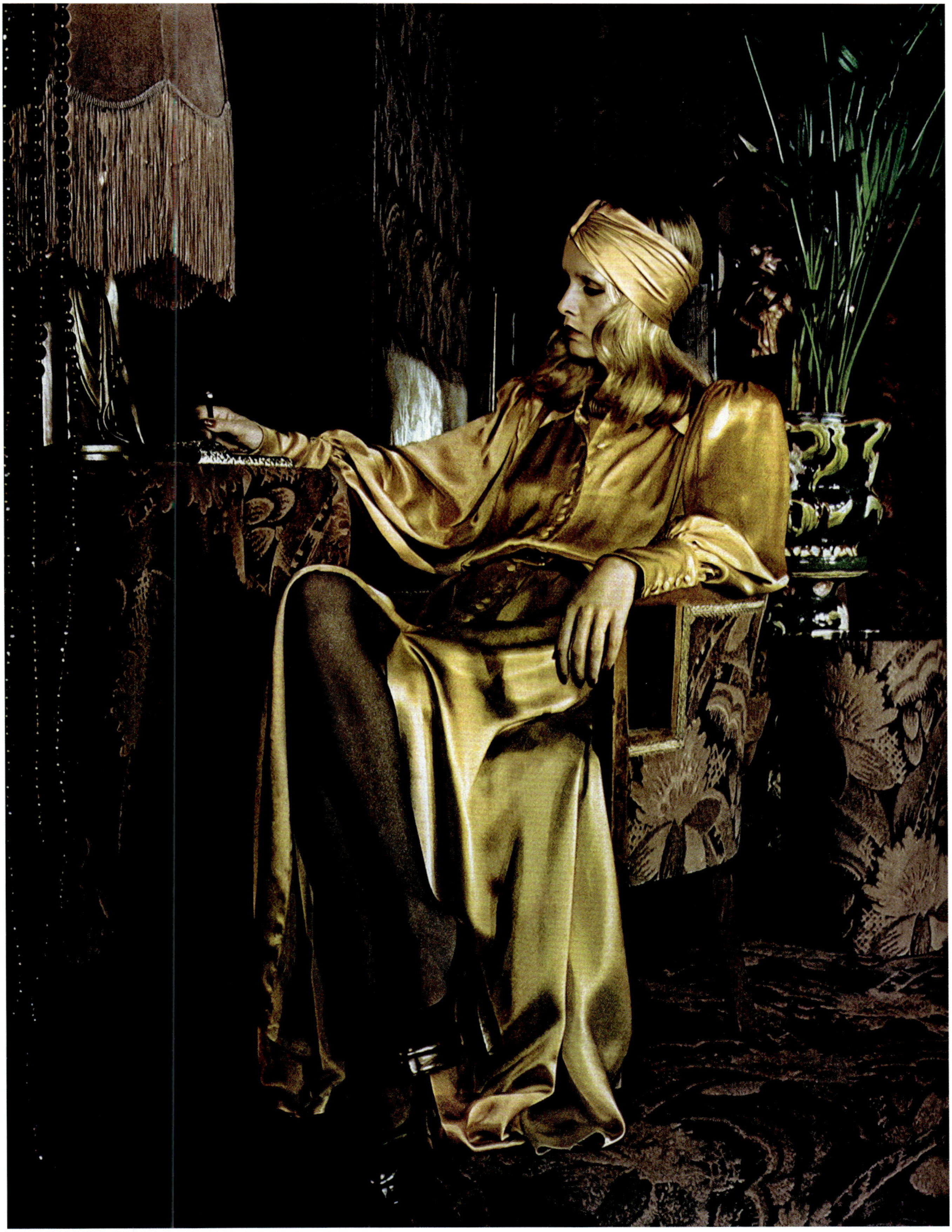

INTRODUCTION
1964–1975
BIBA

"Fashion is a mass phenomenon,
but it feeds on the individual.
These true representatives of
fashion are often those whose
surprising originality leads them
to a very private outward
expression of themselves"

Cecil Beaton, 1971

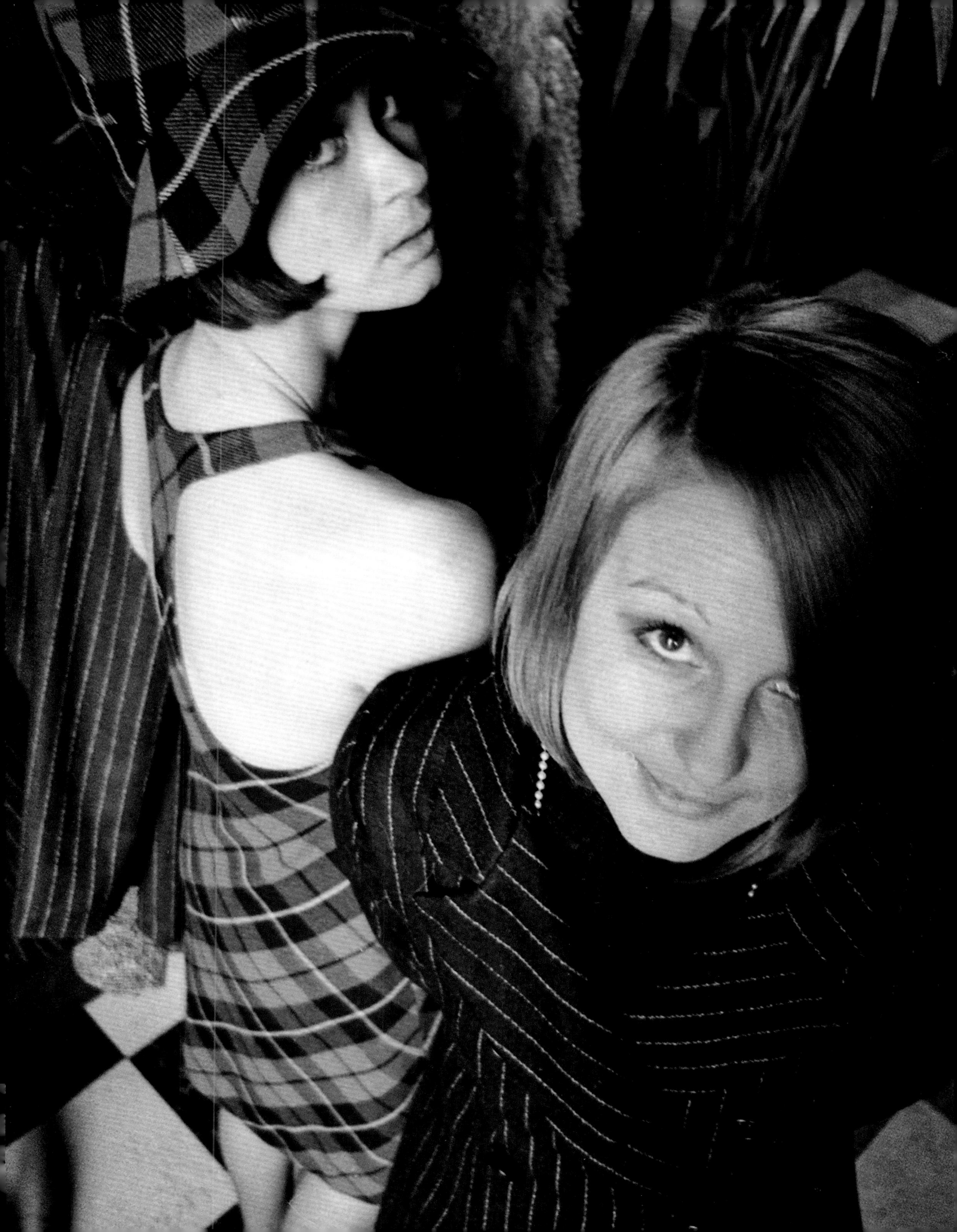

The story of Biba is the story of Barbara Hulanicki, its founder and creative force. It begins in 1963 with Barbara dressing the girl on the street and culminates, in just ten short years, in a lifestyle brand, through which individuals could eat, sleep and breathe Biba. More than just a fashion house, Biba was an expression of Barbara Hulanicki's life and a manifestation of her desire to live in a world of her own making.

At the deeply impressionable age of 12, Barbara's father, the Polish diplomat Witold Hulanicki, was abducted from their family home in Jerusalem and assassinated. He was killed alongside a Polish journalist in early 1948, and, although it is not known who was responsible for his death, Barbara believes it may have been under the instructions of the then newly established Polish communist government. Witold's death became a defining moment in Barbara's life. It catapulted her into adulthood, and into the role of the emotional head of a tight-knit family, caring for her two younger sisters and her devastated mother. It was a role that Barbara never relinquished.

Witold had been working for the British consulate in Palestine, and, while his job had taken the family to Jerusalem, his death brought them to England. They eventually settled in the seaside resort of Brighton to be close to Barbara's wealthy aunt. Aunt Sophie was Barbara's mother's sister; she was a domineering character and felt that she needed to take responsibility for the 'proper' upbringing of her sister's girls. Living under the 'benevolence' of Aunt Sophie – whose lifestyle was rooted in the elite world of pre-war Europe, dressing for the times of the day from her vast array of couture garments and costly jewellery – Barbara grew to resent the economic power 'Auntie' held over her family. Tensions between the two remained throughout their lives. Yet although Barbara's father's death changed the course of her life, it was Auntie's influence that coloured her career. Barbara inherited from

PREVIOUS PAGE Barbara Hulanicki and model in Abingdon Road Biba, 1965

BELOW LEFT Witold Hulanicki holding Barbara as a baby, Poland, c.1937

BELOW RIGHT 'The Smile of Success', 18-year-old Barbara Hulanicki one of three winners of the *Evening Standard* fashion design competition, 1955

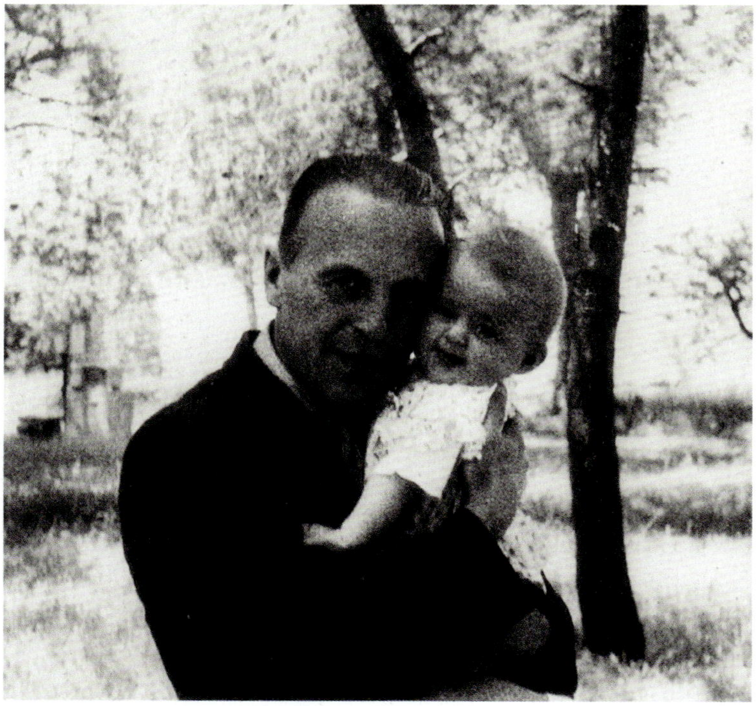

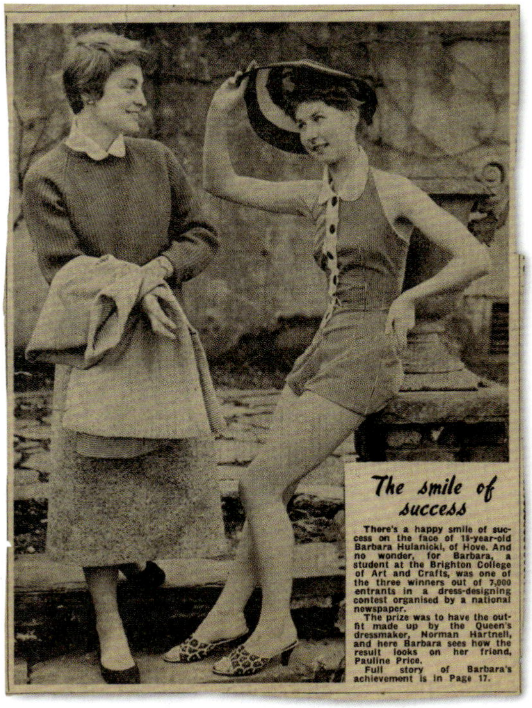

The smile of success

There's a happy smile of success on the face of 18-year-old Barbara Hulanicki, of Hove. And no wonder, for Barbara, a student at the Brighton College of Art and Crafts, was one of the three winners out of 7,000 entrants in a dress-designing contest organised by a national newspaper.

The prize was to have the outfit made up by the Queen's dressmaker, Norman Hartnell, and here Barbara sees how the result looks on her friend, Pauline Price.

Full story of Barbara's achievement is in Page 17.

RIGHT Fashion illustration, woman in black outfit and pearls, Barbara Hulanicki, 1955–60

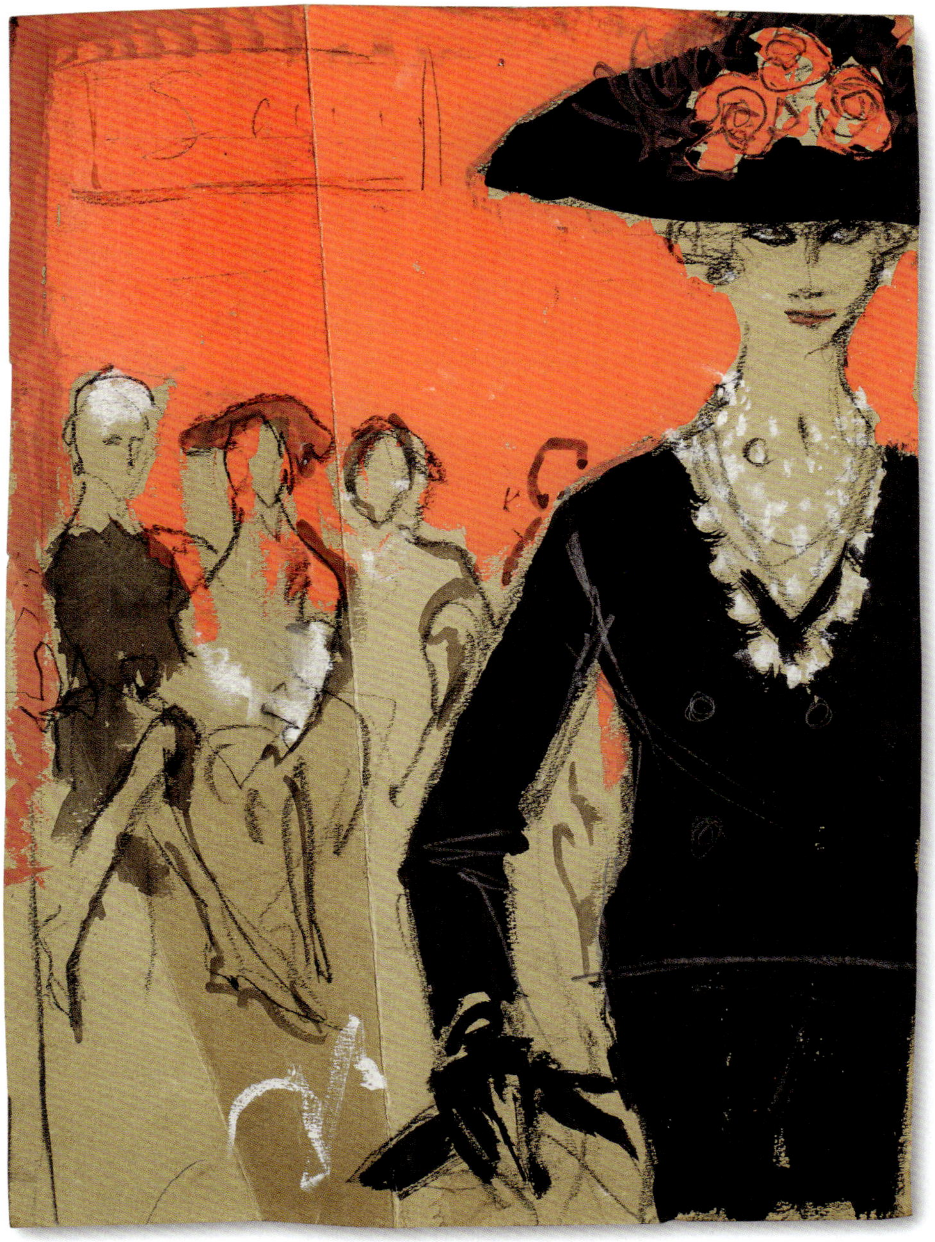

Auntie a love of dressing well, in fully accessorised outfits, as well as a colour palette of dark, Art Nouveau shades. These were influences that would go on to feature heavily at Biba.

Attending a private school in the nearby town of Worthing (paid for by Auntie), Barbara excelled at art, and the solitary pursuit of drawing became a haven from the outside world. Winning numerous awards for her drawings while at school, her skills would take her on to study fashion and art at Brighton Art School (now the University of Brighton). While a student there, Barbara entered and won a fashion design competition run by the *Evening Standard* newspaper. Inspired by her celluloid idol, Audrey Hepburn, Barbara created a beach outfit in striped cotton with a white Eton collar. When interviewed at the time, Barbara said somewhat presciently: 'I think we need more gay, teenage clothes in the shops ... At my age we need comfortable and colourful clothes, don't you think?'[1]

In the late 1950s her skills in drawing gave Barbara her first career: working as a fashion illustrator in London for the advertising agency Helen Jardine Artists. She quickly established herself as a freelance fashion illustrator covering the couture shows in London and Paris for publications including *Women's Wear Daily*, *Vogue* and *Harper's Bazaar*, as well as working for the leading journalists of the day, such as Barbara Griggs at the *Evening Standard* and Felicity Green at the *Daily Mirror*.

Women's fashion of the 1950s was dictated by Parisian couture: from the original haute couture outfits worn by the economic elite to the formal copies of couture 'models' sold in high-end department stores and the inexpensive imitations sold en masse at the lower end of the market. The look was sophisticated and mature, with the bar set by Christian Dior in 1947 following the launch of his couture house and his 'New Look' collection. Restrictions on the use of precious textiles during the war years were lifted in the post-war period, and French fashion designers unapologetically indulged in the use of fabric, with a Dior day dress requiring 15 metres of material. France's couture industry was vital to the recovery of the French economy (the launch of Dior was funded by the French textile manufacturer Boussac), and women of all ages and spending power aspired to be attired in metres of fabric.

"As one of the most in-demand fashion illustrators of the late 1950s and early 1960s, Barbara's work brought her into close contact with couture and the couturiers of the day"

In Britain, rationing officially finished in 1954, almost a decade after the end of the Second World War, and the extended deprivations of war brought their own new look to British fashion in the 1950s. Simple, slim-line and youthful fashions emerged in the work of young London designers; an inventive necessity as well as a reaction to the dominance of French couture. Mary Quant opened her boutique, Bazaar, on the King's Road in London, in 1955, bringing a young silhouette to women's fashion not seen since the 1920s. John Stephen equally revolutionised menswear, opening his first boutique in 1957 on a then-unremarkable street in London's Soho: Carnaby Street. Both were heralds of a new mood in fashion, playing a role in the genesis of the Swinging Sixties, which positioned London as *the* creative fashion capital of the world, a title it holds to this day.

As one of the most in-demand fashion illustrators of the late 1950s and early 1960s, Barbara's work brought her into close contact with the couturiers of the day. Her work in this milieu also created a gradual awareness of how out of step the established fashion industry was with the emerging world of youth culture. In 1963, while still working as a fashion illustrator, Barbara and her husband, Stephen Fitz-Simon ('Fitz'), established Biba's Postal Boutique. The mail-order company, which took its name from the nickname of Barbara's youngest sister, Biruta, sold inexpensive women's and children's clothing through advertisements taken out in national newspapers.

1964 was a pivotal year in the career of Barbara Hulanicki. In February, British *Vogue* devoted a double-page feature to her work as a fashion artist, acknowledging her success in the field of fashion illustration and noting her love of well-made, durable fashion. The accompanying photograph showed Barbara wearing a gold-mesh Chanel sweater, 'bought some time ago in the thirties by her mother and worn hard ever since'.[2] In May, Barbara's life was transformed when *Daily Mirror* journalist Felicity Green introduced Barbara to her readers: 'This is Barbara. Now she's a dress manufacturer as well as a fashion artist.'[3] The article included the offer of a low-priced pink gingham dress and matching headscarf available through Biba's Postal Boutique.

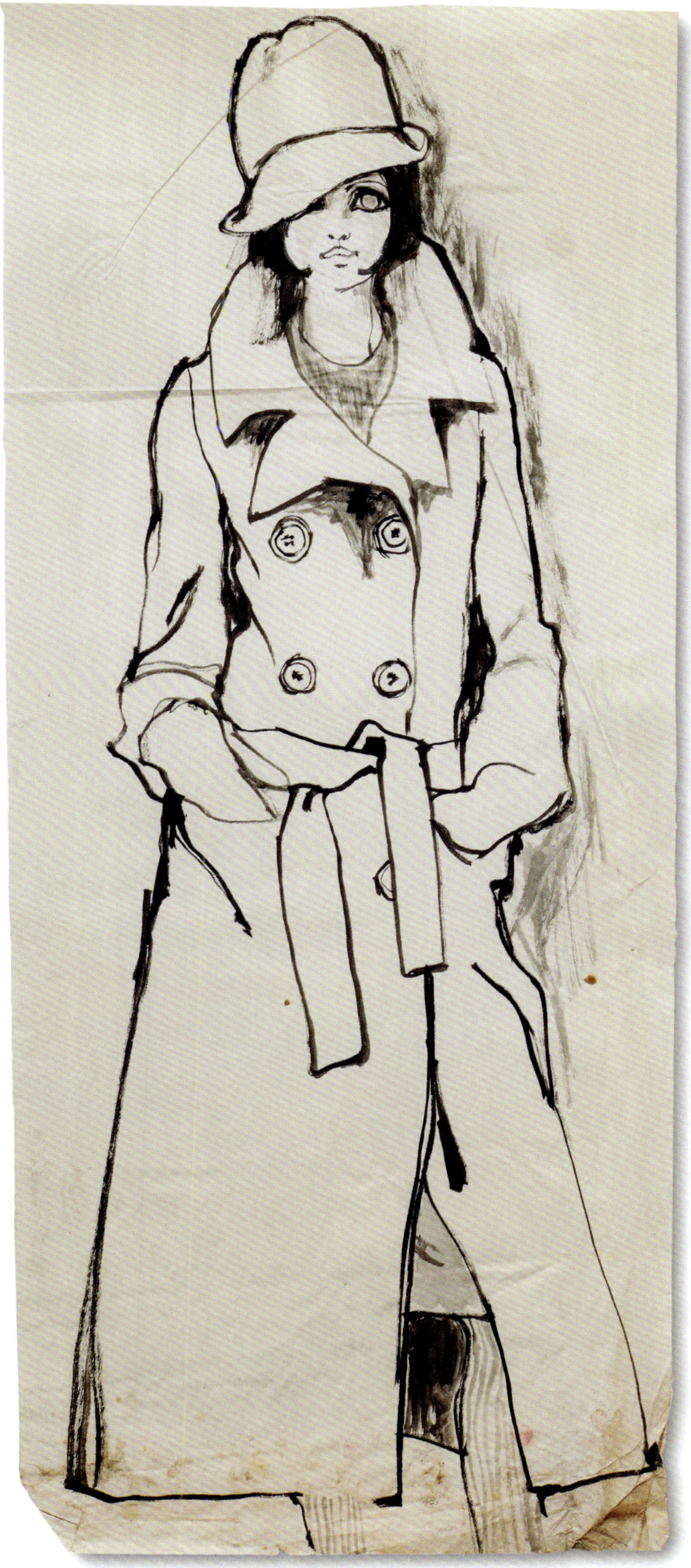

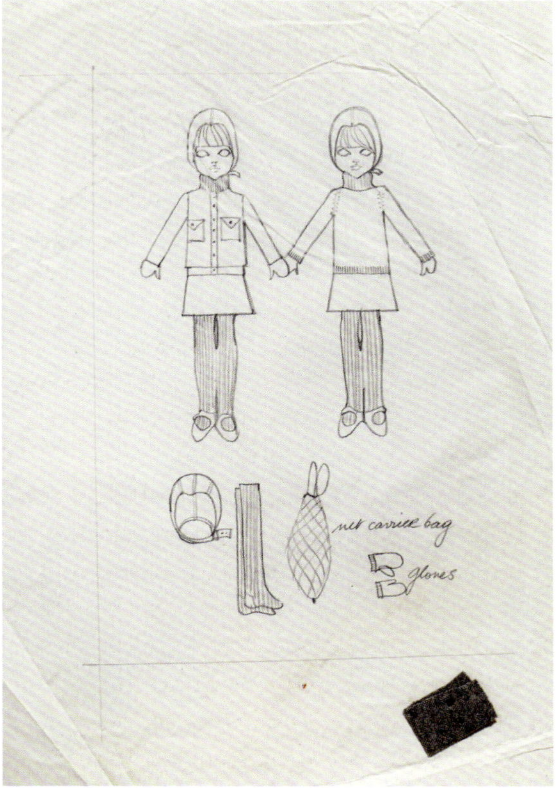

LEFT Fashion illustration, woman in trench coat and matching hat, Barbara Hulanicki, c.1963

ABOVE Design for a fully coordinated children's wear outfit and matching accessories, with fabric swatch, Barbara Hulanicki, c.1963

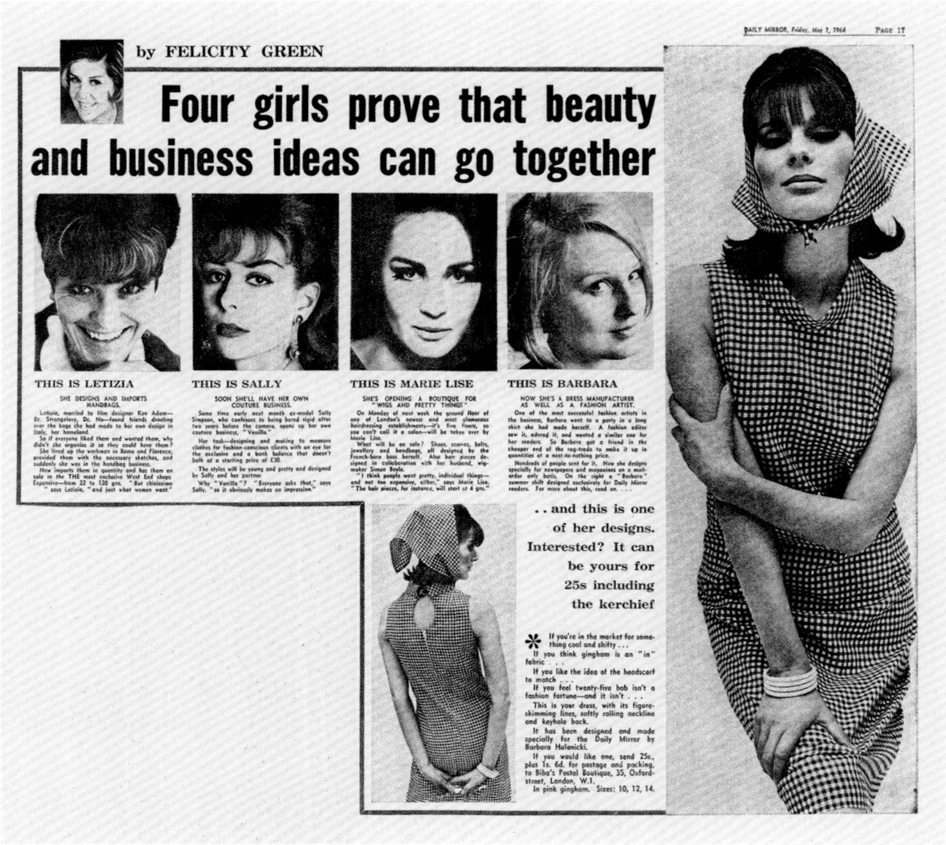

DAILY MIRROR, Friday, May 1, 1964 PAGE 17

by FELICITY GREEN

Four girls prove that beauty and business ideas can go together

THIS IS LETIZIA

SHE DESIGNS AND IMPORTS HANDBAGS.

Letizia, married to film designer Ken Adam—Dr. Strangelove, Dr. No—found friends drooling over the bags she had made to her own design in Italy, her homeland.

So if everyone liked them and wanted them, why didn't she organise it so they could have them?

She lined up the workmen in Rome and Florence, provided them with the necessary sketches, and suddenly she was in the handbag business.

Now imports them in quantity and has them on sale in the THE most exclusive West End shops. Expensive—from 22 to 120 gns. "But chicissimo" says Letizia, "and just what women want."

THIS IS SALLY

SOON SHE'LL HAVE HER OWN COUTURE BUSINESS.

Some time early next month ex-model Sally Simpson, who confesses to being bored rigid after two years before the camera, opens up her own couture business, "Vanilla."

Her task—designing and making to measure clothes for fashion-conscious clients with an eye for the exclusive and a bank balance that doesn't balk at a starting price of £30.

The styles will be young and pretty and designed by Sally and her partner.

Why "Vanilla"? "Everyone asks that," says Sally, "so it obviously makes an impression."

THIS IS MARIE LISE

SHE'S OPENING A BOUTIQUE FOR "WIGS AND PRETTY THINGS"

On Monday of next week the ground floor of one of London's newest and most glamorous hairdressing establishments—it's five floors, so you can't call it a salon—will be taken over by Marie Lise.

What will be on sale? Shoes, scarves, belts, jewellery and handbags, all designed by the French-born boss herself. Also hair pieces designed in collaboration with her husband, wig-maker Simon Boyle.

"I think people want pretty, individual things—and not too expensive, either," says Marie Lise. "The hair pieces, for instance, will start at 4 gns."

THIS IS BARBARA

NOW SHE'S A DRESS MANUFACTURER AS WELL AS A FASHION ARTIST.

One of the most successful fashion artists in the business, Barbara went to a party in a long skirt she had made herself. A fashion editor saw it, adored it, and wanted a similar one for her readers. So Barbara got a friend in the cheaper end of the rag-trade to make it up in quantities at a next-to-nothing price.

Hundreds of people sent for it. Now she designs specially for newspapers and magazines on a mail-order only basis. On the right a "Barbara" summer shift designed exclusively for Daily Mirror readers. For more about this, read on. . . .

. . and this is one of her designs. Interested? It can be yours for 25s including the kerchief

* If you're in the market for something cool and shifty . . .

If you think gingham is an "in" fabric . . .

If you like the idea of the headscarf to match . . .

If you feel twenty-five bob isn't a fashion fortune—and it isn't . . .

This is your dress, with its figure-skimming lines, softly rolling neckline and keyhole back.

It has been designed and made specially for the Daily Mirror by Barbara Hulanicki.

If you would like one, send 25s., plus 1s. 6d. for postage and packing, to Biba's Postal Boutique, 35, Oxford-street, London, W.1.

In pink gingham. Sizes: 10, 12, 14.

LEFT Press cutting, Felicity Green, 'Four Girls Prove that Beauty and Business Ideas Can Go Together', featuring Barbara Hulanicki, *Daily Mirror*, 1 May 1964

Shot by society photographer John French and modelled by Paulene Stone, the dress sold for 25 shillings, cheap even by 1964 standards. Barbara's design of a stylish, inexpensive, cotton day dress and headscarf was created to be worn during what turned out to be an unprecedentedly long and hot British summer. It sold 17,000 copies, confirming Barbara's intuitive understanding of the 1960s market for youthful fashions at affordable prices. The phenomenal number of sales – which became a manufacturing nightmare, as Barbara and Fitz desperately scoured the country for enough gingham to fulfil the deluge of orders – was not merely a result of good marketing. Barbara had created the right dress at the right time, and it was at that moment that her freelance illustration career took a back seat and Biba became Barbara's primary focus.

The pink gingham dress became the template for Barbara's design philosophy of selling up-to-the-minute clothing at low prices. As she said some years later: 'I didn't want to make clothes for kept women, I wanted to make clothes for people in the street, and Fitz and I always tried to get prices down, down, down.'[4] Its success also gave Barbara the confidence to create Biba as a bricks-and-mortar store, and in September 1964 the first Biba boutique opened on a quiet residential street, Abingdon Road in Kensington.

Barbara's career as a fashion illustrator had taught her that strong outlines and an avoidance of fussy detail made for clearer illustrations in newsprint reproductions. This philosophy became the blueprint for Biba designs of bold silhouettes, with decorative elements created through the print and fabric choices. Initially designing and selling simple mini dresses and matching accessories, with shoes supplied by Moya Bowler, Barbara soon employed old friend and former fellow student from

Brighton Art School, Anne Behr, as a pattern cutter. With a growing technical team realising Barbara's designs, the Biba boutique was quickly filled with dresses, coats, shoes, hats and accessories in matching fabrics, giving customers the opportunity to wear the 'Biba look'.

One of the first great successes at the Abingdon Road boutique was a pinstripe trouser suit, released in the autumn of their opening year. The ubiquity of the miniskirt in the story of 1960s women's fashion has overshadowed the significance of the trousers suit, which equally gave women physical freedom and ownership over their own bodies. Exposing one's legs in a miniskirt, while considered racy, was within the bounds of acceptable wear for women; to cover them with trousers was widely considered to be a fashion too far. However, as an article in the *Daily Mail* declared: 'Like it or not – and many men don't – trousers for girls are here to stay.'[5] Worn by Julie Christie in the film *Darling* (1965), for Barbara this trouser suit was more than a moment in fashion: it was a tangible tribute to her father, as her final memory of him was him wearing a similar brown pinstripe suit.

The past proved fertile ground for inspiration for Barbara, and not just her own personal history. The earliest Biba clothes were inspired by historical fashions and designs, from the late nineteenth-century prints of the work of designers such as Augustus Welby Pugin to the satin-weave slip dresses of the 1930s. The revival of Art Nouveau in the post-war years reached its peak in the first half of the 1960s and became

BELOW LEFT Exterior of Abingdon Road Biba boutique with John McConnell logo, c.1964

BELOW RIGHT Interior of Abingdon Road Biba boutique, May 1965

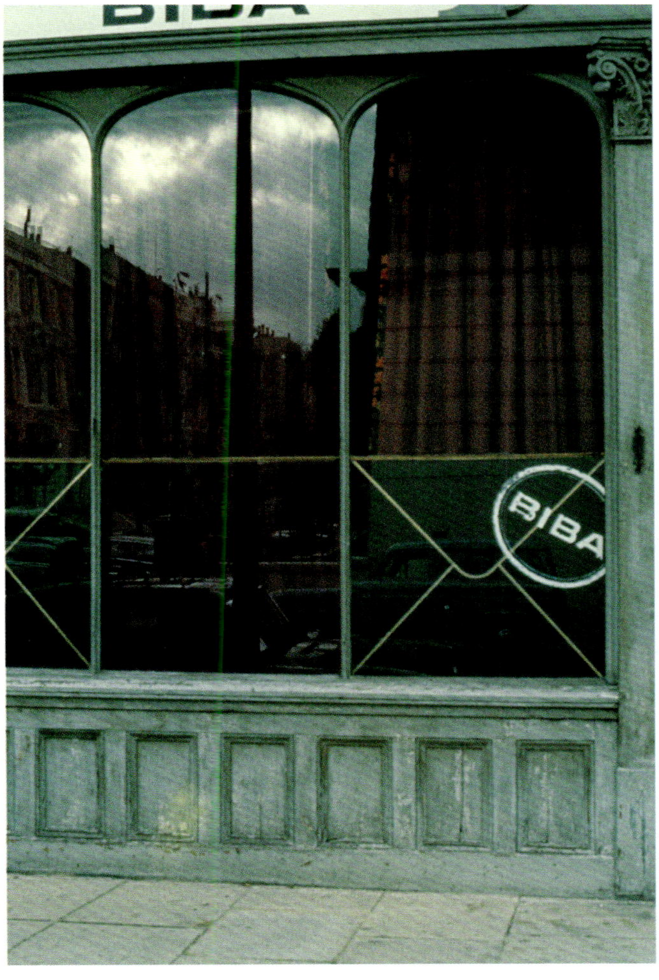

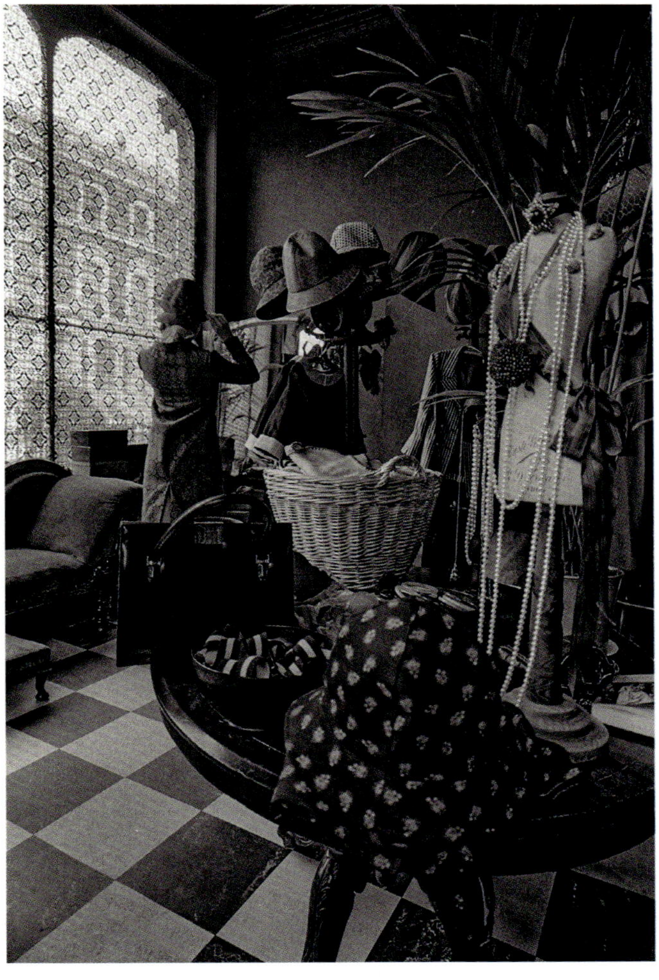

a significant influence on Biba, remaining so for the duration of the company. It was a style that Barbara loved, and Biba's most famous logo, the Celtic knot designed by John McConnell, took its inspiration from Art Nouveau designs of the late 1800s.

Art Nouveau colours – those found in the works of nineteenth-century artists and designers such as Alphonse Mucha, Gustav Klimt and Charles Rennie Mackintosh – became the quintessential Biba shades: brown, rust, plum, green and bilberry. Such hues were not only used in the clothing ranges but were also adopted across all Biba products as the company developed accessories, wallpapers, cosmetics and foodstuffs. They were also the colours Barbara associated with her aunt Sophie. Known by Barbara as 'Auntie colours', it was a term that both paid homage to, and demonstrated ownership over, an individual who had figured so vividly in her teenage years and influenced her understanding of and attitude towards fashion.

From the first success of the pink gingham dress to the final days of Biba, the sourcing of fabric was a continual challenge. Barbara observed: 'We were always desperate for something different. We'd always had hundreds of fabric reps coming into Biba and we produced thousands of in-house prints.'[6] Before Barbara established strong working relationships with British textile manufacturers such as Burgess, Ledward & Co. and Tootal, fabrics were acquired over the counter at department stores at retail prices. Classic Biba fabrics were crepe, marocain, Flanesta and crepe de Chine, reflecting Barbara's love of historical design, particularly of the 1930s. Early difficulties in sourcing fabrics influenced Barbara's decision to limit a design of 500 copies in any one fabric, which eliminated large runs in one textile design while also giving the Biba shops a freshness with the display of new stock.

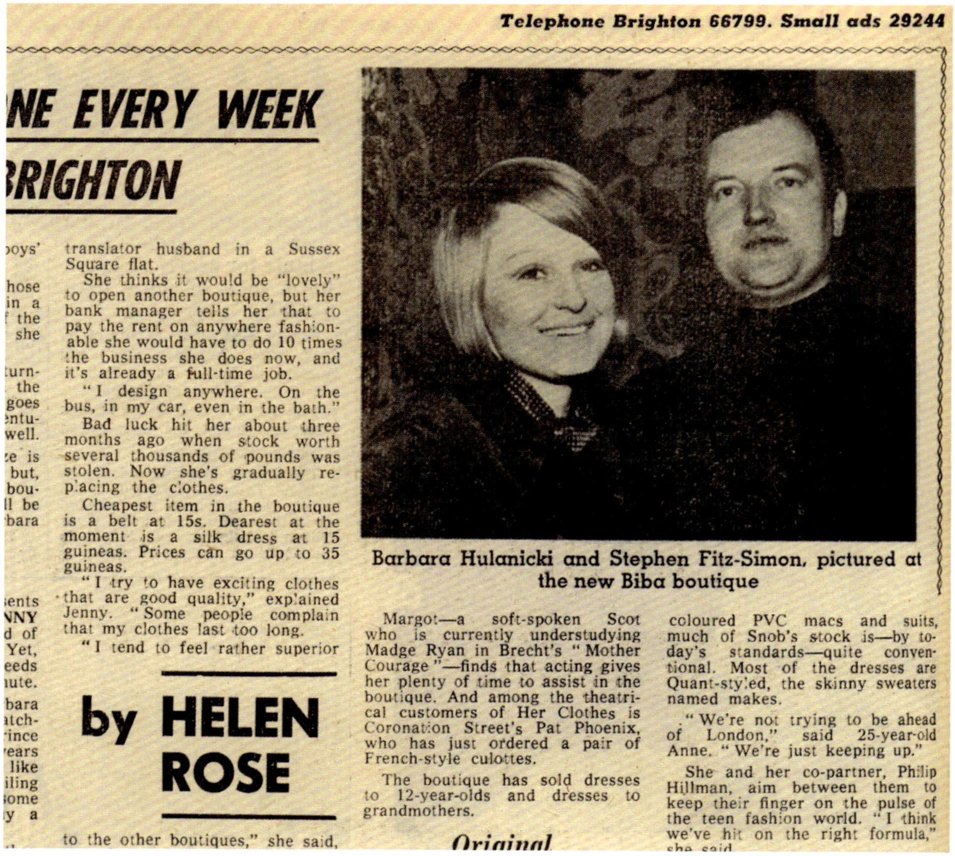

Telephone Brighton 66799. Small ads 29244

NE EVERY WEEK
RIGHTON

translator husband in a Sussex Square flat.

She thinks it would be "lovely" to open another boutique, but her bank manager tells her that to pay the rent on anywhere fashionable she would have to do 10 times the business she does now, and it's already a full-time job.

"I design anywhere. On the bus, in my car, even in the bath."

Bad luck hit her about three months ago when stock worth several thousands of pounds was stolen. Now she's gradually replacing the clothes.

Cheapest item in the boutique is a belt at 15s. Dearest at the moment is a silk dress at 15 guineas. Prices can go up to 35 guineas.

"I try to have exciting clothes that are good quality," explained Jenny. "Some people complain that my clothes last too long.

"I tend to feel rather superior

by HELEN ROSE

to the other boutiques," she said,

Barbara Hulanicki and Stephen Fitz-Simon, pictured at the new Biba boutique

Margot—a soft-spoken Scot who is currently understudying Madge Ryan in Brecht's "Mother Courage"—finds that acting gives her plenty of time to assist in the boutique. And among the theatrical customers of Her Clothes is Coronation Street's Pat Phoenix, who has just ordered a pair of French-style culottes.

The boutique has sold dresses to 12-year-olds and dresses to grandmothers.

Original

coloured PVC macs and suits, much of Snob's stock is—by today's standards—quite conventional. Most of the dresses are Quant-styled, the skinny sweaters named makes.

"We're not trying to be ahead of London," said 25-year-old Anne. "We're just keeping up."

She and her co-partner, Philip Hillman, aim between them to keep their finger on the pulse of the teen fashion world. "I think we've hit on the right formula," she said.

LEFT Press cutting, Barbara and Fitz at the Brighton Biba boutique, *Evening Argus*, 4 November 1965

Biba's instant success saw it become a destination for fashion-savvy teenagers and young women, but from its beginnings Biba was much more than just low-cost fashion. The boutique had a nightclub-like atmosphere with dark interiors, busy with merchandise, music and customers. Clothing and accessories hung from Victorian bentwood hat stands, with changing rooms a makeshift affair as customers tried on outfits communally behind freestanding folding screens, which invariably collapsed under the weight of all of the clothes thrown on top of them. An Art Nouveau-inspired wallpaper covered the walls, and curtains obscured the outside world. As Barbara said: 'From day one of the first Biba I was never quite certain which came first, the clothes or the interiors.'[7]

Twiggy, Jane Asher, Cilla Black and Cathy McGowan were all avid fans of Biba and provided an almost constant presence in the media through newspaper stories, teenage magazines such as *Rave* and *Fabulous 208* and television programmes such as *Ready, Steady, Go!*. With the shop open six days a week from 9am until 8pm, Biba attracted a wide range of customers from schoolgirls to young professional women, and with dresses selling for under three pounds almost anyone could become part of the growing Biba story.

"Abingdon Road's constant stream of customers soon rendered the boutique too small for the growing business, and after 12 months Barbara and Fitz began looking for larger premises in London"

The success of Abingdon Road prompted Barbara to establish a second boutique in her old home town of Brighton. In a prime location on Queen's Road – a road which leads directly from the train station to the seafront – it was intended as the first of many Biba boutiques to open across the country in a plan to take Biba to every high street in Britain.

The Queen's Road boutique opened in November 1965. It was a strategic business move to open in the autumn as Fitz understood that coats, at four times the price of a dress, meant more money in the tills of a newly opened venture. Indeed, all the Biba stores were to open in either autumn or winter. The local newspaper, the *Evening Argus*, reported that Biba brought 'a "little Carnaby Street" look to Brighton ... Inside the shop it's like a cross between a jungle and a cavern. Purple Art Nouveau wallpaper (hand-printed specially for her) blooms over the walls.'[8]

As much as the Brighton boutique was a canny business move, it also represented a more profound personal statement. With an upstairs apartment, Barbara and Fitz spent weekends by the sea, shopping in the many antique shops across town, acquiring mirrors, furniture and plant pots for use in the London store. Brighton brought Barbara geographically closer to her family, and the new boutique served to illustrate to Auntie Barbara's success as a businesswoman, and one who was independently wealthy.

Abingdon Road's constant stream of customers soon rendered the boutique too small for the growing business, and after 12 months Barbara and Fitz began looking for larger premises in London. Biba on Church Street, Kensington, opened in February 1966, in a store four times the size of Abingdon Road. While at Abingdon Road, Biba had become representative nationally of 'Swinging London', and its move to larger premises garnered news stories nationwide. The Youthquake in London fashion soon swept the world, and, after *Time* magazine's visit to the Church Street store in 1966, Biba came to be regarded as the epicentre of the London scene internationally.

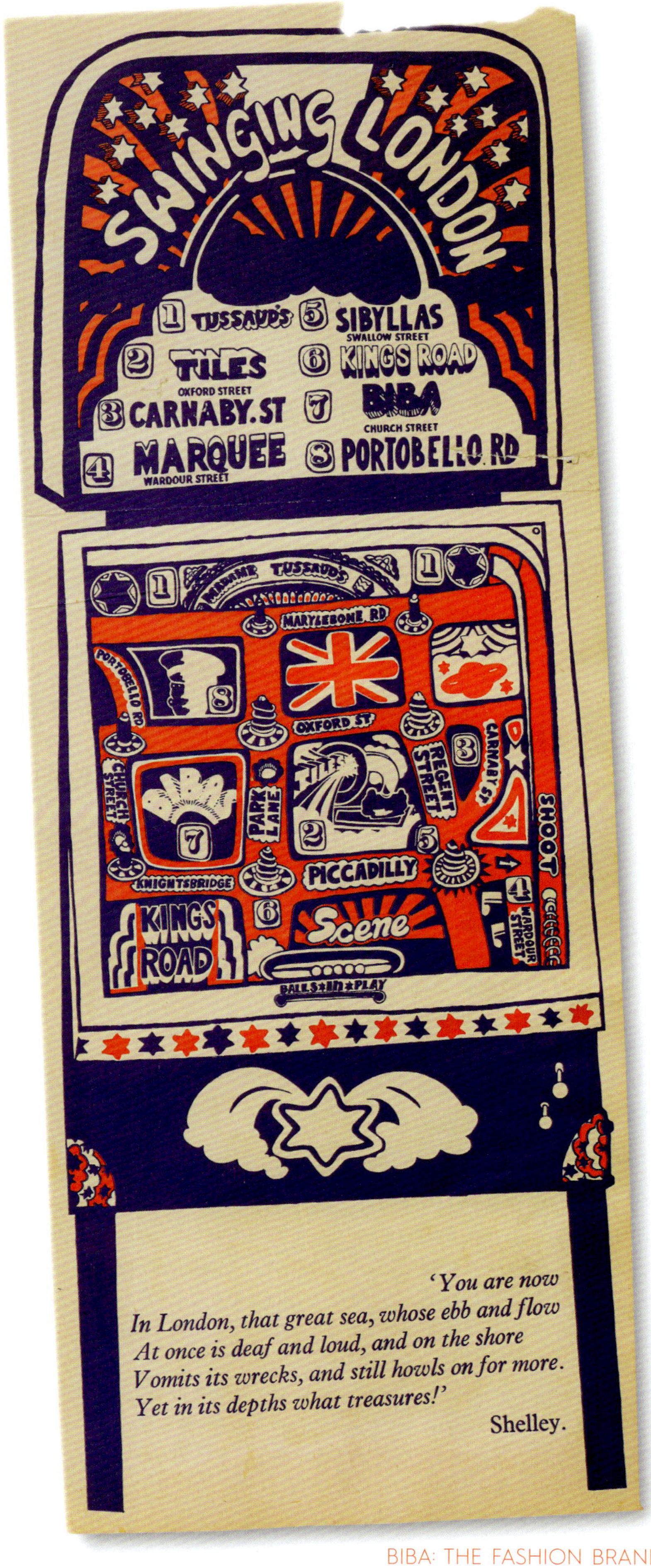

Poster advertising 'Swinging London', c.1967

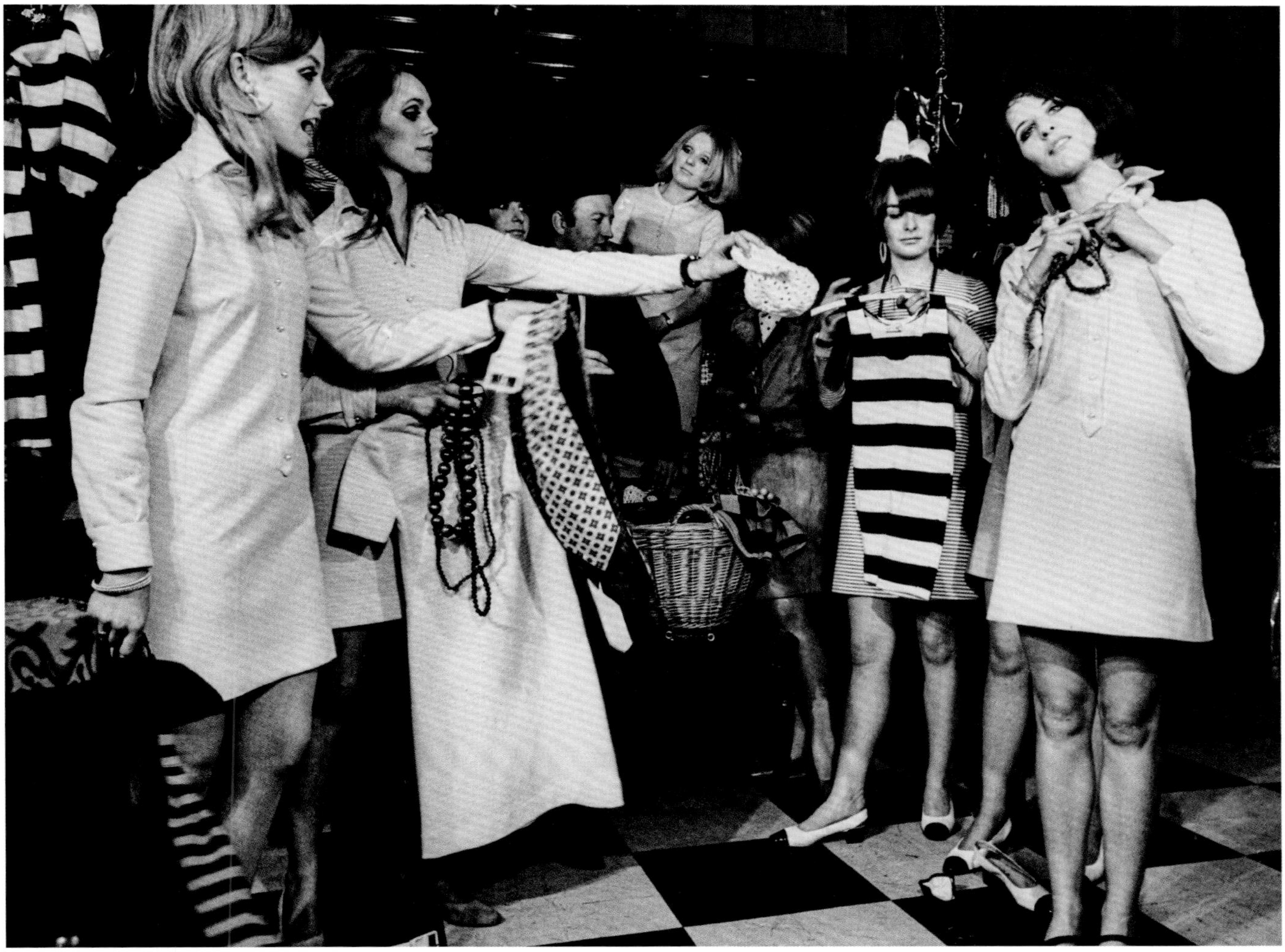

ABOVE Interior of Church Street Biba boutique, six members of staff with Fitz and Barbara at centre, *c.*1966

A triple-fronted shop, the windows of the Church Street store were decked with Art Nouveau-inspired Biba logos and the exterior was painted in black and gold, colours adopted from the funeral parlour located on the opposite side of the road. The interiors were decorated with red and gold wallpaper, and the wall-to-wall mahogany shelving, retained from the building's previous life as a grocer, was filled with Biba clothing. With retail space on the ground floor, a large communal changing room was located in the basement. The cramped spaces of the first Biba boutique had necessitated the makeshift communal changing rooms, but their success in allowing for a faster turnover of customers by eliminating queues for single-occupancy changing rooms, and the fact that they acted as a deterrent to potential thieves, saw them becoming a permanent fixture, both at Biba and across the retail sector more broadly. As the *Sun* newspaper reported in 1967: 'Shops are beginning to fight back in the shoplifting war ... It has been a well-known trick for girls to take several dresses off the rails and then, in the privacy of a changing cubicle, slip one in their bag.'[9]

Barbara now offered her customers extended ranges of womenswear, with Biba selling a wider choice of dresses, coats and accessories including hats, shoes, handbags and tote bags, jewellery and even wigs. Church Street Biba also began selling a small selection of t-shirts, which Barbara sold specifically for Fitz, but which soon developed from basic separates into the first Biba menswear range, encompassing suits and accessories.

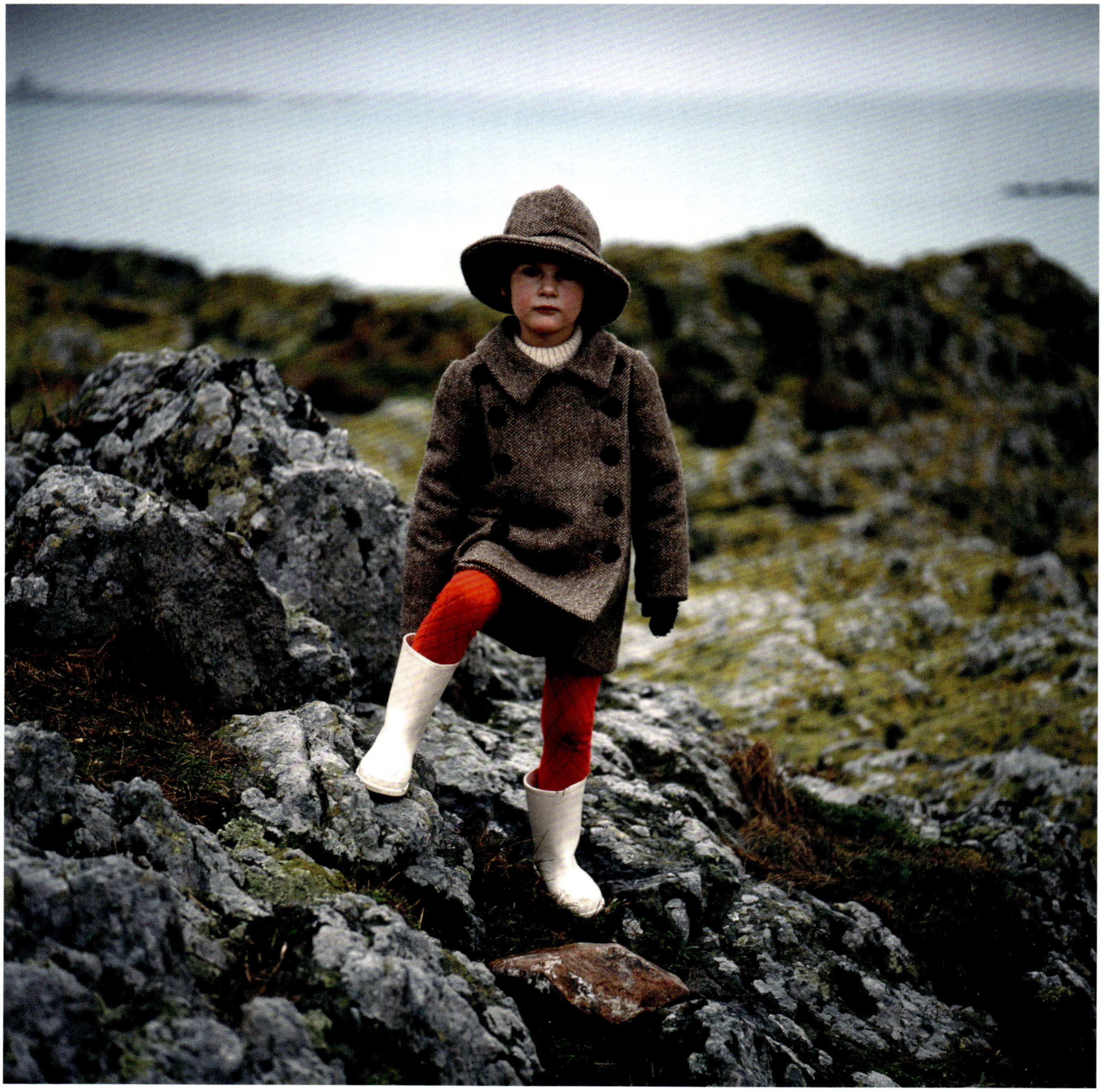

Tessa, aged four, wearing Biba children's wear, photographed by Robert Hallmann, 1969

In June 1967 Barbara and Fitz's son Witold was born and with him came the birth of Biba children's wear. Unlike typical children's clothing found on the high street, Barbara's designs were scaled-down versions of adult clothing. As Barbara observed of her younger customers: 'They have minds of their own. At three they come in to us and choose everything, even their hats. They know what they want.'[10] With an almost exclusively female workforce, Barbara also catered to the needs of other young mothers within the wider 'Biba family' by creating a crèche in the workrooms, perhaps the first of its kind anywhere within a workplace.

Understanding the busy lives of all post-war women, Barbara relaunched the mail-order catalogues, taking good-quality, inexpensive fashion to women across the UK. The Biba shop in Brighton had been intended as the vehicle to take Biba nationwide, but managing the Brighton boutique was problematic. It had become a magnet for Brighton's underworld and, since Barbara was largely based in London, she was unable to oversee the day-to-day running of the store. With a heavy heart, in 1966, Barbara made the decision to close the Brighton boutique. With the closure came the end of the dream of having Biba boutiques nationwide, and the Brighton boutique would be the only Biba store to open outside of London. The relaunched catalogues did, however, take Biba nationwide, but in a manner that Barbara was able to fully oversee.

"The first catalogue was launched in April 1968 and brought fashion into the lives of tens of thousands of women for the first time"

The first of the new mail-order catalogues was launched in April 1968 and brought fashion into the lives of tens of thousands of women for the first time. An instant success, one blouse sold 14,000 copies in the first week. A further five catalogues were produced over an 18-month period. This gave Barbara the opportunity to create a collection of clothes and to present her complete Biba vision: clothing, hair, make-up, accessories, attitude. Up to that point, Biba had been largely ignored by the glossy fashion press of the day due to its low price point; the catalogues became a vehicle by which Barbara could create her own editorial-style images, working with the best photographers of the period including Helmut Newton, Harri Peccinotti and Sarah Moon.

The catalogues themselves were designed to fit through a letter box without bending or folding, bringing Barbara's Biba vision faultlessly to eager customers. John McConnell, the designer of the catalogues, said of their success that 'within a few years the figures were phenomenal, and it changed the [mail-order] business totally'.[11]

Church Street Biba also launched the first non-clothing Biba product: a diary for 1967. Black with a gold Biba logo on the cover, it marked the beginning of the many thousands of Biba products that would be designed and developed by Barbara over the next eight years, all packaged in the distinctive black and gold Biba colours. Biba diaries included recommendations of London restaurants and shops to visit, demonstrating the emerging influence of Biba beyond its own shop walls and suggesting that, more than the clothes on your back, Biba was also the company you kept.

One of the boldest moves by Barbara was the introduction of Biba couture in January 1969. The fashion journalist Liz Smith, a friend of Barbara's and former Biba employee, created a front cover and six-page fashion story for the launch of the range, declaring: 'A week before the Paris couturiers launch their collections the *Observer* magazine presents the newest name in British couture ... Biba.'[12]

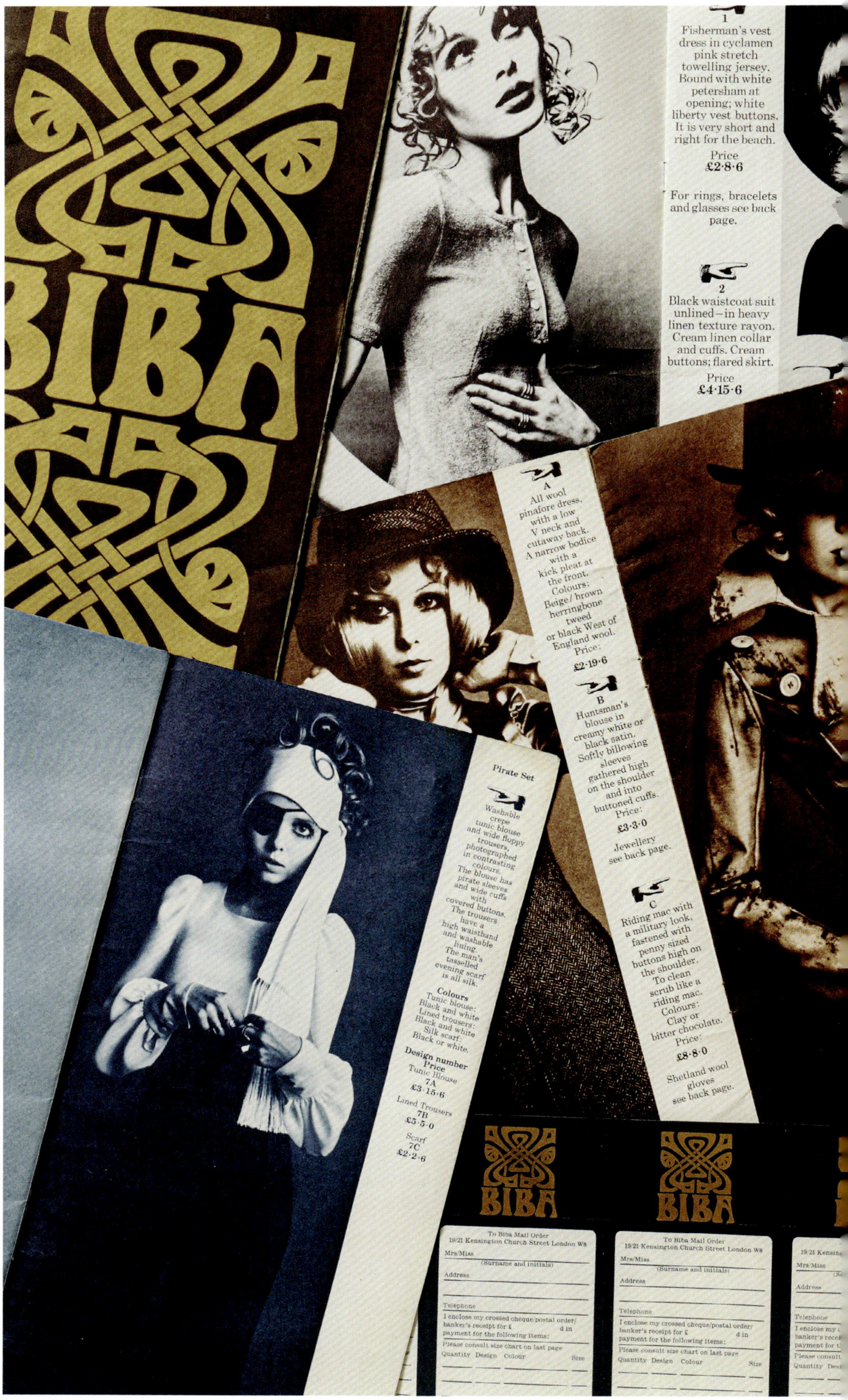

Montage of four of the Biba catalogues, 1968–9

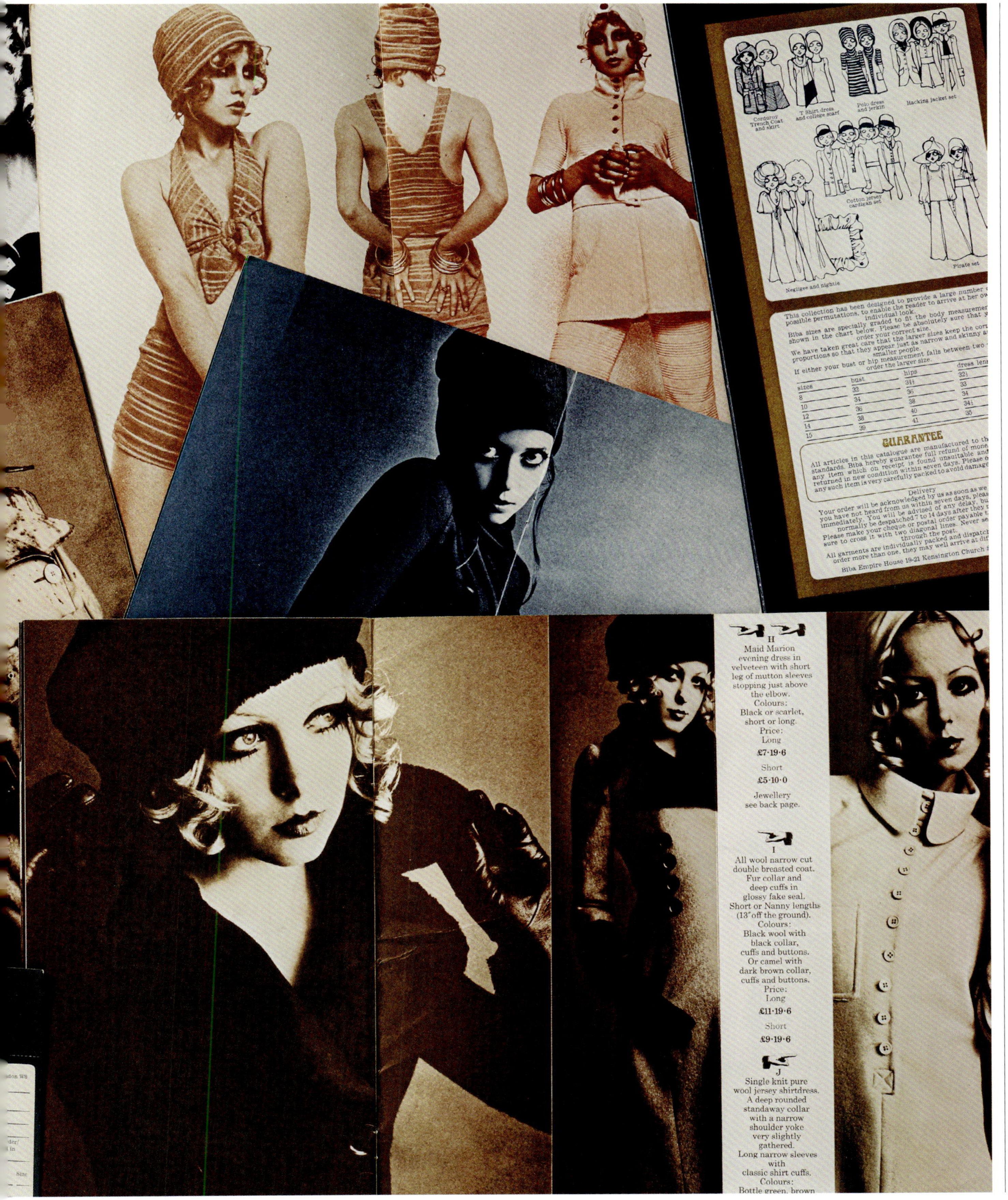
Corduroy Trench Coat and skirt
T Shirt dress and college scarf
Polo dress and jerkin
Hacking jacket set
Cotton jersey cardigan set
Pirate set
Negligee and nightie
This collection has been designed to provide a large number
possible permutations, to enable the reader to arrive at her
individual look.
Biba sizes are specially graded to fit the body measureme
shown in the chart below. Please be absolutely sure that
order your correct size.
We have taken great care that the larger sizes keep the
proportions so that they appear just as narrow and skinny
smaller people.
If either your bust or hip measurement falls between two
order the larger size.
sizes
8
10
12
14
15
bust
32
34
36
38
39
hips
34½
36
38
40
41
dress
32½
33
34
34½
35
GUARANTEE
All articles in this catalogue are manufactured to
standards. Biba hereby guarantee full refund of
any item which on receipt is found unsuitable and
returned in new condition within seven days.
any such item is very carefully packed to avoid
Delivery
Your order will be acknowledged by us as soon as we
you have not heard from us within seven days,
immediately. You will be advised of any delay,
normally be despatched 7 to 14 days after they
Please make your cheque or postal order payable
sure to cross it with two diagonal lines. Never
through the post.
All garments are individually packed and
order more than one, they may well arrive at
Biba Empire House 19-21 Kensington Church
H
Maid Marion
evening dress in
velveteen with short
leg of mutton sleeves
stopping just above
the elbow.
Colours:
Black or scarlet,
short or long.
Price:
Long
£7·19·6
Short
£5·10·0
Jewellery
see back page.
I
All wool narrow cut
double breasted coat.
Fur collar and
deep cuffs in
glossy fake seal.
Short or Nanny lengths
(13" off the ground).
Colours:
Black wool with
black collar,
cuffs and buttons.
Or camel with
dark brown collar,
cuffs and buttons.
Price:
Long
£11·19·6
Short
£9·19·6
J
Single knit pure
wool jersey shirtdress.
A deep rounded
standaway collar
with a narrow
shoulder yoke
very slightly
gathered.
Long narrow sleeves
with
classic shirt cuffs.
Colours:
Bottle green, brown

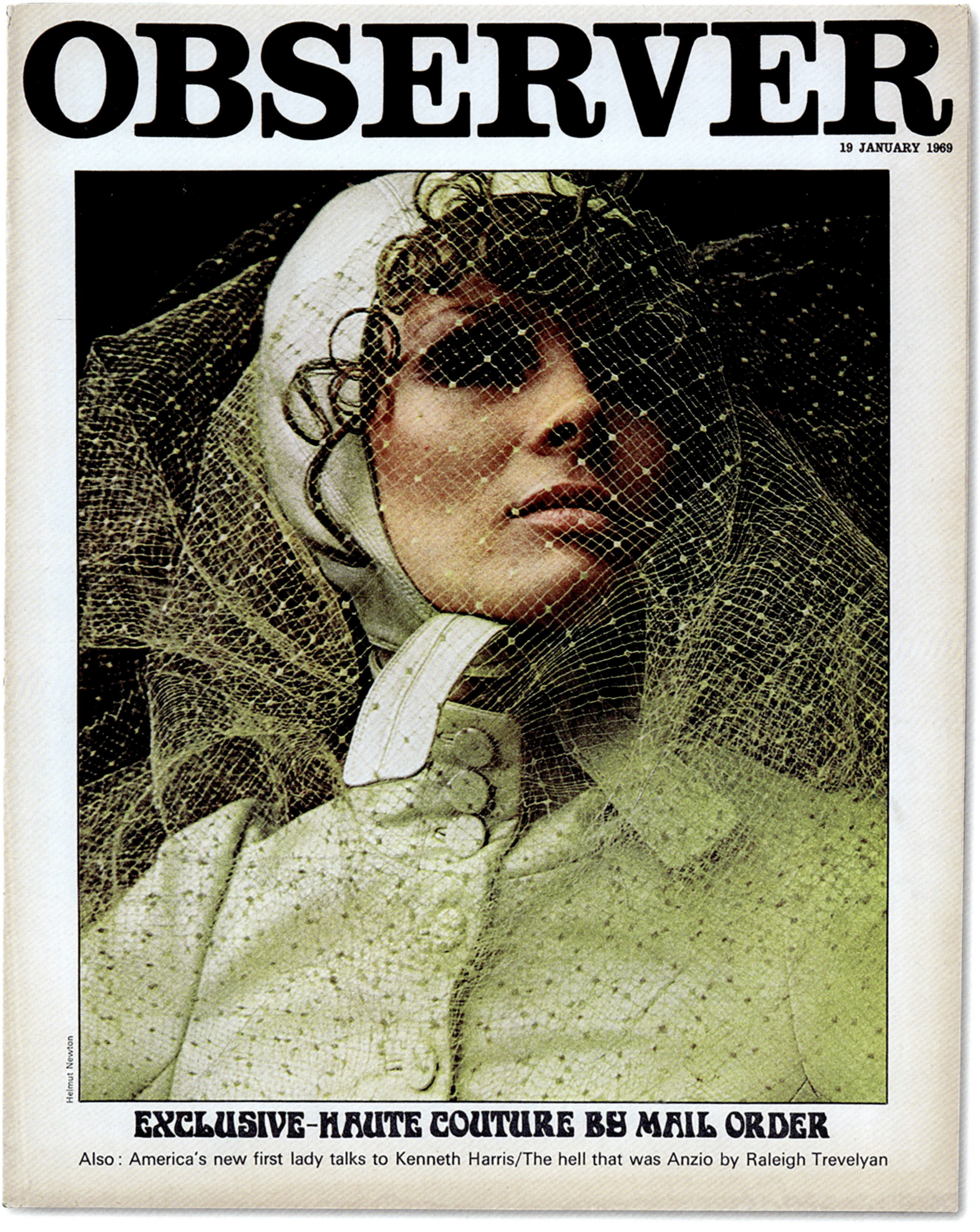
OBSERVER
19 JANUARY 1969
Helmut Newton
EXCLUSIVE-HAUTE COUTURE BY MAIL ORDER
Also: America's new first lady talks to Kenneth Harris/The hell that was Anzio by Raleigh Trevelyan

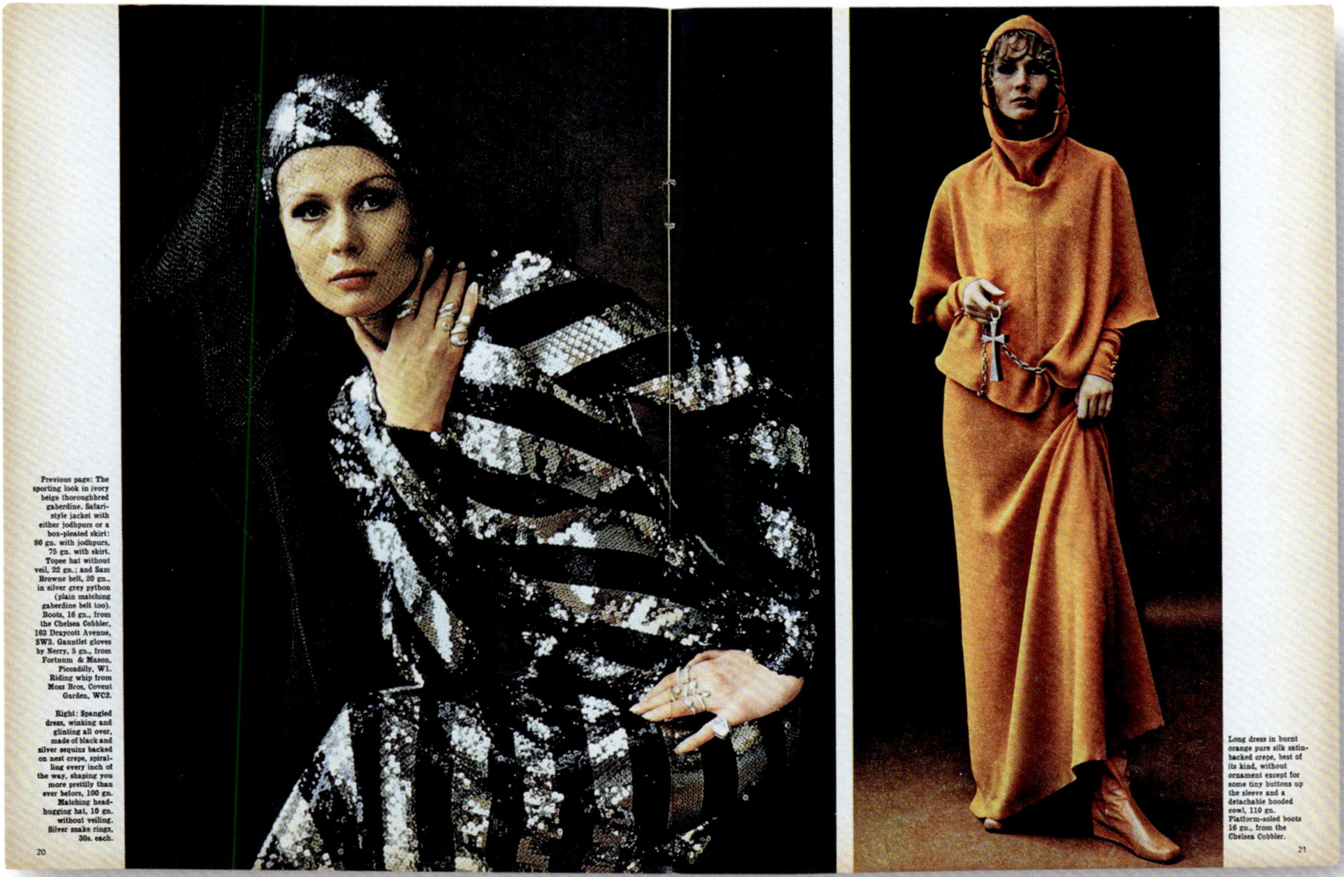

Previous page: The sporting look in ivory beige thoroughbred gaberdine. Safari-style jacket with either jodhpurs or a box-pleated skirt: 80 gn. with jodhpurs, 75 gn. with skirt. Topee hat without veil, 22 gn.; and Sam Browne belt, 20 gn., in silver grey python (plain matching gaberdine belt too). Boots, 16 gn., from the Chelsea Cobbler, 163 Draycott Avenue, SW3. Gauntlet gloves by Nerry, 5 gn., from Fortnum & Mason, Piccadilly, W1. Riding whip from Moss Bros, Covent Garden, WC2.

Right: Spangled dress, winking and glinting all over, made of black and silver sequins backed on nest crepe, spiralling every inch of the way, shaping you more prettily than ever before, 100 gn. Matching head-hugging hat, 10 gn. without veiling. Silver snake rings, 30s. each.

20

Long dress in burnt orange pure silk satin-backed crepe, best of its kind, without ornament except for some tiny buttons up the sleeve and a detachable hooded cowl, 110 gn. Platform-soled boots 16 gn., from the Chelsea Cobbler.

21

LEFT & ABOVE Press cutting, 'Haute Couture By Mail Order', *Observer Magazine*, 19 January 1969

A progression on from the catalogues, the couture range allowed Barbara to design new collections using luxury fabrics such as leather, silk and fur.[13] Created as a mail-order service, customers for Biba couture chose their outfits from a small selection of designs and sent their measurements to Biba for making up. A couture department opened in 1969 inside the next Biba store on Kensington High Street, but with prices at 50 pounds – around ten times the cost of the standard Biba range – couture Biba lasted just 18 months, closing in the summer of 1971.

Although the couture range was not successful commercially, Biba's next move proved to be one that brought customers from across three continents, and which made the company one of the most profitable per square foot in the world: 'The Biba department store is Biba's first step into the world of the big store, and their final step out of the world of the darkened boutique ... Biba has grown up.' Thus declared the Biba press release for the opening of the new store.

As a department store, Biba gave its customers the freedom to furnish their homes and fill their wardrobes. Opening in September 1969, the new store was located in a large retail space that had become vacant on Kensington High Street following the collapse of the Cyril Lord carpet business the preceding year. The modernist interiors of the carpet showroom were replaced with original Victorian wooden interiors reclaimed from the local St Paul's boys' school, which had recently been demolished, alongside Art Nouveau-inspired decor. The influence of Art Deco also emerged at Biba for the first time, with the mirror-clad shoe department based on the 1920s Paris apartment in L'Hôtel of the actress and singer Mistinguett.

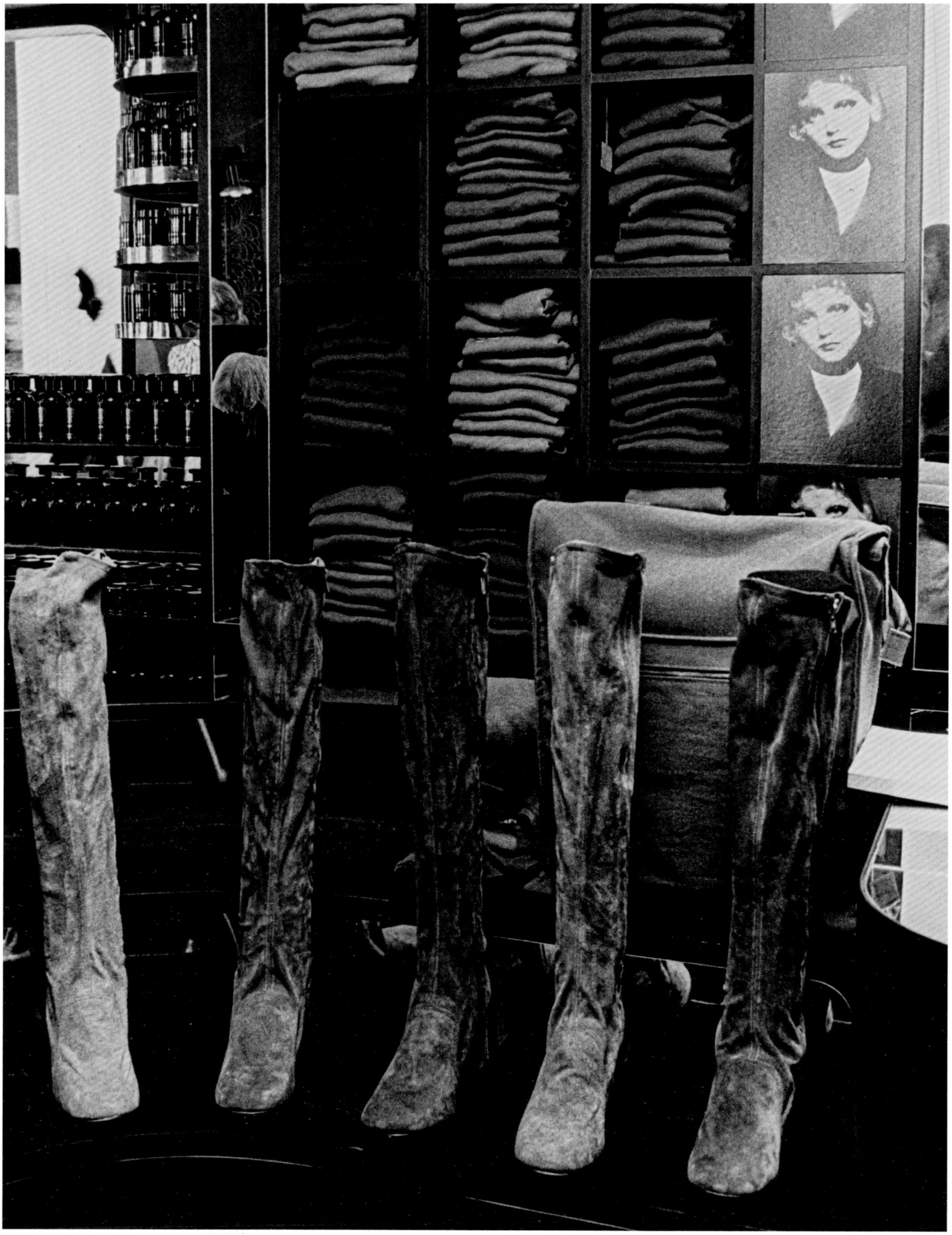

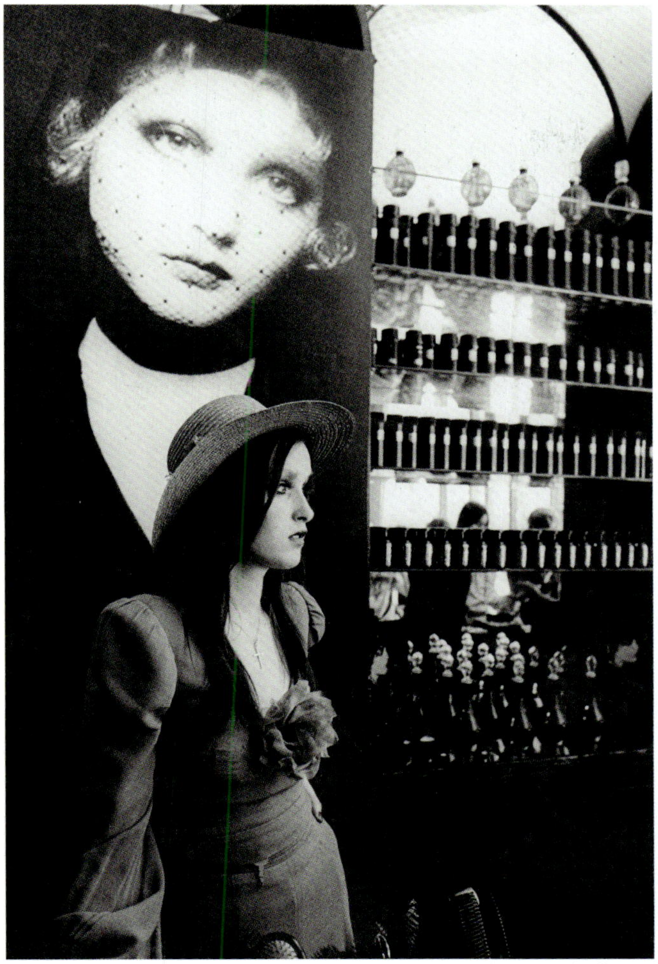

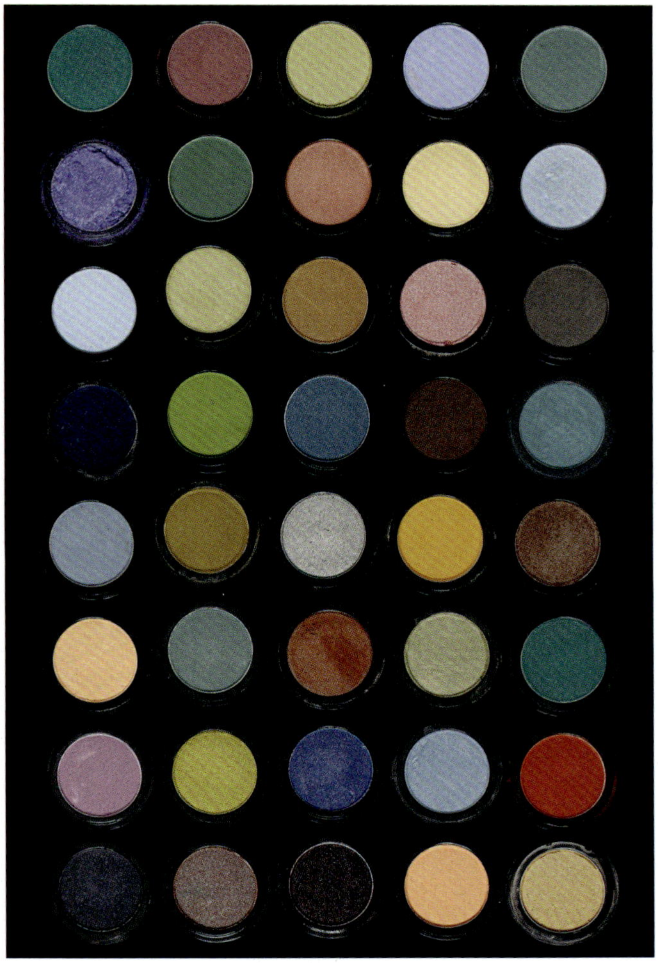

LEFT Biba boots, c.1969

ABOVE LEFT Young woman in Biba, Kensington High Street, c.1971

ABOVE RIGHT Biba cosmetics, powder eyeshadows showing a range of the Biba colours, c.1972

The 'grown-up' store reflected the grown-up customer. The Biba dolly bird had matured into the Biba woman. Barbara observed of this change that: 'As time went by my Biba girl became more dreamy and untouchable. Her long straight hair turned into a halo of golden ringlets, her cheeks were hollowed by brown powder and her lips stained with sepia lipstick.'[14] Sex and sexuality were the new mood at Biba, and Barbara's designs for womenswear reflected the confidence of her new woman. With more than a nod to the fashions of the 1930s, Biba sold floor-length, low-cut dresses revealing the body through construction and clinging fabrics such as satin, devoré and chiffon. Now with homes of their own, the Biba woman could furnish them with Biba wallpapers, bed linen, lamps and lampshades, cushions and tableware, all in the distinctive Biba colours. The 9,000-square-foot retail space offered the complete look for the individual and for the home.

It was at Kensington High Street that Barbara created the most iconic of all Biba clothing, the Biba boot. Boots were the footwear of the 1960s, and Barbara designed one of the most coveted of them all at the end of the decade. Launched in 1969, the tight-fitting, knee-high, zip-up boots would continue in production until the end of Biba. With seasonally appropriate styles and variations of the design, they were created in leather, satin-weave cotton, canvas and suede, and with the heels changing from Louis (medium height, with a narrow waist and splayed foot) to a higher and slimmer version. The popularity of the boots prompted an expansion of the footwear department at Biba, relocating to a considerably larger space on the lower ground floor.

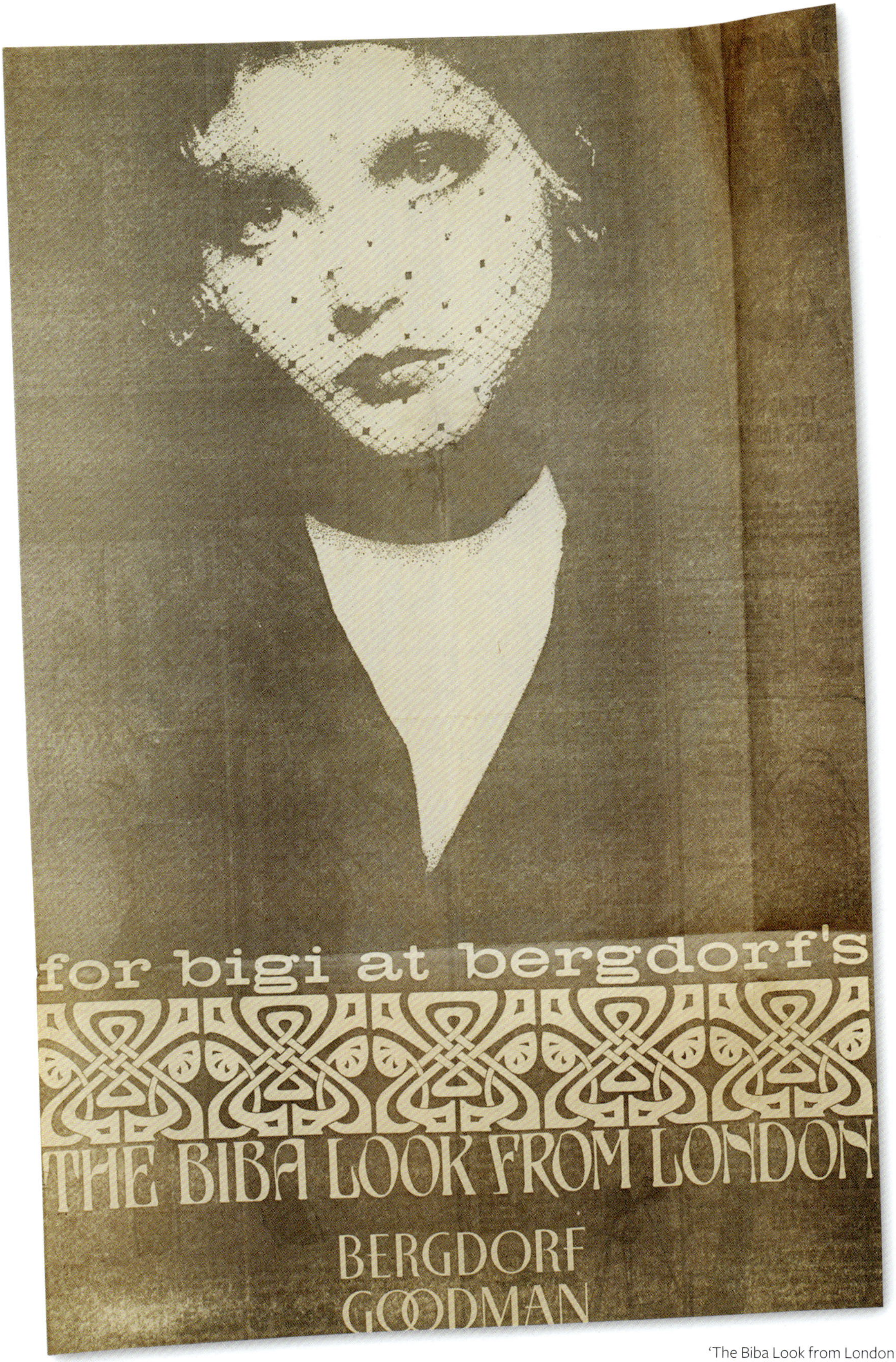

'The Biba Look from London at Bergdorf Goodman', *New York Times*, 7 February 1971

The success of the Biba boot was quickly followed by the phenomenon of Biba cosmetics. From the earliest days of Biba, Barbara wanted to introduce a range of cosmetics, allowing customers to create the complete Biba look: 'First you've got the dress, then the tights, then the shoes, then the hat and then you get to the face ... and nothing.'[15] Launched in 1970, Biba cosmetics became *the* most successful range of Biba products. Sold in-store at the shop on Kensington High Street, Biba cosmetics were also available nationwide through the 300 or so high-street shops of Dorothy Perkins, with whom Biba had gone into business in 1969. Within two years of its launch, Biba cosmetics were sold in over 30 countries and across three continents.

Barbara said in 1974: 'People thought I was mad to bring out make-up when the market was already crowded. But it was crowded with twenty-five different pale blues and twenty-five pale pinks. There was nothing around to go with the kind of dirty, sludgy colours I was using.'[16] Barbara's instincts also saw Biba become the first company to create a full range of cosmetics for Black girls (and boys), with *19* magazine declaring: 'Now, after years of having to compromise with whatever make-up was available on the market, dark-skinned girls can look forward to their own range of make-up ... hot from the bright-thinking Biba laboratories.'[17] Biba was also the first company to launch a range of cosmetics for men. By 1974 the turnover of Biba cosmetics just for the Japanese market was almost one million pounds, and so lucrative were the cosmetics that they continued to be sold by Dorothy Perkins after the demise of Biba and into the 1980s.

Biba's expansion into new markets saw it cross the Atlantic with the launch of Biba womenswear in America. Through the journalist, and friend of Barbara's, Rosemary McMurtry, arrangements were made for Barbara to create a range of Biba textiles to be sold nationwide through Macy's department store and made up at home with McCall's paper patterns. A fashion story by Biba's in-house photographer Sarah Moon and model Ingrid Boulting was shot in Paris in the penthouse offices of the Printemps store and featured as an exclusive in *Seventeen* magazine, promoting Biba to America's youth.

BELOW Architect's drawing for proposed Derry & Toms department store, Bernard George, c.1932

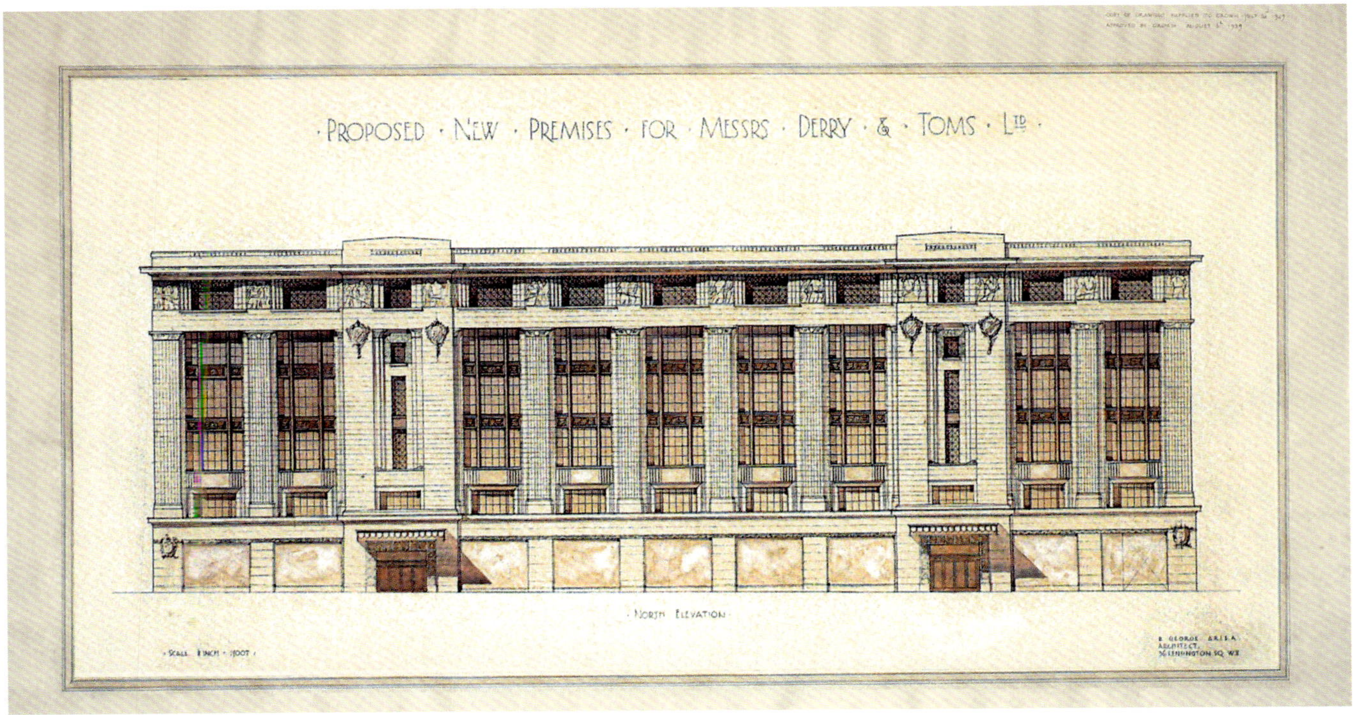

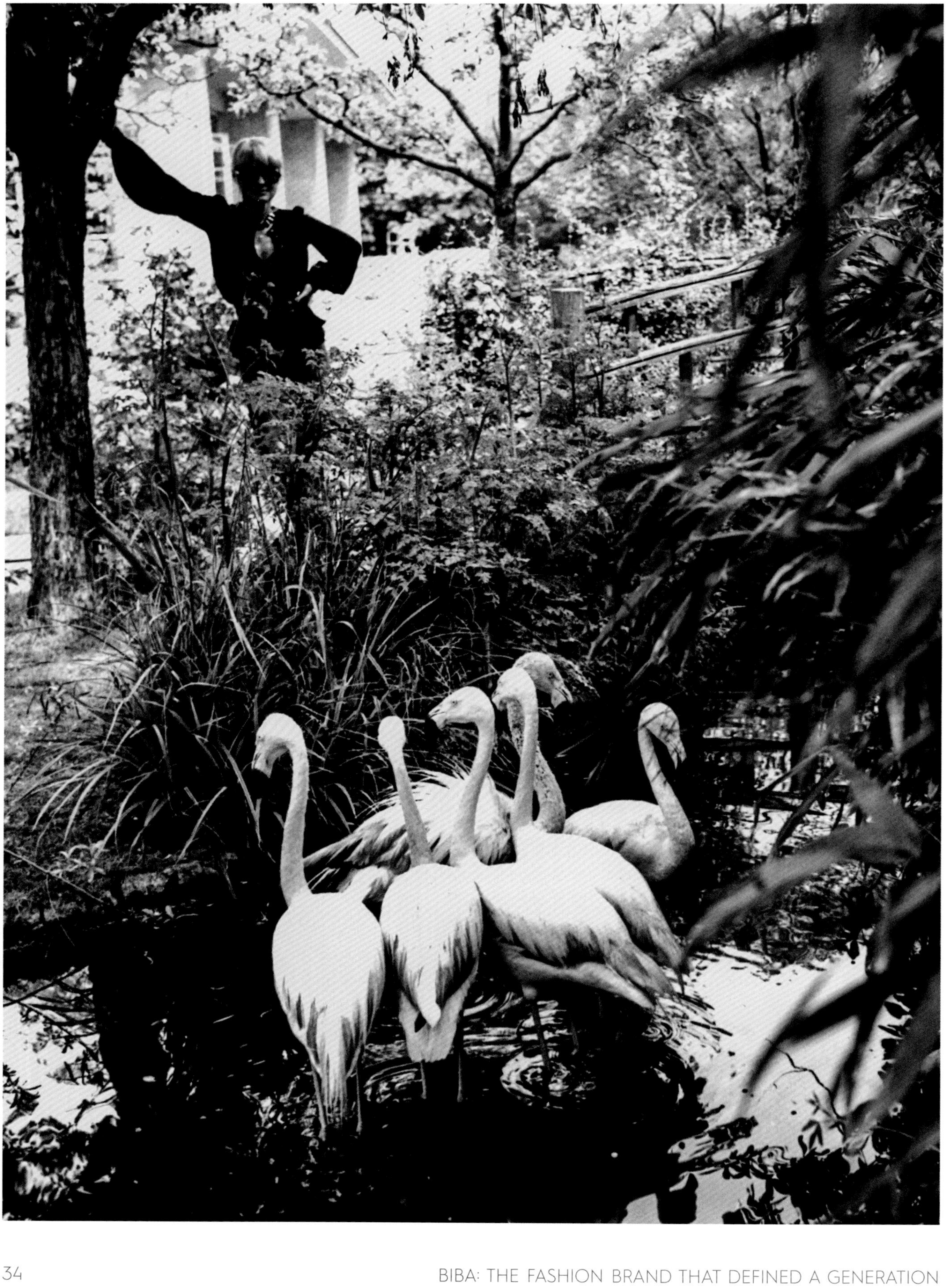

OPPOSITE Barbara Hulanicki on the roof garden of Derry & Toms, photographed by Desmond O'Neill, 1974

RIGHT Biba tinned food, including Biba baked beans, design by Whitmore-Thomas, 1974

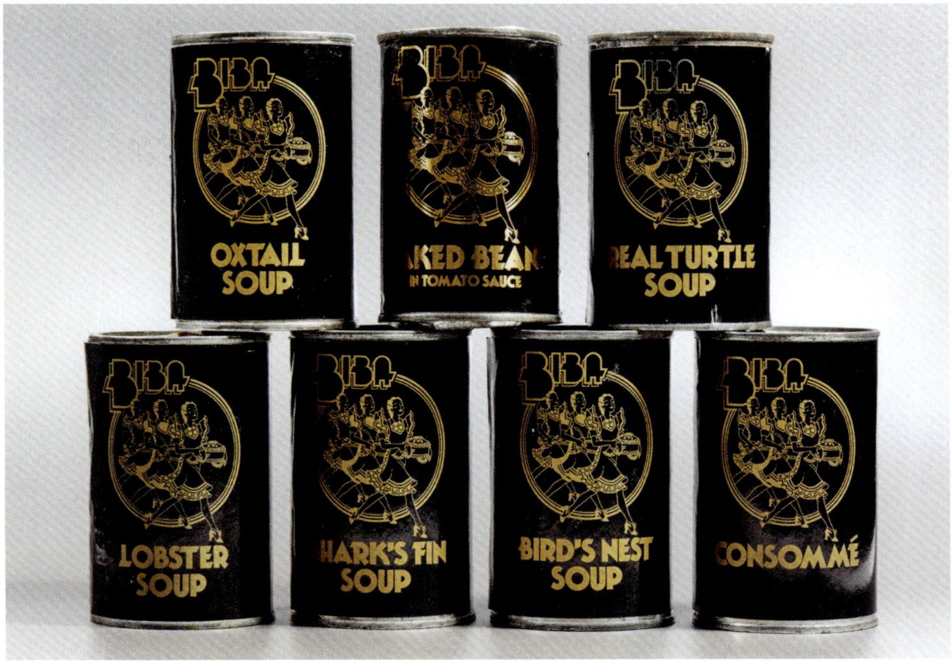

Rosemary McMurtry also introduced Barbara to a fashion buyer at the New York department store Bergdorf Goodman, and in 1971 Biba opened with huge success as a small department within the store.

Biba's ongoing and increasing successes both in Britain and internationally brought the company a high public profile and much attention, some unwanted. The anti-capitalist group The Angry Brigade – who believed that women were slaves to fashion, that Biba led fashion and therefore blowing up Biba would liberate women – exploded a bomb at Biba on May Day 1971. Thankfully no one was injured. Rather than liberating women, Barbara saw the act as an affront to the intelligence of women and their freedom to choose: after all, not *all* women wore Biba.

Around the same the time that Biba was being bombed, Barbara and Fitz had acquired the lease on the seven-storey department store Derry & Toms on Kensington High Street. Built in the early 1930s, it was heralded at the time as 'a monument to the emancipation of women and a tribute to her influence'.[18] It was this tradition that Barbara aimed to uphold with the acquisition of the store, with the latest, and final, incarnation of Biba.

The future of Derry & Toms was uncertain in the first years of the 1970s. Situated in a prime location, on a desirable London thoroughfare, there were rumours that it was to be pulled down and redeveloped, a fate that befell its two neighbouring department stores – Pontings, built in 1900, was pulled down in the mid-1970s, and Barkers, which was conceived and partially built in conjunction with Derry & Toms, was substantially redeveloped in the 1980s.

With the acquisition of the lease by Barbara and Fitz, Derry & Toms was reborn as Big Biba, and with its history at the heart of its rebirth it was once again a place to see, and to be seen. It catered in food for the home and dining out, furniture and fittings for every room in the house and products for home and garden. Biba had become the world's first lifestyle label, and, from new-born babies to adulthood, it provided for almost all of life's necessities.

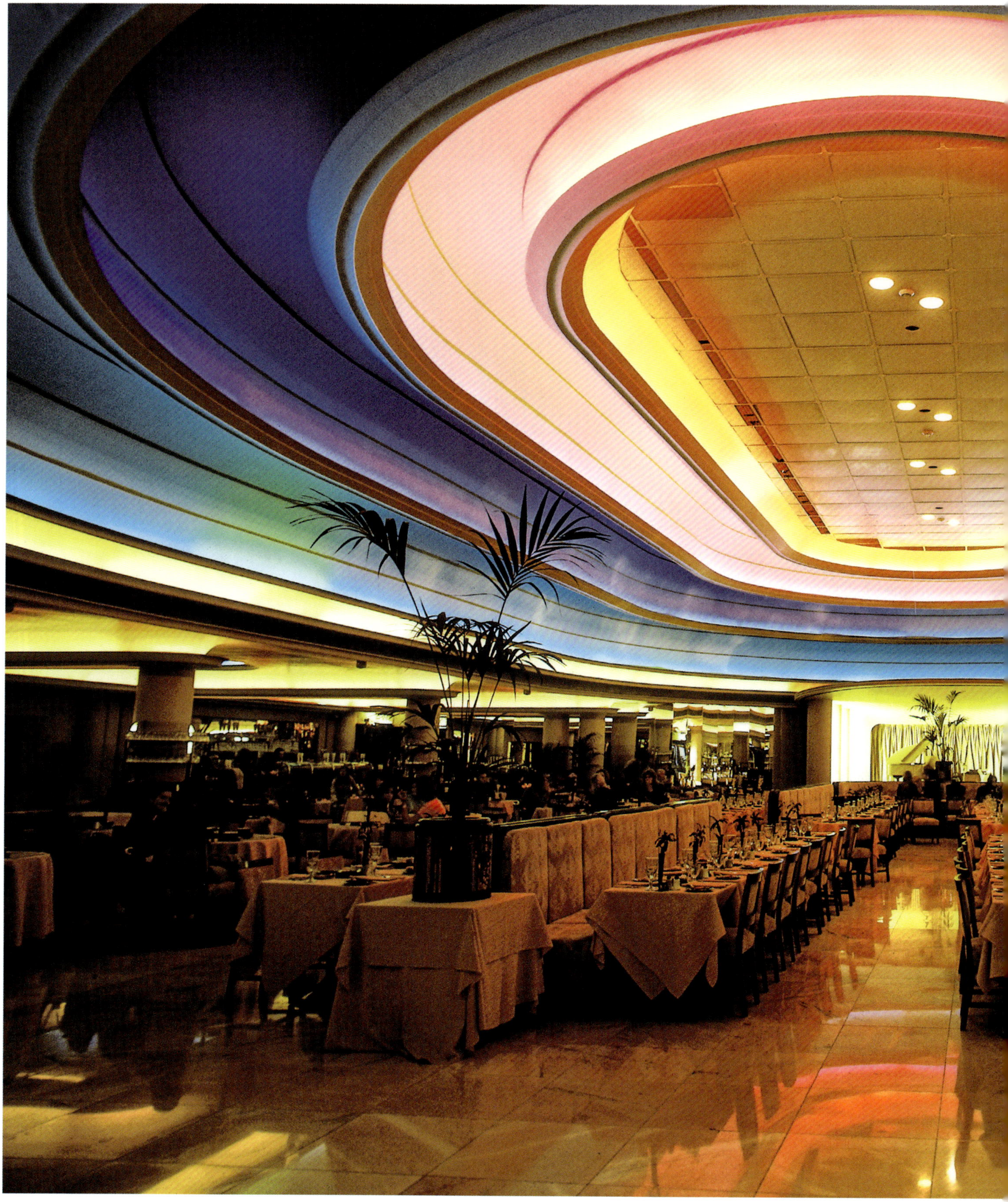

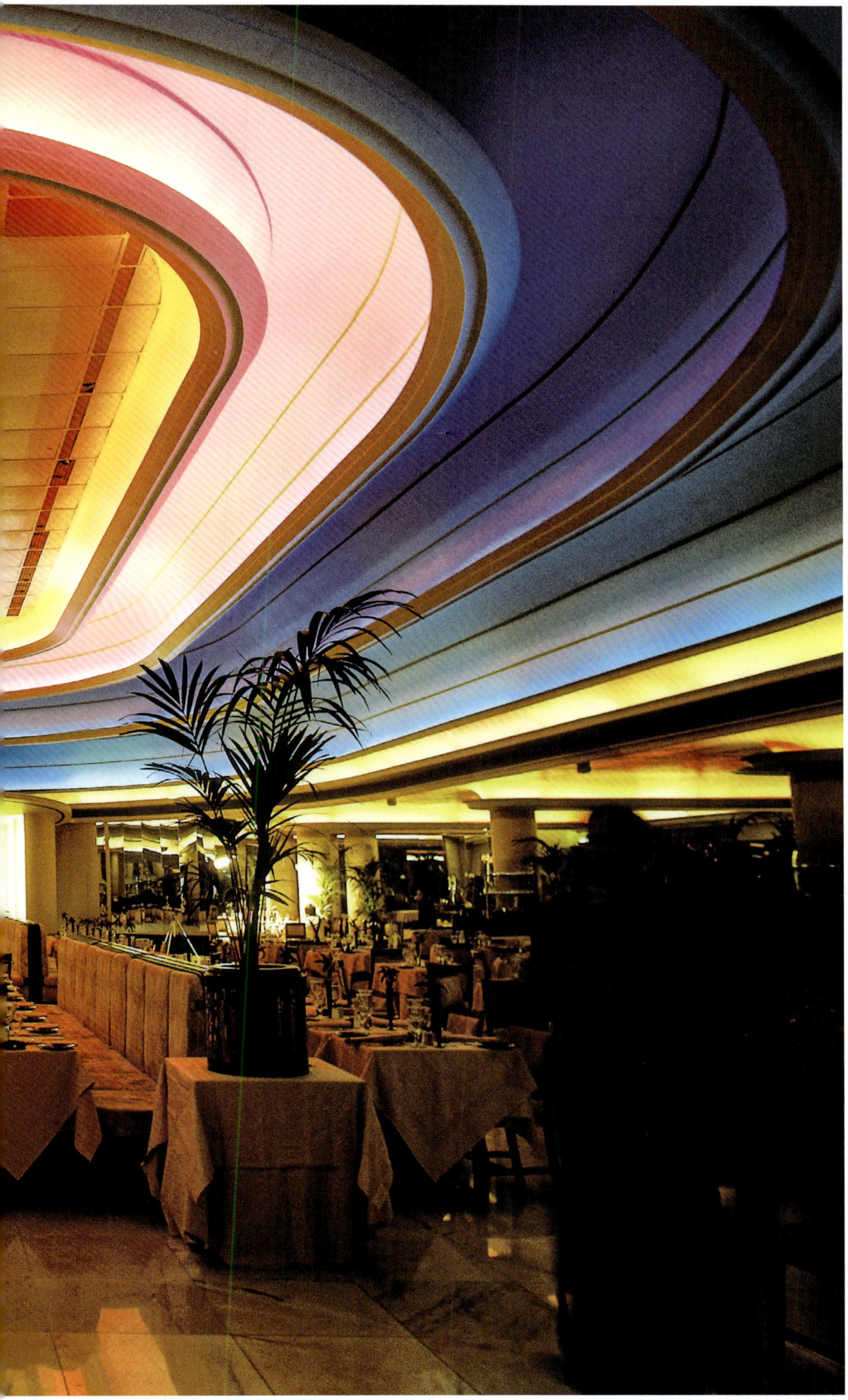

Rainbow Room restaurant, Big Biba, 1973

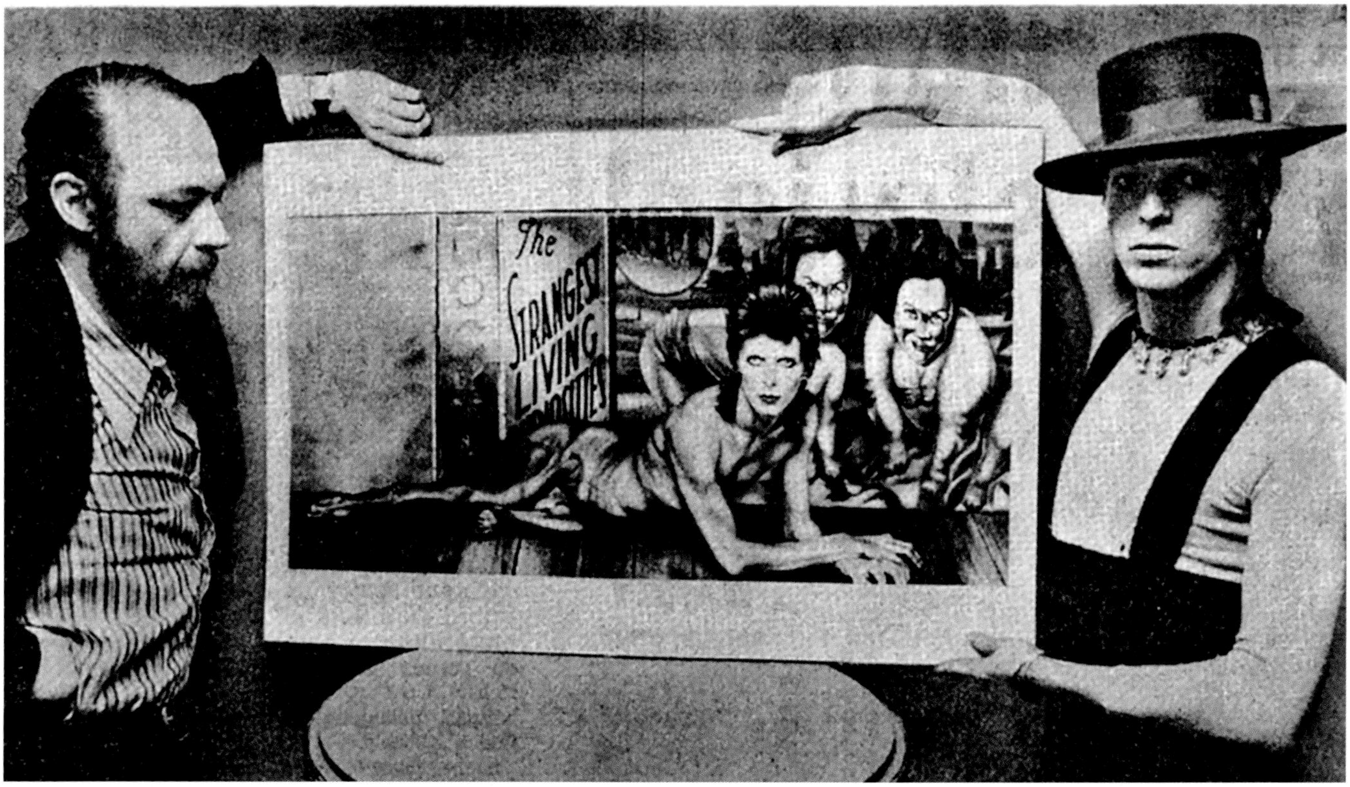

Opening in September 1973, Big Biba was proclaimed by the press to be 'the most beautiful store in the world', with newspapers ranging from Kensington's *Estate Times* to the *Japan Times* covering the story of its launch.[19] As custodians of Derry & Toms, Biba was retail as theatre, with its 15 departments created as sets, built by the same company who made stages for the James Bond films. Each department had its own visual identity, from Victoriana to Pop Art, Art Nouveau and Art Deco, with Big Biba selling not just products but experiences, providing visitors with new sights, sounds, smells, feelings and tastes.

Ten times the size of the previous store, the food department sold Biba camembert, wine, fresh fish and, most famously, Biba baked beans (in reality, tins of Heinz baked beans dressed in Biba). Customers could see exhibitions of artists' work, visit the beauty parlour, take afternoon tea in the largest roof garden in Europe and wander through its three themed gardens. Visitors to the 500-seat Rainbow Room restaurant could eat lunch from an ever-changing menu, and in the evening watch live bands from Biba's house band, Manhattan Transfer, with their take on 1930s lounge music, to the proto-punk band the New York Dolls.

Glam rock reached the height of its success at the same time as the opening of Big Biba and the store became the unofficial hub of glam music, attracting the stars of the scene including Freddie Mercury (whose girlfriend, Mary Austin, had been a Biba girl since the late 1960s), Bryan Ferry, Marc Bolan and David Bowie. Although most of the pop stars of the period were men, their look came straight out of the Biba's womenswear: satin blouses, fur coats, sequin jackets and cosmetics. In contrast to the effeminacy of the glam era, Biba menswear struck a more traditional note, with Barbara saying at the time, 'we found that conventional [men's] clothes sell best ... it is always the safe, sombre colours that go. Black sells so quickly it usually looks as if we don't stock it.'[20]

ABOVE David Bowie and Guy Peellaert, exhibition of Peellaert's work in Big Biba, 1974

OPPOSITE Big Biba closing-down sale, September 1975

The whole of the third floor was dedicated to menswear including boys' clothes, with the entire first floor, known as the Biba floor, given over to the foundation of Biba's success: womenswear. Children's wear was found on the second floor, with the ground floor devoted to cosmetics. The sheer size of the new store inspired Barbara to create a tongue-in-cheek newspaper for the store's opening, illustrating on which floors each department could be found.

Sadly, the spectacle was not to last. The end came quickly, with Big Biba surviving just two years, ceasing to trade on 27 September 1975. The acquisition of Dorothy Perkins, and therefore Biba, by the property company British Land, created tensions in the management and running of Biba, as individuals who didn't understand the Biba vision were brought in to run the company on more traditional retailing lines. Barbara lost the rights to the Biba name, and the final chapter in the Biba story was an auction at Bonhams of the store's fixtures and fittings.

Biba merchandise had become memorabilia.

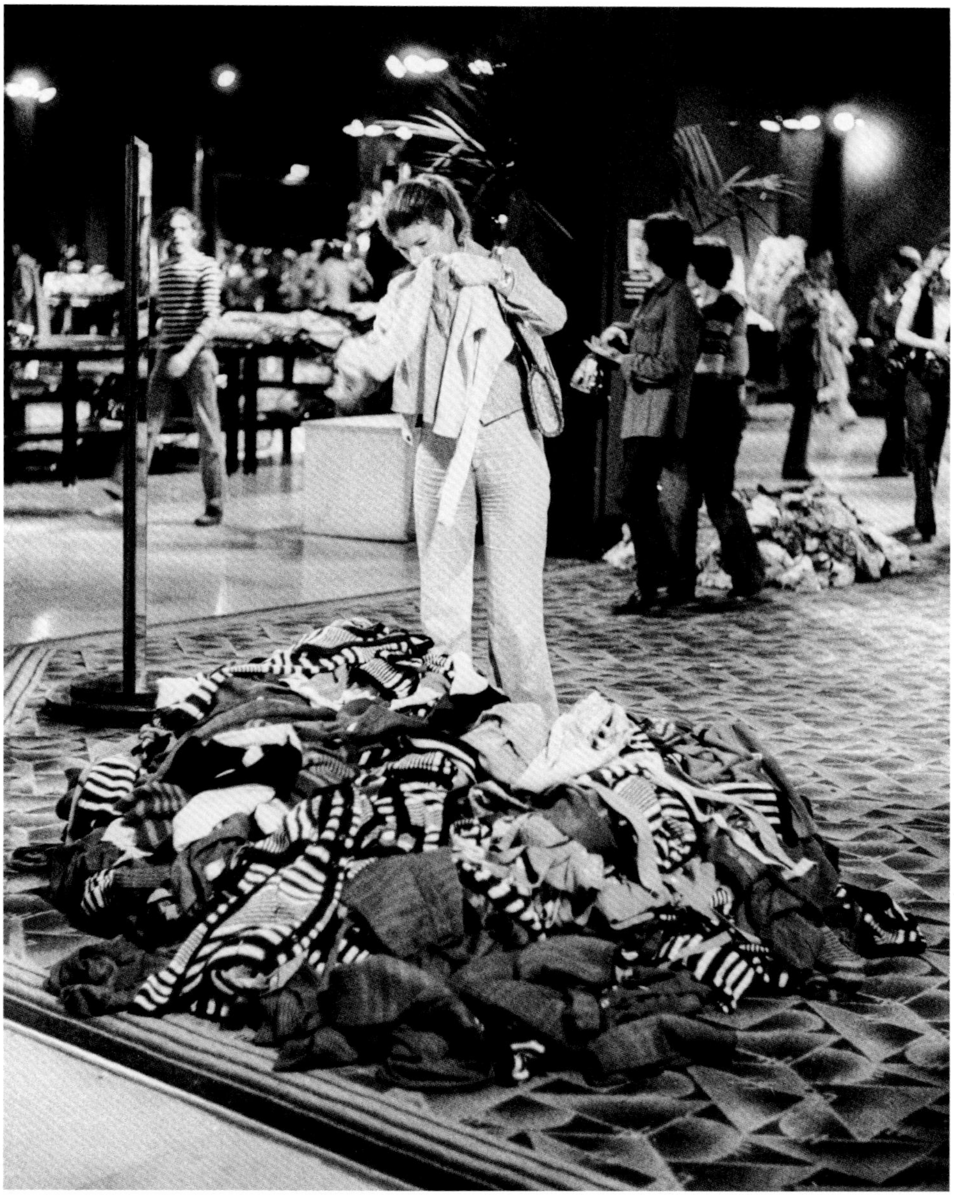

NOTES

1 Page, Irene, 'A Norman Hartnell Model for Student Barbara', *Evening Argus*, undated, np.
2 *Vogue*, February 1964, pp. 51–2.
3 Green, Felicity 'Four Girls Prove that Beauty and Business Ideas Can Go Together', *Daily Mirror*, 1 May 1964, np.
4 Turner, Alwyn W., 2007, *The Biba Experience* (London: ACC Art Books), p. 13.
5 'Girls Will Be Boys!', *Daily Mail*, 24 March 1966, np.
6 Interview with Barbara Hulanicki by the author, 2013.
7 Thomas, Steve and Alwyn W. Turner, 2011, *Welcome to Big Biba: Inside the Most Beautiful Store in the World* (Suffolk: ACC Art Books), p. 5.
8 'Boutiques Boom', *Evening Argus*, 4 November 1965, p. 14.
9 'Dear Customer, You Are Now Being Watched', *Sun*, 12 June 1967, np.
10 'Biba, Biba, Biba', *Daily Mail*, 24 January 1974, np.
11 Interview with John McConnell by the author, 2013.
12 Smith, Liz, 'Haute Couture Goes Mail Order', *Observer*, 19 January 1969, np.
13 Barbara had created coats using real fur in 1965 and 1966, but, due to the unsuitability of fur in creating the skinny Biba look, it was abandoned in favour of the more flexible fake fur material.
14 Hulanicki, Barbara, *From A to Biba: The Autobiography of Barbara Hulanicki* (London: V&A Publishing, 2007), p. 106.
15 Interview with Barbara Hulanicki by the author, 2013.
16 'The Rise and Rise of the Biba Girl', *Petticoat*, 24 November 1974, np.
17 'Black ... Is Beautiful', *19*, 1973, np.
18 'What the 30s Did For Biba', *Irish Independent*, 23 October 1973, np.
19 'Biba Fever', *The Sunday Mirror*, 6 September 1973, np.
20 'What Fits Fitz, Fits Biba', *Evening Standard*, 10 July 1974, p. 2.

CHAPTER ONE

BEFORE BIBA

"I didn't want to end up as a woman who went to Ascot, wore gorgeous things and was just there as a decorative thing for her husband"

Barbara Hulanicki

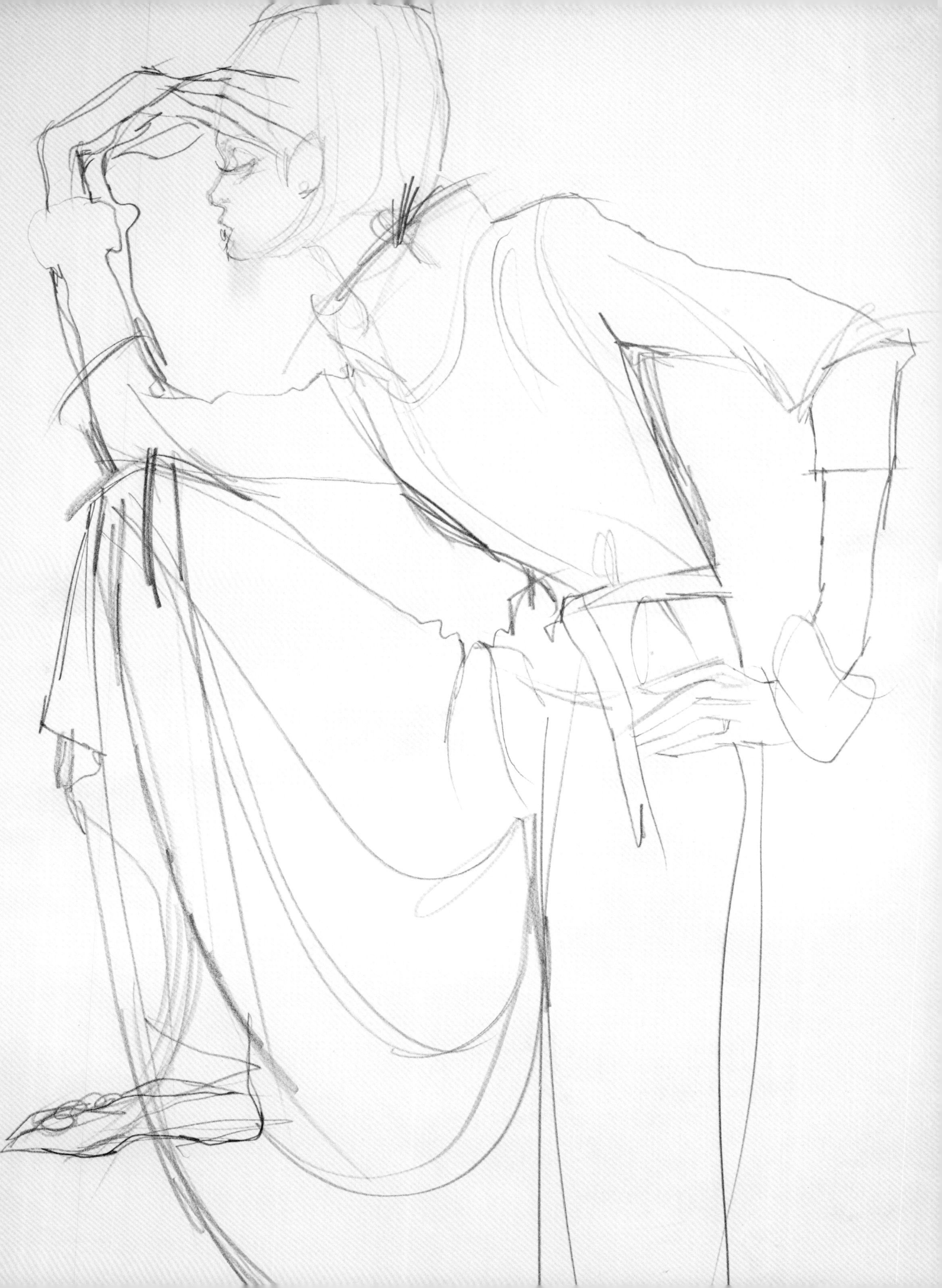

BARBARA HULANICKI AND MARTIN PEL IN CONVERSATION

MARTIN PEL Where do you think your interest in clothes and fashion comes from?

BARBARA HULANICKI We grew up in Palestine, and because of the Second World War we couldn't really buy anything, so we would draw things and sew them ourselves. My mother was amazing; she was forever making things: clothes, toiletries, things for the home. I think the only thing she didn't make was shoes. My father would go away on trips to Persia, or wherever, and he would bring back tons of clothes for my mother. He'd bring one thing in ten colours! Lebanon was fantastic because they had French clothes; they had these incredible shoes with platforms. So, there were always clothes, and I always had a serious interest in clothes, but as a child I couldn't get my hands on anything.

MP You moved to Brighton after your father was killed and lived with your aunt Sophie, with whom you had a difficult relationship. Can you talk a little more about that?

BH I did love her terribly, but she was so mean. She was always nagging, she never stopped. She meant well, I guess, but you can't do that to children all of the time. We didn't dare open our mouths. I had my father's strength, but my sisters had a tough time.

Aunt Sophie became a huge influence on Biba, once I got over the situation and got her cobwebs out of my head. She dressed well, chinchilla, never mink because mink was cheap. It had to be sable, chinchilla, fox. She would wear veils, hats, glove stretchers, the whole thing, and she would have these wonderful hairstyles, held in place with hairpins – not hairclips – that matched her hair. I used to pray, 'I hope she doesn't make me do that with my hair.' I did wear some of Auntie's clothes when she wasn't looking, but I never gave her the satisfaction of letting her know, as she would have said, 'I told you so.' Oh, poor Auntie!

MP Tell me how you got into fashion illustration?

BH I don't remember how I heard of Helen Jardine Artists, which was my first job in fashion illustration. They would send me out to some crummy little advertising agencies that did corsets – underwear doing the Gaultier kind of thing. Then I got a job with J. Walter Thompson, that was a really big agency at the time. I spent about three years going to all the shows. Unlike today, the shows went on for hours. All the models were very snotty, all except one, Christine Tidmarsh, who was fantastic. She was obviously a swimmer and a tennis player, and she had shoulders and muscles. She would come bounding down the runway, always doing Dior black dresses, and everybody would say, 'Oh, thank god! Here she comes', because without her it was so boring.

I would get the commission before I went, but I still had to pay for my ticket, travel and for a hotel. At the show the editor would book with the model she wanted me to draw and then it was a private thing between the model and me. The model would come and stand for me and wriggle and huff and puff because I was so young. I could

PREVIOUS PAGE Fashion illustration, original line drawing, Barbara Hulanicki, 1962–4

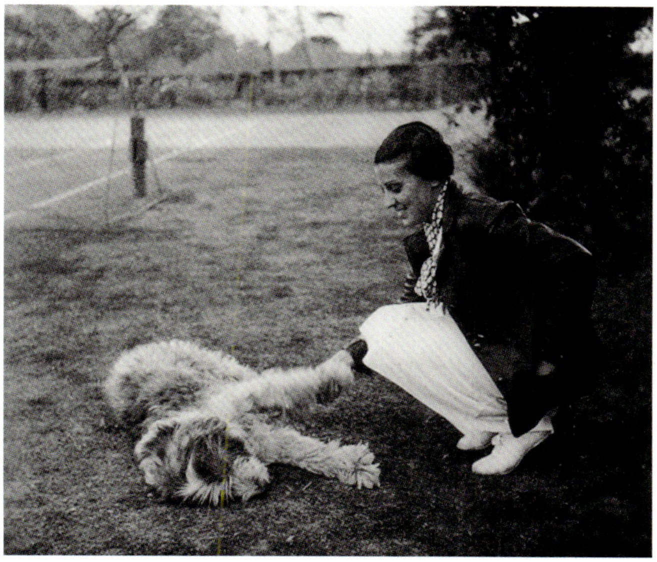

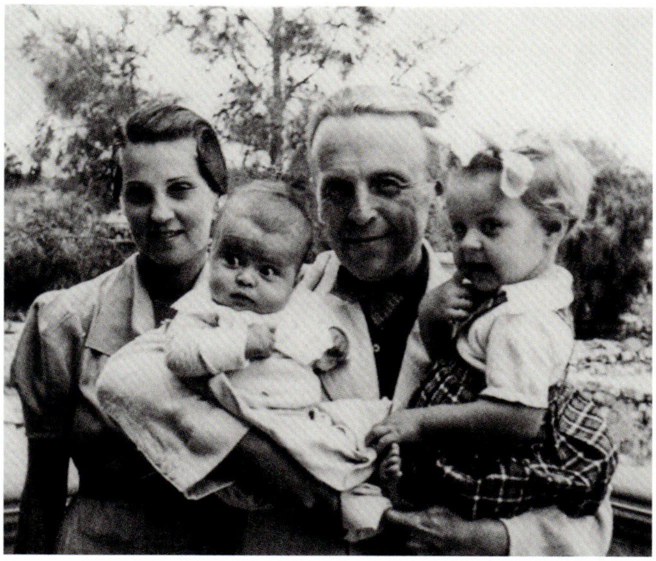

ABOVE LEFT Barbara's mother, Victoria Hulanicki, c.1935

ABOVE RIGHT Barbara's parents, Victoria and Witold Hulanicki, with Barbara and younger sister, Beatrice, c.1940

tell they were often thinking, 'What the hell is she doing here?!' All they wanted was the cash; you had to give them cash at the end of the sketching. You had to work really fast; it was very good training, like learning lines – it would train your visual memory. Because everything was drawn for print reproduction it had to be very simple, since usually they would only use a line and one colour, which was black. You wouldn't do half tones. The only time you might do half tones was for magazines.

MP How did that influence you and your career?

BH I was still working for *Women's Wear Daily* (*WWD*) in the early 1960s and going to people like the designer Michael (Donnellan) of Carlos Place. He was doing quite nice things, as were Hardy Amies and Norman Hartnell. I would draw their collections for *WWD*. I will never forget John Fairchild, Michael and Hardy Amies giving me such a lecture because I didn't get the shape right of Michael's concave front. You always felt you were learning a lot.

The more I saw, the more I was convinced that I was right in trying to get away from the kind of clothes that Auntie and Mother would wear, sort of cocktail clothes. I didn't want to end up as a woman who went to Ascot, wore gorgeous things and was just there as a decorative thing for her husband. There weren't a lot of clothes to choose from – today there is so much – and you were lucky if you could pick out one thing that you loved. All you wanted was maybe a top, or a skirt, or the shoes, you just wanted that one element of an outfit. Foale and Tuffin were the beginning for me; I used to dream about their things. 21 Shop in Woollands Brothers department store started doing young designers. Vanessa Denza, who was the buyer there, was really clever. Foale and Tuffin were just dreamy. I'll never forget, I had a black and white checked suit from them, everything was light and easy. I went to *WWD* and Mary Neal asked what I was wearing as it had a horseshoe neck, which was way ahead of its time. There was another designer called Kiki Byrne; she was amazing. I will never forget seeing a black dress by her – my first black dress – and my heart was pounding.

I studied design at Brighton Art School for two years, but I could see that I was going to have to go into a workroom and just pick up pins for about 20 years before I could design. I never thought I would be able to start my own business because I couldn't pattern cut, well not properly. I remember my teacher, Joanne Brogden (who eventually became head of the Royal College of Art), said to me: 'I can't believe you've passed. I can't believe it. This dress has flap pockets but there are no pockets underneath, just the flaps!' She said that I was much better at drawing so should 'go and draw'.

Years later I met Fitz. He was really on the ball and said to me, 'You've got to stop doing that [fashion illustration]. It's all going to come to an end.' Because he worked in advertising, he could see that photography was coming in. They were starting to use photography for the shows, so he told me I had to get back into designing. I would never have done the designing without him; it was too much. You can't just design dresses and that's it. There has got to be something to go with them, the production side.

"I never thought I would be able to start my own business because I couldn't pattern cut, well not properly"

Fitz went and got to know all the manufacturers, and they loved him. Mr Savva was wonderful. He was a Greek Cypriot and didn't speak any English, which was a bit difficult, but he got on really well with Fitz and he was really patient. I really don't know how we found him; he fell into our lives. Everybody fell into our lives!

MP Was the gingham dress – the first item for Biba's Postal Boutique – one of your big lessons?

BH Oh yes. We had to have the fabric sitting there, which was an investment, and then we'd send it to the manufacturer and hope he didn't screw it up, because if he cut it wrong it was our investment going down the drain. It was a learning curve. I mean, you learn very fast. Say you're doing a jersey, and it was all beautiful in the sample length and stretchy, and then your fabric comes in and it doesn't stretch at all, you have to carry the can. You just have to send it out and hope for the best. It's awful. We got 17,000 orders of the gingham dress and only had about 60 returned, which was amazing. Then the idiot Fitz and his marketing genius – I could have killed him – sent out a leaflet with the orders, 'and now you can buy it in pale blue'. It was still 25 shillings, cheap even in those days.

BELOW The Royal Drawing Society, certificates awarded to Barbara Hulanicki, 1950 and 1952

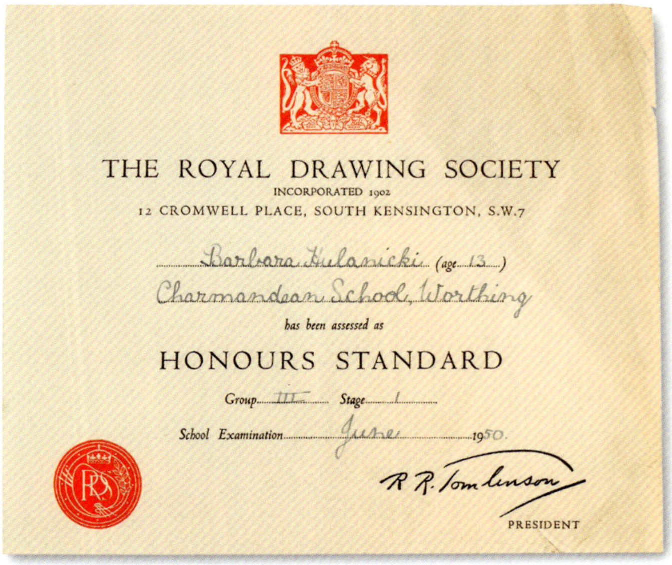
THE ROYAL DRAWING SOCIETY
INCORPORATED 1902
12 CROMWELL PLACE, SOUTH KENSINGTON, S.W.7
Barbara Hulanicki (age 13)
Charmandean School, Worthing
has been assessed as
HONOURS STANDARD
Group III Stage 1
School Examination June 1950
R R Tomlinson
PRESIDENT

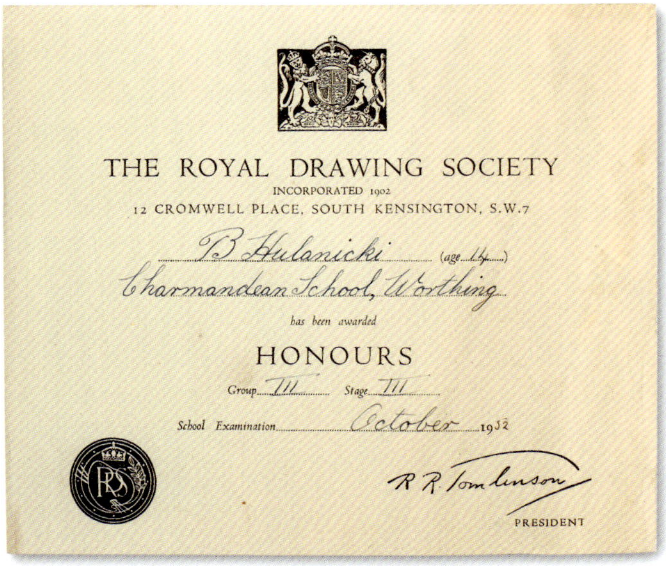
THE ROYAL DRAWING SOCIETY
INCORPORATED 1902
12 CROMWELL PLACE, SOUTH KENSINGTON, S.W.7
B Hulanicki (age 14)
Charmandean School, Worthing
has been awarded
HONOURS
Group III Stage III
School Examination October 1952
R R Tomlinson
PRESIDENT

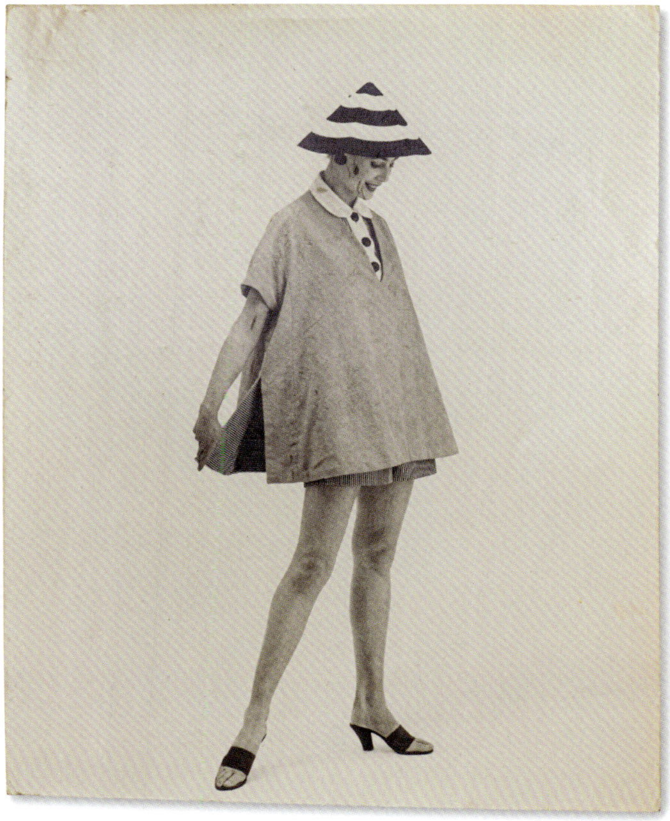

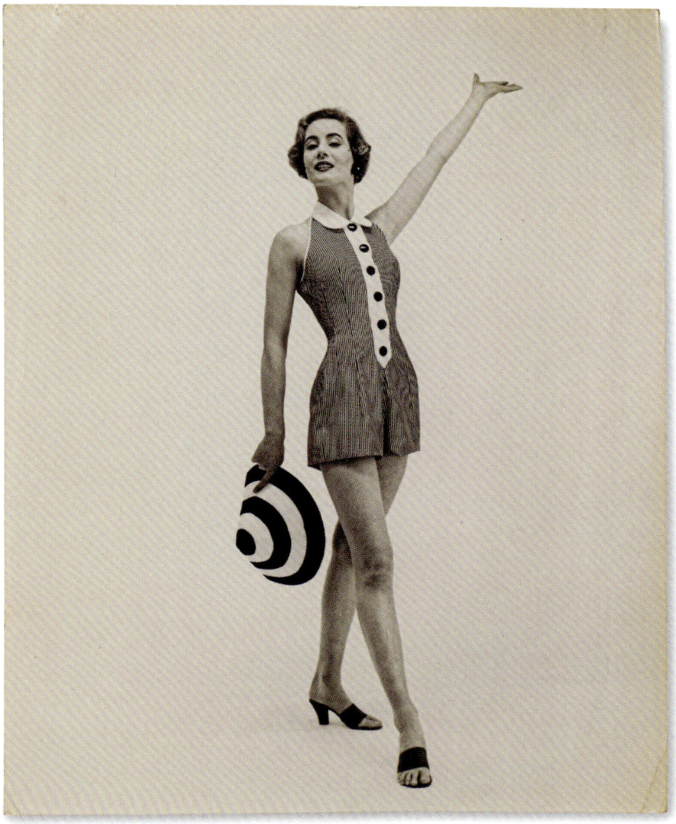

ABOVE LEFT & RIGHT Model wearing Barbara's winning design for the beachwear section of a fashion competition held by the *Evening Standard* newspaper, 1955

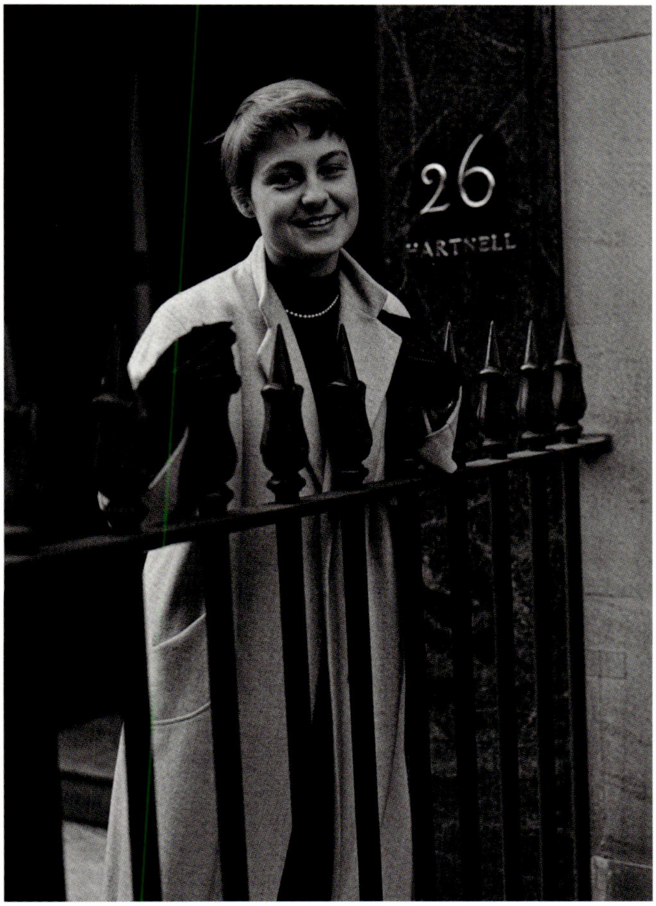

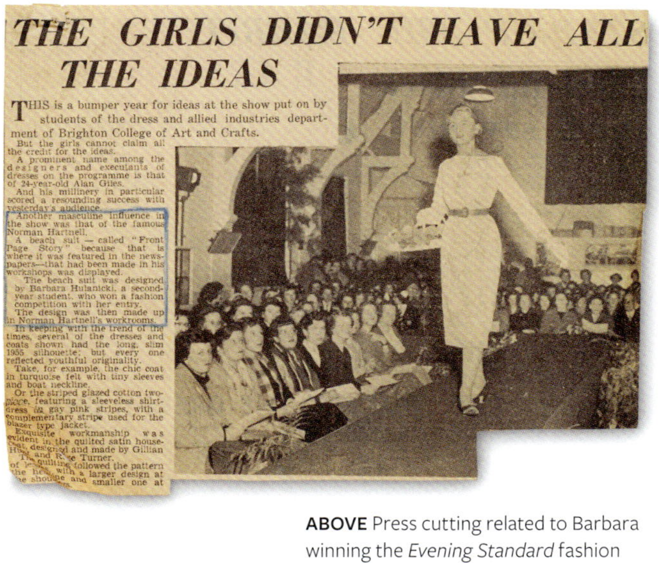

THE GIRLS DIDN'T HAVE ALL THE IDEAS

THIS is a bumper year for ideas at the show put on by students of the dress and allied industries department of Brighton College of Art and Crafts.

But the girls cannot claim all the credit for the ideas.

A prominent name among the designers and executants of dresses on the programme is that of 24-year-old Alan Giles.

And his millinery in particular scored a resounding success with yesterday's audience.

Another masculine influence in the show was that of the famous Norman Hartnell.

A beach suit — called "Front Page Story" because that is where it was featured in the newspapers—that had been made in his workshops was displayed.

The beach suit was designed by Barbara Hulanicki, a second-year student, who won a fashion competition with her entry.

The design was then made up in Norman Hartnell's workrooms.

In keeping with the trend of the times, several of the dresses and coats shown had the long, slim 1955 silhouette; but every one reflected youthful originality.

Take, for example, the chic coat in turquoise felt with tiny sleeves and boat neckline.

Or the striped glazed cotton two-piece, featuring a sleeveless shirt-dress in gay pink stripes, with a complementary stripe used for the blazer type jacket.

Exquisite workmanship was evident in the quilted satin house-coat, designed and made by Gillian H[illegible] and R[illegible]e Turner.

The quilting followed the pattern of [illegible] the he[illegible], with a larger design at the shou[illegible] and smaller one at

ABOVE Press cutting related to Barbara winning the *Evening Standard* fashion competition, 1955

LEFT Barbara Hulanicki visiting the Norman Hartnell couture house on Bruton Street, London, as part of the prize for winning the *Evening Standard* fashion competition, 1955

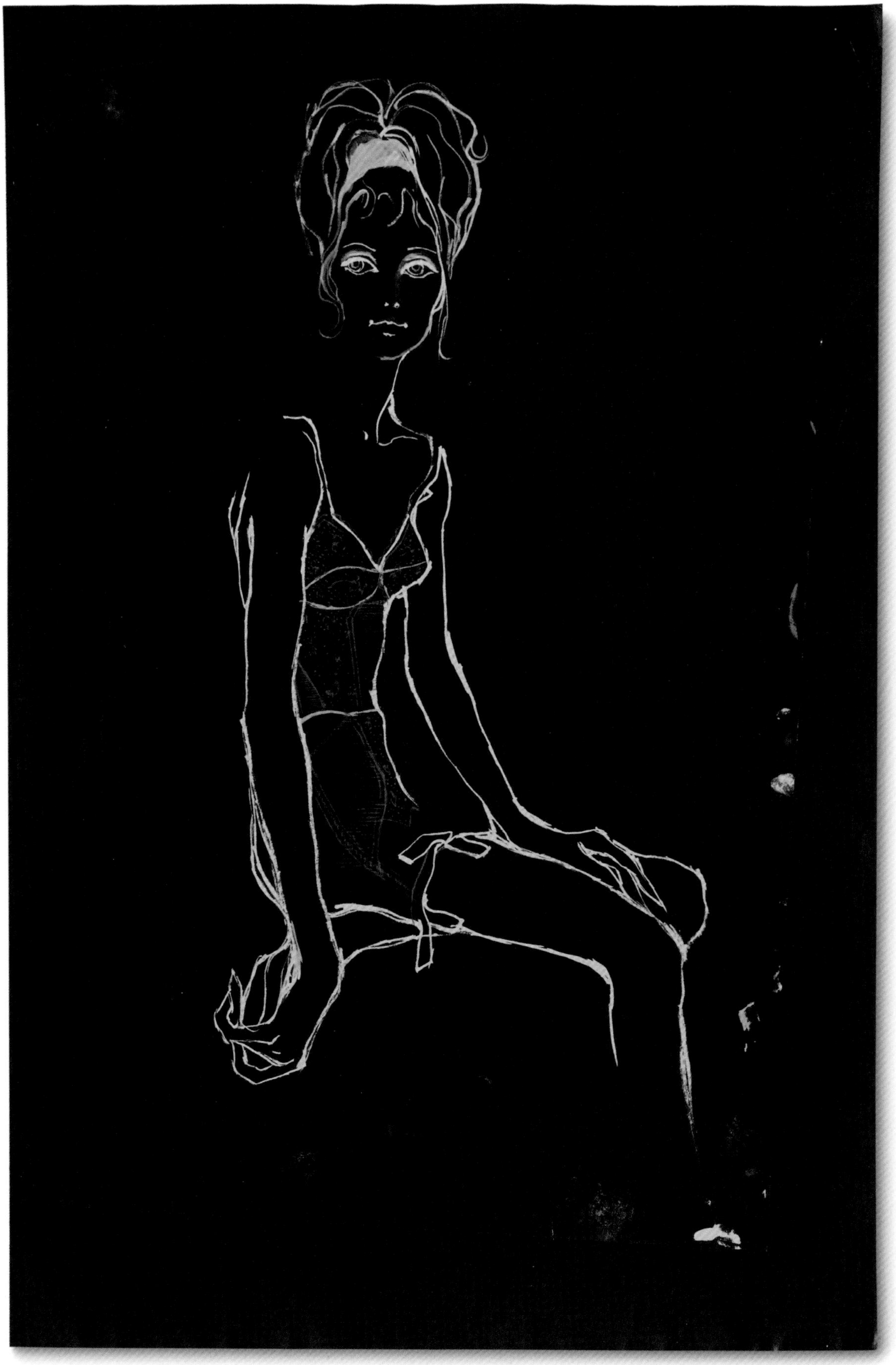

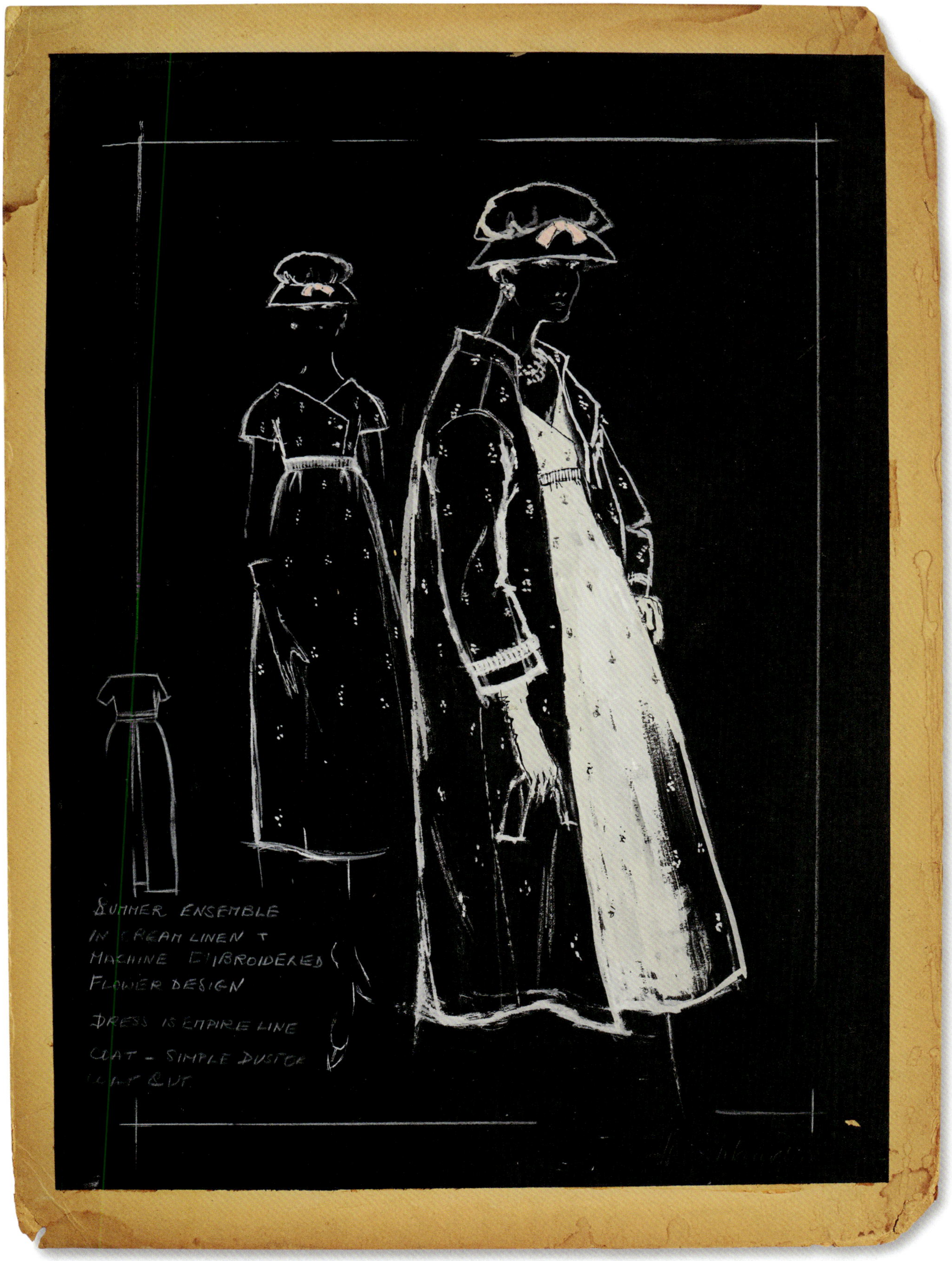

OPPOSITE & ABOVE Early fashion illustrations for Helen Jardine Artists, gouache, Barbara Hulanicki, c.1955–6

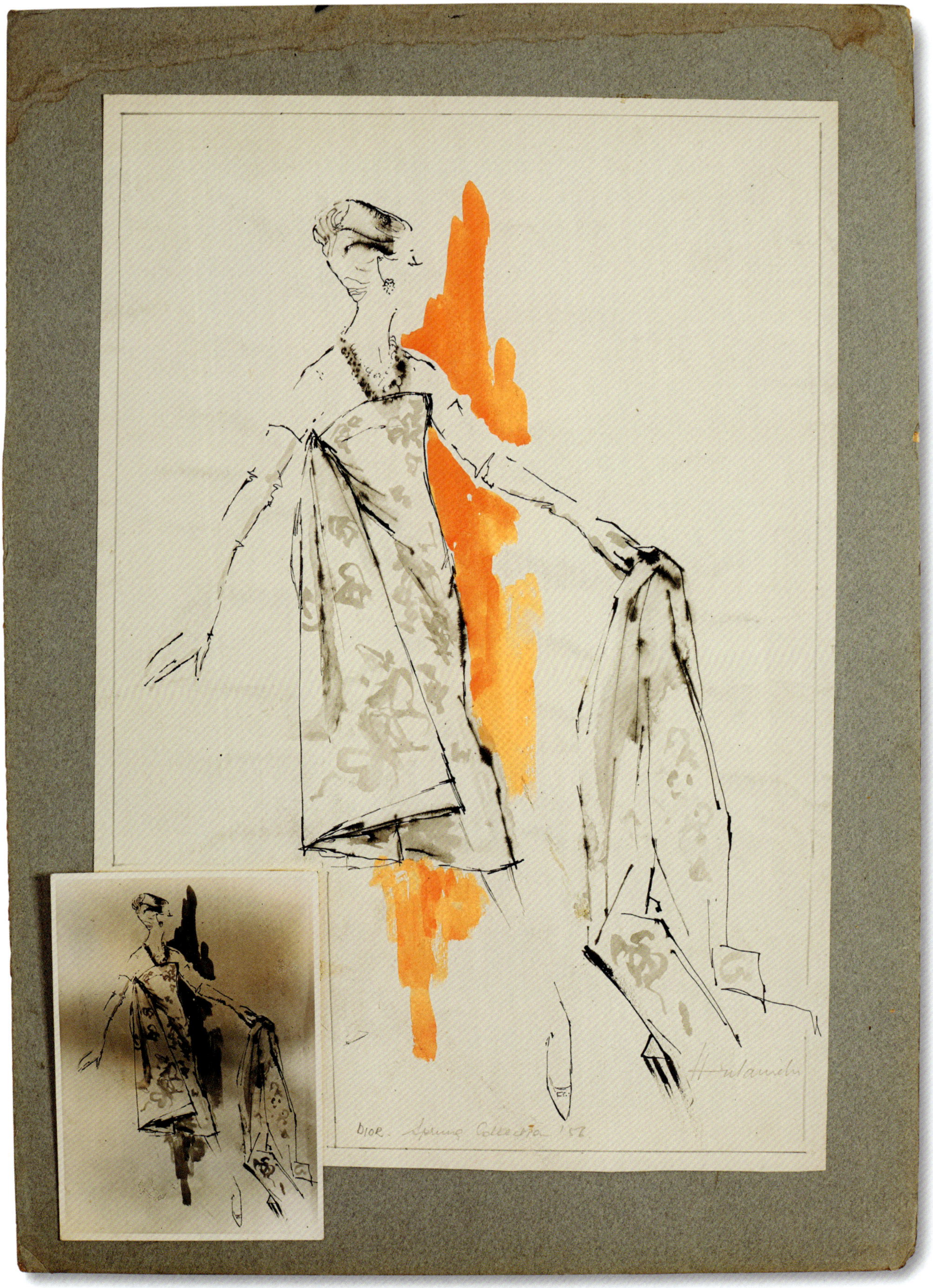
DIOR. Spring Collection '58

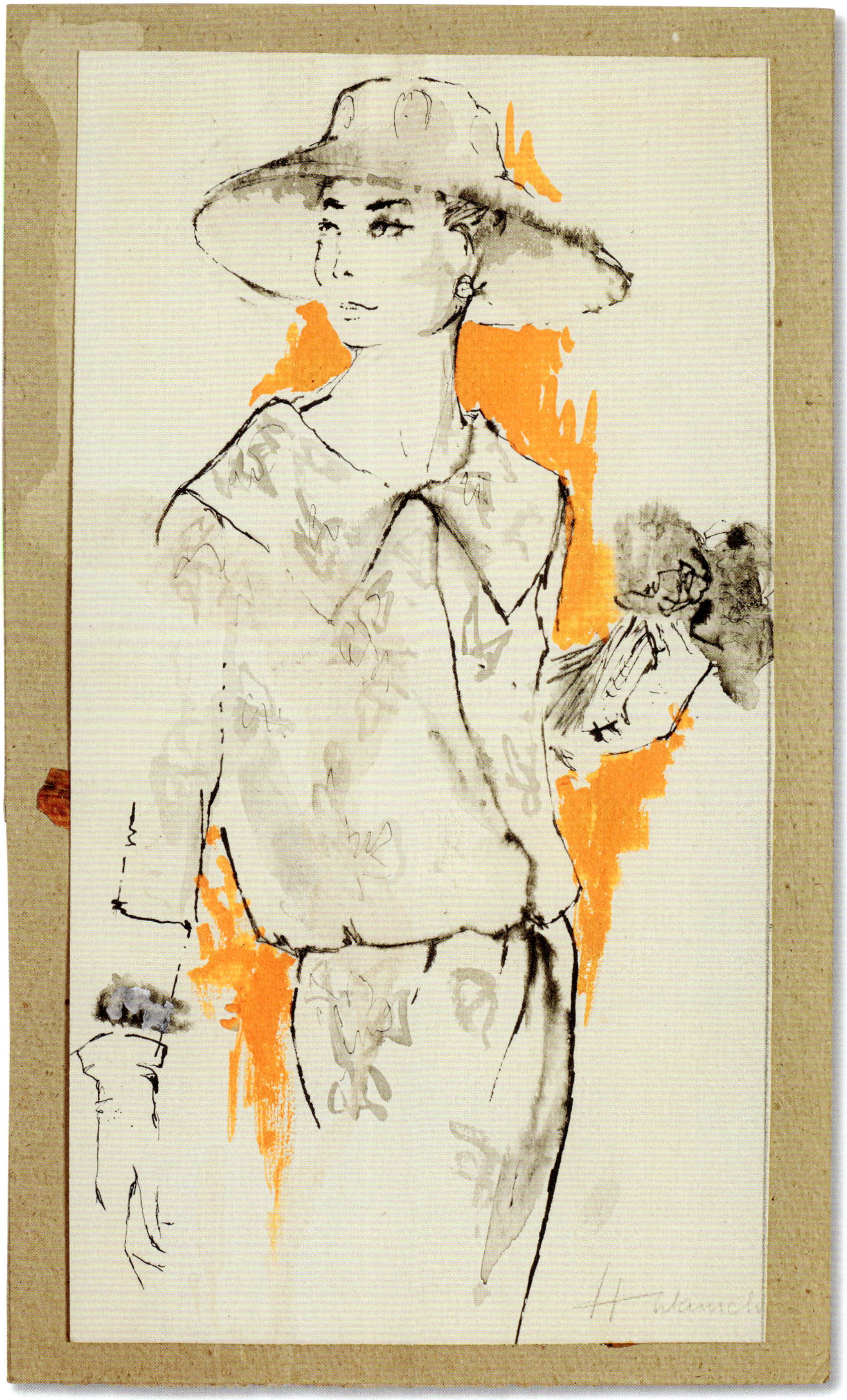

OPPOSITE & RIGHT
Fashion illustrations, ink and watercolour, Barbara Hulanicki, late 1950s

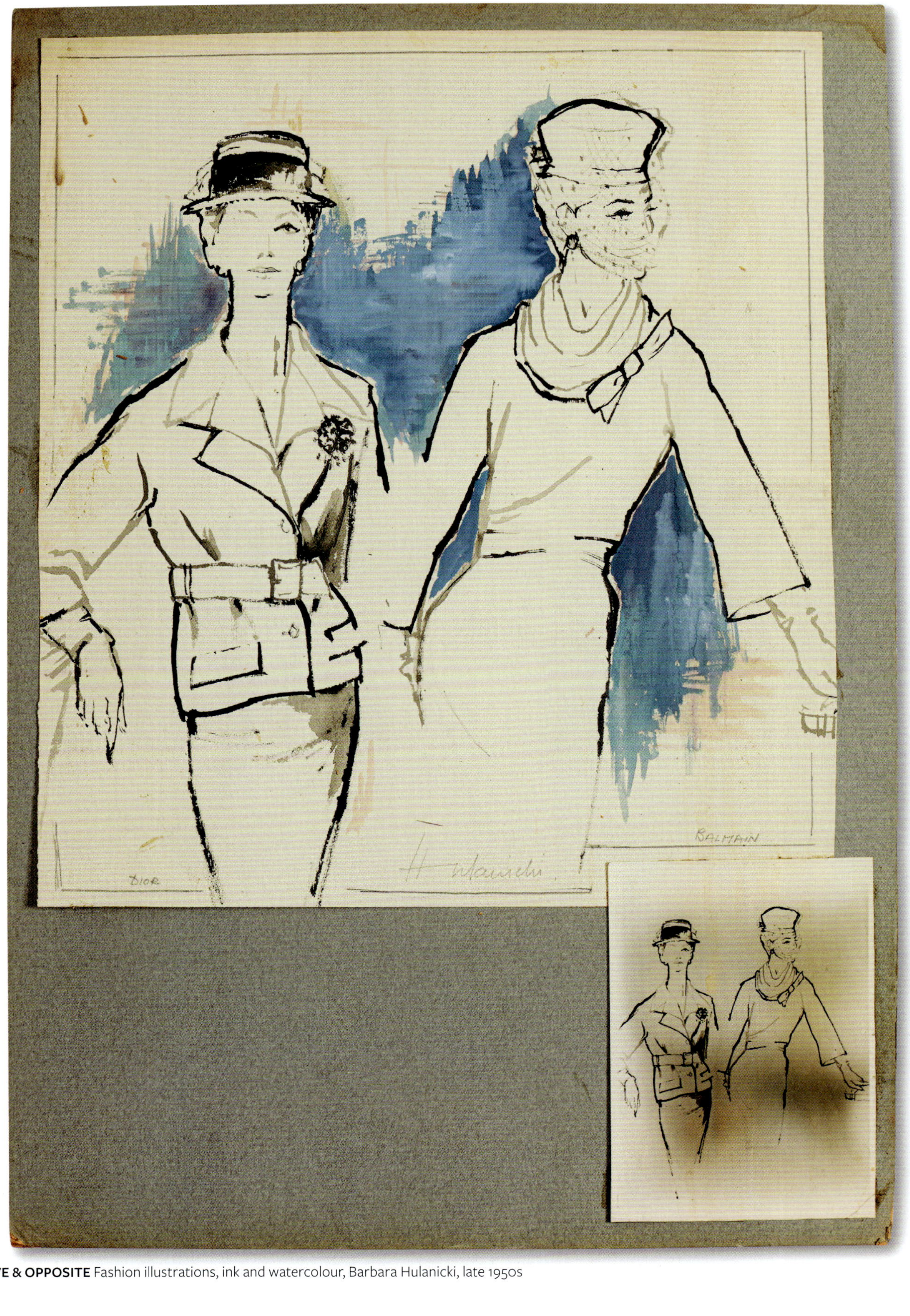

ABOVE & OPPOSITE Fashion illustrations, ink and watercolour, Barbara Hulanicki, late 1950s

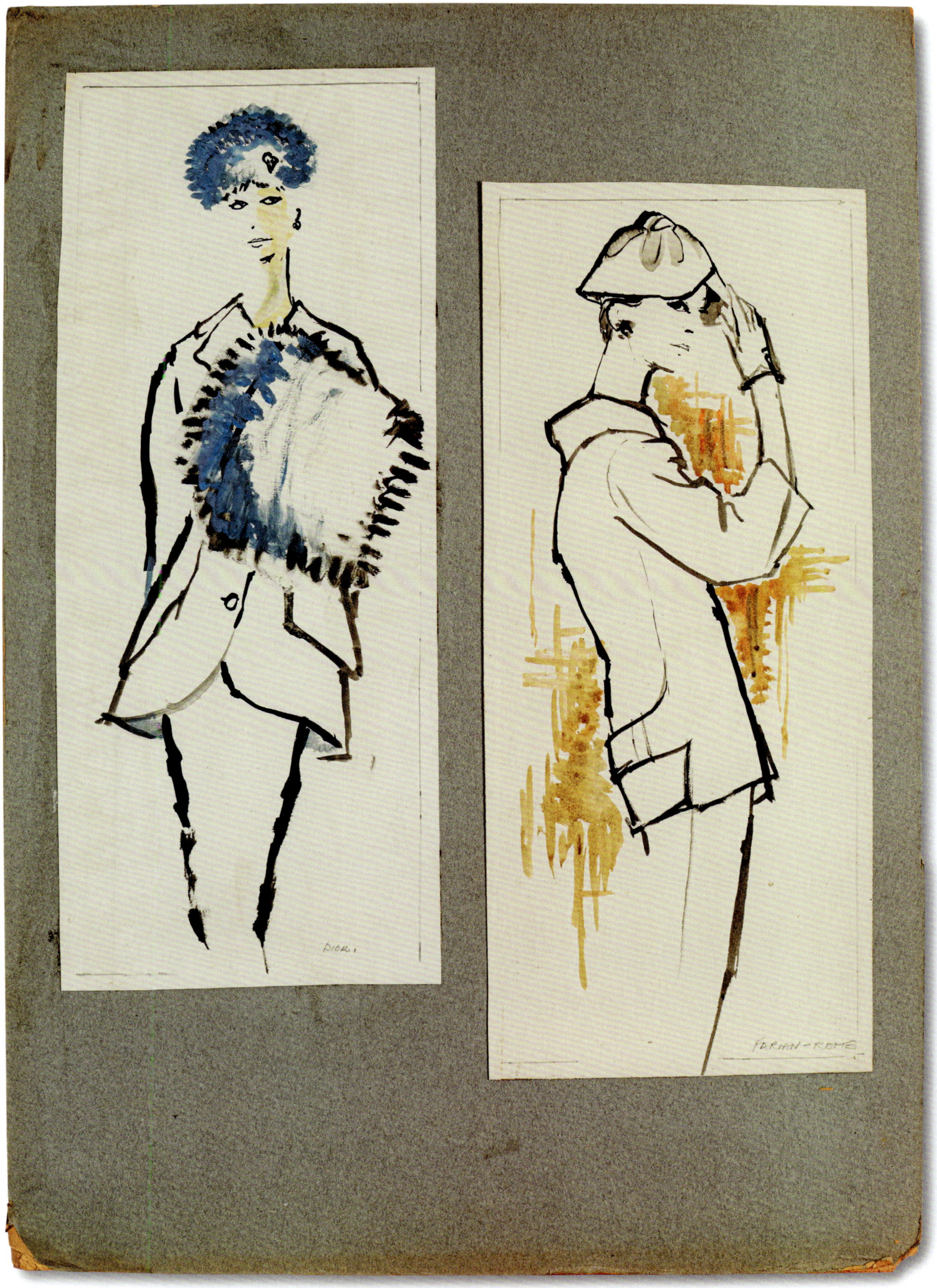
DIOR.
FABIAN-ROME

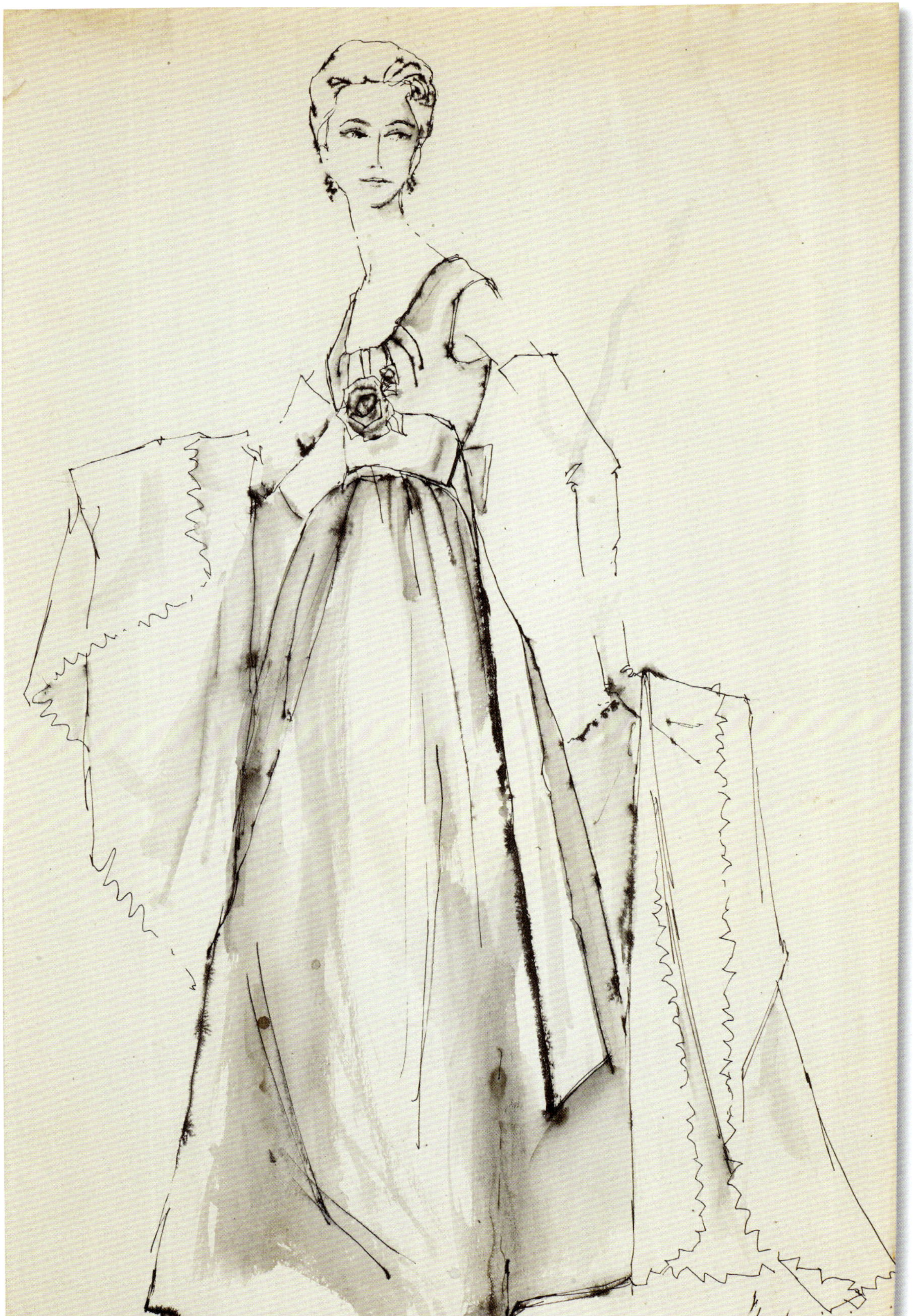
Hulanicki.

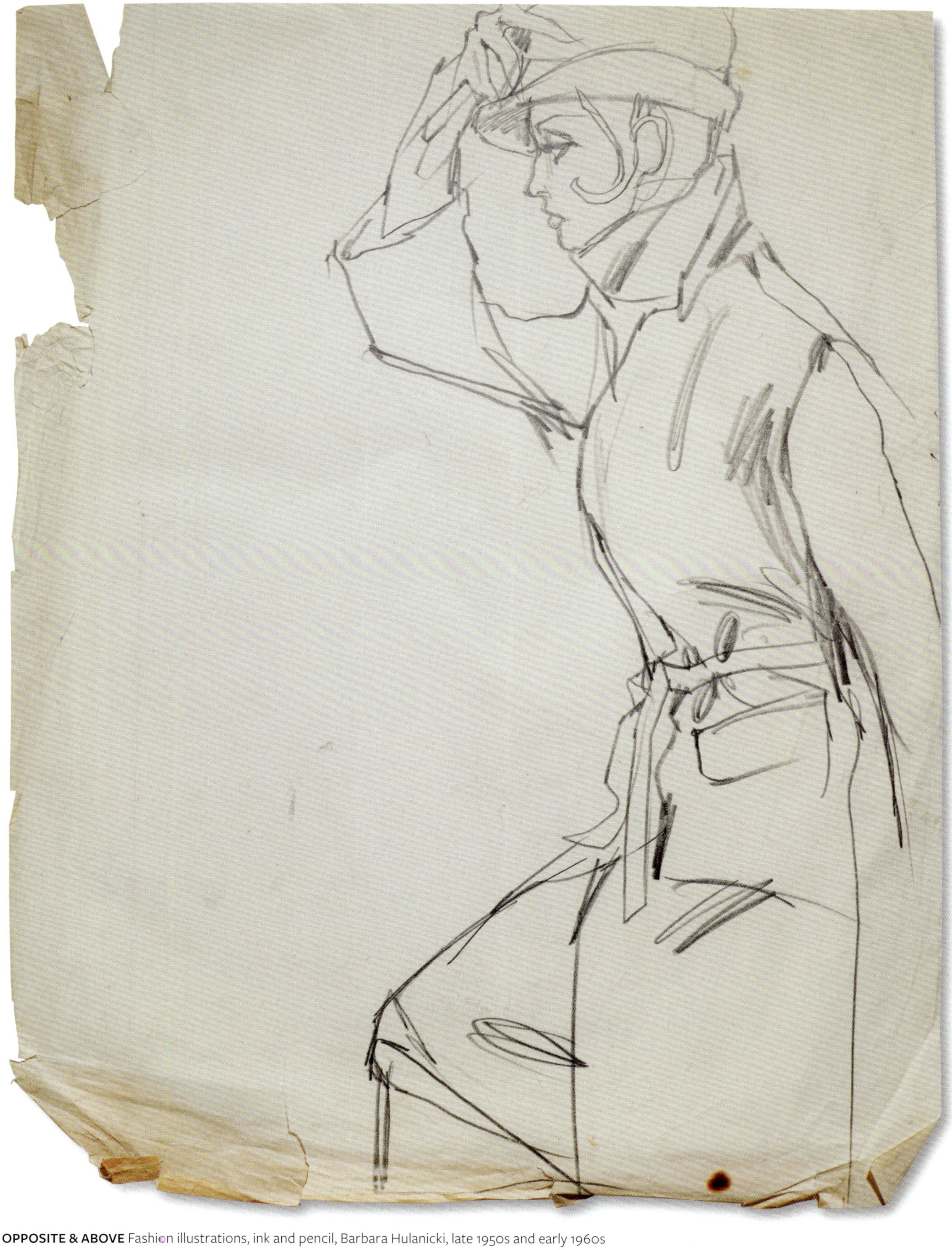

OPPOSITE & ABOVE Fashion illustrations, ink and pencil, Barbara Hulanicki, late 1950s and early 1960s

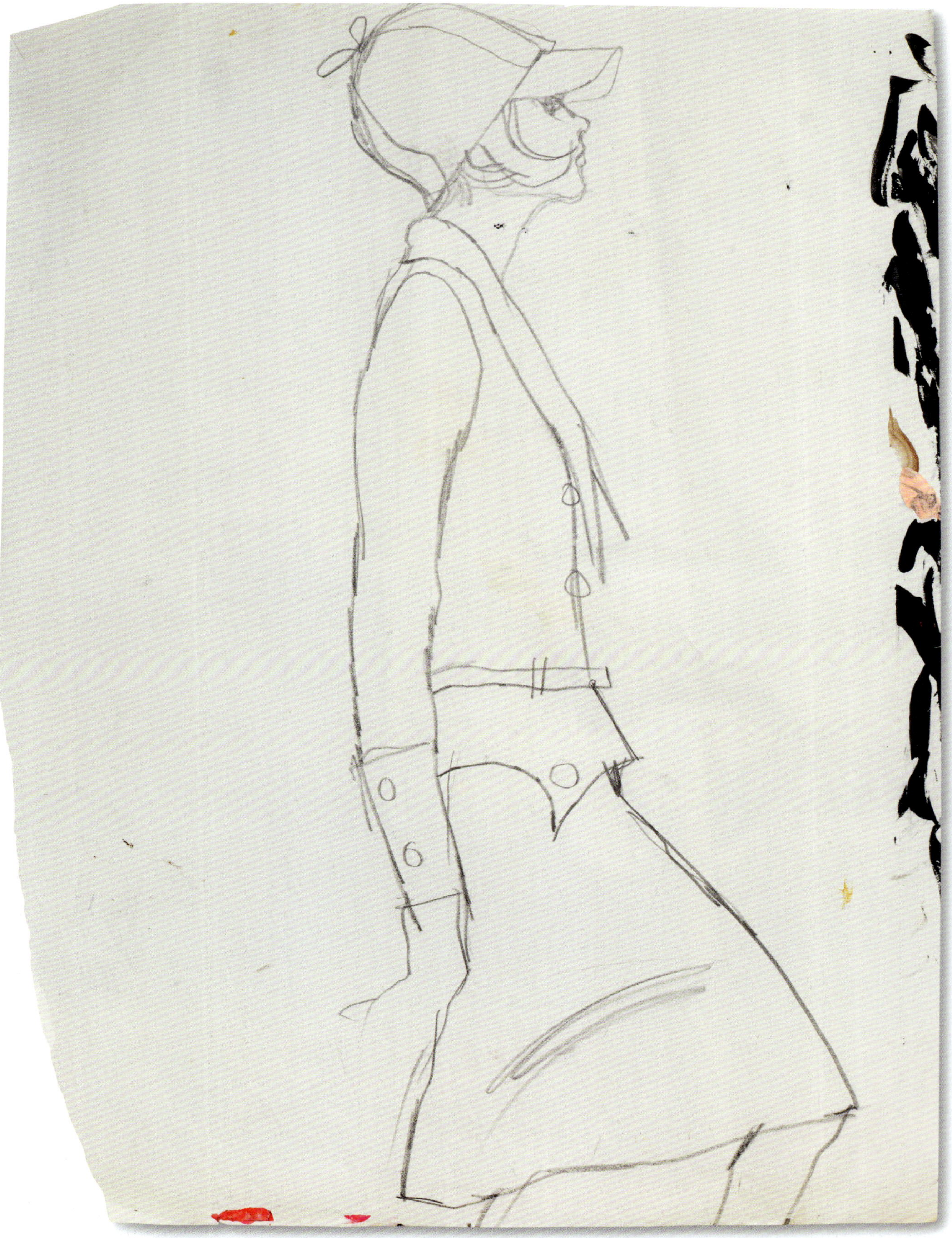
Fashion illustration, pencil and gouache, Barbara Hulanicki, early 1960s

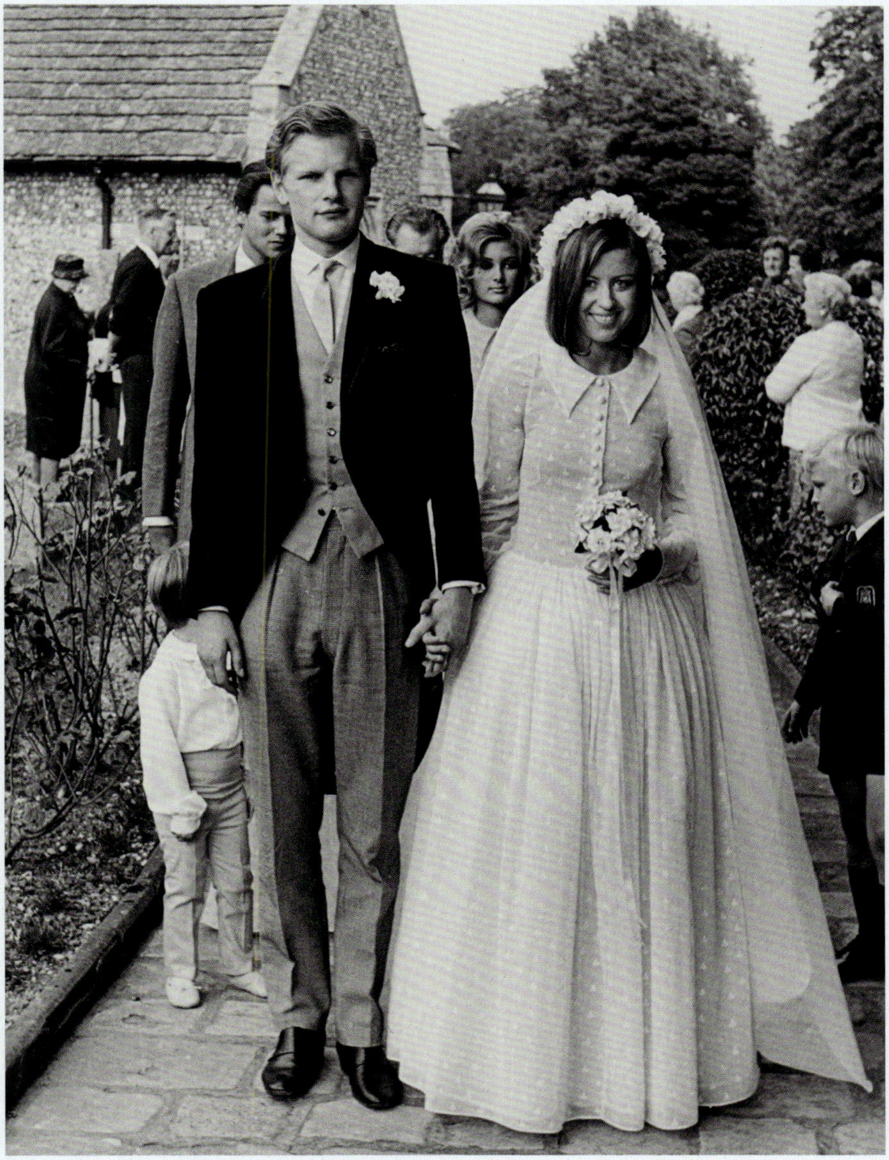

JENNIE PEEL

~ FASHION AND PR ASSISTANT

Jennie Peel on her wedding day wearing a dress designed by Barbara Hulanicki and made at Biba, 1967

I first met Barbara in the 1950s when she came to a party at our family home as she and Peter, my brother, were dating at the time. She was a student at Brighton Art School, and she stunned us all. I had certainly never seen anyone so chic, beautiful and fun before. She was always laughing – a great giggler – and we became lifelong friends.

Sometime later Barbara married Fitz and they started their own design company. She had been asked by Felicity Green, journalist at the *Daily Mirror*, to design the now-famous pink gingham shift dress and matching scarf, which was featured in the paper. Sales took off from day one, and I received a panicked call from Barbara and Fitz asking me to help out as they had received 8,000 orders by post on the first day. What was to follow were days (and nights) working to process all the orders – some without payments and many asking for sizes that we didn't do. The orders eventually reached 17,000. We spent hours sorting and laughing so much. Biba was born.

In the second half of the 1960s, I worked at the *Daily Express* as a fashion assistant. Biba was an editorial gift, with new Biba stories every day: the publication of the beautifully photographed catalogue produced four times a year, the trip to Zermatt to cover the opening of a Biba ski boutique, or a new delivery of the now-famous knee-high Biba boots, which everybody wanted and would queue for hours to buy.

I later went to work in PR, and our offices were opposite the Biba shop in Church Street. Biba staff star-spotters would alert us to who was in the shop, and we'd run across and hide behind the hat stands to have a peak! We saw Brigitte Bardot and Marianne Faithfull to name just two.

How lucky we all were to be there at the birth of Biba and to have such wonderful memories. I feel so lucky to have a lifelong and very special friendship with Barbara.

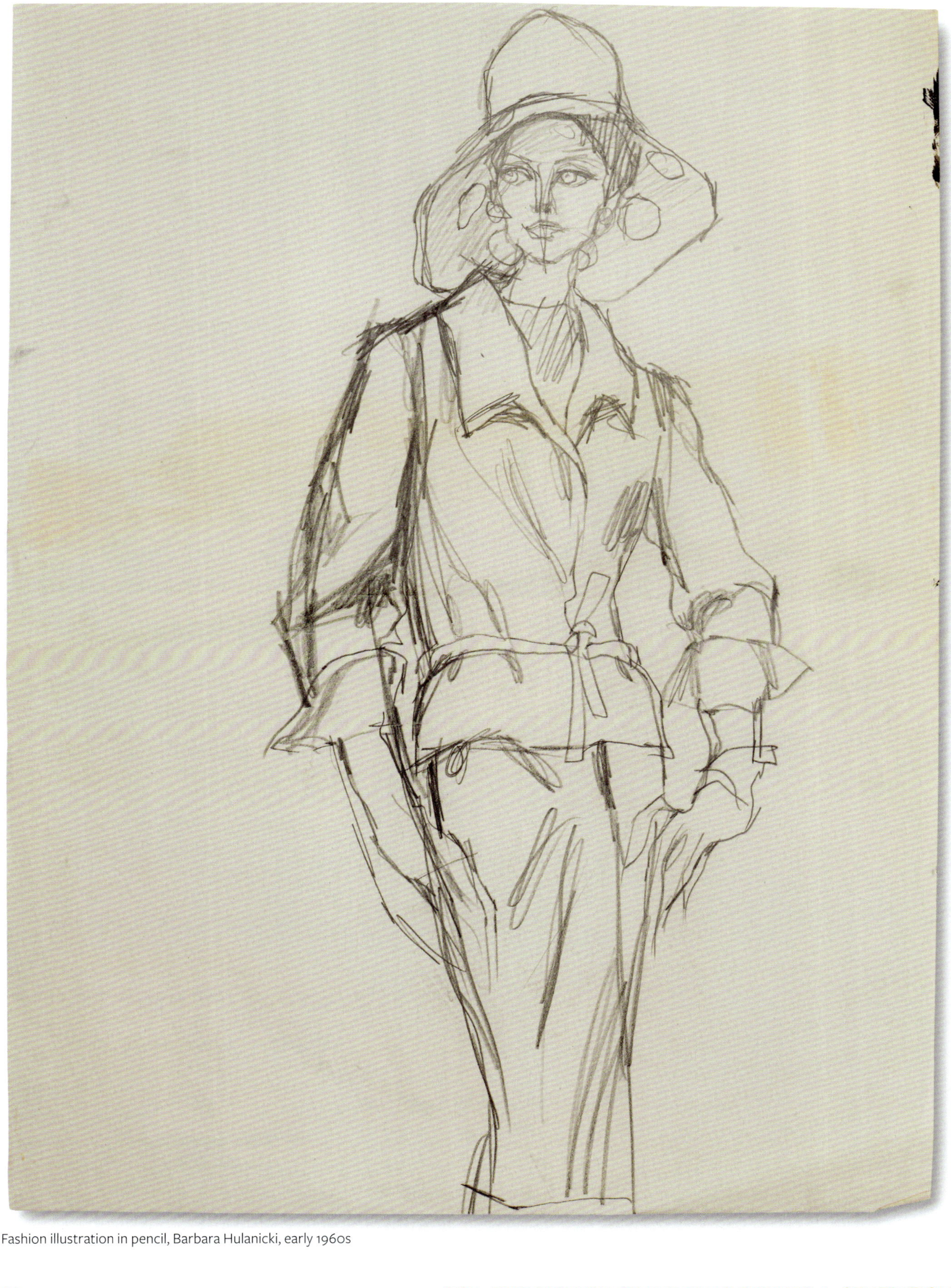

Fashion illustration in pencil, Barbara Hulanicki, early 1960s

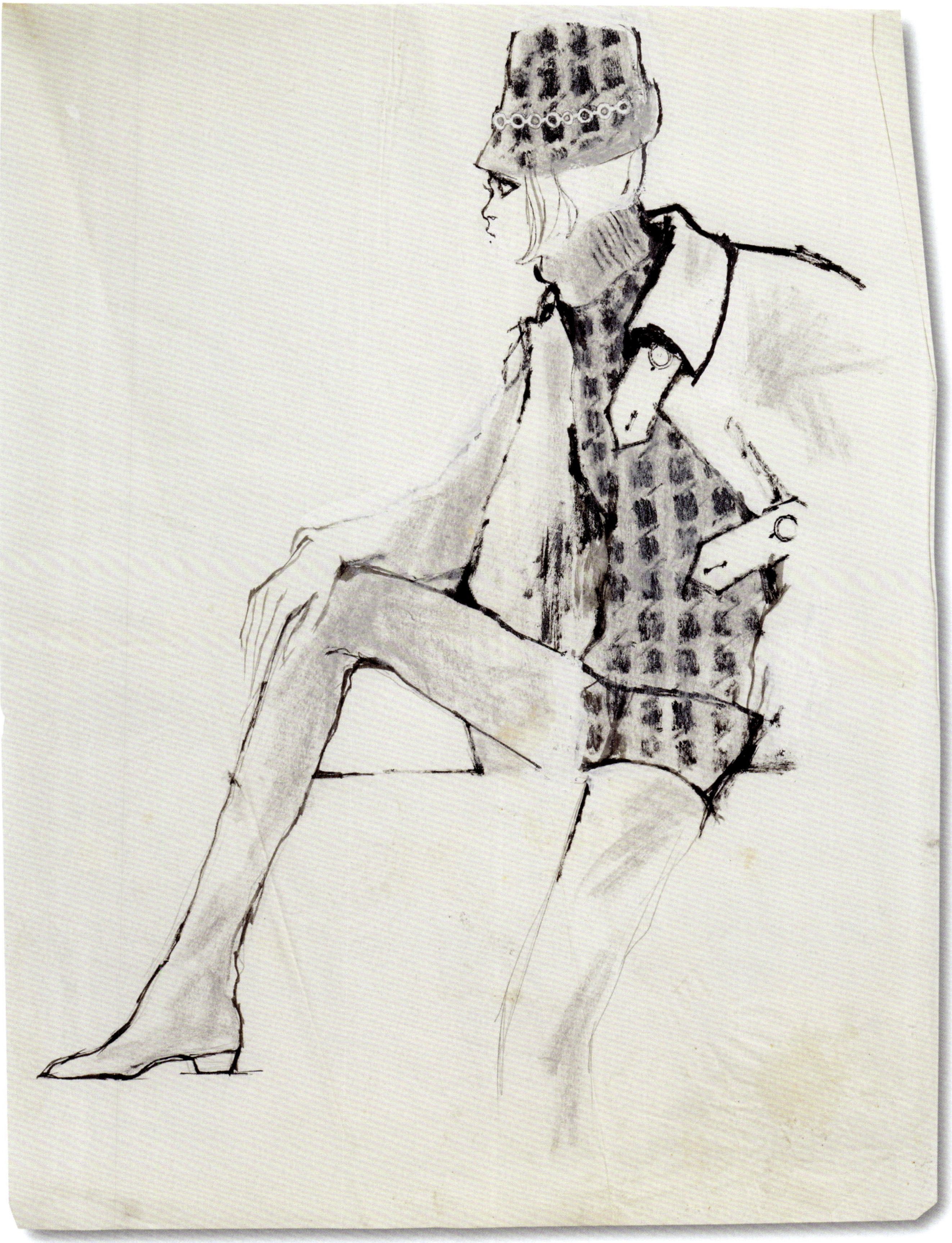

Fashion illustration for editorial (see p. 58), watercolour and gouache, Barbara Hulanicki, c.1963

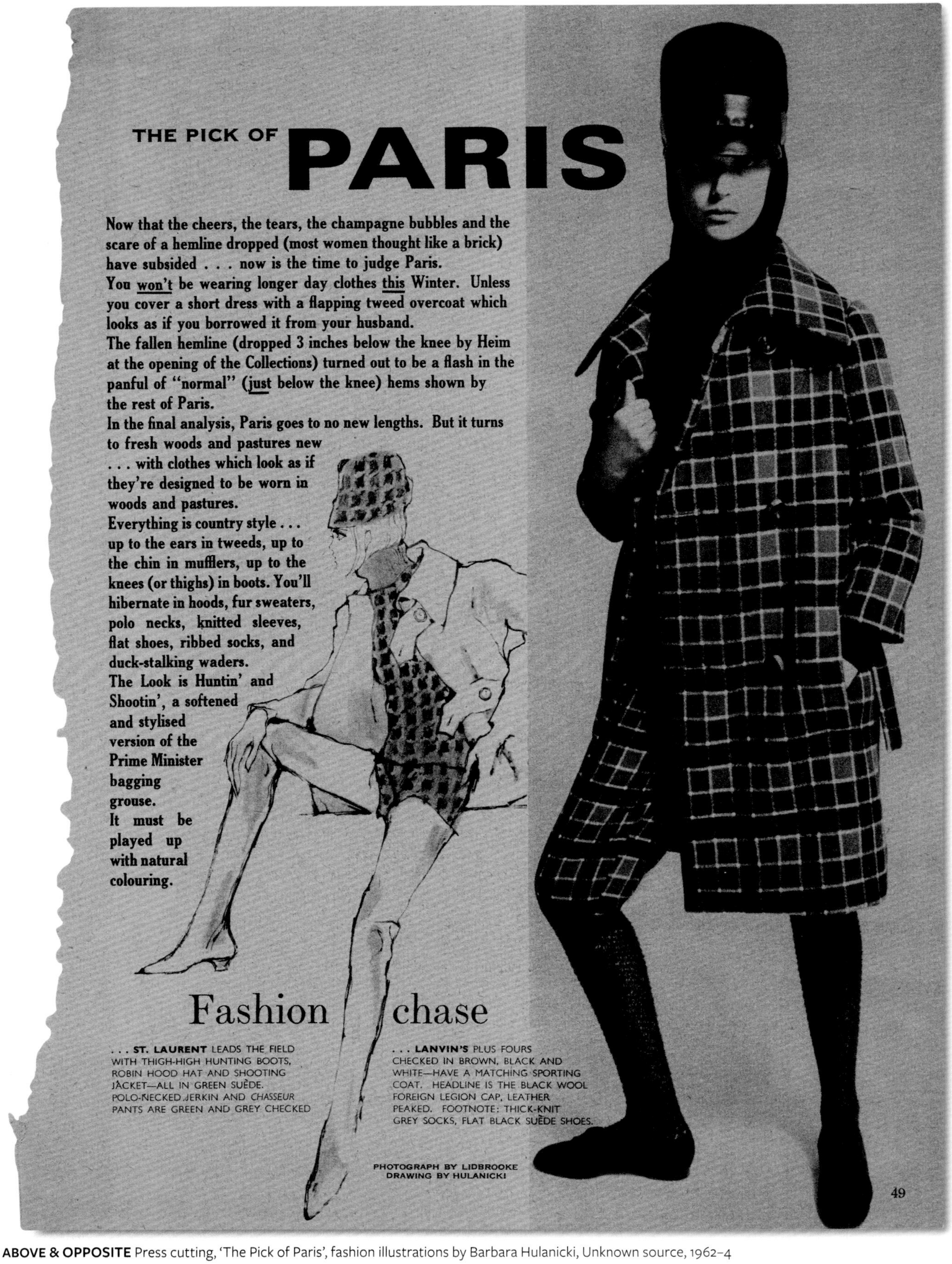

THE PICK OF **PARIS**

Now that the cheers, the tears, the champagne bubbles and the scare of a hemline dropped (most women thought like a brick) have subsided . . . now is the time to judge Paris.

You won't be wearing longer day clothes this Winter. Unless you cover a short dress with a flapping tweed overcoat which looks as if you borrowed it from your husband.

The fallen hemline (dropped 3 inches below the knee by Heim at the opening of the Collections) turned out to be a flash in the panful of "normal" (just below the knee) hems shown by the rest of Paris.

In the final analysis, Paris goes to no new lengths. But it turns to fresh woods and pastures new . . . with clothes which look as if they're designed to be worn in woods and pastures.

Everything is country style . . . up to the ears in tweeds, up to the chin in mufflers, up to the knees (or thighs) in boots. You'll hibernate in hoods, fur sweaters, polo necks, knitted sleeves, flat shoes, ribbed socks, and duck-stalking waders.

The Look is Huntin' and Shootin', a softened and stylised version of the Prime Minister bagging grouse.

It must be played up with natural colouring.

Fashion chase

. . . **ST. LAURENT** LEADS THE FIELD WITH THIGH-HIGH HUNTING BOOTS, ROBIN HOOD HAT AND SHOOTING JACKET—ALL IN GREEN SUÈDE. POLO-NECKED JERKIN AND *CHASSEUR* PANTS ARE GREEN AND GREY CHECKED

. . . **LANVIN'S** PLUS FOURS CHECKED IN BROWN, BLACK AND WHITE—HAVE A MATCHING SPORTING COAT. HEADLINE IS THE BLACK WOOL FOREIGN LEGION CAP, LEATHER PEAKED. FOOTNOTE: THICK-KNIT GREY SOCKS, FLAT BLACK SUÈDE SHOES.

PHOTOGRAPH BY LIDBROOKE
DRAWING BY HULANICKI

49

ABOVE & OPPOSITE Press cutting, 'The Pick of Paris', fashion illustrations by Barbara Hulanicki, Unknown source, 1962–4

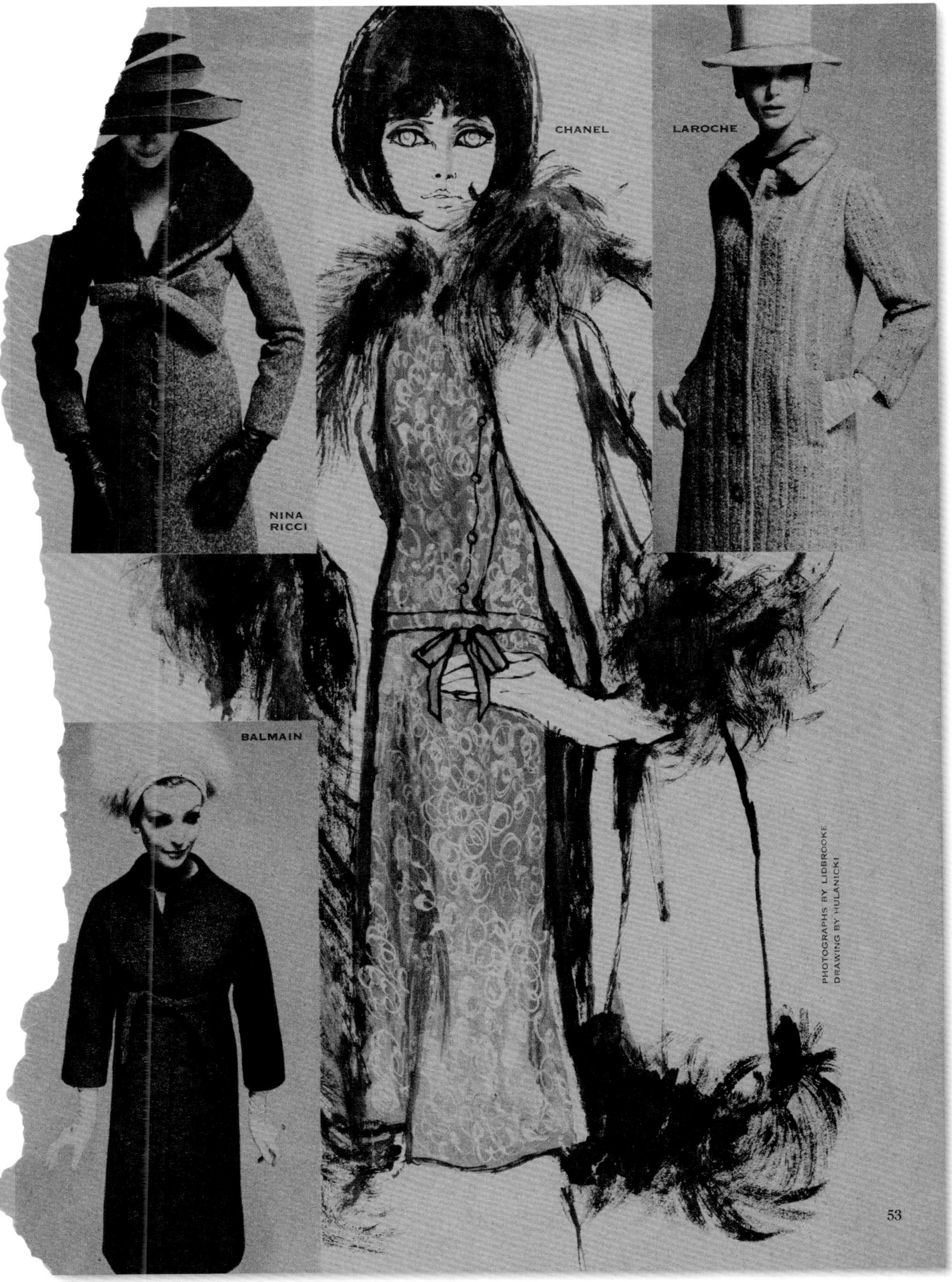
CHANEL
LAROCHE
NINA
RICCI
BALMAIN
PHOTOGRAPHS BY LIDBROOKE
DRAWING BY HULANICKI
53

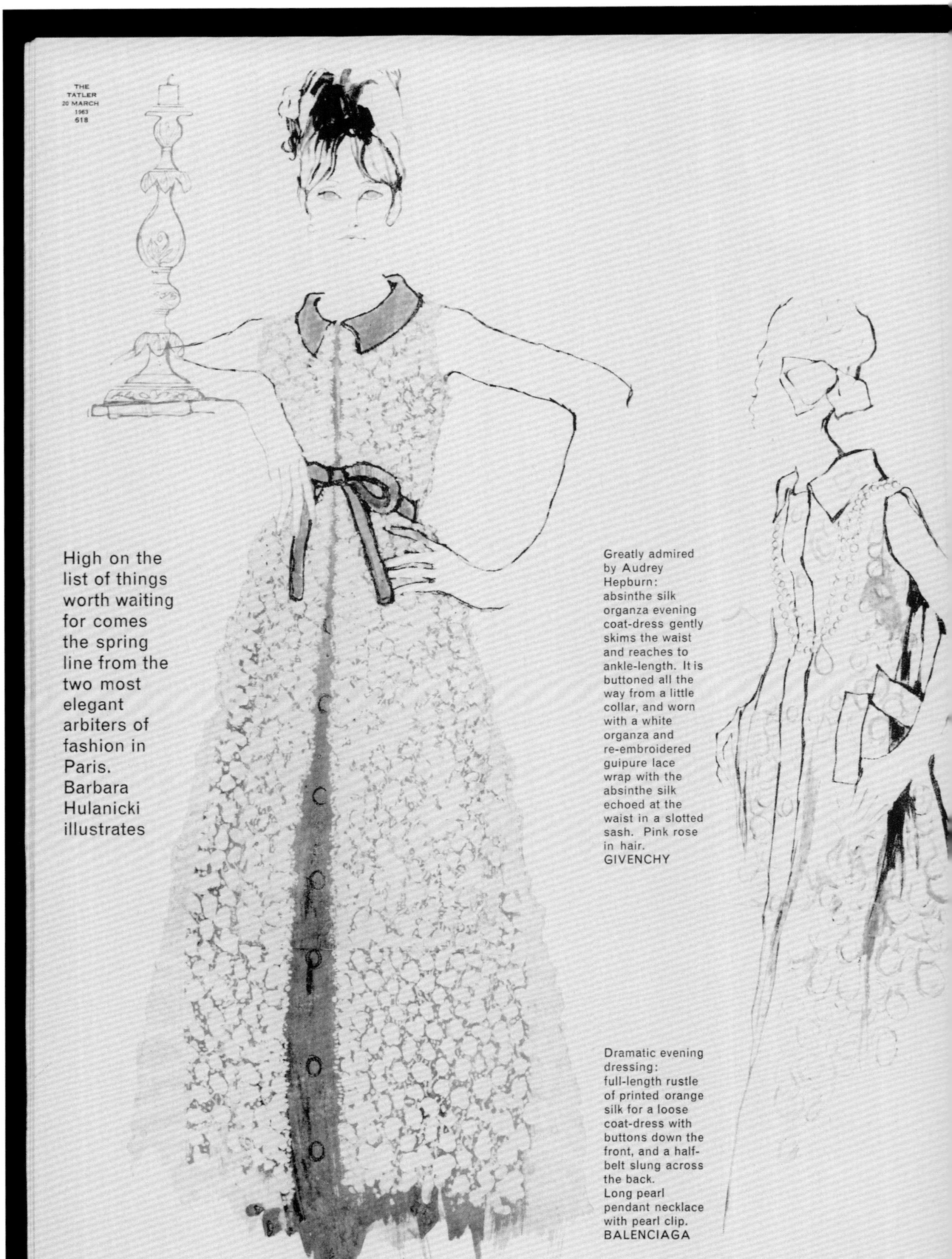

THE TATLER
20 MARCH
1963
618

High on the list of things worth waiting for comes the spring line from the two most elegant arbiters of fashion in Paris. Barbara Hulanicki illustrates

Greatly admired by Audrey Hepburn: absinthe silk organza evening coat-dress gently skims the waist and reaches to ankle-length. It is buttoned all the way from a little collar, and worn with a white organza and re-embroidered guipure lace wrap with the absinthe silk echoed at the waist in a slotted sash. Pink rose in hair.
GIVENCHY

Dramatic evening dressing: full-length rustle of printed orange silk for a loose coat-dress with buttons down the front, and a half-belt slung across the back.
Long pearl pendant necklace with pearl clip.
BALENCIAGA

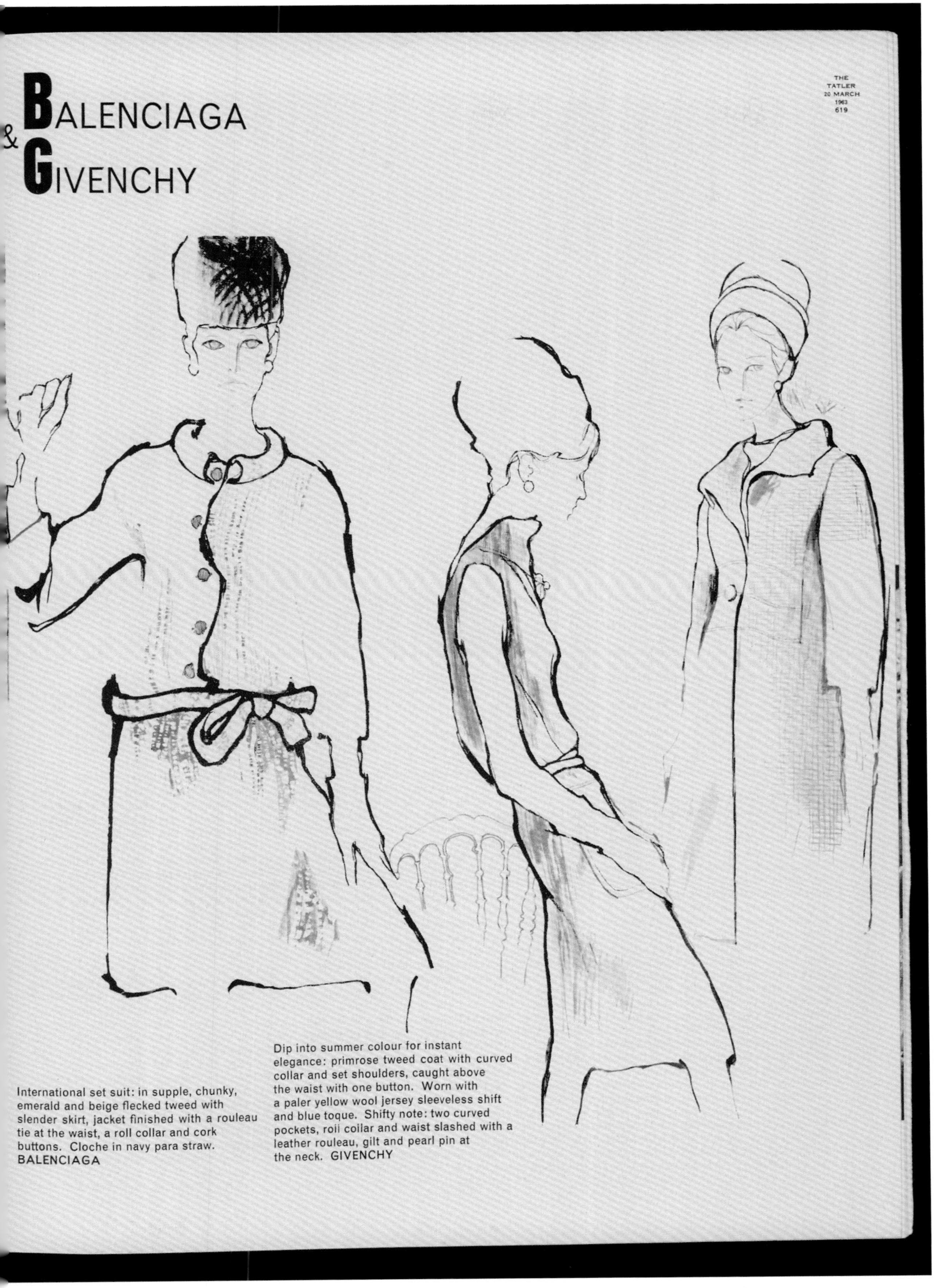

THE TATLER 20 MARCH 1963 619

BALENCIAGA & GIVENCHY

International set suit: in supple, chunky, emerald and beige flecked tweed with slender skirt, jacket finished with a rouleau tie at the waist, a roll collar and cork buttons. Cloche in navy para straw. BALENCIAGA

Dip into summer colour for instant elegance: primrose tweed coat with curved collar and set shoulders, caught above the waist with one button. Worn with a paler yellow wool jersey sleeveless shift and blue toque. Shifty note: two curved pockets, roii coilar and waist slashed with a leather rouleau, gilt and pearl pin at the neck. GIVENCHY

Press cutting, fashion illustrations, 'Balenciaga & Givenchy', by Barbara Hulanicki, *Tatler*, March 1963

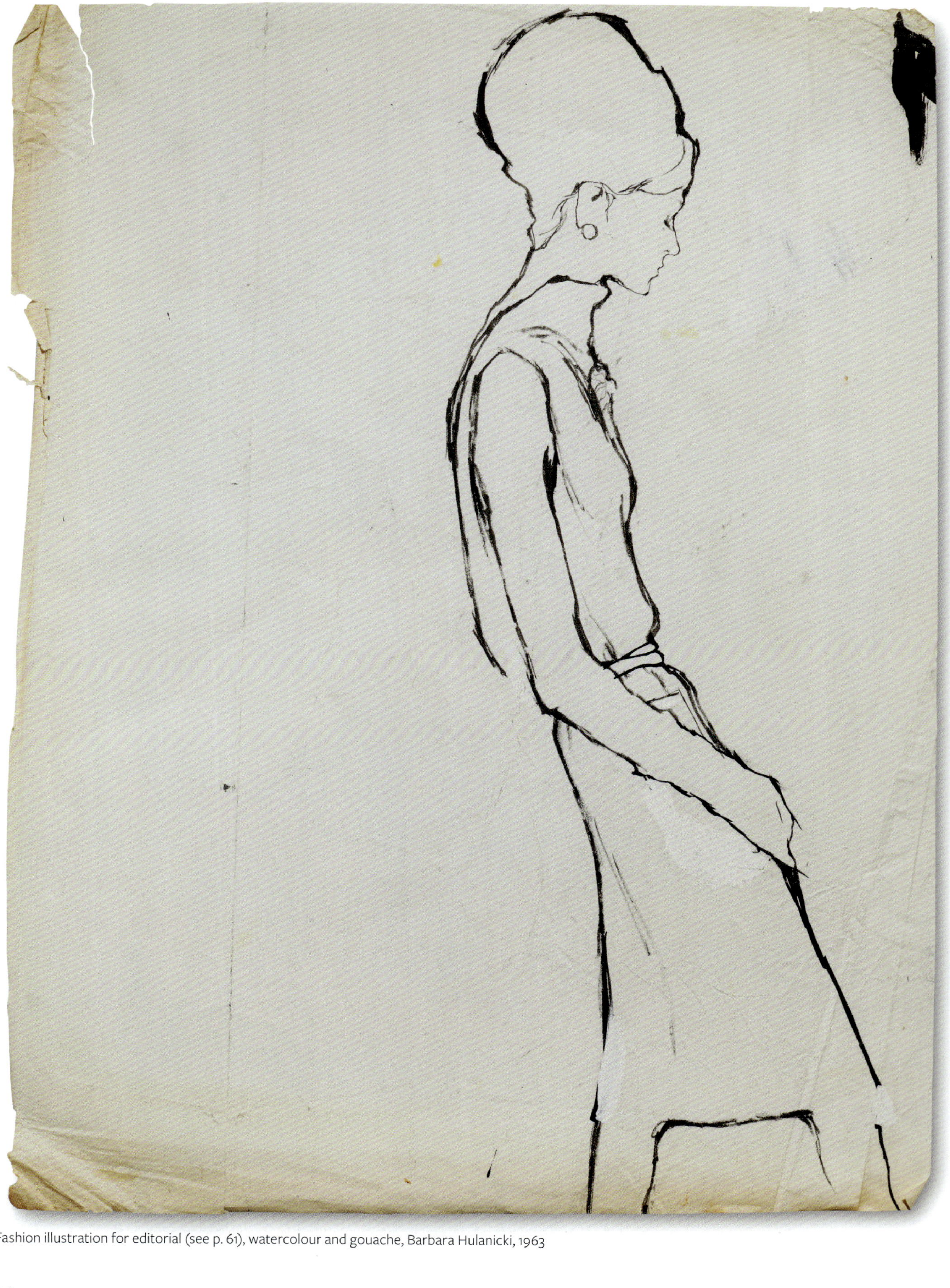

Fashion illustration for editorial (see p. 61), watercolour and gouache, Barbara Hulanicki, 1963

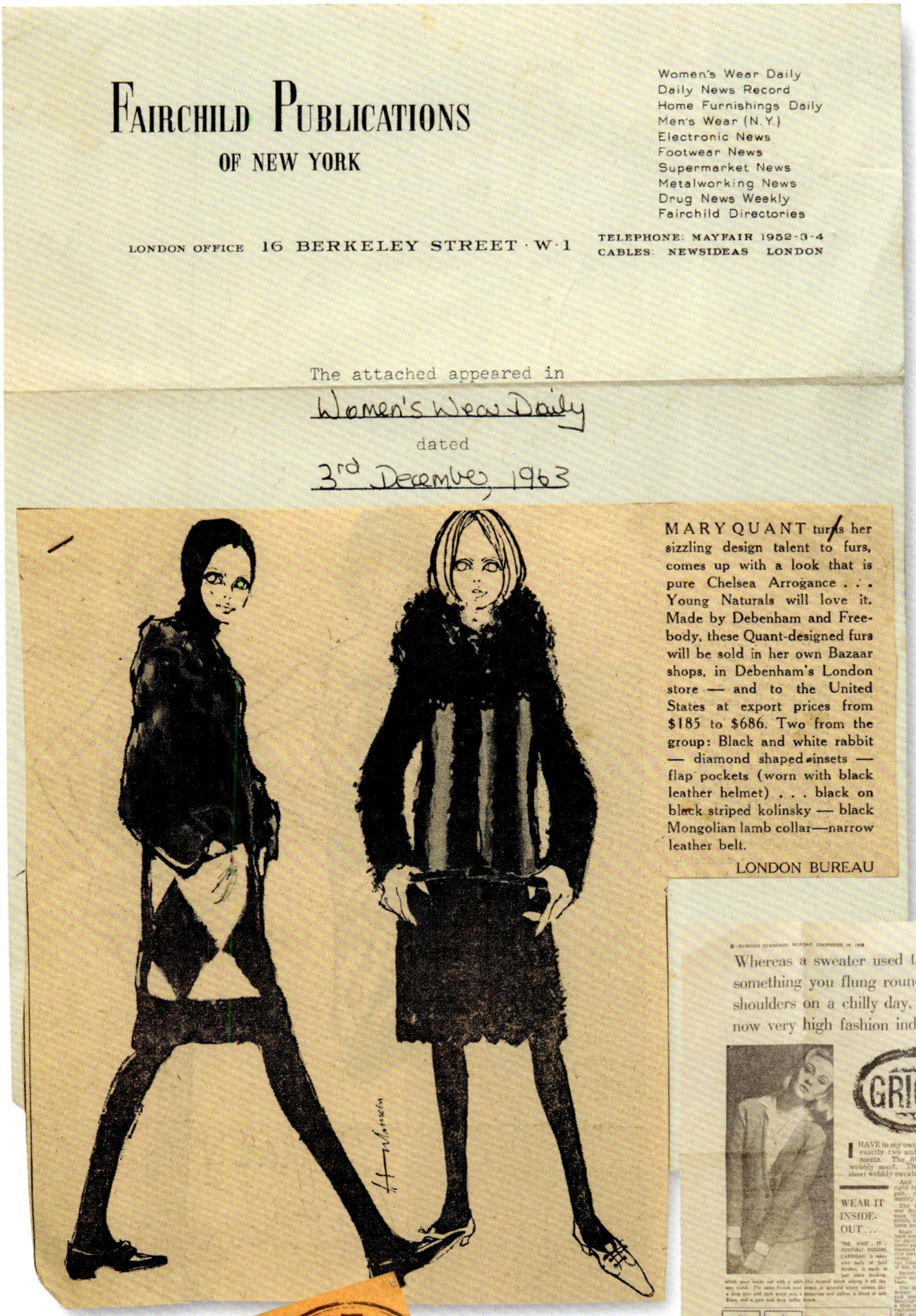

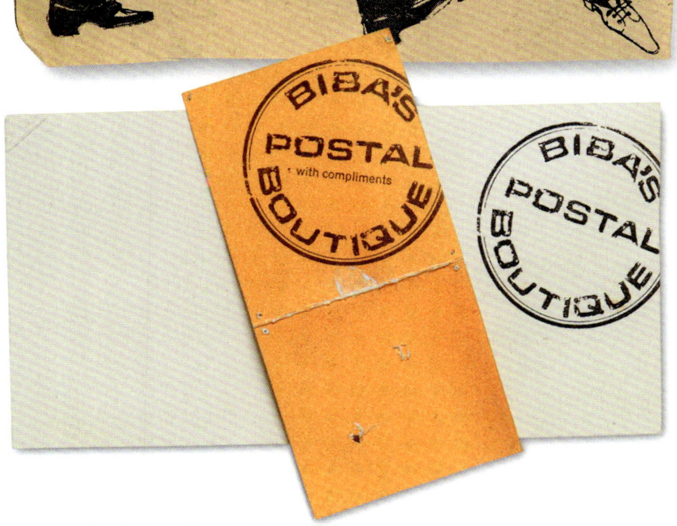

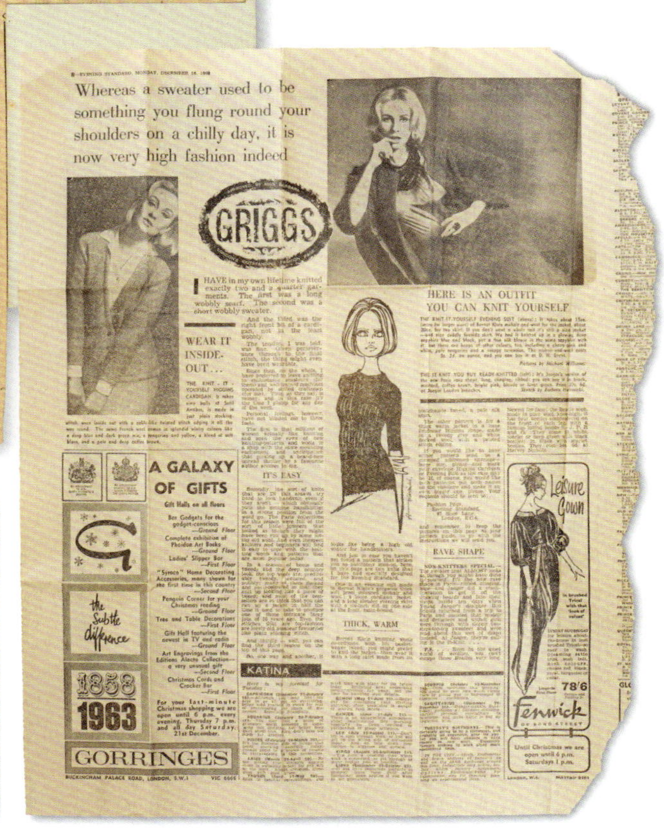

LEFT Press cutting, 'Mary Quant', fashion illustration by Barbara Hulanicki, *Women's Wear Daily*, 3 December 1963

BELOW LEFT Biba Postal Boutique business cards, designed by John McConnell, 1963

BELOW RIGHT Press cutting, central fashion illustration by Barbara Hulanicki, *Evening Standard*, 16 December 1963

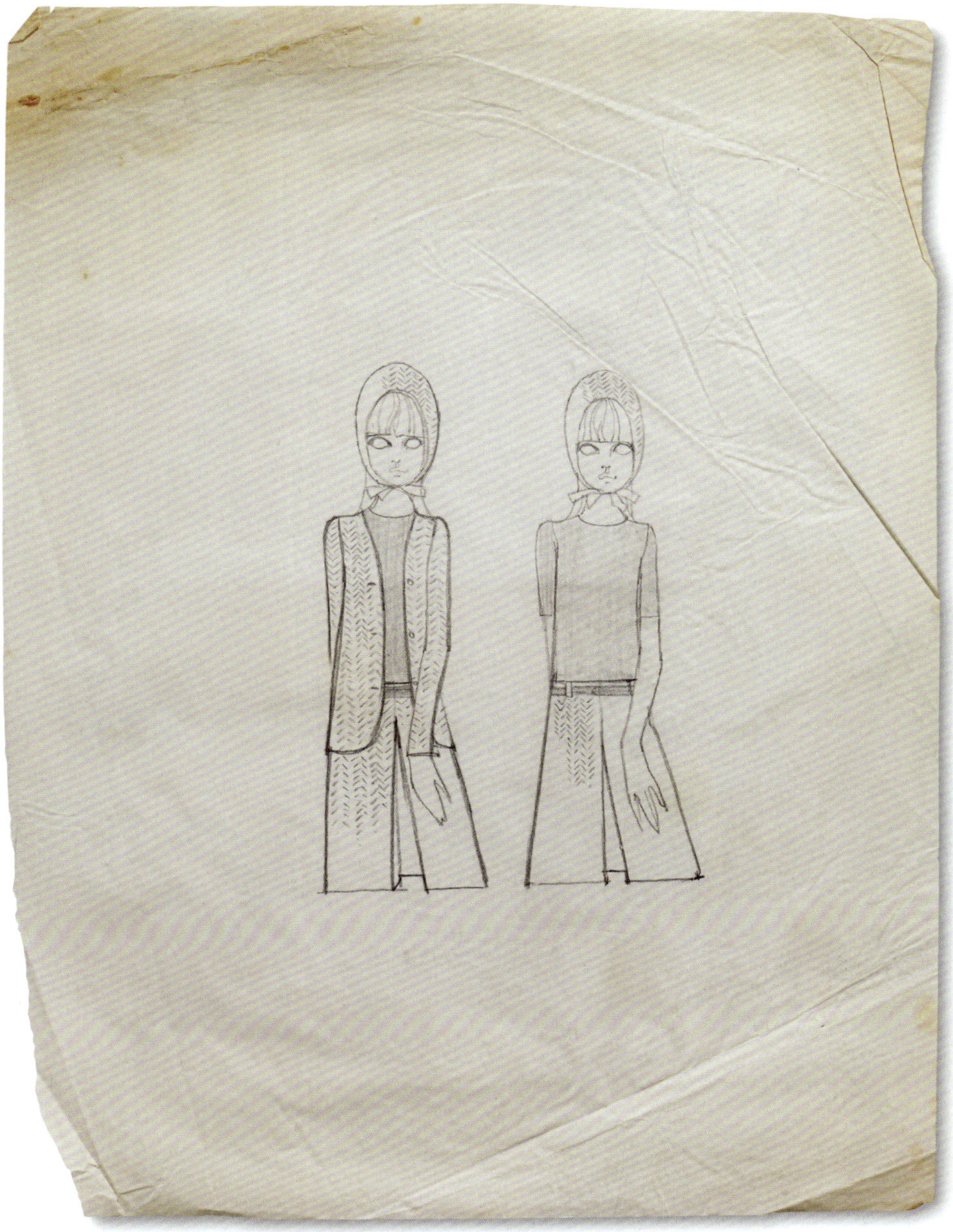

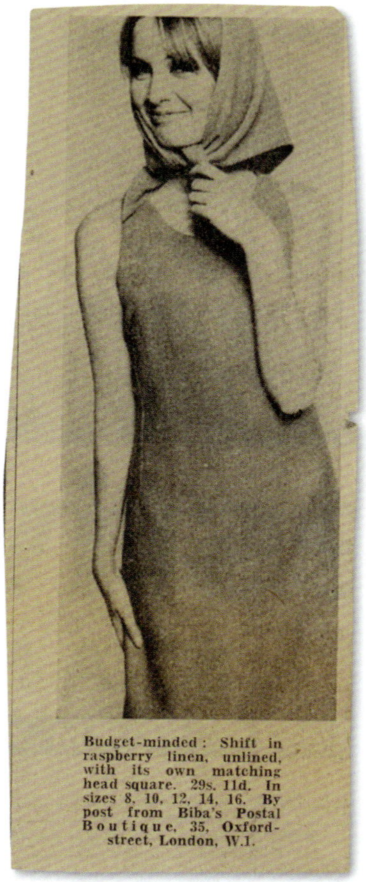

Budget-minded: Shift in raspberry linen, unlined, with its own matching head square. 29s. 11d. In sizes 8, 10, 12, 14, 16. By post from Biba's Postal Boutique, 35, Oxford-street, London, W.1.

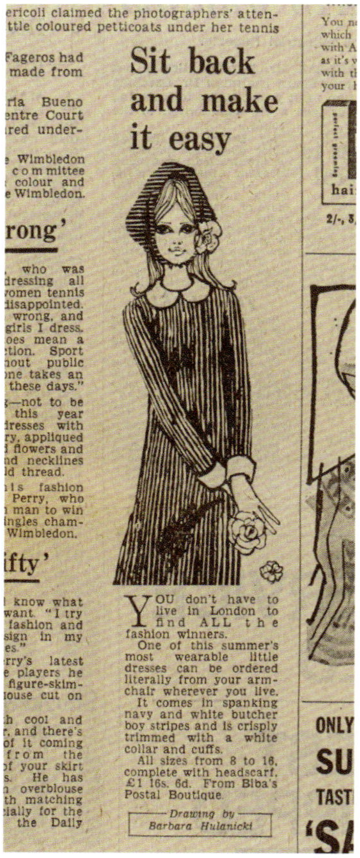

ericoli claimed the photographers' atten-
ttle coloured petticoats under her tennis

Fageros had
made from

ria Bueno
entre Court
red under-

e Wimbledon
committee
colour and
e Wimbledon.

rong'

, who was
dressing all
women tennis
disappointed.
wrong, and
girls I dress.
oes mean a
tion. Sport
hout public
ne takes an
these days."
—not to be
this year
dresses with
ry, appliqued
flowers and
nd necklines
ld thread.
ls fashion
Perry, who
man to win
ingles cham-
Wimbledon.

ifty'

know what
want. "I try
fashion and
sign in my
es."
rry's latest
e players he
figure-skim-
louse cut on

h cool and
r, and there's
of it coming
from the
of your skirt
s. He has
n overblouse
th matching
ially for the
the Daily

Sit back and make it easy

YOU don't have to live in London to find ALL the fashion winners.

One of this summer's most wearable little dresses can be ordered literally from your armchair wherever you live.

It comes in spanking navy and white butcher boy stripes and is crisply trimmed with a white collar and cuffs.

All sizes from 8 to 16, complete with headscarf, £1 16s. 6d. From Biba's Postal Boutique.

Drawing by Barbara Hulanicki

ABOVE Designs in pencil for skirt suit and matching headwear for Biba Postal Boutique, Barbara Hulanicki, c.1963

ABOVE RIGHT Press cutting, shift dress in raspberry linen with matching headscarf, Unknown source, 1964

RIGHT Press cutting, 'Sit Back and Make it Easy', dress and matching headscarf in navy and white cotton with white collar and cuffs from Biba Postal Boutique with illustration by Barbara Hulanicki, Unknown source, c.1963

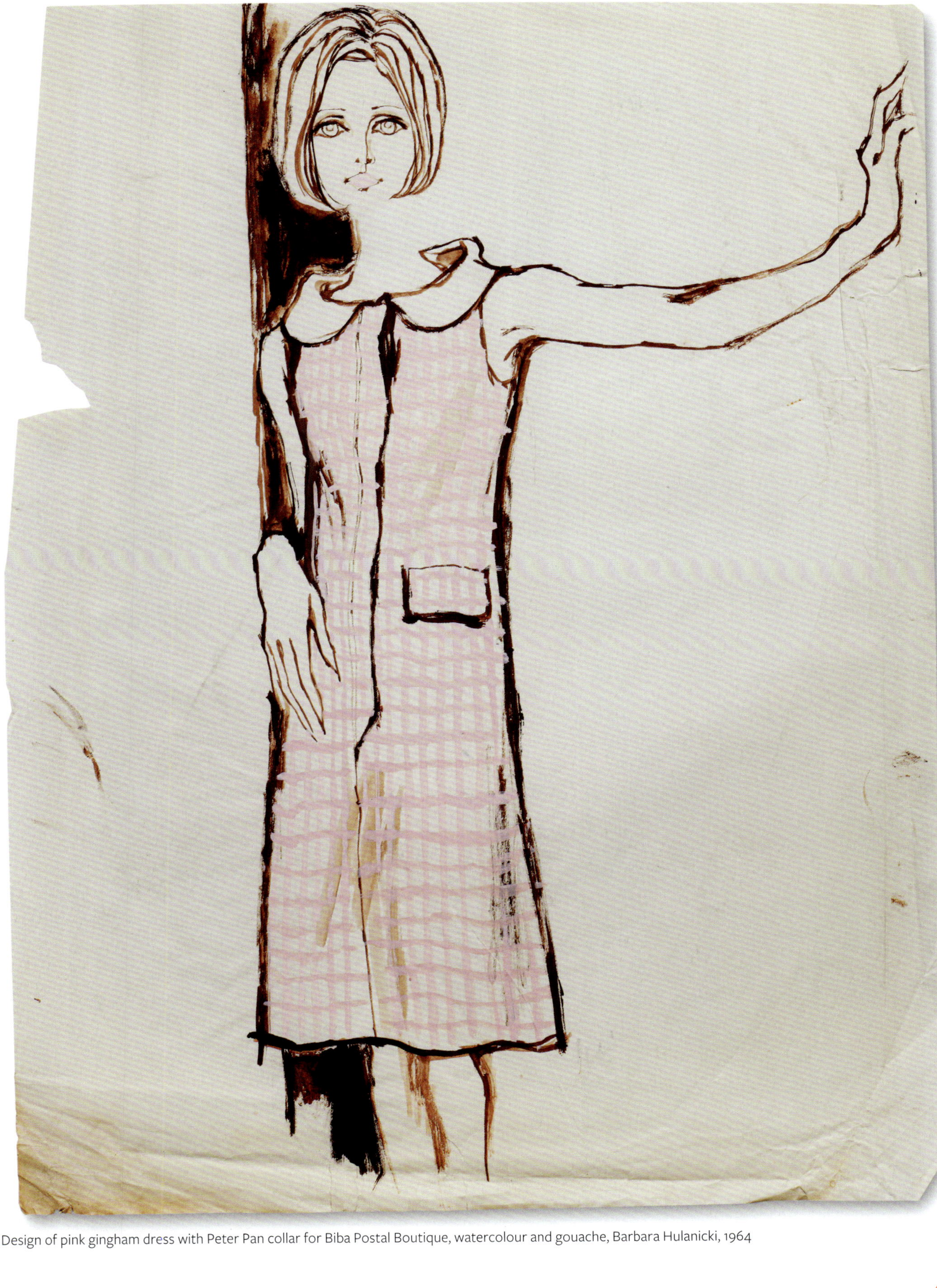

Design of pink gingham dress with Peter Pan collar for Biba Postal Boutique, watercolour and gouache, Barbara Hulanicki, 1964

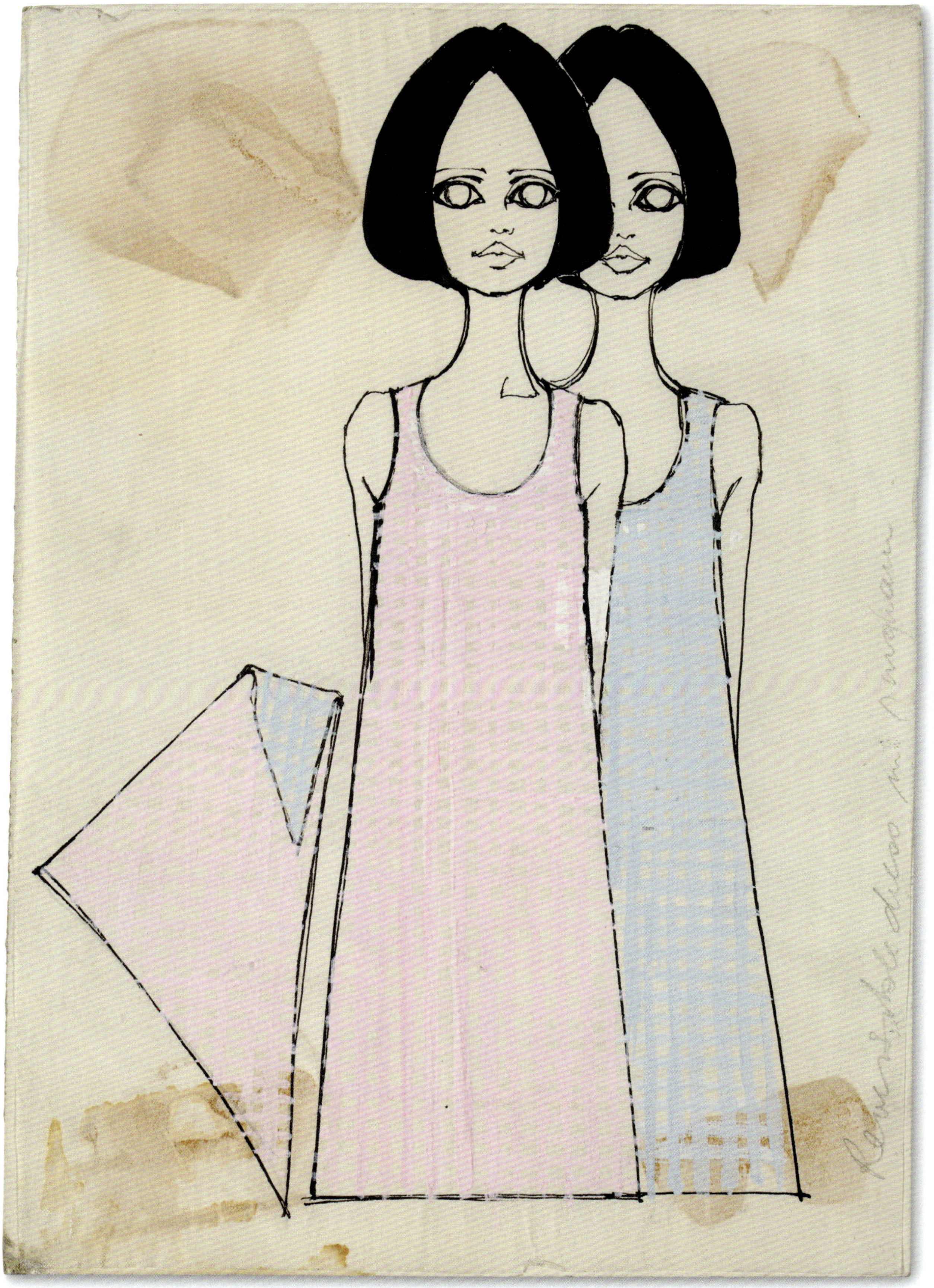

Design of pink gingham dress with matching headscarf for Biba Postal Boutique, watercolour and gouache, 1964

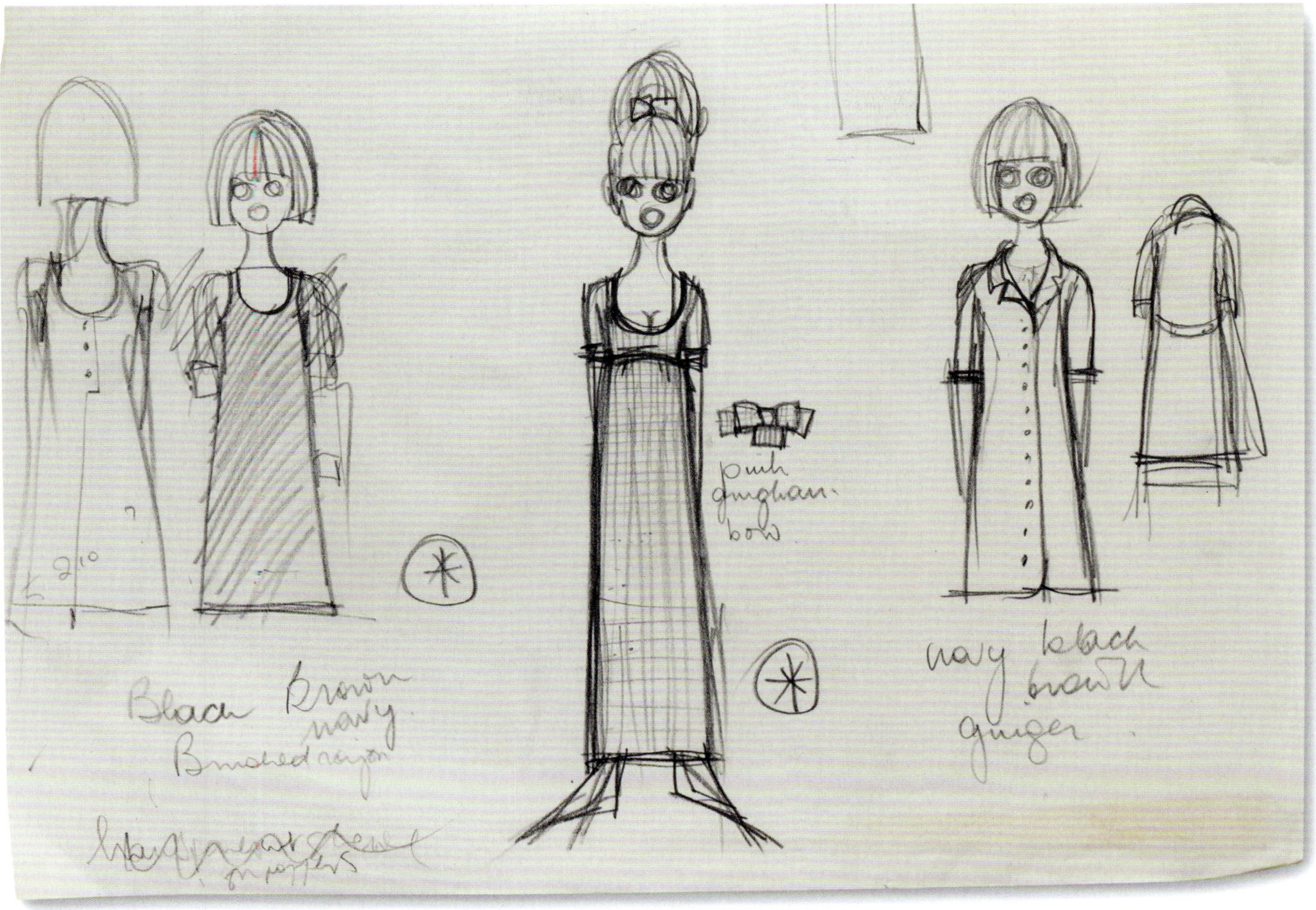

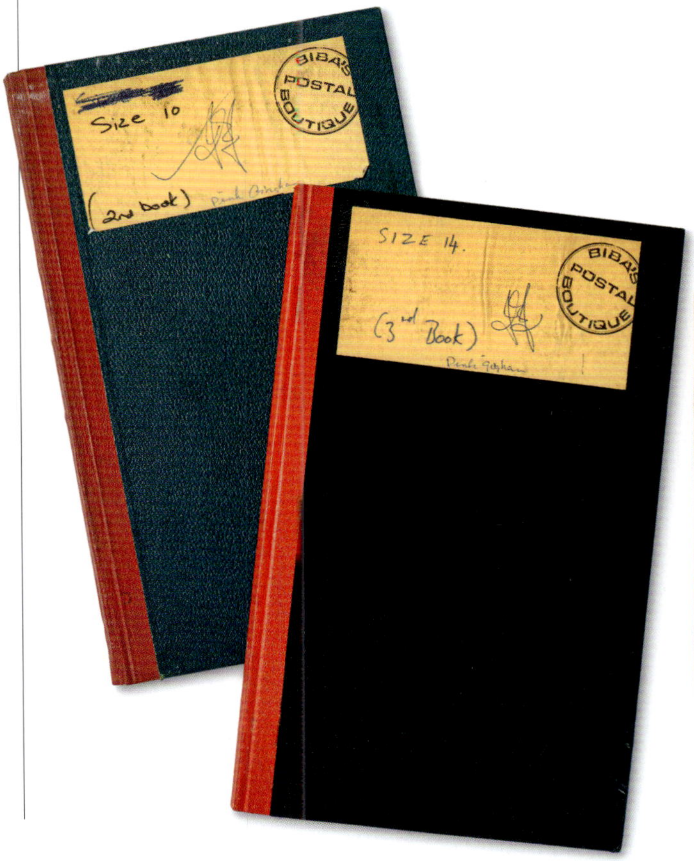

ABOVE Design of dresses including pink gingham dress with matching hair bow, pencil, Barbara Hulanicki, 1964

LEFT Order books for pink gingham dress, 1964

BELOW Original paper pattern, early Biba designs including gingham dress, 1964

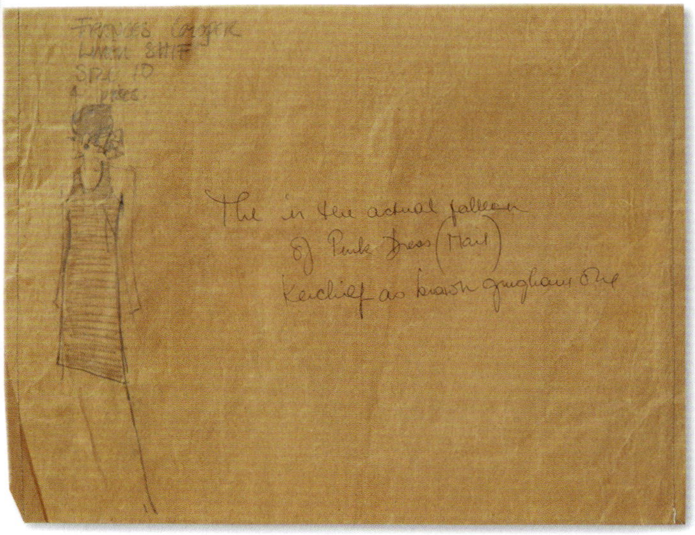

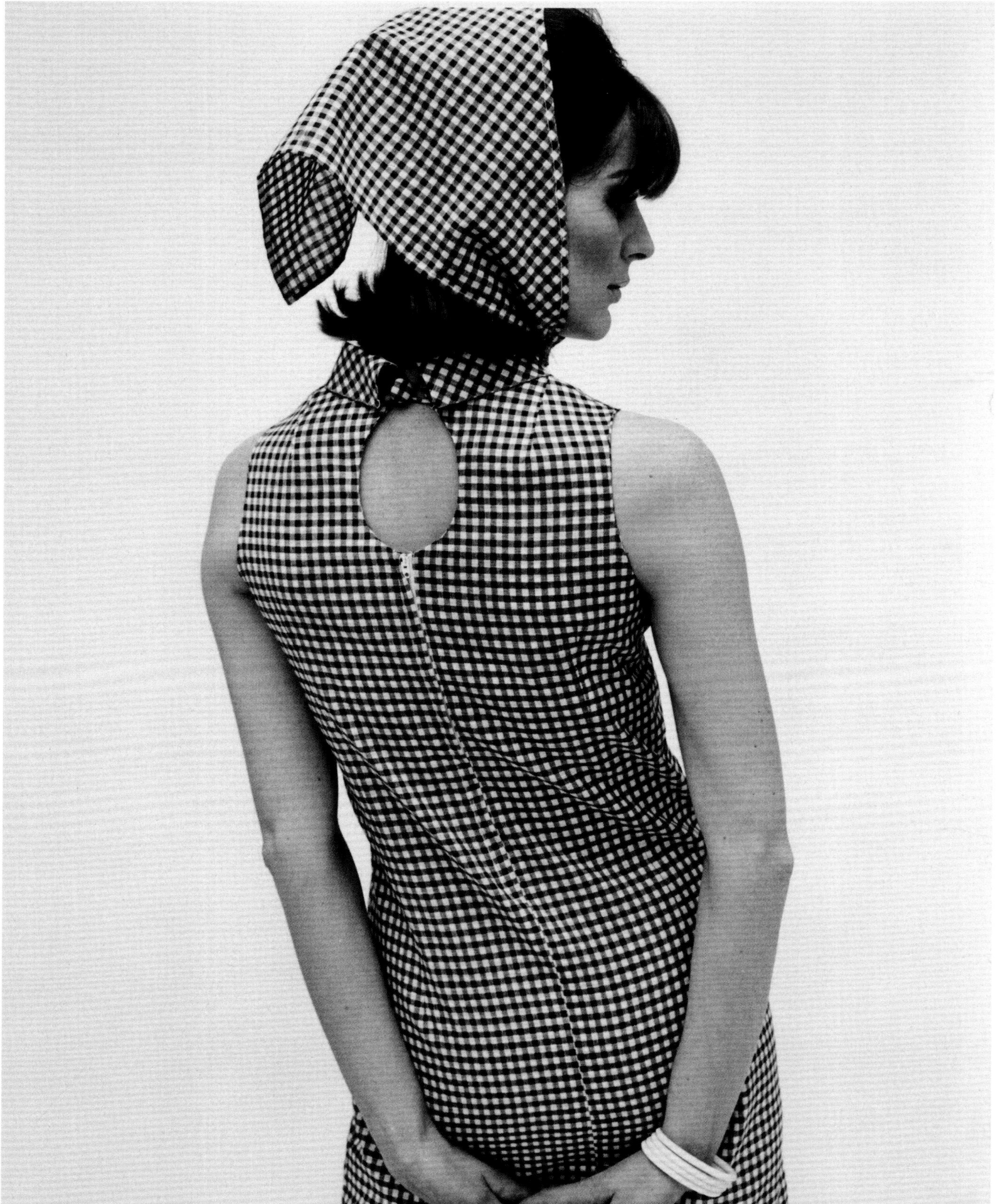

Paulene Stone modelling pink gingham dress, photographed by John French, 1964

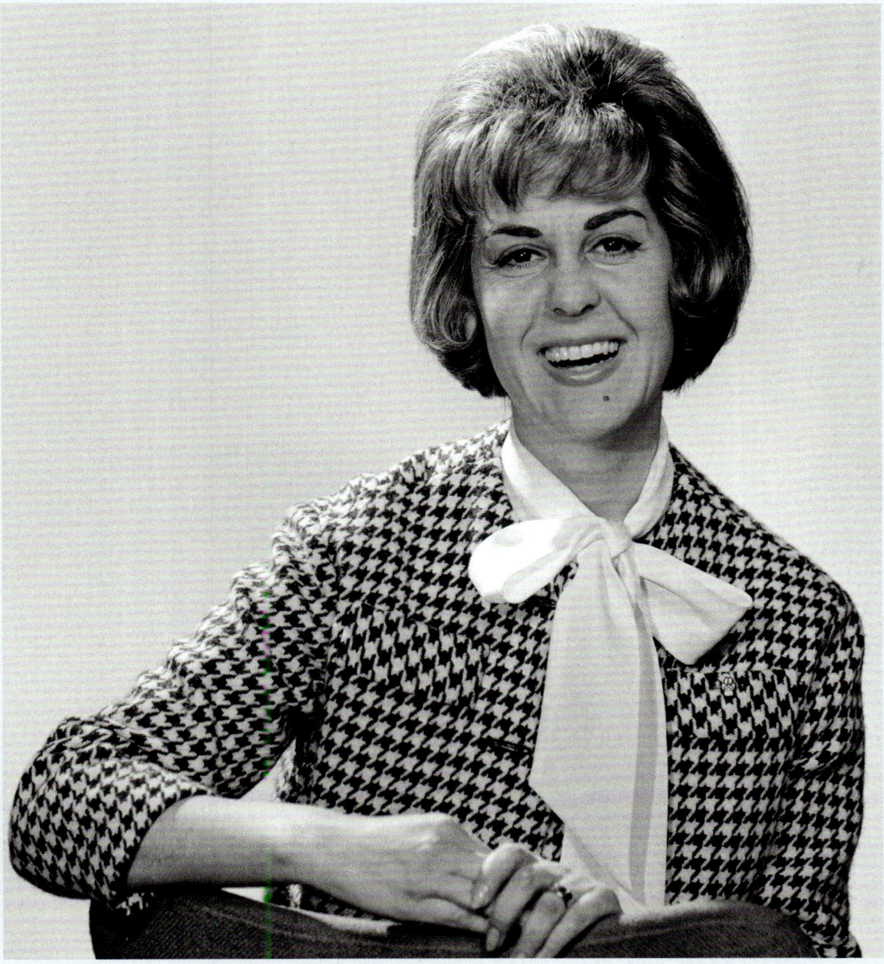

FELICITY GREEN

~

JOURNALIST

Felicity Green, editor of the *Daily Mirror* and one of the first journalists to recognise the importance of the emerging youth market, c.1962

Barbara Hulanicki first came into my *Daily Mirror* life when she was a freelance fashion illustrator. The drawings she did were delightful, and her female figures were a mirror image of Barbara herself: neat and trim, with swinging bobbed hair. Very trendy. Very 1960s.

After several visits – impressing me more and more each time by her understated, but very definite sense of style – I wanted to find a way to offer her look to *Mirror* readers.

I had this idea. I asked Barbara to design a dress that looked like her. Barbara designed a gingham dress of utter simplicity, which I thought would appeal to *Mirror* readers. I decided that the dress – photographed by John French on Paulene Stone, one of the top models of the time – should be offered to *Mirror* readers by mail order for 25 shillings, and thus the famous gingham dress was born. I dramatically underestimated its appeal: it sold 17,000 copies, and Britain ran out of pink gingham.

It not only made history in the fashion world, but also made a big name for Biba.

But there is more to Barbara Hulanicki than just one gingham dress. Her Biba history may have started there, but her fashion invention and ingenuity continue to flourish, and today Barbara remains an international fashion name. She transformed shops into boutiques. She turned dressing rooms for ladies into unisex hang-outs for boys and girls who just wanted to try on her clothes and didn't care if they were showing their knickers or taking off their trousers. Barbara's Biba broke every fashion rule in the book. She made fashion more exciting than it had ever been before and, I am prepared to say, more exciting than it has been ever since.

CHAPTER TWO

1964–1966 ABINGDON ROAD

"When you're 24,
nothing is a gamble.
You're just so optimistic
about everything"

Barbara Hulanicki

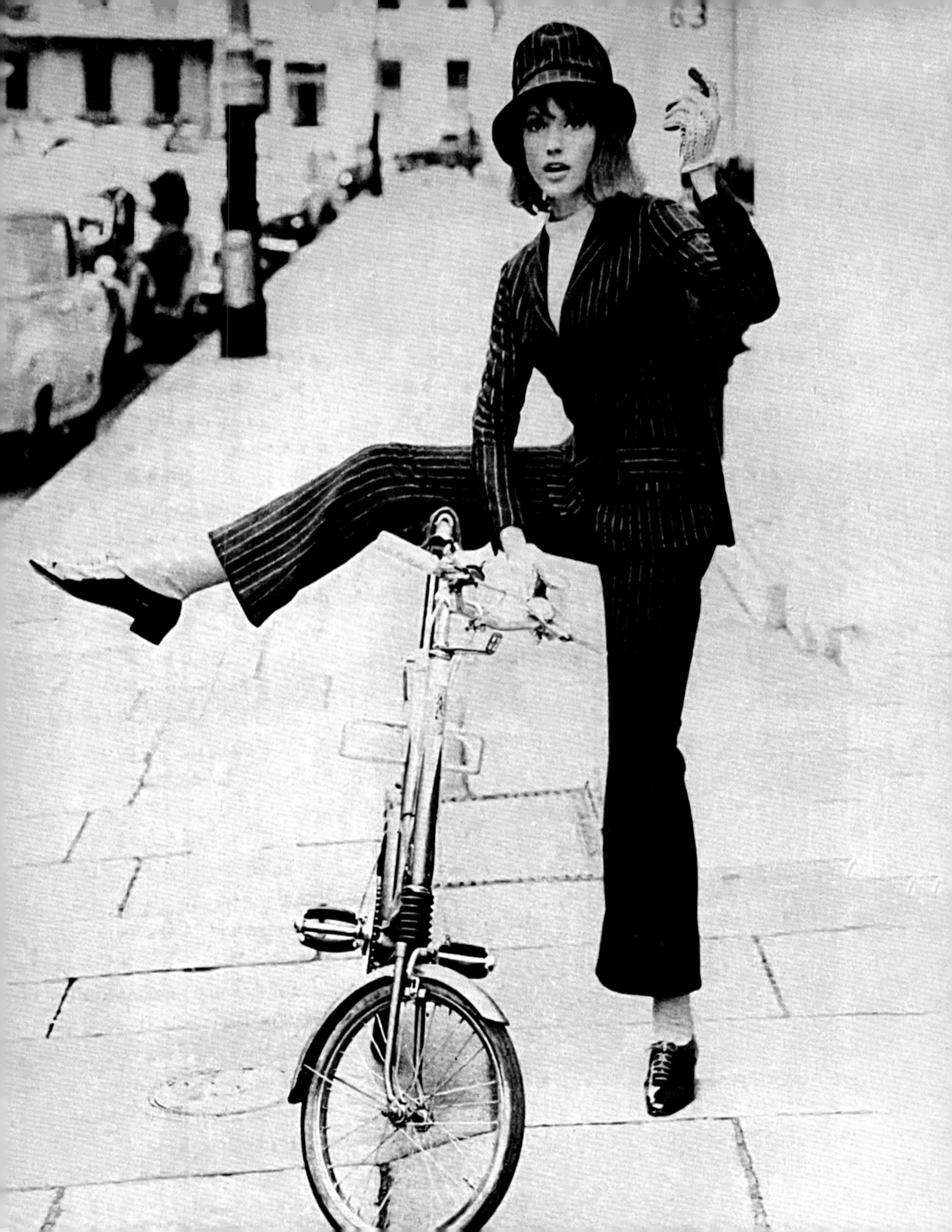

MARTIN PEL You opened the first Biba shop in 1964 in Abingdon Road, Kensington. Did you think it was a gamble?

BARBARA HULANICKI When you're 24, nothing is a gamble. You're just so optimistic about everything. In our flat on Cromwell Road, we had all these leftover garments from the Biba Postal Boutique, so I rang up all the secretaries of the people I was working for and said we were having a sale. We were inundated; that's what really started the shop. People came from miles around, and, even though it was a one-day sale, people continued to come over all the time, even though everything had gone by then. Everything was always organic. Our accountant thought it was a gamble. Fitz thought, 'Oh, I don't know; I don't know whether I can still work and run a shop', as we were both still working full-time.

We used to have Royal College of Art students cut the first patterns, and they were really bad at cutting. We had one pattern – a smock with bell sleeves – and we had to do it in thousands of fabrics. Fitz and I used to go to Pontings – the department store on Kensington High Street, a fantastic place – and we got to know the people there. They had a great fabric department. They took us to the storeroom, this whole office full of 1930s fabrics. It was incredible. We used to unroll these fabrics and they were faded, but we used a lot of that stuff. It was like a goldmine. We had all these fabrics to use, so we just had one style produced in all these fabrics. I had to get my mother up quickly from Brighton for the opening of our shop, and we went and bought tons of braid and things for her to sew on just to make everything look different because there was only the one style. I was at art school with Anne Behr, who was an illustrator and painter, and she really understood everything I wanted, and so she joined us as a pattern cutter.

MP Was there a big difference owning the shop?

BH With a shop you are right there, you've got your finger on the pulse. It's your decision to put something in the shop and it's the decision of the customer if they are going to buy it. It's fair play on both sides, and the feedback is immediate; you get an instant reaction. When you have a shop, you have a better sense of what is going to sell and what isn't. Everyone is on the same wavelength, because of what they're reading, or seeing on the streets, or in the cinema – although it's more difficult now because there are so many different avenues and so many different markets. The only thing you don't know is how something will do if it's completely new. I will never forget our first long t-shirt, which Vedonis in Leicester did for us. It was a wonderful company, which made all these amazing Victorian undergarments – all men's knickers with buttons made in wonderful jersey. When the long t-shirts first came into the shop there was silence; they were on the shelf, and nothing happened. Fitz was about to dump them, and then Ernestine Carter, a journalist for *The Sunday Times*, came into the shop and featured them in her pages. Then they just flew out and the whole t-shirt thing took off.

MP You mention Ernestine Carter. What were the journalists like in the early days?

BH Terrifying. I was terrified of Ernestine Carter and Lady Rendlesham, who was editor for *Queen* magazine. She came in and wanted white plastic Courrèges boots

PREVIOUS PAGE The first Biba trouser suit, brown pinstripe, 1964

printed with something. Can you imagine taking on those boots, plastic boots, when you can't even make a trouser pattern?! These old dowagers. The ones we really loved were Norma Moriceau at *19* and *Petticoat* magazines, Barbara Griggs at the *Evening Standard*, Jill Butterfield at *Nova* magazine and of course Felicity Green at the *Daily Mirror*, but she was frightening.

MP Is it true that there was no sign above the first Biba boutique to begin with?

BH The first shop was so beautiful. It was all peeling paint, and I didn't want to repaint it at all until slightly later. We put panels in the window with the Biba logo on them and then took them down because we didn't like them. It made no difference. It got still fuller even with no name.

We always opened in September because that's when you can make a lot of money selling coats – the price of a coat is about four times that of a dress. We always sold everything right on the nose – we never sold clothes too early or too late in the season. Swimsuits would be sold when it got hot, coats would be sold when it was cold. Our biggest coat sales were in December when everybody else had stopped selling coats and we used to score like mad. The market was instant for that age group, as they wanted it there and then. They didn't want to wait as they didn't look to the future in any way. The future was nothing.

"We put panels in the window with the Biba logo on them and then took them down because we didn't like them. It made no difference. It got still fuller even with no name"

Inside, the shop was supposed to look like a drawing room or nightclub. There were two huge windows and a lot of light coming in, so we had curtains made up. I think they were purple. We sold a dress on mail order in the same fabric, and when we ran out of fabric we had to take the curtains down to use them! We had lace in the windows to obscure the light, and the first winter the interiors were all painted a dark, navy blue. When spring came, I panicked thinking 'they will never come into this darkness', so poor Fitz had to paint all the Victorian ceilings white, which he did overnight. It's funny, but when you look at the taste of that age group it's very *Dracula*. You go through that stage of being drawn to darkness, perhaps because you're brought up in the light.

MP Biba was known for its distinctive colour palette from the beginning.

BH They were Art Nouveau colours, very Alphonse Mucha and Gustav Klimt, artists of that period. They were the colours I loved. Everything else was so grungy, and people wore old things, sort of Harris Tweed style. If you look at an English garden there are lots of purples, lots of pink and lots of lilac. It hadn't struck me until I came back to London more recently that every garden is just completely purple and pink. Now I know why the English are so into those colours.

MP And in 1965 you opened a Biba in Brighton.

BH That was a beautiful little house. I thought we were going to do lots of little stores all over the country until we opened that one; never again. Thank goodness we tried it out there because it was easy to get to. It's another business doing lots of shops. All of your energies are too dispersed; for both of us, it was more important that we had all of our energy invested in one thing. But even though the Brighton store became a worry, I thought it was lovely and I wouldn't let it go for a long time. After that experience, we had to think of other ways to expand Biba, without having shops dotted around the country.

MP Meanwhile, Biba in Abingdon Road became a celebrity hang-out.

BH Vicki Wickham, who was the producer of *Ready, Steady, Go!*, had seen us in *Honey* magazine. She was always pushing everybody towards us. I went to see Cathy McGowan – the presenter of *Ready, Steady, Go!* – at the studios in Holborn, and we got on like a house on fire. She liked my man's watch and I liked her style. She was amazing looking and had a great figure, with long legs. Terribly elegant, she had incredible taste for someone her age. She also had lovely hair, which was by Leslie Russell at Smile. Everybody went to Leslie in that age group; it was all word of mouth. I remember Cathy taking me to see Mick Jagger and Keith Richards; she said, 'You've got to meet this fantastic chap, I really fancy him.' We went and met them on *Ready, Steady, Go!*. Little shy boys, the whole lot of them. Fitz said that Mick Jagger always used to be in the Abingdon Road store. Chrissie Shrimpton (sister of Jean Shrimpton) was his girlfriend, and he used to come in with her – she was very beautiful, a very nice girl. Twiggy would come in too. Twiggy was amazing and just looked incredible in everything ... but especially Biba!

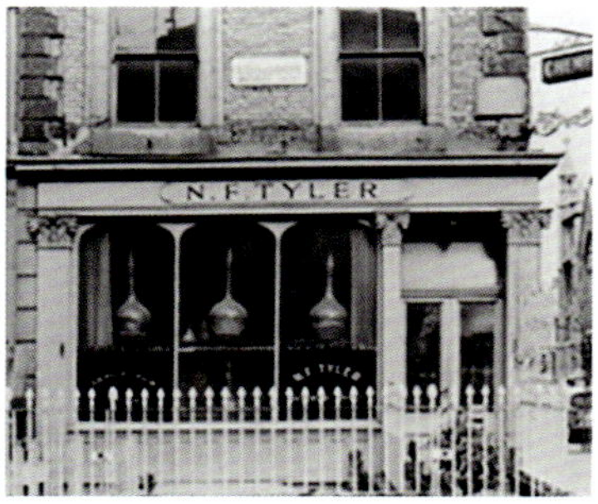

ABOVE N. F. Tyler, chemist's shop, 87 Abingdon Road, Kensington, c.1950s. This is the building that would become the first Biba boutique.

BELOW Biba, first boutique, 87 Abingdon Road, Kensington, c.1964

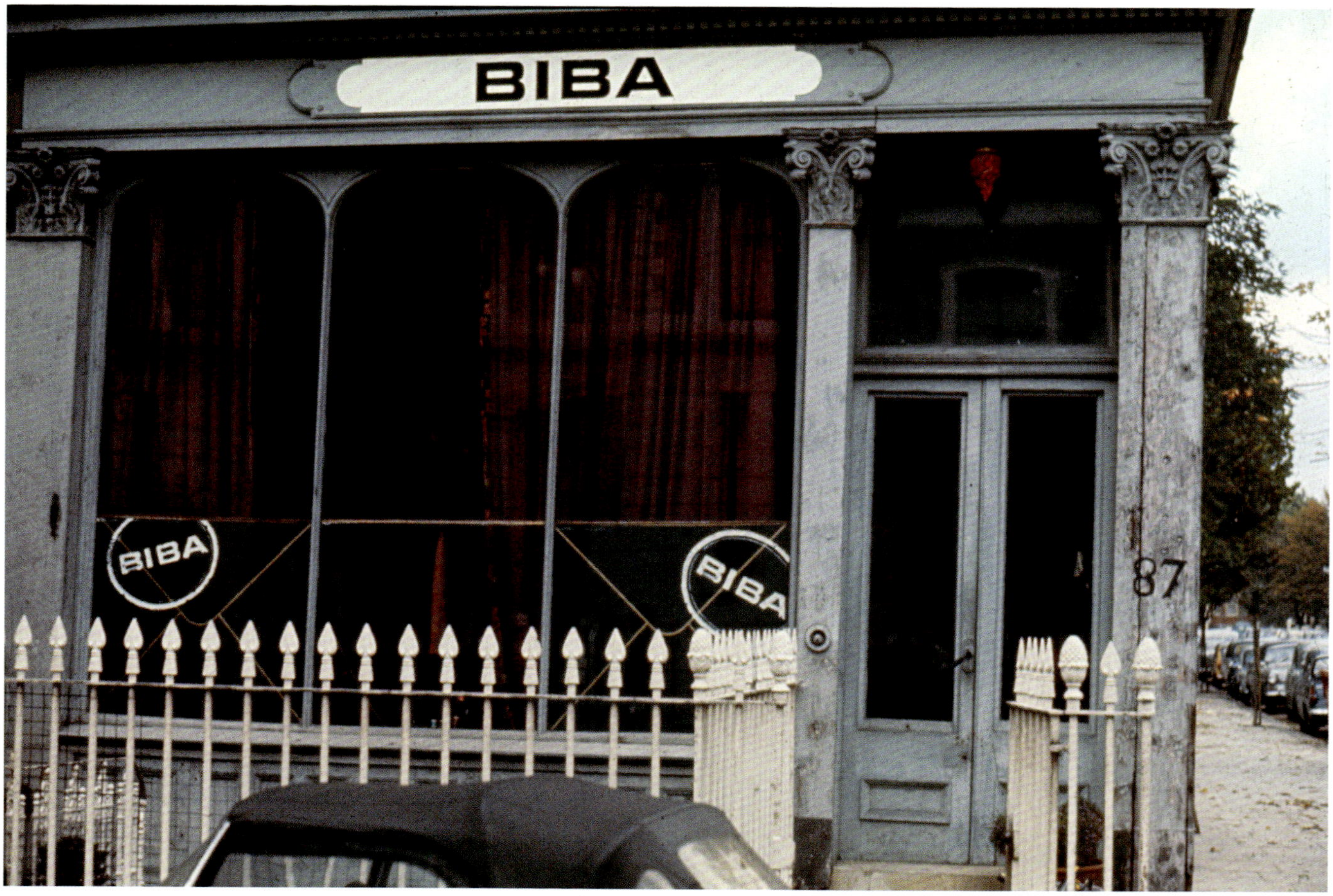

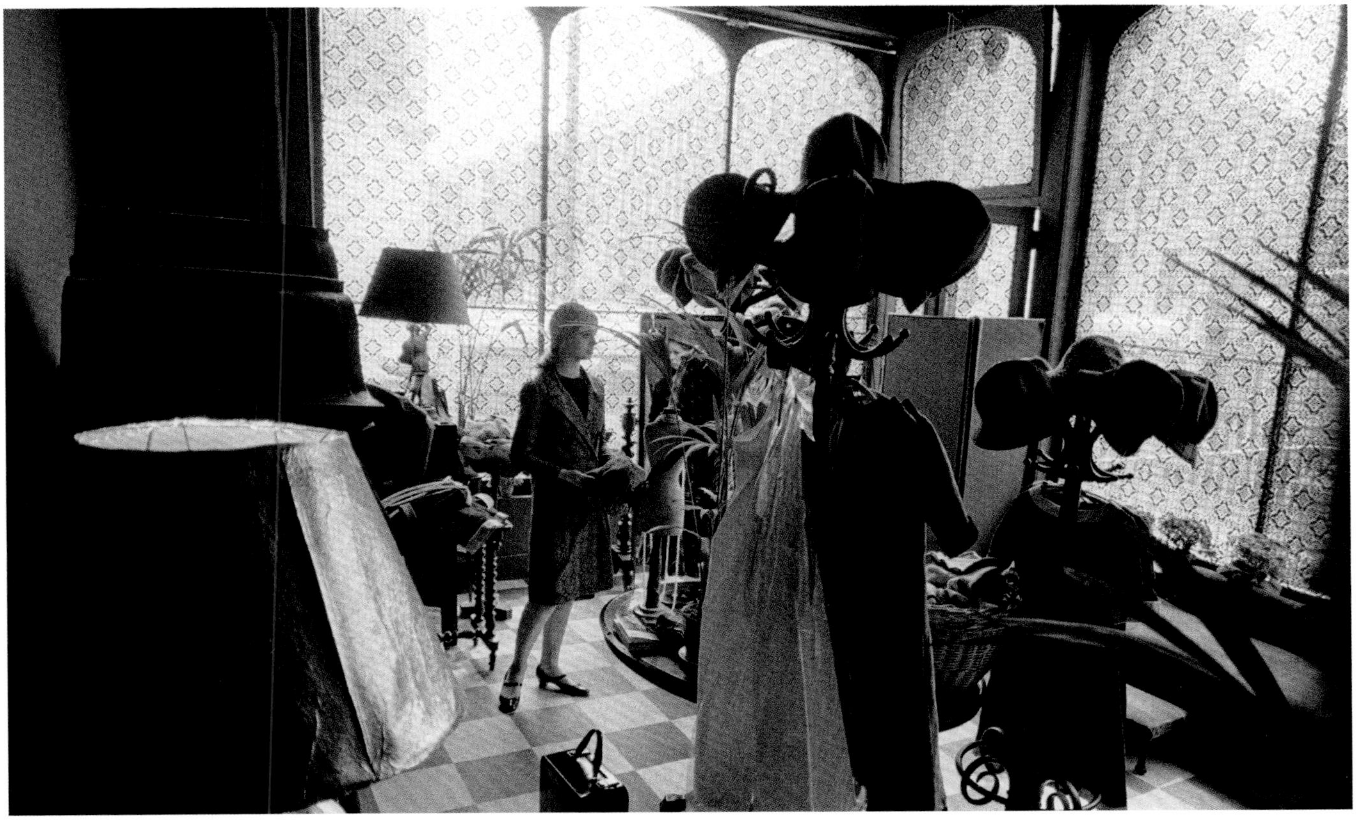

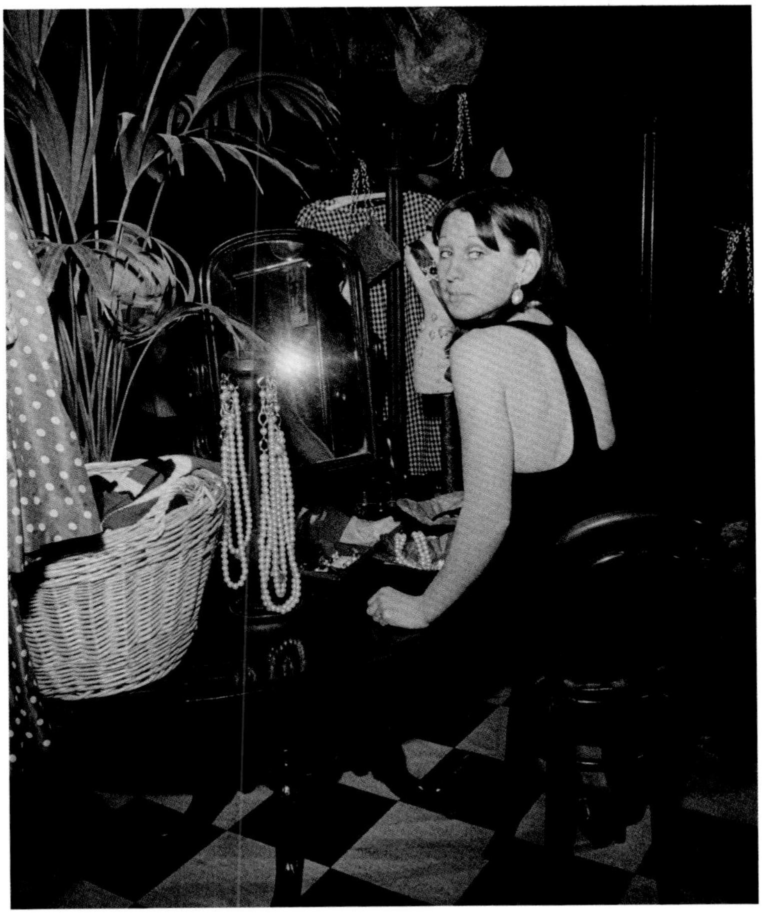

ABOVE Biba, Abingdon Road, interior, 1965

LEFT Biba, Abingdon Road, interior, c.1964

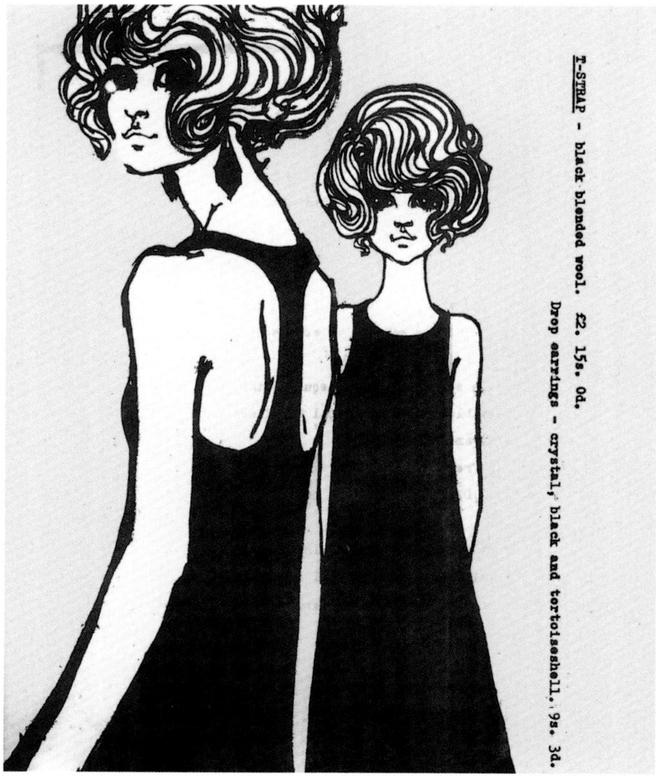

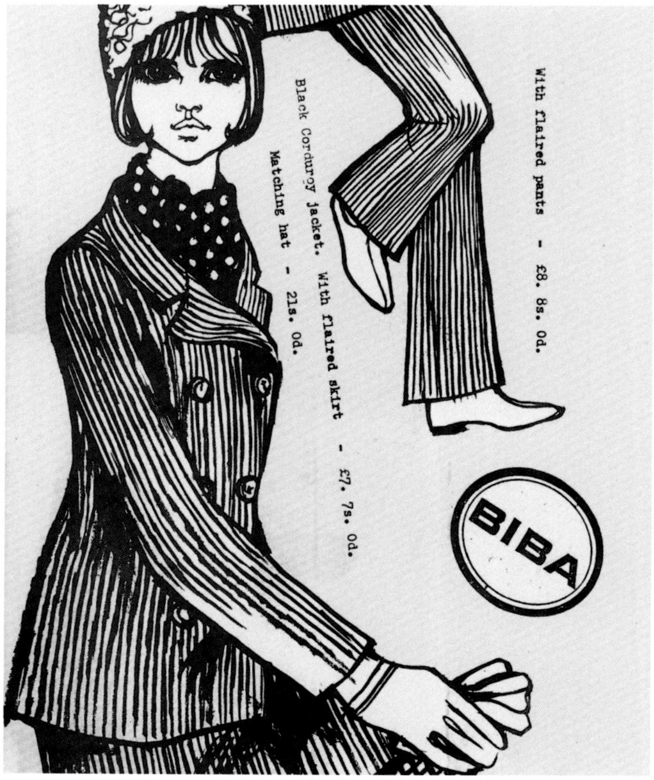

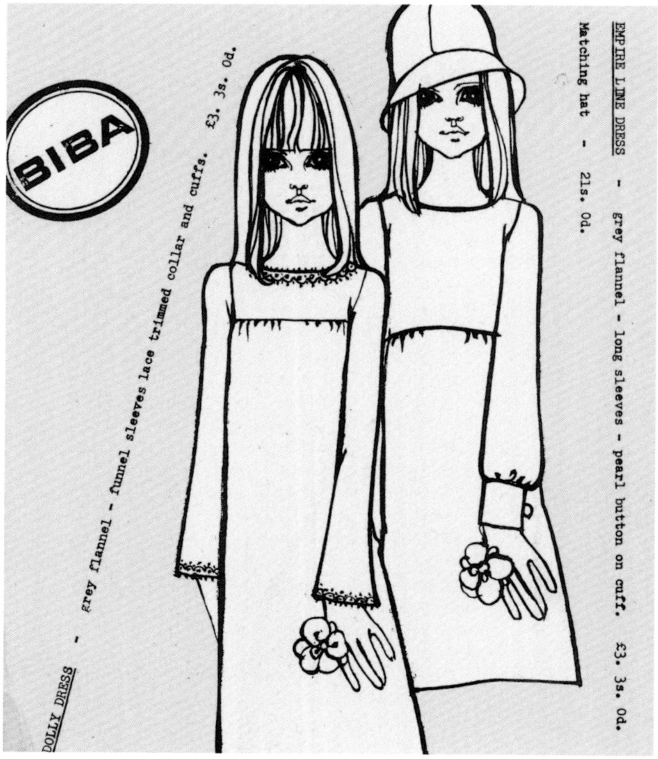

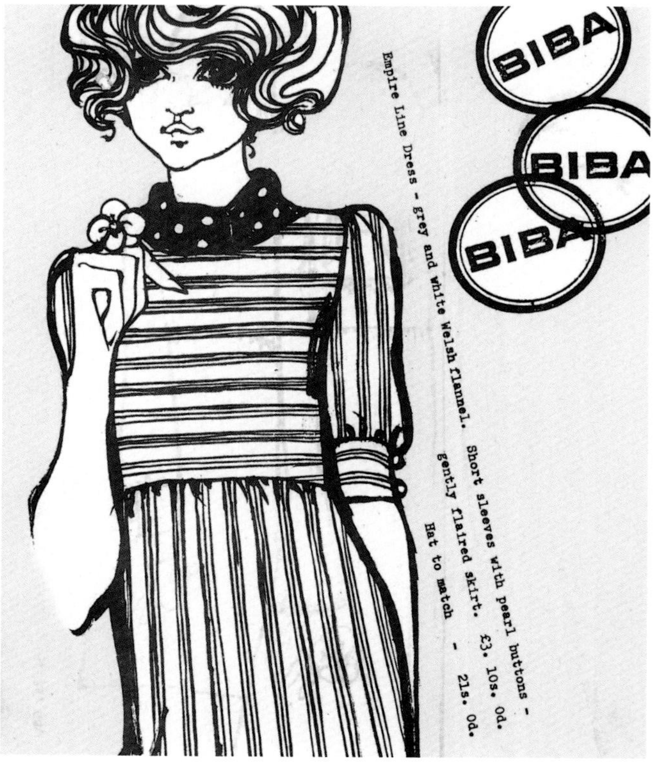

Early Biba catalogue, illustrations by
Barbara Hulanicki, 1964

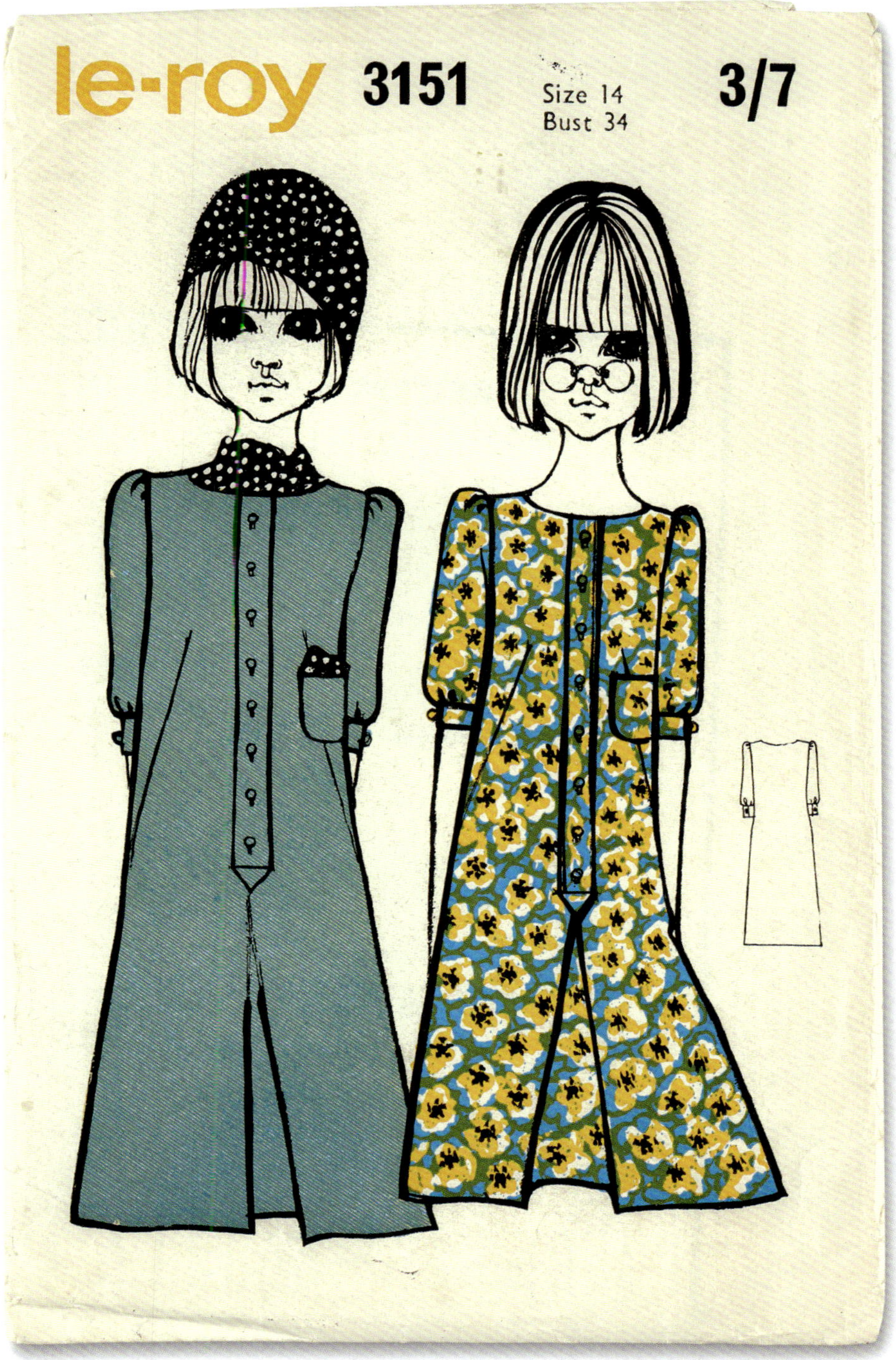

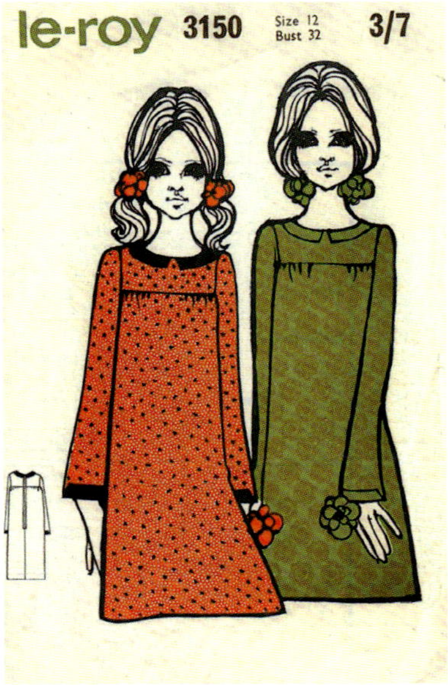

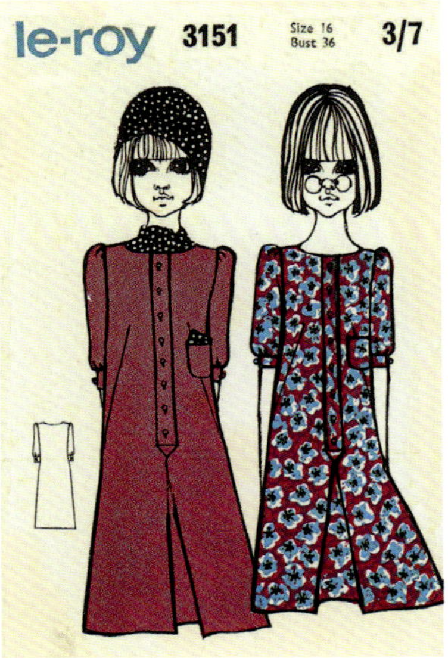

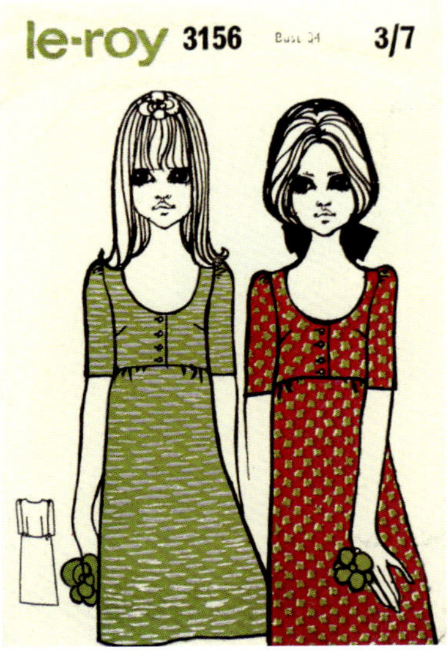

Le-Roy paper pattern, cover illustrations by Barbara Hulanicki, 1964–5

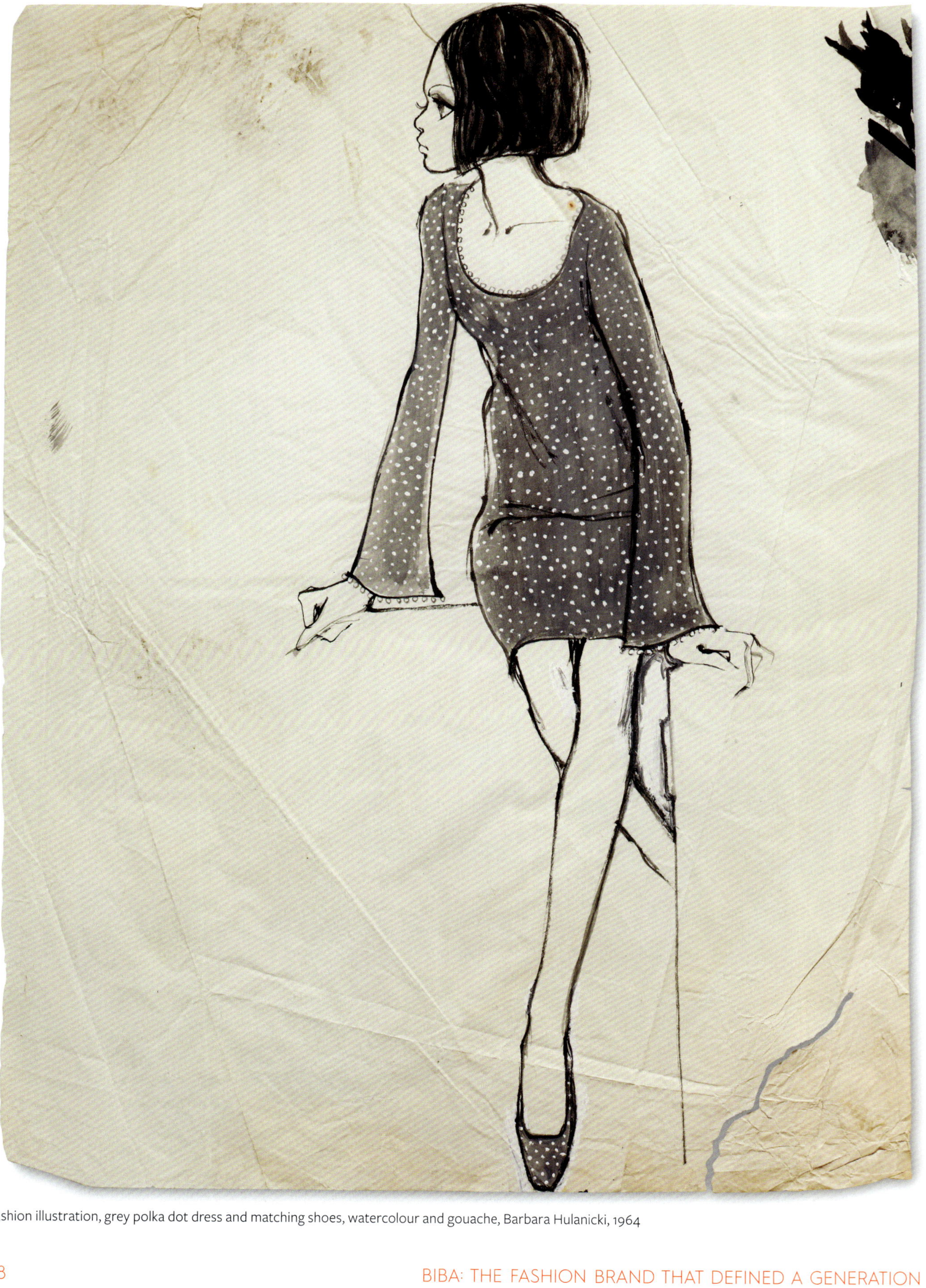

Fashion illustration, grey polka dot dress and matching shoes, watercolour and gouache, Barbara Hulanicki, 1964

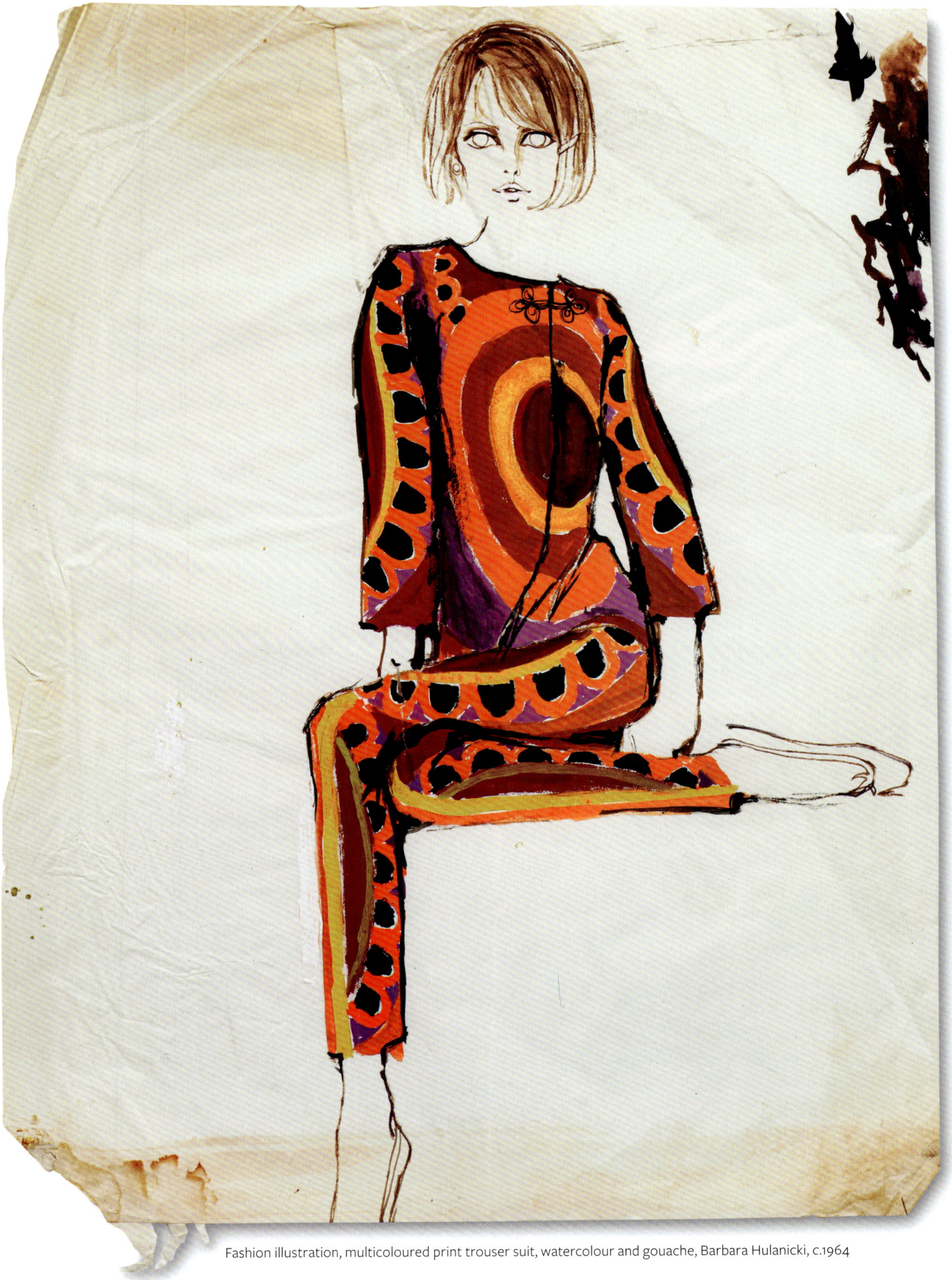

Fashion illustration, multicoloured print trouser suit, watercolour and gouache, Barbara Hulanicki, c.1964

SARAH PLUNKET
~
BIBA STORE MANAGER

I was always interested in clothes. Helping a seamstress from a young age taught me a lot and gave me the confidence to make my own clothes. I was lucky enough to work at the British couture house Bellville et Cie in my late teens, which was my first experience with beautiful clothes.

In late 1963 I left Bellville to go on a trip around Europe with a girlfriend. In the end we didn't visit many places as we ran out of money! It was, however, a lot of fun and we ended up on the island of Capri. On arriving home, I had a message from my friend, the fashion journalist Liz Dixon, who said that Barbara Hulanicki, a good friend of hers, was looking for a manager for the new shop that she and her husband Stephen ('Fitz') were opening.

After ringing Barbara and having had a good chat we arranged to meet. On arrival I walked down the stairs to their basement workrooms in Motcomb Street where, as it happens, I had worked at Bellville previously. Barbara and Fitz were very interesting, great fun and very excited about the first Biba shop.

It was only later that it struck me how lucky I'd been to be interviewed by, and chosen to work with, Barbara and Fitz. Their enthusiasm was infectious from the first day I walked up the steps into the very first Biba shop on Abingdon Road.

It was hectic getting the shop ready for opening. Two pretty young girls came in every evening to ask for a job, but Barbara and Fitz said they could only afford to pay one. In the end I persuaded them to take on both girls, which turned out to be a great success. Soon afterwards Barbara met my cousin Rosie, and she also began working at Biba, which she continued to do for many years.

Once Abingdon Road opened there were queues outside every day, with customers waiting to explore all the fabulous coats, dresses, hats, feather boas and jewellery, which came from a Mr McCardy who lived in the shop's basement. Quite often, in those early days, Twiggy and her friends arrived in their school uniforms.

> "There were queues outside every day, with customers waiting to explore all the fabulous coats, dresses, hats, feather boas and jewellery"

My role was to always be on hand and to get on with whatever needed to be done, while also keeping an eye on all the customers. I usually arrived at 8 in the morning and stayed until closing time which, at weekends, was late as you had to wait for the last customer to leave and then tidy and prepare everything for the next day. A lot of coffee drinking went on, with chat and laughter, but there were also dramas, such as one occasion when a load of dresses arrived with their sleeves sewn on back-to-front!

Two years after the Abingdon Road Biba opened, the time arrived when a bigger place had to be found. Although the prospect was daunting for us all, Barbara and Fitz found a rather special building, which seemed ideal, and soon everyone was so excited for the new Biba on Church Street.

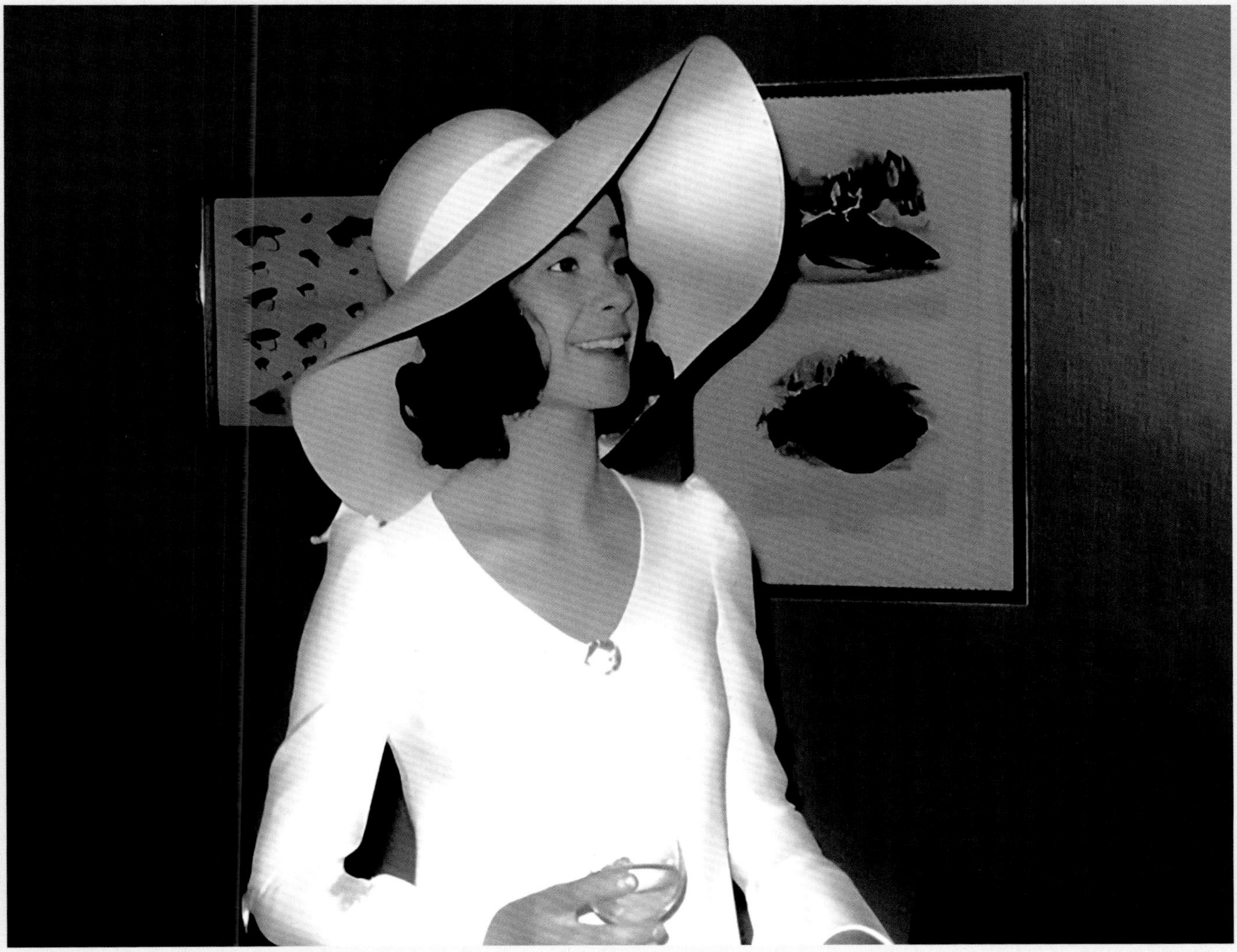

Sarah Plunket in her wedding dress designed by Barbara Hulanicki with a hat by Nancy at Bellville et Cie, 1968

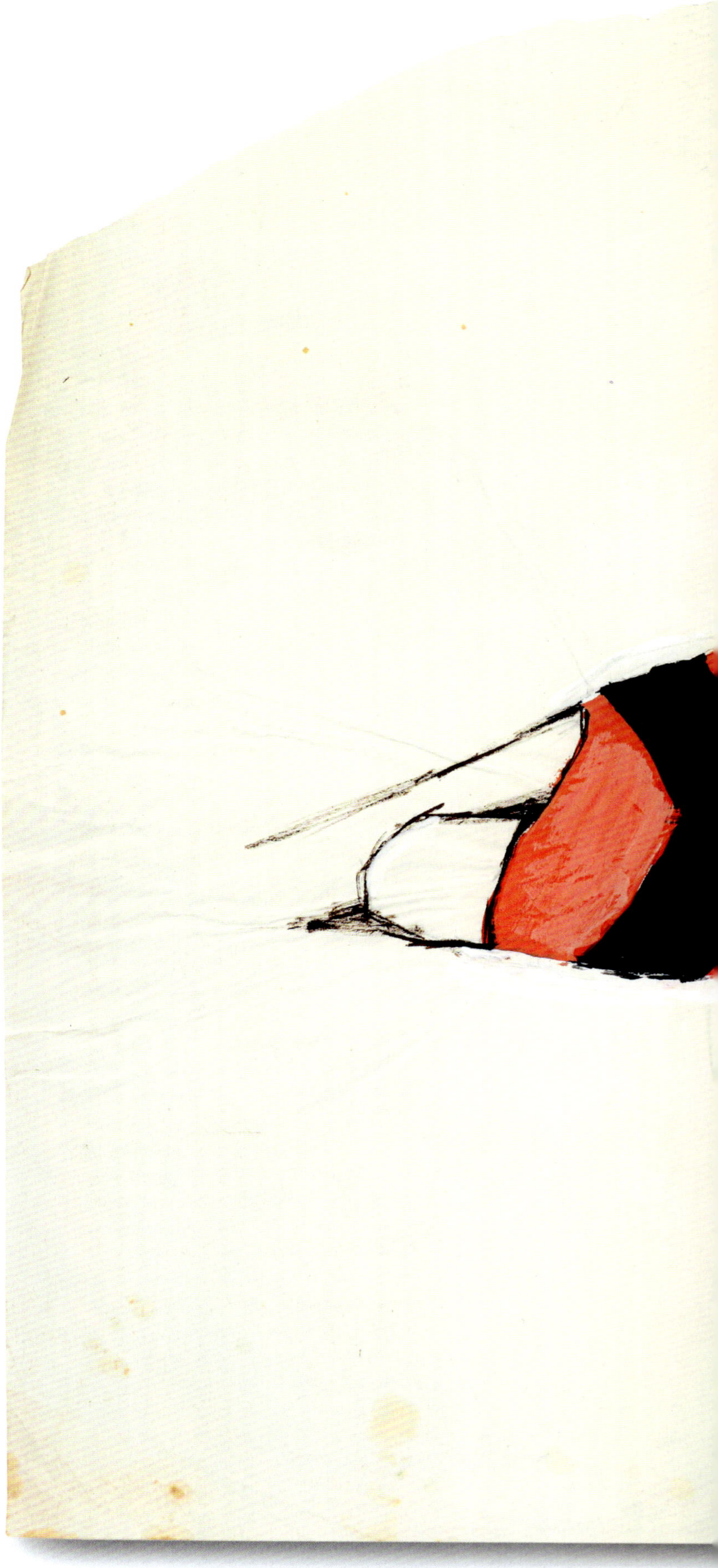

Fashion illustration, green, black and red dress with matching hat and accessories, watercolour and gouache, Barbara Hulanicki, c.1964

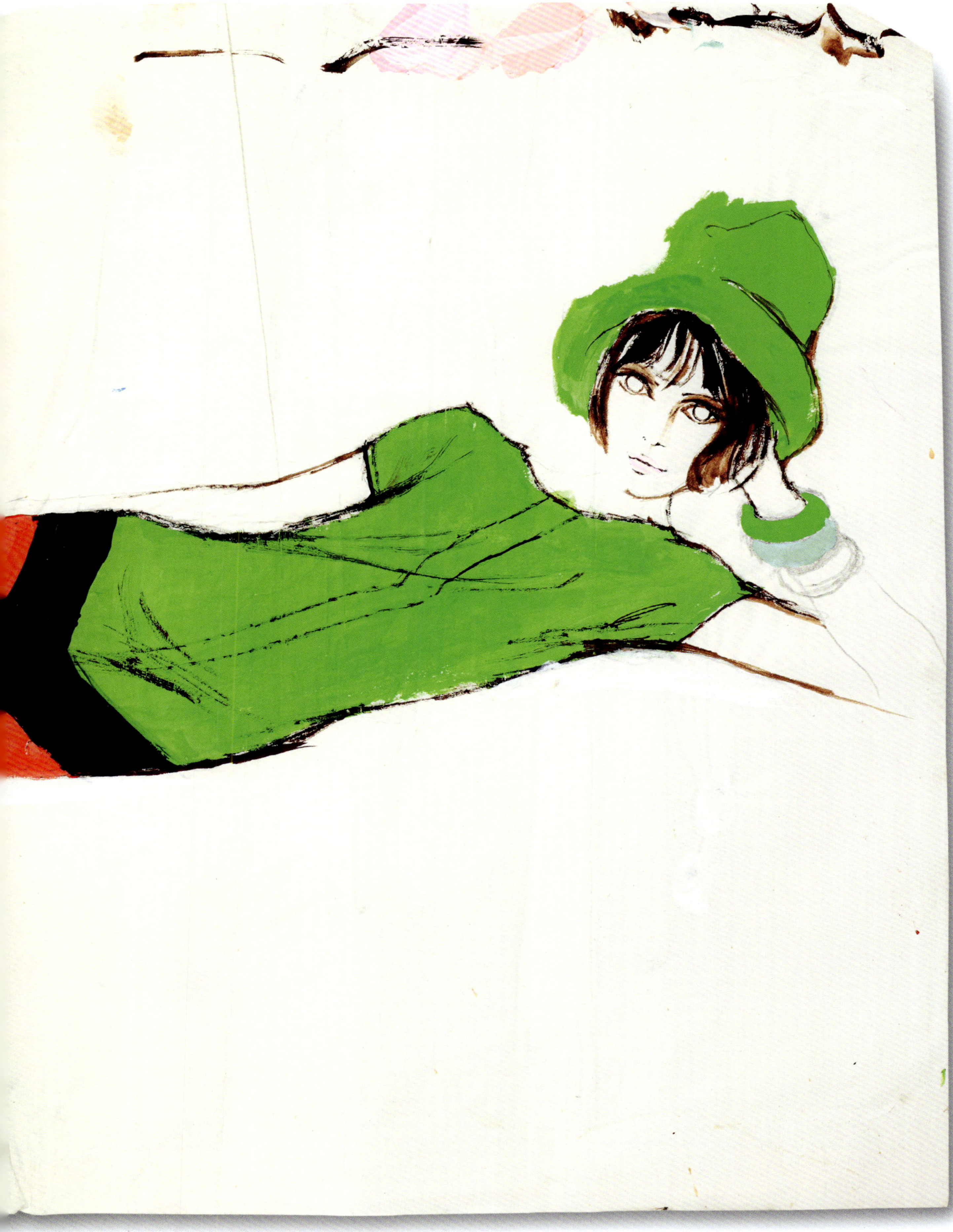

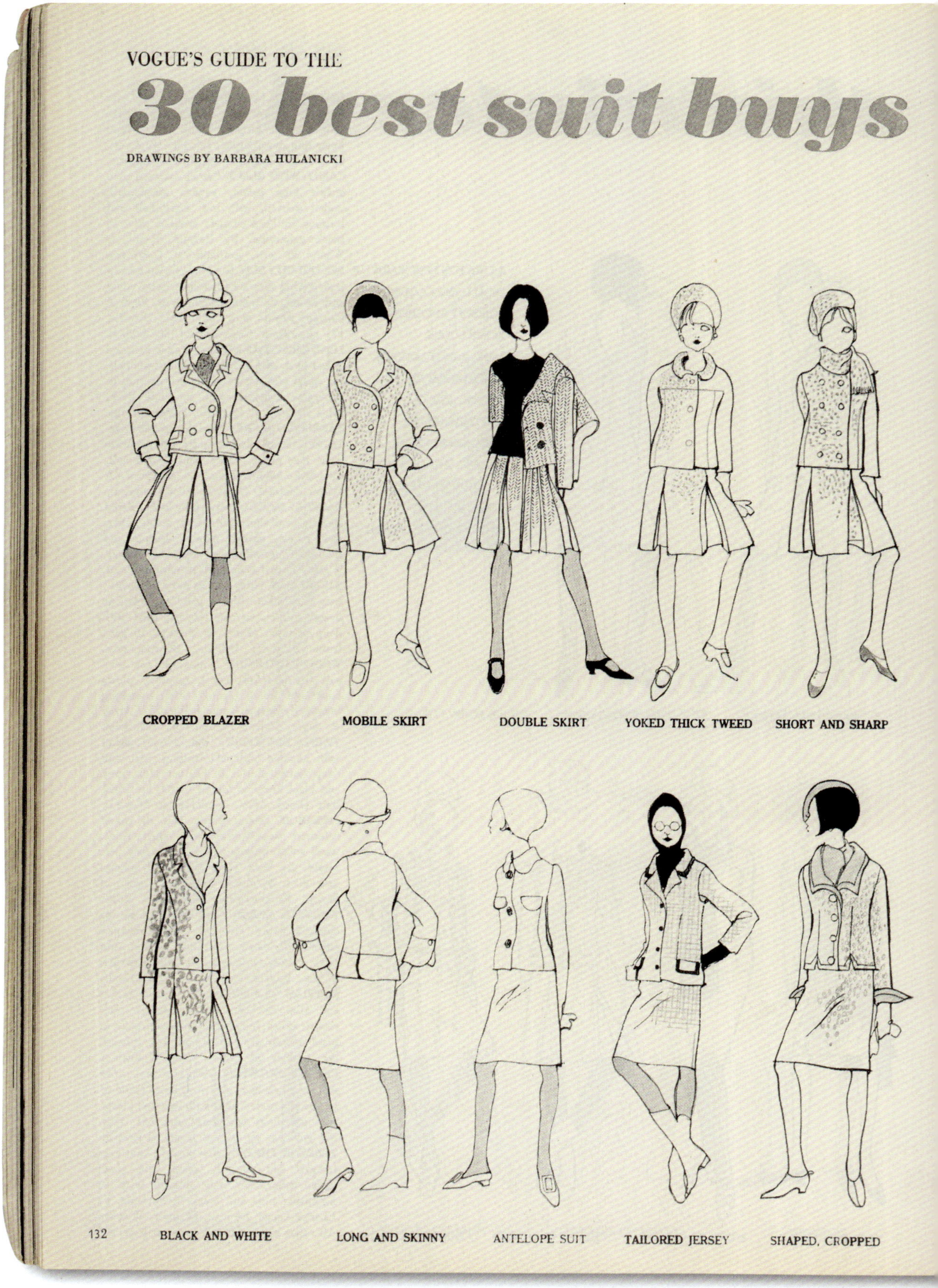
VOGUE'S GUIDE TO THE
30 best suit buys
DRAWINGS BY BARBARA HULANICKI
CROPPED BLAZER
MOBILE SKIRT
DOUBLE SKIRT
YOKED THICK TWEED
SHORT AND SHARP
132
BLACK AND WHITE
LONG AND SKINNY
ANTELOPE SUIT
TAILORED JERSEY
SHAPED, CROPPED

Press cutting, '30 Best Suit Buys this Winter', fashion illustrations by Barbara Hulanicki, *Vogue*, October 1964

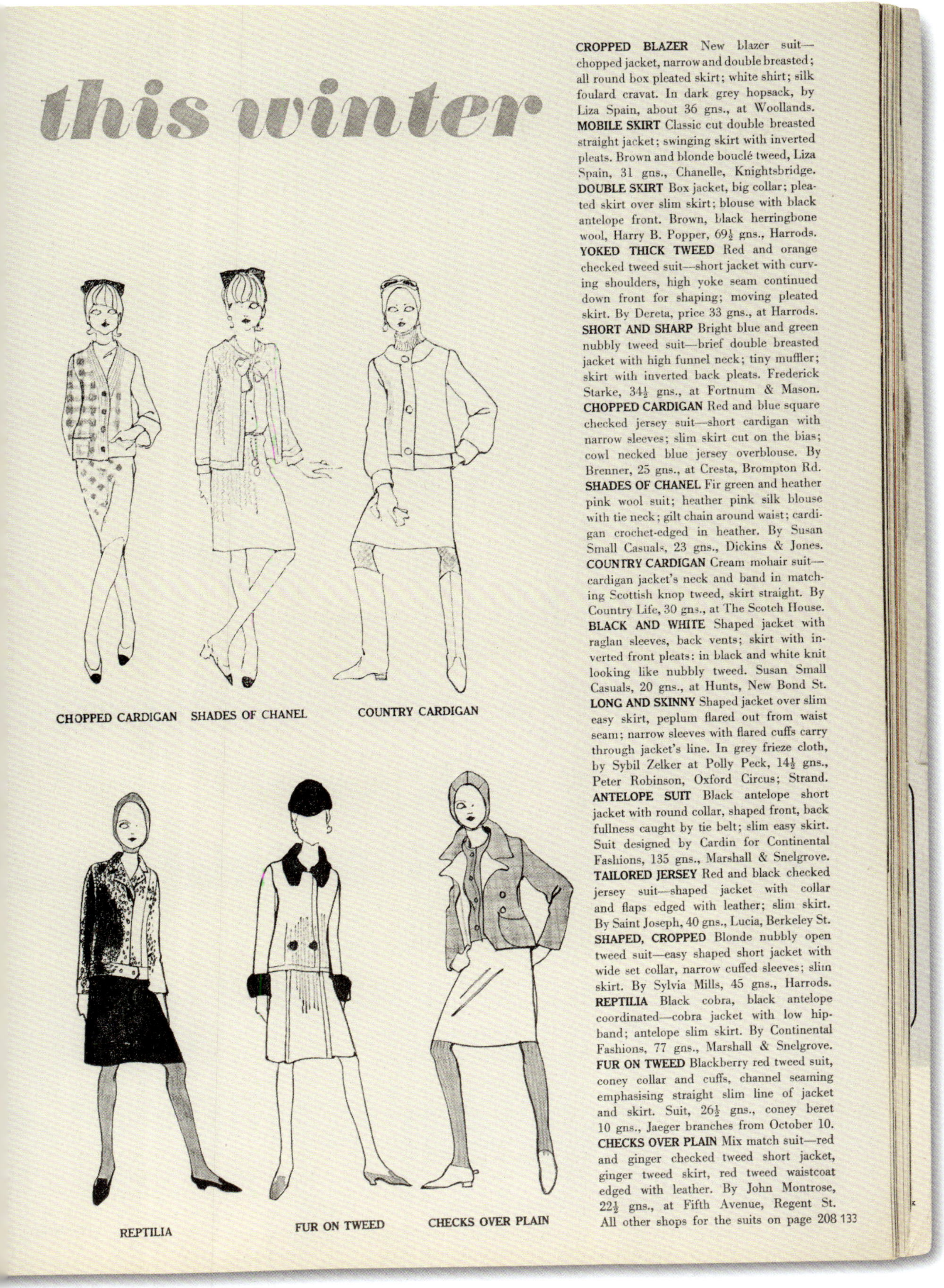

this winter

CHOPPED CARDIGAN SHADES OF CHANEL COUNTRY CARDIGAN

REPTILIA FUR ON TWEED CHECKS OVER PLAIN

CROPPED BLAZER New blazer suit—chopped jacket, narrow and double breasted; all round box pleated skirt; white shirt; silk foulard cravat. In dark grey hopsack, by Liza Spain, about 36 gns., at Woollands. **MOBILE SKIRT** Classic cut double breasted straight jacket; swinging skirt with inverted pleats. Brown and blonde bouclé tweed, Liza Spain, 31 gns., Chanelle, Knightsbridge. **DOUBLE SKIRT** Box jacket, big collar; pleated skirt over slim skirt; blouse with black antelope front. Brown, black herringbone wool, Harry B. Popper, 69½ gns., Harrods. **YOKED THICK TWEED** Red and orange checked tweed suit—short jacket with curving shoulders, high yoke seam continued down front for shaping; moving pleated skirt. By Dereta, price 33 gns., at Harrods. **SHORT AND SHARP** Bright blue and green nubbly tweed suit—brief double breasted jacket with high funnel neck; tiny muffler; skirt with inverted back pleats. Frederick Starke, 34½ gns., at Fortnum & Mason. **CHOPPED CARDIGAN** Red and blue square checked jersey suit—short cardigan with narrow sleeves; slim skirt cut on the bias; cowl necked blue jersey overblouse. By Brenner, 25 gns., at Cresta, Brompton Rd. **SHADES OF CHANEL** Fir green and heather pink wool suit; heather pink silk blouse with tie neck; gilt chain around waist; cardigan crochet-edged in heather. By Susan Small Casuals, 23 gns., Dickins & Jones. **COUNTRY CARDIGAN** Cream mohair suit—cardigan jacket's neck and band in matching Scottish knop tweed, skirt straight. By Country Life, 30 gns., at The Scotch House. **BLACK AND WHITE** Shaped jacket with raglan sleeves, back vents; skirt with inverted front pleats: in black and white knit looking like nubbly tweed. Susan Small Casuals, 20 gns., at Hunts, New Bond St. **LONG AND SKINNY** Shaped jacket over slim easy skirt, peplum flared out from waist seam; narrow sleeves with flared cuffs carry through jacket's line. In grey frieze cloth, by Sybil Zelker at Polly Peck, 14½ gns., Peter Robinson, Oxford Circus; Strand. **ANTELOPE SUIT** Black antelope short jacket with round collar, shaped front, back fullness caught by tie belt; slim easy skirt. Suit designed by Cardin for Continental Fashions, 135 gns., Marshall & Snelgrove. **TAILORED JERSEY** Red and black checked jersey suit—shaped jacket with collar and flaps edged with leather; slim skirt. By Saint Joseph, 40 gns., Lucia, Berkeley St. **SHAPED, CROPPED** Blonde nubbly open tweed suit—easy shaped short jacket with wide set collar, narrow cuffed sleeves; slim skirt. By Sylvia Mills, 45 gns., Harrods. **REPTILIA** Black cobra, black antelope coordinated—cobra jacket with low hipband; antelope slim skirt. By Continental Fashions, 77 gns., Marshall & Snelgrove. **FUR ON TWEED** Blackberry red tweed suit, coney collar and cuffs, channel seaming emphasising straight slim line of jacket and skirt. Suit, 26½ gns., coney beret 10 gns., Jaeger branches from October 10. **CHECKS OVER PLAIN** Mix match suit—red and ginger checked tweed short jacket, ginger tweed skirt, red tweed waistcoat edged with leather. By John Montrose, 22½ gns., at Fifth Avenue, Regent St. All other shops for the suits on page 208

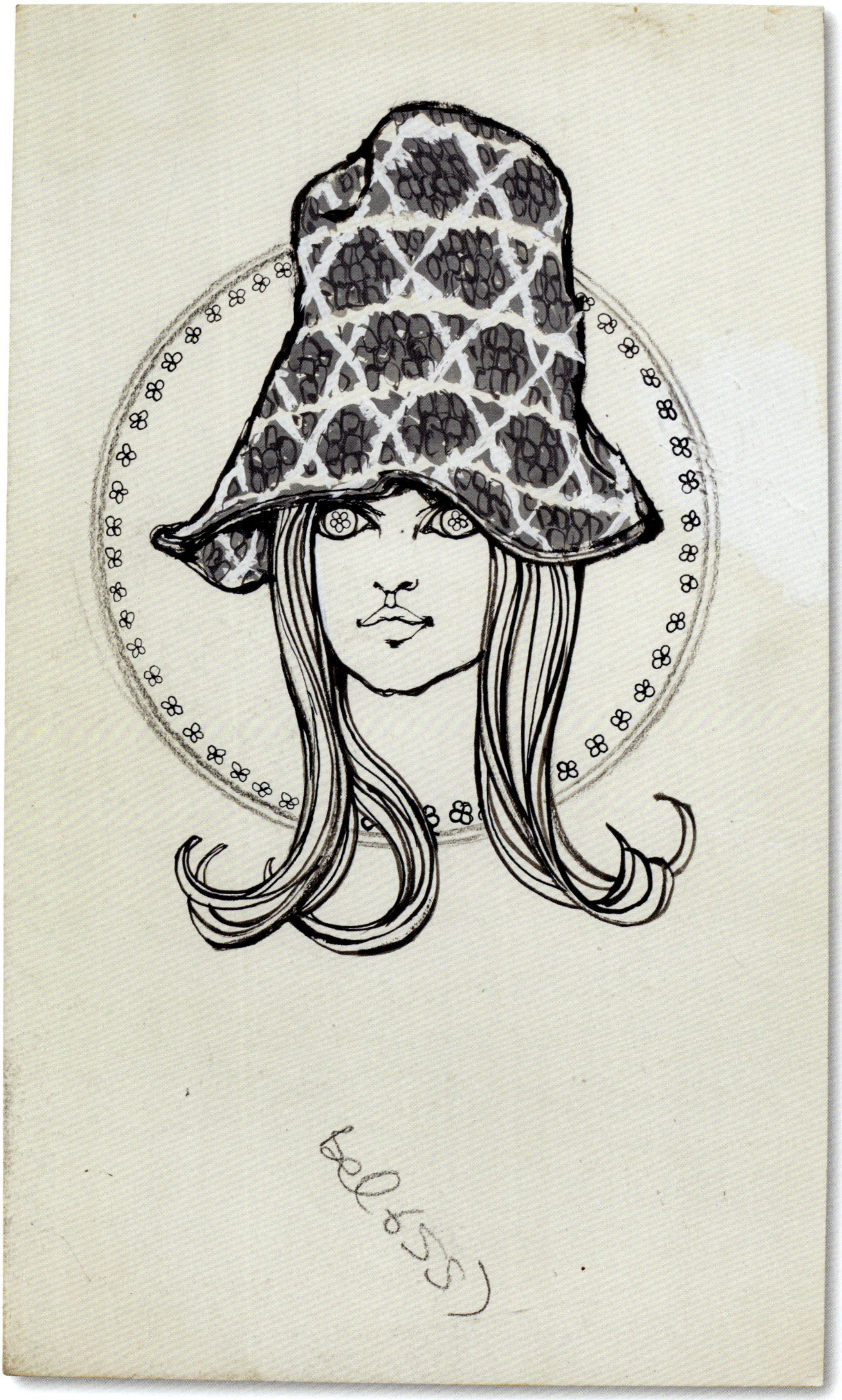

Fashion illustration, girl with bucket hat and flower iris eyes, watercolour and gouache, Barbara Hulanicki, 1964

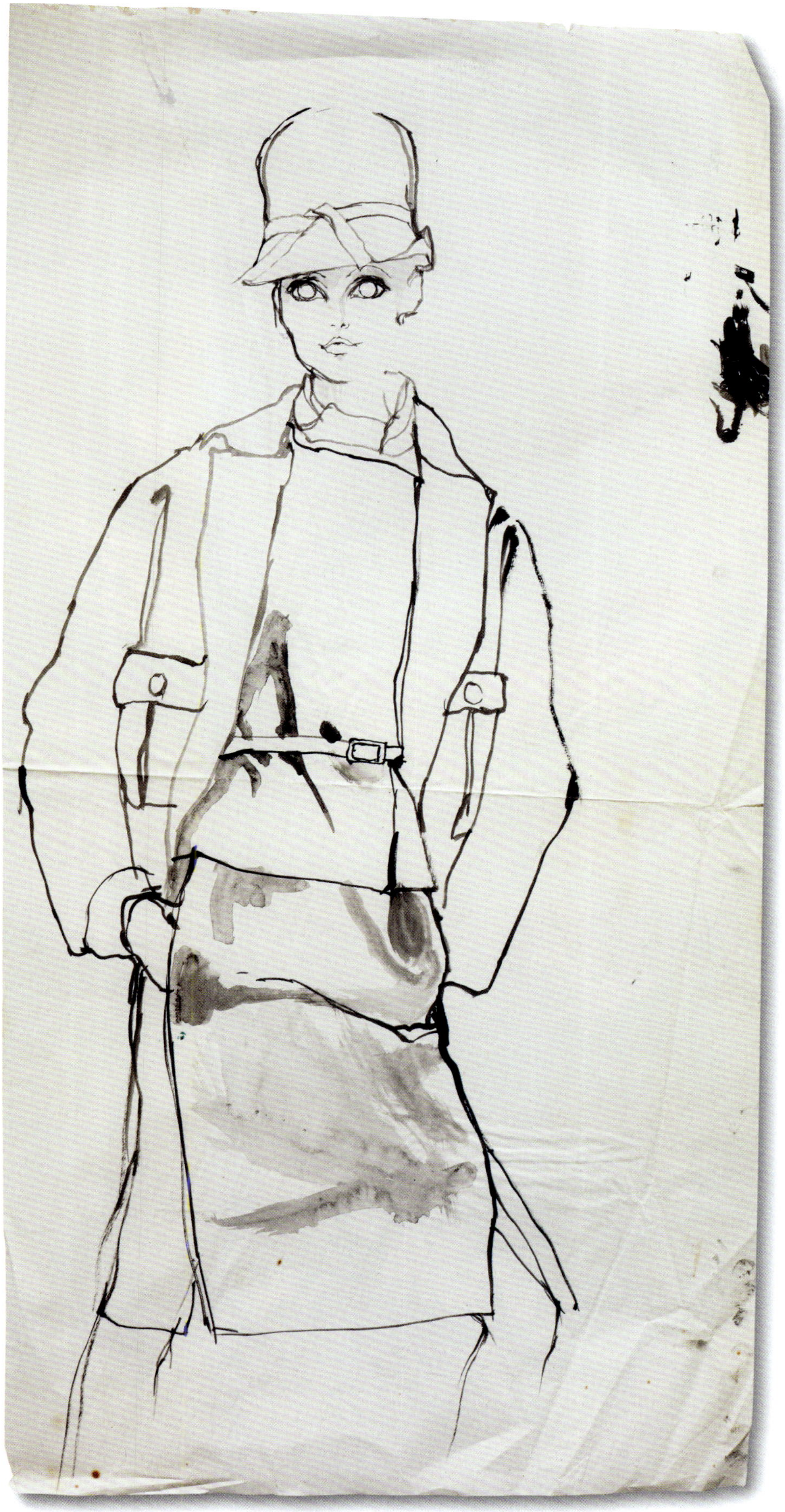

Fashion illustration, woman in belted blouse, skirt, jacket and matching hat, watercolour and gouache, Barbara Hulanicki, c.1964

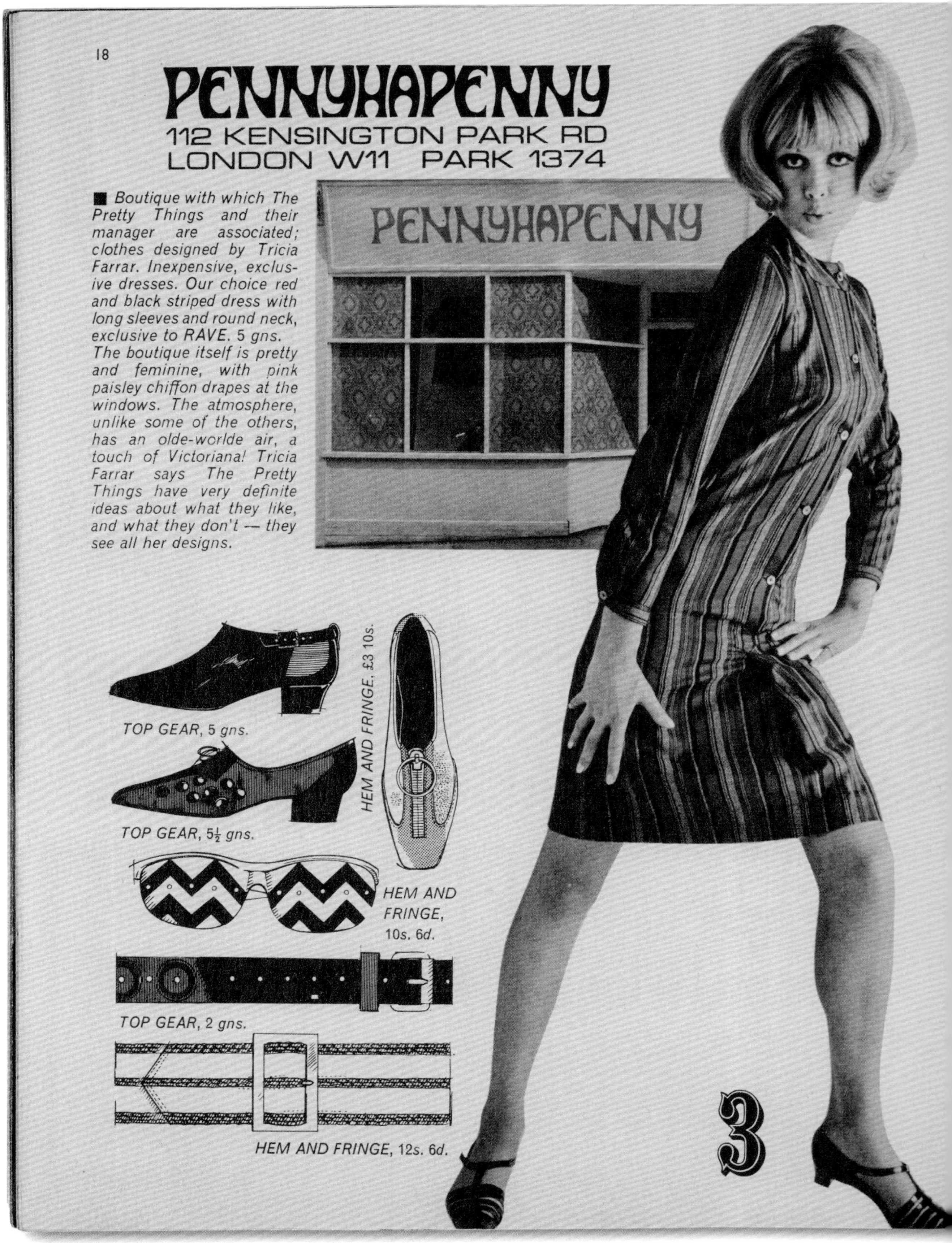

18

PENNYHAPENNY

112 KENSINGTON PARK RD
LONDON W11 PARK 1374

■ *Boutique with which The Pretty Things and their manager are associated; clothes designed by Tricia Farrar. Inexpensive, exclusive dresses. Our choice red and black striped dress with long sleeves and round neck, exclusive to RAVE. 5 gns. The boutique itself is pretty and feminine, with pink paisley chiffon drapes at the windows. The atmosphere, unlike some of the others, has an olde-worlde air, a touch of Victoriana! Tricia Farrar says The Pretty Things have very definite ideas about what they like, and what they don't — they see all her designs.*

Biba, Abingdon Road, feature in *Rave* magazine, September 1965

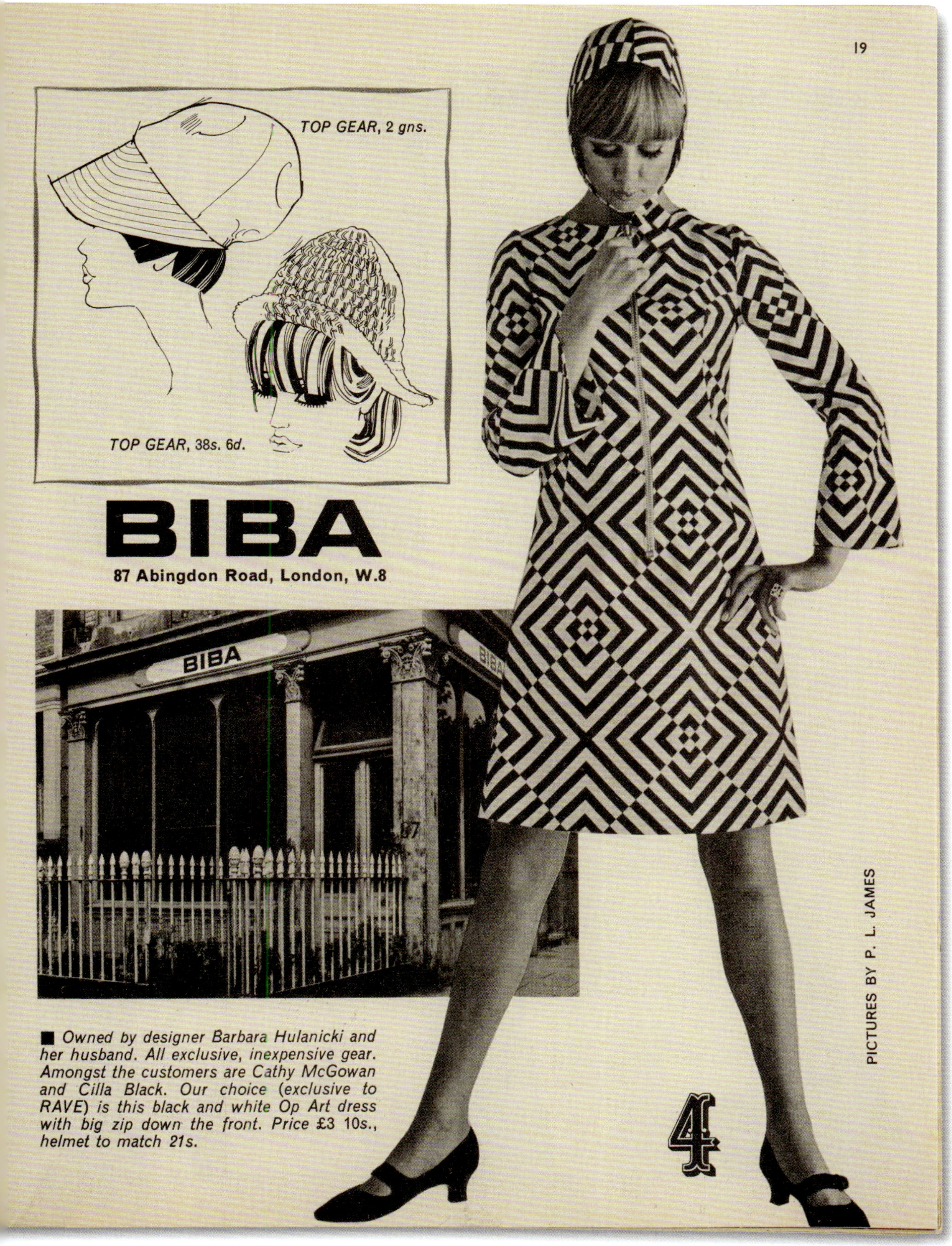

19

TOP GEAR, 2 gns.

TOP GEAR, 38s. 6d.

BIBA

87 Abingdon Road, London, W.8

BIBA

■ *Owned by designer Barbara Hulanicki and her husband. All exclusive, inexpensive gear. Amongst the customers are Cathy McGowan and Cilla Black. Our choice (exclusive to RAVE) is this black and white Op Art dress with big zip down the front. Price £3 10s., helmet to match 21s.*

4

PICTURES BY P. L. JAMES

Fleetway Publications Ltd

FLEETWAY HOUSE
FARRINGDON STREET
LONDON E.C.4

Telegrams: Fleetmags, London, E.C.4
TELEPHONE: CENTRAL 8080

NP/140

25th August, 1965.

Miss Barbara Hulaniki,
Biba's Boutique,
89a Abingdon Road,
London W.8.

Dear Barbara,

Unfortunately I do not know your new home address. On Monday night we came back late from Cambridge feeling very tired and dispirited and found the front door blocked by something the size, shape and weight of a sub-machine gun wrapped in polythene. When we carried it inside we found it was an extravagant, gorgeous, and delightful mass of flowers which are now filling the flat so that it smells like a garden. As the card said, "Lots of love, Barbara", I am sure they came from you. It was a marvellous surprise which staggered and delighted both of us. Thank you very much.

The second half is more business-like. Would you confirm this caption as soon as possible and assure me that the swim suit will be available next summer? "A flag-striped Helanca swimsuit designed by Barbara Hulaniki, with a flamboyant red zipper, 3 gns., at Biba's Boutique, 89a Abingdon Road, W.8. (Postage extra)".

We will get round to printing merchandise credit slips when we really know the name of the magazine.

Love

Maggie

honey FLEETWAY HOUSE · FARRINGDON STREET · LONDON · E·C·4 PHONE · CENTRAL 8080

TELEGRAMS FLEETMAGS CENT LONDON

13th December, 1964.

Miss Barbara Hulanicki,

87, Abingdon Road,

London, W.8.

Barbara dear,

I do, do, do, apologise for being such an eternity with this letter....trying to fly around all my appointments and photograph the March issue, in the face of the Christmas shopping crowds has been more than my human frame could stand .....I am quite horizontal with exhaustion.....anyway...I have now got all the odds and ends I said I would let you have...when was it? 1066 or was that some other happening!

First of all....handbags....the pretty crushed kis bags which Paris is promoting are by a firm called Jeanne Bernard in Paris.

The fabric firm I thought that was very good in London was Dig-o-loom....Dick and Goldschmidt, 32-34, Gt. Pulteney Street, London, W.1 Mrs. Cynthia Reed the P.R.O and general factotem there is a sweet, knowledgeable and helpful woman.

Cheapish manufacturing furriers ...whose names I have managed to glean from my papa at his office...are as follows....please check in the directory that they are absolutely correct before tripping along....I may have got them down a little wrong over the phone ..it was rather a bad line.

Seigal...323, City Road.
A. Roberts, 1-2 Stuart Street ....BIS 8289
S. Benjamin, Middlesex Street.
A. &. D Hope, 41, Farringdon Road, London, E.C.1.
E. Lucas and Sons, 35, Paul Street, E.C.2.
G. Gough, 1-2 Little Montague Court, Little Brittain, E.C.1.

I do sincerely hope this is all of some use to you...let me know if there is anything else I can do...I promise to do it more quickly next time...

FLEETWAY PUBLICATIONS LTD

Vanity Fair

CHESTERGATE HOUSE VAUXHALL BRIDGE ROAD LONDON SW1 Tel. Victoria 2331

Editor
Phyllis Bayley van Thal

Proprietors
The National Magazine Company Limited

Dear Barbara.

You really are very sweet to send me such a heavenly bouquet of flowers. And such an enormous one too. Thank you very much indeed. You've no idea how much it helped to cheer up a horrid week.

I have tried to get you on the telephone without success, hence the delay.

But will be in touch soon and will no doubt see you before long.

Yours

Marjorie Bowra

The information and any recommendation is given strictly on terms that the Publishers accept no liability whatsoever, neither can they accept responsibility for any act or omission or any negligence on the part of the persons, Firm or Corporation recommended

THE OBSERVER
1791
The Observer Limited
22 TUDOR STREET
LONDON, E.C.4

TELEPHONE:
FLEET STREET 0202

Tuesday.

Dear Barbara,

How very sweet of you to send me the dear little spectacles! They are marvellous – I must get lenses put in the ones that stay on my nose.

The black cut-out dress from Biba is in this Sunday (unless something awful happens in between): do let me know when you have a lot of new stuff in the shop, I am a great fan of Biba's.

Love from Georgina

KAREN

KAREN teen-togs

PHONE PRESTWICH 6020

60 BURY OLD ROAD · WHITEFIELD · MANCHESTER

15th October, 1965.

Miss B. Hulanicki,
Biba's Boutique,
87, Abingdon Rd.,
LONDON, W.8.

Dear Miss Hulanicki,

My sister and I have recently - in August of this year - opened a really attractive and up-to-the-minute boutique here in Manchester.

We are both great admirers of your trend-setting clothes, and as to our knowledge you have no retail outlet for them in the North, we wondered if you would be interested in coming to some arrangement whereby we could feature your things at Karen.

We do advertise a great deal, and the shop, in many ways a trend-setter [redacted] itself, has attracted a good deal of attention already. We feel sure that some sort of tie-up could only be mutually beneficial.

If you are interested, I shall be in London on the 8th and 9th November, when I could call and see you, tell you more about ourselves, and we could discuss the matter further.

I look forward to hearing from you, and meanwhile wish you continued success in your marvellous enterprise.

Yours sincerely,

Adele Rose

(for KAREN teen-togs)

KAREN ROSE LTD. DIRECTORS: ADELE ROSE. MONTAGUE M. ROSE. DOROTHY ROSE

Mark Simon Trends Ltd.,
(pending acceptance)
8a Gloucester Avenue,
London N.W.1.

MSW/BYH

9th November, 1965.

Biba's Boutique,
87 Abingdon Road,
London W.8.

Dear Sirs,

I am planning to open a ladies' fashion boutique in Leicester, the first of its type in the Midlands, and am wondering if you would be interested in supplying made up skirts, suits, trouser suits, dresses and accessories, etc., for sale when I open.

This is a largely unexploited area with a large free spending potential market and I am sure we could both profit from a mutually suitable arrangement.

If we could perhaps meet at your convenience, I would be most grateful. An early reply would be much appreciated.

Yours faithfully,

M. S. Williams

Mark S. Williams.

Biba,
87 Abingdon Road,
London. W.8.

Dear Miss Hulanicki,

I have just returned from living in London and have opened a boutique selling way-out young clothes. I brought quite a few samples with me from England, including one or two of your garments bought retail, and have had a great reaction from these here.

I would therefore very much like to import more of your garments, hats & accessories too. There is a great interest here in English fashion as seen in English magazines, but, apart from Mary Quant, very little is available and I believe there would be a great demand if it were.

Perhaps you would be kind enough to send me your latest catalogue and I could choose styles from that to start with. I have kept my A/c in London with Barclays Bank, Station Road Harrow, so immediate payment to you would be no problem.

I hope you will be able to help me -
Yours faithfully,

Pat Connaughton

OPPOSITE Letters demonstrating the relationship between journalists and Barbara Hulanicki in the first year of the Biba boutique, 1964–5

ABOVE & RIGHT Letters to Biba from boutique owners asking advice and stocking Biba clothes, 1965

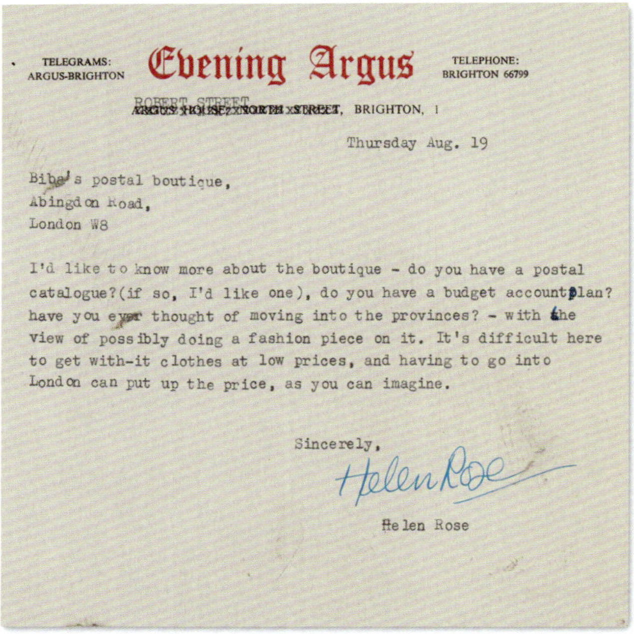

TELEGRAMS: ARGUS-BRIGHTON

Evening Argus

TELEPHONE: BRIGHTON 66799

ROBERT STREET
~~ARGUS HOUSE, NORTH STREET~~, BRIGHTON, 1

Thursday Aug. 19

Biba's postal boutique,
Abingdon Road,
London W8

I'd like to know more about the boutique - do you have a postal catalogue? (if so, I'd like one), do you have a budget account plan? have you ever thought of moving into the provinces? - with the view of possibly doing a fashion piece on it. It's difficult here to get with-it clothes at low prices, and having to go into London can put up the price, as you can imagine.

Sincerely,

Helen Rose

Helen Rose

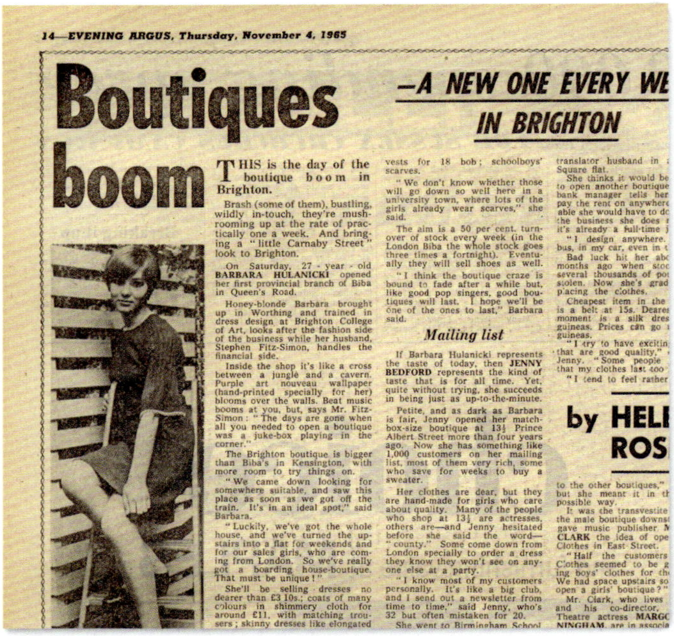

14—EVENING ARGUS, Thursday, November 4, 1965

Boutiques boom —A NEW ONE EVERY WE[…] IN BRIGHTON

THIS is the day of the boutique boom in Brighton.

Brash (some of them), bustling, wildly in-touch, they're mushrooming up at the rate of practically one a week. And bringing a "little Carnaby Street" look to Brighton.

On Saturday, 27-year-old **BARBARA HULANICKI** opened her first provincial branch of Biba in Queen's Road.

Honey-blonde Barbara brought up in Worthing and trained in dress design at Brighton College of Art, looks after the fashion side of the business while her husband, Stephen Fitz-Simon, handles the financial side.

Inside the shop it's like a cross between a jungle and a cavern. Purple art nouveau wallpaper (hand-printed specially for her) blooms over the walls. Beat music booms at you, but, says Mr. Fitz-Simon: "The days are gone when all you needed to open a boutique was a juke-box playing in the corner."

The Brighton boutique is bigger than Biba's in Kensington, with more room to try things on.

"We came down looking for somewhere suitable, and saw this place as soon as we got off the train. It's in an ideal spot," said Barbara.

"Luckily, we've got the whole house, and we've turned the upstairs into a flat for weekends and for our sales girls, who are coming from London. So we've really got a boarding house-boutique. That must be unique!"

She'll be selling dresses no dearer than £3 10s.; coats of many colours in shimmery cloth for around £11, with matching trousers; skinny dresses like elongated vests for 18 bob; schoolboys' scarves.

"We don't know whether those will go down so well here in a university town, where lots of the girls already wear scarves," she said.

The aim is a 50 per cent. turnover of stock every week (in the London Biba the whole stock goes three times a fortnight). Eventually they will sell shoes as well.

"I think the boutique craze is bound to fade after a while but, like good pop singers, good boutiques will last. I hope we'll be one of the ones to last," Barbara said.

Mailing list

If Barbara Hulanicki represents the taste of today, then **JENNY BEDFORD** represents the kind of taste that is for all time. Yet, quite without trying, she succeeds in being just as up-to-the-minute.

Petite, and as dark as Barbara is fair, Jenny opened her match-box-size boutique at 13½ Prince Albert Street more than four years ago. Now she has something like 1,000 customers on her mailing list, most of them very rich, some who save for weeks to buy a sweater.

Her clothes are dear, but they are hand-made for girls who care about quality. Many of the people who shop at 13½ are actresses, others are—and Jenny hesitated before she said the word—"county." Some come down from London specially to order a dress they know they won't see on anyone else at a party.

"I know most of my customers personally. It's like a big club, and I send out a newsletter from time to time," said Jenny, who's 32 but often mistaken for 20.

She went to Birmingham School […]

translator husband in […]
Square flat.

She thinks it would be […]
to open another boutique […]
bank manager tells her […]
pay the rent on anywhere […]
able she would have to do […]
the business she does […]
it's already a full-time j[…]

"I design anywhere. […]
bus, in my car, even in t[…]

Bad luck hit her abo[…]
months ago when stoc[…]
several thousands of po[…]
stolen. Now she's grad[…]
placing the clothes.

Cheapest item in the […]
is a belt at 15s. Deares[…]
moment is a silk dres[…]
guineas. Prices can go […]
guineas.

"I try to have excitin[…]
that are good quality," […]
Jenny. "Some people […]
that my clothes last too […]

"I tend to feel rather […]

by HEL[…] ROS[…]

to the other boutiques," […]
but she meant it in th[…]
possible way.

It was the transvestite […]
the male boutique downst[…]
gave music publisher M[…]
CLARK the idea of ope[…]
Clothes in East Street.

"Half the customers […]
Clothes seemed to be g[…]
ing boys' clothes for th[…]
We had space upstairs so […]
open a girls' boutique?" […]

Mr. Clark, who lives […]
and his co-director, […]
Theatre actress **MARGO[…]**
NINGHAM, are in associa[…]

ABOVE LEFT Letter to Biba from Brighton journalist Helen Rose of the *Evening Argus* enquiring about Biba clothing and a move to Brighton, 1965

ABOVE RIGHT Press cutting, 'Boutiques Boom', *Evening Argus*, 4 November 1965

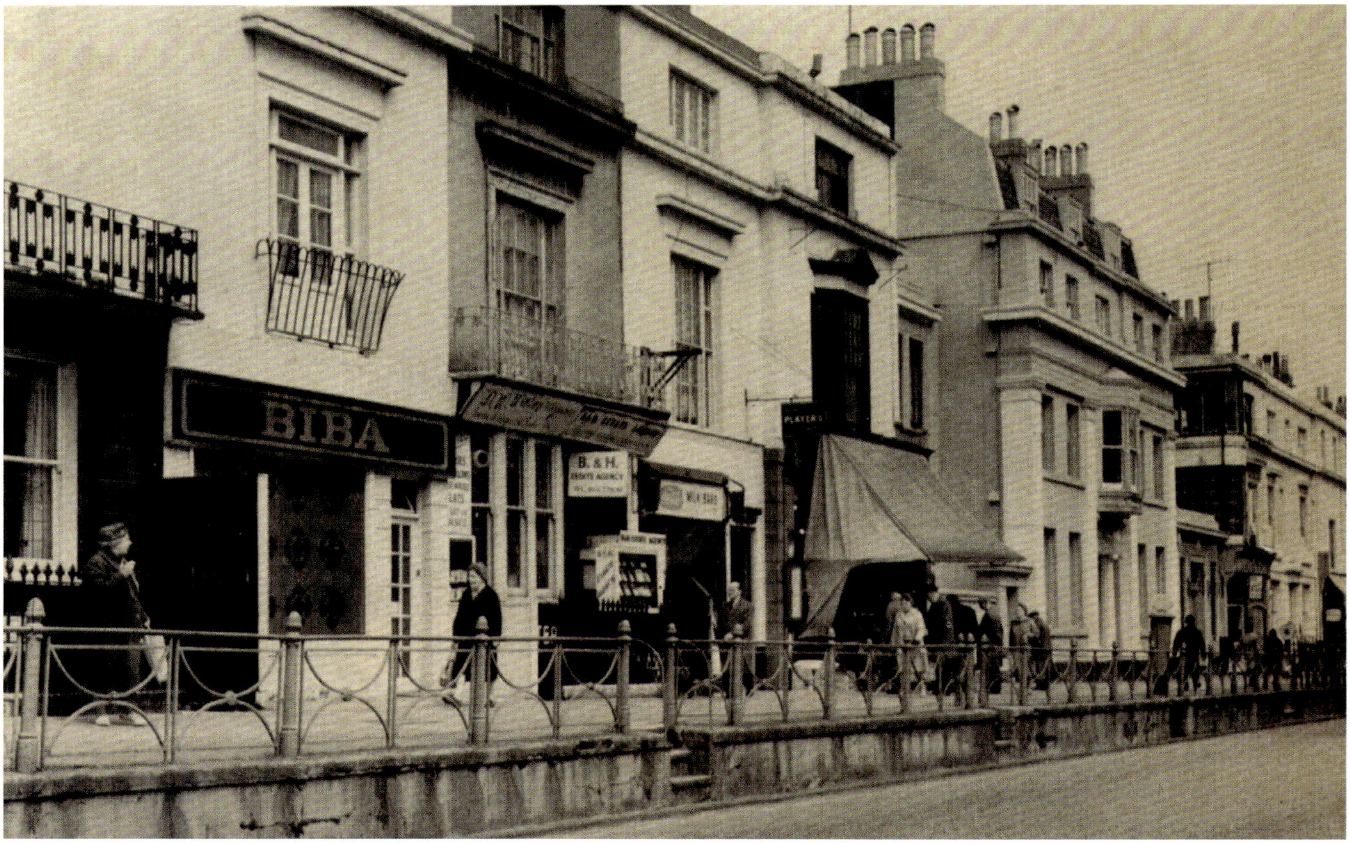

ABOVE Exterior of Brighton Biba boutique, 21 Queens Road, 1965–6

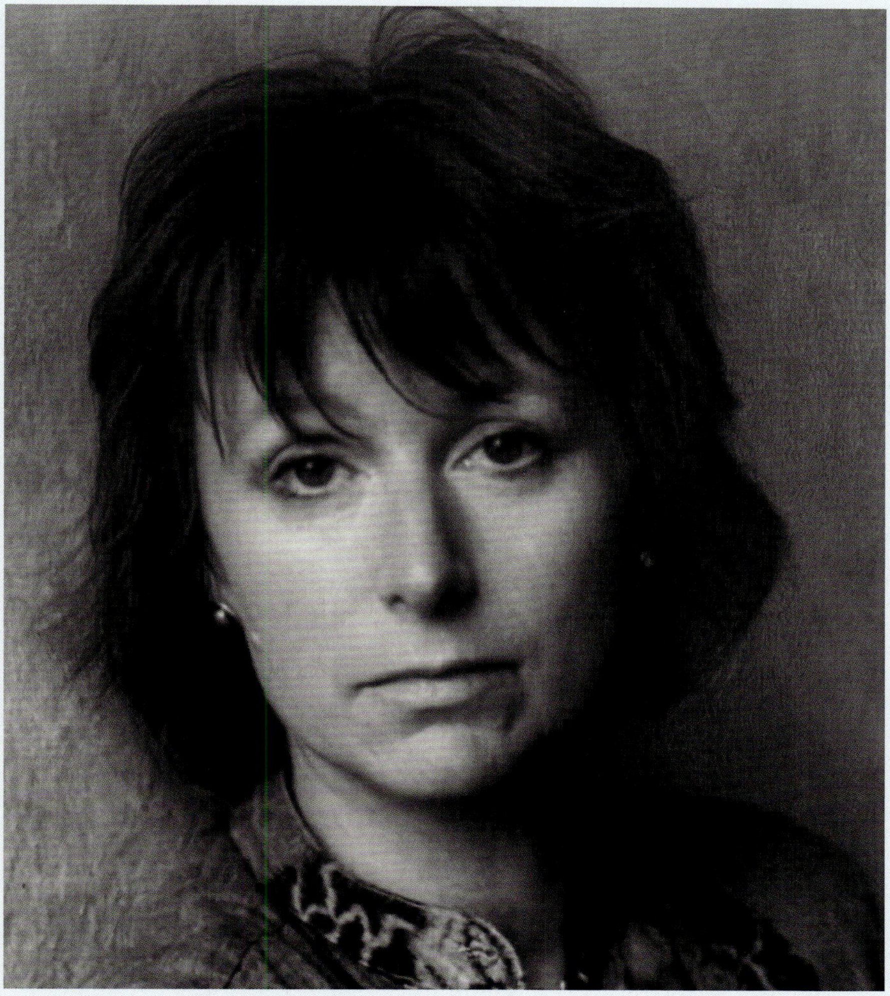

ROSIE MARKES
~
ASSISTANT TO BARBARA HULANICKI

Rosie Bartlett (née Markes), late 1970s

I began working at Biba in 1964. My cousin Sarah, who was already working at Biba in Abingdon Road, rang me up to ask if I would like a job at Biba as Barbara's assistant. I jumped at the idea and met Barbara the next day. We got on very well and there was no question of an interview or references; she liked the skirt I was wearing and the Mini I was driving, so I got the job! All I knew about the role was that I would be a helpful right hand to her. I had admired her drawings as a young girl and had spent a lot of time tracing them, so I was very excited.

The shop was tiny: dresses, coats, hats and feather boas were all hung on hat stands; a screen to change behind, and music playing all day long. It looked fabulous – extraordinary – and very different to anything else. It was unique; you couldn't find any other tiny little boutiques with palm trees in them! It was a new and exciting way to shop and an instant hit with the girls.

Barbara was fantastic to work with. She did beautiful drawings of her designs, and we would go to the workroom for her to okay the calico samples, which I had to model, before they were sent to the outworkers. We were often out and about, 'getting inspired'. We thought we were working very hard!

As Biba became successful, the fabric reps were eager to supply materials and we would have a lot of cloth specially dyed in certain colours: every shade of berry – raspberry, blackberry, bilberry – as well as lots of browns and shades of purple. It was all go! And then there was the move to Kensington Church Street, which was even more exciting and successful.

I stayed with Barbara until 1968 and have many wonderful memories of working with her and the beautiful shops she created. She remains a great friend and inspiration to me.

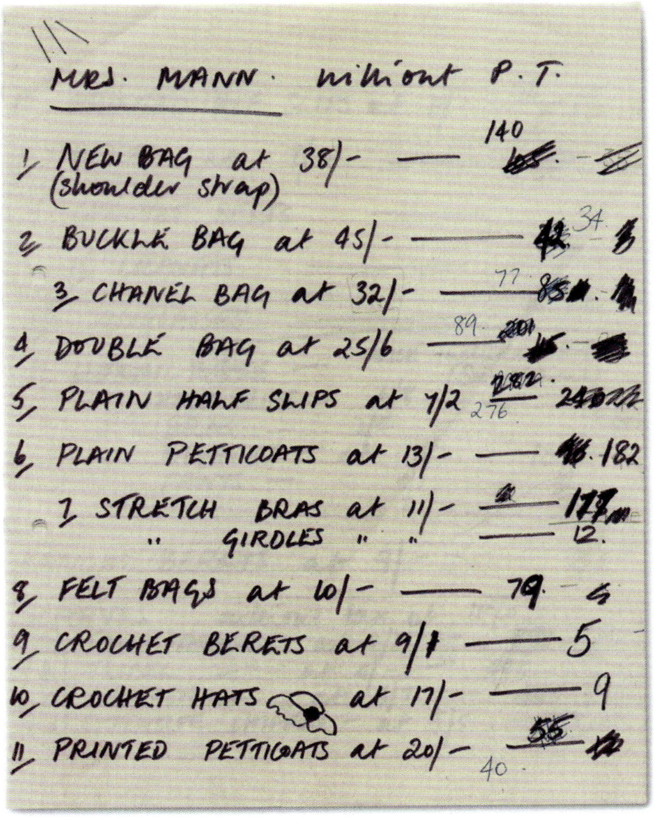

MRS. MANN. without P.T.

1, NEW BAG at 38/- — 140
(shoulder strap)
2, BUCKLE BAG at 45/- — 34
3, CHANEL BAG at 32/- — 77
4, DOUBLE BAG at 25/6 — 89
5, PLAIN HALF SLIPS at 7/2 — 276
6, PLAIN PETTICOATS at 13/- — 182
7, STRETCH BRAS at 11/- — 177
" GIRDLES " " — 12.
8, FELT BAGS at 10/- — 79
9, CROCHET BERETS at 9/- — 5
10, CROCHET HATS at 17/- — 9
11, PRINTED PETTICOATS at 20/- — 55 40

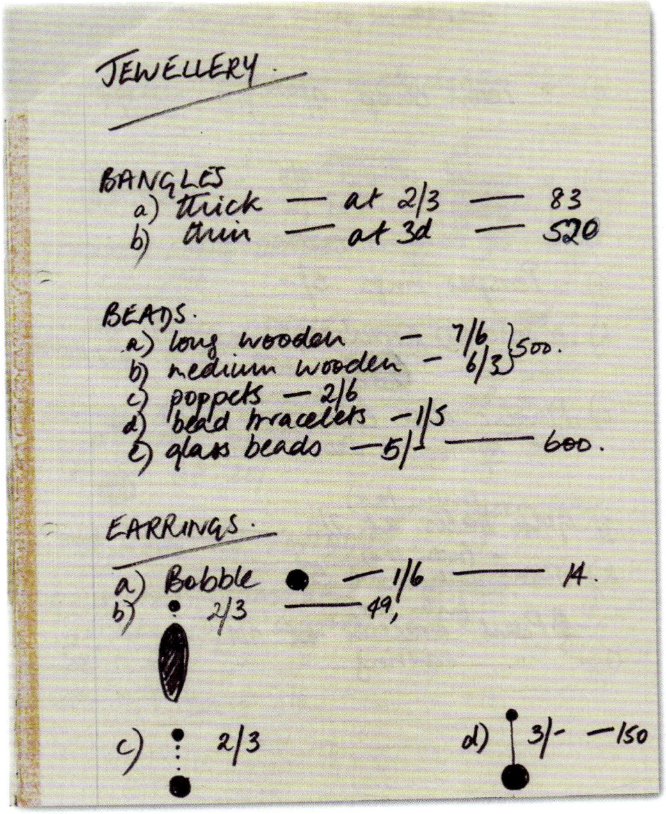

JEWELLERY.

BANGLES
a) thick — at 2/3 — 83
b) thin — at 3d — 520

BEADS.
a) long wooden – 7/6
b) medium wooden – 6/3 } 500.
c) poppets — 2/6
d) bead bracelets – 1/5
e) glass beads – 5/- — 600.

EARRINGS.
a) Bobble — 1/6 — 14.
b) 2/3 — 49,
c) 2/3
d) 3/- – 150

ABOVE LEFT & RIGHT Handwritten lists of Biba clothing and accessories with prices in pounds, shillings and pence, 1965

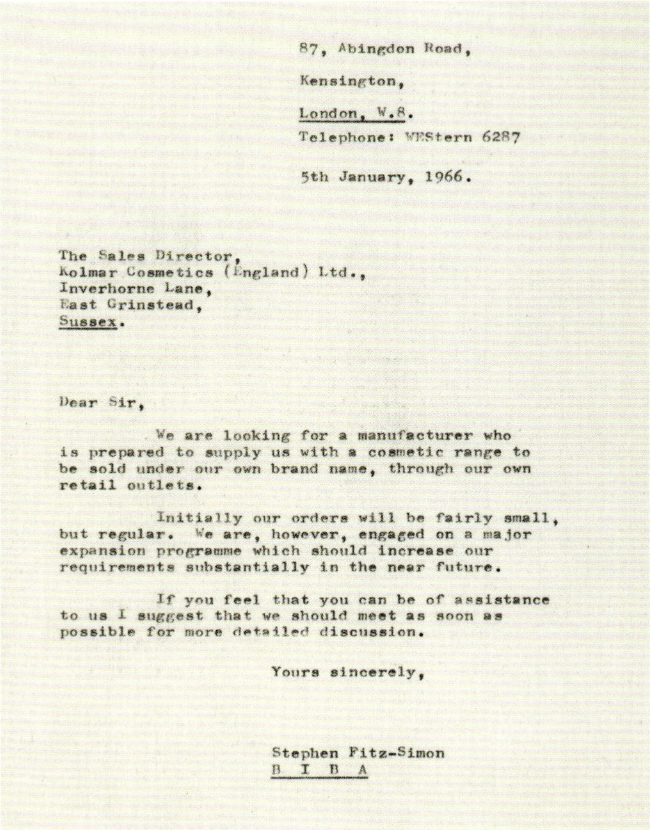

87, Abingdon Road,
Kensington,
London, W.8.
Telephone: WEStern 6287

5th January, 1966.

The Sales Director,
Kolmar Cosmetics (England) Ltd.,
Inverhorne Lane,
East Grinstead,
Sussex.

Dear Sir,

We are looking for a manufacturer who is prepared to supply us with a cosmetic range to be sold under our own brand name, through our own retail outlets.

Initially our orders will be fairly small, but regular. We are, however, engaged on a major expansion programme which should increase our requirements substantially in the near future.

If you feel that you can be of assistance to us I suggest that we should meet as soon as possible for more detailed discussion.

Yours sincerely,

Stephen Fitz-Simon
B I B A

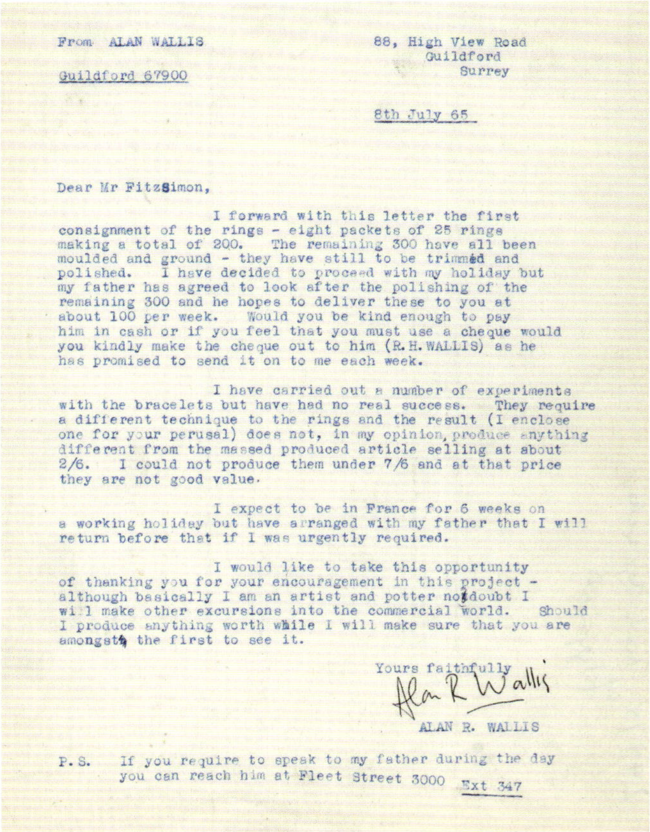

From ALAN WALLIS
Guildford 67900

88, High View Road
Guildford
Surrey

8th July 65

Dear Mr FitzSimon,

I forward with this letter the first consignment of the rings - eight packets of 25 rings making a total of 200. The remaining 300 have all been moulded and ground - they have still to be trimmed and polished. I have decided to proceed with my holiday but my father has agreed to look after the polishing of the remaining 300 and he hopes to deliver these to you at about 100 per week. Would you be kind enough to pay him in cash or if you feel that you must use a cheque would you kindly make the cheque out to him (R.H. WALLIS) as he has promised to send it on to me each week.

I have carried out a number of experiments with the bracelets but have had no real success. They require a different technique to the rings and the result (I enclose one for your perusal) does not, in my opinion, produce anything different from the massed produced article selling at about 2/6. I could not produce them under 7/6 and at that price they are not good value.

I expect to be in France for 6 weeks on a working holiday but have arranged with my father that I will return before that if I was urgently required.

I would like to take this opportunity of thanking you for your encouragement in this project - although basically I am an artist and potter no doubt I will make other excursions into the commercial world. Should I produce anything worth while I will make sure that you are amongst the first to see it.

Yours faithfully
Alan R Wallis
ALAN R. WALLIS

P.S. If you require to speak to my father during the day you can reach him at Fleet Street 3000 Ext 347

ABOVE LEFT & RIGHT Letters to and from manufacturers of Biba goods, 1965–6

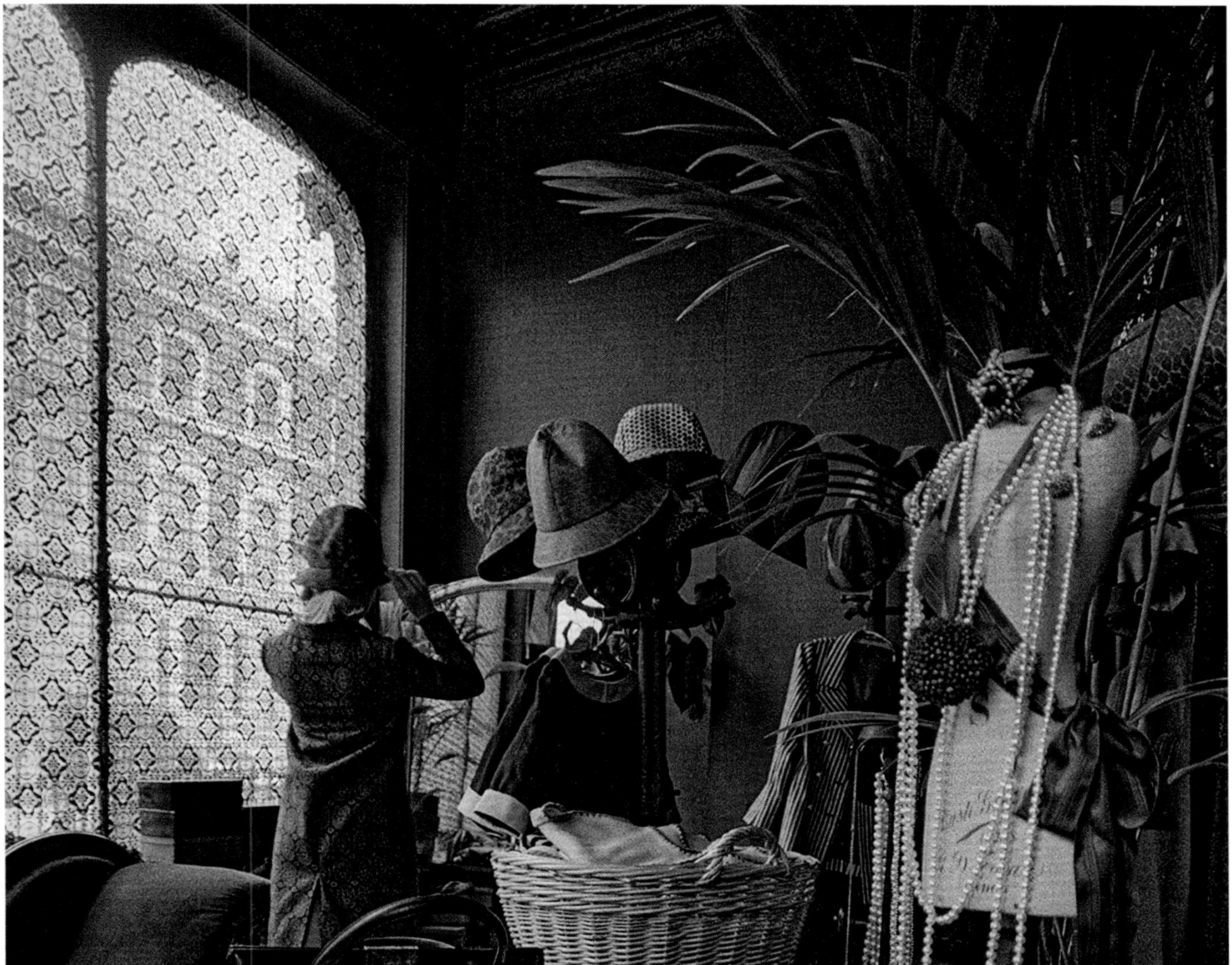

Biba, Abingdon Road, interior, 10 May 1965

CHAPTER THREE

1966–1969 CHURCH STREET

"I didn't want my name up front. I didn't want it to distract from Biba. I just wanted Biba, Biba, Biba"

Barbara Hulanicki

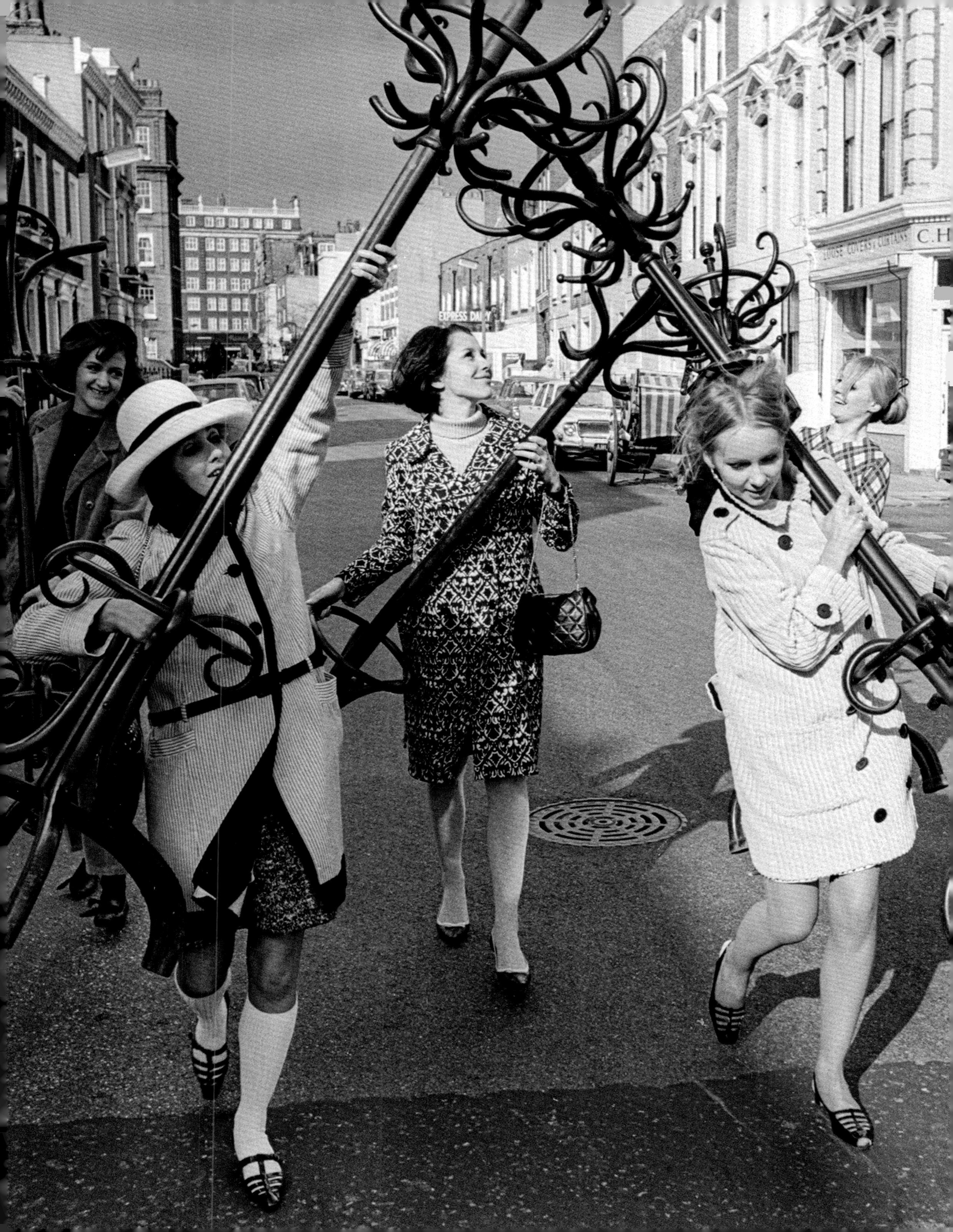
EXPRESS
C.H

MARTIN PEL In 1966 you moved Biba from Abingdon Road to Church Street, Kensington.

BARBARA HULANICKI Well, Abingdon Road was bursting at the seams, and it was almost impossible to sell anything because customers couldn't get to the till. We got a loan from the bank for a thousand pounds via our bank manager, who really loved us because of all of our cash flow. He thought a bigger shop might be a bit of a risk, but on opening day it was packed.

We didn't really advertise, but we did a photoshoot of the Biba girls in a van and running up the street with clothes rails and hat stands for the new Biba on Church Street. That was the idea of Cathy McGowan's agent, I think. He said, 'I'm going to get a truck and get the girls in it', and I thought, 'What a stupid idea.' After it made all the papers, I thought, 'Ah, well done. What a clever guy!' You see it was terrible to be seen to be advertising. It was better that things spread by word of mouth. People were looking all the time, desperate to find decent clothes as there was so little about. When the delivery would come into Church Street on a Saturday morning, customers would be waiting for something in particular that somebody had told somebody about. Customers would ask, 'What's coming in?', and Sarah Plunket would let them know, as we roughly knew from what was being cut. I remember Mr Savva once sent in a blouse instead of a dress because it was quicker to make, and Fitz and I were so scared as the customers were toughies. We were sitting there waiting, thinking, 'They're going to kill us!'

MP Sixties London exploded while you were at Church Street, with Biba at the centre of it all.

BH It took *Time* magazine for Swinging London to go global. In 1966 they were photographing all around London and I was supposed to talk to them, but I didn't want to. I never used to do interviews because I didn't want my name up front. I didn't want it to distract from Biba. I just wanted Biba, Biba, Biba.

When the *Time* article came out it was just amazing – the whole world was suddenly interested. But mainstream America didn't take it very seriously. I don't think a lot of them knew what to make of it, but the younger generation of Americans understood and were mad for it. For Europeans, London was like, 'Whoa!' They were coming over like mad, every weekend: the Italians, the French, the Germans, the whole lot, you know, because it was swinging – Portobello Road, clubs, girls in minis and Minis! Yeah, it was huge. And the exchange rate was amazing, so they would fill up their bags with stuff. It was huge business. About that time there were some rag traders who registered the Biba name in France, which is why we couldn't open in Paris. They had a Biba shop and they used to come to Biba to see what we were doing. Fitz would say, 'I don't care, as long as they keep buying the stuff.'

MP Explain the Church Street shop to me.

BH The Church Street interiors were bright: wallpaper in red and orange, matched for a while by the clothes. A textile designer walked into the shop one day with a collection and we bought everything; all these weird prints that we called cloud print. Her stuff

PREVIOUS PAGE Biba girls carrying hat stands from Abingdon Road to Church Street Biba, 1966

was really good, and it was like an explosion in the shop. When Fitz saw it, he said 'Crickey, I hope it sells!'

The shop itself should have been preserved because we kept all the original shelving. There was the bus stop outside, and all the old ladies used to wait in the shop. I had a table where I kept all these old hairpins and clips so they could steal them. I deliberately put them there so they could steal them because they were pensioners. I'd say to the staff, 'Don't watch them; let them do it!' I loved that table.

MP Biba was famous for communal changing rooms.

BH That came about at Abingdon Road. At first, we had individual screens with a mirror, but they were always falling down so we had screens put up and people used to change behind them. They would throw clothes over the top, and, after a certain number of clothes, the screen would fall down, but the customers wouldn't take any notice and would just keep changing. Things got so crowded that nobody could move – it was only 500 square feet – and we had this little mezzanine, so we were going to do changing rooms with cubby holes. We got as far as putting the mirrors up – big, old mirrors because they were cheap – and people just ran in and started changing. We decided we could save money by not putting the partitions in, and that's how it stayed.

"It was swinging – Portobello Road, clubs, girls in minis and Minis!"

MP It was at Church Street Biba that you created the now-iconic Biba catalogues. How did they come about?

BH We did catalogues really early on, before the first shop. They were illustrated with drawings, which were xeroxed and pinned together and sent out to customers who bought from the Biba Postal Boutique, or who contacted us through newspapers featuring Biba. Once we started selling from the shop, the catalogues became a nuisance. Much later, the photographic catalogues became a nuisance as well!

There was a big gap between the illustrated catalogues and the photographic ones. The minute we opened the shops there was a different frame of mind, because we were on our feet all the time and I couldn't sit down and concentrate on drawing. It was just a completely different way of working. By the time of the Abingdon Road shop, I was sick and tired of drawing; that's why I asked Moira Macgregor to do the drawings, which were wonderful. And I think I did one. Then we used photographs.

MP Whose idea was it to do photographic catalogues?

BH Oh mine! I always, always wanted to do photographic catalogues because I didn't want to draw. Fitz thought it was time to do catalogues again because we were growing and growing. I was so thrilled because I love photography and I just wanted to be able to put the Biba look down on paper.

MP To create your own editorial?

BH Yes, exactly. Power! When we launched the Biba couture range, Helmut Newton shot the story for the *Observer*. The journalist Liz Smith used to work for us; she was the second Biba girl after Sarah Plunket, and was terribly beautiful. I said to her, 'I'd

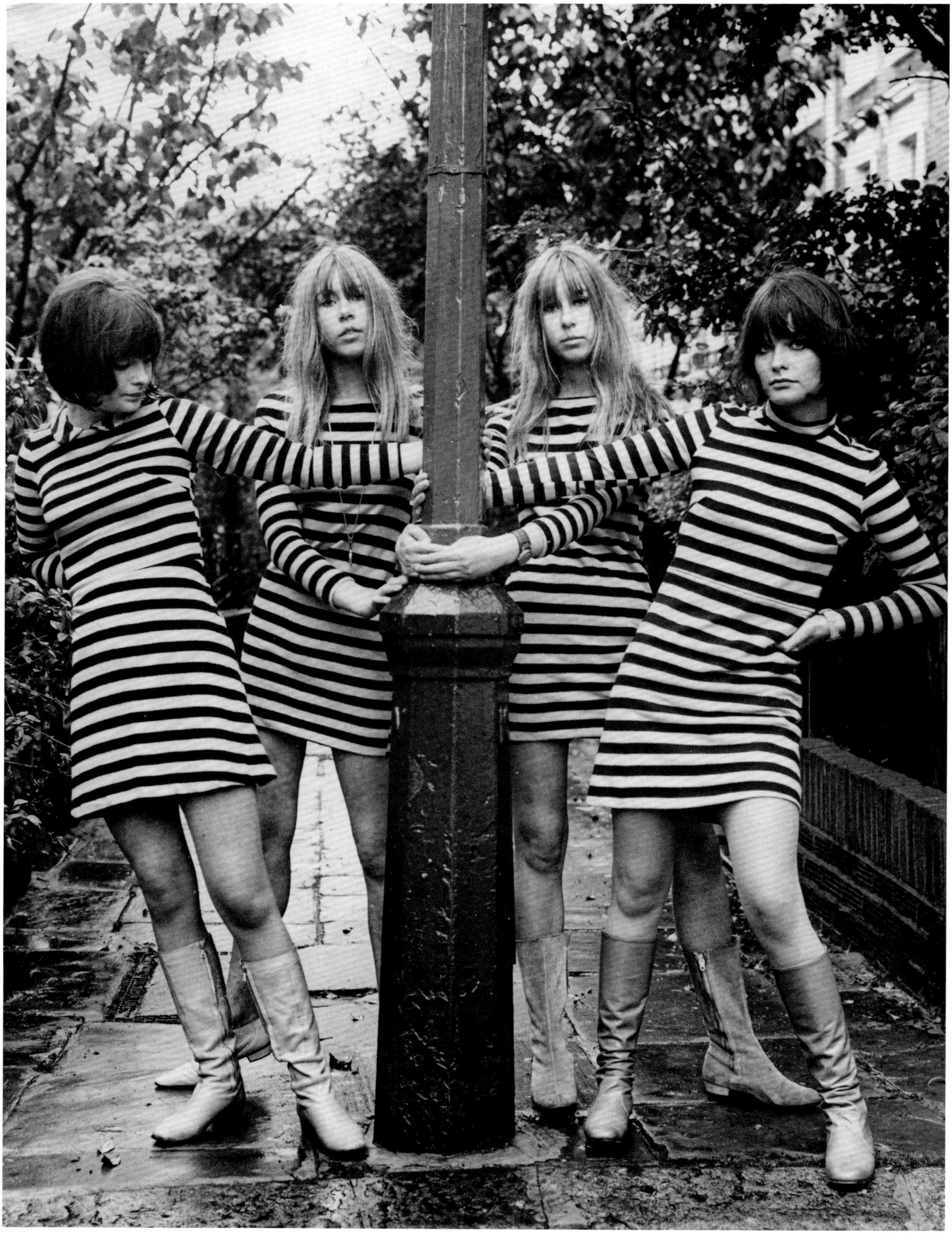

do anything to work with Helmut Newton again', and she said 'Okay, I'll ask him', and he happily agreed. I saw him years later and he asked me, 'Why didn't you ask me to do more? I loved working for Biba.' I told him that I didn't dare!

With the catalogue you could do it your way. The photographer Donald Silverstein did the first catalogue for us. He was a hero of mine because he did all these amazing photographs for *Queen* magazine when he was working for them. I thought they were incredible; he used lenses that made the head look really big and the body went out to nothing. And his lighting was amazing, absolutely amazing – I loved it. I remember Wally Rose, who was in the real smutter trade, supplying clothing through catalogues, and for him everything depended on the photography. He would come down to see Fitz and ask how many items we'd sold from our catalogues. He'd say, 'You've sold so much of this one ... and you can only see the collar!' He couldn't quite get that people were buying into a look.

"I didn't want to talk down to any Biba customers just because of their age, or where they came from. Biba was for everyone"

The model, Madelaine Smith, was so gorgeous with her hair with the ringlets in the front. I mean, we never even tested her. The look with the turban, that came from my aunt Sophie. When Auntie was travelling across India on her honeymoon, the heat was so sticky and she had these ringlets, so she would tuck them in under her turbans. So, I did turbans, and we had them in all colours; they sold like mad. The couture range at Church Street was Auntie. Once I had got over her, I could see the beauty in the clothes she wore and her attitude to dress. I also wanted to elevate the whole thing. I wanted to use more expensive fabrics and a lot of sequins, because Biba clothes were all simple shapes.

MP Your aunt Sophie had a significant influence on Biba, and 'Biba' was the nickname of your youngest sister. Did other close family members influence Biba?

BH Well, we began selling menswear at Church Street because Fitz needed clothing! We started with t-shirts, those ones with little buttons all the way down, by Vedonis I think. Victorian t-shirts. And then I became pregnant, which was a nice surprise after six years of marriage, and so we began selling children's wear for our son, Witold. Children's clothes were so horrible at that time, and everyone was desperate for something interesting, but there was nothing to buy. Nobody was doing decent children's clothes; there was just the high-waisted, very old English sort of things for kids. It would probably be lovely now, rompers with three daisies on, but I never looked as it was depressing. Later at Biba, we built a little house with everything at a child's height so *they* could pick things out, not the mother. I didn't want to talk down to any Biba customers just because of their age, or where they came from. Biba was for everyone.

OPPOSITE The 'Biba Twins' dressed in Biba for a photoshoot; from left to right: Rosie Young, Michelle Hellier, Nicole Hellier, Susy Young, 1966

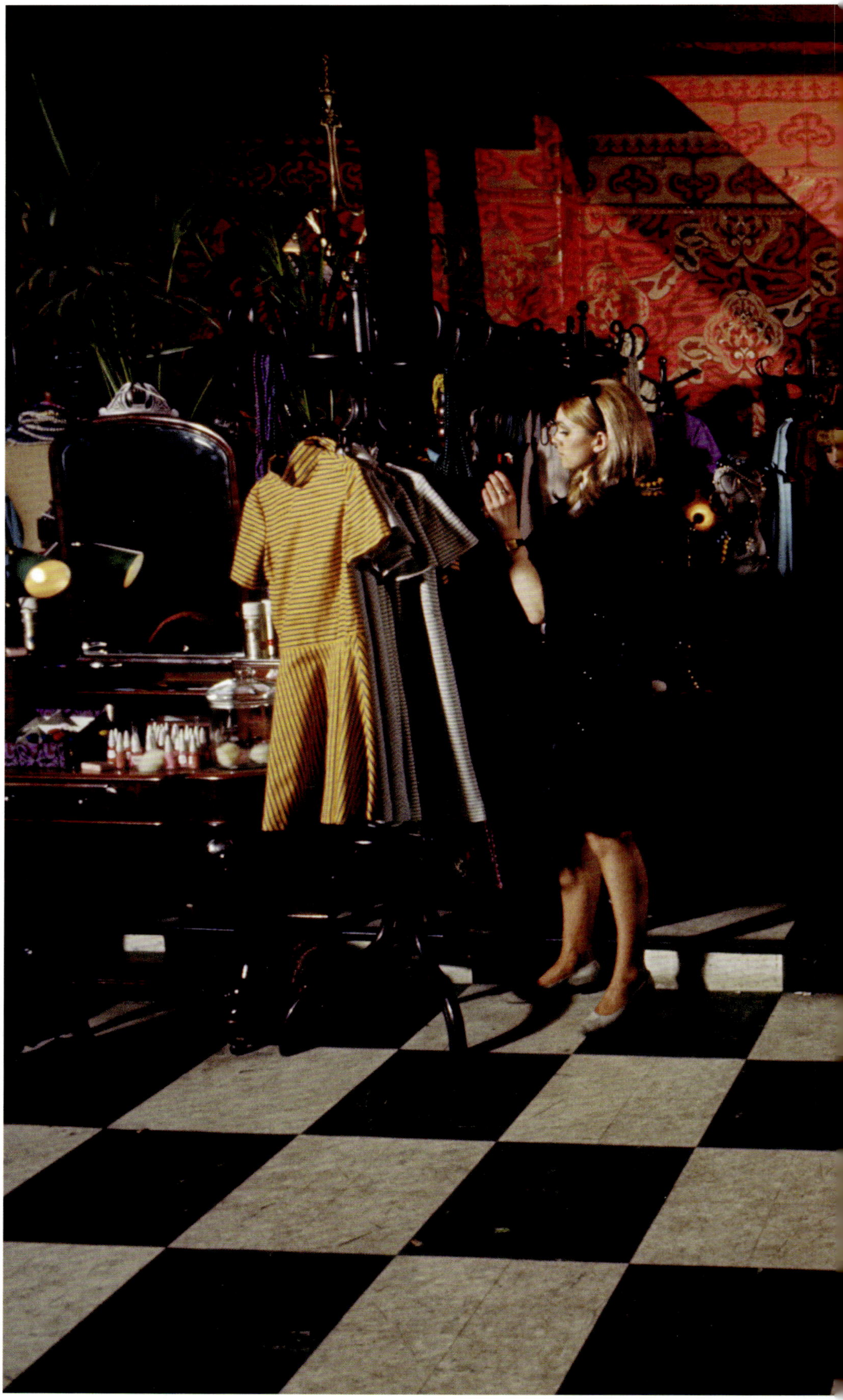

Interior of Biba, Church Street, January 1966

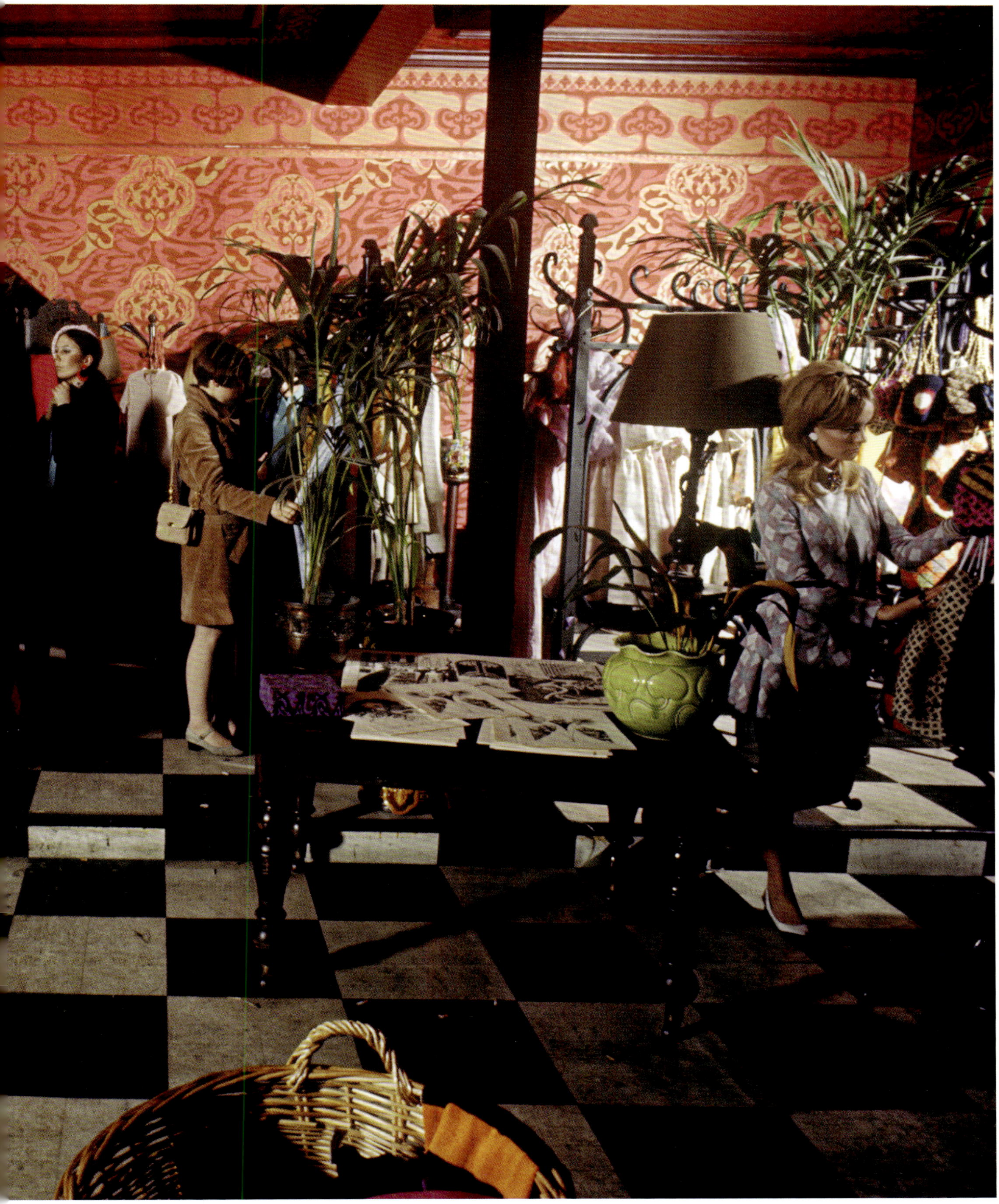

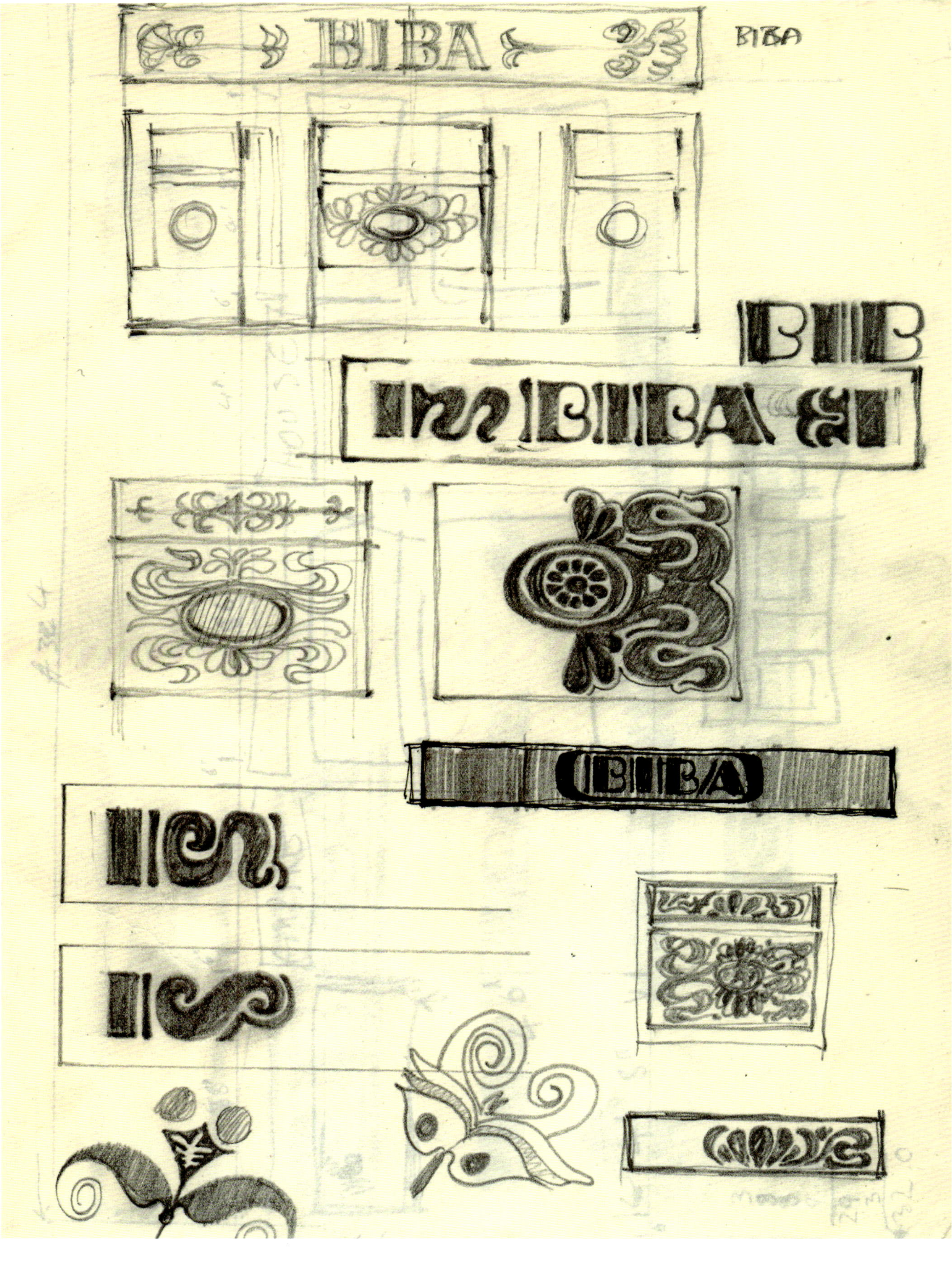
BIBA
BIBA
BIBA
BIBA

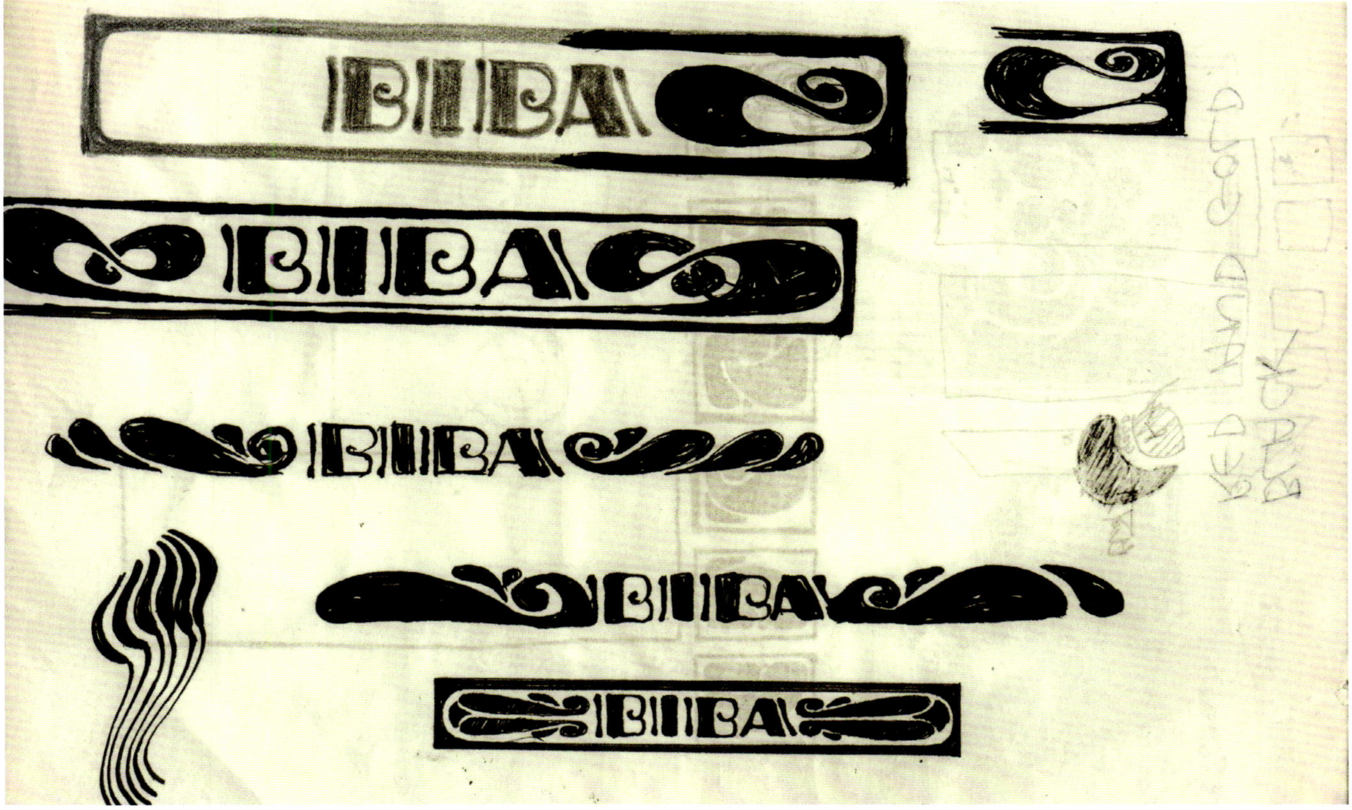

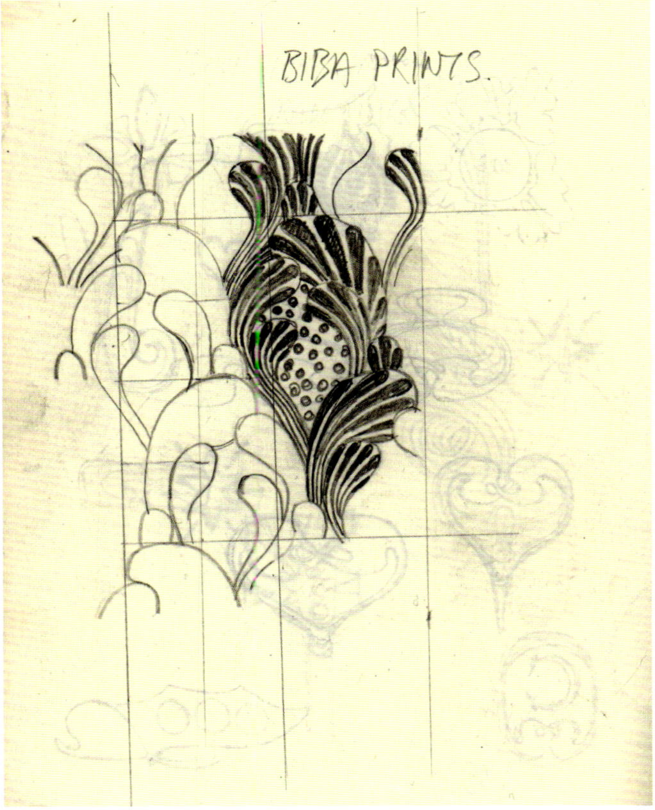

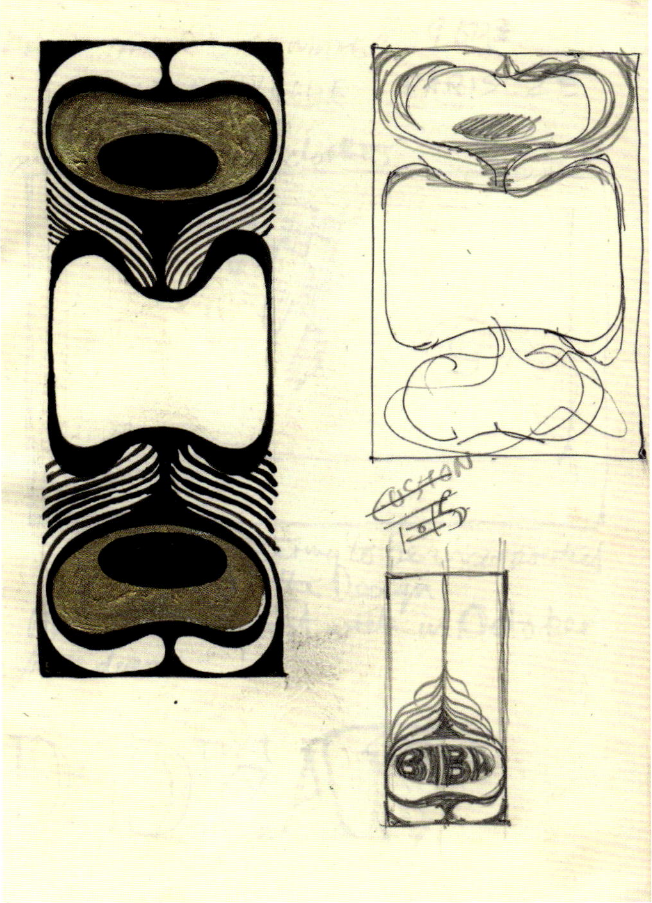

OPPOSITE & TOP Designs for Biba shop front and signage, Church Street, Antony Little, 1965

ABOVE LEFT & RIGHT Designs for Biba logos and textiles, Antony Little, 1965

ROSIE YOUNG ~ BIBA TWIN

It was 1965, and my twin sister Susy and I began to feel a need to leave the comfort and security of our home by the sea in Dorset for the bright lights of London. Not long after we arrived, Susy spotted an ad in the *Evening Standard* mentioning Biba – possibly the first real boutique, certainly the coolest. It was moving from its small shop in Abingdon Road to bigger premises on Church Street and was looking for shop girls. Susy immediately applied. I had already secured a job at Harvey Nichols in the 'Inexpensive Shoe' department – it was a world away from Biba and I was envious.

Susy, having been accepted by Biba, asked if I could join her. Being identical twins and not bad looking, we fitted the bill, and thus began the best job we could have picked for those heady days. Shop girls became glamorous. We were to join the whole Swinging Sixties scene, which included photographers, designers, artists, pop stars, actors, models and hairdressers. There we were, at the centre of it all. We became unconventional shop girls, known as the 'Biba Twins', and much photographed as such, appearing in prestigious magazines of the day – national and international – as well as in a film by David Bailey. We were not models, but as attractive twins we were in demand from photographers who took us to different locations to exploit this new trend.

"Everyone who was anyone went to Biba"

Everyone who was anyone went to Biba. Among the many famous names who visited the Church Street shop, the two people who perhaps caused the biggest stir were Princess Anne and Brigitte Bardot, an icon even then, accompanied by the French musician Sacha Distel. Other well-known stars, too many to mention by name, came in regularly.

I once led a complaint about the taking away of some holiday entitlements for us all and, ironically, was promoted to 'personnel manager' as a result. One of my few claims to fame in that role was the sacking of a young Anna Wintour.

The changing room beneath the ground floor of the shop was a large, undivided space. Any amount of clothes could be taken in to try on by enthusiastic shoppers, desperate to buy as much as they could. Whole outfits in those days were not expensive, particularly as they were skimpy and well fitting. Much was bought but also, at the end of each day, discarded items were left, knee deep, covering the floor of the large room. All of this had to be tidied away in preparation for the next, equally busy, day.

Biba was unique, unconventional and casual – never run of the mill. Music played continuously, and there were usually people sitting on the velvet cushions in the window taking in the vibe rather than shopping. There was a long counter with an old-fashioned till – money was collected hourly, stuffed into a paper bag and taken to the office. On one memorable occasion, a customer, buying a feather boa, was given the bag bursting with our hourly take instead of the one containing the boa.

One Christmas, as the Biba fame spread, a hotelier living in the Swiss town of Zermatt decided to take Biba to Switzerland, building an uncompromising replica of the Church Street shop, which included papering the walls with the original wallpaper and all the clothes and accessories. It even included the shop girls – we were thrilled to be there. A band, The End, was also shipped in from London and so evenings were spent dancing, drinking and flirting. Any spare time was spent skiing and tobogganing.

Many years later, I met Barbara, and afterwards she sent me an email saying that Susy and I were 'the spirit of early Biba'.

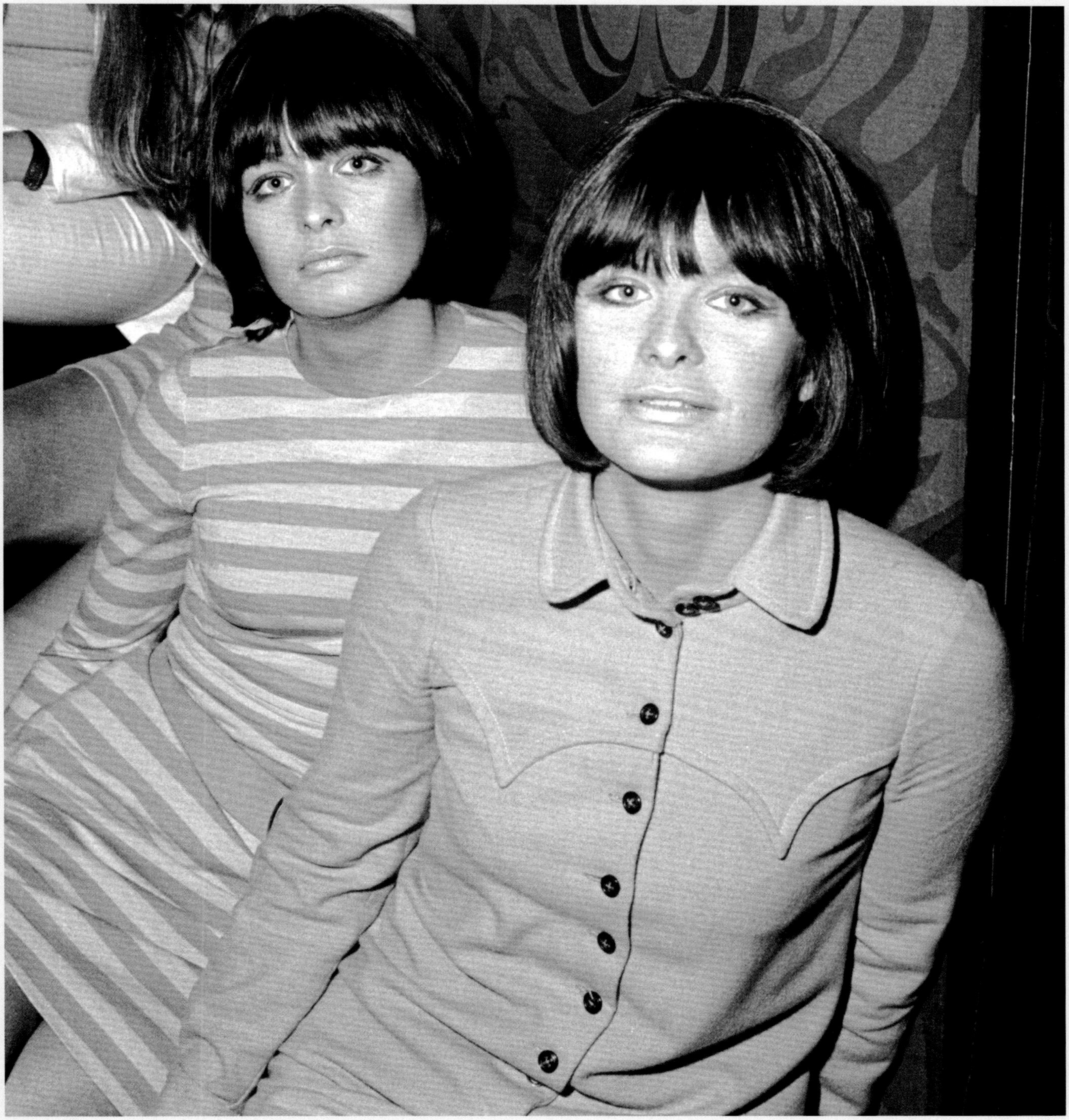

Twin sisters Rosie and Susy Young
in Biba, Church Street, photographed
by Caroline Gillies, 1966

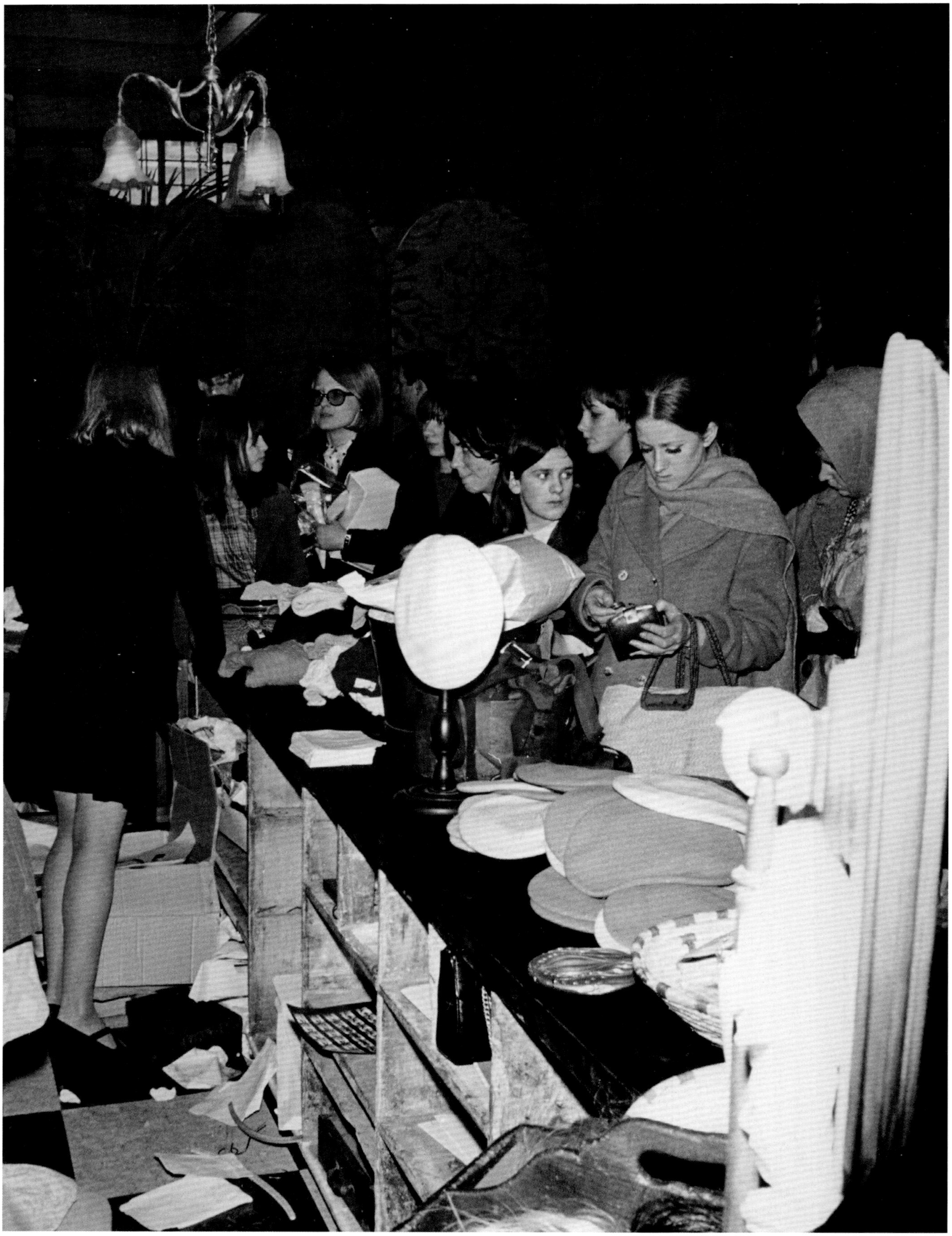

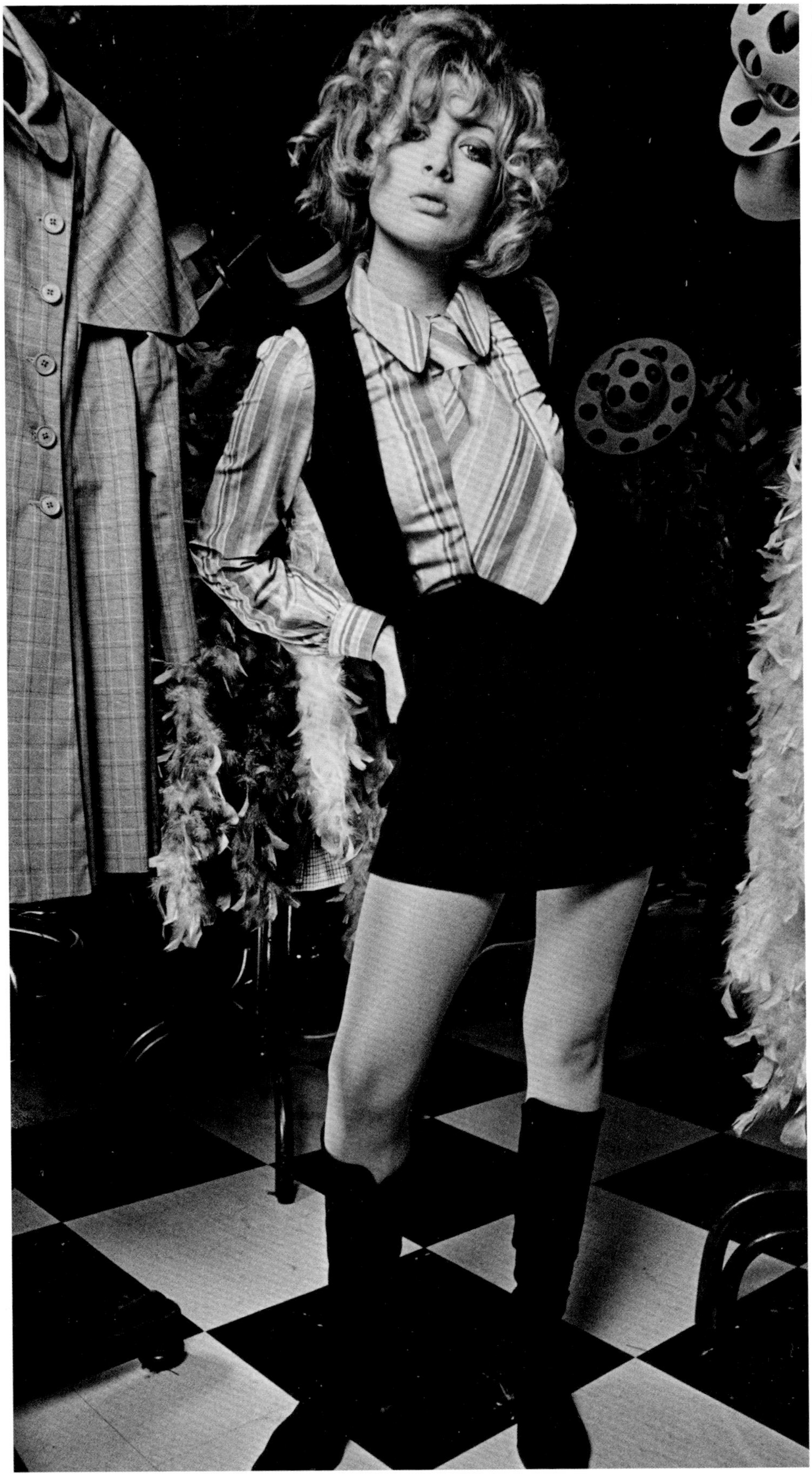

OPPOSITE Biba, Church Street, interior, Barbara Hulanicki standing by the counter wearing glasses, c.1966

RIGHT Woman modelling in Biba, Church Street, 1967

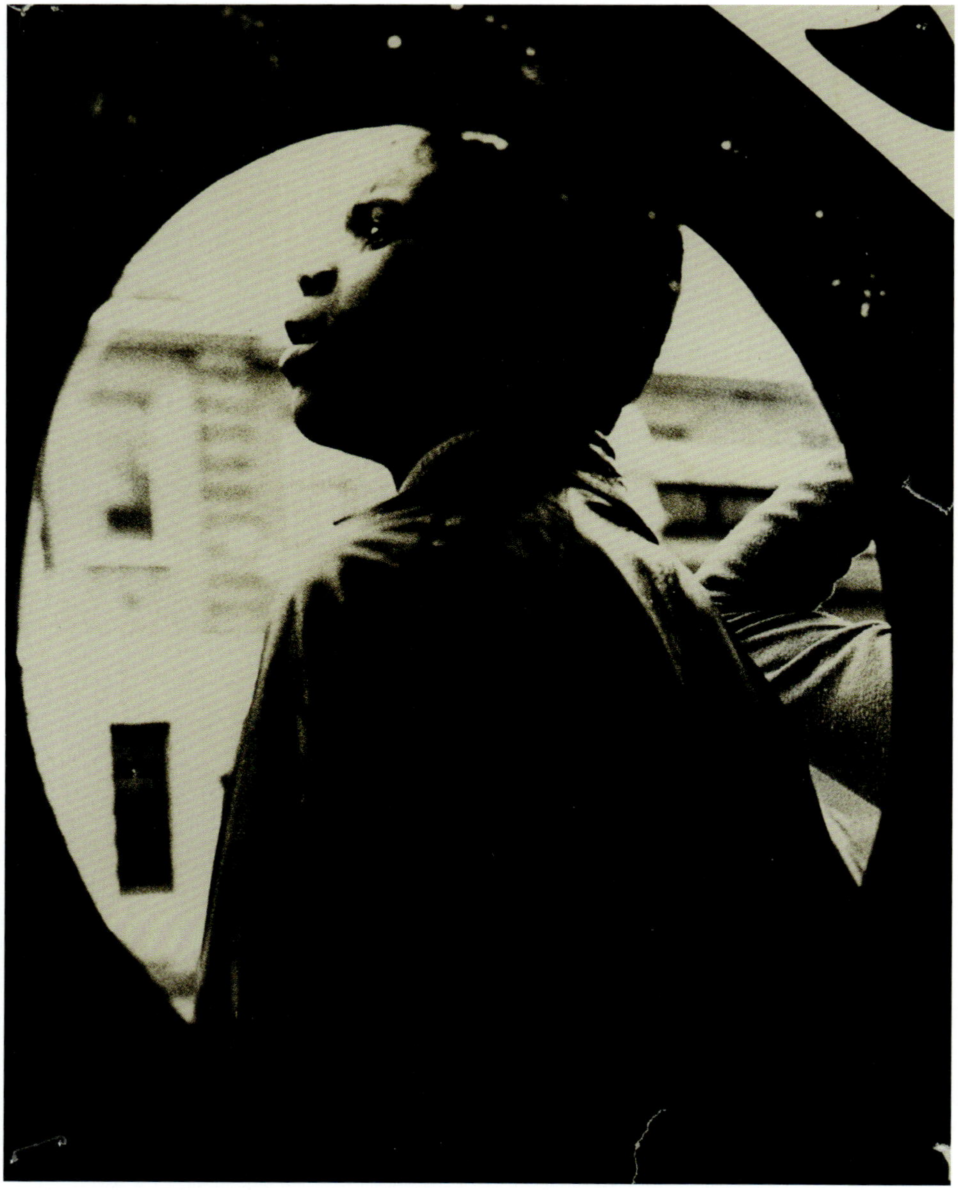

ABOVE Man on Church Street seen through the window of Biba, *c.*1967

OPPOSITE TOP LEFT Letter to Fitz from Hicks, Arnold & Co. regarding trademarking the Biba name in America, 27 July 1966

OPPOSITE TOP RIGHT Letter from the property company Knight, Frank & Rutley regarding Biba's expansion to Paris, 8 February 1967. Biba had hoped to open a boutique in Paris but were unable to use the name as another company had registered 'Biba' and had opened a boutique in the city.

OPPOSITE BOTTOM LEFT & RIGHT Floor plans for a property in Paris, 1967. This three-storey shop at 7 rue Grégoire de Tours was suggested to Barbara and Fitz as one option for the Paris Biba.

FINK & PAVIA

ATTORNEYS AND COUNSELLORS AT LAW

63 WALL STREET
NEW YORK, N.Y. 10005
HANOVER 2-6996
CABLE "PAVIALAW"

GEORGE M. PAVIA
DAVID A. BOTWINIK
DANIEL O. DECHERT
THEODORE S. SIMPSON
DONALD J. SISKIND
MURRAY MOGEL
JORDAN E. RINGEL
JEROME I. DANK

VIA FILIPPO TURATI 3
MILAN, ITALY
TEL: 653508-665460
CABLE "ELPAVIA"

RICCARDO GORI-MONTANELLI
BRUNO R. PAVIA
AVV. ENRICO L. PAVIA
AVV. GIUSEPPE ANSALDO
MEMBERS OF ITALIAN BAR ONLY

RECEIVED
01 AUG 1966
Ans'd..............

NEW YORK, July 27, 1966

Hicks, Arnold & Co.
25 Southampton Street
Strand
London, W.C.2

Gentlemen:

We have examined the questions presented in your letter of July 14th and we have consulted with our patent and trademark counsel. Our answers follow:

Trademarks are registerable in the United States in a Federal registry in Washington, D. C. In order to register a trademark in the United States on the Federal Register, your client must either be using the mark "BIBA" as a trademark in the United States or client must have obtained a trade mark registration of trademark in Great Britain. The registration of the name in the London Registry of Business Names is not a sufficient basis for obtaining registration in the United States.

In the event that your client has registered the mark "BIBA" as a trademark with the British Patent Office, then in order to apply for registration in the United States, it will be necessary for you to obtain and forward to us a certified copy of the British registration and a certificate from the British Patent Office stating that such registration is still in full force and effect. In addition, we will require eight (8) labels bearing the mark "BIBA" as actually affixed to the goods or containers for the goods. Upon receipt of these documents and specimens, an application for registration can be prepared.

In the event that no registration has been obtained in Great Britain, then we strongly urge that an application for registration be filed there forthwith and that upon filing such application for registration, you forward to us a certified copy of the application and the eight labels. If we file in the United States within six months of your filing in Great Britain, we can obtain the benefit of your British filing date.

Of course, another alternative to lay the groundwork for an application for registration in the United States would be to import some merchandise bearing the mark "BIBA" into the United States at this time. If such a course of action is

KNIGHT, FRANK & RUTLEY
20 HANOVER SQUARE, LONDON, W.1

PETER C. OLDFIELD, O.B.E., M.A. (OXON), F.A.I.
GEOFFREY C. L. GAY, F.R.I.C.S., F.A.I.
GERARD P. HELLER, F.R.I.C.S., F.A.I.
SAMUEL K.H. GOODENOUGH, M.A. (OXON), F.R.I.C.S.
GEOFFREY J. AKROYD,
STANLEY F. H. GLYNN, F.A.L.P.A.
RICHARD B. DAVIS, F.R.I.C.S., F.A.I.
BRIAN W. HATCHER, F.A.I.
STANLEY G. BAKER, F.R.I.C.S., F.A.I.
JEREMY G. HAWORTH, M.A. (OXON), A.R.I.C.S., A.A.I.
DAVID W. GARDNER, A.R.I.C.S.
PETER H. A. KEARON, A.R.I.C.S.
WILLIAM F. ANDERSON, A.R.I.C.S.
ARNOLD W. JAMES, A.A.I.A., F.B.A.A., A.A.L.P.A.
JACK E. GUY, F.A.I., F.A.L.P.A.
ROBERT G. RUTTY, F.A.L.P.A.
ROWLAND T. ENTWISTLE, F.A.L.P.A.
HEREFORD:
JOHN G. WORDSWORTH, O.B.E.
CONSULTANTS:
WILLIAM CUNNINGHAM, F.A.L.P.A.
CHARLES A. H. STENHOLM, F.R.I.C.S.

Telephone:
MAYfair 8171
Telegrams and Cables:
Knitefrank, London, W.1

Your Reference:

Our Reference: TCO'R/eos

8th February, 1967.

Dear Sir,

Further to your meeting with our Mr. Menzies we are writing to thank you for instructing us to find you a shop in Paris. We would confirm that should we be successful, our commission becomes payable by you, according to the scale laid down by the Royal Society of Chartered Surveyors, that is to say 10% on the first years rent, and on any premium, 5% on the first £1000 and 2½% on the residue.

We have written to our associates in Paris and as soon as we have heard from them we will contact you again.

Yours faithfully,

Knight, Frank & Rutley

INTERNATIONAL DEPARTMENT

Mr. Fitzsimon,
Biba House,
Kensington Church Street,
LONDON, W.8.

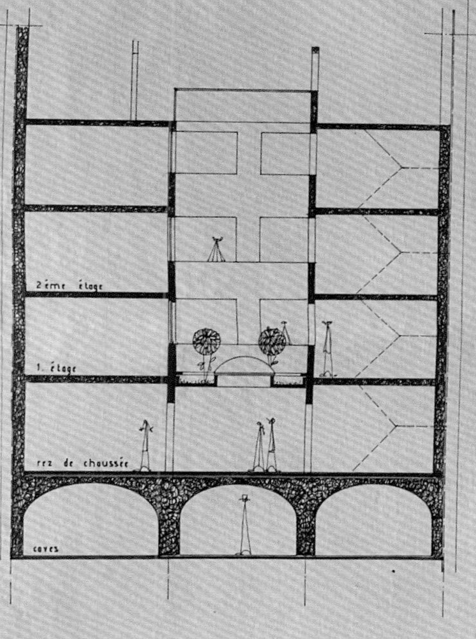

COUPE immeuble 7 rue grégoire de tours.

Rue Grégoire de Tours

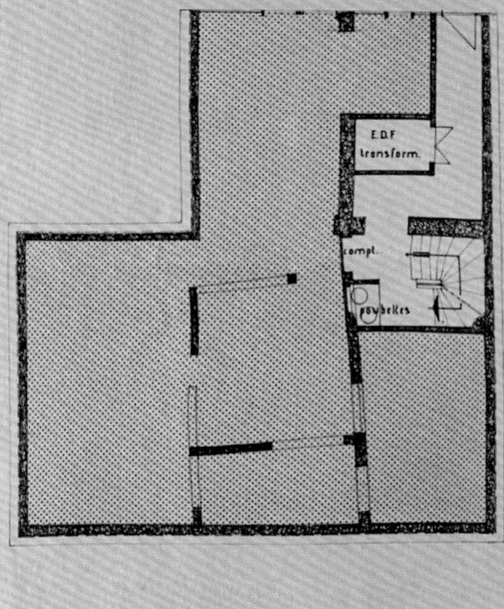

Rez de Chaussée SOLUTION 5

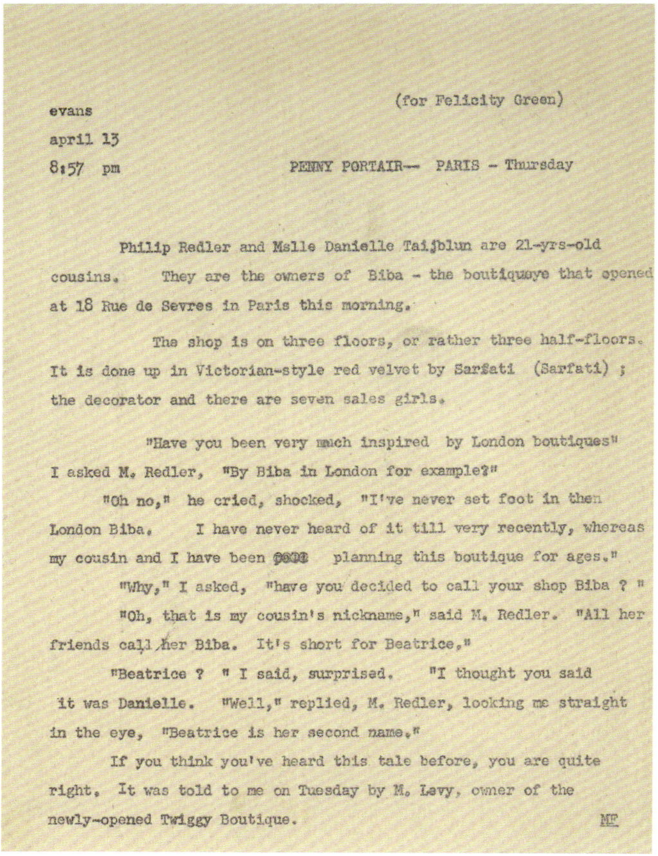

evans (for Felicity Green)
april 13
8:57 pm PENNY PORTAIR-- PARIS - Thursday

Philip Redler and Mslle Danielle Taijblun are 21-yrs-old cousins. They are the owners of Biba - the boutiquseye that opened at 18 Rue de Sevres in Paris this morning.

The shop is on three floors, or rather three half-floors. It is done up in Victorian-style red velvet by Sargati (Sarfati) ; the decorator and there are seven sales girls.

"Have you been very much inspired by London boutiques" I asked M. Redler, "By Biba in London for example?"

"Oh no," he cried, shocked, "I've never set foot in then London Biba. I have never heard of it till very recently, whereas my cousin and I have been [illegible] planning this boutique for ages."

"Why," I asked, "have you decided to call your shop Biba ? "

"Oh, that is my cousin's nickname," said M. Redler. "All her friends call her Biba. It's short for Beatrice."

"Beatrice ? " I said, surprised. "I thought you said it was Danielle. "Well," replied, M. Redler, looking me straight in the eye, "Beatrice is her second name."

If you think you've heard this tale before, you are quite right. It was told to me on Tuesday by M. Levy, owner of the newly-opened Twiggy Boutique. MF

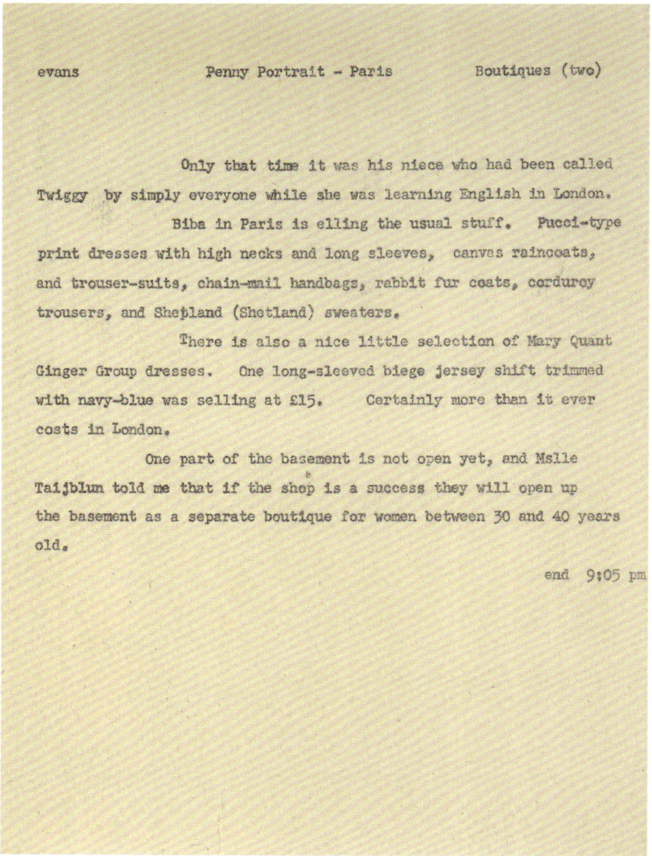

evans Penny Portrait - Paris Boutiques (two)

Only that time it was his niece who had been called Twiggy by simply everyone while she was learning English in London.

Biba in Paris is elling the usual stuff. Pucci-type print dresses with high necks and long sleeves, canvas raincoats, and trouser-suits, chain-mail handbags, rabbit fur coats, corduroy trousers, and Shepland (Shetland) sweaters.

There is also a nice little selection of Mary Quant Ginger Group dresses. One long-sleeved biege jersey shift trimmed with navy-blue was selling at £15. Certainly more than it ever costs in London.

One part of the basement is not open yet, and Mslle Taijblun told me that if the shop is a success they will open up the basement as a separate boutique for women between 30 and 40 years old.

end 9:05 pm

ABOVE News story written by journalist Felicity Green, Biba name already trademarked in Paris, 13 April 1967

BELOW LEFT & RIGHT Paris Biba business card and press cutting detailing opening of a Biba boutique, 1967

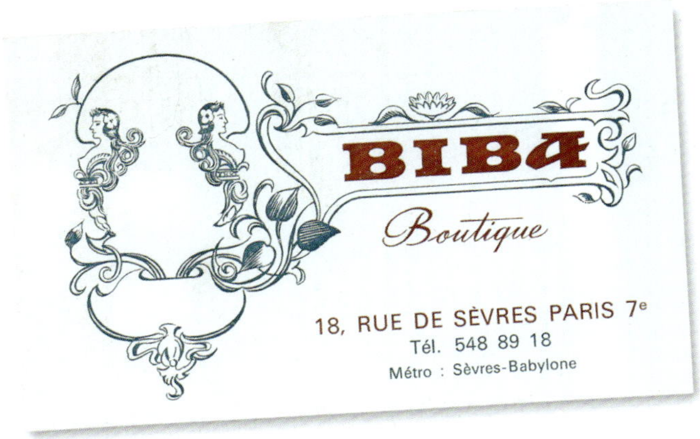

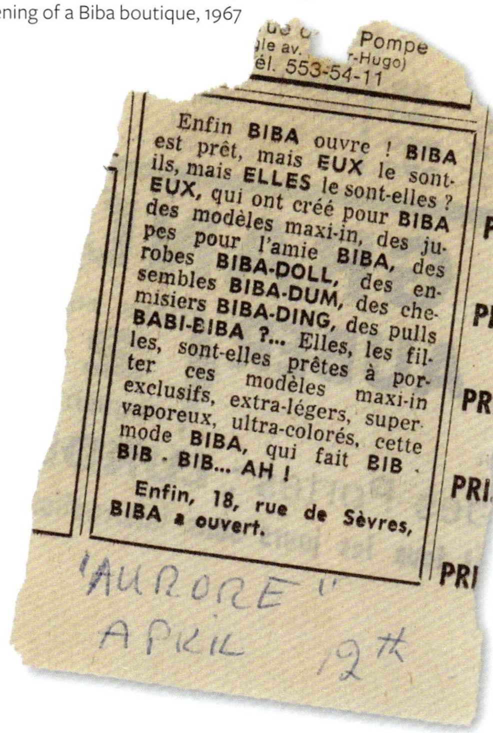

Enfin BIBA ouvre ! BIBA est prêt, mais EUX le sont-ils, mais ELLES le sont-elles ? EUX, qui ont créé pour BIBA des modèles maxi-in, des jupes pour l'amie BIBA, des robes BIBA-DOLL, des ensembles BIBA-DUM, des chemisiers BIBA-DING, des pulls BABI-BIBA ?... Elles, les filles, sont-elles prêtes à porter ces modèles maxi-in exclusifs, extra-légers, super-vaporeux, ultra-colorés, cette mode BIBA, qui fait BIB . BIB . BIB... AH !

Enfin, 18, rue de Sèvres, BIBA a ouvert.

'AURORE'
APRIL 12th

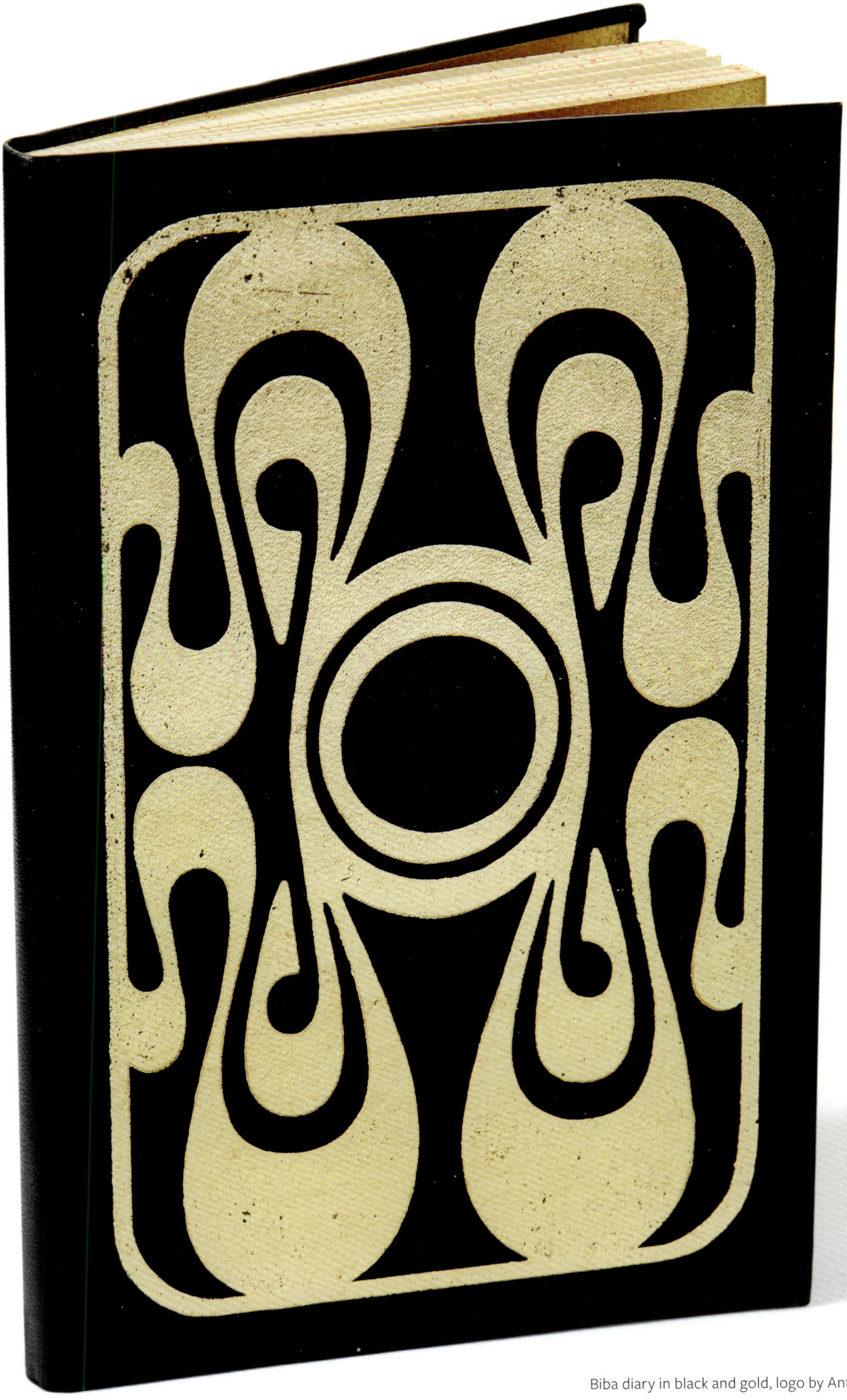

Biba diary in black and gold, logo by Antony Little, 1967

ELEANOR POWELL

~

STORE MANAGER

‘I am standing here in Church Street, Kensington, because I forgot the keys to the store’, would probably be the most apt explanation for this photograph! I’m afraid I can’t remember who the photographer was, why I did it, or why the photo became so representative of the time.

The Church Street store was special. Our first shop after Abingdon Road. The clothes were superb, of course – and cut beautifully by a somewhat forgotten Anne Behr – and the atmosphere was uplifting, with the promise of a little decadence. Biba Church Street offered affordable great design and fun; a modern-day take on the elegance of the 1930s and 1940s. This was a moment when the worlds of fashion and music had become harmoniously intertwined creating an incredibly exciting time to be young. Biba was street-savvy and business was incredible.

“Music was always essential to Biba, creating much of the atmosphere conducive to good sales. From Mozart to Queen, from Hungarian gypsy music to Billie Holiday”

There were many stories linked to the store. One such was the arrival of the late Michael Winner one busy Saturday. He parked his Rolls Royce halfway up the pavement outside, and he and his entourage marched confidently in, stating that he wished to film in the shop the following Saturday afternoon as ‘background’ for his next film. I politely told him that we could never disturb our customers with a film crew, especially on our busiest day of the week. He thought we should be eternally grateful for the publicity, but, when he was told what our likely Saturday turnover would be, he turned tail and stormed off in a puff of cigar smoke, never to be seen again.

Later came the Kensington High Street store, featuring Biba cosmetics and the famous suede boots, which sold out on a twice-daily basis, with queues along the High Street for almost two blocks. I still miss those boots.

Music was always essential to Biba, creating much of the atmosphere conducive to good sales. From Mozart to Queen, from Hungarian gypsy music to Billie Holiday it elevated moods.

Without the demise of Biba, I may not have had a successful career in the film industry. It was a regular Biba customer who purchased our clothes for her Caribbean boutique who alerted her co-chairman husband when he was looking for someone to assist with world sales of his production called *The Deer Hunter*. Of course, I said yes.

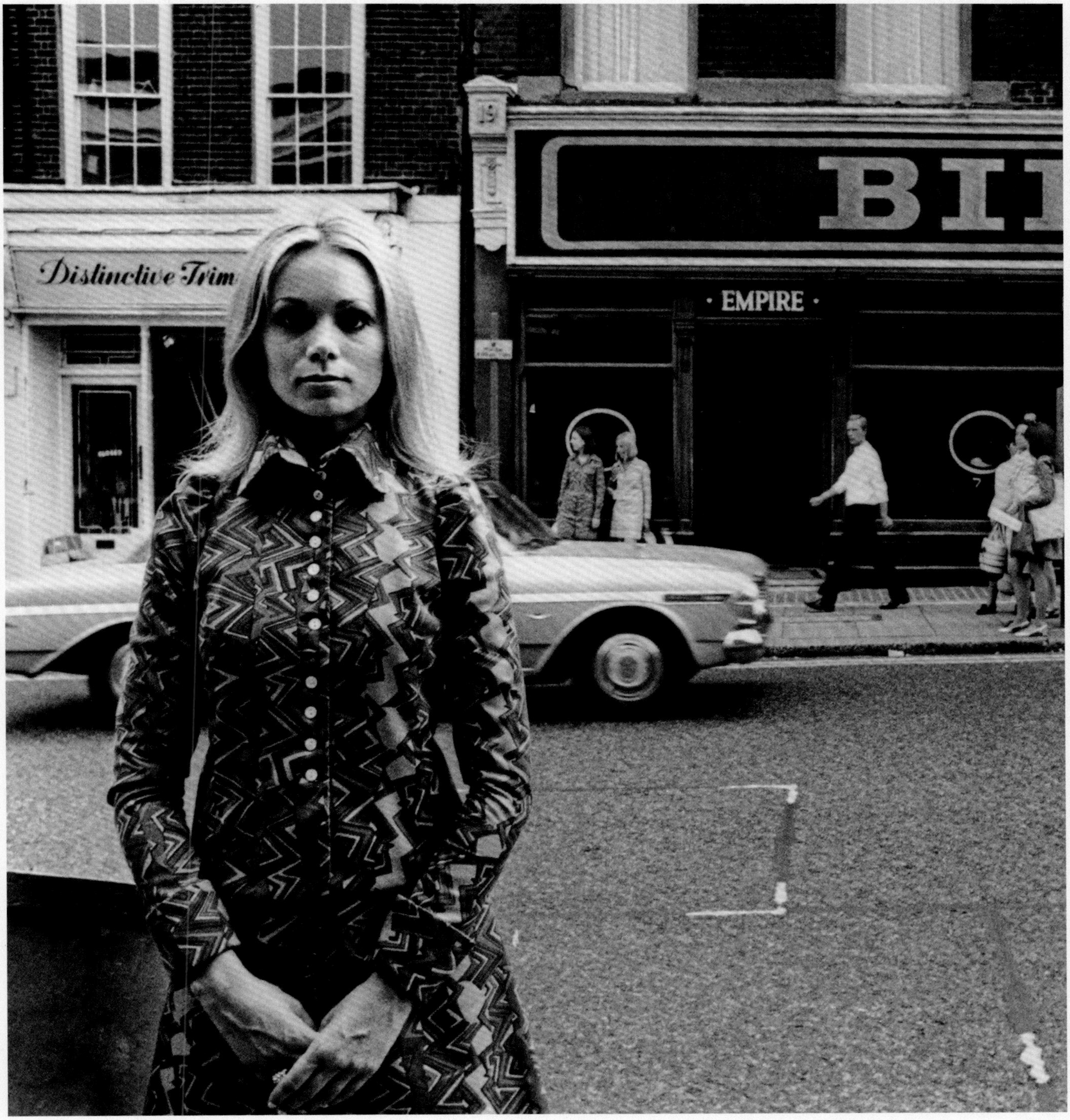

Eleanor Powell in front of Biba, Church Street, c.1967

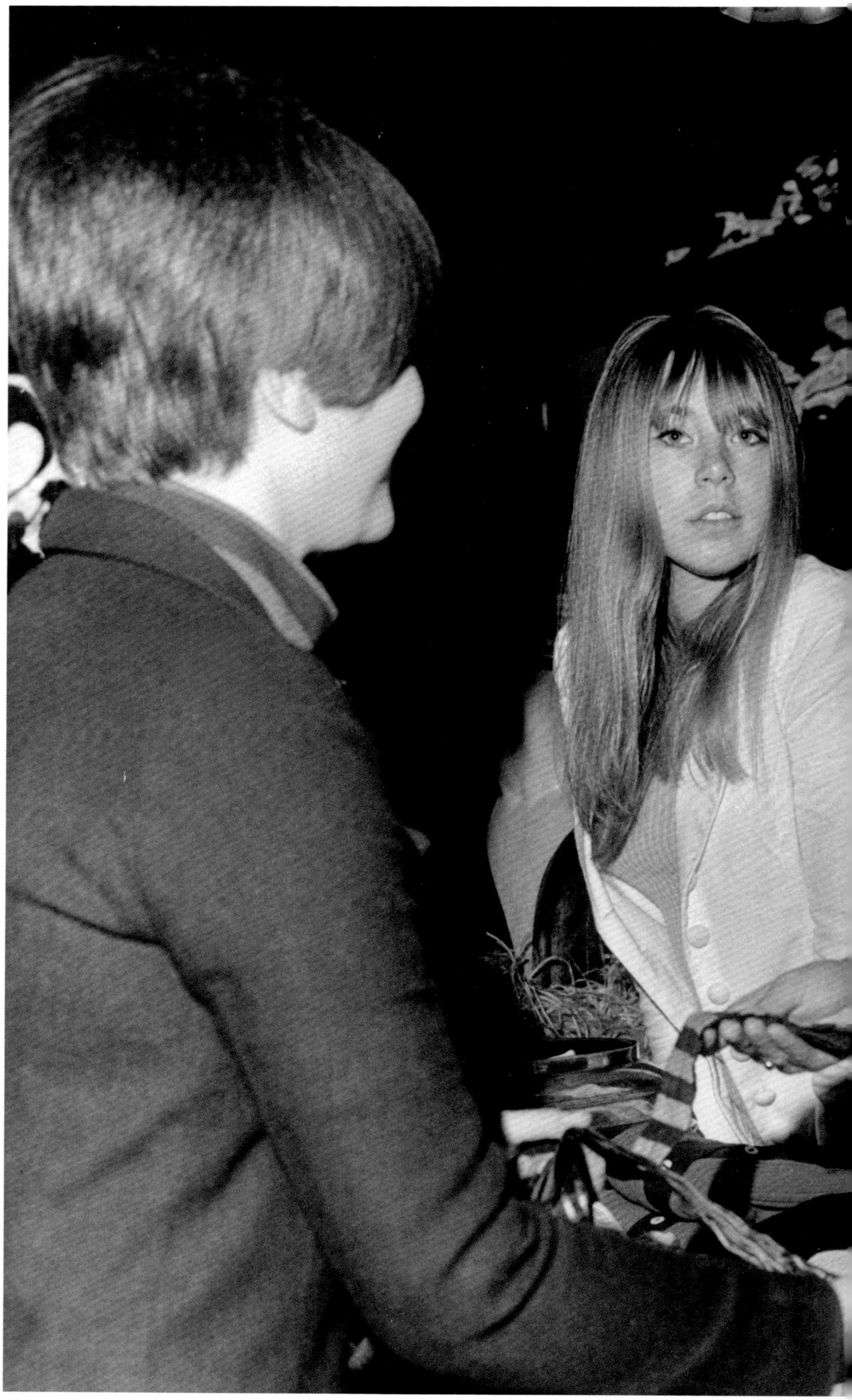

Biba twins (from right to left) Michelle Hellier, Susy Young, Rosie Young, Nicole Hellier serving a customer in Biba, Church Street, photographed by Caroline Gillies, 1966

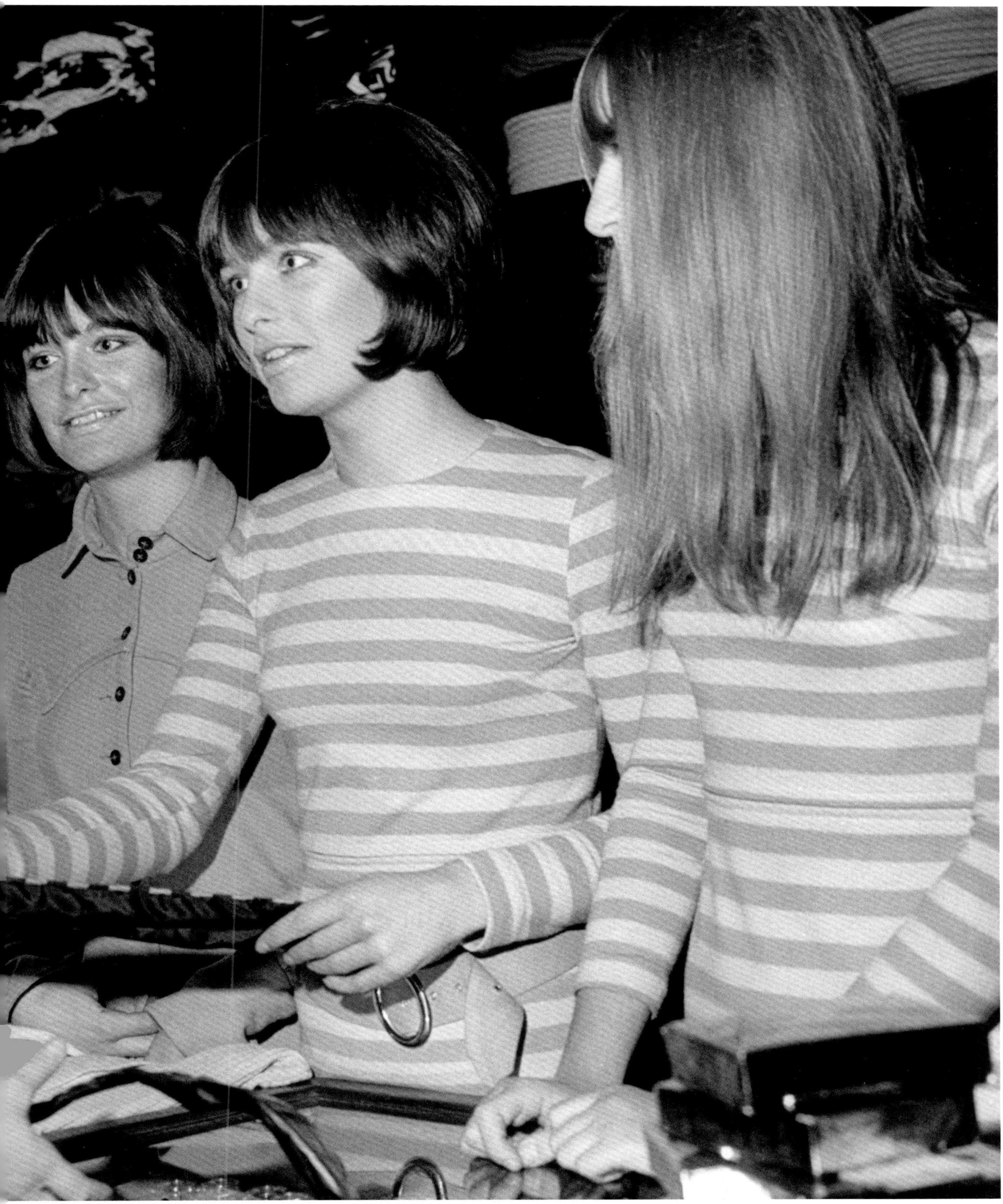

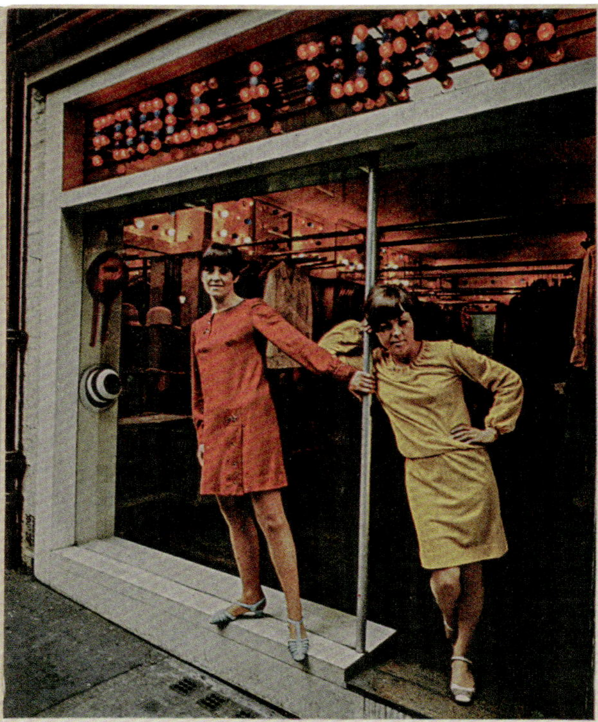

Carnaby Street is What's Happening in London fashion; two top happeners are Sally Foale and Marion Tuffin.

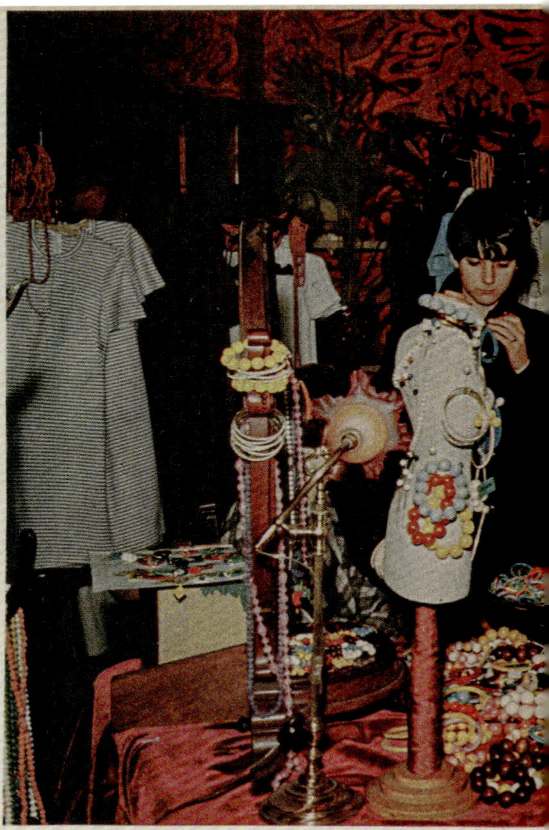

Big among boutiques is Biba's on Kensington Church Street. "Biba" is the nickname of the proprietress' sister.

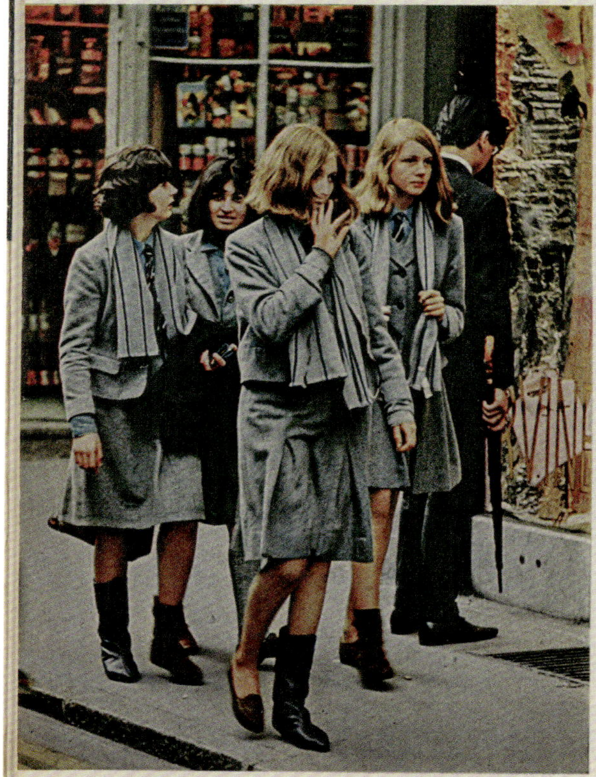

Uniformed schoolgirls, tramping purposefully into Carnaby Street, break the monotony by swapping boots.

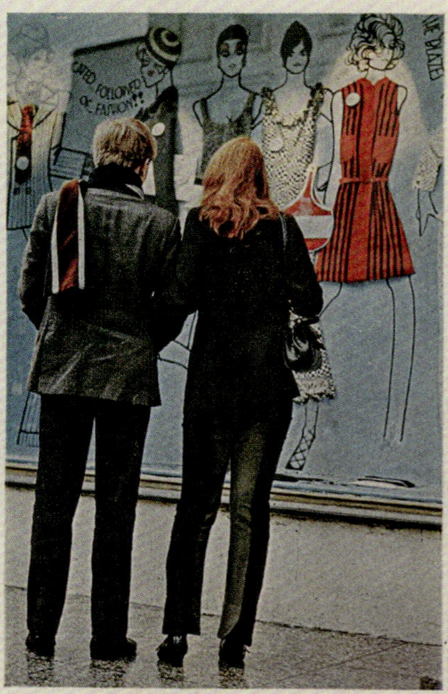

JOHN READER

Companionably suited, a mixed mod twosome browses past a shop in King's Road, Chelsea.

'London, the Swinging City', featuring Biba, *Time* magazine, 15 April 1966

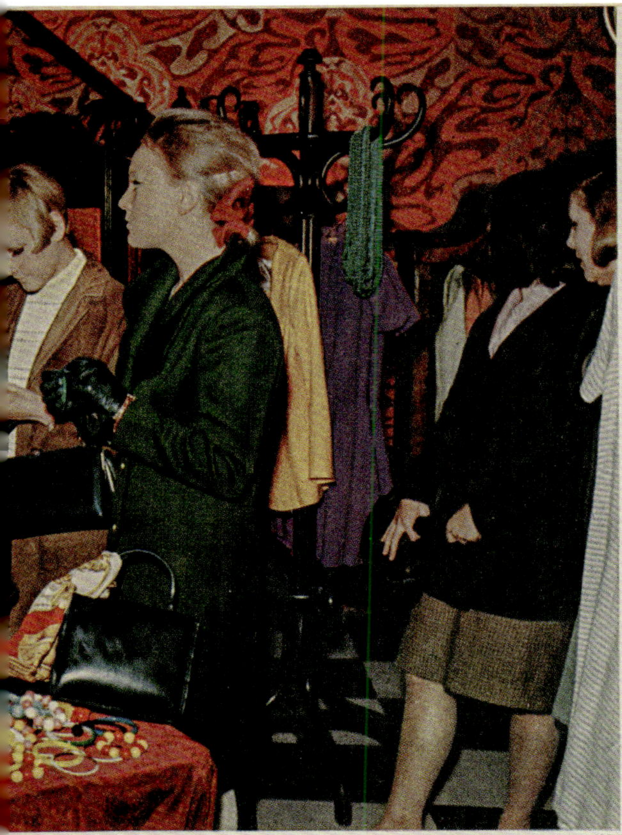

PHOTOGRAPHS BY BEN MARTIN

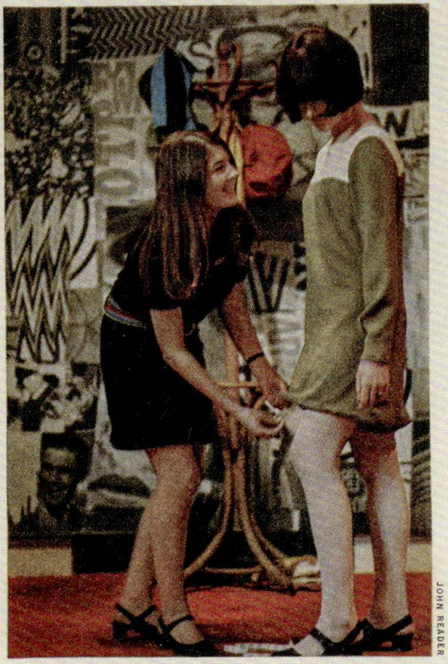

JOHN READER

Mavis Tapley, at 21 designer-in-chief of Hem and Fringe in Pimlico, minimizes a miniskirt.

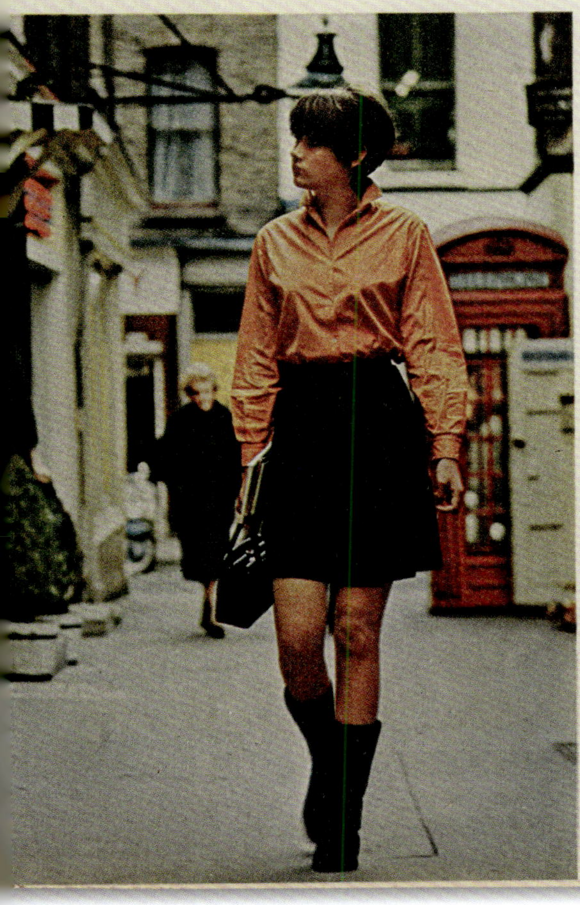

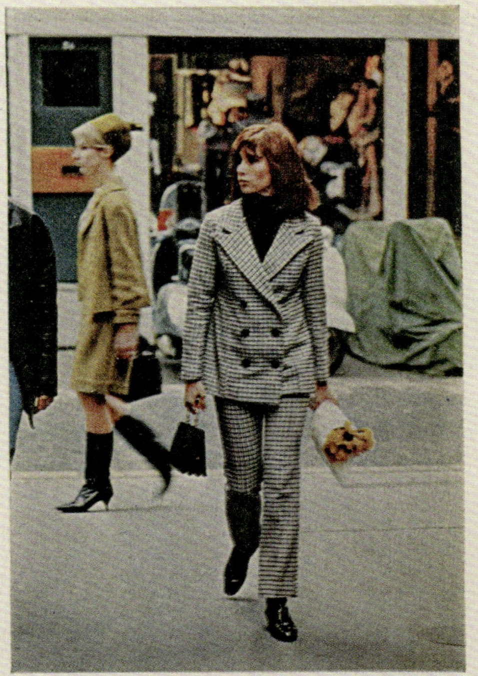

One of the hottest spring looks on Carnaby Street is the bell-bottomed trouser outfit, with daffodils.

Miniskirts are for dancing, walking and girl watching. Sitting in them takes practice.

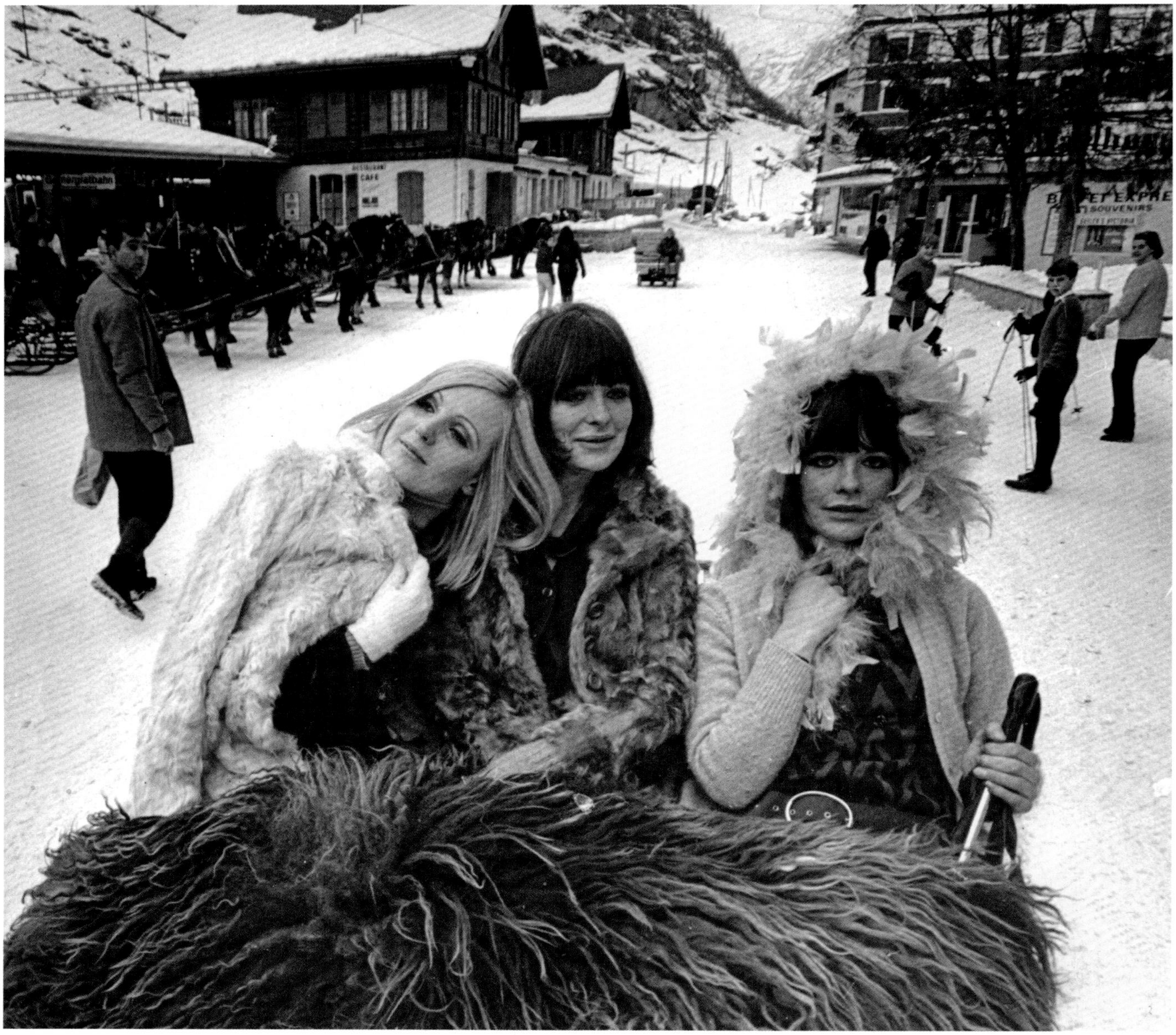

ABOVE Biba girls in the Swiss ski-resort Zermatt, Rosie Young and Susy Young shown centre and right, 1967

OPPOSITE 'It's Gear on the Rocks ...', *London Looks*, 14 January 1967

IT'S GEAR ON THE ROCKS...

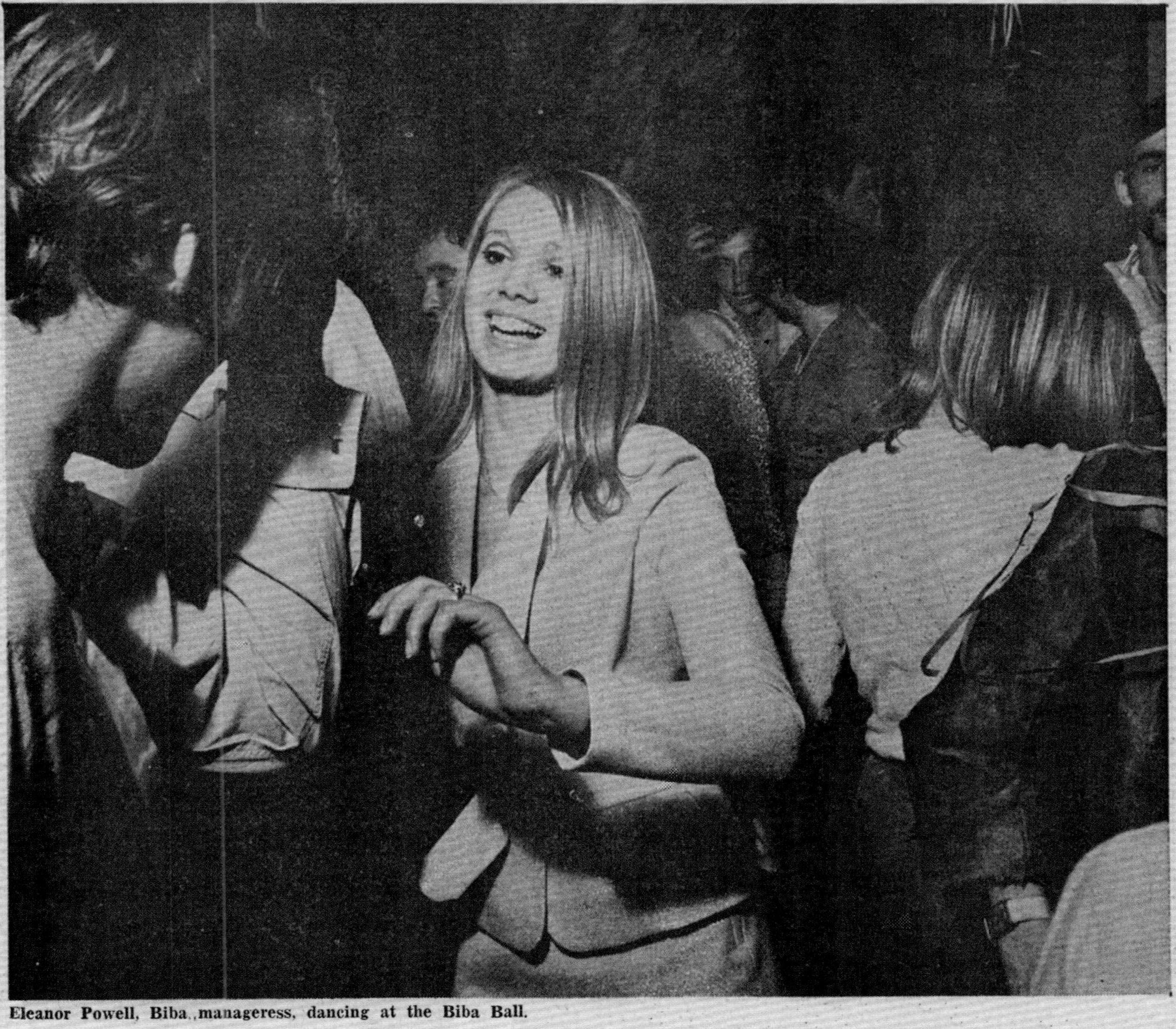

Eleanor Powell, Biba, manageress, dancing at the Biba Ball.

THE LAST of the Biba birds flew home this week, after a London fashion blitz on Zermatt, the Swiss ski resort. For two weeks, people from the Biba shop in Kensington Church Street spearheaded a London fashion campaign, established a "branch" shop there, and led residents and tourists in aprés-ski nightlife at a specially-opened club. JOHN PROSSER was there to take the pictures for *London Look*.

American skier Carl Iveson originated the fashion fortnight. He is based at the Hotel Post, in Zermatt, and asked the Biba people to fly out and open a store for the New Year holiday season. They agreed immediately, and flew out a team of girls, and all the Biba gear, including the distinctive clothes-racks, wallpaper and decor. The finished store in Zermatt was an exact replica of the Kensington Church Street Shop.

The team was headed by Biba general manager Sarah Plunkett and manageress Eleanor Powell. The girls who took over Biba clothes – including lots of silver, glitter dresses and fur coats – were twins Rosie and Suzy Young, Kim Willmott, Eva Molnar, Susan Dennis, Irena Stachurska and Mary Austin.

John Williams, of the British Army ski team, volunteered to parade the streets with a sandwich-board, reading "Visit Biba at the Hotel Post."

The Zermatt Biba store was soon ready for business, with the familiar Biba wallpaper, mirrors, potted palms and merchandise. There was a run on all the fashion lines, including the famous Biba hats.

The club was specially opened to tie in with the fashion

MADELAINE SMITH

~ BIBA MODEL

One winter's day in 1965 I was serving a customer in my capacity as a Saturday odd-job girl in the west London department store I worked long hours in. I was in charge of sweaters in every shade of lilac, fuchsia and purple, wildly popular colours at the time, and specially shrunk woollen ribbed creations that were called skinny sweaters. I became mesmerised by a customer, particularly by her fashionable mode of dress. As I gazed at the vision before me, I realised that I coveted the short black dress this beautiful girl was wearing. This was the beginning of the era of the miniskirt and dress, purchased from the Biba fashion boutique on Abingdon Road, no less. That day I made a pact with myself to sneak out of school on Monday, remove the navy uniform and secrete it inside my school bag and catch a bus to Abingdon Road.

When I alighted from the number 27 bus in Kensington the following Monday, I was wearing a bright pink Dollyrockers dress, purchased from Harrods for my birthday. Scrunched in my hand was the brown paper envelope with my latest wages – just shy of a pound after deductions. The original Biba shop was on a sliver of a street unchanged since Victorian times. The premises, formerly a chemist, were dark and small. Purple feather boas hung from Victorian hat stands, and The Beach Boys blared across the street from the open doorway. Two indifferent blonde assistants flitted about from time to time, wasting no energy on charm. I crept inside and grabbed a pink, candy-striped dress of soft, brushed cotton cloth with capped sleeves and pearl buttons at the neckline. It was so short that cream tights became an essential. Biba dresses scarcely covered anything!

"Biba was an experience, not so much a shop"

I returned to Biba again, the first day after leaving school, to beg the management to give me a job. A job was found, and in July 1967 I took the District line train from my home in Kew Gardens to their new premises on Kensington Church Street. Biba hours were long, but the wages were generous: eight pounds a week plus a free dress of my choosing. The clothes were so bright and lurid that tourists came in droves. Velvet banquettes lined the windows, and cigarette-puffing boyfriends draped themselves for the duration. Biba was an experience, not so much a shop.

One task was to be sent into the basement communal changing room to look for shoplifters. It was almost impossible to pick them out, particularly as we had to sit on the floor and gaze up into the gloom. After six weeks I was getting dangerously bored. Under my arm I carried a book downstairs – I had been battling with Dostoevsky's *The Brothers Karamazov*. Then there came a tap on my shoulder. I distinguished the kindly features of Barbara's assistant, who held a most senior position and was obviously watching me carefully. Her suggestion was that I give a week's notice because she felt that I wasn't cut out for this life!

A week later I was back at Biba to show all my friends a series of fashion photographs taken by the photographer John Cowan. I had been vaguely in the background of these pictures and wearing beautiful Biba clothes, 1967 style. As a result, John Cowan's assistant, Richard Dawkins, took a series of test shots of me because it was thought that I should try my hand – or face! – as a model. Barbara was in the back room on this particular day and requested that I come through and show her the photos. She asked if I would accept a very generous payment of approximately 60 pounds for two days' work and be the model for her first photographic Biba catalogue. Several Sundays were now devoted to a naked Madelaine having pieces of material sewn together on her! The garments were tailor-made: a navy and white spotted suit, slithery satin negligee, a terry-towelling beach dress and much more besides. Then, days later, the joyful mayhem, the thumping jazz, the smoke-filled rooms of a basement studio in Riding House Street in central London. Donald Silverstein was our photographer, dressed head-to-toe in black leather, pointing his camera up into my torso to produce a dream-like fantasy more akin to film than photography.

The result was a black and gold fold-out book of delights that I treasure to this day.

OPPOSITE Madelaine Smith modelling for the first photographic Biba catalogue, photographed by Donald Silverstein, 1968

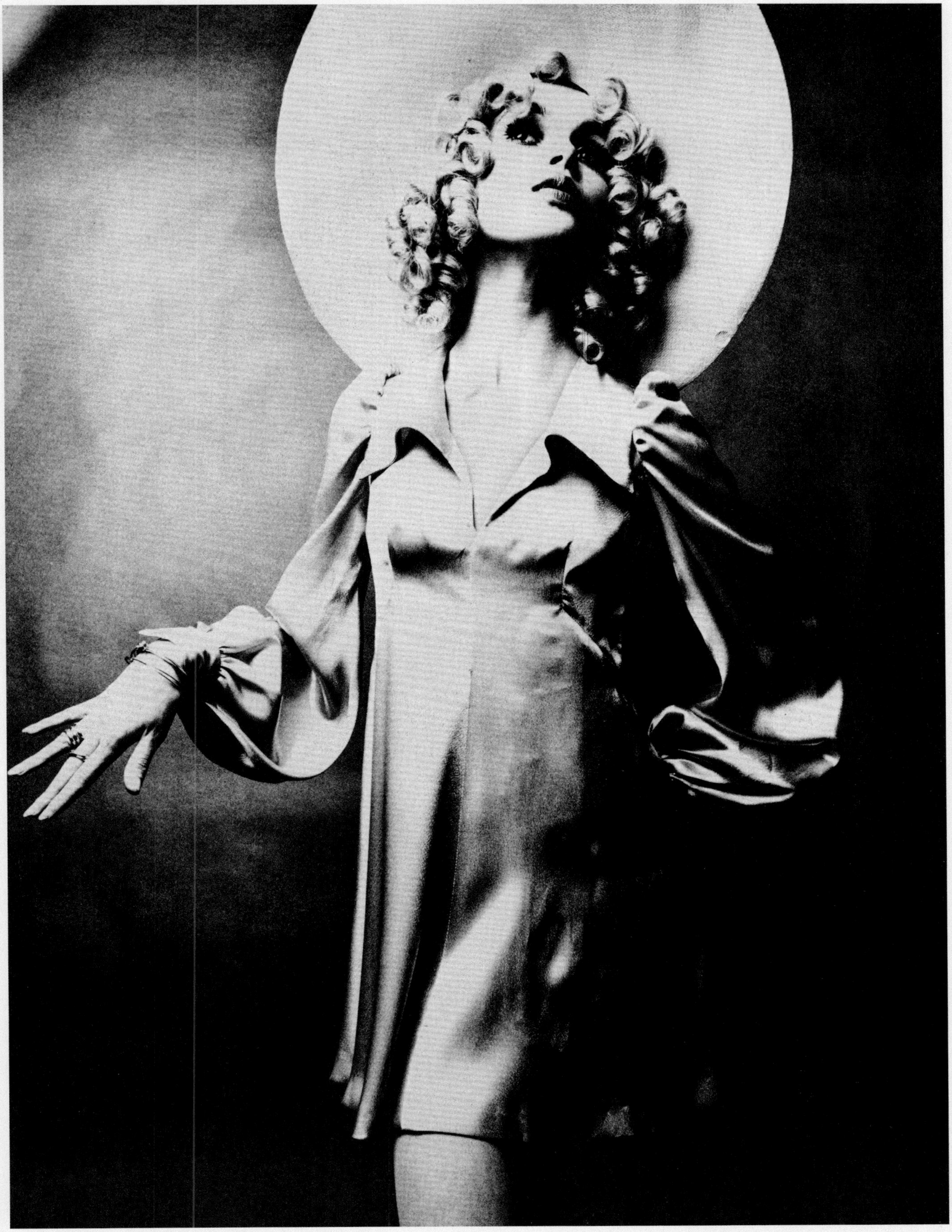

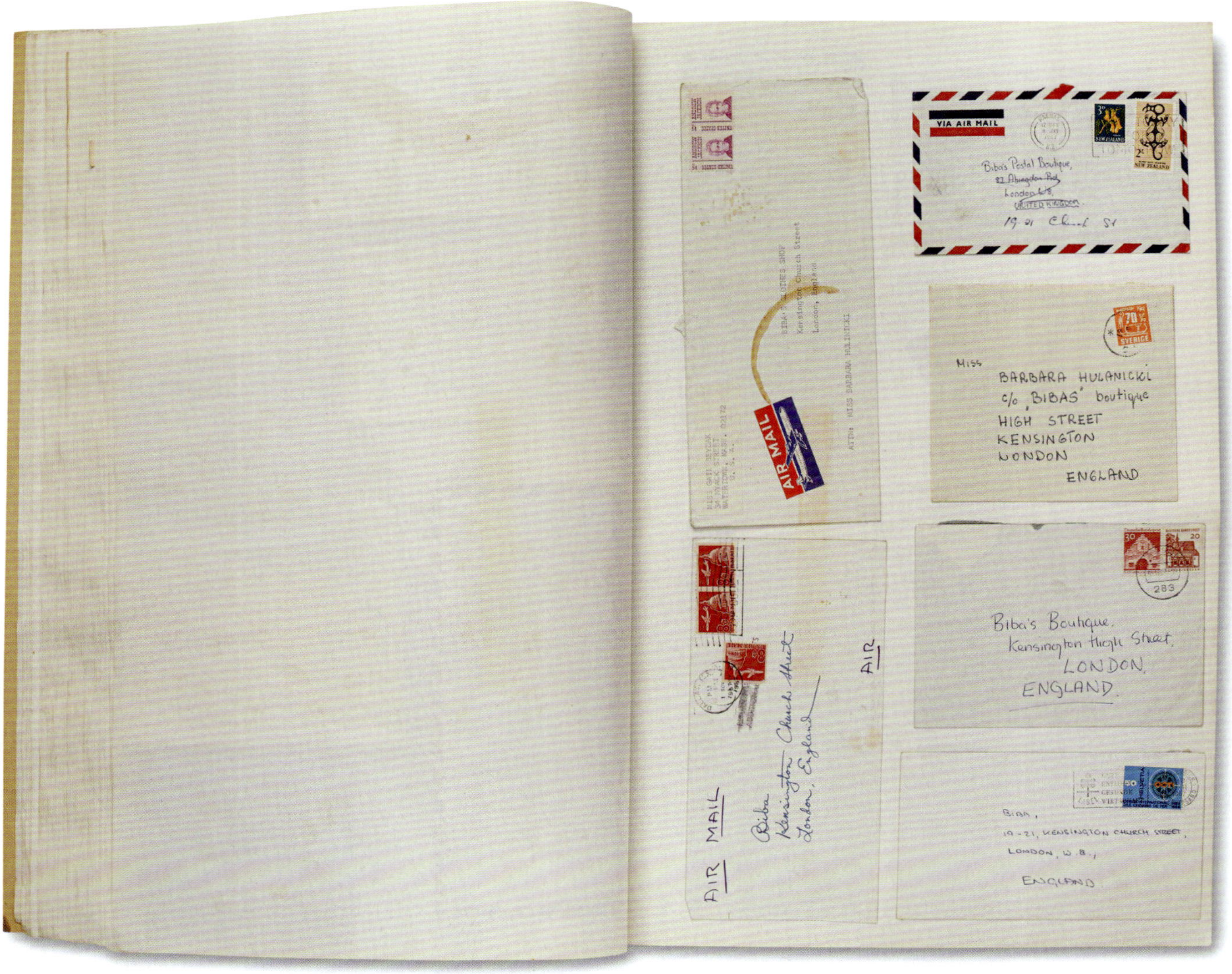

ABOVE & OPPOSITE Letters to Biba and Barbara Hulanicki from overseas Biba fans, 1967

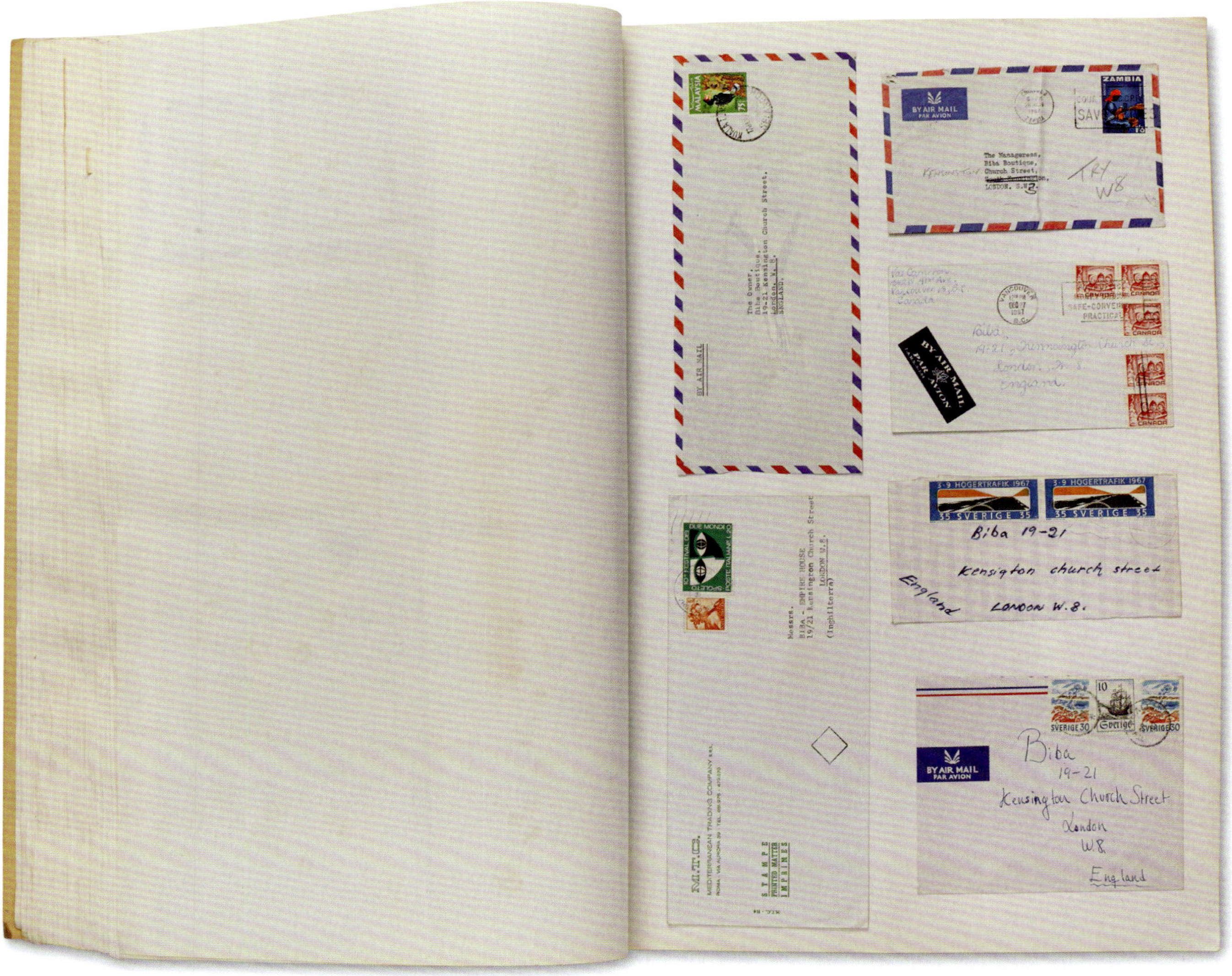
MALAYSIA
BY AIR MAIL
ZAMBIA
BY AIR MAIL
PAR AVION
The Manageress,
Biba Boutique,
Church Street,
LONDON. W.8.
TRY
W8
BY AIR MAIL
PAR AVION
CANADA
3-9 HÖGERTRAFIK 1967
35 SVERIGE 35
Biba 19-21
Kensigton church street
England
LONDON W.8.
SPOLETO
DUE MONDI
POSTE ITALIANE
Messrs.
BIBA - EMPIRE HOUSE
19/21 Kensington Church Street
LONDON W.8.
(Inghilterra)
MEDITERRANEAN TRADING COMPANY
STAMPE
PRINTED MATTER
IMPRIMÉ
SVERIGE 30
Sverige
BY AIR MAIL
PAR AVION
Biba
19-21
Kensington Church Street
London
W.8.
England

ANN CALLENDER & ASSOCIATES LTD

23 Old Burlington St.,
W.1

AC/VA

23rd February , 1967

Stephen Fitz-Simon
Biba
Empire House,
19-21 Kensington Church St.,
W.8.

Dear Fitz:

Thank-you for your letter regarding the CATHY MCGOWAN section in the G.U.S. catalogue. I would like to confirm the points you made in your letter as follows:-

Biba will supply initial designs/fabrics for the Cathy McGowan section in the G.U.S. catalogue for a flat fee of £500, payable on receipt of the sketches. This agreement will become operative in Autumn, 1967.

This arrangement supersedes the previous agreement, whereby you receive 50% of the royalties due to Cathy McGowan Enterprises Ltd. for the sale of designs through the catalogue sections with which you were involved. However, on all the catalogues prior to the one on which you are working, the original agreement still stands: i.e. you will receive 50% of the royalties as soon as they are paid to Cathy McGowan Enterprises Ltd.

Yours sincerely,

Ann Callender

Ann Callender Associates,
23 Old Burlington St.,
W.1

21st February, 1967

Dear Miss Callender,

I would be obliged if you would send me a letter of confirmation, with reference to our telephone conversation of this morning.

As I understand it, the situation between BIBA and CATHY McGOWAN ENTERPRISES LTD, is now as follows:-

BIBA will supply initial designs/fabrics for the Cathy McGowan section in the G.U.S. catalogue for a flat fee of £500, payable on receipt of the sketches.

This agreement will become operative for the catalogue on which we are at present engaged; i.e. Autumn 1967.

This arrangement supersedes our previous agreement, whereby we receive 50% of the royalties due to Cathy McGowan Enterprises Ltd., for the sale of designs through the catalogue sections with which we were involved. However, on all catalogues prior to the one upon which we are working, the original agreement still stands; i.e. we will receive 50% of the royalties as soon as they are paid to Cathy McGowan Enterprises Ltd.

I hope the above summarizes the situation accurately, and I look forward to your letter of confirmation.

Yours sincerely,

S.C. Fitz-Simon
B I B A

Ann Callender Associates,
23 Old Burlington St., W.1

23rd June, 1967

Dear Ann,

Thank-you for your letter. There seems to be some misunderstanding re. our most recent agreement of the Dennis Day/G.U.S. catalogue designs.

The relevant paragraph of our new agreement is contained in my letter to you of 1st February, and is as follows:-

- "BIBA will supply initial designs/fabrics for the Cathy McGowan section in the G.U.S. catalogue for a flat fee of £500, payable on receipt of the sketches.

This agreement will become operative for the catalogues on which we are at present engaged; i.e. Autumn 1967.

This arrangement supersedes our previous agreement, whereby we receive 50% of the royalties due to Cathy McGowan Enterprises Ltd., for the sale of designs through the catalogue sections with which we were involved. However, on all catalogues prior to the one on which we are working, the original agreement still stands; i.e. we will receive 50% of the royalties as soon as they are paid to Cathy McGowan Enterprises Ltd." -

So far we have received two payments from Cathy McGowan Enterprises Ltd., the first being the advance payment of £500 and the second one being the first full payment from the initial catalogue of some £2,000.

As I understand this is the payment from Dennis Day to your company at about this time which will be based on the turnover of the first catalogue and part of the second.

As I see it, we still have probably three of four further payments to come in respect of catalogues with which we were involved at a fifty-fifty basis with Cathy McGowan Enterprises Ltd.

I would be most grateful if you would confirm that such is the case and if you would give me some indication as to the timing and likely amount of these payments.

Yours sincerely,

S.C. Fitz-Simon

Correspondence between Biba and Ann Callender Associates regarding the supply of clothing designs and textiles to Cathy McGowan Enterprises Ltd for sale through G.U.S. catalogue business, 1967

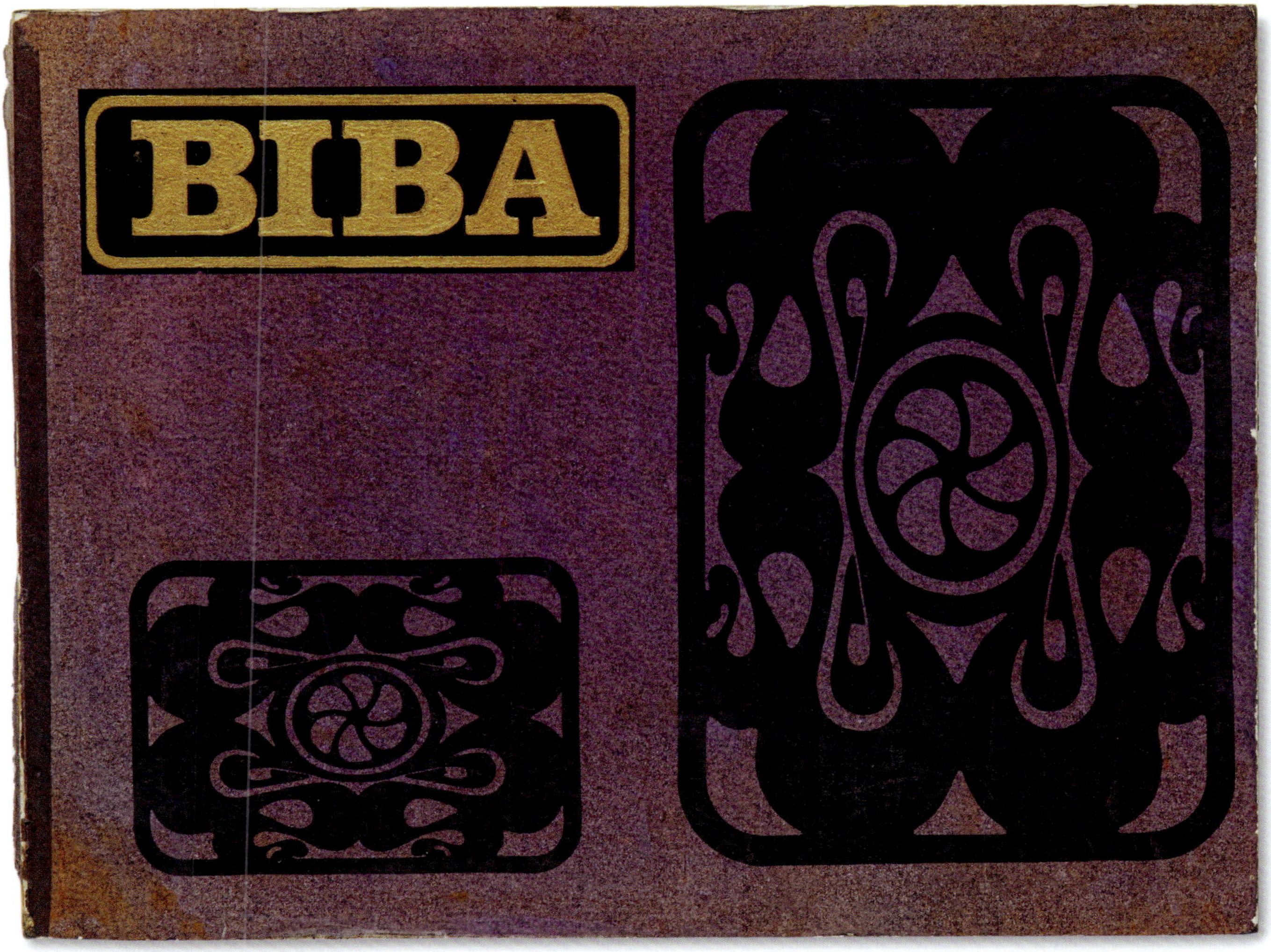

Mock-up of the initial design for the front cover of the first photographic Biba catalogue, Antony Little, 1967

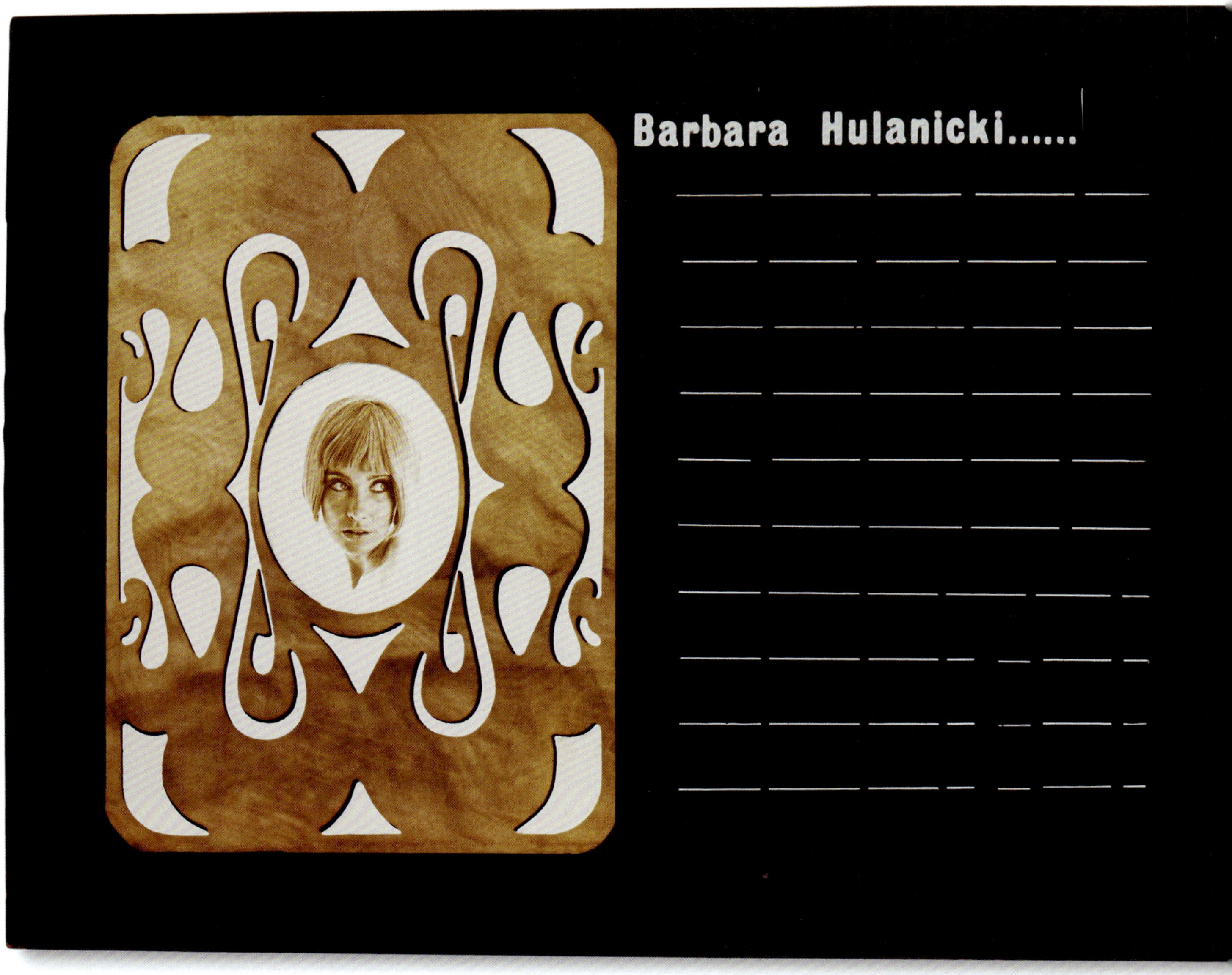

ABOVE & OVERLEAF Mock-up of pages for the first photographic Biba catalogue, Antony Little, 1967. This design never went into production.

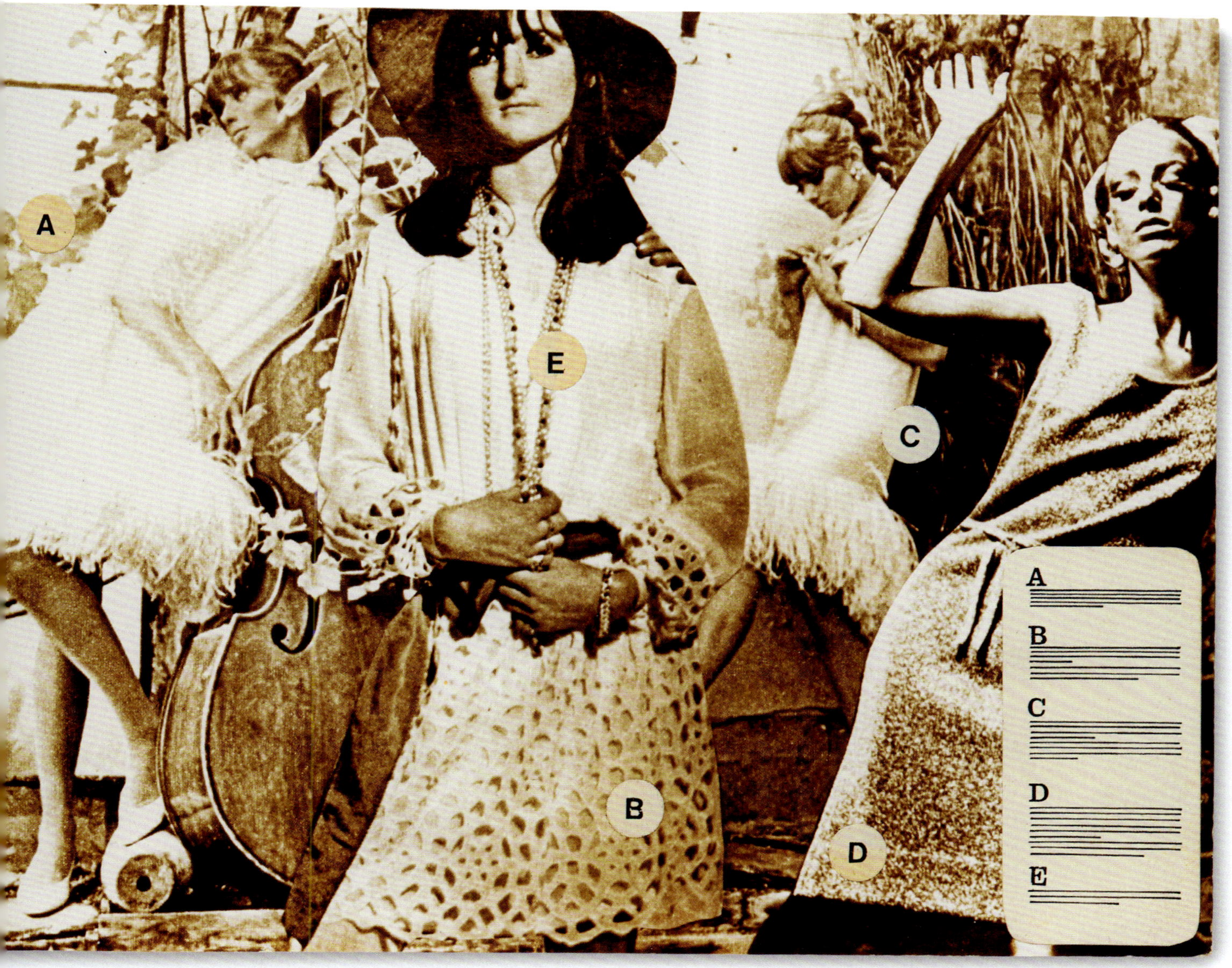
A
E
C
B
D
A
B
C
D
E

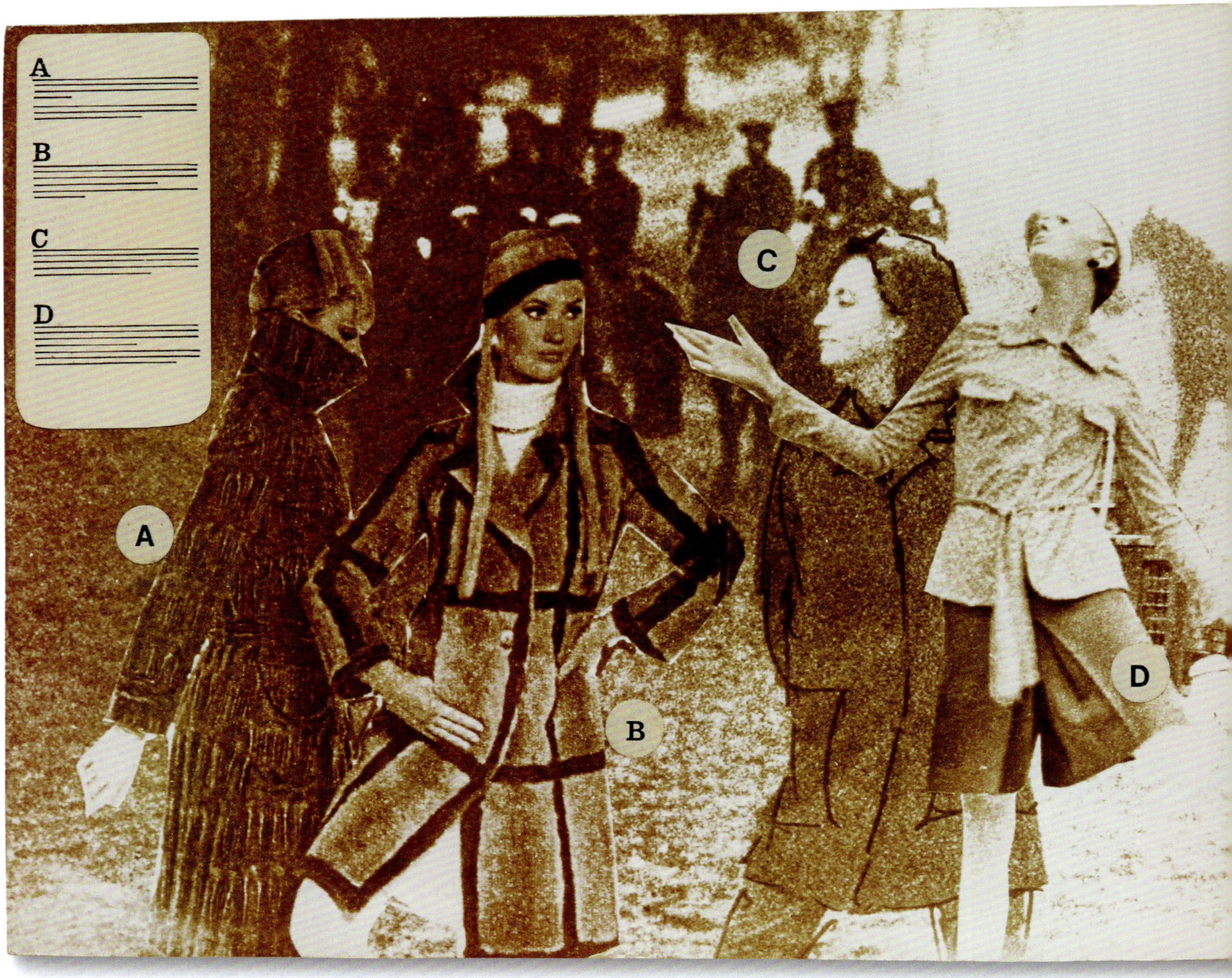
A
B
C
D

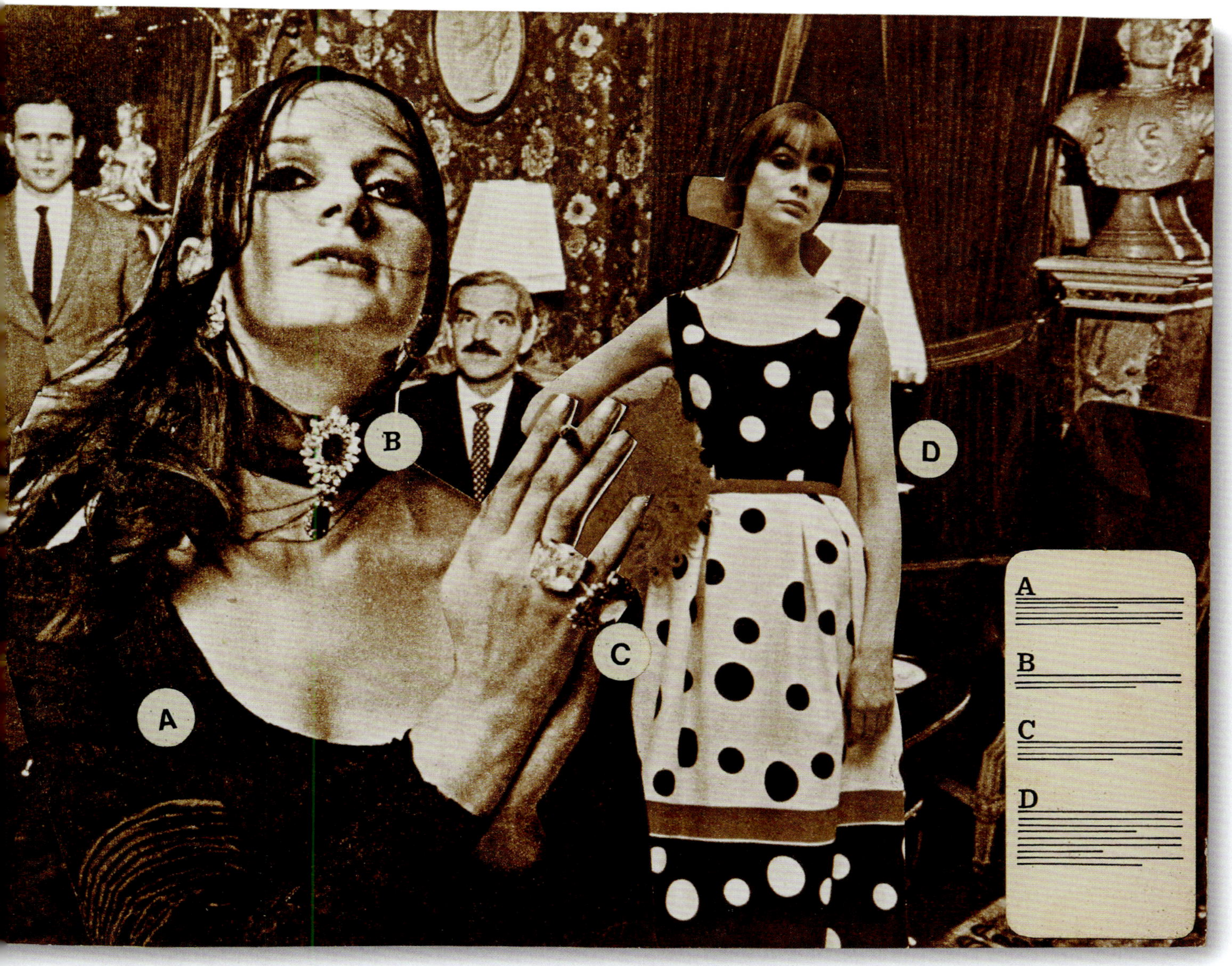
B
D
C
A
A
B
C
D

RIGHT Design ideas by Barbara Hulanicki, including clothing for the first photographic Biba catalogue, c.1967

BELOW Press cutting, launch of the first photographic Biba catalogue, *The Sunday Times*, 31 March 1968

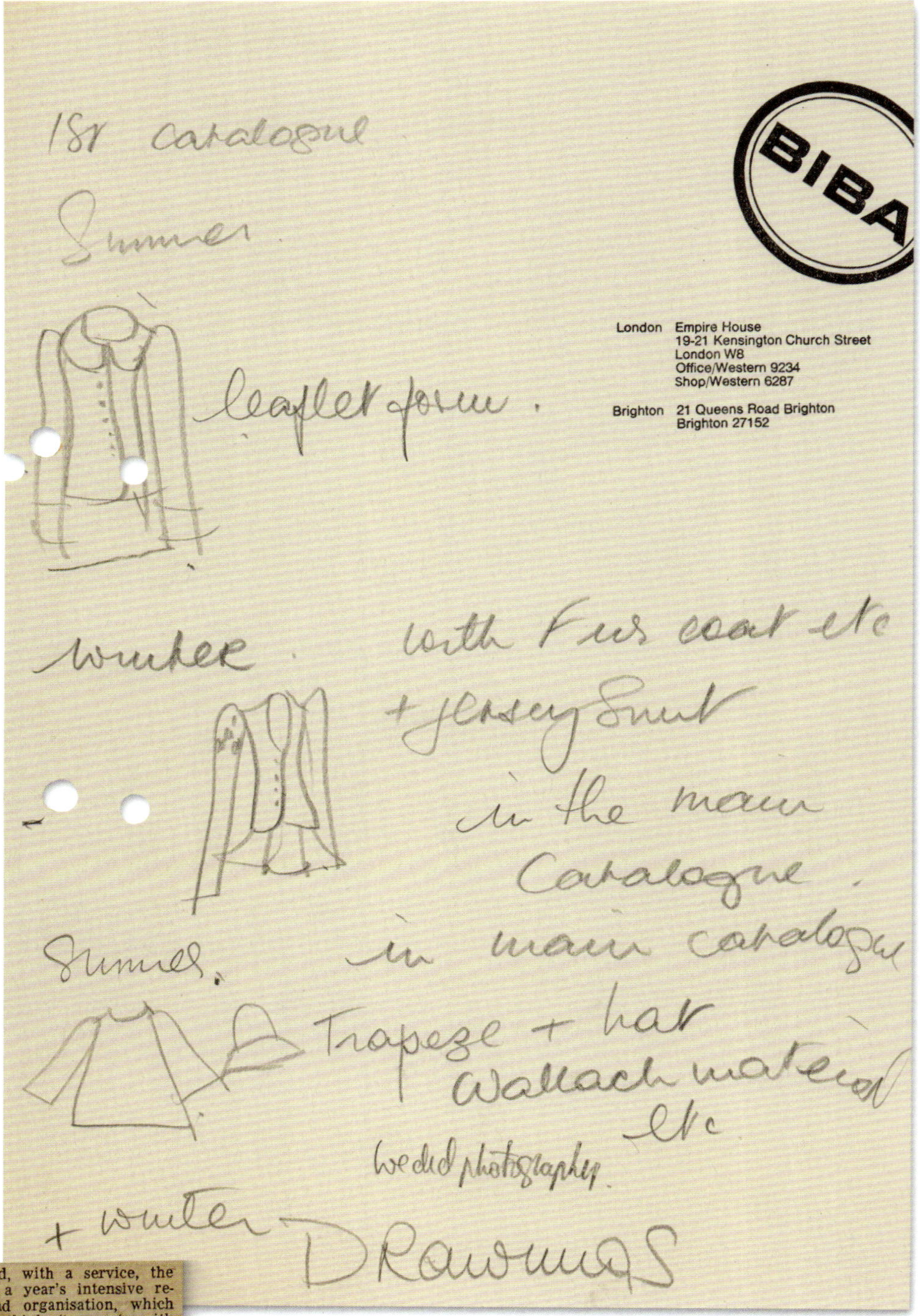

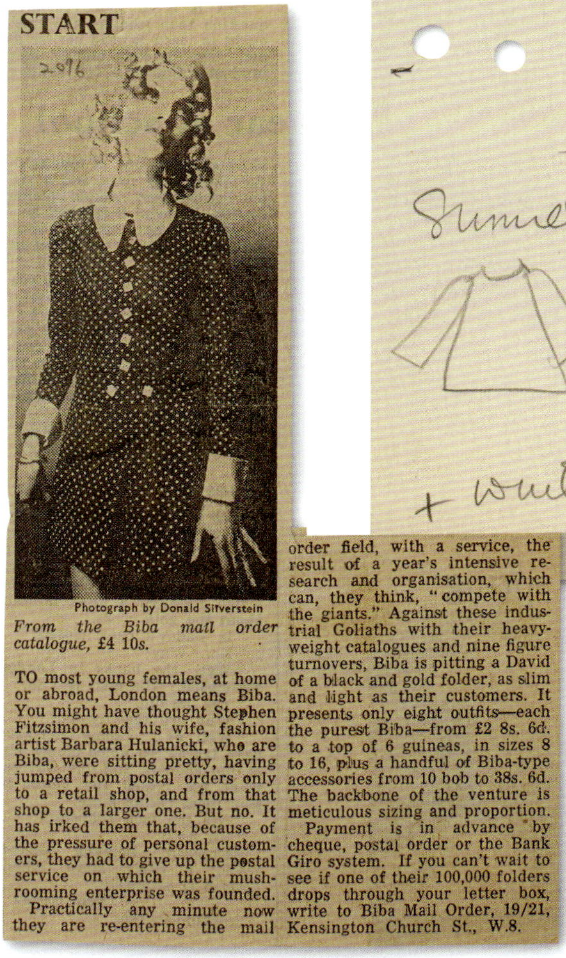

START

Photograph by Donald Silverstein

From the Biba mail order catalogue, £4 10s.

TO most young females, at home or abroad, London means Biba. You might have thought Stephen Fitzsimon and his wife, fashion artist Barbara Hulanicki, who are Biba, were sitting pretty, having jumped from postal orders only to a retail shop, and from that shop to a larger one. But no. It has irked them that, because of the pressure of personal customers, they had to give up the postal service on which their mushrooming enterprise was founded.

Practically any minute now they are re-entering the mail order field, with a service, the result of a year's intensive research and organisation, which can, they think, "compete with the giants." Against these industrial Goliaths with their heavyweight catalogues and nine figure turnovers, Biba is pitting a David of a black and gold folder, as slim and light as their customers. It presents only eight outfits—each the purest Biba—from £2 8s. 6d. to a top of 6 guineas, in sizes 8 to 16, plus a handful of Biba-type accessories from 10 bob to 38s. 6d. The backbone of the venture is meticulous sizing and proportion.

Payment is in advance by cheque, postal order or the Bank Giro system. If you can't wait to see if one of their 100,000 folders drops through your letter box, write to Biba Mail Order, 19/21, Kensington Church St., W.8.

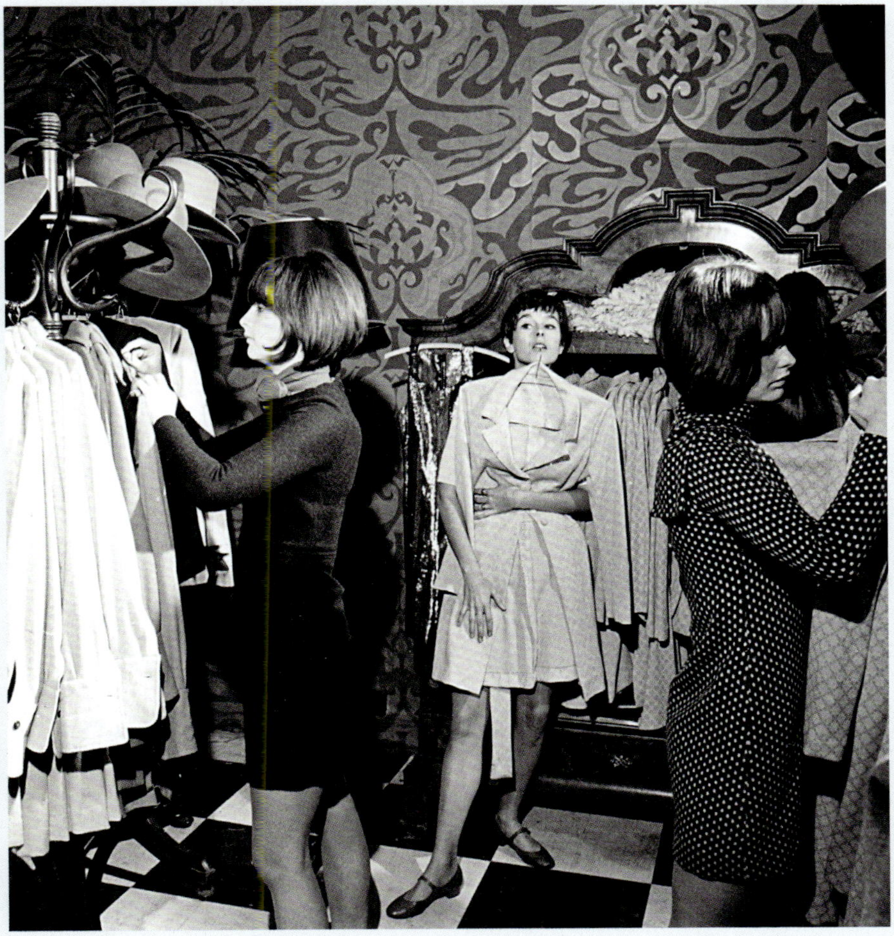

ROSIE MARKES ~ ASSISTANT TO BARBARA HULANICKI

Interior of Biba, Church Street, with Rosie and Susy Young and unknown woman in the middle, c.1967

Biba Church Street was very exciting, a wonderful shop. Tony Little did the outside and Julie Hodges did the wallpapers – it was beautiful. There were hat stands all over the place, with clothes hanging from them. You could just go in and sit on the sofa and watch the world go by; it was fascinating, like a sort of theatre.

Customers were girls from the high street, shop girls. They would come up and go crazy in their lunch hour, spending all their wages. Little dolly birds, they used to be called, with their long hair, fringes and black eye make-up. I remember there was a big communal changing room downstairs. It was great fun, with everyone throwing clothes all over the place. I think there was a lot of shoplifting, but Barbara didn't seem to mind – she thought it was rather a compliment.

And then the celebrities would come in: Brigitte Bardot, Mia Farrow, Yoko Ono. I was in the office with Barbara and the shop girls came in to say that Yoko Ono was in, so I went out to see her and asked if she needed anything. She told me that she wanted 'to buy a dress for my exhibition tonight'. We did sometimes lend clothes, so she picked a dress that she was happy with, and I let her take it. I can't remember if she signed anything, perhaps I didn't do the paperwork properly. In any case, Yoko went off with her dress, and on television that evening there she was, doing her performance art, sitting on the stage with the dress being cut up. All I could think was, 'Oh my god ... that's the dress I've lent her. Fitz will be furious!' I knew I'd be in trouble the next day. I went to see Fitz and said, 'I'm so sorry about the dress', and I remember Fitz saying, 'That was three pounds fifty!' She didn't pay for it, and she cut it up! You think she would have said something!

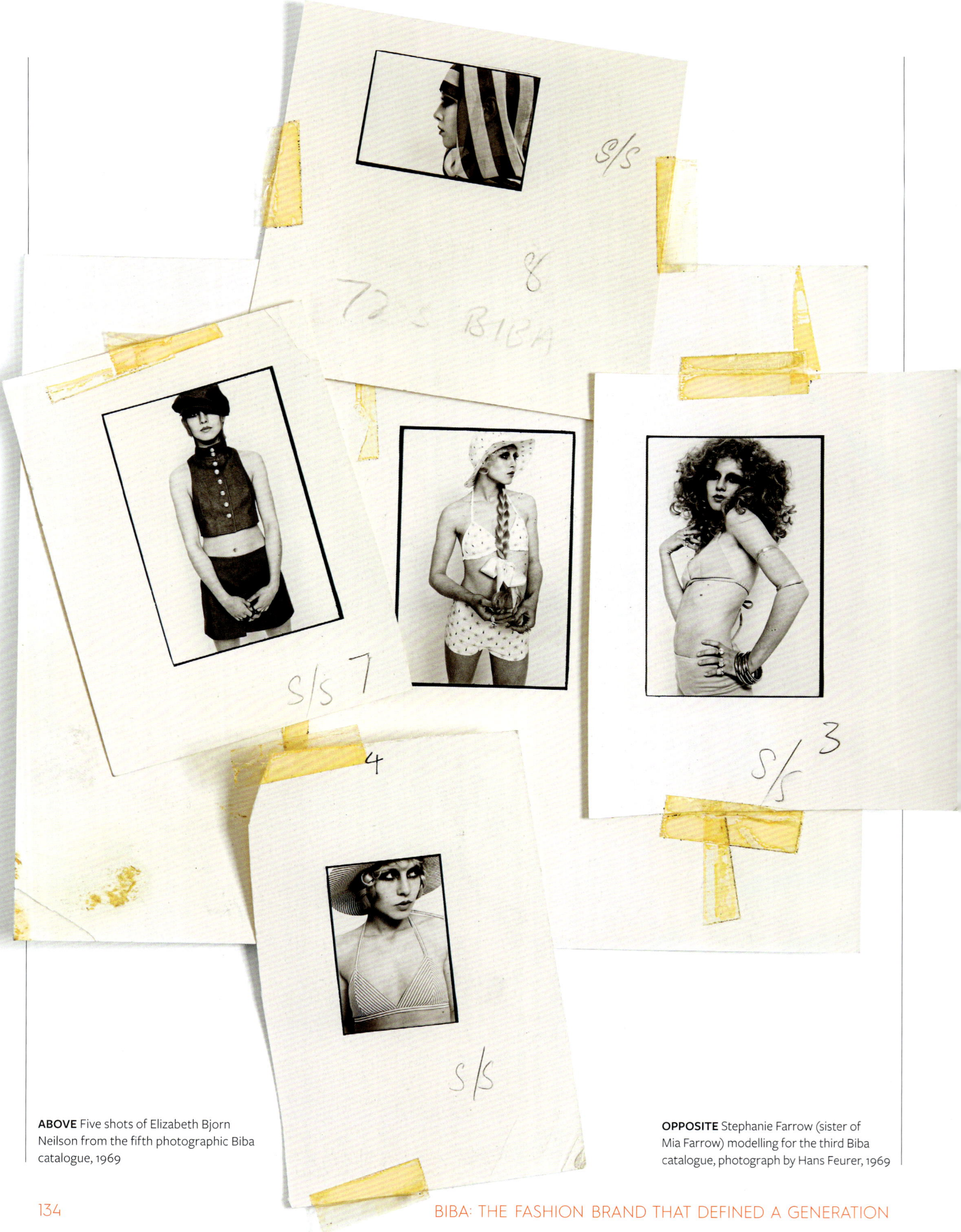

ABOVE Five shots of Elizabeth Bjorn Neilson from the fifth photographic Biba catalogue, 1969

OPPOSITE Stephanie Farrow (sister of Mia Farrow) modelling for the third Biba catalogue, photograph by Hans Feurer, 1969

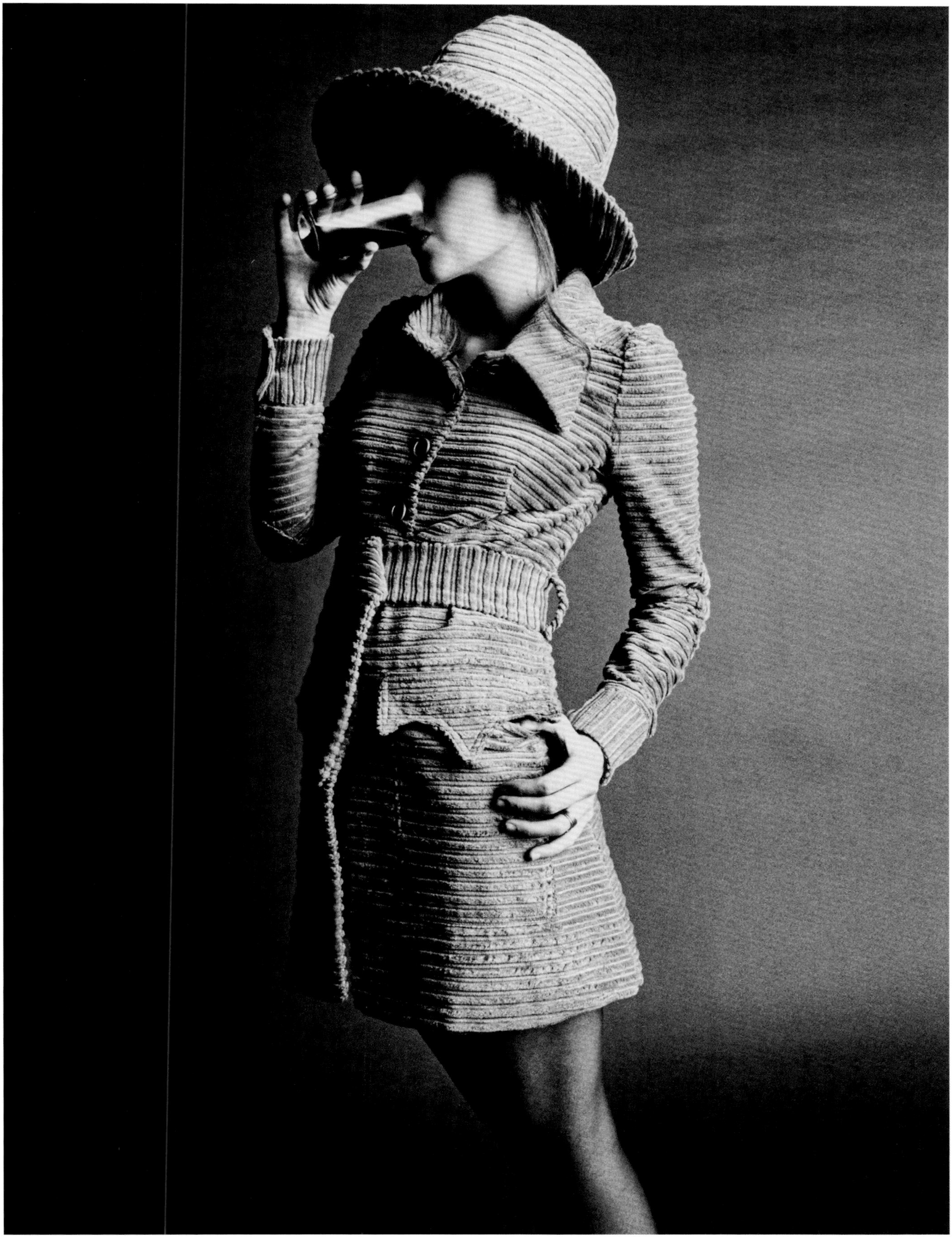

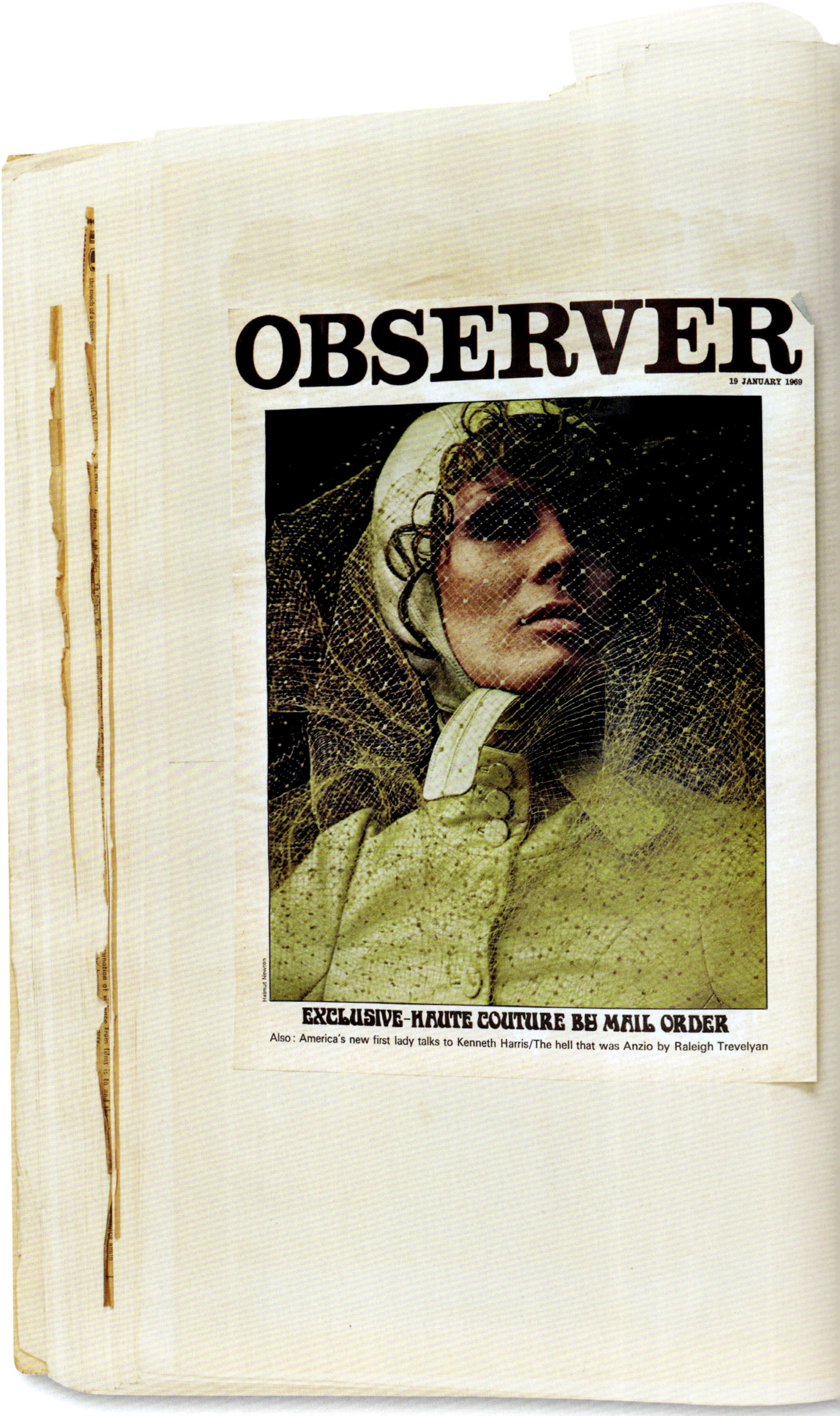
OBSERVER
19 JANUARY 1969
EXCLUSIVE-HAUTE COUTURE BY MAIL ORDER
Also: America's new first lady talks to Kenneth Harris/The hell that was Anzio by Raleigh Trevelyan

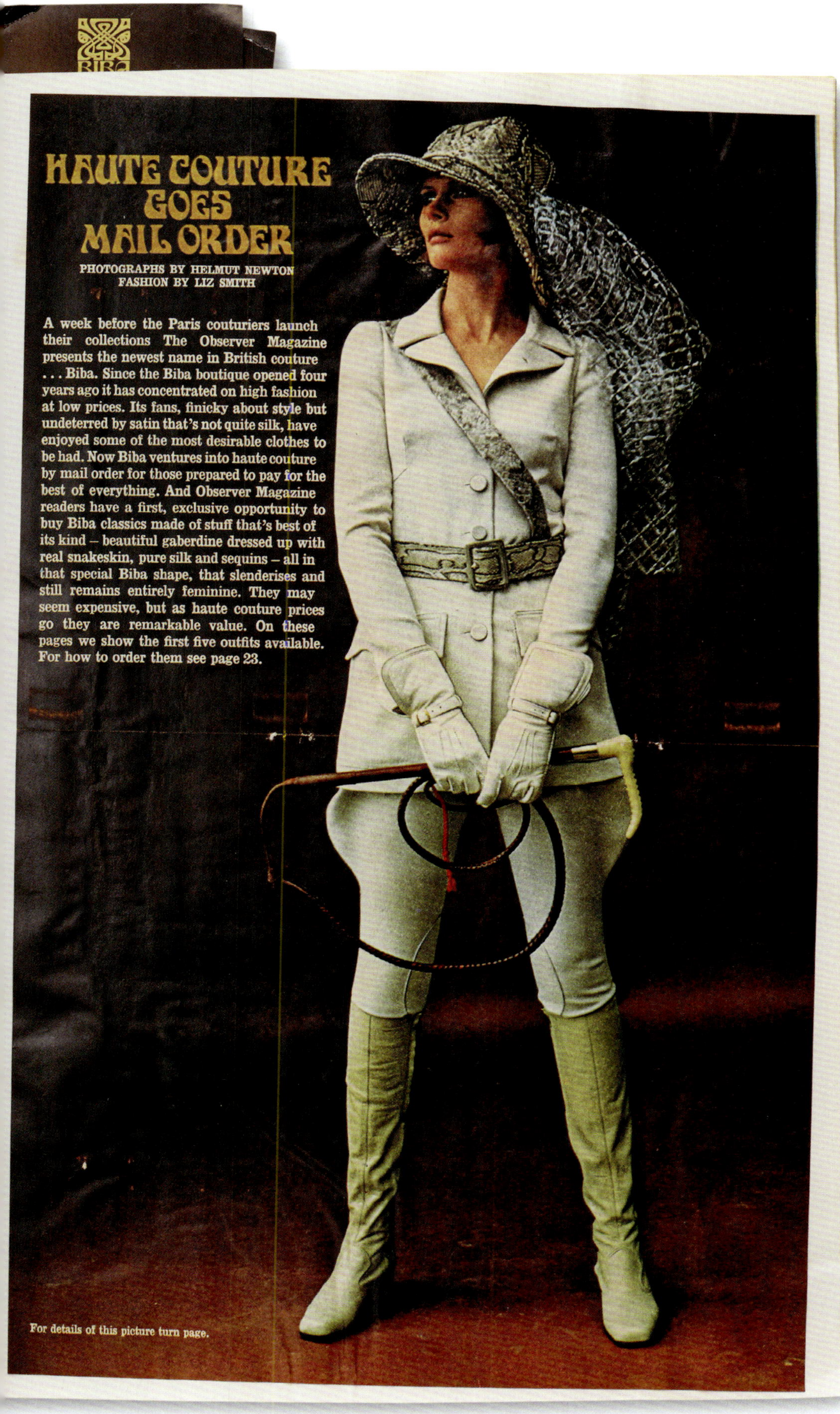

HAUTE COUTURE GOES MAIL ORDER

PHOTOGRAPHS BY HELMUT NEWTON
FASHION BY LIZ SMITH

A week before the Paris couturiers launch their collections The Observer Magazine presents the newest name in British couture . . . Biba. Since the Biba boutique opened four years ago it has concentrated on high fashion at low prices. Its fans, finicky about style but undeterred by satin that's not quite silk, have enjoyed some of the most desirable clothes to be had. Now Biba ventures into haute couture by mail order for those prepared to pay for the best of everything. And Observer Magazine readers have a first, exclusive opportunity to buy Biba classics made of stuff that's best of its kind – beautiful gaberdine dressed up with real snakeskin, pure silk and sequins – all in that special Biba shape, that slenderises and still remains entirely feminine. They may seem expensive, but as haute couture prices go they are remarkable value. On these pages we show the first five outfits available. For how to order them see page 23.

For details of this picture turn page.

OPPOSITE, ABOVE & OVERLEAF Biba couture range launched in the *Observer Magazine* with photographs by Helmut Newton, 19 January 1969

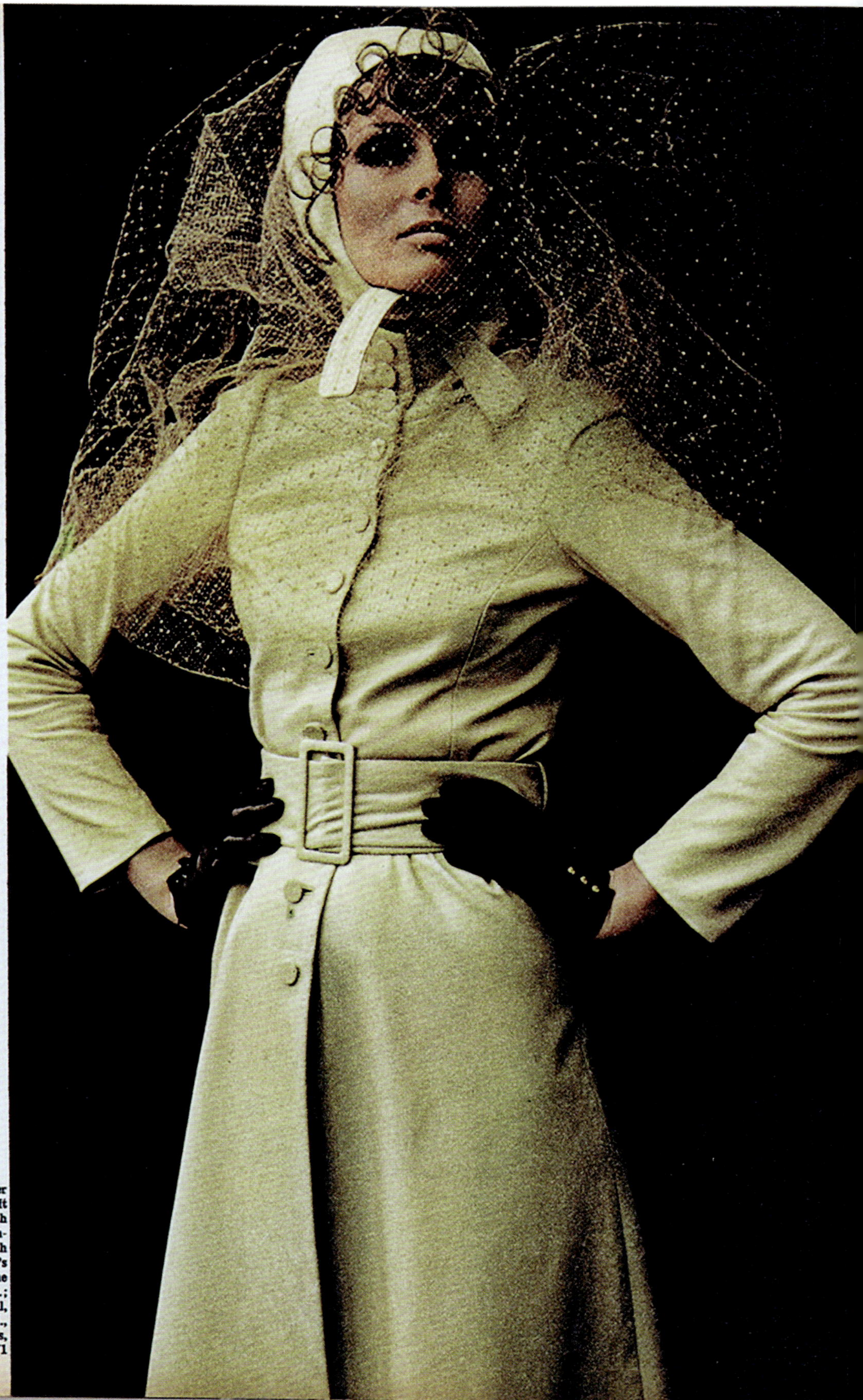

Vanilla cape leather coat, wonderfully soft and supple, which buttons up to a high-banded collar, with matching aviator's helmet tied under the chin. Coat, 120 gn.; helmet, without veil, 14 gn.; gloves, 59s. 6d., by Nerry from Harrods, Knightsbridge, SW1

22

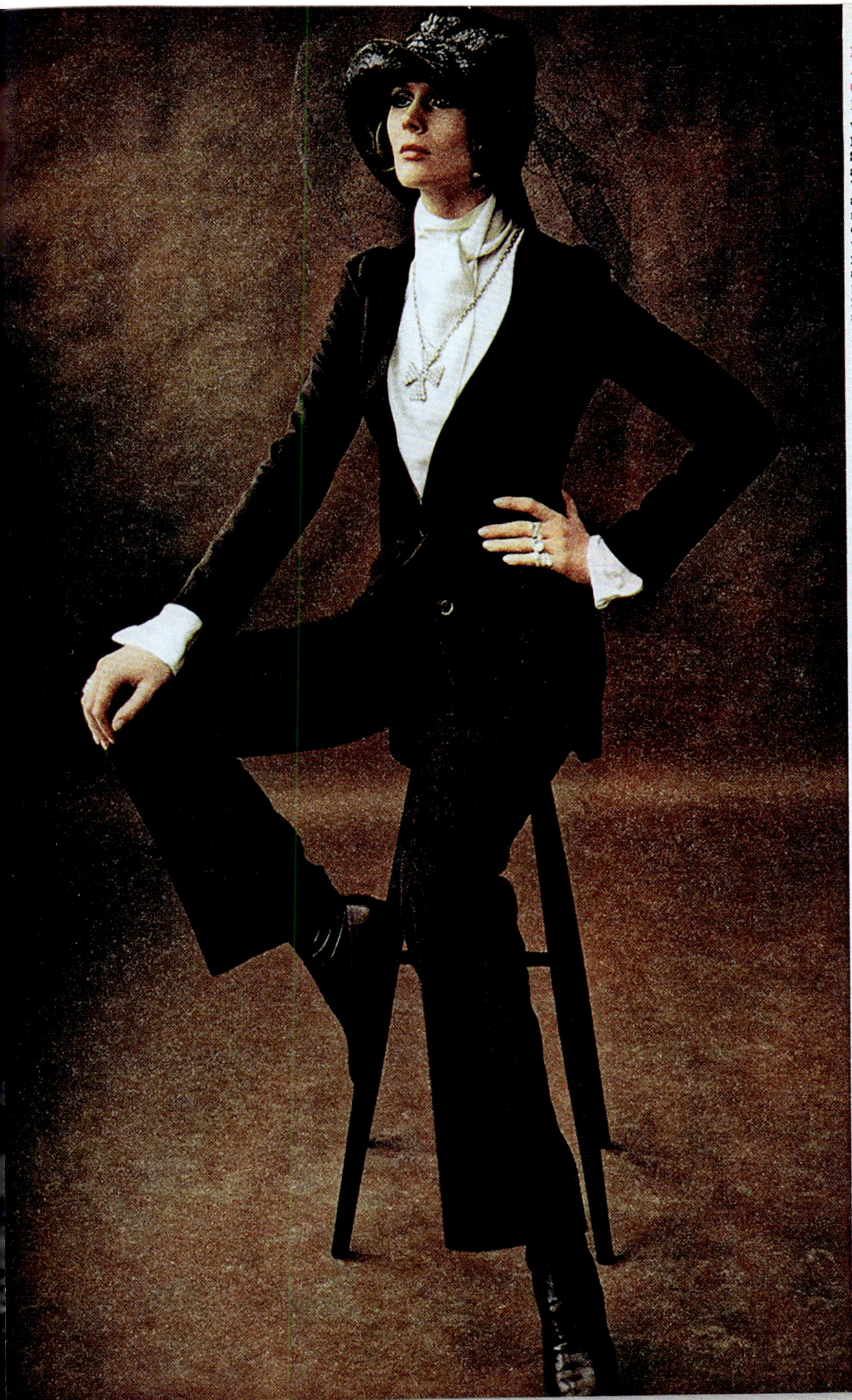

HOW TO GET A BIBA COUTURE OUTFIT BY POST

Write to Biba Ltd, 19 Kensington Church Street, London W 8, for a special order form. With it you will get a very detailed measurement chart to complete. It is vital, writes Liz Smith, that you are measured accurately (get a competent person to do it for you). Then send off the order form with £15 deposit.
You will be sent a toile of the garment made to your measurements, together with a cutting of the fabric. Alterations can be made on the toile, and it's up to you to ensure it fits exactly the way you want. You will be sent a special chart on which to note any alterations.
Finally, send back the approved toile together with the balance of the price, and the dress, suit or coat will be made up for you in the couture fabric.
Each garment will be cut to individual measurements out of couture cloth, with perfect buttonholes, hand sewn zips and linings of silk.

Chocolate brown whipcord trousers and shapely cardigan jacket, 60 gn. Cream crepe-de-chine blouse with stock tied softly at the neck, 25 gn. Silver rings, 30s. each; fake diamond ring, 30s. Plummy brown snakeskin hat, 25 gn. Boots, 16 gn., from the Chelsea Cobbler. Hair by Valerie, at Cheveux, Abingdon Road, W8

23

CHAPTER FOUR

1969–1973 KENSINGTON HIGH STREET

"Fitz had found the shop
on Kensington High Street,
and we thought, 'Oh God,
it looks dreadful', but it
was amazing inside"

Barbara Hulanicki

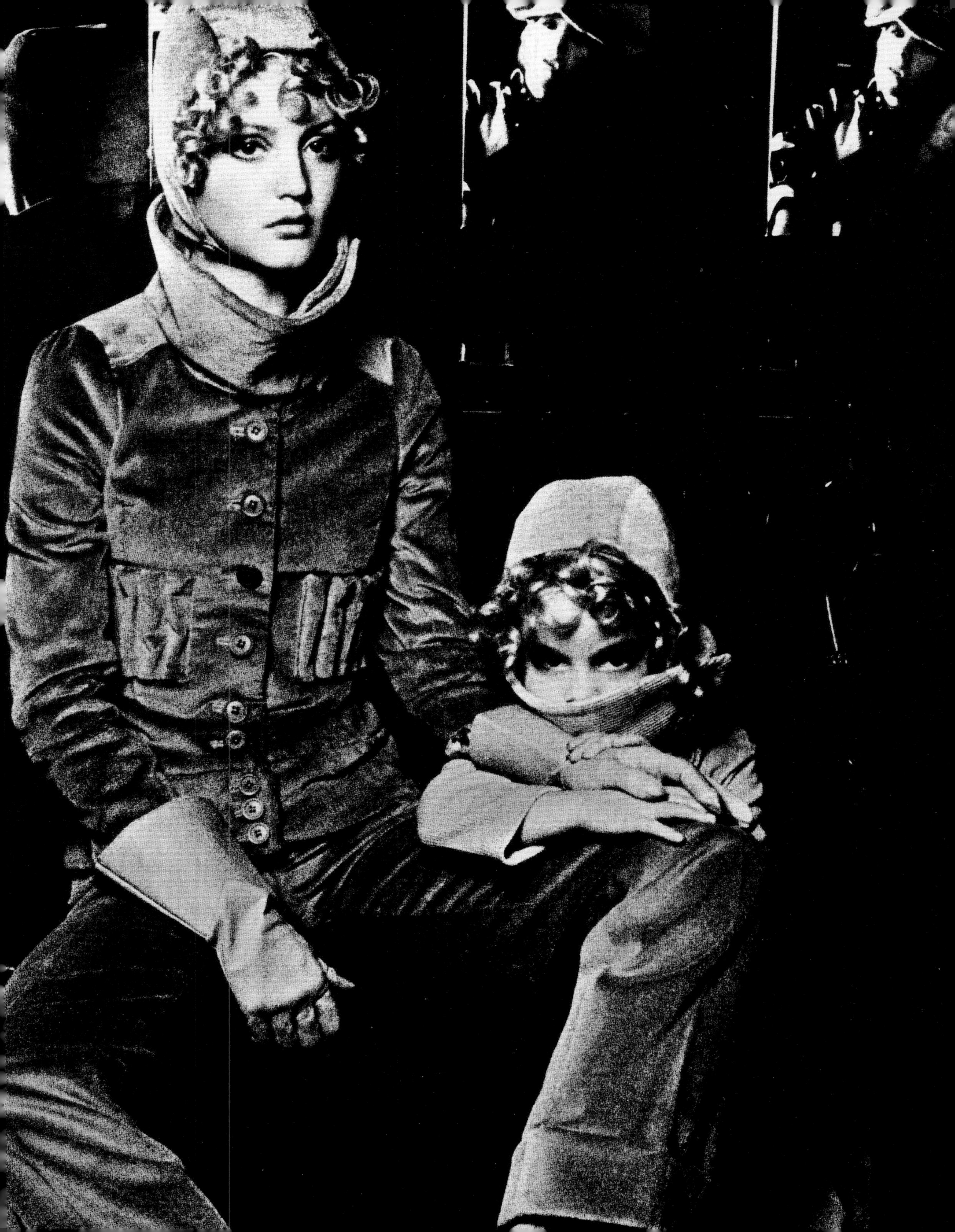

MARTIN PEL At Kensington High Street Biba became a department store.

BARBARA HULANICKI It was a natural progression to become a department store. Everybody by then had their babies and they were getting homes. We needed more space at Biba because it was bulging. Fitz had found the shop on Kensington High Street, and we thought, 'Oh god, it looks dreadful', but it was amazing inside.

In terms of the decor, to be honest, I'm not sure if the shops were an extension of my home or my home was an extension of the shops! I used to collect Victorian pedestals and pots. We had the whole shop full of them at one stage, and then they slowly broke because they were ceramic. That was another thing about having a shop, you could go shopping for junk. It's like the mirrors in the Church Street changing rooms, you could get them for nothing. Nobody wanted them. If you went to Brick Lane at 5 in the morning and dug through all the rubbish, you would find fantastic antiques. We had all these statues cast from old sculptures. There was a guy in Westbourne Grove, Nick Haywood, and he had them all cast for us, and manufactured in London, and then we used them for decor in Big Biba. Everybody was on the same wavelength. Everybody went to The Lacquer Chest in Kensington, up the road on Church Street; we all rushed in to see what they had. For the household range, we researched and found a manufacturer who made lace bedspreads, another who made lampshades and another for pillows. We told them what we wanted, and they made it for us.

We created the shoe department at the Kensington High Street store because we were selling so many shoes. Then we moved the shoe department from upstairs to downstairs as we were selling so many boots. We wanted to increase the space so there was more room for people to try on. I think I wanted to put something else upstairs – probably handbags and tights. The mirrored design came from the Mistinguett hotel apartment of L'Hôtel in Paris. It was meant to be like a stage set; the idea was that people looked at the shoes in these mirrored seats and they could see themselves all over.

From the beginning of Biba, the shoe sales were big business, and our shoes were sold at really good prices. We always had the one thing. Fitz used to say, you zero in on one thing and do it properly in lots of colours and at a good price, so you don't have too much stray stuff. I just had to do the boots and they went on for years and then we had tons and tons of platforms. Tons and tons! It was a huge business.

MP And then there was the Biba cosmetics range.

BH The cosmetics were an absolute must. You've got the dress, the shoes, the hat, you've got everything, and there's no face. Fitz found Kolmar cosmetics, a big company in East Grinstead that was making cosmetics for other people. When we went to see them they were rude to us! I wanted sepia lipstick and there were all these men sitting around giving excuses as to why they couldn't produce it because *they* didn't think it would sell. I wanted to say, 'Excuse me, I'm paying and I want it.' Eventually they produced about 60 lipsticks all in one colour and sent them down in terrible packaging; they all sold out in under an hour. We were in business, and Kolmar started to listen to us.

Our make-up was really high pigment, and the colours were designed to go with the clothes. There would be the basic colours, and then we would bring out a capsule

PREVIOUS PAGE Ingrid Boulting and child in Biba, photographed by Sarah Moon, 1970

collection for a particular season. There was the basic range and then something like 'Pop', which had blue lipstick, blue eyeshadow, blue powder, blue eyelashes and a blue wig, which would have been in and out.

MP In 1971 Biba went to America.

BH Rosemary McMurtry, the editor of *Seventeen* magazine, came to see us at Church Street. We thought she was fabulous, and we became great friends. She put us on to Colette Toohey, who was at the Bergdorf Goodman department store in New York, and who asked us if we would like to sell at Bergdorf's. They gave us about 600 square feet on the BG floor, a boutique-y sort of floor. We had almost carte blanche to put in what we wanted, so we did everything that was coordinated: the boots, clothes, tights, cosmetics. It was really great, and we did it for a few years.

Around the same time, we did the promotion with Macy's department store. Macy's sold Biba printed textiles, which we were already doing in England, and McCall's did the paper pattern. I didn't realise it was going to be so big. Macy's rolled it out to all their stores, and it became huge. Rosemary did a big fashion story for *Seventeen*, and the photographer Sarah Moon managed to get these wonderfully huge rooms at the top of Printemps department store for the shoot. It was this fantastic penthouse where the directors used to have their sitting room.

"You've got the dress, the shoes, the hat, you've got everything, and there's no face"

MP How long had you been doing your own fabrics?

BH We'd been doing our own fabrics right from the beginning. Burgess, Ledward & Co. supplied the fabric for the 1964 gingham dress, and we were big time with them because we paid our bills. They brought this chap out of retirement as I kept asking for all the vintage stuff: crepe, crepe de Chine, Flanesta, which was a sort of copy of a Liberty wool but in rayon – everything was in rayon – and he would develop all the old fabrics for us. These were completely out of fashion, so they were digging out all of this old stock. These were all base fabrics. The prints we would either design in-house or we would use old archive prints and do them in all the colourways. If we wanted 23 colours, we would have people sitting there copying and painting out sheets of colour to send to the manufacturer. Pantone was only in its early days at that time and not as readily available, so we had to create the colours ourselves. We would have to get the colour exactly right as the manufacturers would go by the colour that we sent them. Then these colours would go to the various manufacturers, and Daphne Bewes would be making sure that all the colours matched across all the different fabrics and products. This was just for one colour, and we had around 23 colours across lots of products. It was quite an amazing set-up when you come to think about it.

We went into partnership with Dorothy Perkins in 1969. At the time it was a family business run by the founder, Alan Farmer, and his son Ian. We had six years with them. We needed financing to move things forward as we were completely cash-flowing everything. With cash-flowing you have to have a certain amount of capital to buy new stock. When we went into partnership, it was an amazing success for Dorothy Perkins financially. The minute we had capital we made them tons of money, and everyone was so happy, it was incredible.

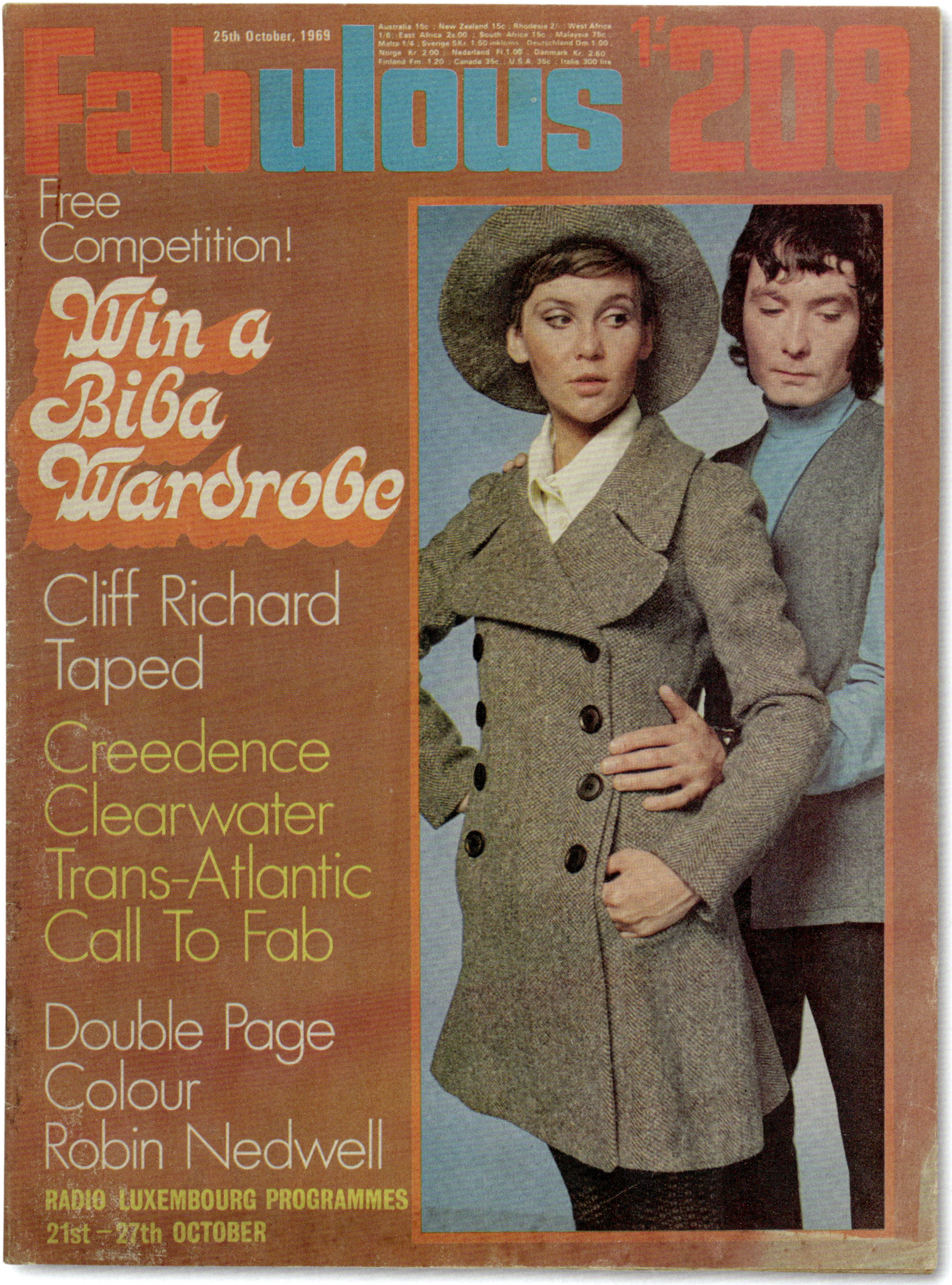

Magazine competition promoting the sixth (and final) photographic Biba catalogue, *Fabulous 208*, 25 October 1969

Win a Biba Wardrobe

Everyone who enters will get a free Biba Catalogue

by HEATHER KIRBY Photographs by ROGER BROWN

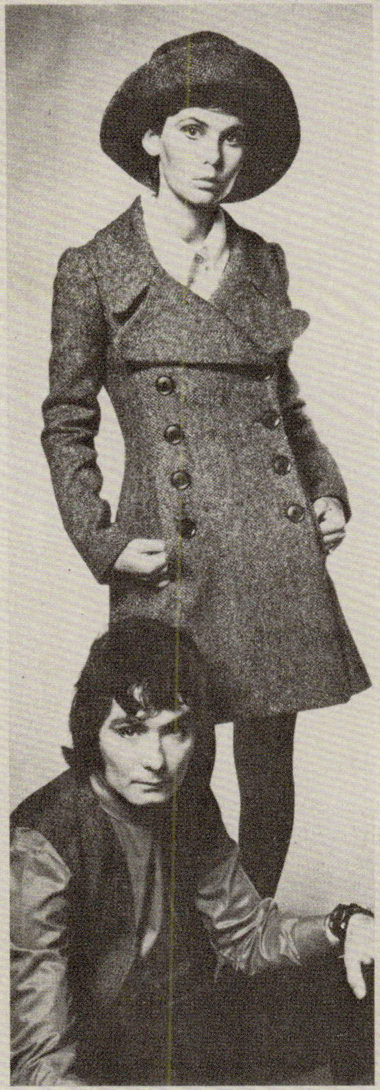

Fab fella is Vince Edwards, one of the stars of *Hair*. Coat, £9 19s. 6d. Blouse, £2 15s. 6d. Hat £1 19s. 6d.

If your idea of Heaven is wearing a Biba wardrobe, then this page is your passport to the Pearly Gates! You can win a whole wardrobe of clothes from the swinging-est boutique in Britain by entering our free competition. All the gear is from Biba's latest catalogue and, as you can see from our cover pic and the ones over the page, they are fantastic.

What is the prize? A wardrobe worth over £47 made up of eight fantastic pieces. The material is pebble herringbone tweed and, besides the browny colour we photographed, there is a lovely bluey shade which you can have if you prefer.

What's it all about? The ankle length coat is lined, double breasted with large revers and slit pockets. The short version is ditto. The jacket is long, lean and fitted and so is the waistcoat. The skirt has a kick pleat and the sharp-cut trousers are funnel shape. The blouse is in Flanesta which is washable, and the hat is lovely and squashy and floppy. What more could a girl ask? Nothing in the whole wide world!

A—Low prices
B—Up-to-the-minute styles
C—Off-beat colours
D—Being able to match everything up
E—The cut
J—The quick changes of style
K—The materials used
L—They are right for my age

Now for the gen on how to win our prize. Listed in the panel above are eight reasons for wanting Biba clothes. All you have to do is put them in order of importance to the average FAB reader.

Fill in your answers on the Free Entry Coupon by writing the *key letters only* of these points in the numbered spaces. For example, if you consider *Off-beat colours* most important of all, write C in the first space; then the letter of your second choice in the next space, and so on for all eight.

Finally, tell us what you think B-I-B-A stands for (it doesn't really stand for anything! But can you think up something appropriate it *could* stand for?). This will be taken into account only in the event of ties.

Off you go then. Complete the coupon all in ink or ball-point, cut it out and post to: FAB 208 Biba Competition, 1-2 Bear Alley, Farringdon Street, London, E.C.4. (Comp.) Entries must arrive not later then Friday, 31st October, 1969.

The winner will be notified and the result published in the earliest possible issue of FAB. All entrants will be sent Biba catalogues in due course.

RULES: There is no entry fee, but each attempt must be completed in ink or ball pen on the coupon cut from FABULOUS 208 and must bear the entrant's full name and address.

Every attempt will be examined and the Prize, as described, will be awarded to the competitor who, in the opinion of the judges, and in any one attempt, lists the eight qualities in the best order of importance. In the event of ties, the suggestions for what BIBA stands for submitted by such tying competitors will be taken into account to decide the winner.

Any entry received after the closing date will be disqualified, as will any received mutilated or illegible, incomplete or containing alterations or with more than one key letter in each space. No responsibility will be taken for entries lost or delayed in the post or otherwise.

The judges' decision, and that of the Editor of FABULOUS 208 in all other matters affecting the competition, will be final and legally binding. No correspondence will be entered into.

The competition is open to all readers in Great Britain, Northern Ireland and the Channel Isles, except employees (and their families) of IPC Magazines Ltd., the printers of FABULOUS 208, or Biba.

FREE ENTRY COUPON

FAB 208 BIBA WARDROBE COMPETITION

1st	
2nd	
3rd	
4th	
5th	
6th	
7th	
8th	

My order of importance for the eight features of Biba clothes is given on the left. I suggest BIBA stands for:

B .... I .... B .... A ....

....

I agree to the rules as final and legally binding.
Full Name ....
Full Address ....

....

.... **Tel. No. (if any)** ....

CIRCLE YOUR SIZE: 8, 10, 12, 14, 15

cut neatly round this line

7

Fashion story in *Fabulous 208*, 25 October 1969

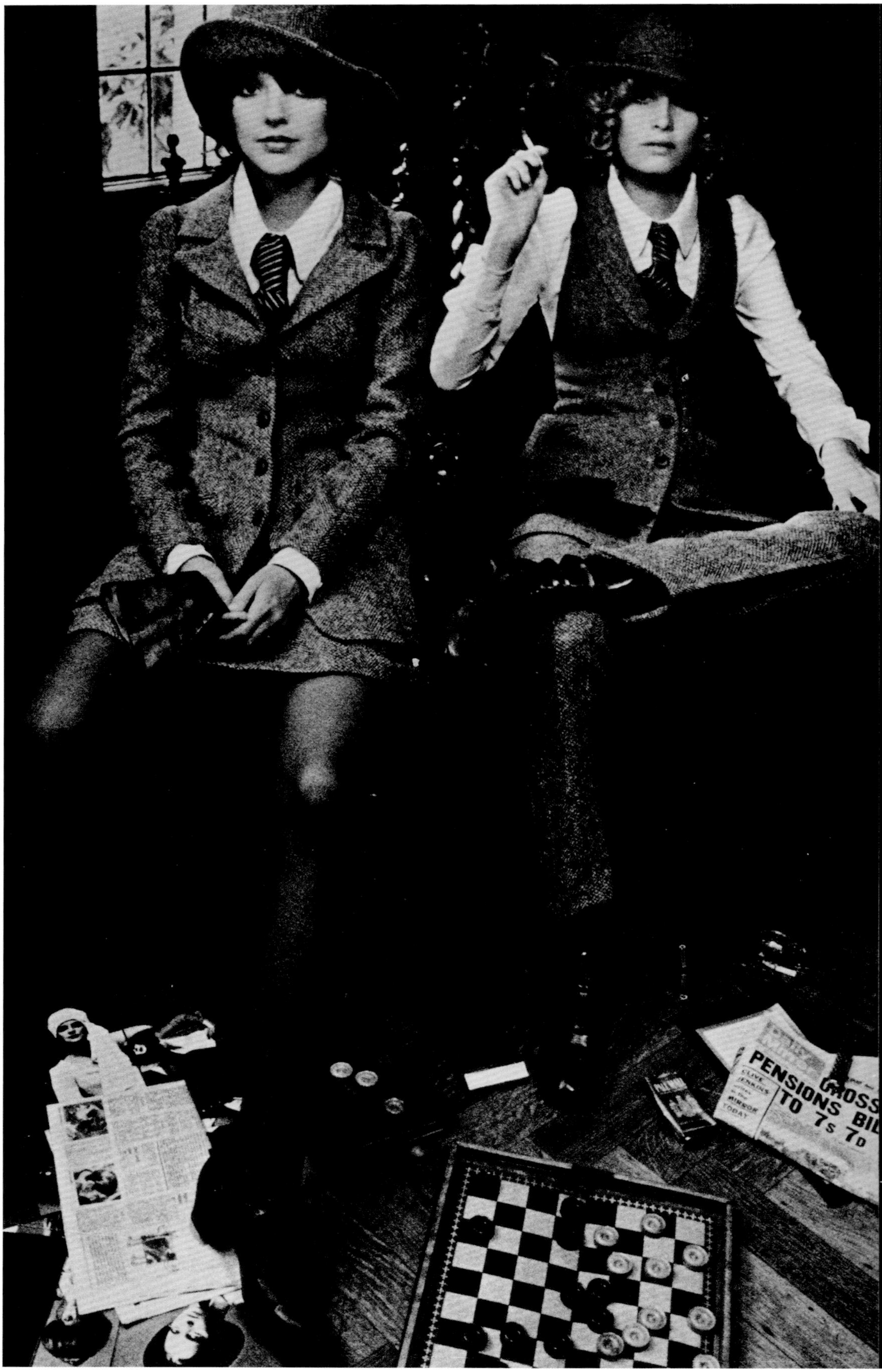
PENSIONS
TO 7s 7D
CLIVE
JENKINS
MIRROR
TODAY

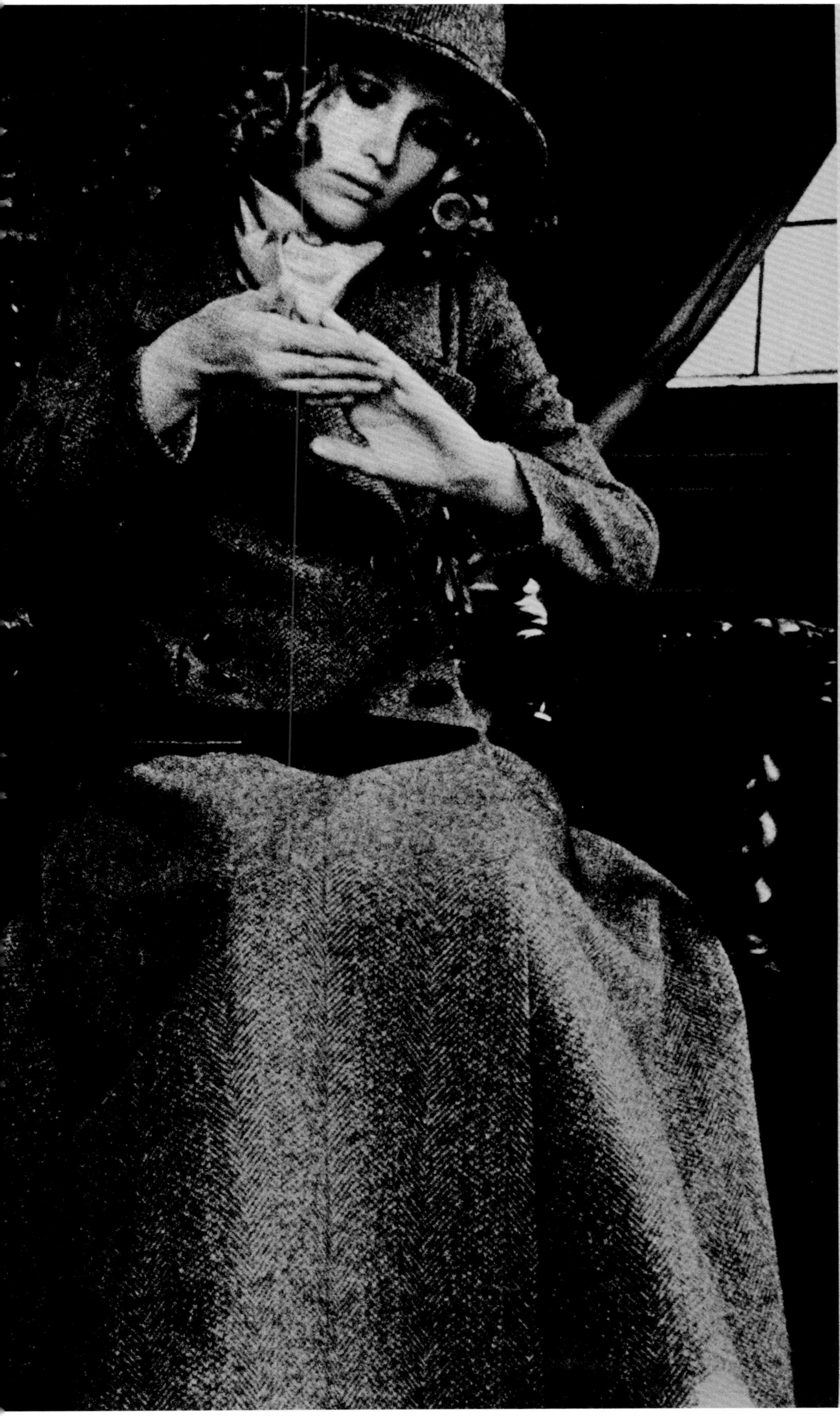

A four piece set in
pebble/herringbone
tweed.
Long, lean fitted jacket,
and equally long and
fitted waistcoat with
rounded revers,
skirt with kick pleat
and funnel shape
trousers.
Dyed to tone with
the tweed
(and golf check outfit
overleaf) a washable
Flanesta shirt.
In identical tweed,
a floor length or short
double breasted
lined coat with
large revers and
slit pockets.

Colours:
Tweeds
Brown/Beige
Dusty Blue/Grey
Shirt:
Biba brown
Black
Airforce blue
Cream

Design Number/Price
Long Coat ·
12A
£13·13·0

Short Coat
12B
£9·19·6

Jacket
12C
£7·15·6

Waistcoat
12D
£4·19·6

Trousers
12E
£3·15·6

Skirt
12F
£2·10·0

Shirt
12G
£2·15·6

Hat
12H
£1·19·6

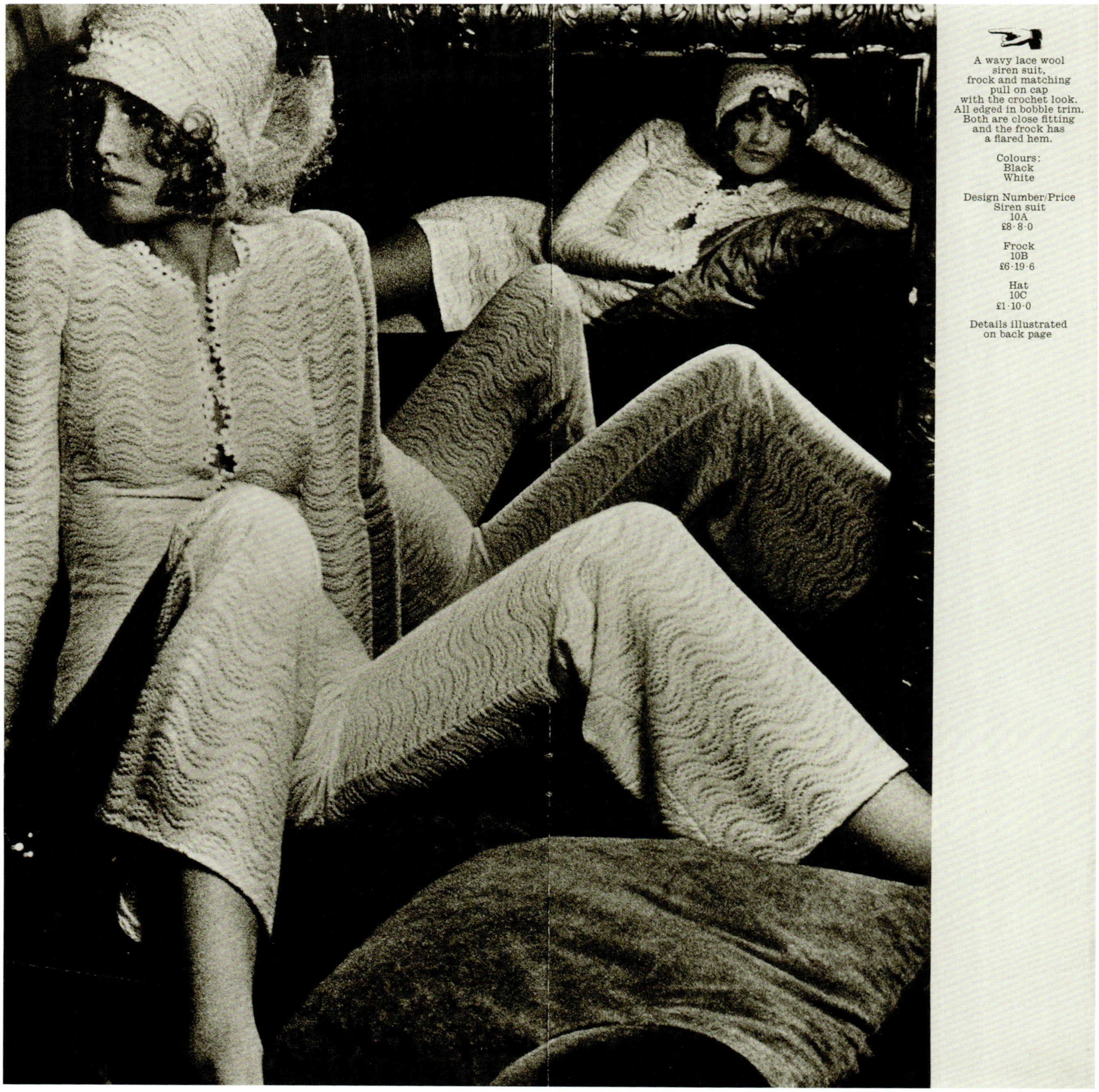

PREVIOUS PAGE, ABOVE & OPPOSITE
Marie Knopka and Quinella modelling for the sixth, and final, photographic Biba catalogue, photographed by Sarah Moon, 1969

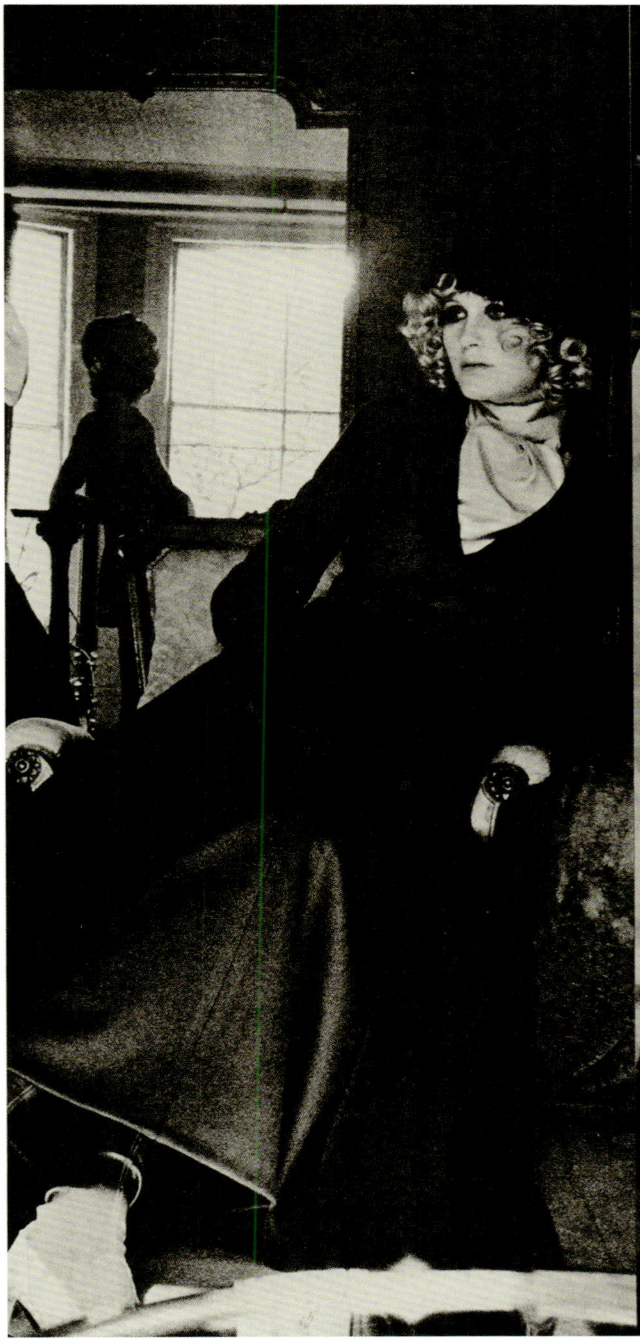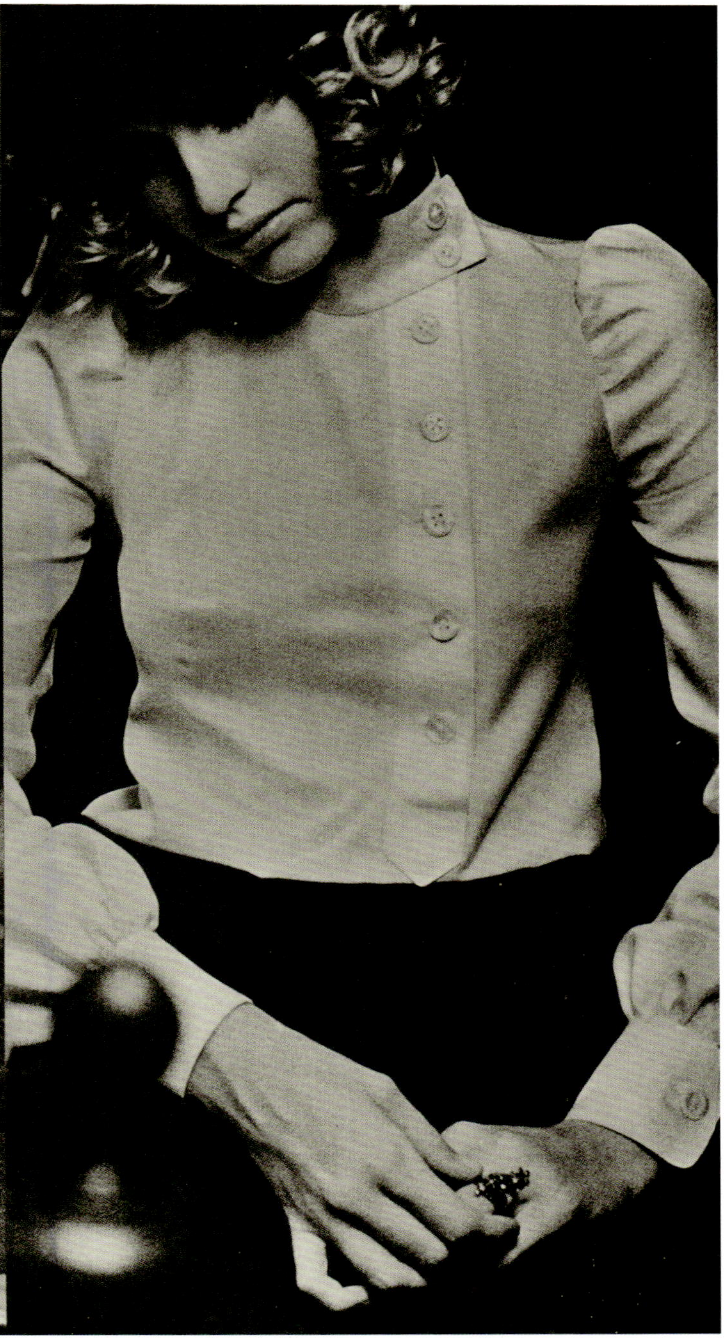

"I remember how Biba was absolutely linked with that time in London, where everything was happening. It was exciting for me to be part of Biba's story, and of course I never forgot how nice it was working with Barbara Hulanicki"

Sarah Moon, Biba photographer, 1969–73

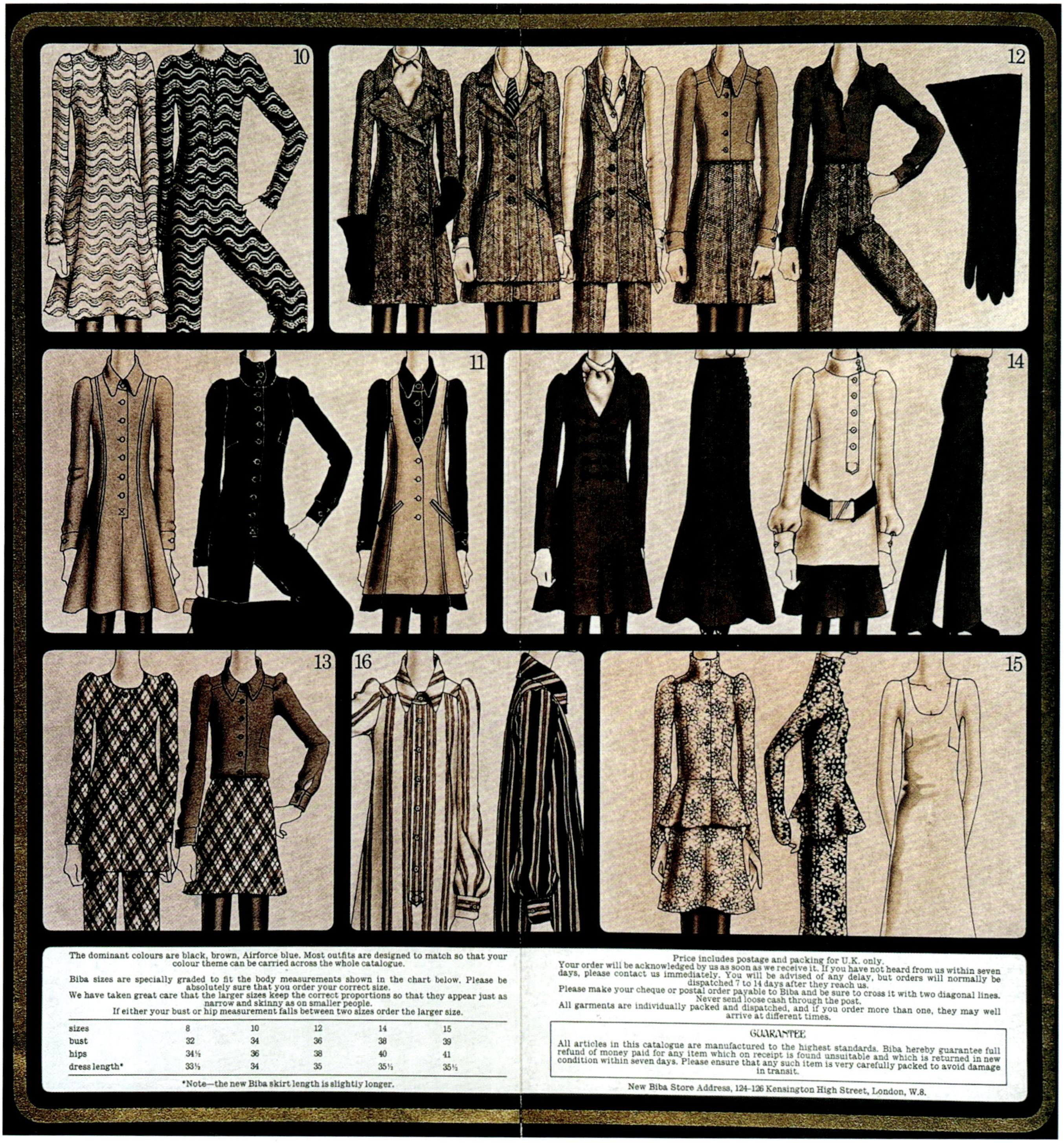

ABOVE Fashion illustrations by Moira Macgregor included in the sixth Biba catalogue, 1969

OPPOSITE Ingrid Boulting and child in the couture department of Biba, 1970

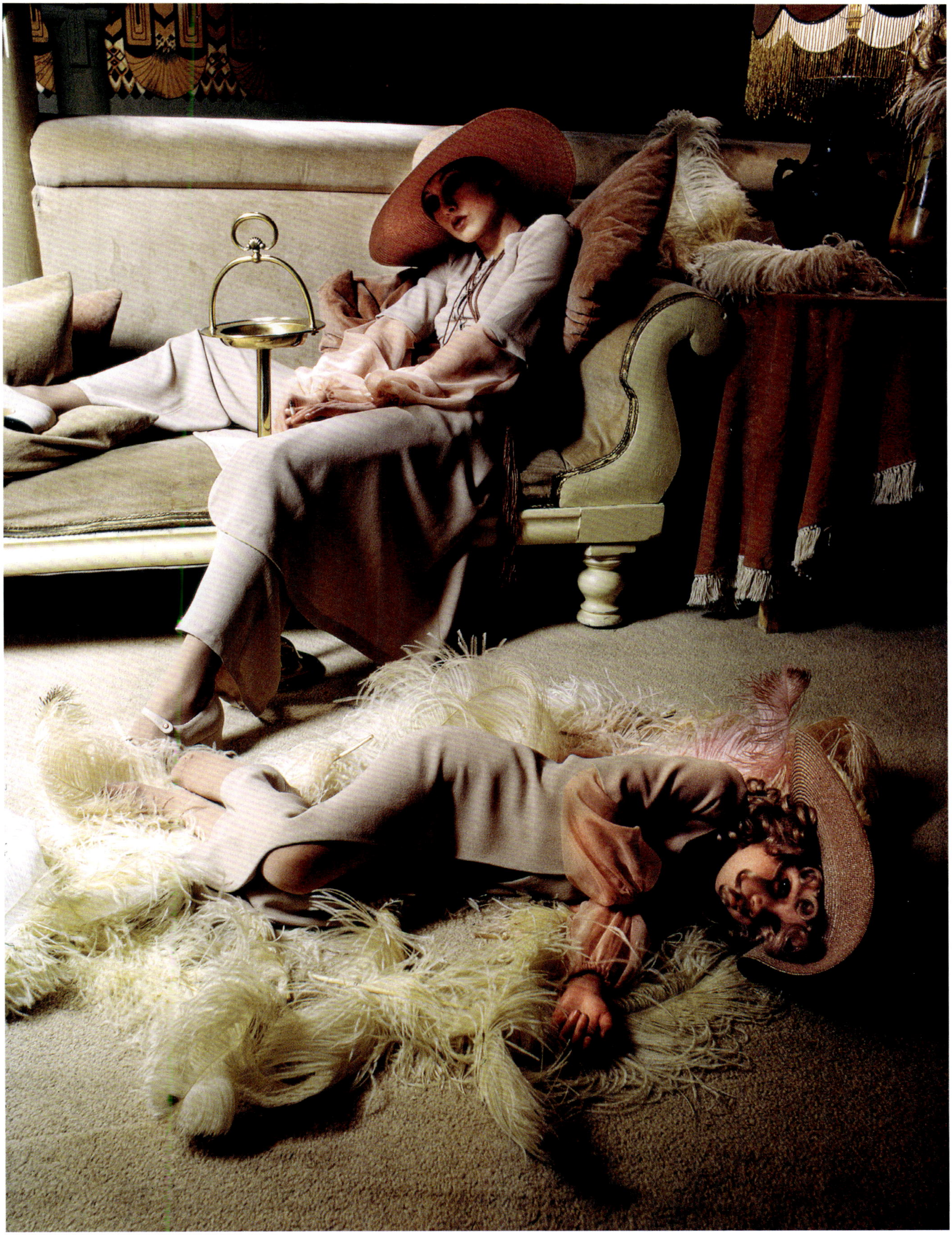

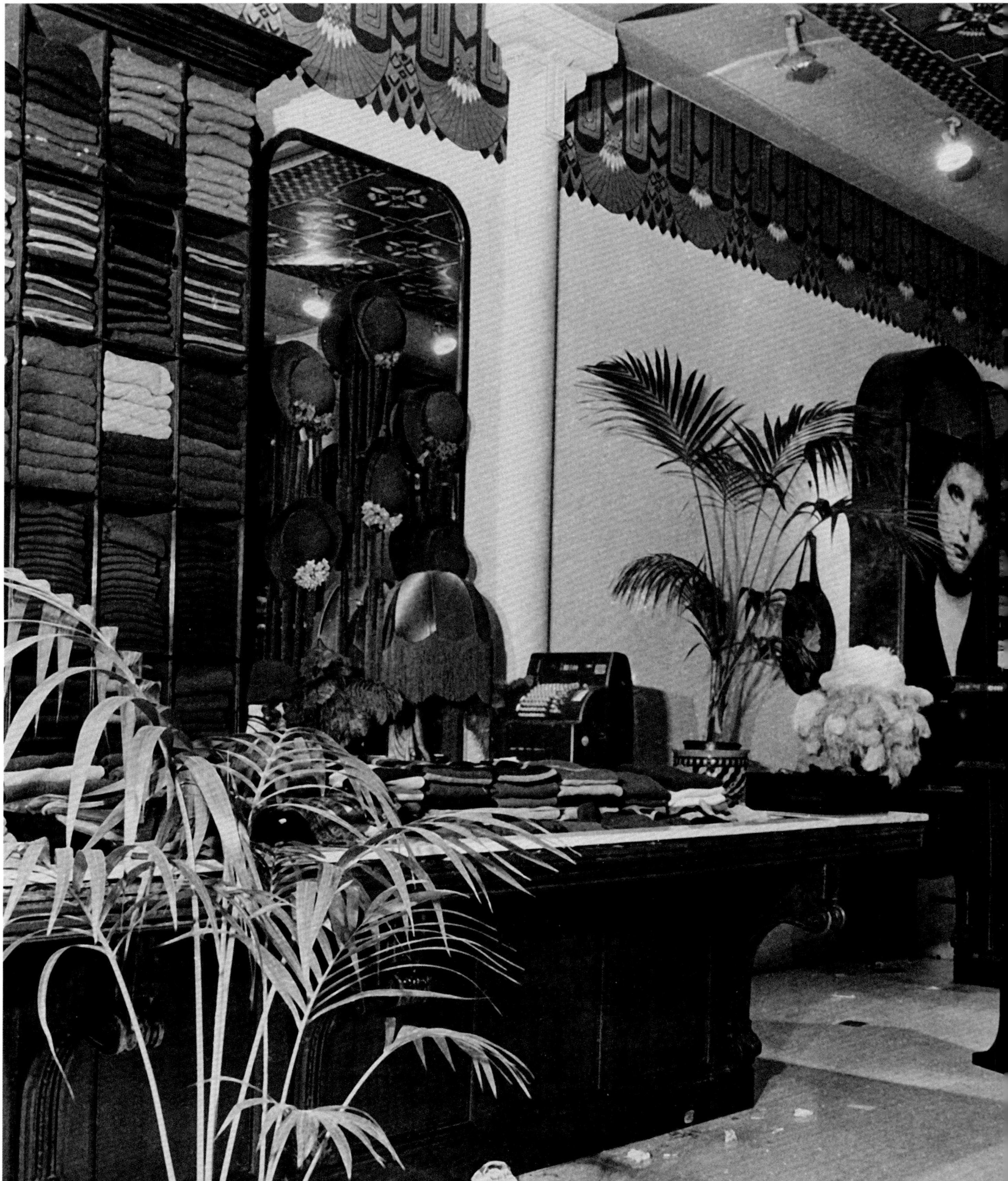

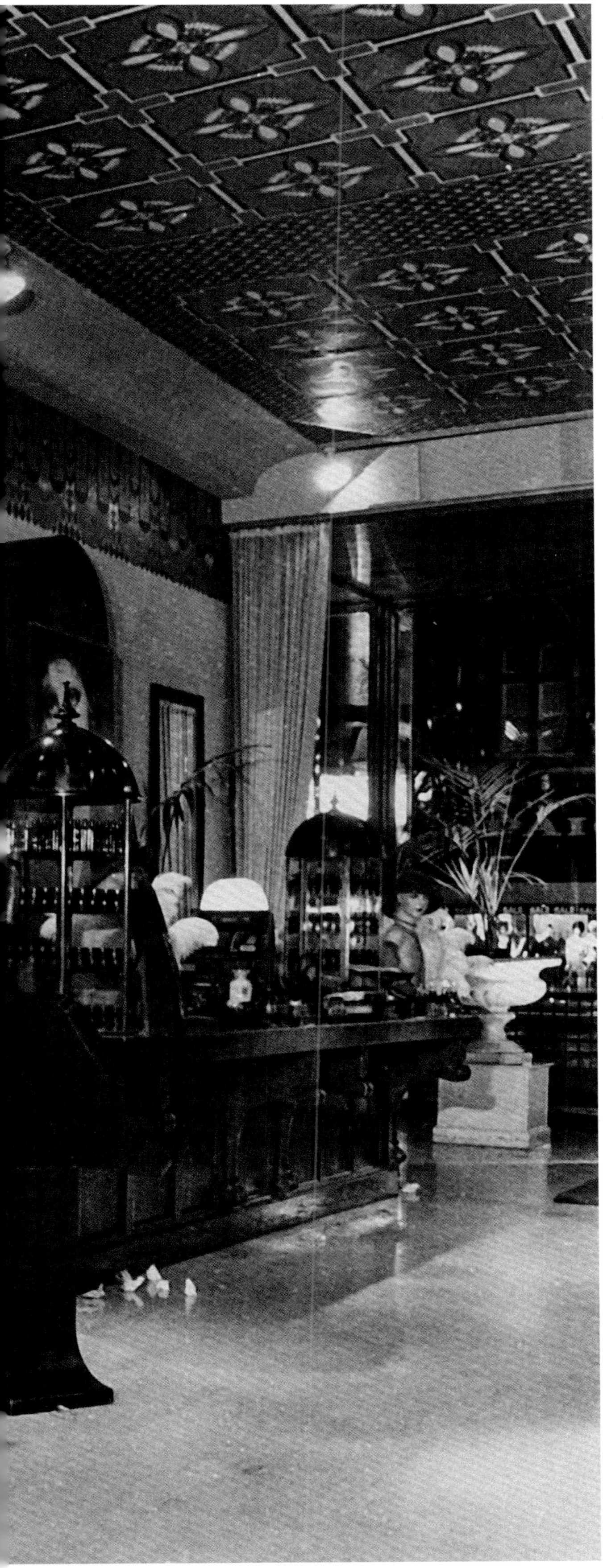

LEFT & OVERLEAF Interiors of Biba, Kensington High Street, showing the wooden interiors reclaimed from the recently demolished boys' school, St Paul's, c.1969

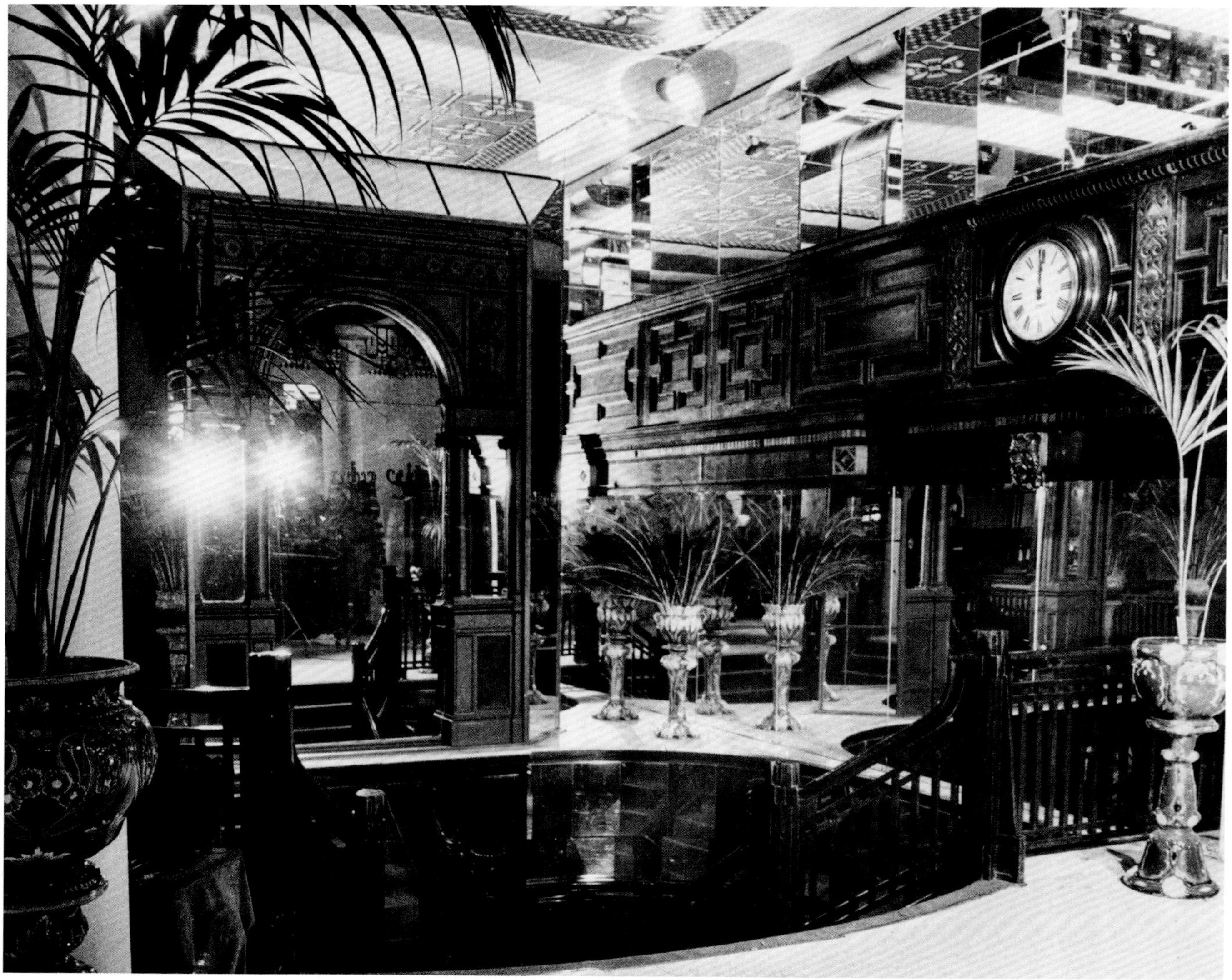

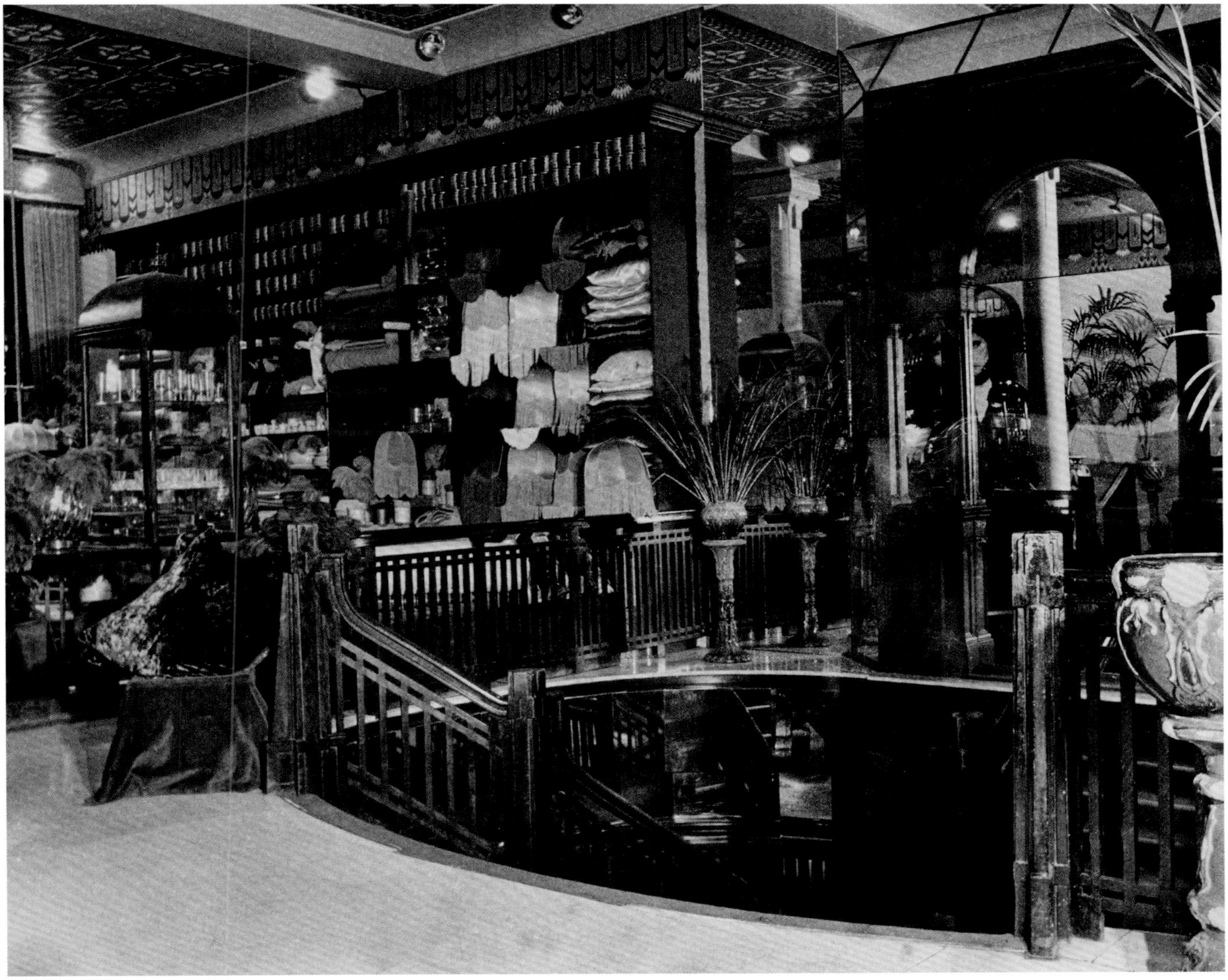

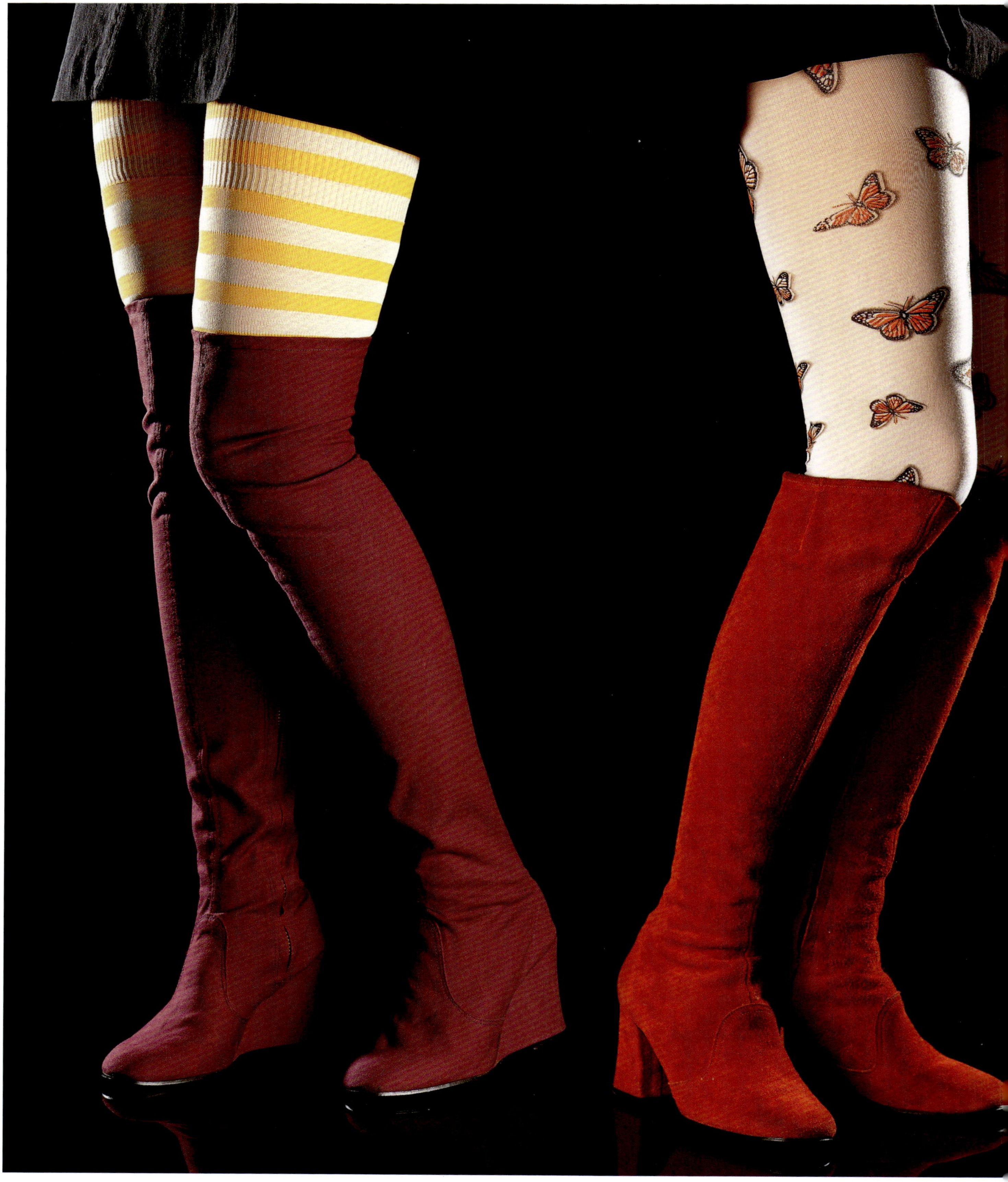

Three pairs of Biba boots, showing variations in length, heel styles and fabrics, 1970–5, photographed by Sian Irvine, 2004

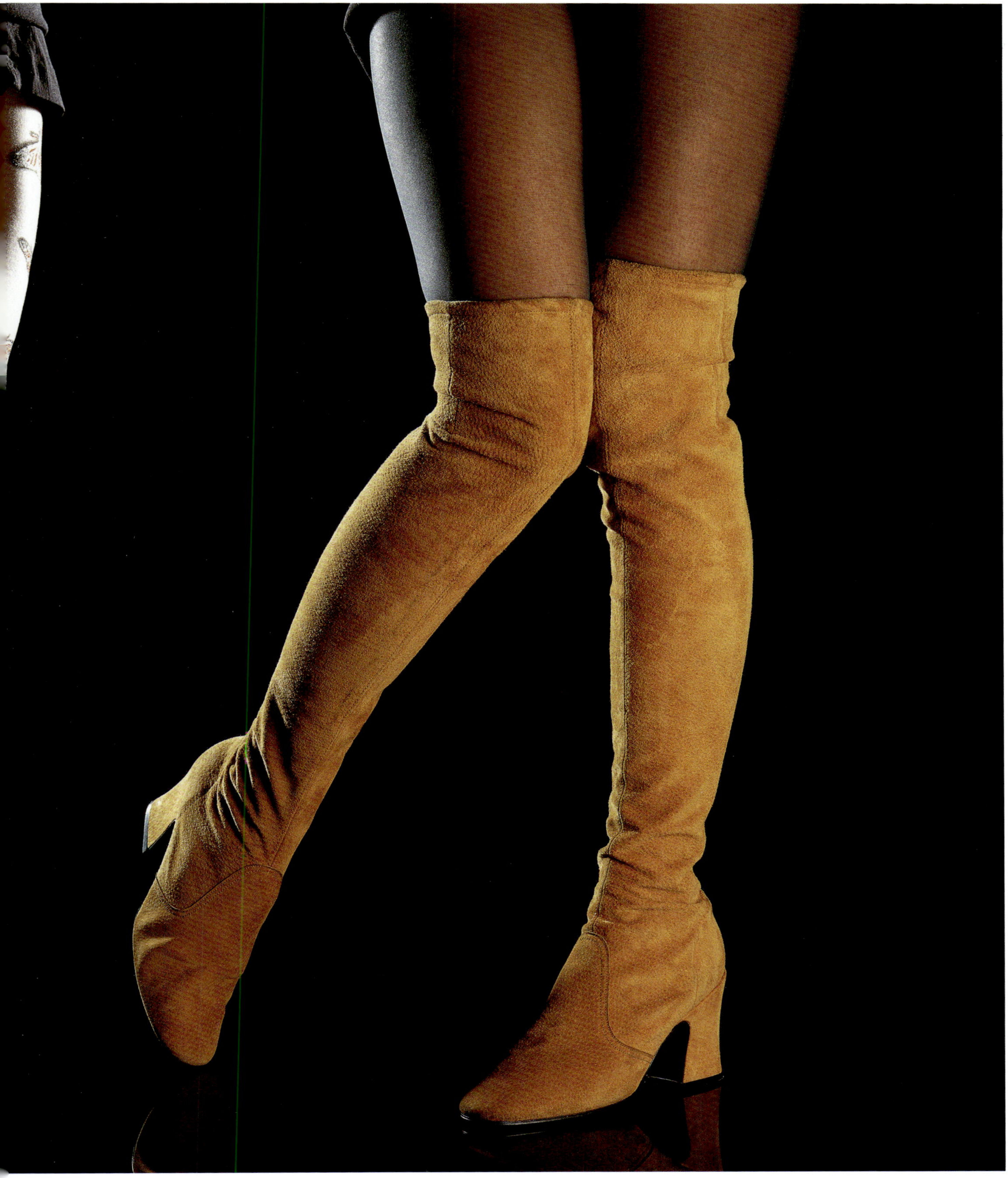

DELISIA HOWARD
~
BIBA COSMETICS BUYER

I joined Biba as a holiday job while I was at university in the 1960s. I'd seen a job advert in the *Evening Standard*, and it promised a clothes allowance with the role. As Biba was the coolest clothes shop I knew, I joined the queue of shop-girl hopefuls in Church Street, with little hope of getting the job as the line was hardly moving. Then the tall, elegant Anne Behr swept in and picked me out (I was dressed rather interestingly!) and took me to Fitz's office (a revelation in fake animal skins) where he gave me a job in the shop. It was a wonderful, dark, exotic souk, where my main functions were to replace the quick-selling stock and to look great in the clothes.

I was plucked out again by Anne Behr, who thought I looked like a size 10. They wanted someone very average to try on the pre-production clothes and I was, apparently, ideal. With Barbara and Anne, I did fittings in every garment they made from then (in 1968) until Biba closed in 1975, no matter what else I was doing. The funniest time I was talking on the telephone to a very exclusive champagne maker in France in my bad French, while practically naked with pins going in everywhere. He kept saying, 'Is that laughter I can hear?'

"Barbara had fulfilled her plan to include cosmetics for all colours of skin and even create a range for men"

I loved Babara as soon as I met her. The office – always communal, with Barbara drawing away at her desk – was the opposite of the shop, all white, with a huge bottle of Mitsouko perfume for general use. Biba was moving around the corner to the first shop on Kensington High Street: Barbara was a genius at finding great places. Cosmetics were going to be part of the expansion and I became the cosmetics buyer.

Barbara's idea was to build up a huge range of colours (at that time you could only get pink for skin and lips!) without discontinuing anything (it's so annoying to be told that there's no call for it). The factory we used also made cosmetics for the company Beauty Without Cruelty, and were incredibly green, although we never publicised the fact. The first range of colours was wild – mulberry, black and blue lipstick, to name just three. At first the factory manager said they wouldn't meet with FDA regulations so it couldn't be done. There were, however, young girls in the laboratory who loved the colours and who managed to formulate them to meet the regulations ... a miracle! Packaging also became a problem, as to create bottles in our own designs would be far beyond our budget. The solution: to use medical/scientific bottles (beautiful) and get them printed with Biba labels. We also offered customers the opportunity to refill perfume bottles (very economical). By the end of Biba, Barbara had fulfilled her plan to include cosmetics for all colours of skin and even create a range for men. The cosmetics were sold at the same mark-up as everything else – 33 per cent – and 'knowledgeable' people in the industry said they wouldn't sell at such low prices. They were wrong.

OPPOSITE Delisia Howard wearing satin Biba blouse, photographed by Barbara Hulanicki, c.1971

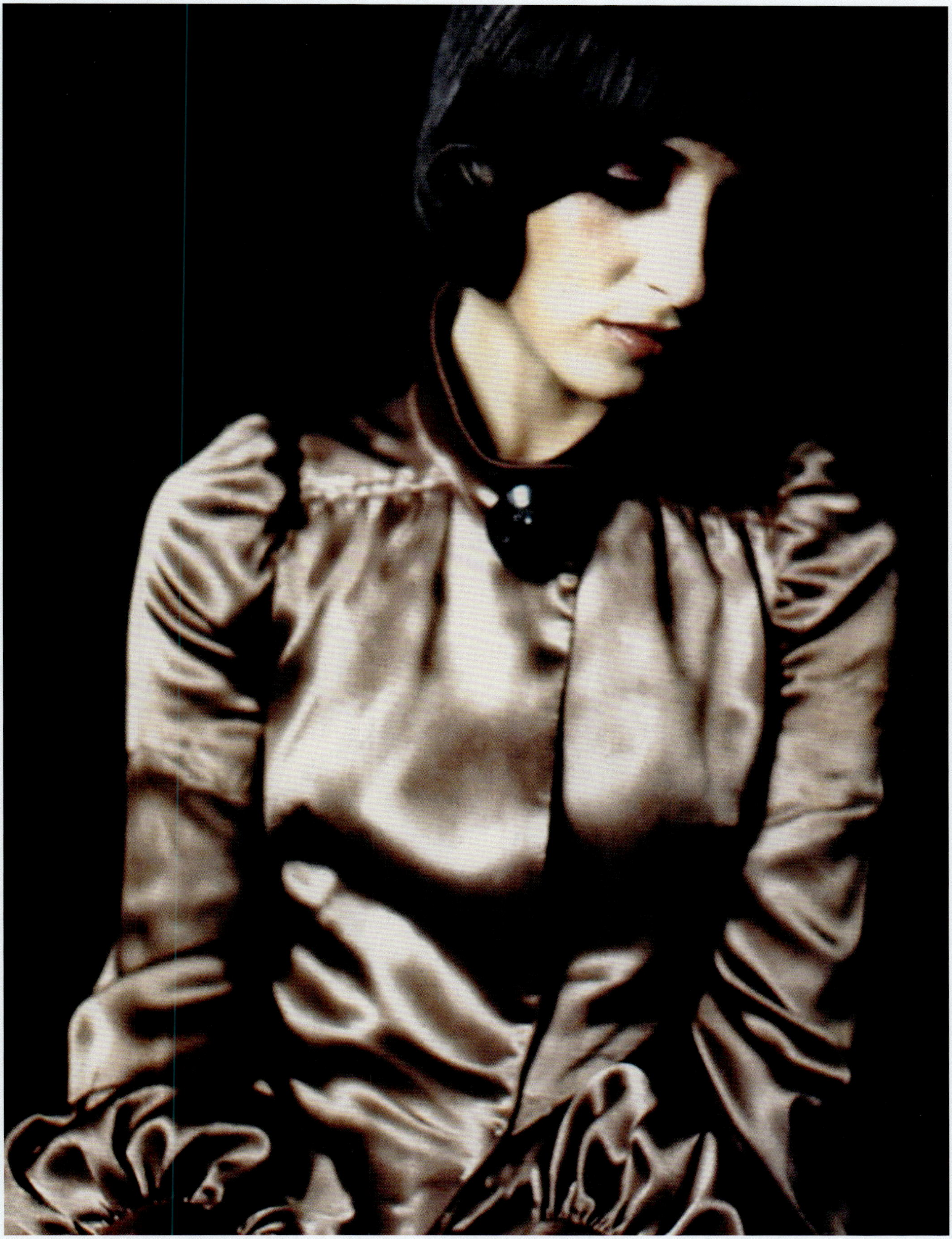

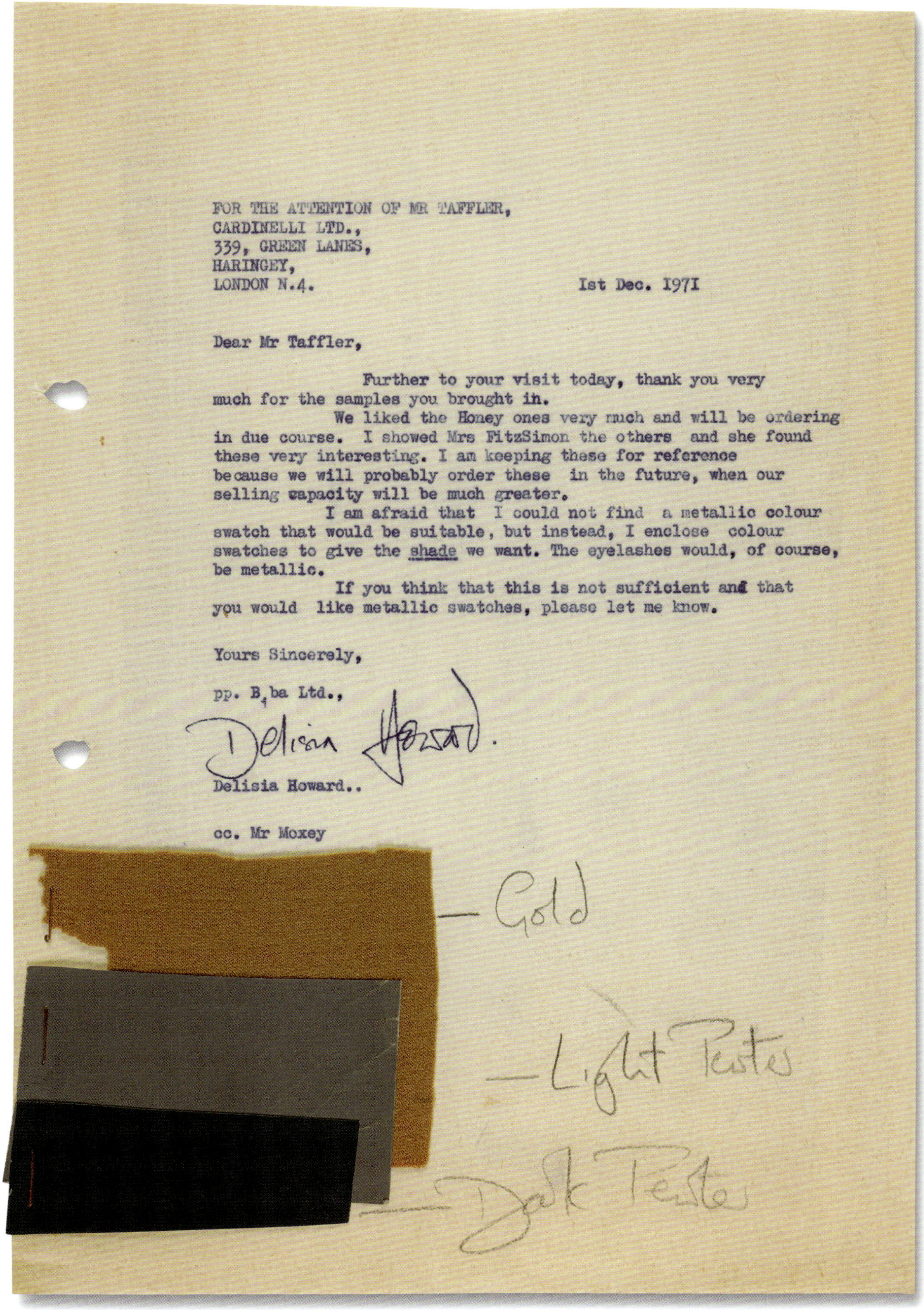

FOR THE ATTENTION OF MR TAFFLER,
CARDINELLI LTD.,
339, GREEN LANES,
HARINGEY,
LONDON N.4.

Ist Dec. I97I

Dear Mr Taffler,

Further to your visit today, thank you very much for the samples you brought in.

We liked the Honey ones very much and will be ordering in due course. I showed Mrs FitzSimon the others and she found these very interesting. I am keeping these for reference because we will probably order these in the future, when our selling capacity will be much greater.

I am afraid that I could not find a metallic colour swatch that would be suitable, but instead, I enclose colour swatches to give the shade we want. The eyelashes would, of course, be metallic.

If you think that this is not sufficient and that you would like metallic swatches, please let me know.

Yours Sincerely,

pp. Biba Ltd.,

Delisia Howard

Delisia Howard..

cc. Mr Moxey

– Gold

– Light Pewter

– Dark Pewter

Correspondence between Delisia Howard and Cardinelli Ltd regarding colours of false eyelashes, 1 December 1971

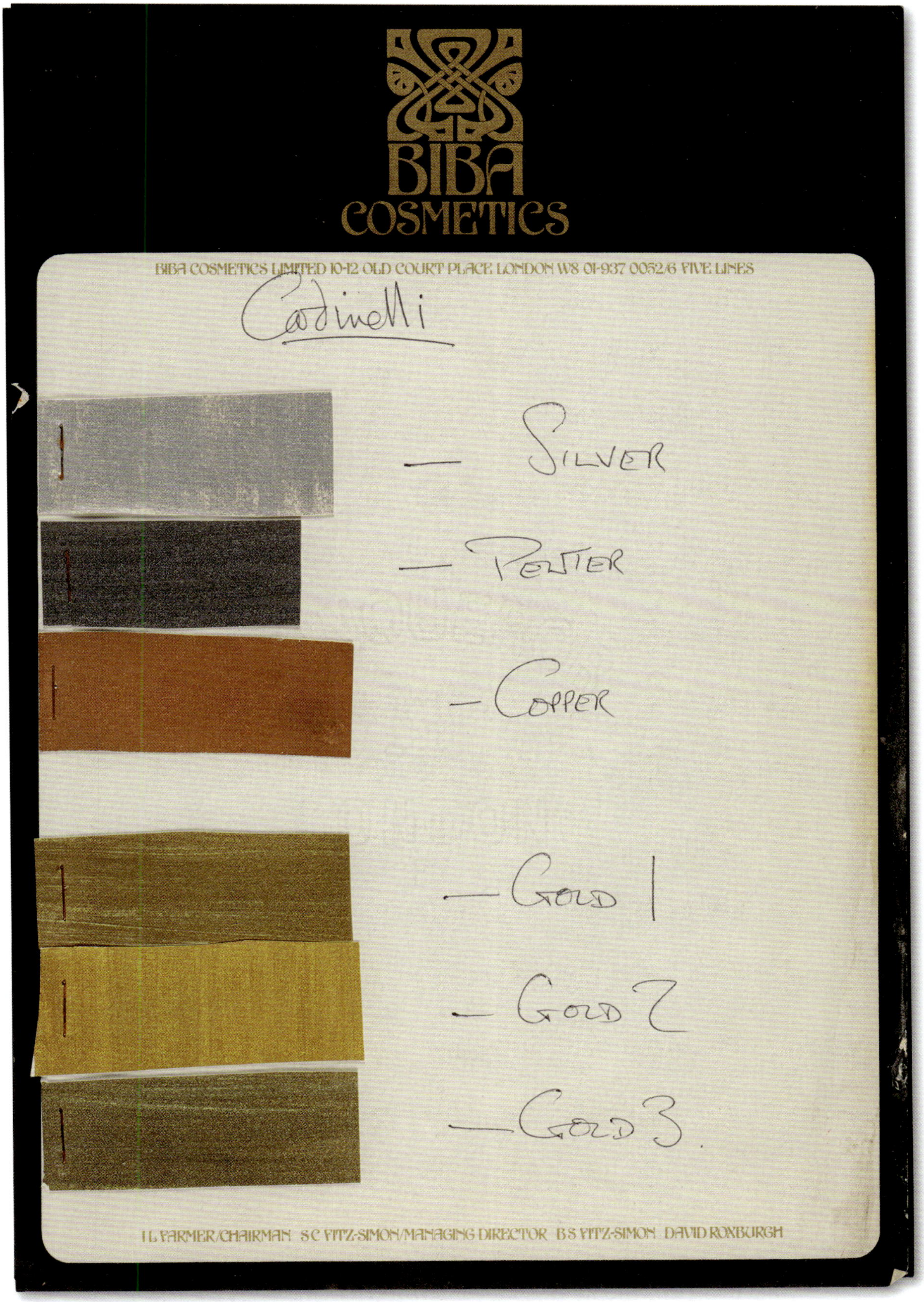

Hand-painted cards sent from Biba to Cardinelli Ltd to colour-match for range of eyelashes, 1971

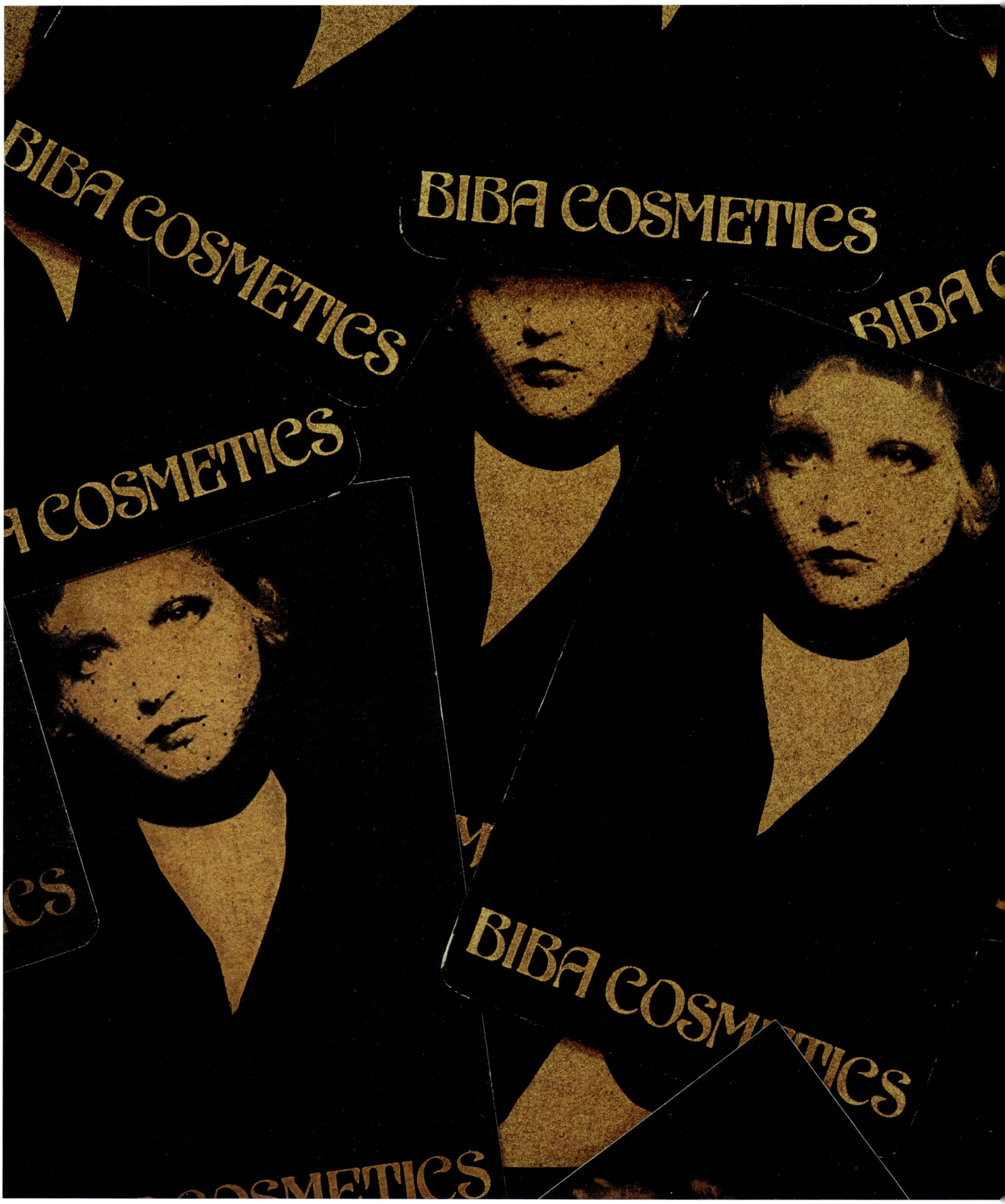
BIBA COSMETICS
BIBA COSMETICS

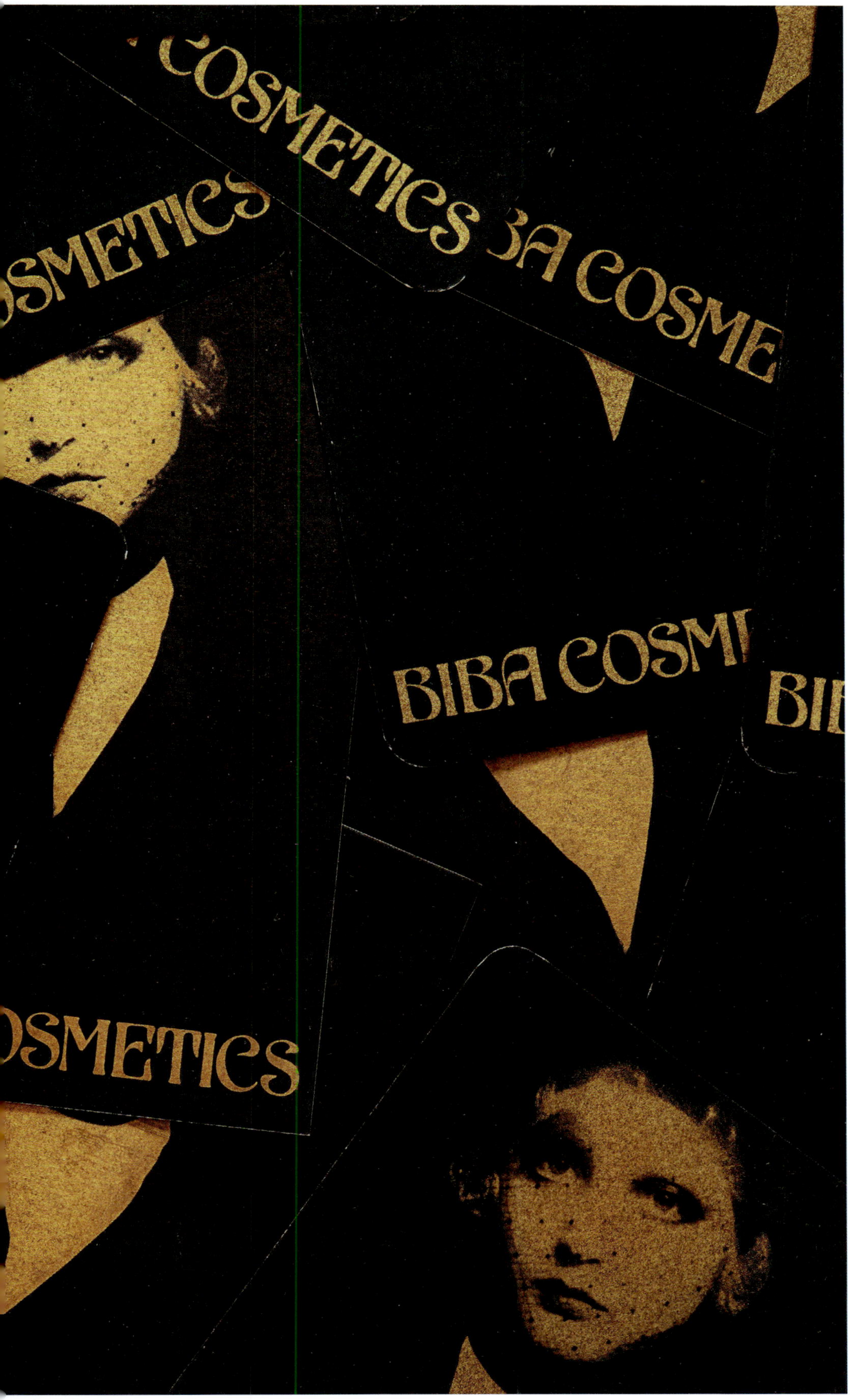

Biba cosmetics advertising cards featuring model Ingrid Boulting, c.1970

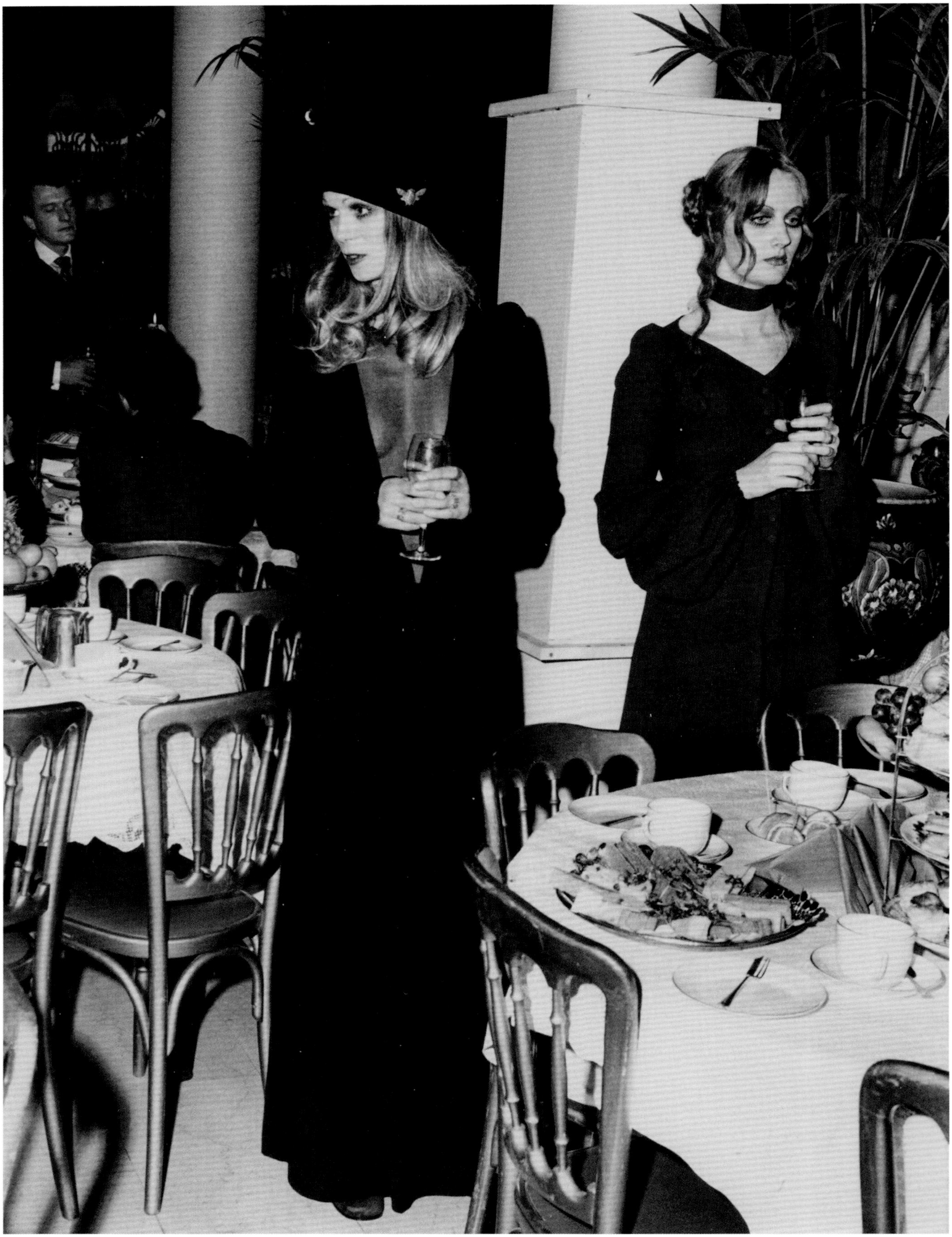

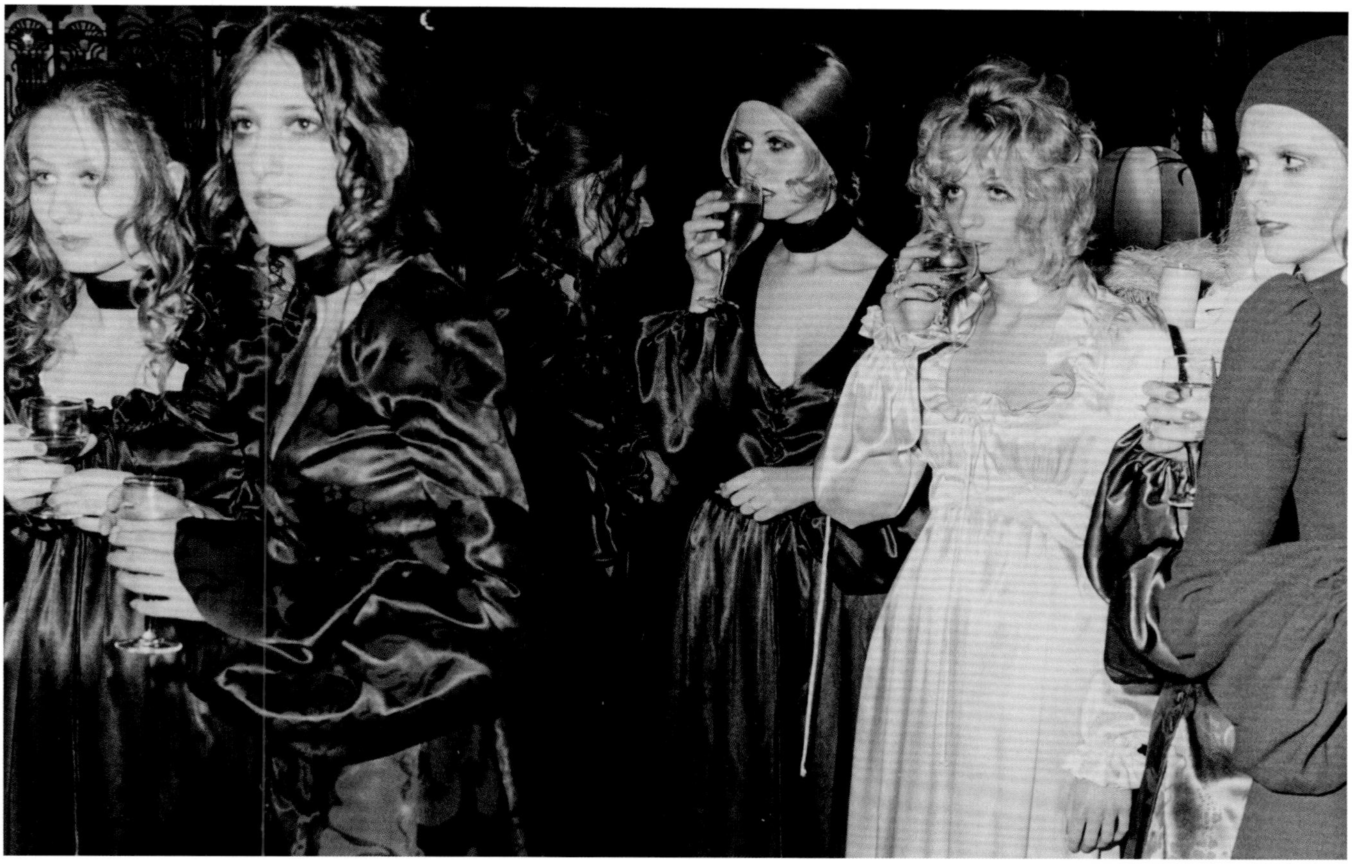

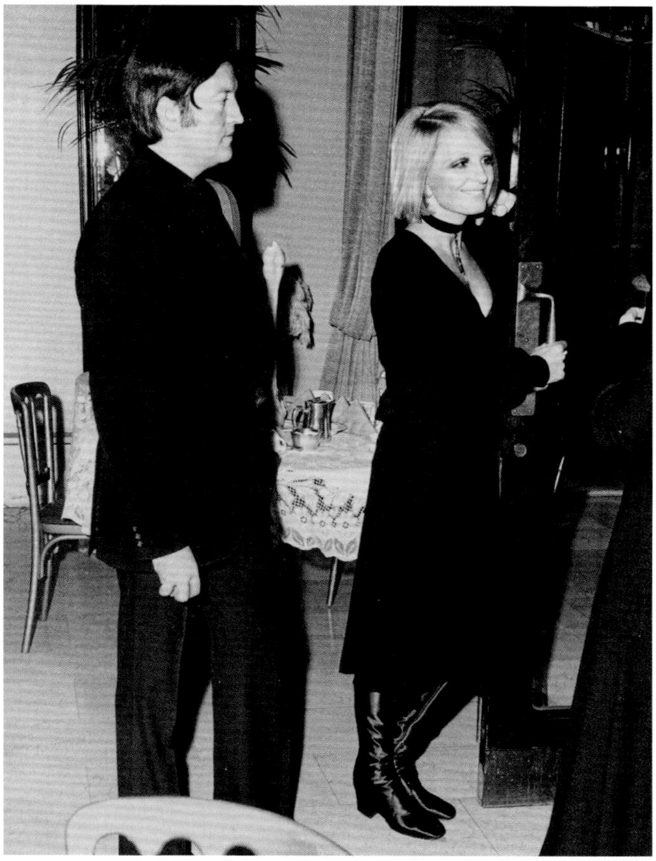

LEFT & ABOVE Biba sales assistants at the tea dance at Biba to launch the cosmetics range, 25 October 1970

RIGHT Barbara and Fitz at the tea party for the launch of Biba cosmetics, Biba, Kensington High Street, 25 October 1970

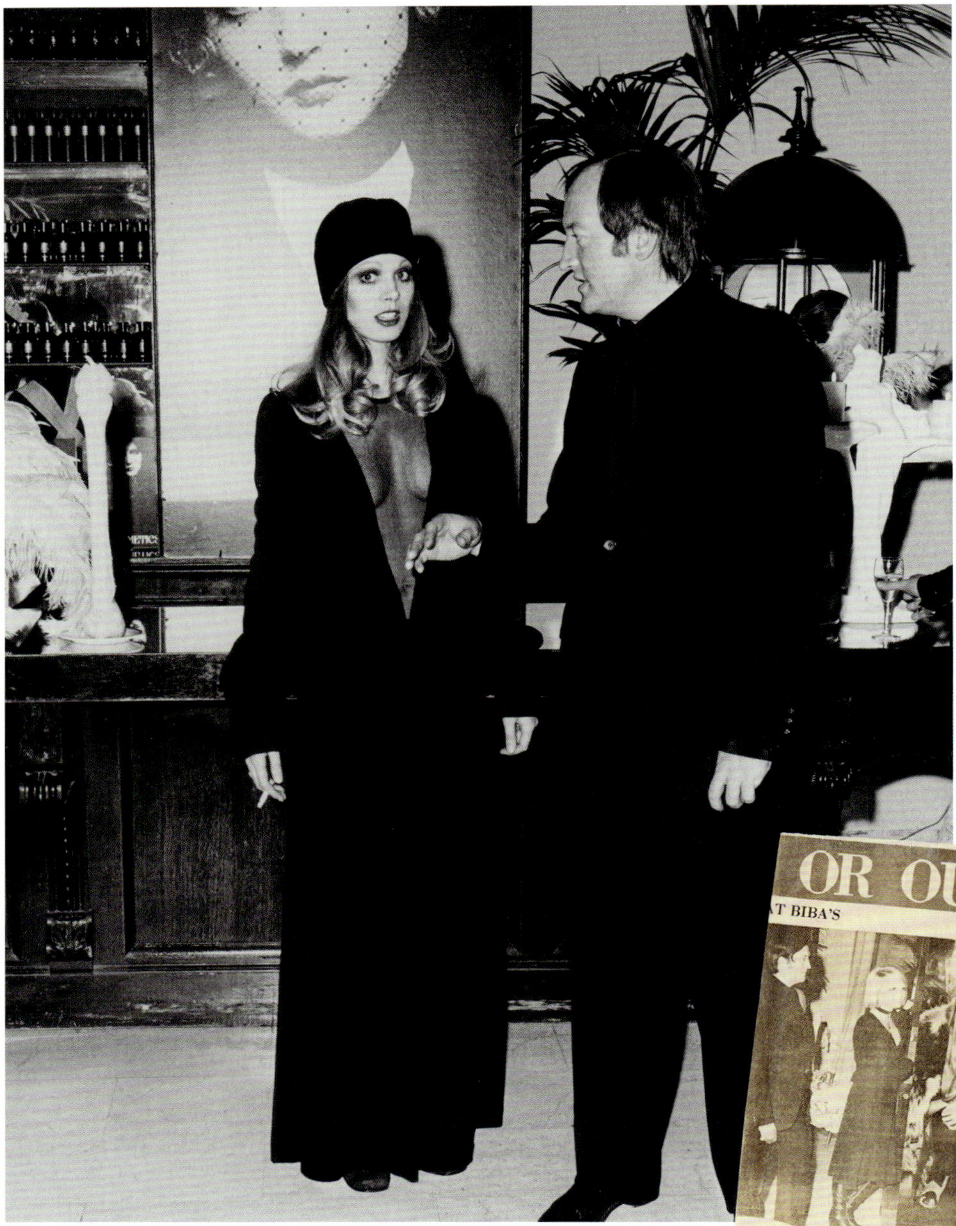

ABOVE & OPPOSITE Tea dance at Biba to launch Biba cosmetics, 25 October 1970

BELOW Press cutting, Biba cosmetics launch party, *Women's Wear Daily*, 1970

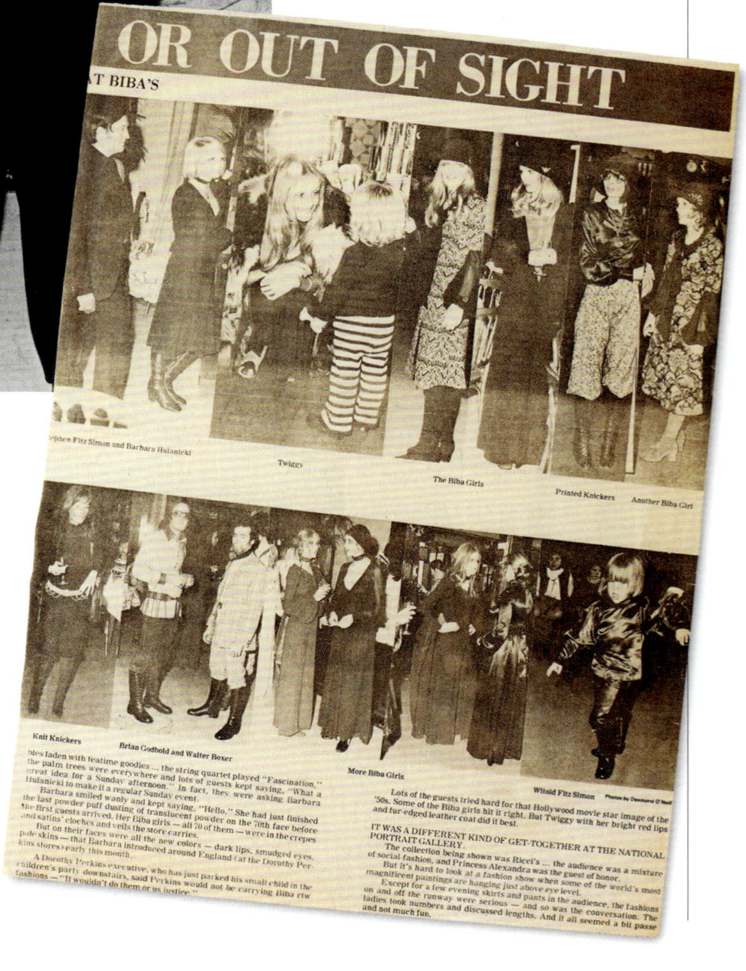

OR OUT OF SIGHT

T BIBA'S

ephen Fitz Simon and Barbara Hulanicki

Twiggy

The Biba Girls

Printed Knickers

Another Biba Girl

Kait Knickers

Brian Godbold and Walter Boxer

More Biba Girls

Witold Fitz Simon

Photos by Desmond O'Neill

bles laden with teatime goodies … the string quartet played "Fascination," the palm trees were everywhere and lots of guests kept saying, "What a great idea for a Sunday afternoon." In fact, they were asking Barbara Hulanicki to make it a regular Sunday event.

Barbara smiled wanly and kept saying, "Hello." She had just finished the last powder puff dusting of translucent powder on the 70th face before the first guests arrived. Her Biba girls — all 70 of them — were in the crepes and satins' cloches and veils the store carries.

But on their faces were all the new colors — dark lips, smudged eyes, pale skins — that Barbara introduced around England (at the Dorothy Perkins stores) early this month.

A Dorothy Perkins executive, who has just parked his small child in the children's party downstairs, said Perkins would not be carrying Biba rtw fashions — "It wouldn't do them or us justice."

Lots of the guests tried hard for that Hollywood movie star image of the '50s. Some of the Biba girls hit it right. But Twiggy with her bright red lips and fur-edged leather coat did it best.

IT WAS A DIFFERENT KIND OF GET-TOGETHER AT THE NATIONAL PORTRAIT GALLERY.

The collection being shown was Ricci's … the audience was a mixture of social-fashion, and Princess Alexandra was the guest of honor.

But it's hard to look at a fashion show when some of the world's most magnificent paintings are hanging just above eye level.

Except for a few evening skirts and pants in the audience, the fashions on and off the runway were serious — and so was the conversation. The ladies took numbers and discussed lengths. And it all seemed a bit passe and not much fun.

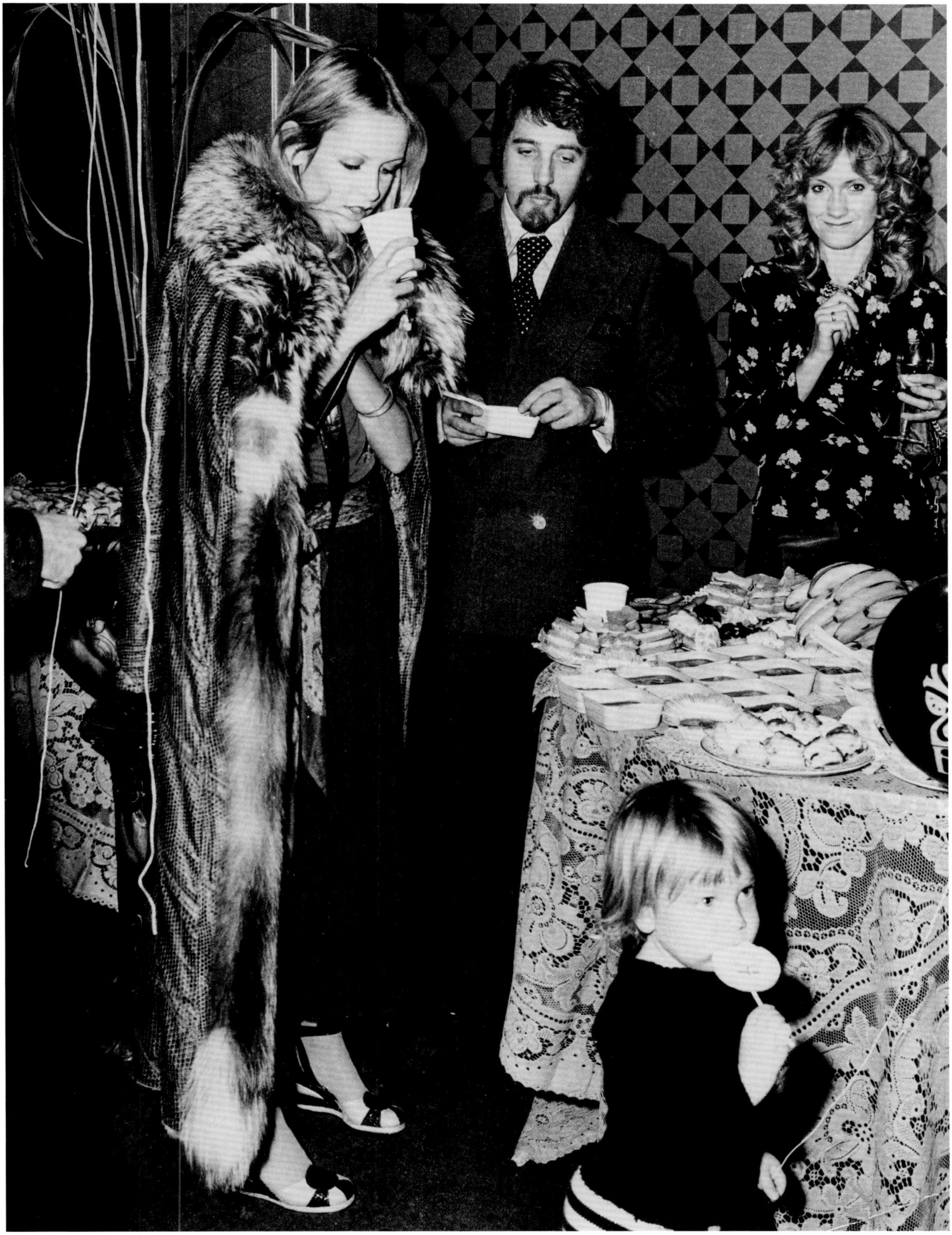

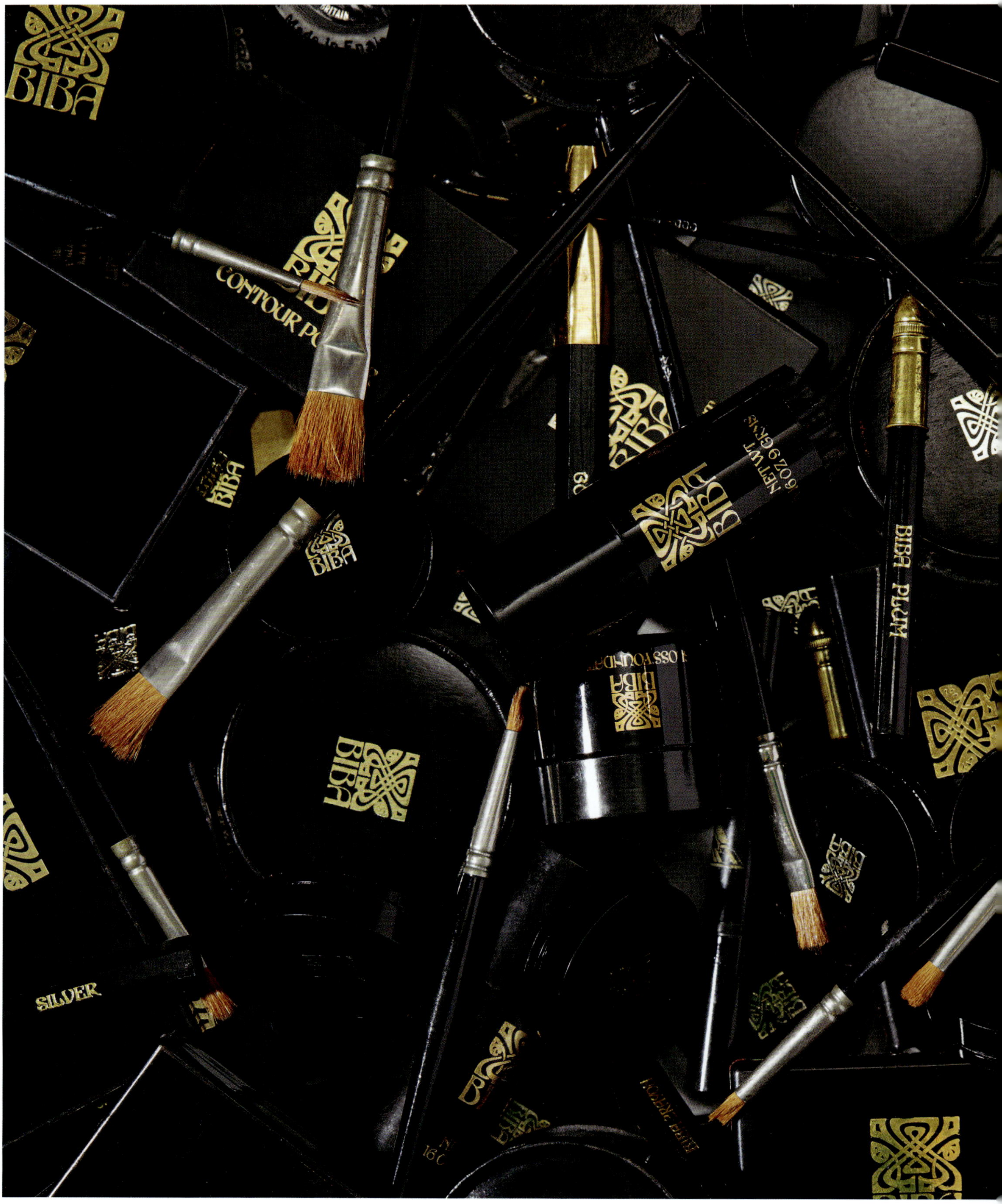
BIBA
SILVER
BIBA PLUM

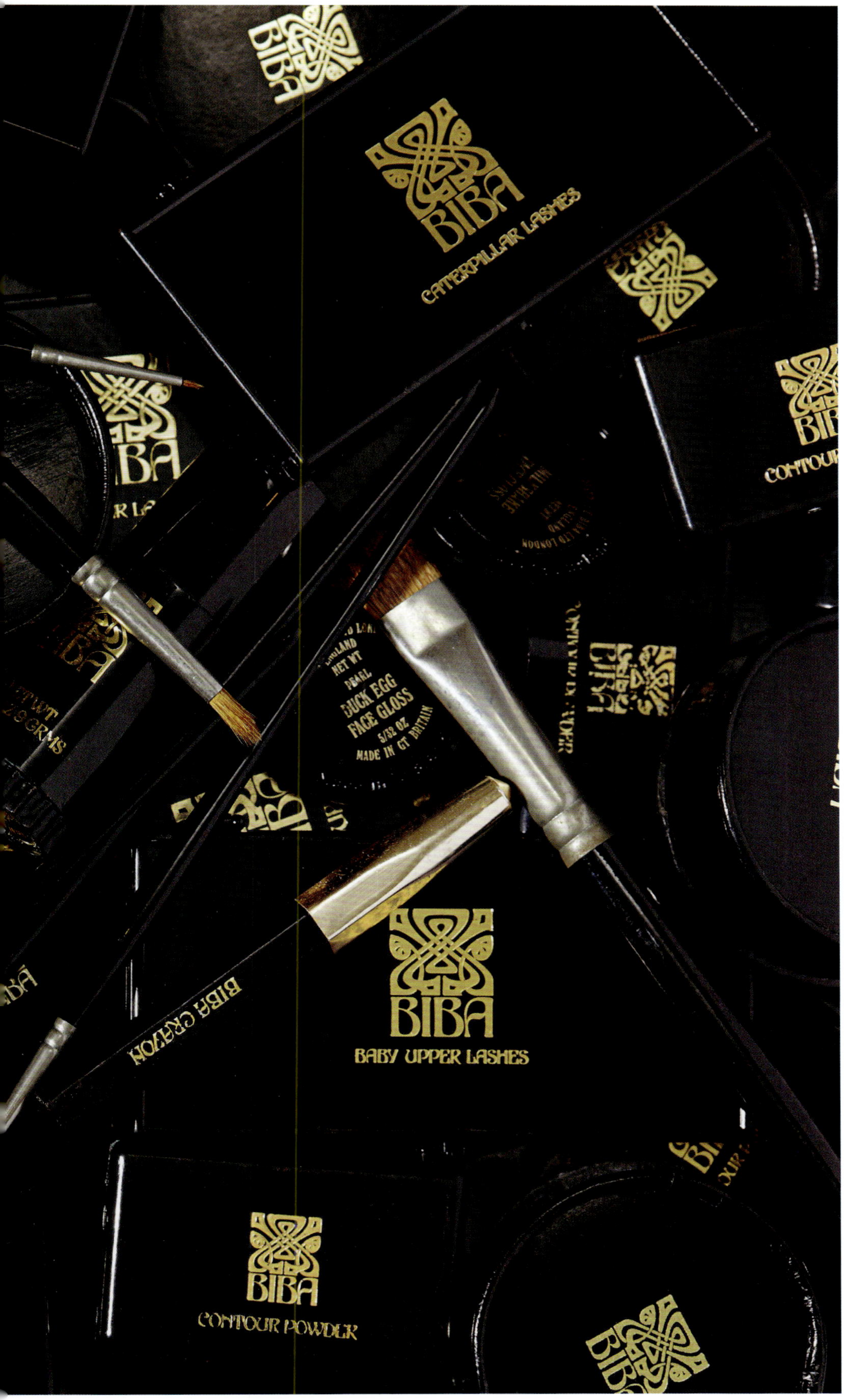

Biba cosmetics range from 1974, found in the Biba archive in 2024

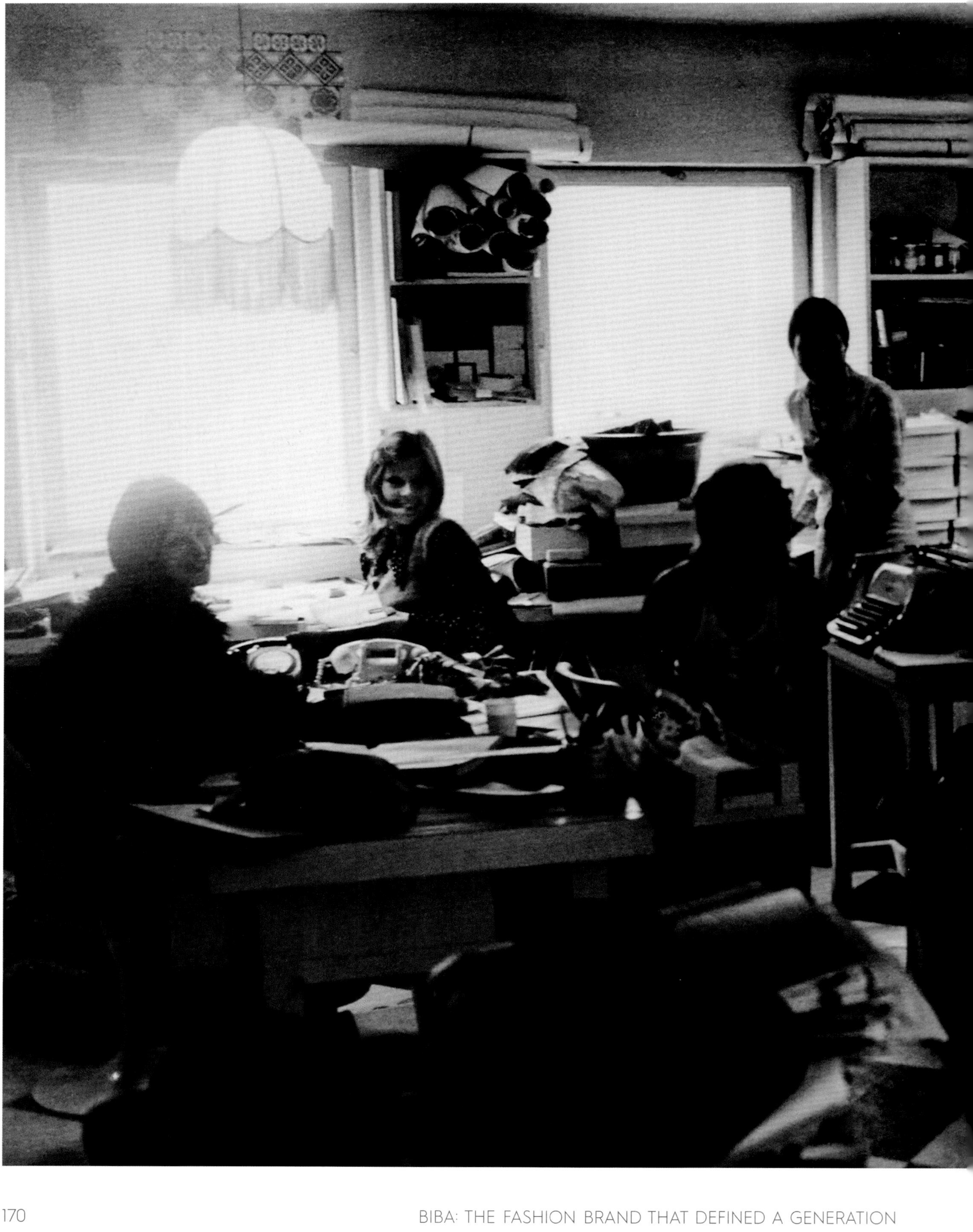

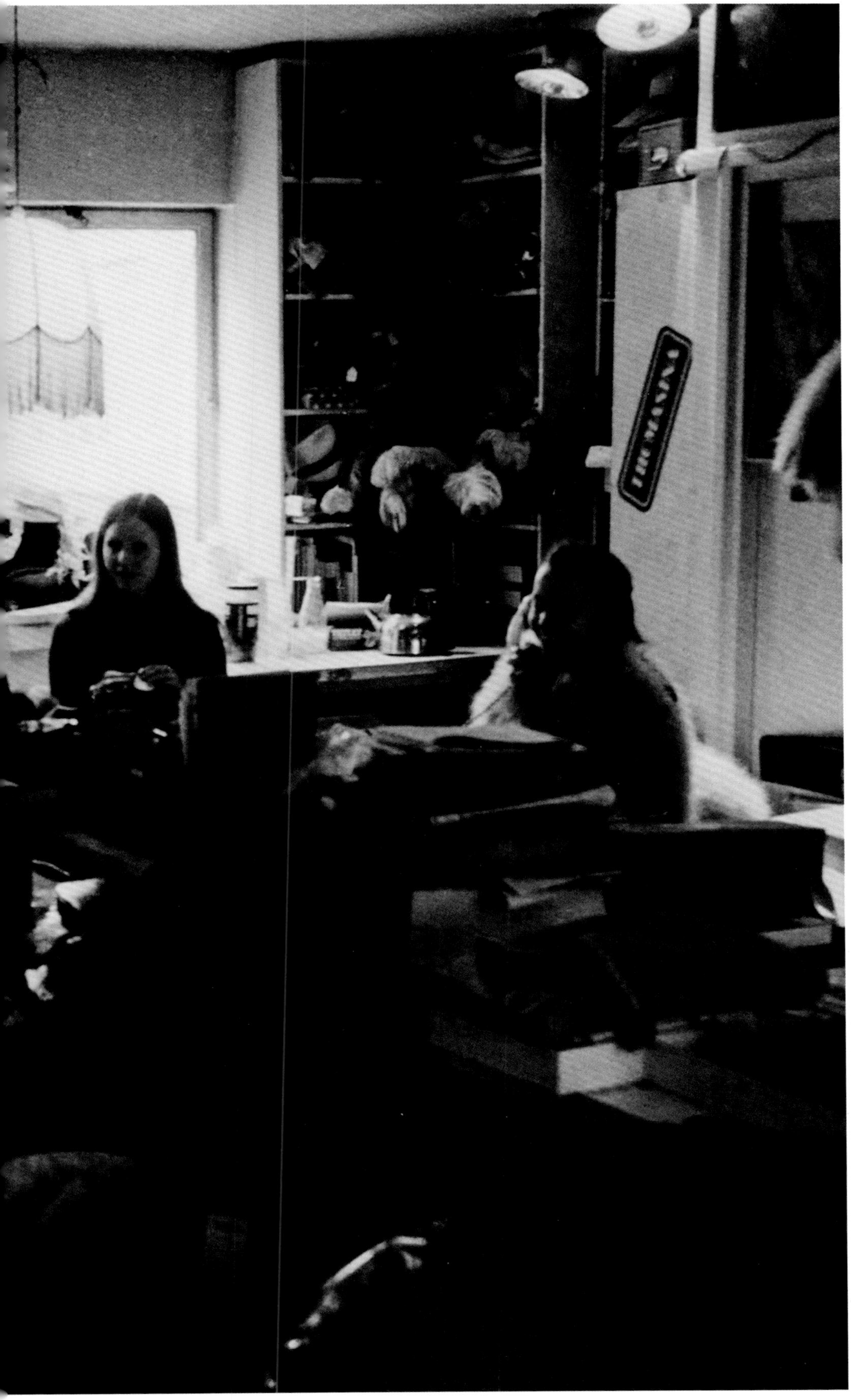

Biba workrooms on Old Court Place, behind Church Street, which were in use until 1973, c.1970. Photograph includes cloth buyer Daphne Black (far left) possibly textile designer Althea McNish (middle, standing), and accessories buyer Eva Molnar (far right).

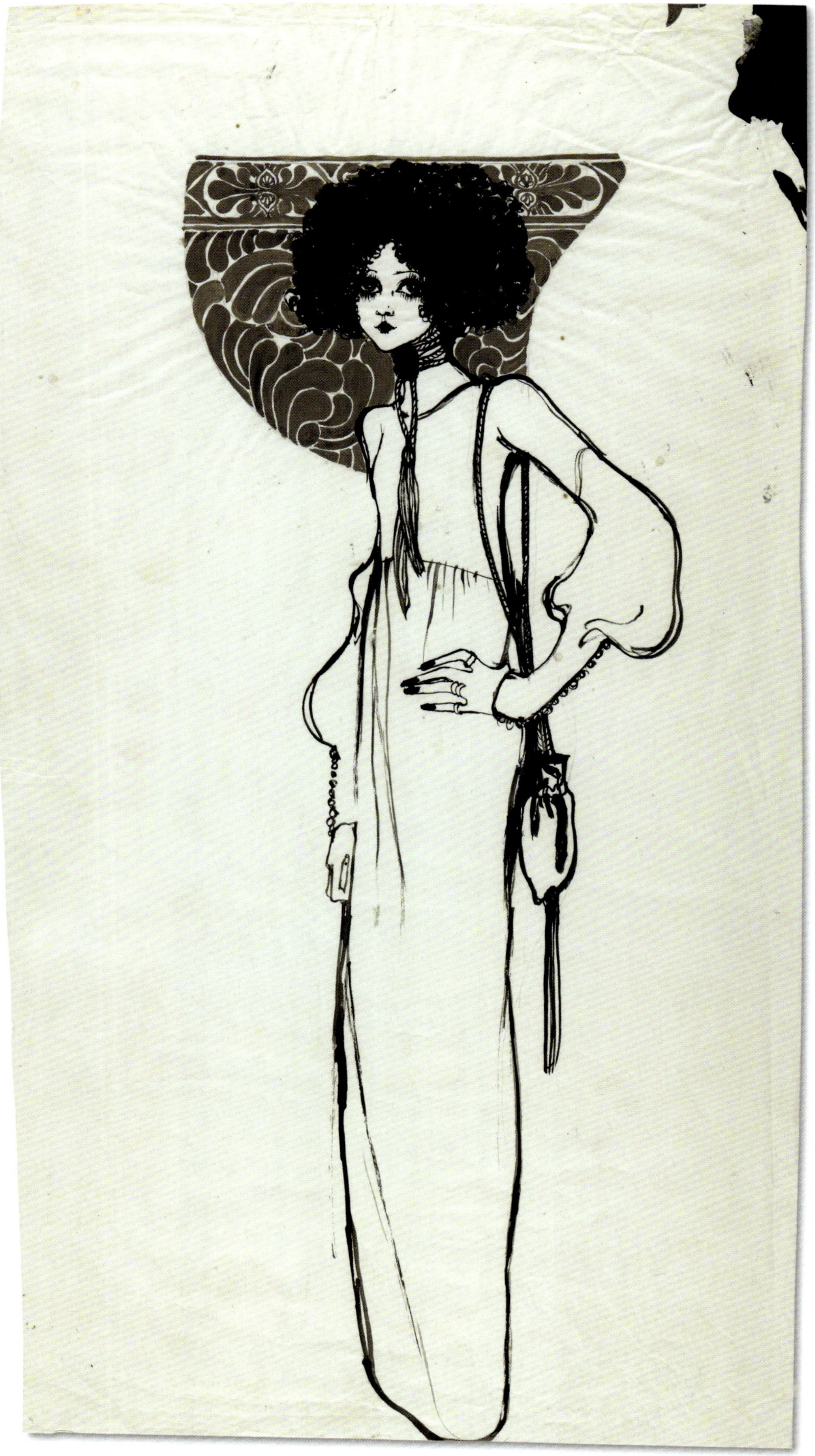

LEFT & OPPOSITE
Fashion illustrations, watercolour and gouache, Barbara Hulanicki, 1971

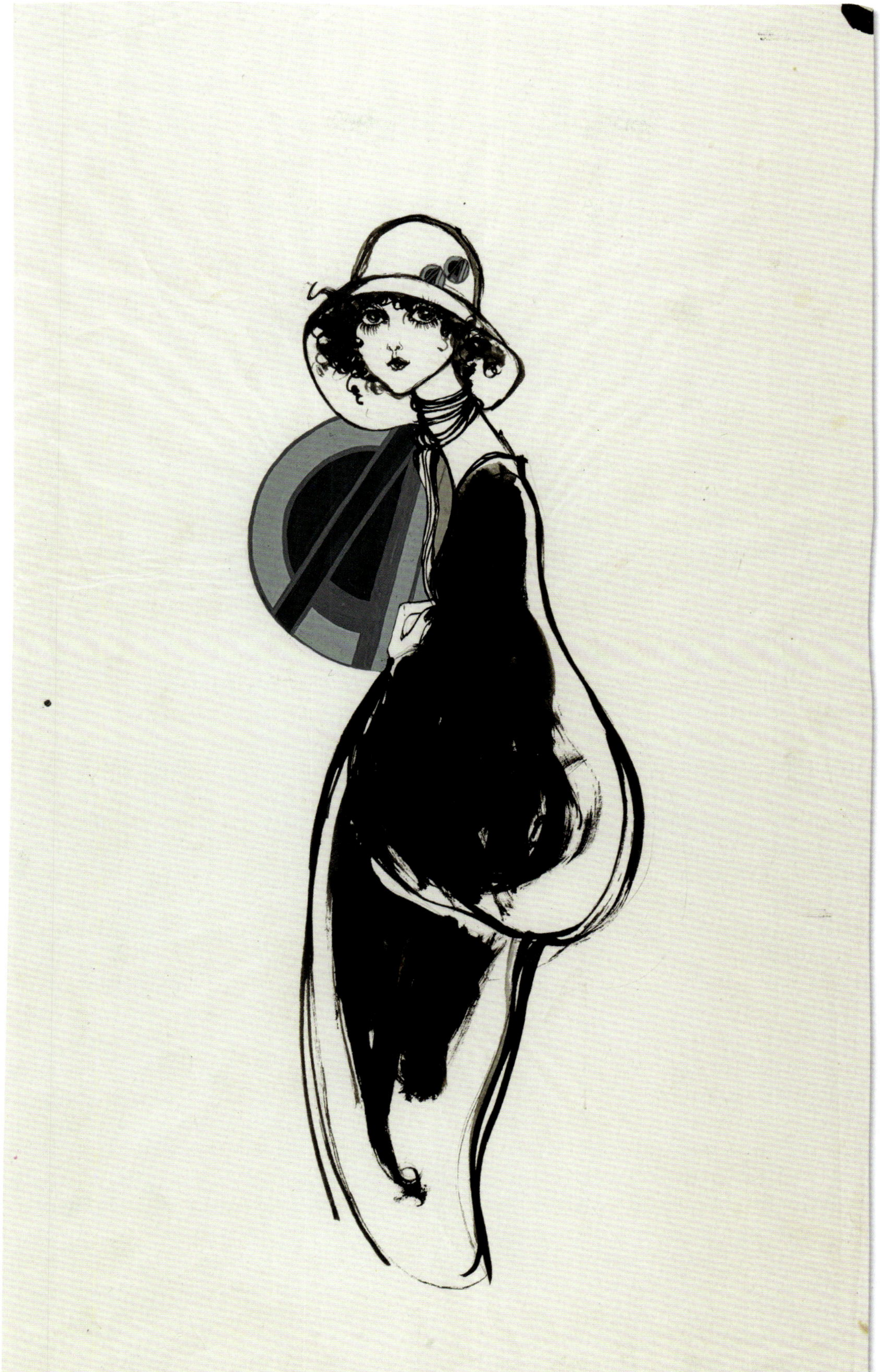

JO DINGEMANS

~ BIBA MODEL

The first time I modelled for our family friend Barbara Hulanicki, I was 10 years old, and I loved it. It was 1960, and Barbara stood me on a small table and placed a hat on my head before sitting down to sketch me. The sketch was for a newspaper, as Barbara was a much sought-after illustrator.

In 1966, aged 16, I worked for a week at the Church Street Biba. I spent my wages on a fabulous pink linen trouser suit, which my father considered rather shocking until he saw the mini dress I had also bought.

In 1967 I flew to São Paulo, Brazil, to take part in an international fashion fair for Biba. I had been modelling in Paris and done a few shows there, so together with pattern cutter Anne Behr and shop manager Eleanor Powell the three of us put on a small fashion show in Brazil, alongside designers from Paris and New York. We collated a soundtrack of British pop and danced our way down the catwalk in the shortest of skirts, jodhpurs, Victorian nightdresses and mobcaps, and the ubiquitous coloured feather boas so synonymous with the Biba look. The press and public loved us, and we were given a week's free holiday in Rio de Janeiro for the coverage we had attracted.

"We put together a soundtrack of British pop and danced our way down the catwalk in the shortest of skirts, jodhpurs, Victorian nightdresses and mobcaps"

In 1969 I went to work for Barbara in the Kensington High Street Biba. Before the new shop opened, she sent me off to buy antiques to decorate it. I had to go because she said if she walked in the price doubled! I loved doing this. Working in the shop was fun too, even though, and unusually for then, it was open until late every evening. Barbara was an exceptionally good photographer, and sometimes on Saturdays she would whisk me from the shop and style me up. This was much more fun than working in the shop all day. Barbara was one of the first to produce everything you needed for the look under one roof. The Biba make-up range matched the dresses, tights, boots and accessories, and Barbara would use the very long, spidery false lashes and the dark green eyeshadows, lipsticks and nail varnishes for the Saturday photographic sessions.

In early 1971 Biba launched their make-up in Printemps, Paris. Biba manager, Kim Wilmot, and I worked hard to get the other brands there to accept us, but they hated the fact that customers could try the product out on our stand (which had not been done before) and we were outselling them, despite – horror of horrors – blue lipstick and green nail enamel.

In 1971 Biba also opened a concession in Bergdorf Goodman in New York. Barbara designed a series of white Victorian nightdresses with matching mobcaps, and she photographed me wearing them with false curls and Biba make-up. The window display at Bergdorf's was devoted to Biba, and Barbara's black and white photographs were enlarged to fill each window.

Later in 1971 Barbara was asked to put on a fashion show by *19* magazine for charity. She asked me to put the looks and models together, and, as we had no budget, I used all the Biba girls and took an alternative funky approach to the styling. I loved the entire process. A few weeks later, I got a phone call from the fashion editor of *19*, Norma Moriceau, asking me if I would like to be her assistant. I said 'Yes!'

Barbara taught me so much and gave me so many great opportunities.

OPPOSITE Jo Dingemans modelling Biba clothes, photographed by Barbara Hulanicki. A series of these photos were used to promote Biba at the New York department store Bergdorf Goodman in 1971 (overleaf).

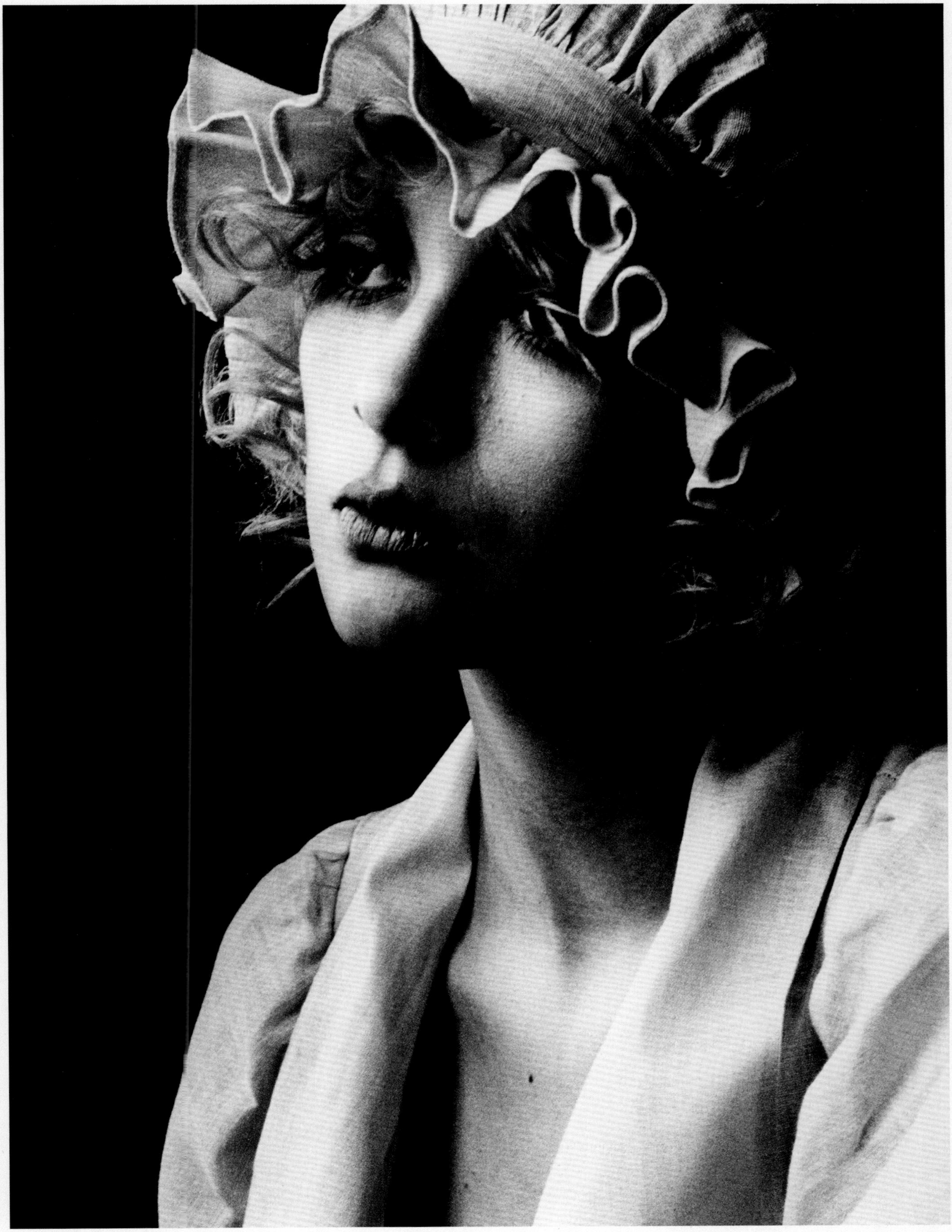

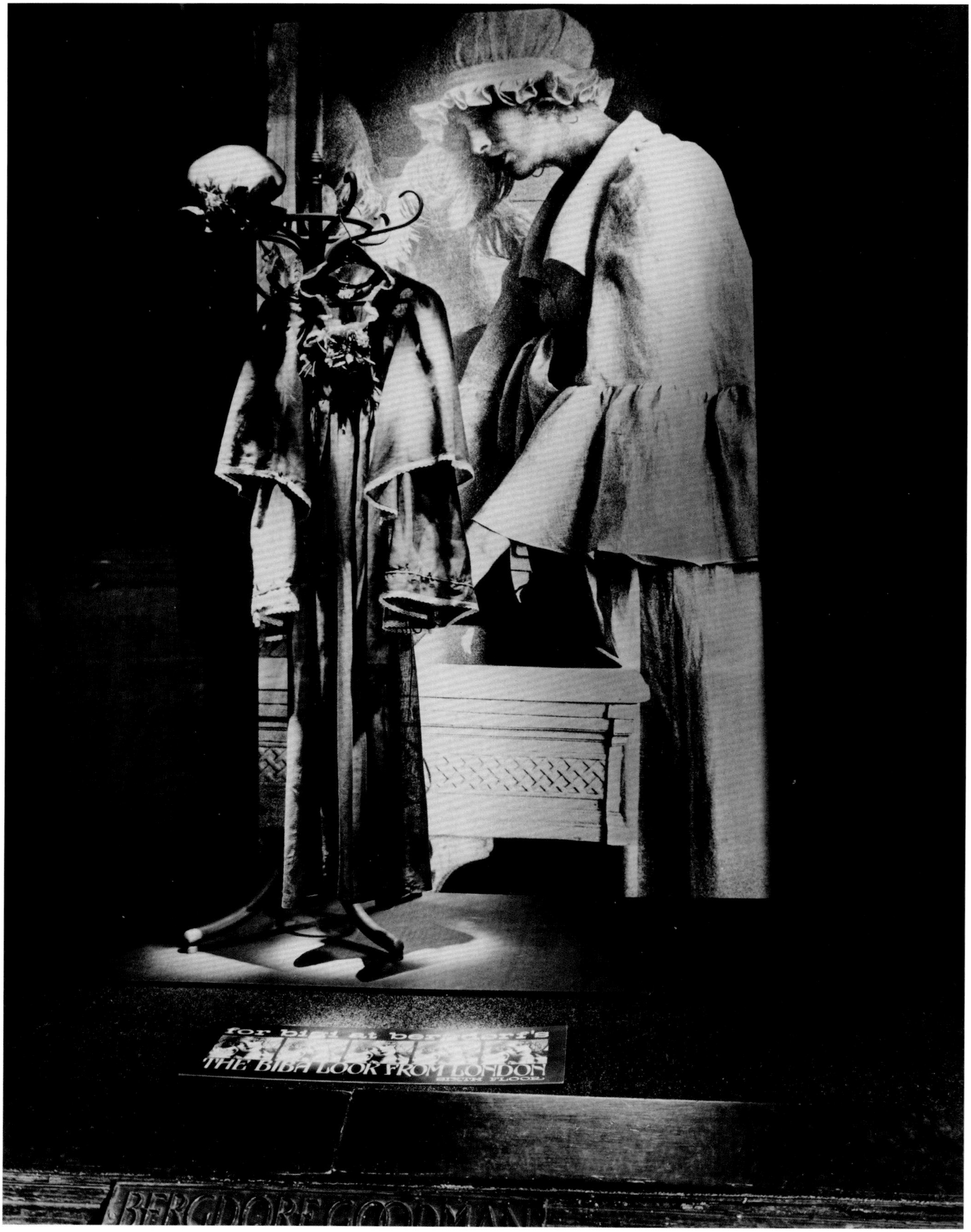

ABOVE & OPPOSITE Bergdorf Goodman windows advertising the newly opened Biba department in the store, photographed by Barbara Hulanicki, 1971

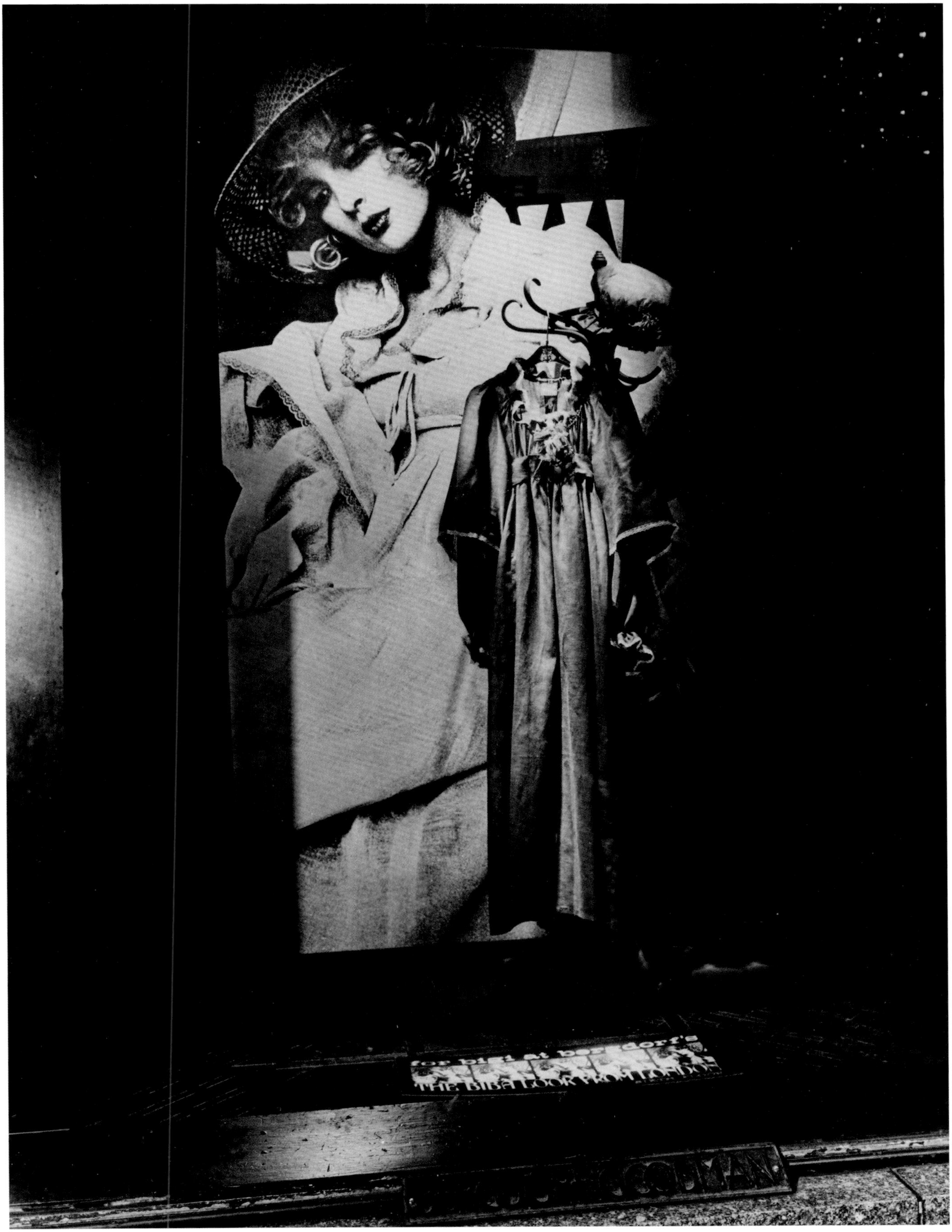
THE BIBA LOOK FROM LONDON

WOMEN'S WEAR DAILY, FRIDAY, DECEMBER 10, 1971

BIBA

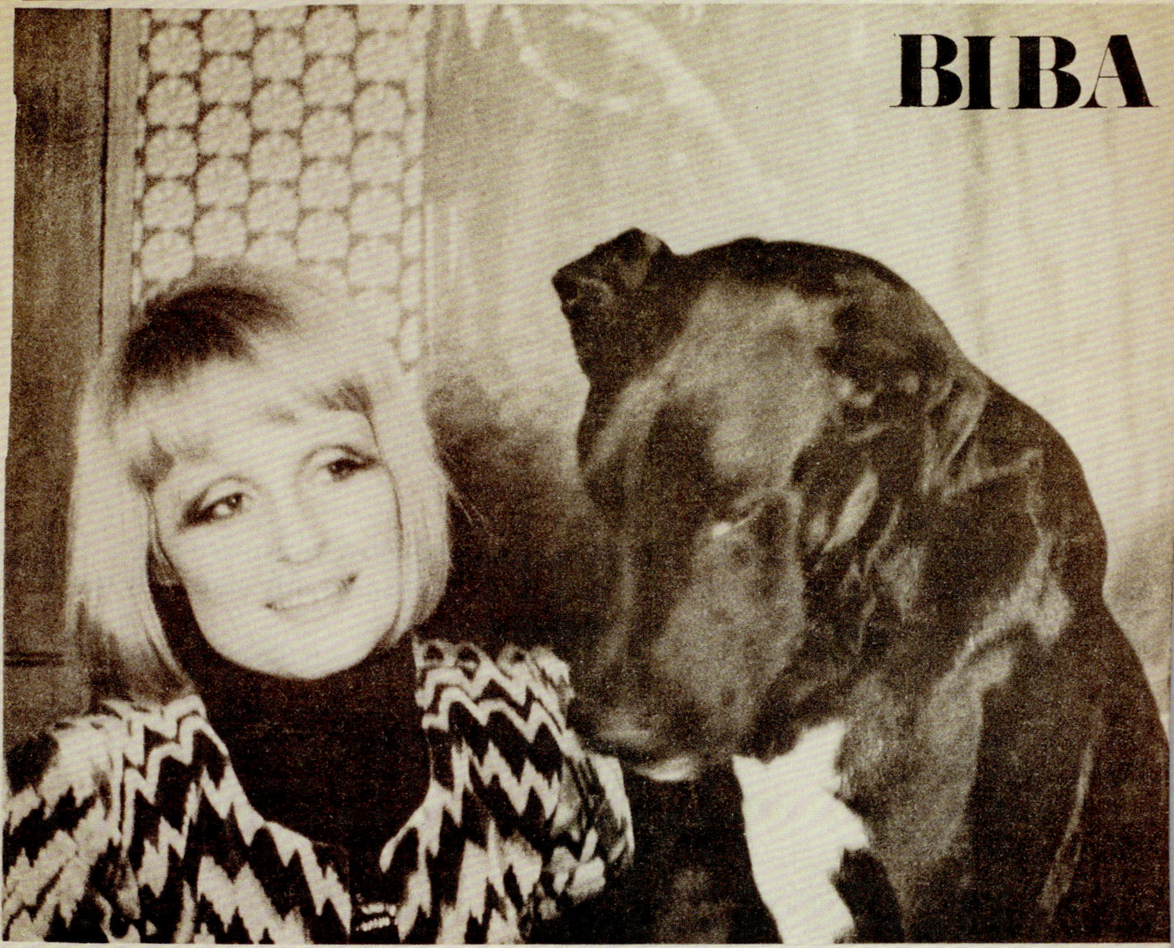

Photo by Desmond O'Neill

Barbara Hulanicki Fitz-Simon,

LONDON — Barbara Hulanicki and Stephen Fitz-Simon have gotten cosmetics down to a science ... without losing the emotional factor.

The husband and wife, owners of Biba, sold cosmetics for three years in their boutique before branching out into the general market one year ago. It's become a big business as evidenced by the Telex machine rattling away in the corner of their dark office off Kensington Church Street. Stephen (known as 'Fitz') wears all black as he sits on the brown couch next to their great Dane, Othello, who is the size of a small pony. Barbara joins him wearing a dark brown and black cut velvet jacket, her eyes outlined above and below with shadow.

"W‹ find it's economical to have a Telex," comments Fitz as he goes over to read a message coming from Italy. "When one of our outlets gets 5,000 more lipsticks than it wants, it can be embarrassing. We don't lose a day with orders this way. I check out what colors are selling wherever we are weekly."

"We had a year of testing them in our store first," explains Barbara. "We did it as a brand because the response was so good. It was more by popular demand."

Apart from the U.K., the biggest customer for their products is Italy. There is a sales office in Milan and they are currently opening five or six outlets a week in Italy according to Fitz.

"We are making a big export effort in Italy," he says. "There are no big department store chains there, so we sell through the boutiques. We have about 70 outlets now — we've been there since last March, but we've opened most in the last two or three months. There's a limit as to how many we can open in a week, but they've really been queuing up for it. We hope to have 150 by next spring and then we'll pause so we can weed out the low volume ones."

Fitz says they're reserving their main European effort until England enters the Common Market so prices can be more competitive.

"We're not such a good buy in Europe now because the tariffs are so high in France and Italy. In Paris we're right up with the cosmetic leaders, but we're not seeking as many outlets as, say, Revlon. It's more of a mass market for them — we have only a small percentage of the total market. We sell in Au Printemps and Vog boutique."

North America is the next area in Fitz-Simons master plan. He hopes to make it a bigger market than Italy and has made a careful study of American merchandising of cosmetics from both the manufacturer's and retailer's point of view.

"We have 20 outlets in the U.S., located in department stores and in the Judy shops in California, but we're holding back until February to do another 20. I'm recruiting executives now and by next summer we hope to have a total of 100 outlets. If fashion people are not in a town it's pointless for us to be there just for distribution sake. It must be controlled — there's a difference between just selling and making money. Cosmetics are an easy field to lose a fortune."

The American market is obviously a place where Fitz has made a careful study and is aware of the possible pitfalls. It is in this merchandising area that the Biba philosophy of selling is most apparent.

"The American Cosmetics marketing jamboree is no longer relevant in terms of marketing — it's disastrous to making profits. Brands seem to die out before they start — it's stupid. We find there are two types of outlets in the U.S. — those who say 'great, we love the Biba makeup' and those who say 'how much money have you got for promotions?' Cosmetics firms are in terror of being kicked out of a fine store because of the status they get. A lot of cosmetics buyers are really screwing them — the volumes cannot pay for the overhead. It's inflated by promotions. Some stores cannot see beyond the next giveaway — we don't believe in this."

Fitz says the customer Biba caters to is not catered to by anyone else so it's a success story immediately.

"We cater to them 100 per cent. They are looking for what we're offering. We bring in the unit and train the girl and then people just begin to arrive — it's very simple. From week one, we're comparable to the leading brand without free gifts and promotions. It would be disastrous for us to do that. Our price is the promotion. Sometimes I'm attacked by people for having such low prices

L'AMOUR

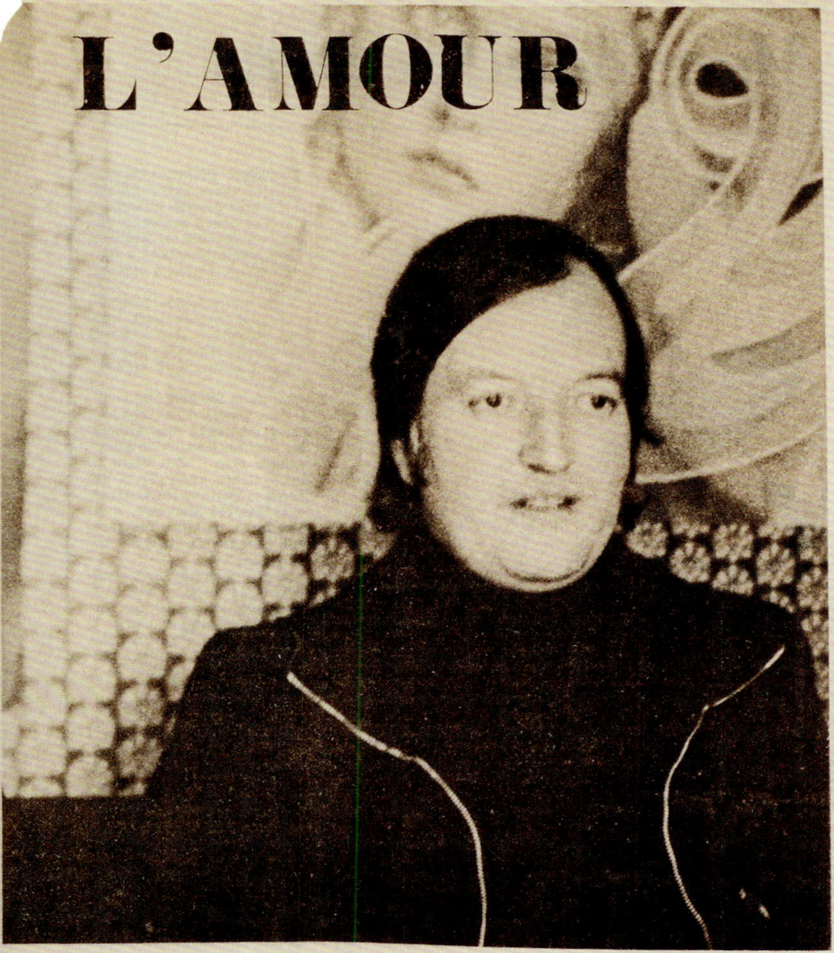

'ello and Stephen Fitz-Simon

— their idea is how much can you get for it instead of how low can I sell it for."

Barbara feels that the Biba customer is aware that in brand shopping she often pays more just for a name.

"Our customer is genuine. She doesn't believe in the phoney status bit. The selling technique is bad in a store when the customer is dying to try a product and the saleswoman is standing there like an ogre. You should feel happy whether you've bought something or not." Fitz also objects to the high pressure sales pitch by salespeople at cosmetics counters.

"Our customer wants to stand at the display unit and make her mind up and not be pursued by a saleslady trying to spray her with something. Girls in London love shopping, and they know the value of things — I'd rather sell them 10 lipsticks than three for the same price. We don't do in-store demonstrations. The girls have the answers to makeup questions if they're asked. But they're not on commission — we don't allow them to be, so they don't push to make an extra $10."

Barbara admits there is a difference in selling to American girls.

"American customers ask a lot of questions about makeup — they're not as experimental as they are here."

The Biba poster of 1971 is expected to sell two million copies according to Fitz. The new one has a softer view of a girl with a pale veil across her face and a Lalique-crystal-lite foreground. The current products selling in the shop are lipsticks, nail polishes and eye makeup in blues, greens and purple hues.

"For spring we're doing softer colors," says Barbara. "When everyone else gets into the darker colors we switch back. We hope to have literally every color under the sun in the range including the blues and greens — it's a paintbox effect. There's no need for cosmetics to be a seasonal thing. The next look for us is to add lots of new colors. We hope to have 50 colors in each product group by spring."

Barbara says the blues and greens are selling well without any adverse reaction either in England or the U.S.

"There's been no reaction to it — there was more hoopla and yelling about the browns and dusty colors when we introduced those. We like anti-publicity."

Stephen agrees: "There's nothing worse than being praised by the wrong people. Up to now we've had too few colors so we're building up a selection. There's no need to take anything off the line."

When new colors are added, it does not detract from sales in the rest of the collection, he adds.

"When we bring out a blue or green, we increase sales in the brown," says Barbara. Fitz grins as he explains why — "A person who comes in and sees the green is so shocked that she buys brown in relief."

The Fitz-Simons are not worried that other cosmetic firms are bringing out dusty browns similar to theirs.

"When companies bring out new colors

they don't really sell them — they use it to bring in customers but they don't go into depth with it. The colors they sell do look brown on the stick but not when they're on. They're terrified about alienating their bread-and-butter market because they're committed to selling the mass market, and if they changed, they'd risk losing customers. We don't expect the mass market to buy our blue lipstick, but our customer will."

The Fitz-Simons say they have no plans to enter the mass market which would require them to compete color for color with other brands.

"We know if we put in pink lipsticks we could sell millions," says Barbara. "But on principal, we won't do it to compete peach for peach, etc."

Someone rings up and tells Fitz that Mary Quant has announced on American TV that she will do blue and green lipsticks. His reaction is to laugh and say, "That's super."

Barbara's theory on color is to create a lipstick to match the color clothes she is making or sometimes vice-versa. The makeup is not a separate entity from rtw.

"Sometimes we do a color for the cosmetics range and then do clothes to go with it. Customers are always looking for eyeshadows, especially to match their clothes. Lipstick is the biggest selling item followed by nail-polish and eye makeup, the real color products. Eyelashes do well in the winter and less in summer — the boom of false lashes is over, but they're still selling well."

The Fitz-Simons are moving into larger offices in February, and they will have a lab to experiment with new product ideas.

"We may do treatment products in the future, but the time is not right now for those type of beauty products," says Barbara.

"Cosmetics are a lighthearted field but it's become solemn and expensive. It shouldn't cost half a week's wages," says Fitz.

Biba is expanding in another direction, too. It's going to become the biggest boutique on Kensington High Street. Fitz, who runs the store with Barbara, says Biba will take over the present site of Derry & Toms Department Store (almost opposite their present boutique) in 1973.

"We've been planning this for five years," Fitz says. House of Fraser, which owns Derry & Toms, sold the store to British Land Company and Dorothy Perkins, which owns a 75 per cent interest in Biba.

"We have no date as to exactly when we open, but we're going to be restoring it. It's a perfect store as it stands now but we're going to renovate it," Fitz-Simon explained. "It was built in 1928 and it has a beautiful exterior and a fabulous roof garden."

The present Biba store will be in operation only until the new site is ready for occupancy. "We'll close it the day before we open the new one," says Stephen. "I'm still working out the space, but it will be about 200,000 feet of selling space, about 400,000 for the total store. The store is on one-and-a-half acres. Some parts of it are not necessary — they're just not relevant to a modern store."

At present, Derry & Toms has a basement, six floors and a roof garden. There is a restaurant on the fifth floor and a roof garden restaurant open during the summer. Stephen says Biba will retain these and enter the restaurant business as well.

"We're going to keep them. The fifth floor Rainbow Room is 1,000 feet of restaurant. We'll be running both ourselves."

The Biba executive offices will move into the new premises but they will have to make a temporary move for two years until the new store is completed, because they have outgrown their present setup on Old Court Street near both stores. Stephen admits the new move will slow up expansion in other areas.

"We'll need our best executives to handle this, so it will slow us up. We will be moving our cosmetics into Bloomingdale's as planned in February, but we'll slow up the rate of expansion in North America. We have a fairly substantial task here and we will need our best people for it."

House of Fraser still owns Barker's on Kensington High Street. — STEFFI FIELDS

Press cutting, 'Biba L'Amour', *Women's Wear Daily*, 10 December 1971

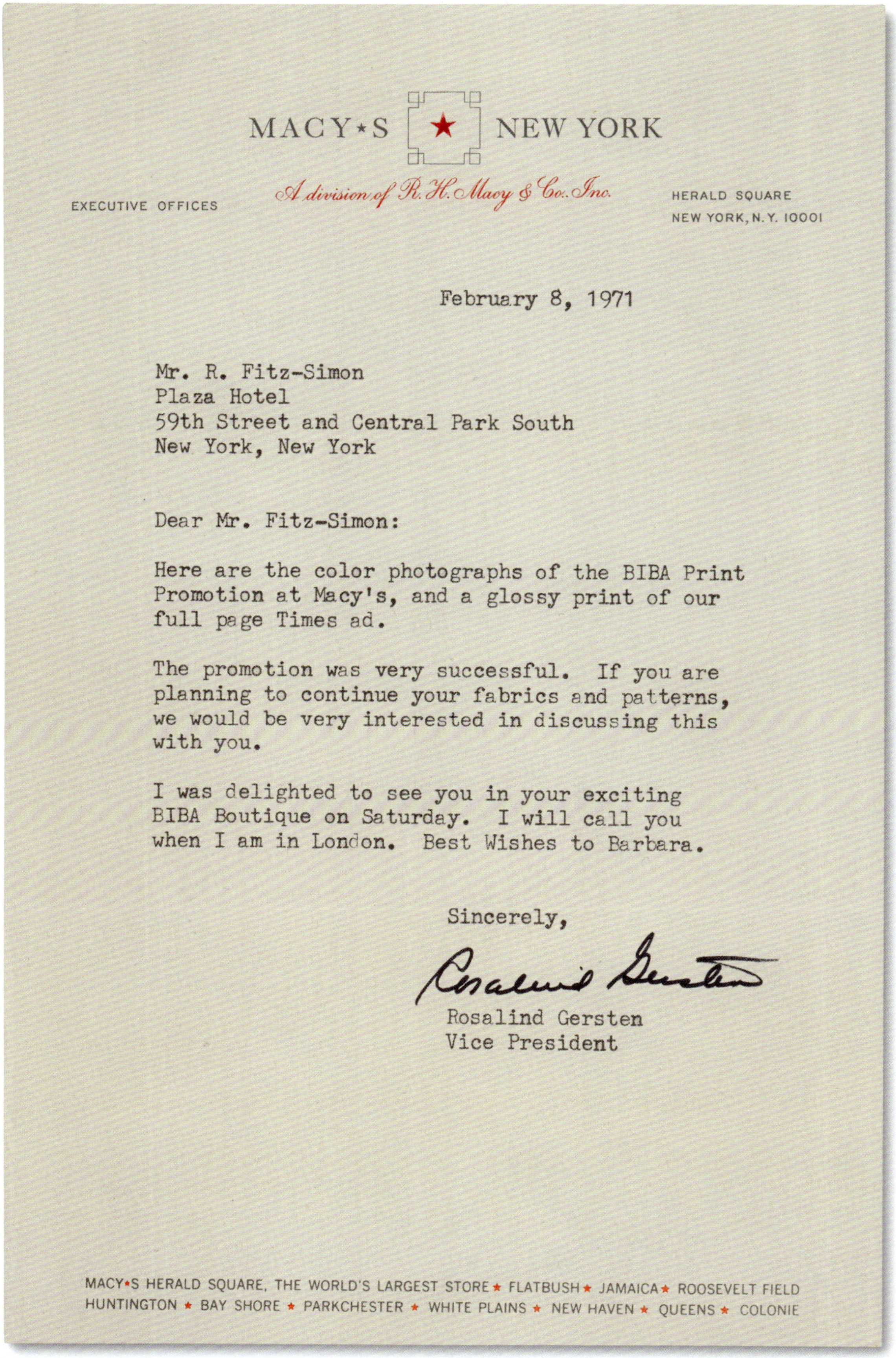

MACY★S NEW YORK

A division of R. H. Macy & Co. Inc.

EXECUTIVE OFFICES

HERALD SQUARE
NEW YORK, N.Y. 10001

February 8, 1971

Mr. R. Fitz-Simon
Plaza Hotel
59th Street and Central Park South
New York, New York

Dear Mr. Fitz-Simon:

Here are the color photographs of the BIBA Print Promotion at Macy's, and a glossy print of our full page Times ad.

The promotion was very successful. If you are planning to continue your fabrics and patterns, we would be very interested in discussing this with you.

I was delighted to see you in your exciting BIBA Boutique on Saturday. I will call you when I am in London. Best Wishes to Barbara.

Sincerely,

Rosalind Gersten

Rosalind Gersten
Vice President

MACY★S HERALD SQUARE, THE WORLD'S LARGEST STORE ★ FLATBUSH ★ JAMAICA ★ ROOSEVELT FIELD
HUNTINGTON ★ BAY SHORE ★ PARKCHESTER ★ WHITE PLAINS ★ NEW HAVEN ★ QUEENS ★ COLONIE

Letter to Fitz from Macy's department store regarding the promotion of Biba at Macy's, 8 February 1971

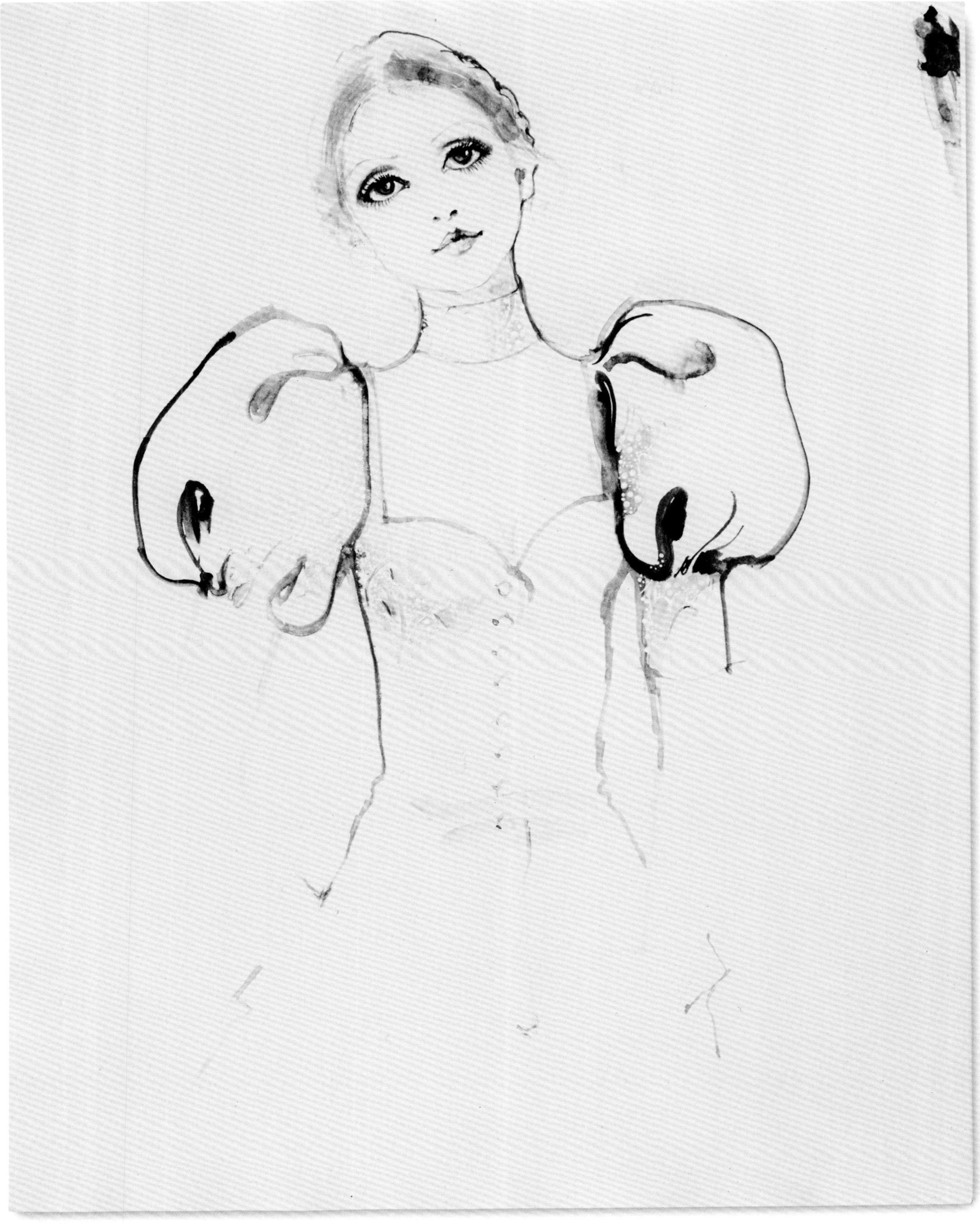

ABOVE & OVERLEAF Photographic reproductions of fashion illustrations created by Barbara Hulanicki to promote Biba in America through Macy's department store, McCall's paper patterns and a fashion story in the teenage girl magazine *Seventeen*, 1971

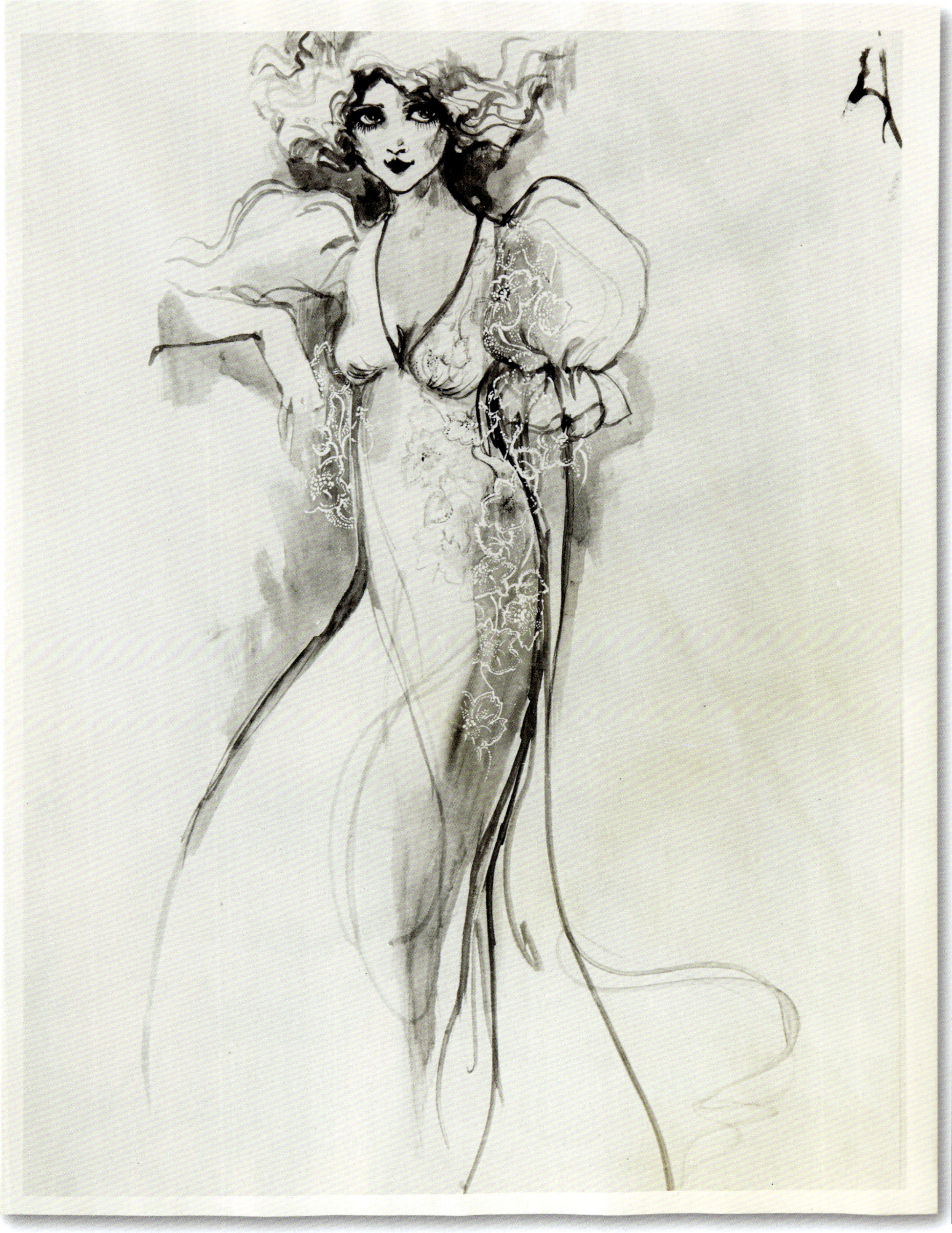

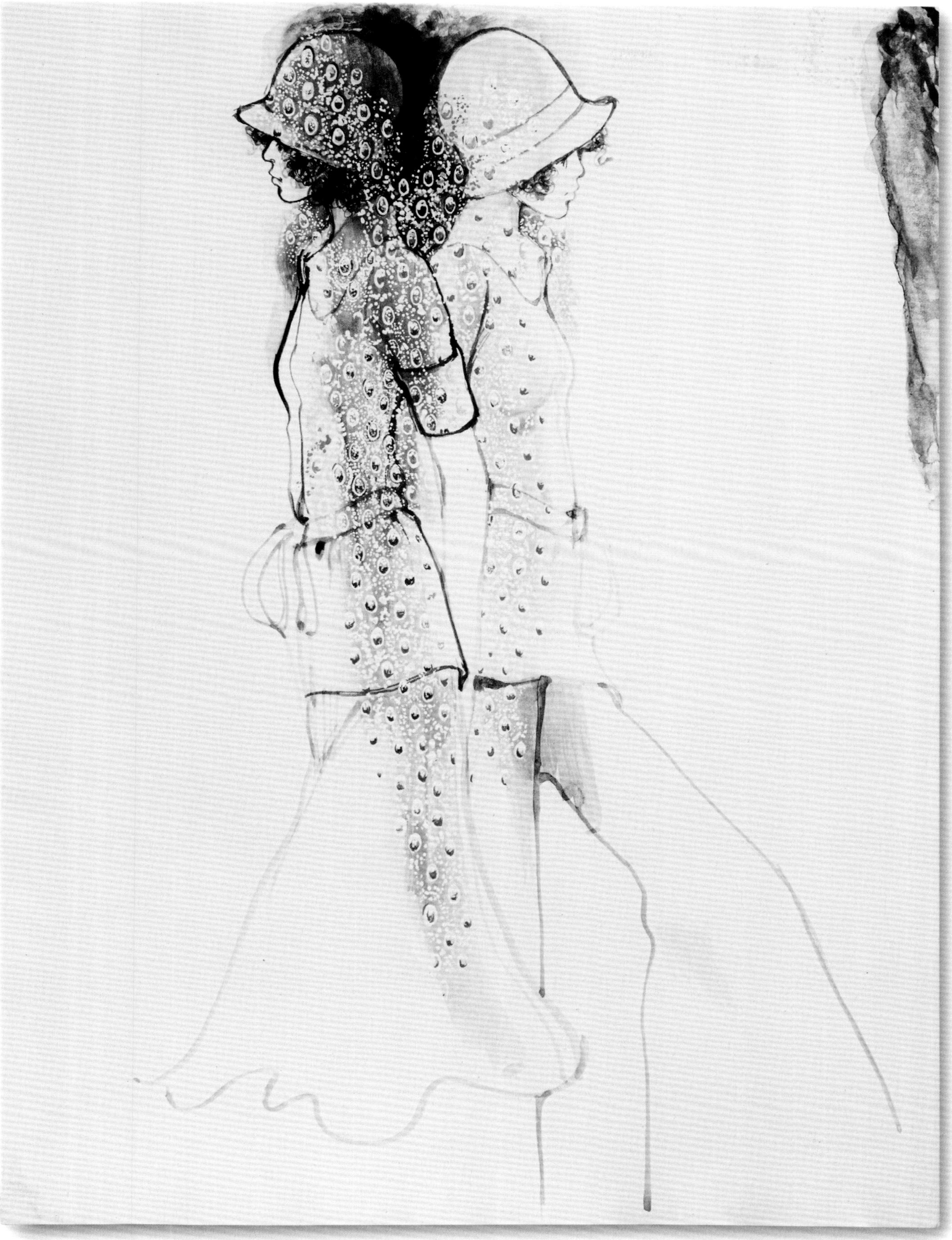

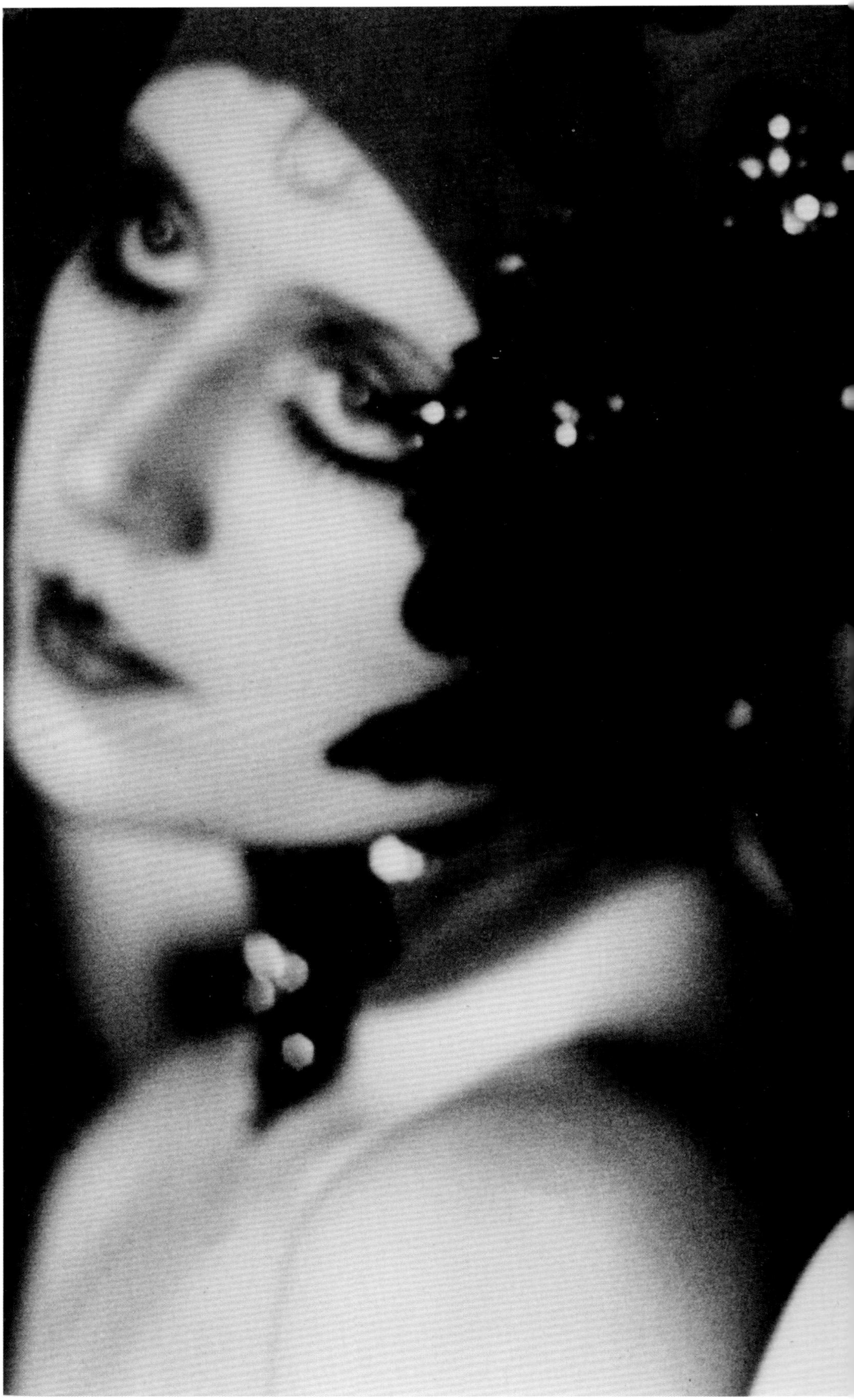

Elizabeth Bjorn Neilson modelling Biba cosmetics, photographed by Barbara Hulanicki, c.1971. Neilson was Witold Fitz-Simon's nanny and the model for the fifth photographic Biba catalogue.

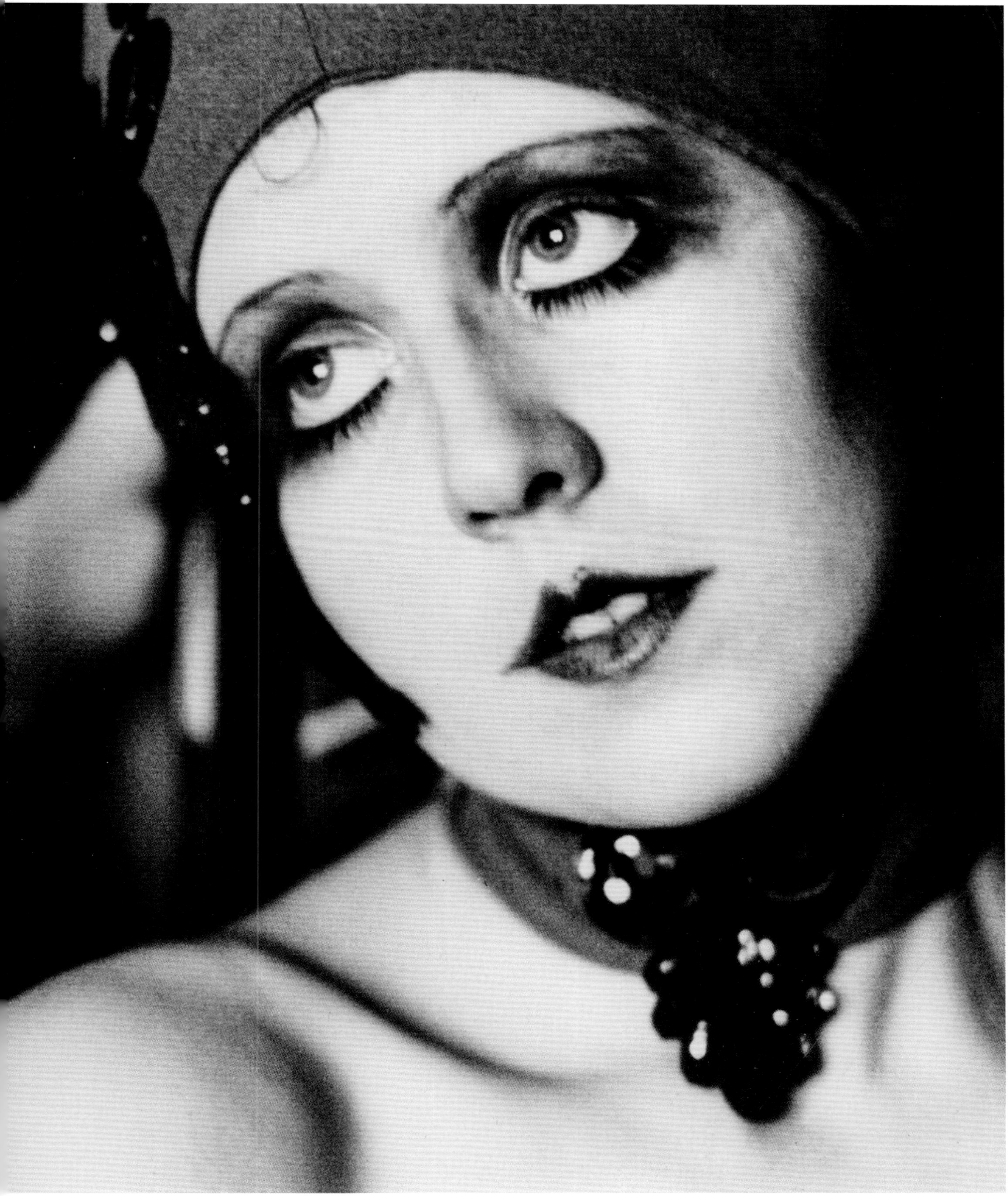

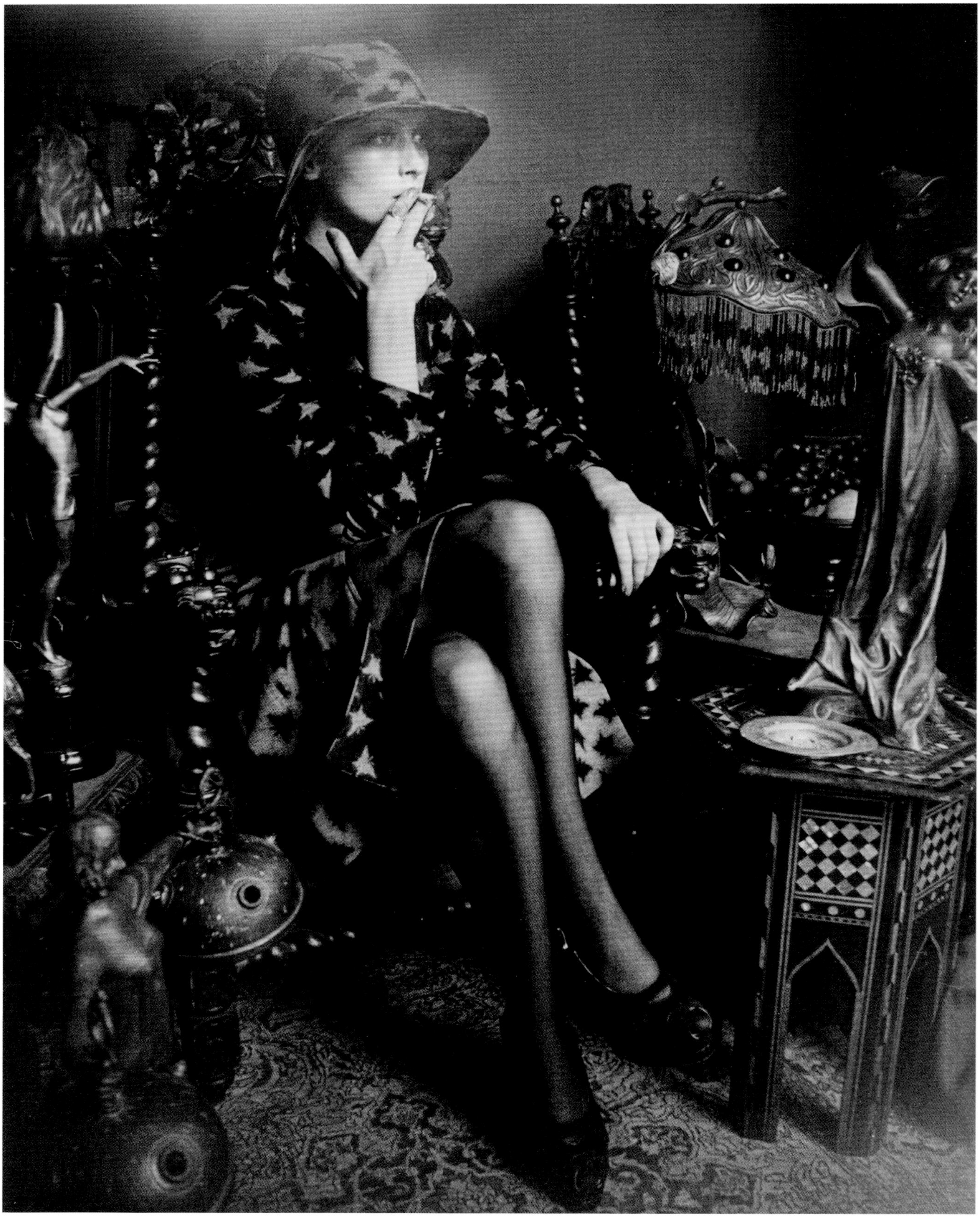

Jo Dingemans modelling Biba surrounded by Art Nouveau and Art Deco objects in Barbara and Fitz's home, photographed by Barbara Hulanicki, *c.*1970. Jo later went on to become fashion editor at *19* magazine.

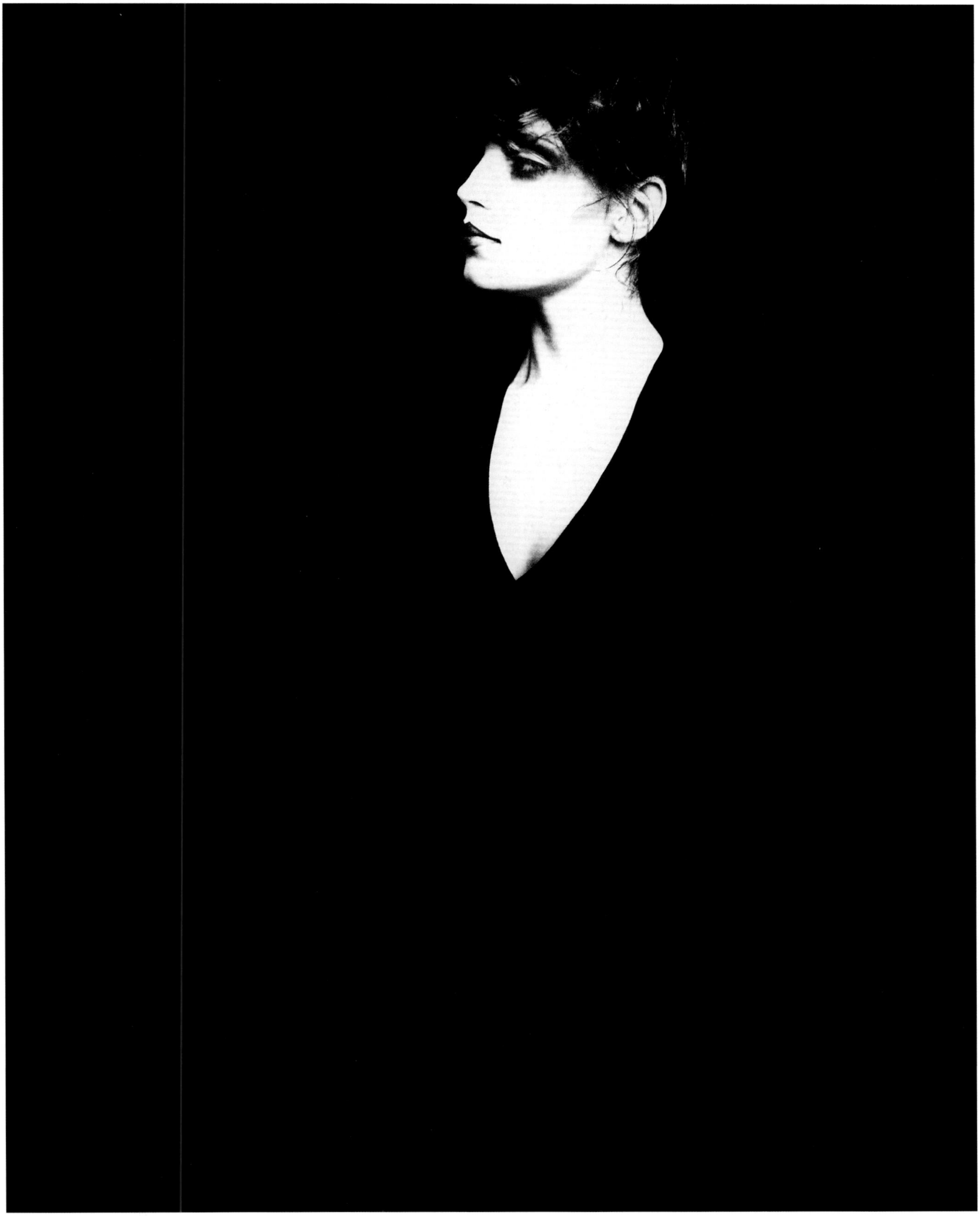

Eva Molnar modelling Biba cosmetics, photographed by Barbara Hulanicki, c.1971.
A variation of this photograph was used to promote Biba cosmetics in-store and in the media.

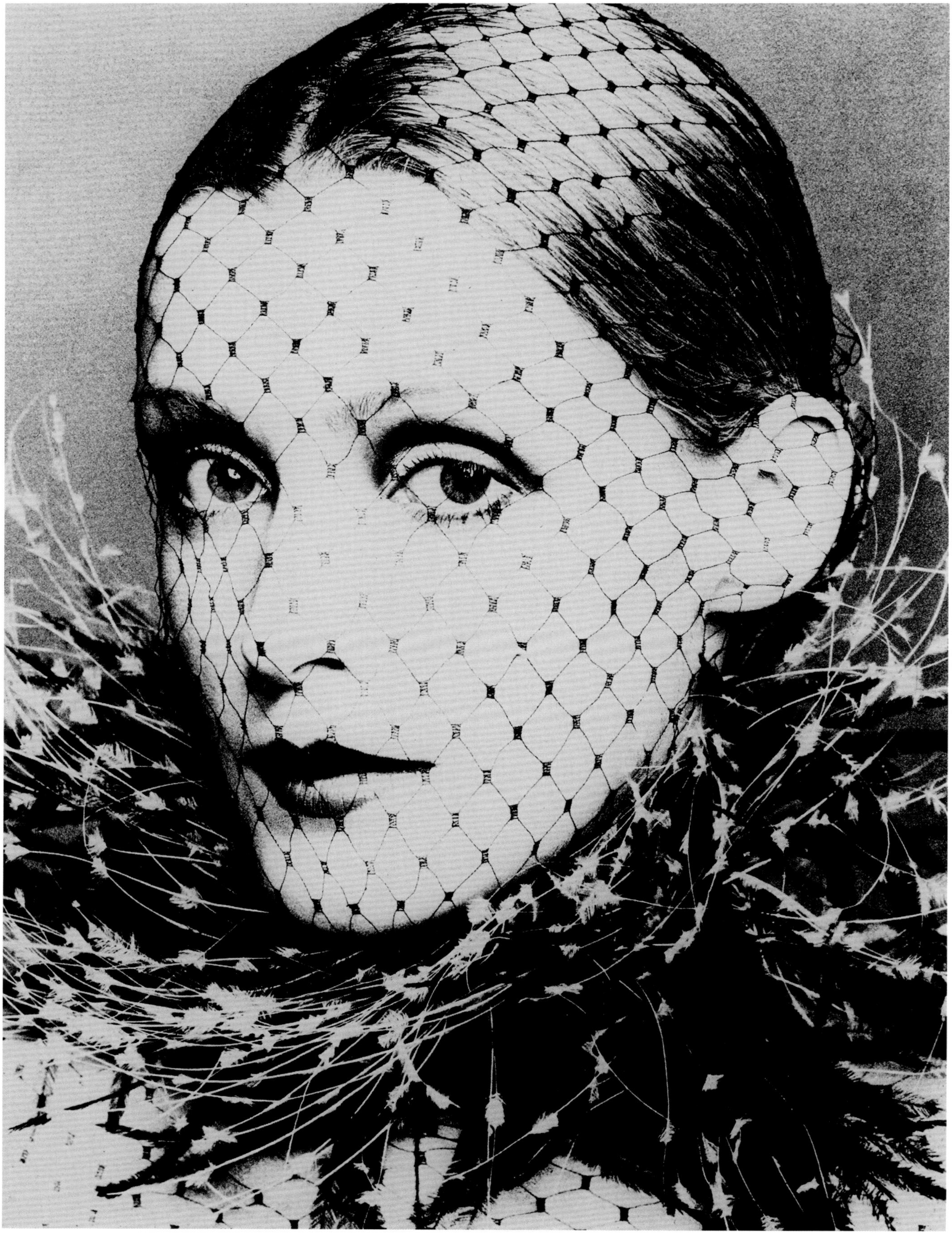

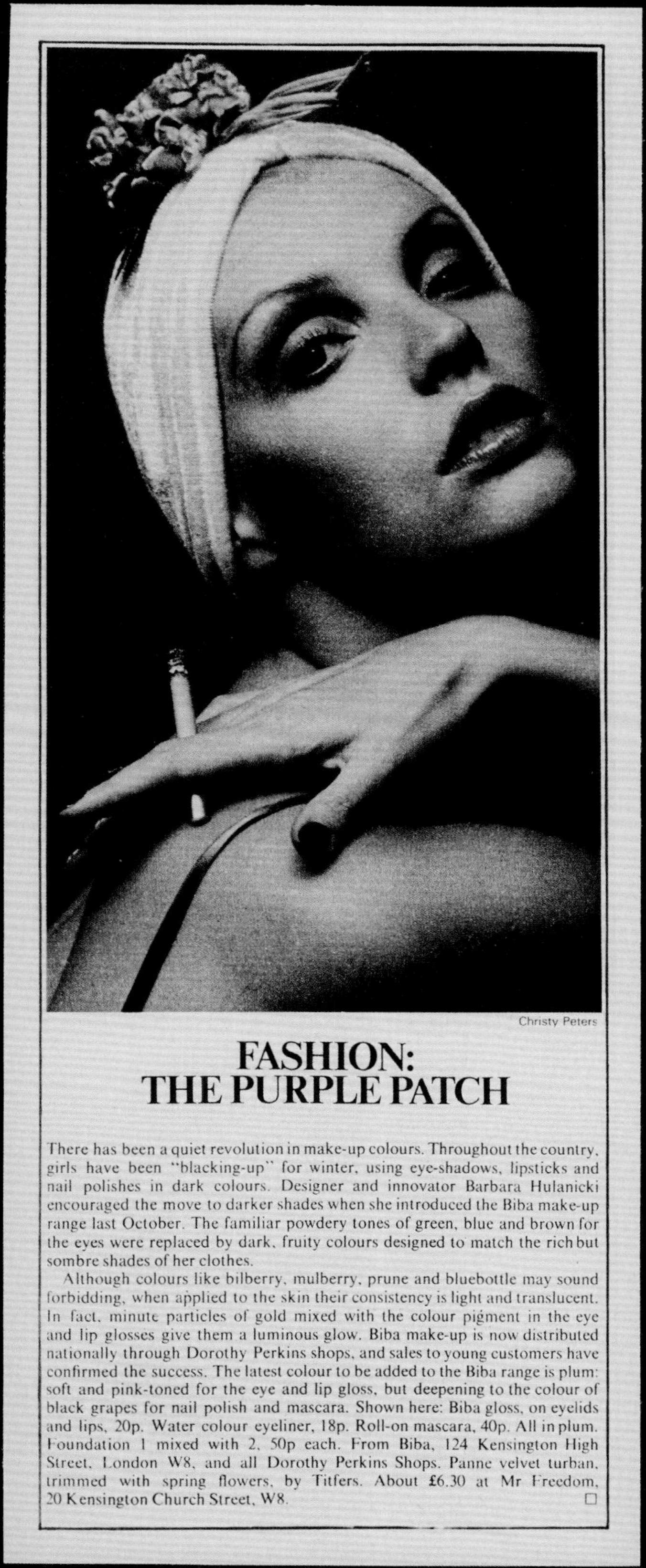

Christy Peters

FASHION: THE PURPLE PATCH

There has been a quiet revolution in make-up colours. Throughout the country, girls have been "blacking-up" for winter, using eye-shadows, lipsticks and nail polishes in dark colours. Designer and innovator Barbara Hulanicki encouraged the move to darker shades when she introduced the Biba make-up range last October. The familiar powdery tones of green, blue and brown for the eyes were replaced by dark, fruity colours designed to match the rich but sombre shades of her clothes.

Although colours like bilberry, mulberry, prune and bluebottle may sound forbidding, when applied to the skin their consistency is light and translucent. In fact, minute particles of gold mixed with the colour pigment in the eye and lip glosses give them a luminous glow. Biba make-up is now distributed nationally through Dorothy Perkins shops, and sales to young customers have confirmed the success. The latest colour to be added to the Biba range is plum: soft and pink-toned for the eye and lip gloss, but deepening to the colour of black grapes for nail polish and mascara. Shown here: Biba gloss, on eyelids and lips, 20p. Water colour eyeliner, 18p. Roll-on mascara, 40p. All in plum. Foundation 1 mixed with 2, 50p each. From Biba, 124 Kensington High Street, London W8, and all Dorothy Perkins Shops. Panne velvet turban, trimmed with spring flowers, by Titfers. About £6.30 at Mr Freedom, 20 Kensington Church Street, W8. □

OPPOSITE & ABOVE Editorials featuring Biba cosmetics and products, Unknown sources, c.1970

LILLI ANDERSON

BIBA HOUSEHOLD DEPARTMENT MANAGER

I grew up in a small village in the south-west of Scotland. I would order the Biba catalogue and pore over the beautiful images inside; they inspired me to make my own versions of the clothes, as I couldn't really afford to buy anything and would have been too impatient waiting if I had placed an order. I visited Glasgow most weekends and would always visit the Dorothy Perkins shop to buy Biba cosmetics. I would be so proud of my purchases inserted into a small Biba bag.

I moved to London in July 1971 and was at last able to visit the Biba store. It was a magical experience, and one which only intensified with each visit as there was always something new to see.

On seeing an advert in the *Evening Standard* for a role as a sales assistant, I went along to the open interview. I was asked to call back later in the week to see if I had been successful but, to my dismay, I heard someone in the background saying I was too short. Instead of taking this comment as defeat, a few months later, when they advertised again, I attended the interview this time wearing much higher platform shoes! To my delight I was accepted and began work at Biba on Kensington High Street in February 1972. Little did I know that this would define my working life.

"I usually had Freddie Mercury, who then had a stall in Kensington Market, for company lounging on a peacock chair waiting for his girlfriend Mary Austin to finish work"

The shop was open weekdays from 9.30am until 8pm, and we worked alternate days either from 9am to 5.30pm or midday until 8pm. On Saturdays, everyone worked from 9am until 5.30pm and then it was all hands to the pump to clear the changing room, which would be knee deep in clothes as there was no limit to the number of items you could try. It was difficult to keep on top of the clothes pile most days but totally impossible on a Saturday. This was how new members of staff spent their first two weeks: clearing the changing room, rehanging garments and returning them to the shop floor, thus making them more familiar with the stock. There were a few rules everyone had to adhere to: wearing false eyelashes and no eating or drinking on the shop floor, but you were allowed to smoke cigarettes.

I was subsequently moved to the household department, which was situated at the entrance to the store opposite the cosmetics counter. The strikingly beautiful girls at the cosmetics counter would be wearing a different coloured crepe outfit – black, rust, pink, blue, green – wearing make-up colours that matched their clothes exactly, showcasing the vast colour range and making a strong statement.

Household was probably seen as the least glamorous department, but after a few days of being a little disappointed I grew to love it. You could forge a real relationship with the customer, who wanted the Biba look for their home. We sold wallpaper and paint colours, lady lamps, fringed lampshades and cushions in either satin or velvet as well as peacock feathers all in the famous Biba colours. Customers could place orders for lampshades, and on Friday evenings I would telephone the customer if their order was ready for collection. One call was to Robert Plant, and I had to speak to every member of Led Zeppelin before I spoke to Robert. On my late nights, I usually had Freddie Mercury, who then had a stall in Kensington Market, for company lounging on a peacock chair waiting for his girlfriend Mary Austin to finish work.

It was great to be able to advise customers how to create the Biba look in their home, translating Barbara's vision of a Biba room. One Saturday afternoon, a customer I had helped a few weeks before entered the shop and shouted, 'Where is that girl who helped me design my room?' My heart sank as I was worried it hadn't worked and that she hated it. To my relief she adored the outcome and wanted my advice for a colour scheme for another room. Not all customers were so agreeable. A man once interrupted me, while I was busy serving another customer, to ask for wallpaper. I directed him to the drawers containing the different designs and colourways of wallpaper, which came in sheets like wrapping paper, making it very easy to hang, and said please help yourself. His rather aggressive reply was, 'I want a Biba girl on her knees counting my sheets of wallpaper.' I responded, 'I'm sorry but you've picked the wrong Biba girl, and if you want to make a complaint please speak to Mary on reception!'

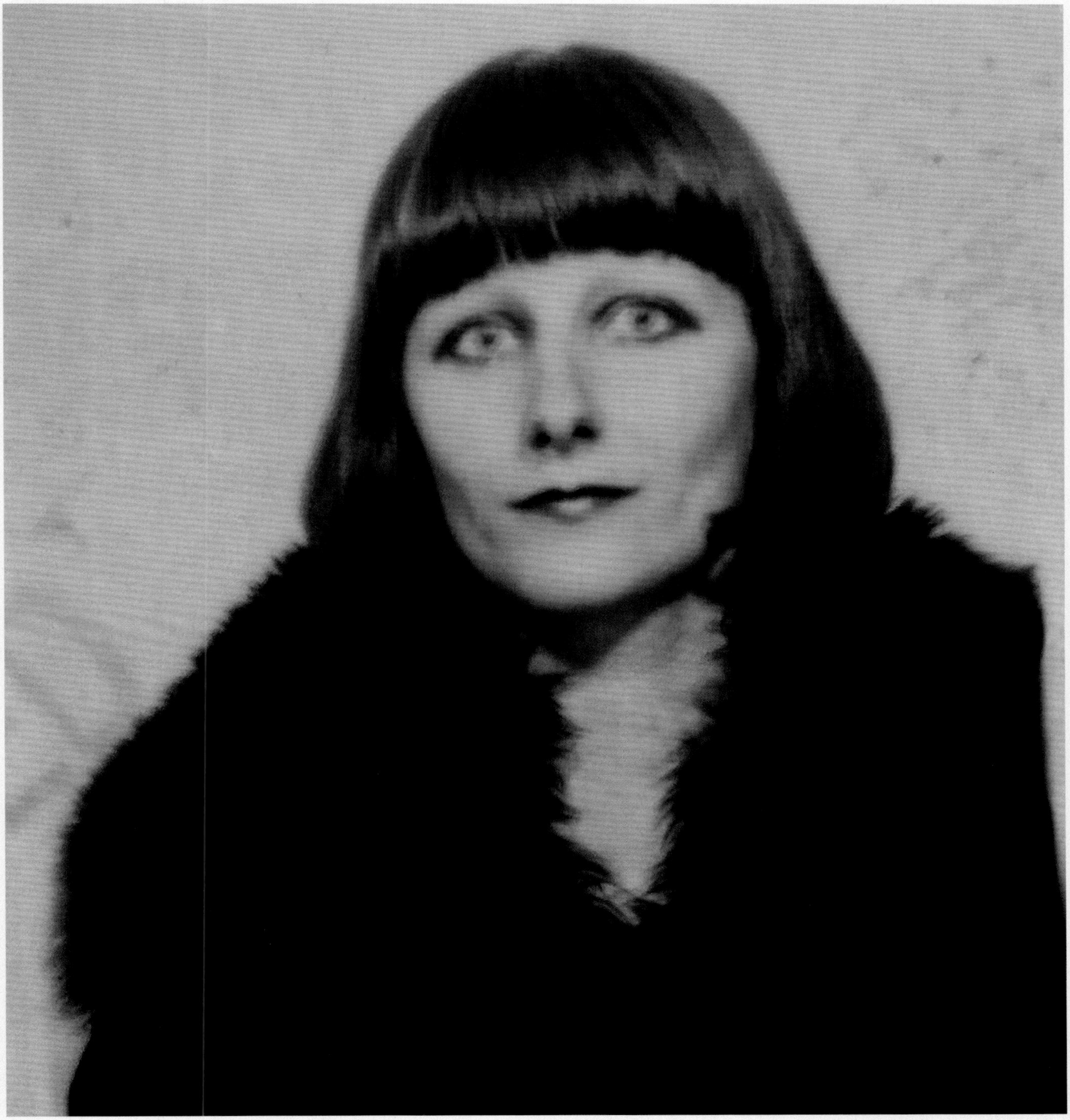

Lilli Anderson wearing Biba coat
and cosmetics, 1975

CHAPTER FIVE

1973–1975

BIG BIBA

"The thing was, with this type of department store, you could go in and not come out again for hours"

Barbara Hulanicki

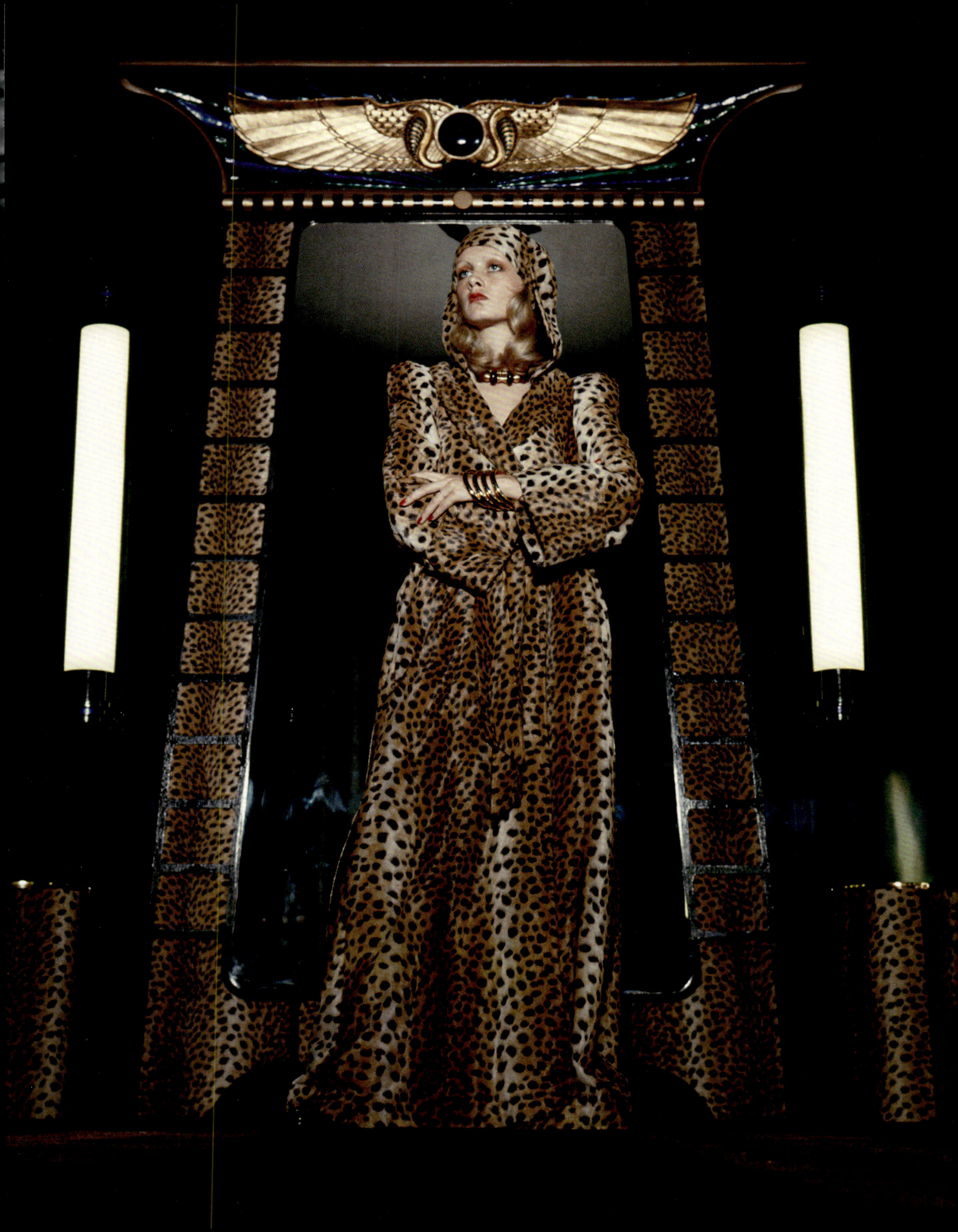

MARTIN PEL You took on the lease of the Derry & Toms department store and created one of the most legendary shops ever to exist.

BARBARA HULANICKI I had fallen in love with the building. It was a ramshackle old building, and it was possibly going to be torn down. Fitz arranged for us to visit. Witold wanted to go up to the rooftop garden to see the flamingos. We went in, and there were all of these incredible lifts with wonderful surrounds; it was so beautiful, I fell in love with the place. We went up to the rooftop garden and I said to Fitz, 'We've got to get this.'

Each floor had to have a different carpet to give it a distinct look and a different feel. We collected swatches from a vintage shop for the carpets and upholstery. The Rainbow Room's was taken from the original carpet, which we had made in a moquette. For the men's department we kept all the old fittings. It was supposed to feel like a man's closet. The office was on the first floor with the clothes, and on the second floor there was a big crèche where the girls could bring their babies. There was also a nurse, which they employed, but we gave them things like fridges and cookers, and all that sort of thing.

We were going to build a cinema, but we had trouble getting the films. In the children's department, which was based on Disney, we were going to do a shop selling Marvel comic character, for Witold. We also had the hairdresser's and beauty parlour, which was actually the beauty parlour from Derry & Toms, with all the original Art Deco panels, where our *visagiste* Régis Huet worked.

The thing was, with this type of department store, you could go in and not come out again for hours. You could spend a whole day in there, which is what they used to do in the 1930s. People would come into London to be made over. You could shop till you dropped. With Big Biba, you didn't have to shop, you could just have a good time. There was even an ice cream parlour!

In May 1974 we opened the rooftop garden, and there was the gardening club with about six or seven people and the gardener, who'd been there since the year dot. He was lovely and really very old. There was also Mr Moorehouse, whom we bought with the building. He was the 'floor walker'. Back in the 1930s, they used to have floor walkers making sure everything was alright across the store. He wanted to be dressed in pinstripes and black, and I think tails. Because the building was so old and he had been there so long, he was the only one who knew where to put the buckets when it rained! We couldn't tell where the drips were going to come from, or on which floor, but he knew.

The thing with Big Biba was that there were no mobile phones (obviously) and no computers like today, so you had to do everything physically. We made it a rule that nobody from the staff should go up in the main lift; we all had to use the side stairs. In order to talk to someone, you might be lucky and get them in the stock room or on the internal phone, if you could find a phone to call on. Otherwise, you had to go and find them. It was very tiring, exhausting. Physically I wasn't used to it, but you do get used to things like that. The worst thing was in the mornings. I used to go in early. Most mornings I'd arrive at about 8 in the morning (we opened at 10am), to find that the cleaners hadn't been. That was a horror story. Oh god, I remember those mornings.

MP Big Biba looks like it was a lot of fun! Were there a lot of parties?

PREVIOUS PAGE Twiggy modelling fake leopard-print outfit in the Egyptian-themed changing rooms of Big Biba, photographed by Justine de Villeneuve, 1973

BH We used to have some parties in Fitz's room. We had dinners all the time. We had one with Bryan Ferry, which Justin de Villeneuve gave with Tony Curtis and Amanda Lear, which was fabulous. We had one for Molly Parkin (who designed our hats) when she was in her red and white period. We also had a New Year's Eve party in the Rainbow Room, which was all pink and black food. That was Andrew Logan. There was a fashion show, and he brought all his guys to do a Miss World thing with guys dressed in drag, Michael Roberts dressed as Diana Ross.

MP You also had lots of genuine performers in the Rainbow Room.

BH Yes, we had lots of live bands in the evenings. The Rainbow Room was a really smelly cafe when Fitz and I went round it the first time. There were all these mice in there and it was roach heaven. We opened it in the day as a restaurant for lunch and there was a bar that was open late in the evenings. The price of the lunches was amazing when you think about it, and it was always packed. We used to do 1,200 lunches every day. We were some of the first to do French and Italian food. We wanted really clean food as the English used to make one awful sauce and shove it on everything on the menu.

"It was so beautiful, I fell in love with the place. We went up to the rooftop garden and I said to Fitz, 'We've got to get this.'"

In the evenings, the Rainbow Room would be for live music. Often, when people came on tour to England, they would come in at the end of the tour because they made some extra money. Agents would bring their bands in. The New York Dolls were fantastic. They came up in the goods lift on their way to the changing rooms before their performance, looking amazing. They were so elegant, with beautiful shoes, sort of Jacqueline Onassis shoes. I was so jealous! They were very quiet, never said anything, very sweet, very nice. CBS did a whole series of concerts with The Kinks, some really famous bands they brought in. Eddie Hunt came – he was young, he was amazing. On Friday nights we used to have all the new, small bands, great people, and they brought the younger crowd in.

We had a 'Fantastic Fifties' evening with the Jive Club in Southend. They came up, and we all learnt how to jive and bebop. Alan Gearing told me that Elvis had not done Las Vegas, but he said that Elvis would apparently only do the Rainbow Room for a comeback. Can you imagine? That would have been something. The Rainbow Room was well known with artists because it was very small – it seated about 500 – and they used to like doing small venues.

We also had a gallery on the side of the Rainbow Room, and we had the artist Guy Peellaert, who did the album covers for David Bowie and The Rolling Stones and the illustrations for the *Rock Dreams* book. We also showed the portraits of Marilyn Monroe by Bert Stern. It was amazing because we got this girl on stage who was a lookalike Marilyn, and she sang all her songs. I wish I had a picture of it. We had David Bowie and Angie Bowie watching this girl. They came and sat there all alone in the Rainbow Room because everyone else was in the gallery.

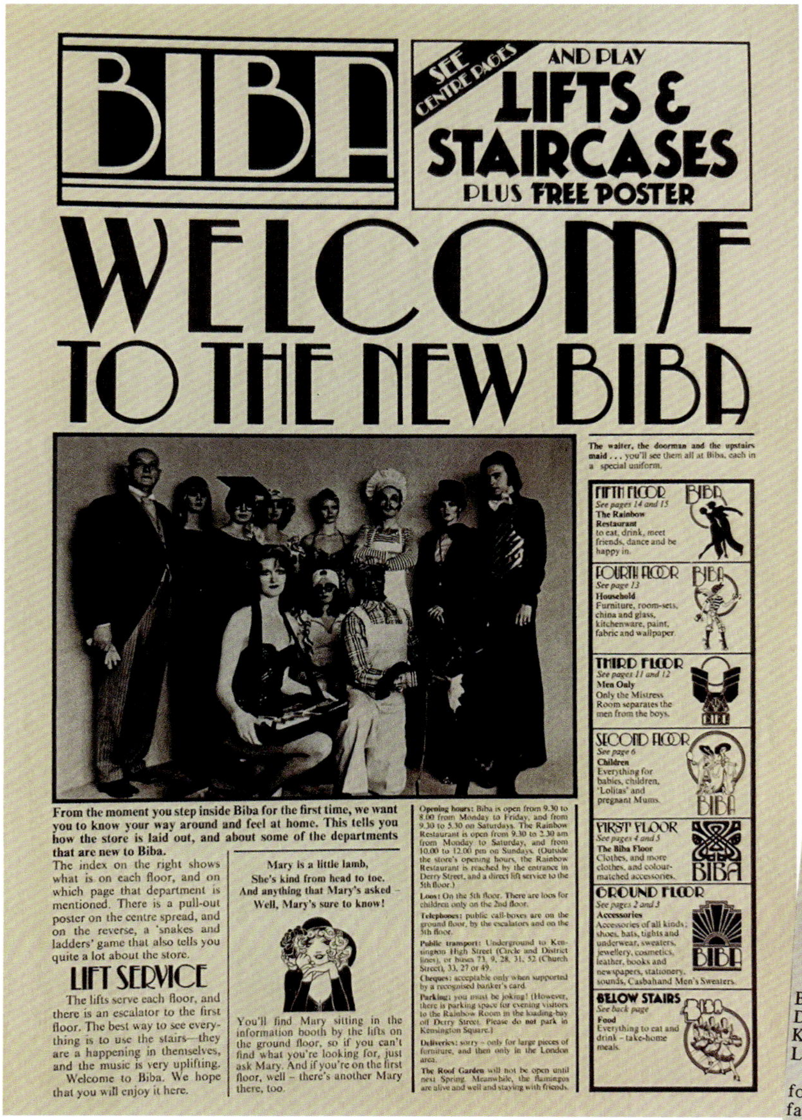

BIBA

SEE CENTRE PAGES AND PLAY LIFTS & STAIRCASES PLUS FREE POSTER

WELCOME TO THE NEW BIBA

The waiter, the doorman and the upstairs maid . . . you'll see them all at Biba, each in a special uniform.

From the moment you step inside Biba for the first time, we want you to know your way around and feel at home. This tells you how the store is laid out, and about some of the departments that are new to Biba.

The index on the right shows what is on each floor, and on which page that department is mentioned. There is a pull-out poster on the centre spread, and on the reverse, a 'snakes and ladders' game that also tells you quite a lot about the store.

LIFT SERVICE

The lifts serve each floor, and there is an escalator to the first floor. The best way to see everything is to use the stairs—they are a happening in themselves, and the music is very uplifting.

Welcome to Biba. We hope that you will enjoy it here.

Mary is a little lamb,
She's kind from head to toe.
And anything that Mary's asked –
Well, Mary's sure to know!

You'll find Mary sitting in the information booth by the lifts on the ground floor, so if you can't find what you're looking for, just ask Mary. And if you're on the first floor, well – there's another Mary there, too.

Opening hours: Biba is open from 9.30 to 8.00 from Monday to Friday, and from 9.30 to 5.30 on Saturdays. The Rainbow Restaurant is open from 9.30 to 2.30 am from Monday to Saturday, and from 10.00 to 12.00 pm on Sundays. (Outside the store's opening hours, the Rainbow Restaurant is reached by the entrance in Derry Street, and a direct lift service to the 5th floor.)

Loos: On the 5th floor. There are loos for children only on the 2nd floor.

Telephones: public call-boxes are on the ground floor, by the escalators and on the 5th floor.

Public transport: Underground to Kensington High Street (Circle and District lines), or buses 73, 9, 28, 31, 52 (Church Street), 33, 27 or 49.

Cheques: acceptable only when supported by a recognised banker's card.

Parking: you must be joking! (However, there is parking space for evening visitors to the Rainbow Room in the loading-bay off Derry Street. Please do **not** park in Kensington Square.)

Deliveries: sorry – only for large pieces of furniture, and then only in the London area.

The Roof Garden will not be open until next Spring. Meanwhile, the flamingos are alive and well and staying with friends.

FIFTH FLOOR *See pages 14 and 15* **The Rainbow Restaurant** to eat, drink, meet friends, dance and be happy in.

FOURTH FLOOR *See page 13* **Household** Furniture, room-sets, china and glass, kitchenware, paint, fabric and wallpaper.

THIRD FLOOR *See pages 11 and 12* **Men Only** Only the Mistress Room separates the men from the boys.

SECOND FLOOR *See page 6* **Children** Everything for babies, children, 'Lolitas' and pregnant Mums.

FIRST FLOOR *See pages 4 and 5* **The Biba Floor** Clothes, and more clothes, and colour-matched accessories.

GROUND FLOOR *See pages 2 and 3* **Accessories** Accessories of all kinds; shoes, hats, tights and underwear, sweaters, jewellery, cosmetics, leather, books and newspapers, stationery, sounds, Casbahand Men's Sweaters.

BELOW STAIRS *See back page* **Food** Everything to eat and drink – take-home meals.

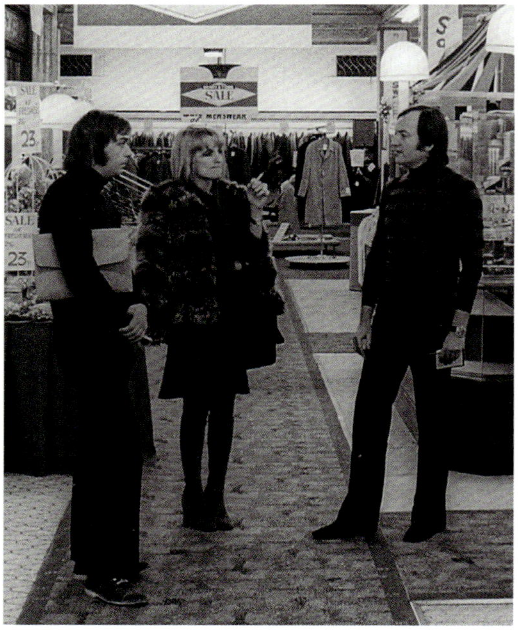

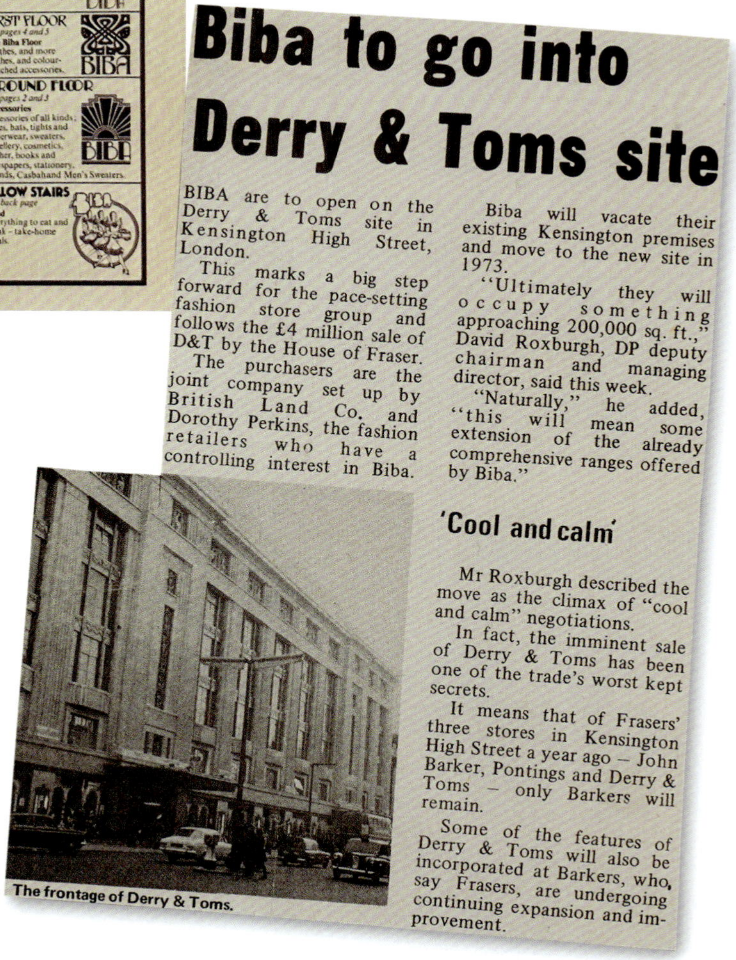

Biba to go into Derry & Toms site

BIBA are to open on the Derry & Toms site in Kensington High Street, London.

This marks a big step forward for the pace-setting fashion store group and follows the £4 million sale of D&T by the House of Fraser.

The purchasers are the joint company set up by British Land Co. and Dorothy Perkins, the fashion retailers who have a controlling interest in Biba.

Biba will vacate their existing Kensington premises and move to the new site in 1973.

"Ultimately they will occupy something approaching 200,000 sq. ft.," David Roxburgh, DP deputy chairman and managing director, said this week.

"Naturally," he added, "this will mean some extension of the already comprehensive ranges offered by Biba."

The frontage of Derry & Toms.

'Cool and calm'

Mr Roxburgh described the move as the climax of "cool and calm" negotiations.

In fact, the imminent sale of Derry & Toms has been one of the trade's worst kept secrets.

It means that of Frasers' three stores in Kensington High Street a year ago – John Barker, Pontings and Derry & Toms – only Barkers will remain.

Some of the features of Derry & Toms will also be incorporated at Barkers, who, say Frasers, are undergoing continuing expansion and improvement.

ABOVE Newspaper created for the launch of Big Biba, Whitmore-Thomas, September 1973

ABOVE RIGHT Barbara, Fitz and Tim Whitmore (designer) in Derry & Toms after acquiring the lease, photograph by Steve Thomas, 1971

RIGHT Press cutting, 'Biba to go into Derry & Toms Site', Unknown source, 1971

RIGHT Mock-up of the newspaper for the launch of Big Biba showing the different floors and departments, Whitmore-Thomas, 1973

BELOW 'Play "Lifts and Staircases" at Big Biba', game, 1973

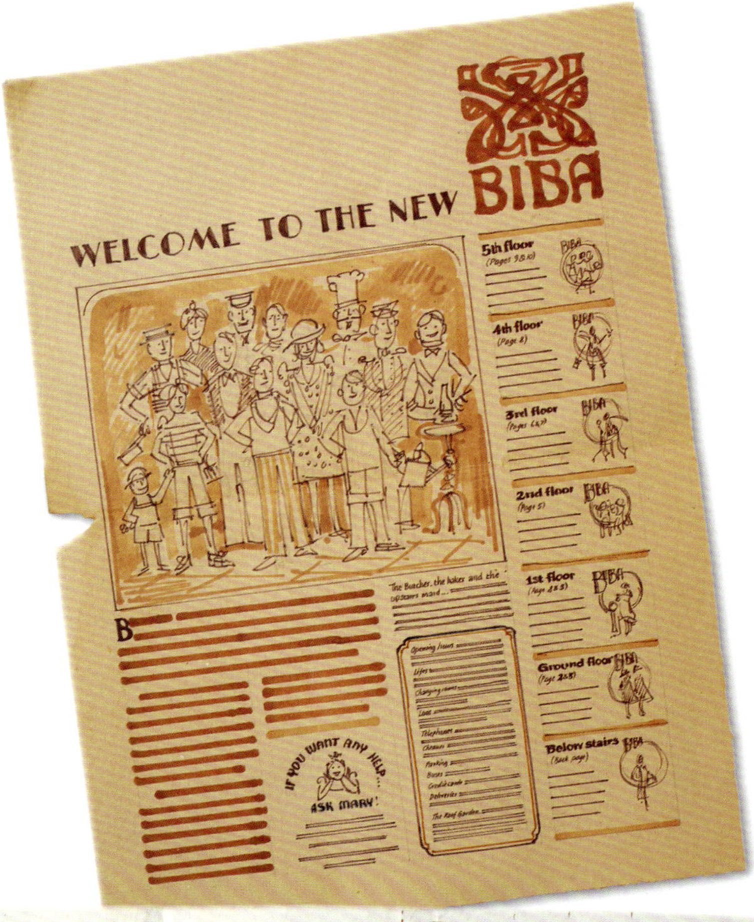

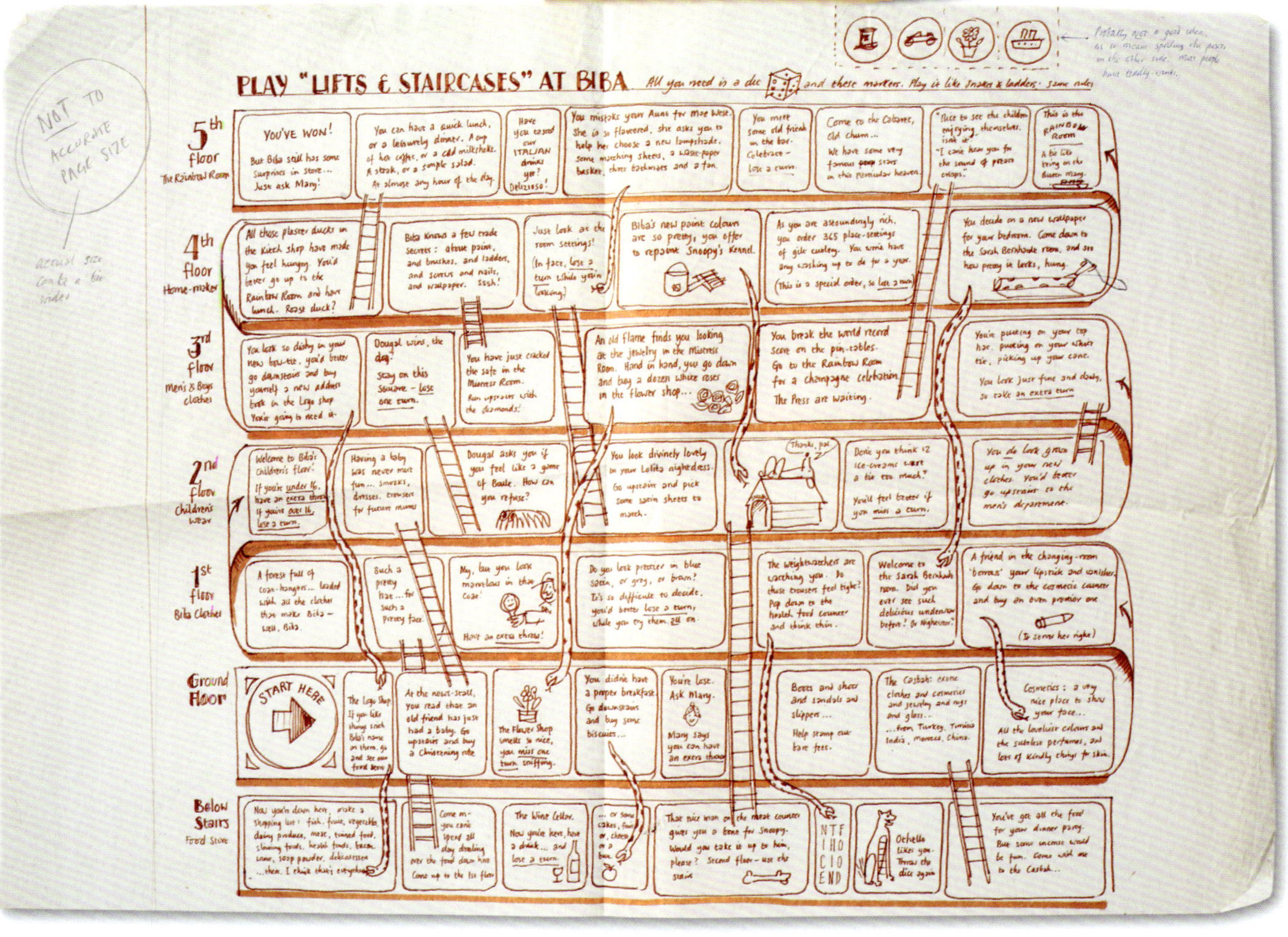

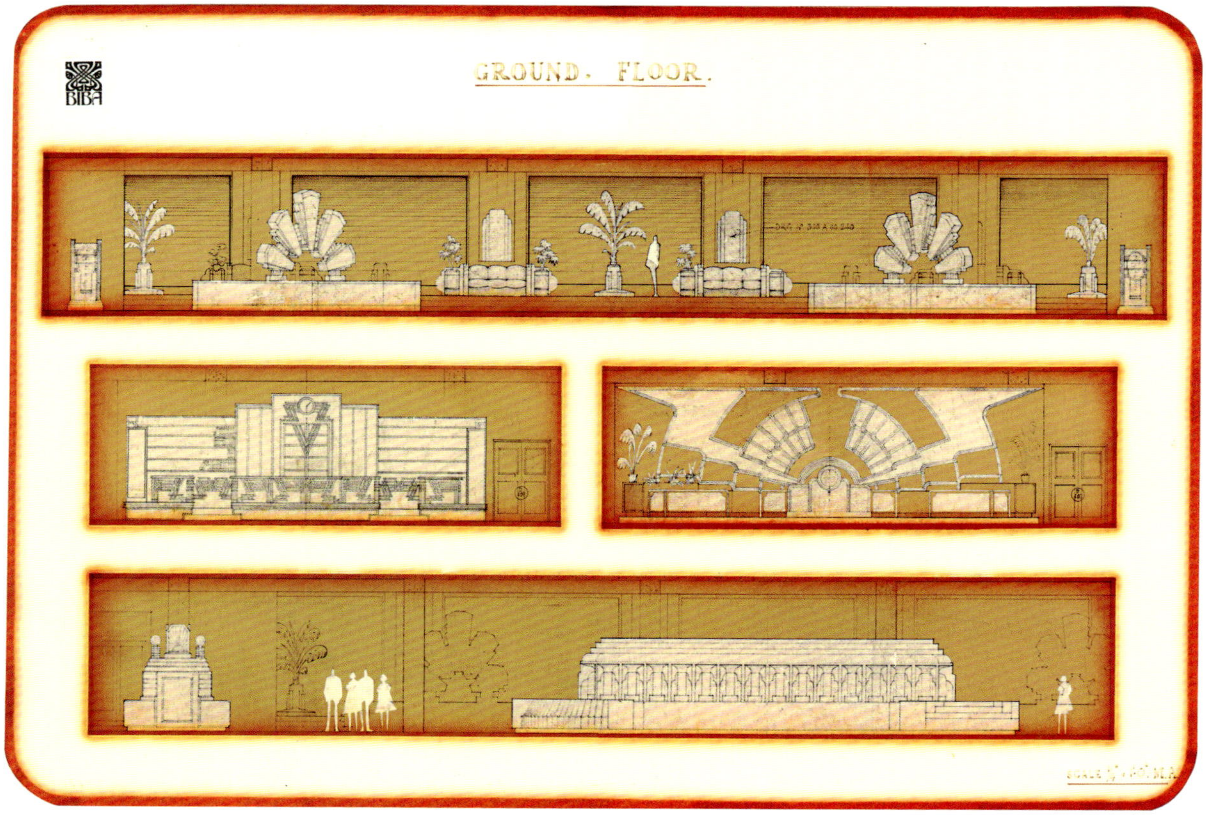

ABOVE Illustration of the retail counters for the ground floor of Big Biba, Markwell Associates Limited, 1973

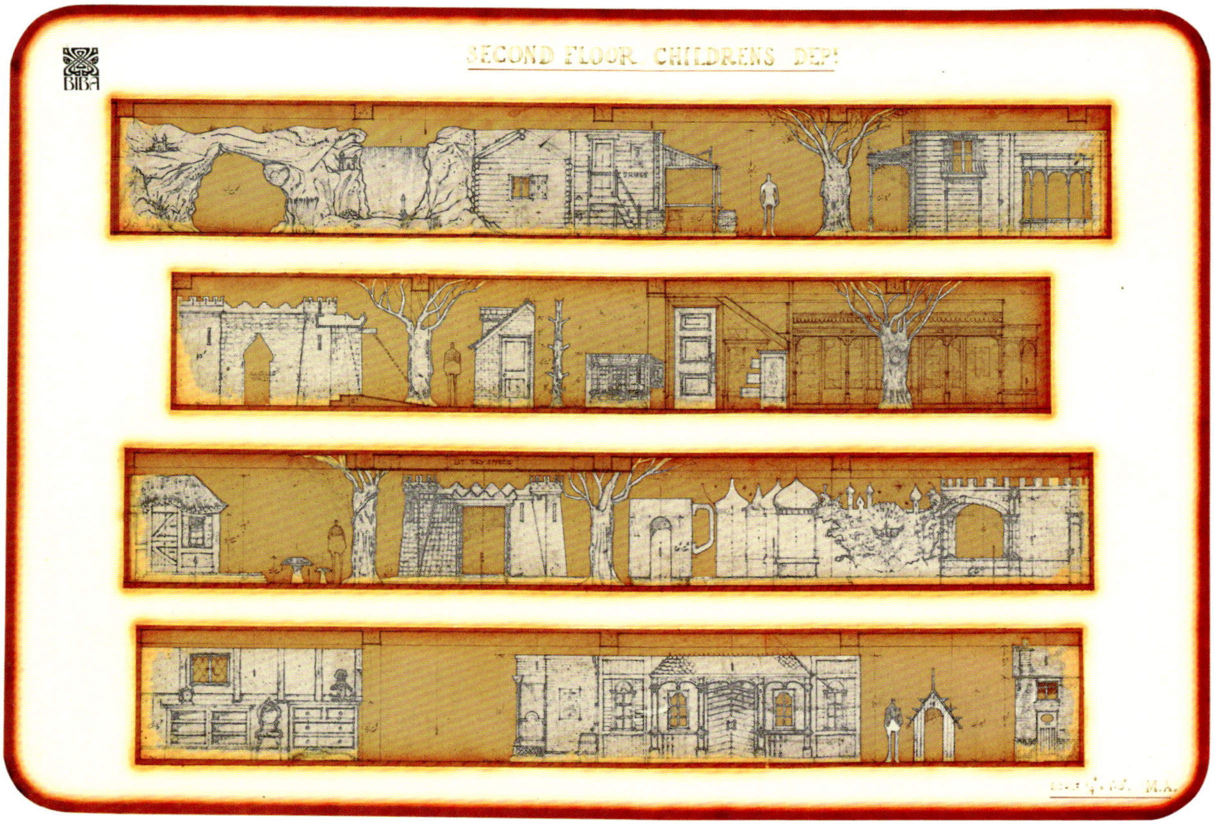

ABOVE Illustration of the children's department on the second floor of Big Biba, Markwell Associates Limited, 1973

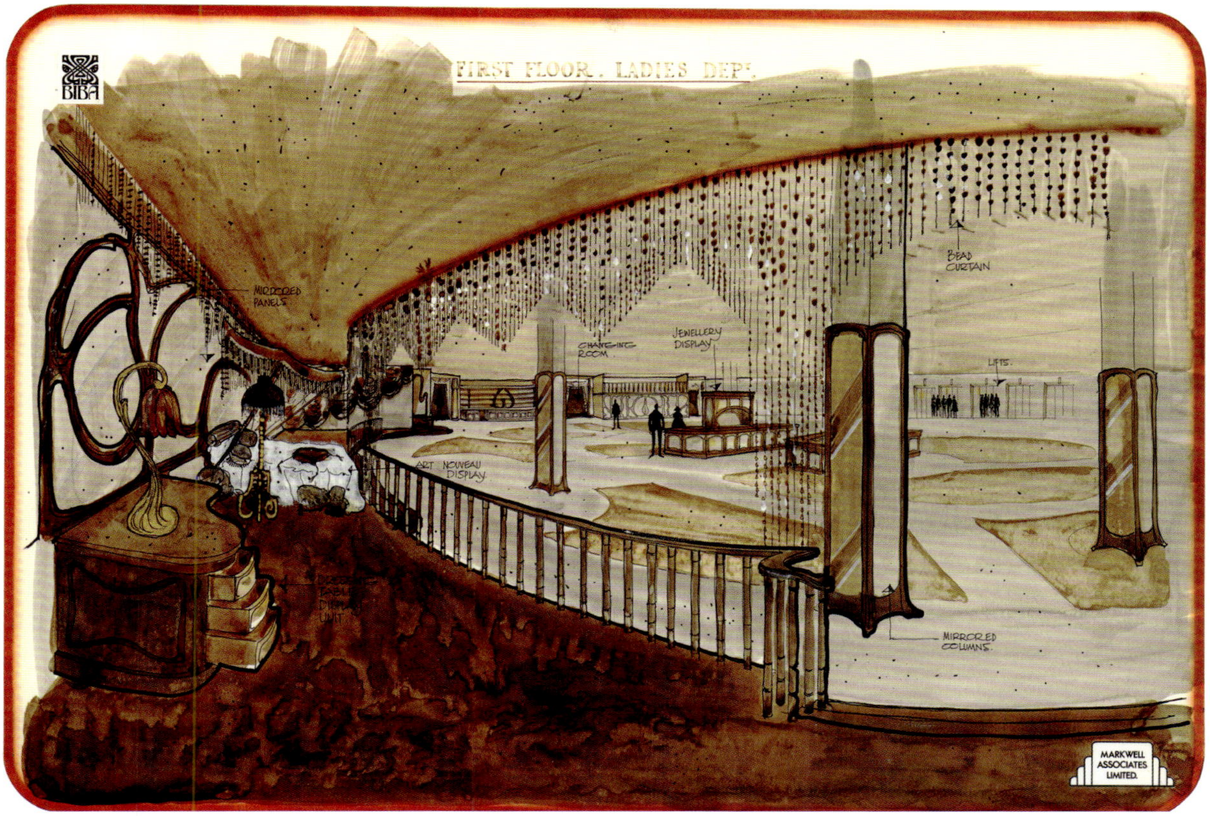

ABOVE Illustration of the potential layout of the womenswear department on the first floor of Big Biba, Markwell Associates Limited, 1973

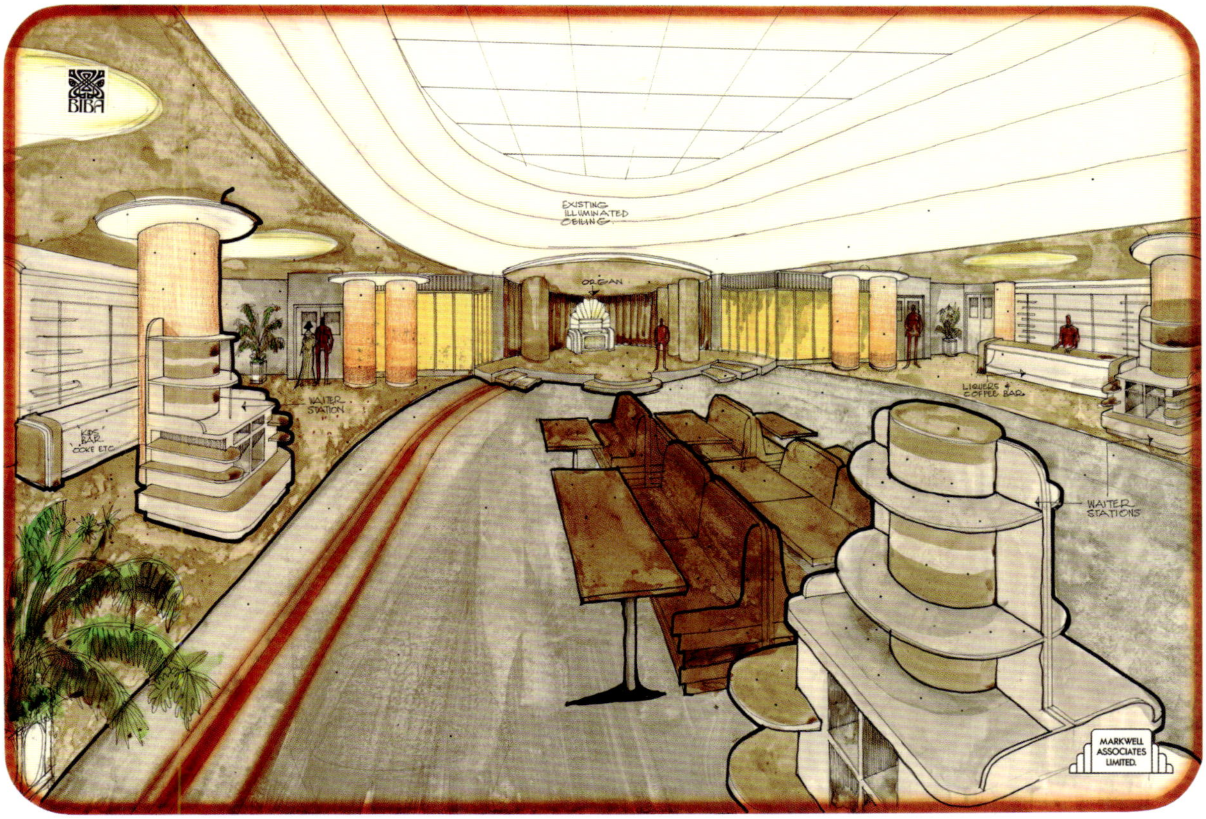

ABOVE Illustration of the potential layout of the Rainbow Room, Big Biba, Markwell Associates Limited, 1973

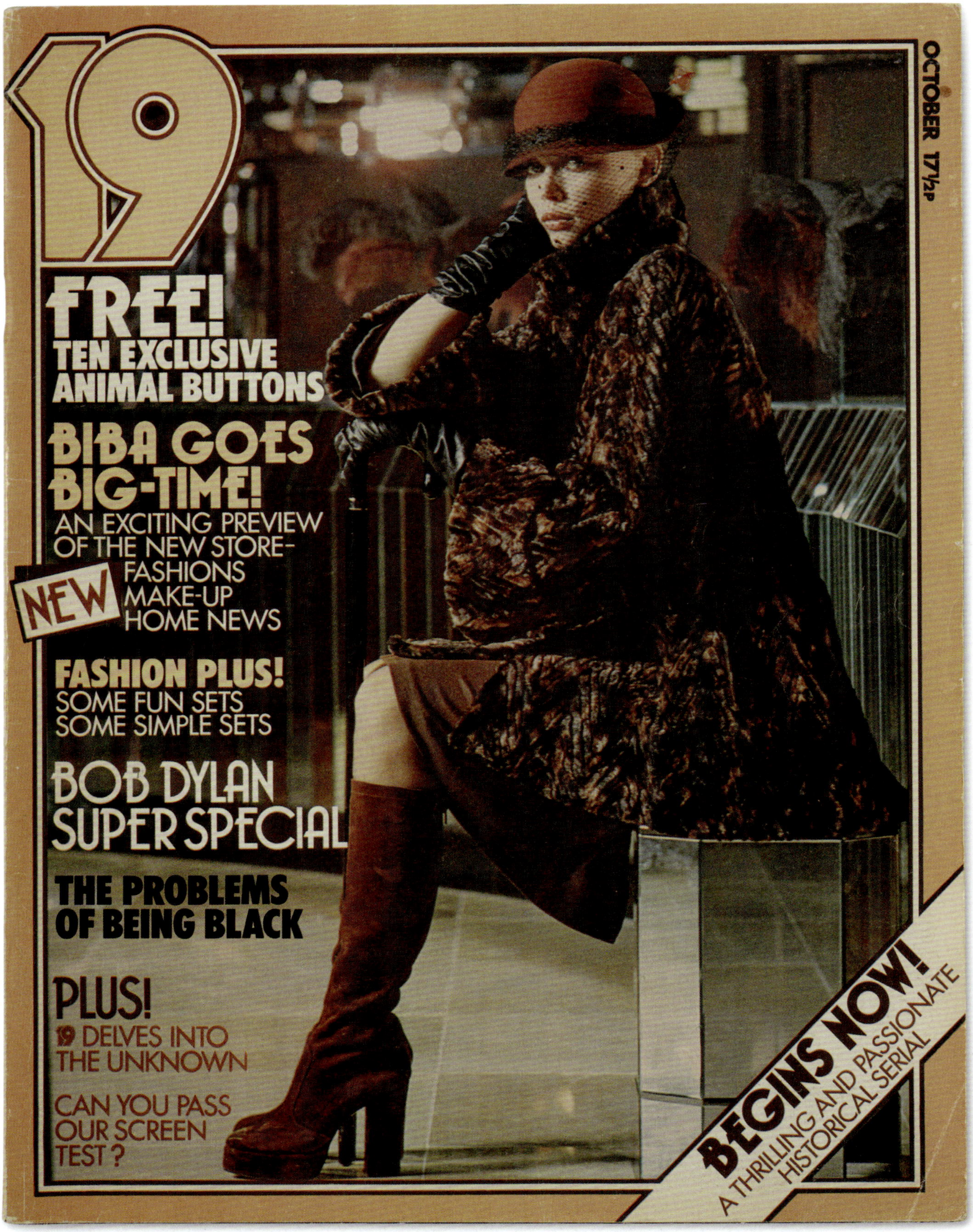

Fashion story shot in Big Biba for *19* magazine, October 1973

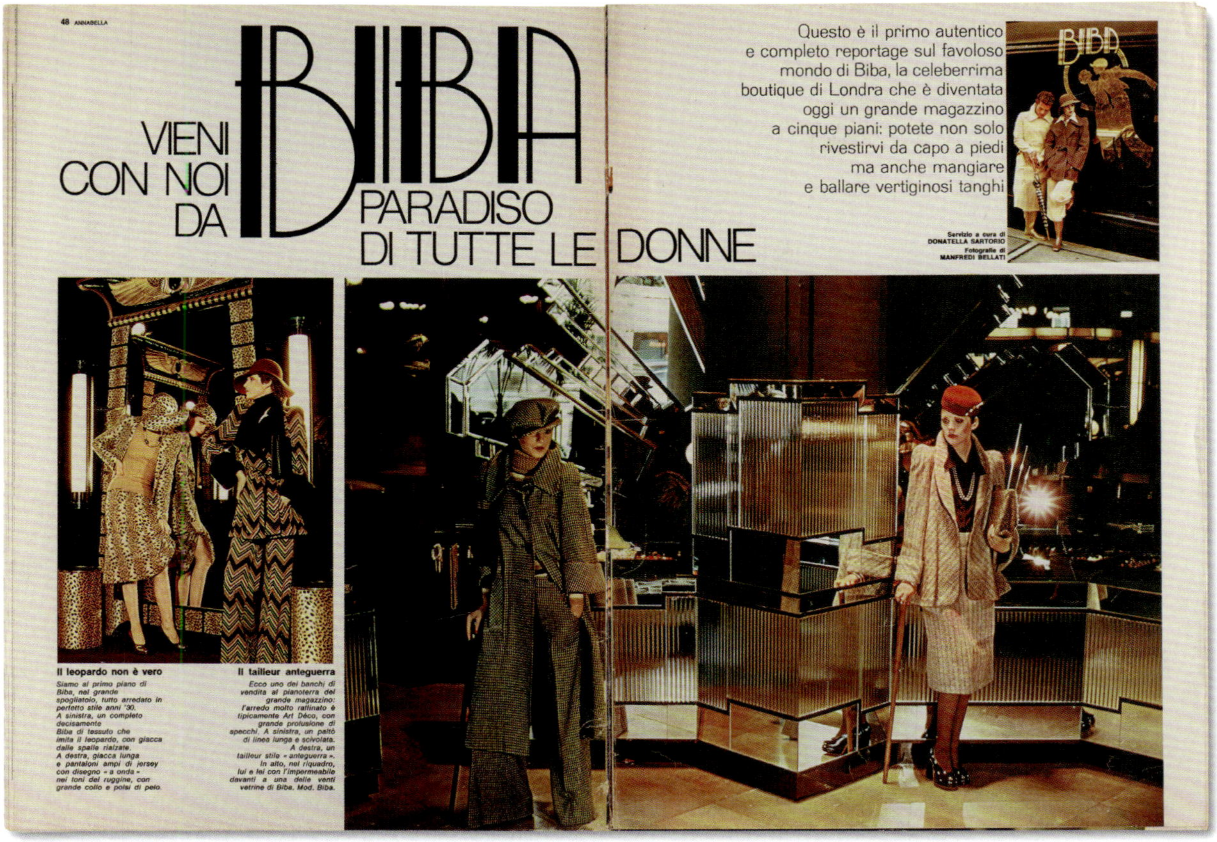

48 ANNABELLA

VIENI CON NOI DA BIBA PARADISO DI TUTTE LE DONNE

Questo è il primo autentico e completo reportage sul favoloso mondo di Biba, la celeberrima boutique di Londra che è diventata oggi un grande magazzino a cinque piani: potete non solo rivestirvi da capo a piedi ma anche mangiare e ballare vertiginosi tanghi

Servizio a cura di DONATELLA SARTORIO
Fotografie di MANFREDI BELLATI

Il leopardo non è vero

Siamo al primo piano di Biba, nel grande spogliatoio, tutto arredato in perfetto stile anni '30. A sinistra, un completo decisamente Biba di tessuto che imita il leopardo, con giacca dalle spalle rialzate. A destra, giacca lunga e pantaloni ampi di jersey con disegno « a onda » nei toni del ruggine, con grande collo e polsi di pelo.

Il tailleur anteguerra

Ecco uno dei banchi di vendita al pianoterra del grande magazzino: l'arredo molto raffinato è tipicamente Art Déco, con grande profusione di specchi. A sinistra, un paltò di linea lunga e scivolata. A destra, un tailleur stile « anteguerra ». In alto, nel riquadro, lui e lei con l'impermeabile davanti a una delle venti vetrine di Biba. Mod. Biba.

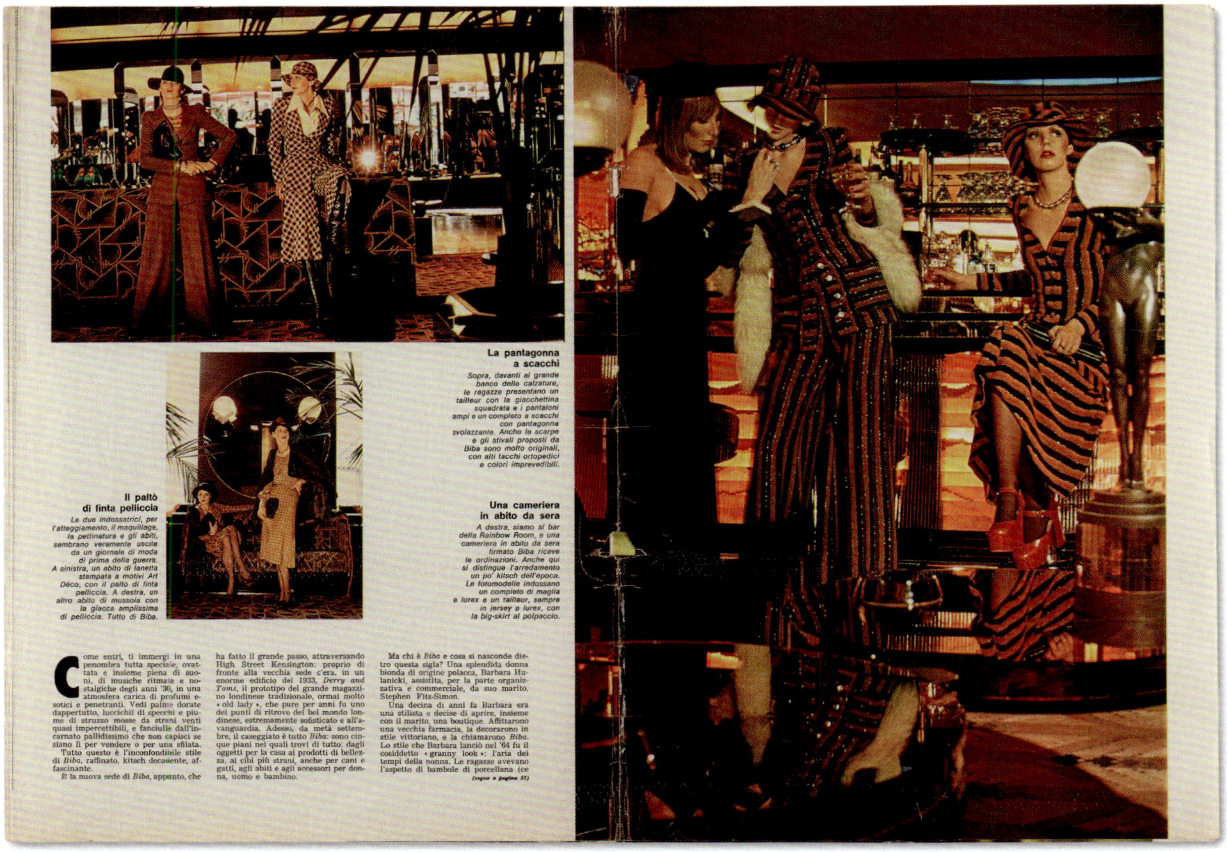

La pantagonna a scacchi

Sopra, davanti al grande banco delle calzature, le ragazze presentano un tailleur con la giacchettina squadrata e i pantaloni ampi e un completo a scacchi con pantagonna svolazzante. Anche le scarpe e gli stivali proposti da Biba sono molto originali, con alti tacchi ortopedici e colori imprevedibili.

Il paltò di finta pelliccia

Le due indossatrici, per l'atteggiamento, il maquillage, la pettinatura e gli abiti, sembrano veramente uscite da un giornale di moda di prima della guerra. A sinistra, un abito di lanetta stampata a motivi Art Déco, con il paltò di finta pelliccia. A destra, un altro abito di mussola con la giacca amplissima di pelliccia. Tutto di Biba.

Una cameriera in abito da sera

A destra, siamo al bar della Rainbow Room, e una cameriera in abito da sera firmato Biba riceve le ordinazioni. Anche qui si distingue l'arredamento un po' kitsch dell'epoca. Le fotomodelle indossano un completo di maglia e lurex e un tailleur, sempre in jersey e lurex, con la big-skirt al polpaccio.

Come entri, ti immergi in una penombra tutta speciale, ovattata e insieme piena di suoni, di musiche ritmate e nostalgiche degli anni '30, in una atmosfera carica di profumi esotici e penetranti. Vedi palme dorate dappertutto, luccichii di specchi e piume di struzzo mosse da strani venti quasi impercettibili, e fanciulle dall'incarnato pallidissimo che non capisci se siano lì per vendere o per una sfilata.

Tutto questo è l'inconfondibile stile di *Biba*, raffinato, kitsch decadente, affascinante.

È la nuova sede di *Biba*, appunto, che ha fatto il grande passo, attraversando High Street Kensington: proprio di fronte alla vecchia sede c'era, in un enorme edificio del 1933, *Derry and Toms*, il prototipo del grande magazzino londinese tradizionale, ormai molto « old lady », che pure per anni fu uno dei punti di ritrovo del bel mondo londinese, estremamente sofisticato e all'avanguardia. Adesso, da metà settembre, il caseggiato è tutto *Biba*: sono cinque piani nei quali trovi di tutto: dagli oggetti per la casa ai prodotti di bellezza, ai cibi più strani, anche per cani e gatti, agli abiti e agli accessori per donna, uomo e bambino.

Ma chi è *Biba* e cosa si nasconde dietro questa sigla? Una splendida donna bionda di origine polacca, Barbara Hulanicki, assistita, per la parte organizzativa e commerciale, da suo marito, Stephen Fitz-Simon.

Una decina di anni fa Barbara era una stilista e decise di aprire, insieme con il marito, una boutique. Affittarono una vecchia farmacia, la decorarono in stile vittoriano, e la chiamarono *Biba*. Lo stile che Barbara lanciò nel '64 fu il cosiddetto « granny look »: l'aria dei tempi della nonna. Le ragazze avevano l'aspetto di bambole di porcellana (ce

(segue a pagina 51)

Fashion story shot in Big Biba for Italian magazine *Annabella*, 19 January 1974

SOPHIE PARKIN

~

DAUGHTER OF BIBA HAT DESIGNER MOLLY PARKIN

Barbara and Biba played as much a part in my childhood education as school. It was elevating going to each of her shops, right through to the extravaganza of the building that had been Derry & Toms on Kensington High Street. For my generation, Big Biba was a place at which to worship. The building itself fulfilled our fantasies of glamour as much as its contents. It was Barbara's attention to detail that made shopping at Biba different to shopping anywhere else; it was from top to toe, and not just your hat to your shoes, but a lifestyle. Who else had thought to call a lingerie department 'The Mistress Room'? It was surreal, live flamingos and giant flower sculptures by artist Andrew Logan adorned the roof garden. Wild, Bill Hailey, The Pointer Sisters, Ian Drury and the New York Dolls, I saw them all perform in the Rainbow Room of Big Biba. Humorous, a Great Dane display of their dog for dog food. It had the pizazz of excitement, enchanting us all – we longed to live there. More, Barbara designed clothes that made everyone feel like a film or rock star, for the price of a shop girl's wallet. She brought fashion to the masses. She gave Britain style and a new colour palette, not only for clothes but for shoes, accessories and make-up (purple lipstick) as well. You cannot underestimate what she did for this country's reputation abroad. Before Barbara, we were the worst-dressed people in Europe; after, we were what Europe craved. Mary Quant might have invented the miniskirt, but Barbara invented the vampy Biba girl, who felt more beautiful and more powerful than any dolly bird!

Anyone who was there could testify to the above, but Barbara and her family were much closer to us. My mother – Molly Parkin – started making matching hats and bags for Biba, along with her friend Maurice (a dresser from the Royal Court theatre) in 1964. Barbara pounced on Mum after she had seen her in the Abingdon Road shop wearing a dark velvet hat made by Maurice. Our front room turned into a sewing factory, and that hat became known as the 'Molly hat'. A year later, Mum's projection into the world of fashion journalism started with *Nova* magazine and ended with *The Sunday Times* and featured Biba continually. Mum and Barbara were creative, hard-working soulmates who loved to laugh. The book launch for mum's first novel was at Biba. I chose my eight-year-old bridesmaid outfit for my Mum's wedding – black satin Goth – from Biba. All my clothes came from Biba. I still wear the fake leopard midi skirt and coat that Barbara designed for Mum in the 1960s. Worn but timeless. Later, when Mum launched her stage career of one-woman raconteur shows, Barbara, back from Brazil, designed all her costumes of balloon-sleeved gowns in glittering whites and striped metallics. It was pure glamour.

Barbara designed clothes that made everyone feel like a film or rock star, for the price of a shop girl's wallet

Both Barbara and Mum were brought up on a diet of movies in post-war Britain, which fed their childhood fantasies of all the lives that could be lived, and they channelled that into their beings.

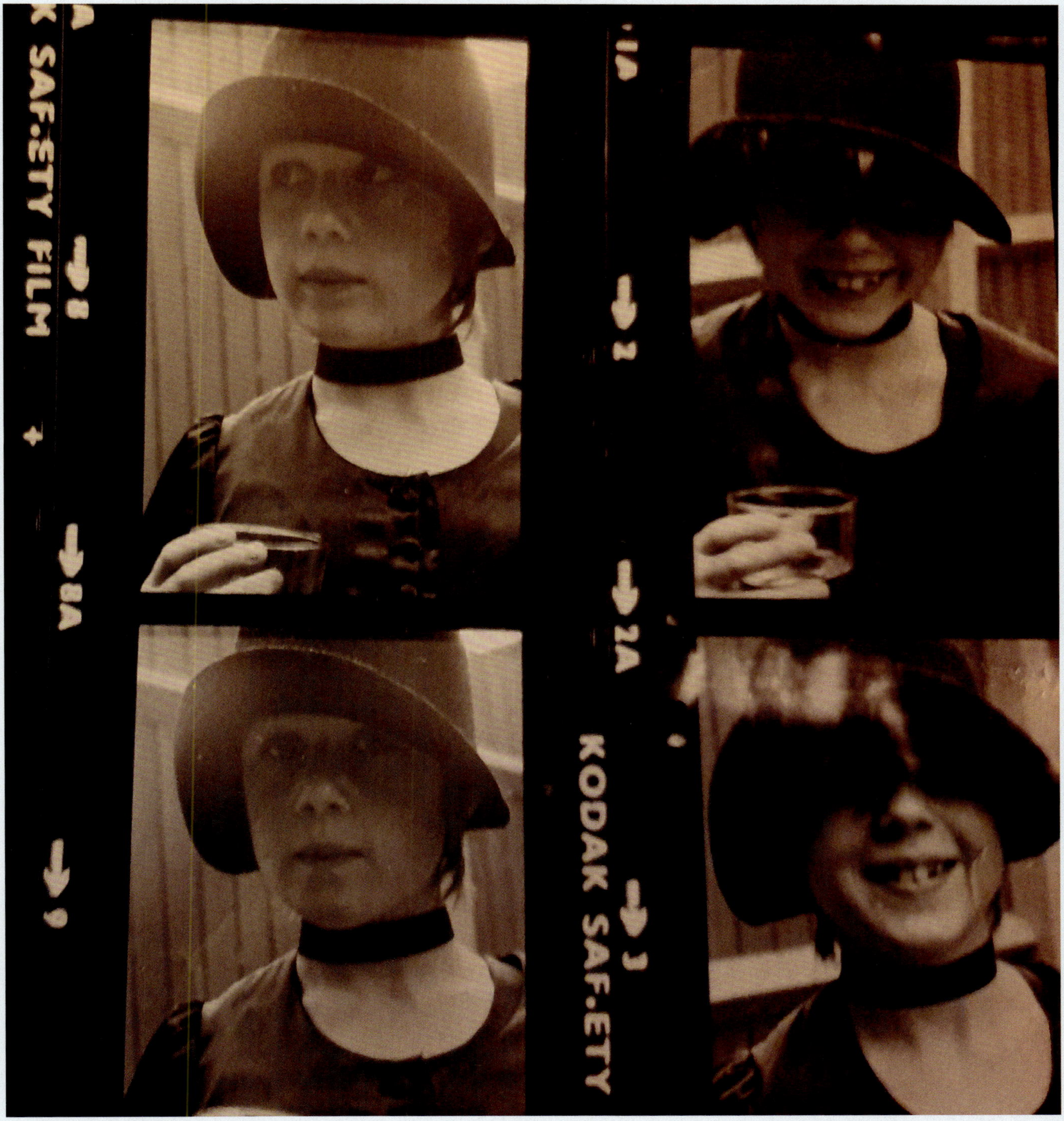

Sophie Parkin in her Biba outfit, worn as a bridesmaid for her mother's wedding, photographed by John Timbers, 1969

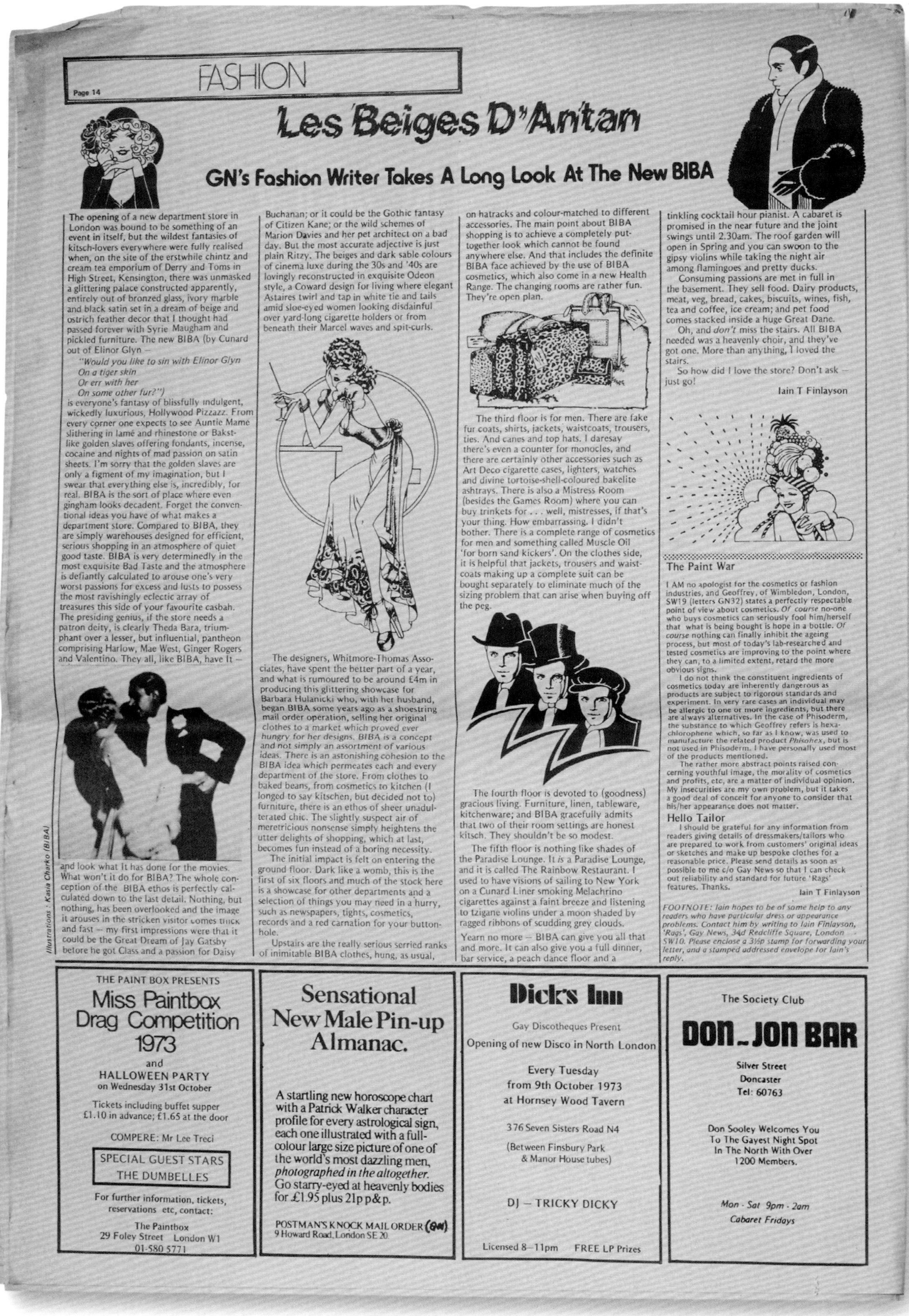

FASHION

Page 14

Les Beiges D'Antan

GN's Fashion Writer Takes A Long Look At The New BIBA

The opening of a new department store in London was bound to be something of an event in itself, but the wildest fantasies of kitsch-lovers everywhere were fully realised when, on the site of the erstwhile chintz and cream tea emporium of Derry and Toms in High Street, Kensington, there was unmasked a glittering palace constructed apparently, entirely out of bronzed glass, ivory marble and black satin set in a dream of beige and ostrich feather decor that I thought had passed forever with Syrie Maugham and pickled furniture. The new BIBA (by Cunard out of Elinor Glyn –

"Would you like to sin with Elinor Glyn
On a tiger skin
Or err with her
On some other fur?")

is everyone's fantasy of blissfully indulgent, wickedly luxurious, Hollywood Pizzazz. From every corner one expects to see Auntie Mame slithering in lamé and rhinestone or Bakst-like golden slaves offering fondants, incense, cocaine and nights of mad passion on satin sheets. I'm sorry that the golden slaves are only a figment of my imagination, but I swear that everything else is, incredibly, for real. BIBA is the sort of place where even gingham looks decadent. Forget the conventional ideas you have of what makes a department store. Compared to BIBA, they are simply warehouses designed for efficient, serious shopping in an atmosphere of quiet good taste. BIBA is very determinedly in the most exquisite Bad Taste and the atmosphere is defiantly calculated to arouse one's very worst passions for excess and lusts to possess the most ravishingly eclectic array of treasures this side of your favourite casbah. The presiding genius, if the store needs a patron deity, is clearly Theda Bara, triumphant over a lesser, but influential, pantheon comprising Harlow, Mae West, Ginger Rogers and Valentino. They all, like BIBA, have It – and look what It has done for the movies. What won't it do for BIBA? The whole conception of the BIBA ethos is perfectly calculated down to the last detail. Nothing, but nothing, has been overlooked and the image it arouses in the stricken visitor comes thick and fast – my first impressions were that it could be the Great Dream of Jay Gatsby before he got Class and a passion for Daisy Buchanan; or it could be the Gothic fantasy of Citizen Kane; or the wild schemes of Marion Davies and her pet architect on a bad day. But the most accurate adjective is just plain Ritzy. The beiges and dark sable colours of cinema luxe during the 30s and '40s are lovingly reconstructed in exquisite Odeon style, a Coward design for living where elegant Astaires twirl and tap in white tie and tails amid sloe-eyed women looking disdainful over yard-long cigarette holders or from beneath their Marcel waves and spit-curls.

Illustrations: Kasia Charko (BIBA)

The designers, Whitmore-Thomas Associates, have spent the better part of a year, and what is rumoured to be around £4m in producing this glittering showcase for Barbara Hulanicki who, with her husband, began BIBA some years ago as a shoestring mail order operation, selling her original clothes to a market which proved ever hungry for her designs. BIBA is a concept and not simply an assortment of various ideas. There is an astonishing cohesion to the BIBA idea which permeates each and every department of the store. From clothes to baked beans, from cosmetics to kitchen (I longed to say kitschen, but decided not to) furniture, there is an ethos of sheer unadulterated chic. The slightly suspect air of meretricious nonsense simply heightens the utter delights of shopping, which at last, becomes fun instead of a boring necessity.

The initial impact is felt on entering the ground floor. Dark like a womb, this is the first of six floors and much of the stock here is a showcase for other departments and a selection of things you may need in a hurry, such as newspapers, tights, cosmetics, records and a red carnation for your buttonhole.

Upstairs are the really serious serried ranks of inimitable BIBA clothes, hung, as usual, on hatracks and colour-matched to different accessories. The main point about BIBA shopping is to achieve a completely put-together look which cannot be found anywhere else. And that includes the definite BIBA face achieved by the use of BIBA cosmetics, which also come in a new Health Range. The changing rooms are rather fun. They're open plan.

The third floor is for men. There are fake fur coats, shirts, jackets, waistcoats, trousers, ties. And canes and top hats. I daresay there's even a counter for monocles, and there are certainly other accessories such as Art Deco cigarette cases, lighters, watches and divine tortoise-shell-coloured bakelite ashtrays. There is also a Mistress Room (besides the Games Room) where you can buy trinkets for . . . well, mistresses, if that's your thing. How embarrassing. I didn't bother. There is a complete range of cosmetics for men and something called Muscle Oil 'for born sand kickers'. On the clothes side, it is helpful that jackets, trousers and waistcoats making up a complete suit can be bought separately to eliminate much of the sizing problem that can arise when buying off the peg.

The fourth floor is devoted to (goodness) gracious living. Furniture, linen, tableware, kitchenware; and BIBA gracefully admits that two of their room settings are honest kitsch. They shouldn't be so modest.

The fifth floor is nothing like shades of the Paradise Lounge. It *is* a Paradise Lounge, and it is called The Rainbow Restaurant. I used to have visions of sailing to New York on a Cunard Liner smoking Melachrino cigarettes against a faint breeze and listening to tzigane violins under a moon shaded by ragged ribbons of scudding grey clouds.

Yearn no more – BIBA can give you all that and more. It can also give you a full dinner, bar service, a peach dance floor and a tinkling cocktail hour pianist. A cabaret is promised in the near future and the joint swings until 2.30am. The roof garden will open in Spring and you can swoon to the gipsy violins while taking the night air among flamingoes and pretty ducks.

Consuming passions are met in full in the basement. They sell food. Dairy products, meat, veg, bread, cakes, biscuits, wines, fish, tea and coffee, ice cream; and pet food comes stacked inside a huge Great Dane.

Oh, and *don't* miss the stairs. All BIBA needed was a heavenly choir, and they've got one. More than anything, I loved the stairs.

So how did I love the store? Don't ask – just go!

Iain T Finlayson

The Paint War

I AM no apologist for the cosmetics or fashion industries, and Geoffrey, of Wimbledon, London, SW19 (letters GN32) states a perfectly respectable point of view about cosmetics. *Of course* no-one who buys cosmetics can seriously fool him/herself that what is being bought is hope in a bottle. *Of course* nothing can finally inhibit the ageing process, but most of today's lab-researched and tested cosmetics are improving to the point where they can, to a limited extent, retard the more obvious signs.

I do not think the constituent ingredients of cosmetics today are inherently dangerous as products are subject to rigorous standards and experiment. In very rare cases an individual may be allergic to one or more ingredients, but there are always alternatives. In the case of Phisoderm, the substance to which Geoffrey refers is hexachlorophene which, so far as I know, was used to manufacture the related product *Phisohex*, but is not used in Phisoderm. I have personally used most of the products mentioned.

The rather more abstract points raised concerning youthful image, the morality of cosmetics and profits, etc, are a matter of individual opinion. My insecurities are my own problem, but it takes a good deal of conceit for anyone to consider that his/her appearance does not matter.

Hello Tailor

I should be grateful for any information from readers giving details of dressmakers/tailors who are prepared to work from customers' original ideas or sketches and make up bespoke clothes for a reasonable price. Please send details as soon as possible to me c/o Gay News so that I can check out reliability and standard for future 'Rags' features. Thanks.

Iain T Finlayson

FOOTNOTE: Iain hopes to be of some help to any readers who have particular dress or appearance problems. Contact him by writing to Iain Finlayson, 'Rags', Gay News, 34d Redcliffe Square, London SW10. Please enclose a 3½p stamp for forwarding your letter, and a stamped addressed envelope for Iain's reply.

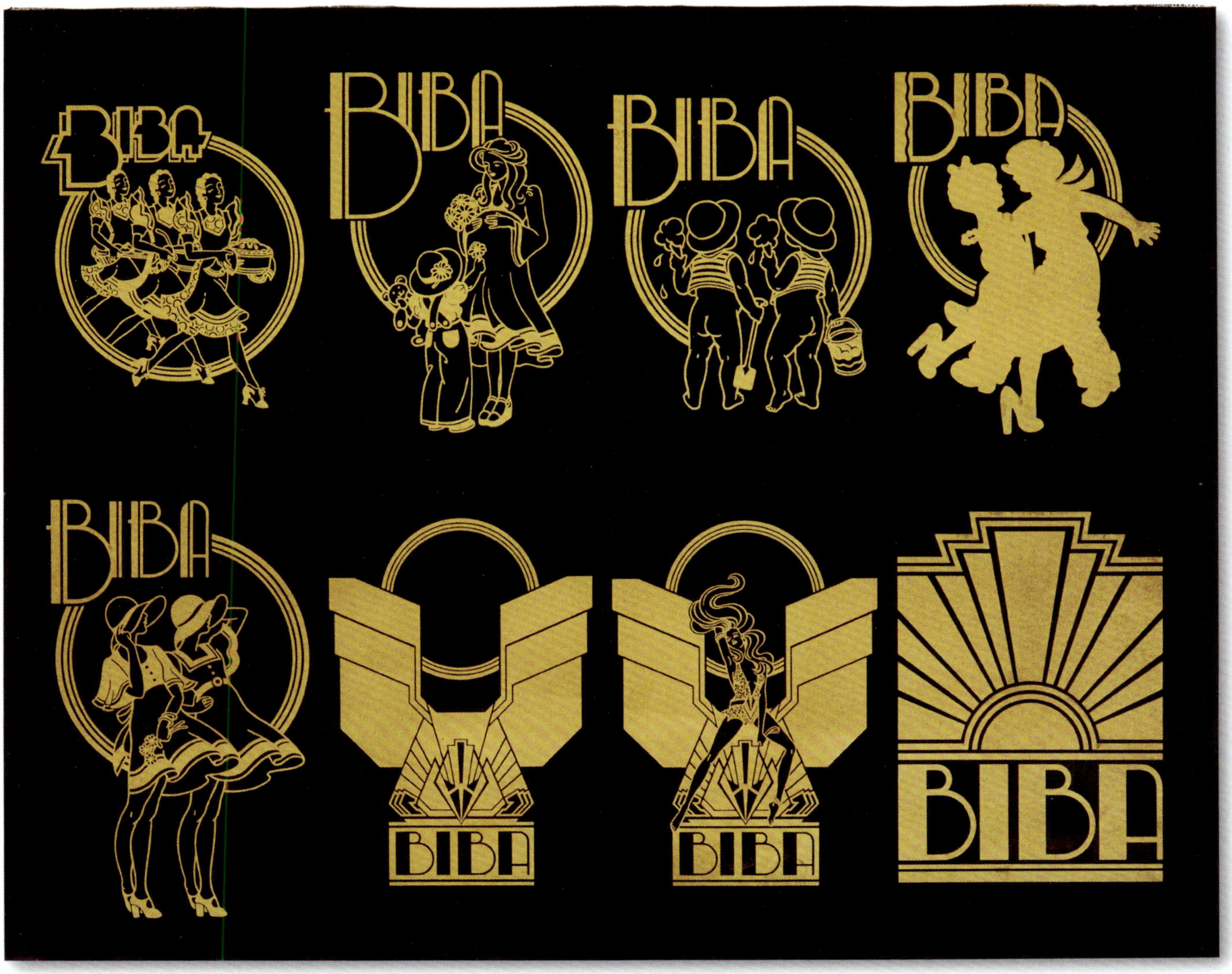

OPPOSITE Review of the opening of Big Biba, *Gay News*, October 1973

ABOVE Poster of eight logos for Big Biba departments, Whitmore-Thomas, 1973

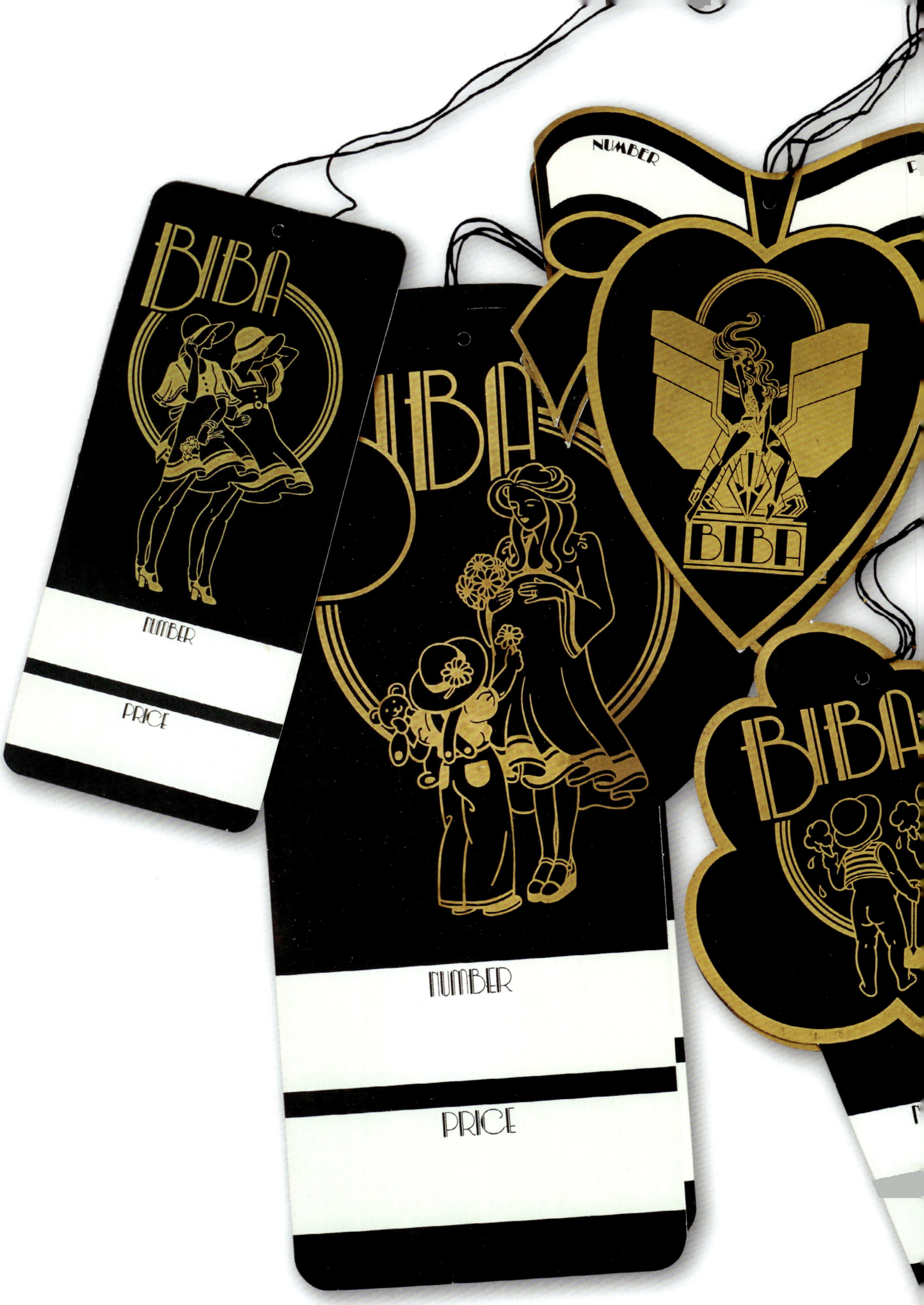
BIBA
NUMBER
PRICE
BIBA
NUMBER
PRICE
NUMBER
BIBA
BIBA

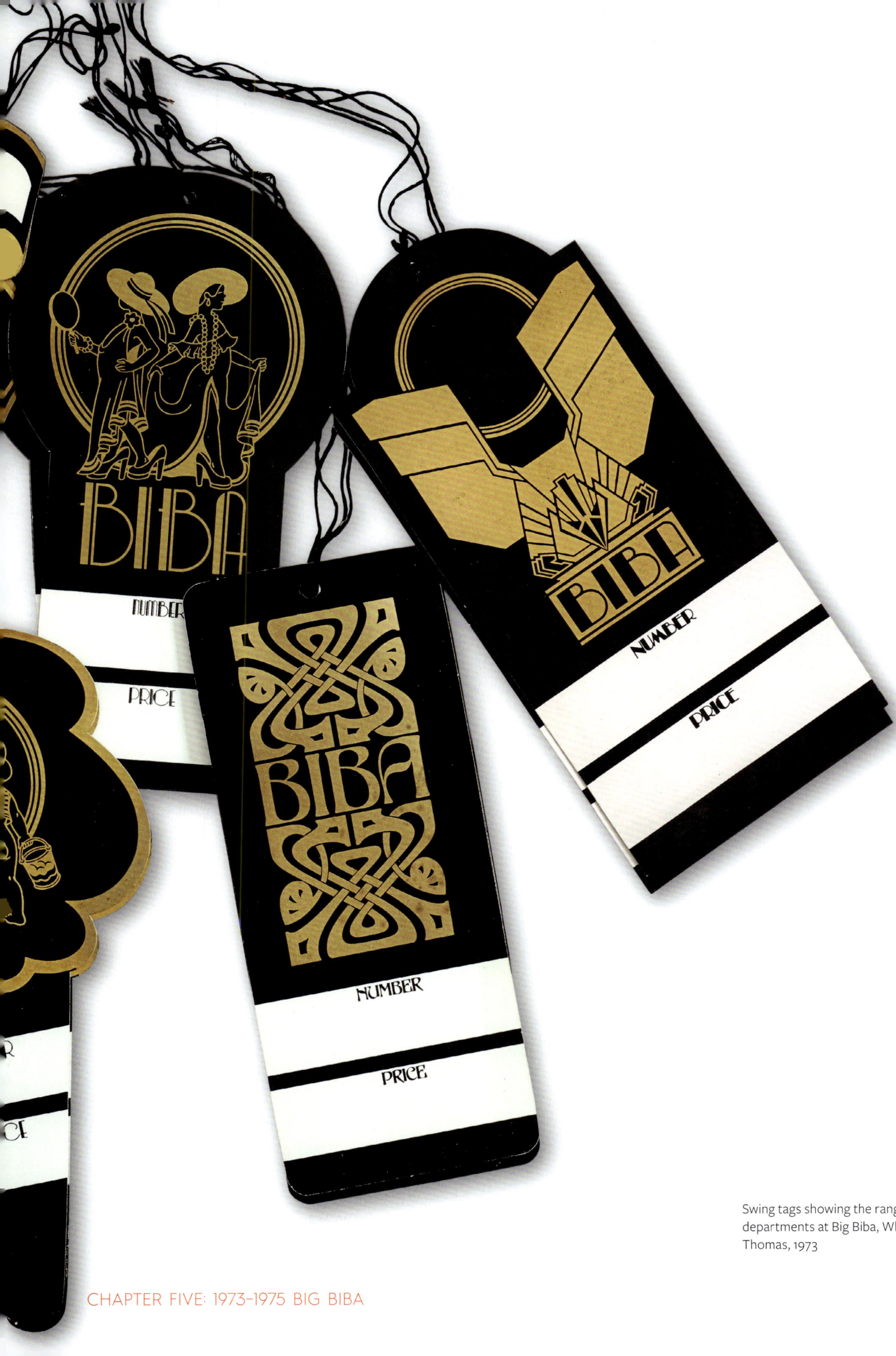

Swing tags showing the range of different departments at Big Biba, Whitmore-Thomas, 1973

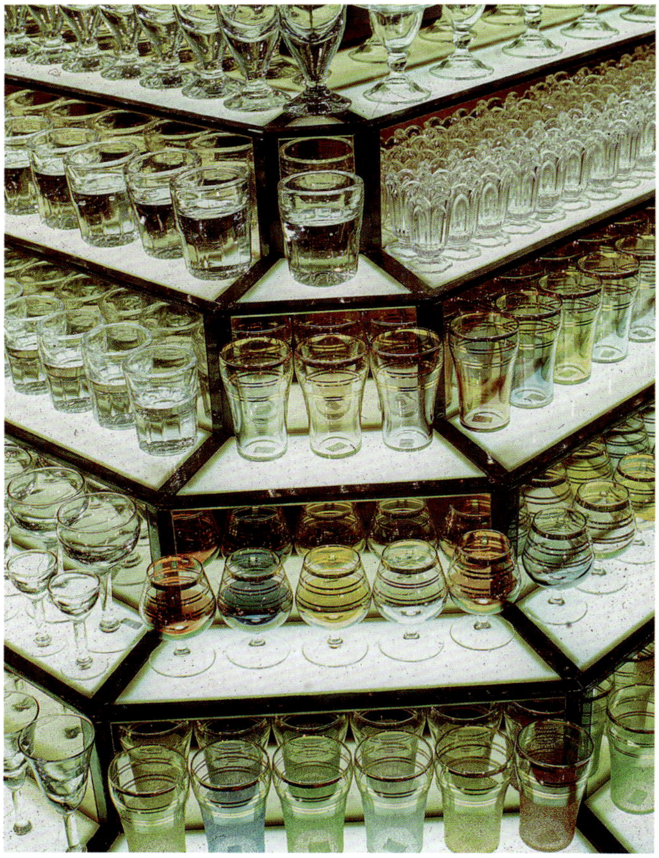

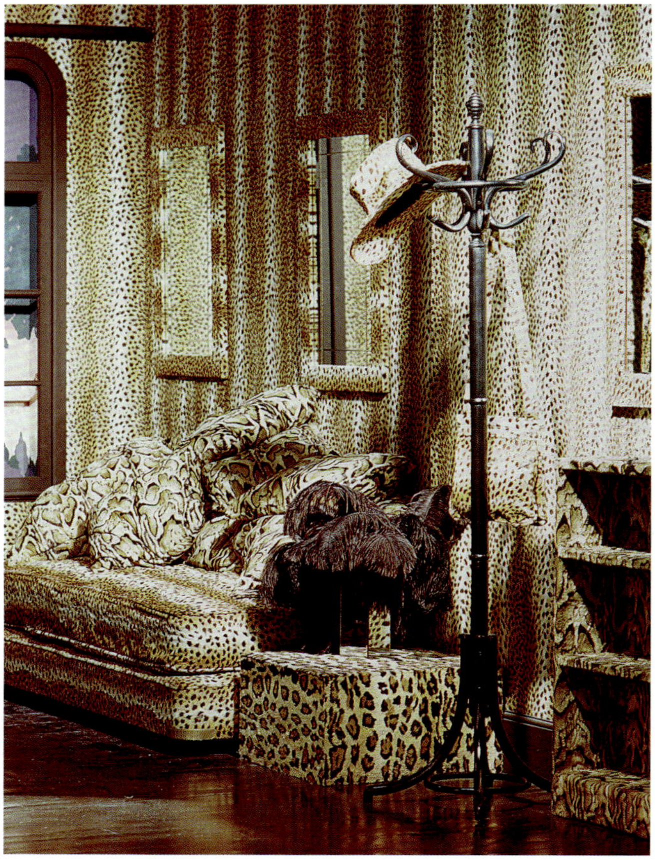

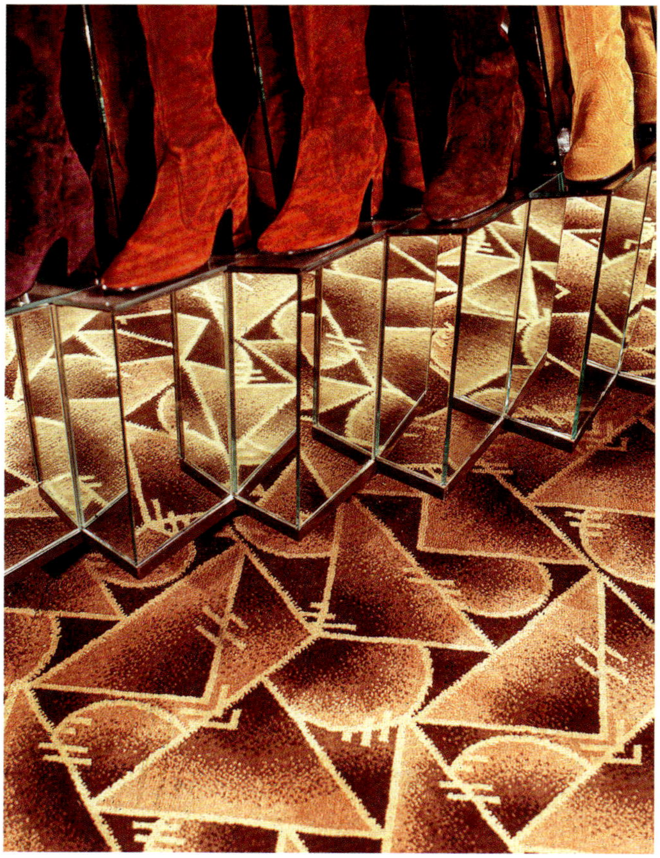

ABOVE, LEFT & OPPOSITE Detail shots of various departments at Big Biba, including the food hall, household and footwear, 1973

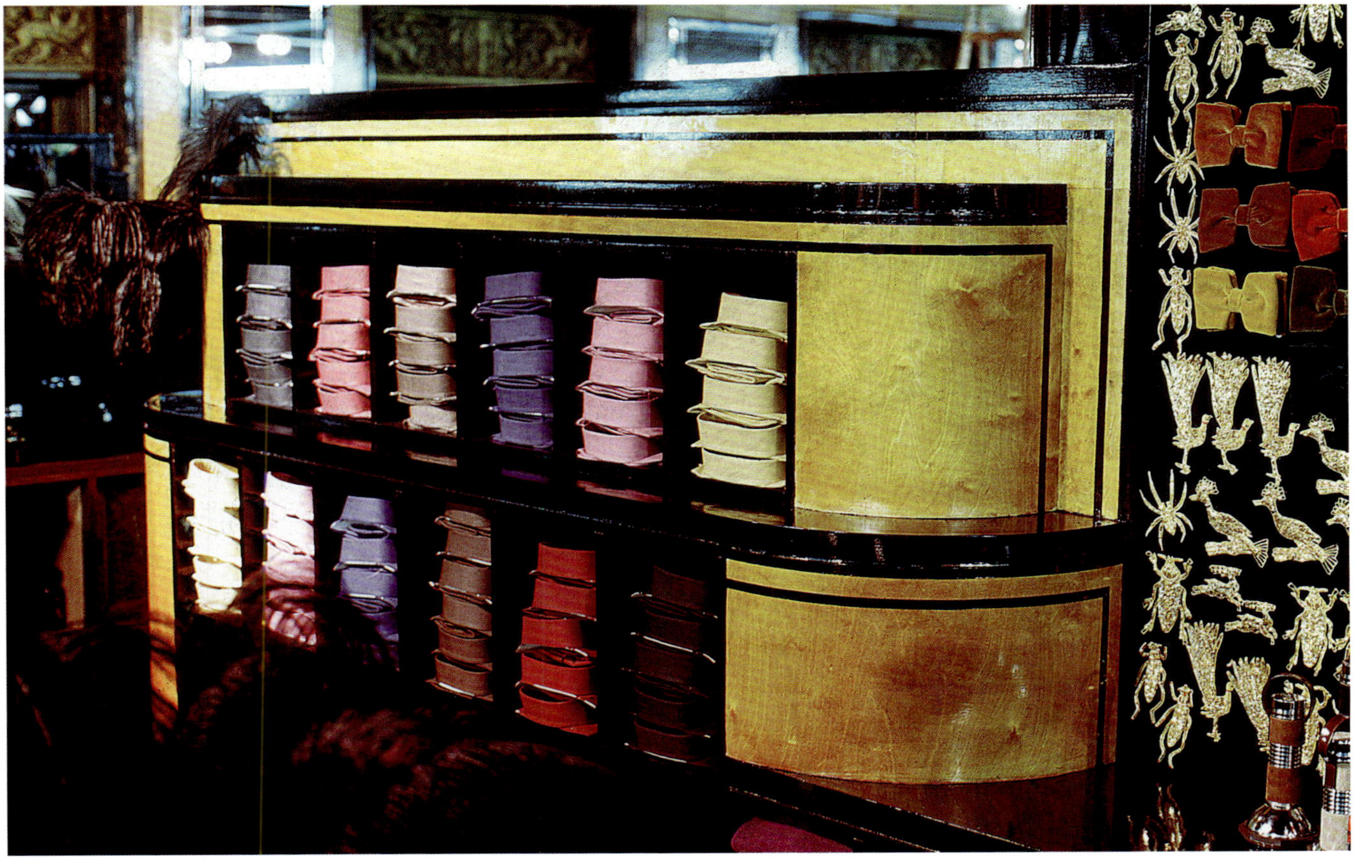

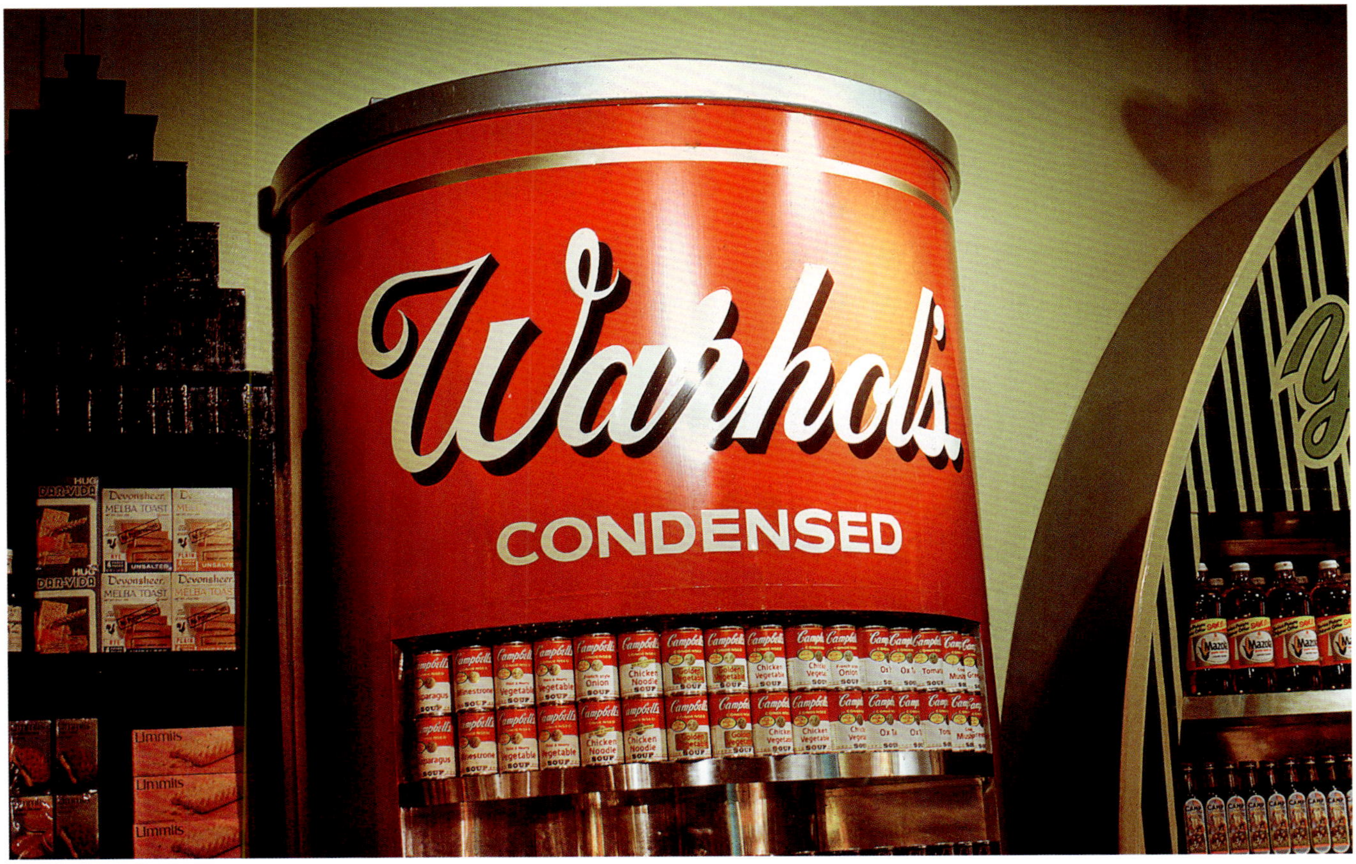
Warhol's
CONDENSED

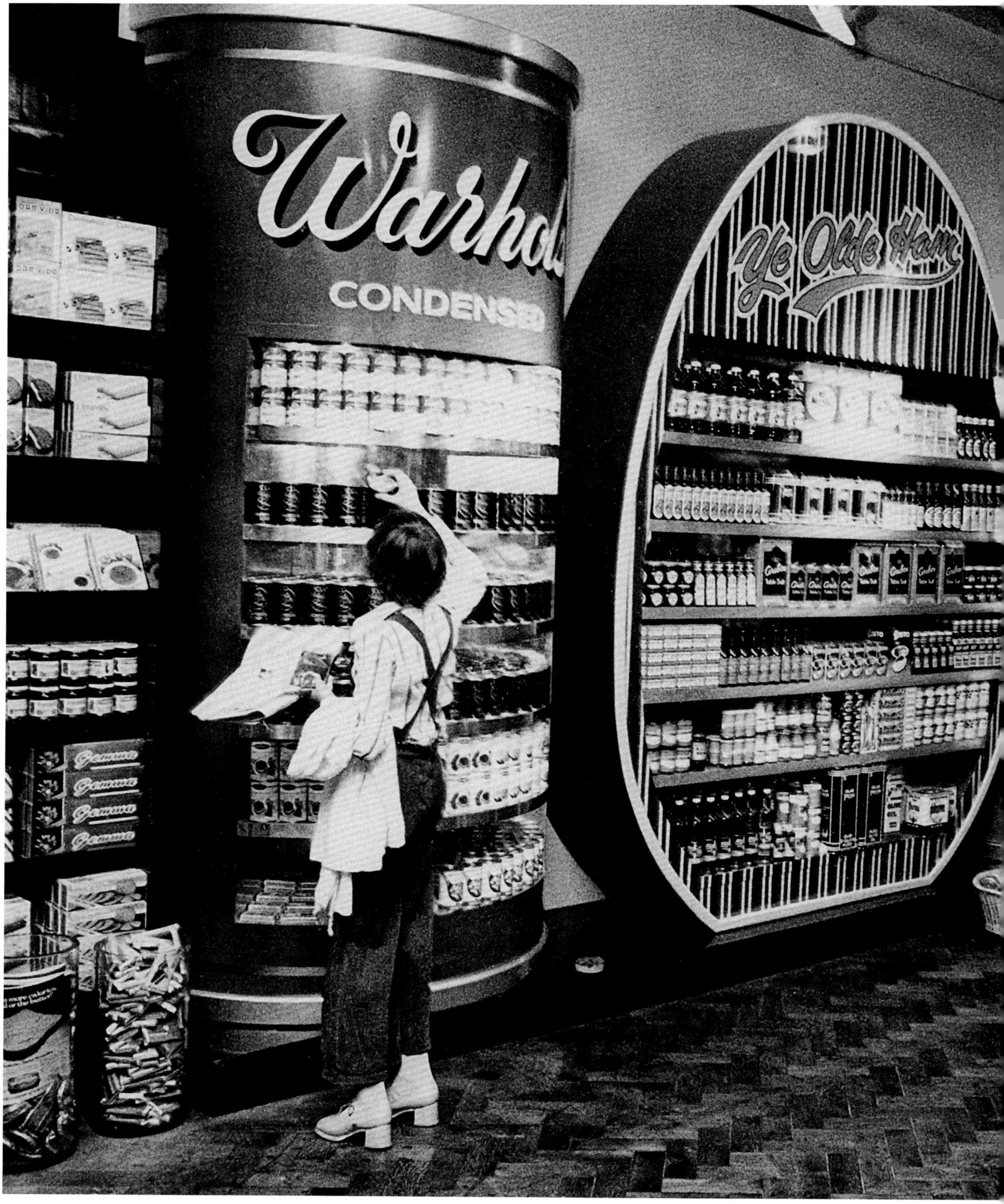
Warhol
CONDENSED
Ye Olde Ham

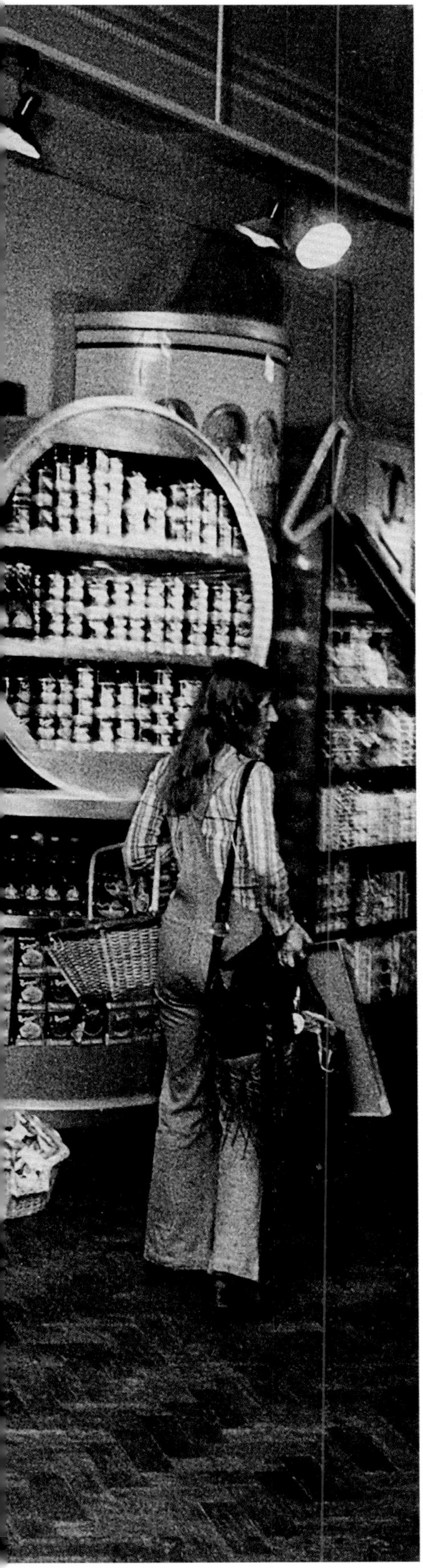

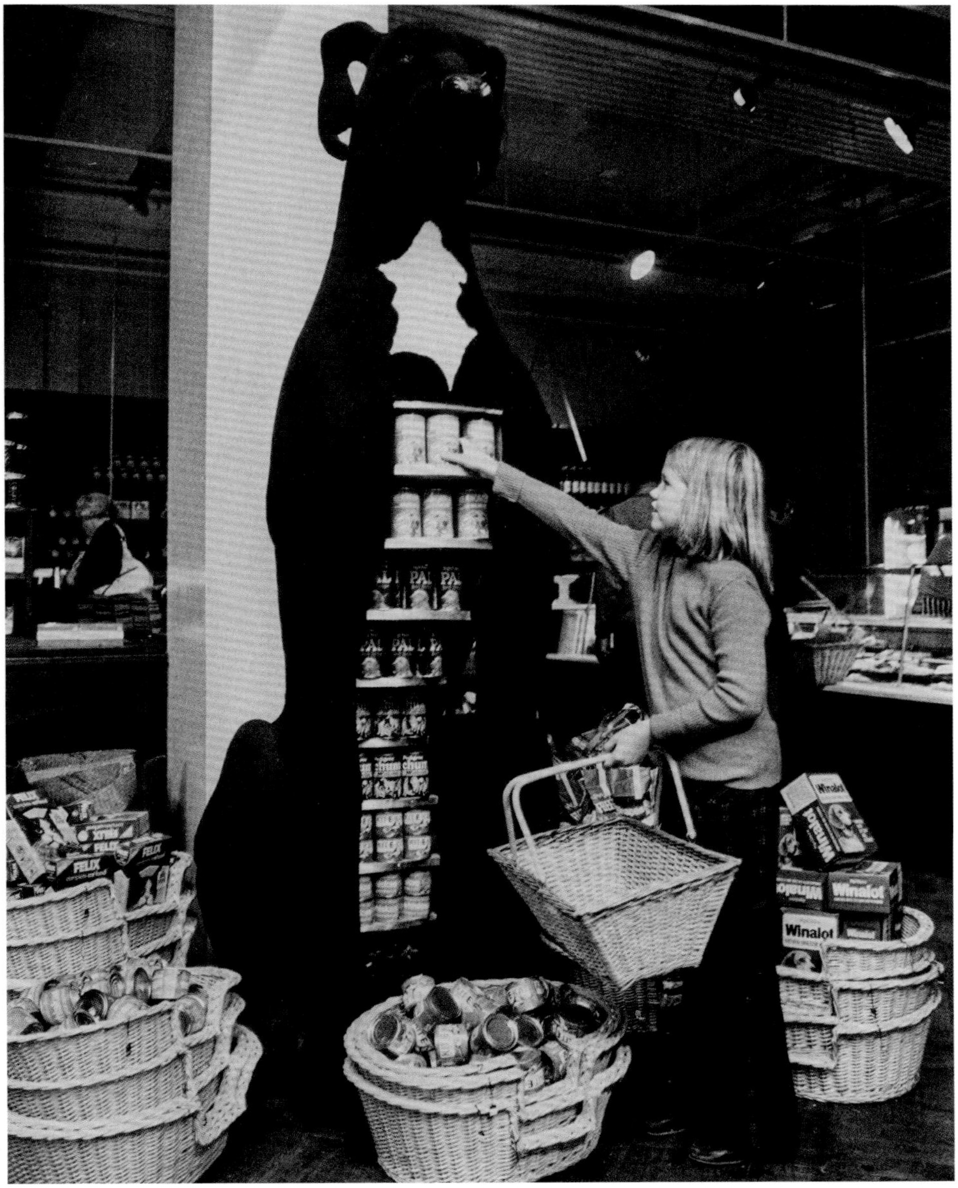

ABOVE Big Biba tinned dog food display stand, modelled on the Fitz-Simons' pet dog Othello, c.1973

LEFT Big Biba food hall with Pop Art-inspired display units of oversized food cans, c.1973

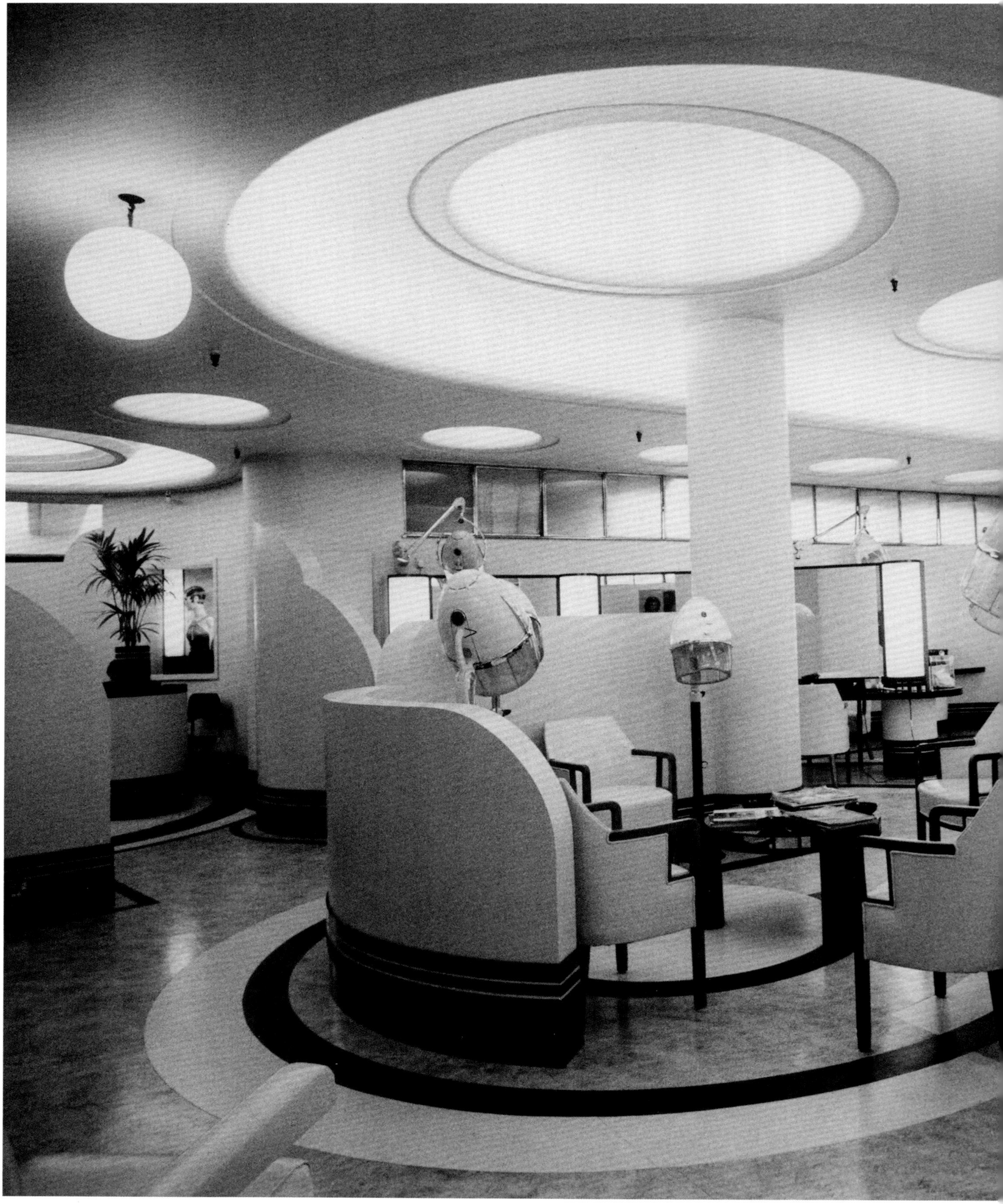

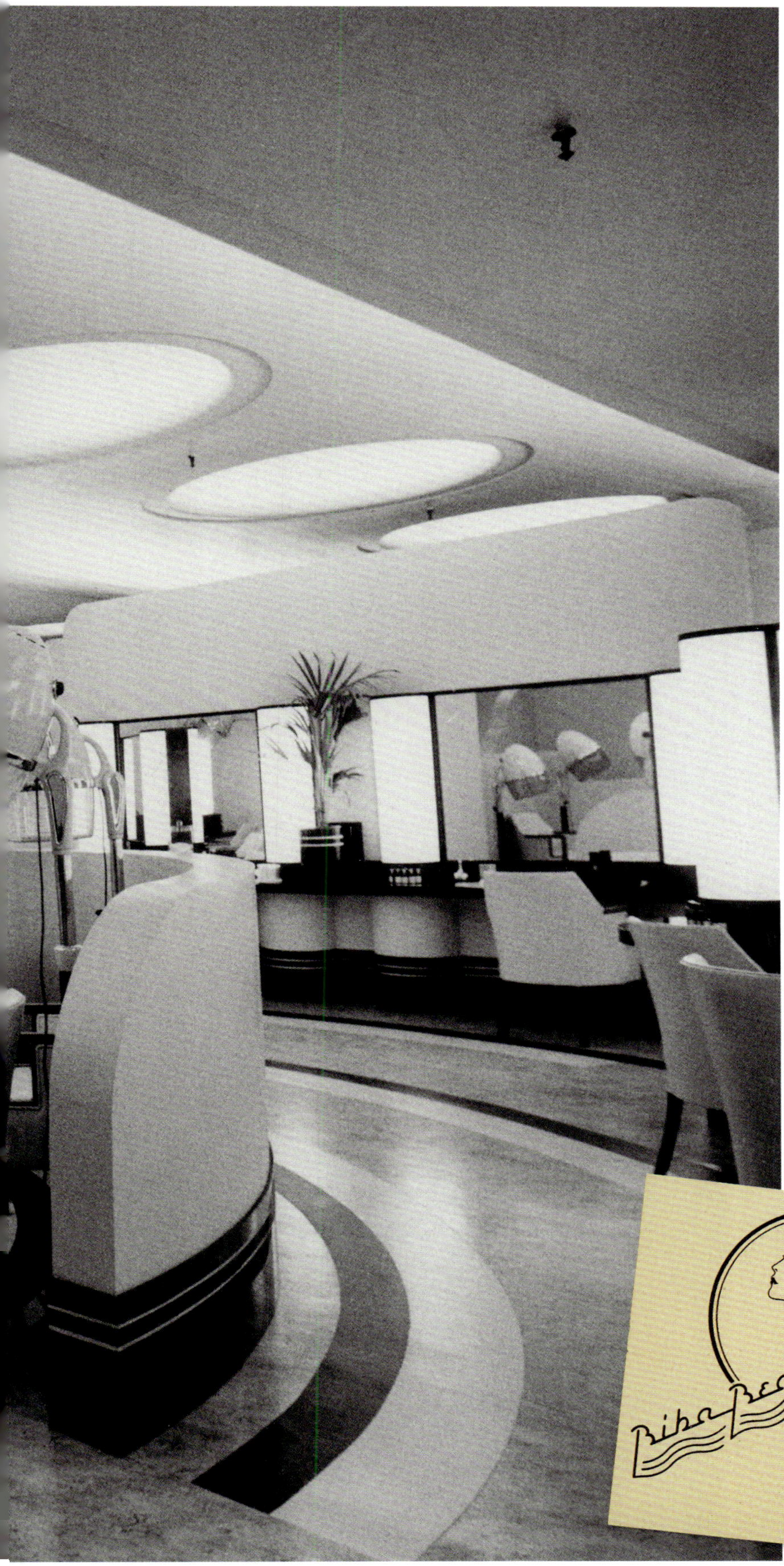

LEFT Big Biba beauty parlour, which opened in 1974 and was located on the third floor, 1974

BELOW Ephemera from the Biba beauty parlour, which was run by in-house *visagiste* Régis Huet

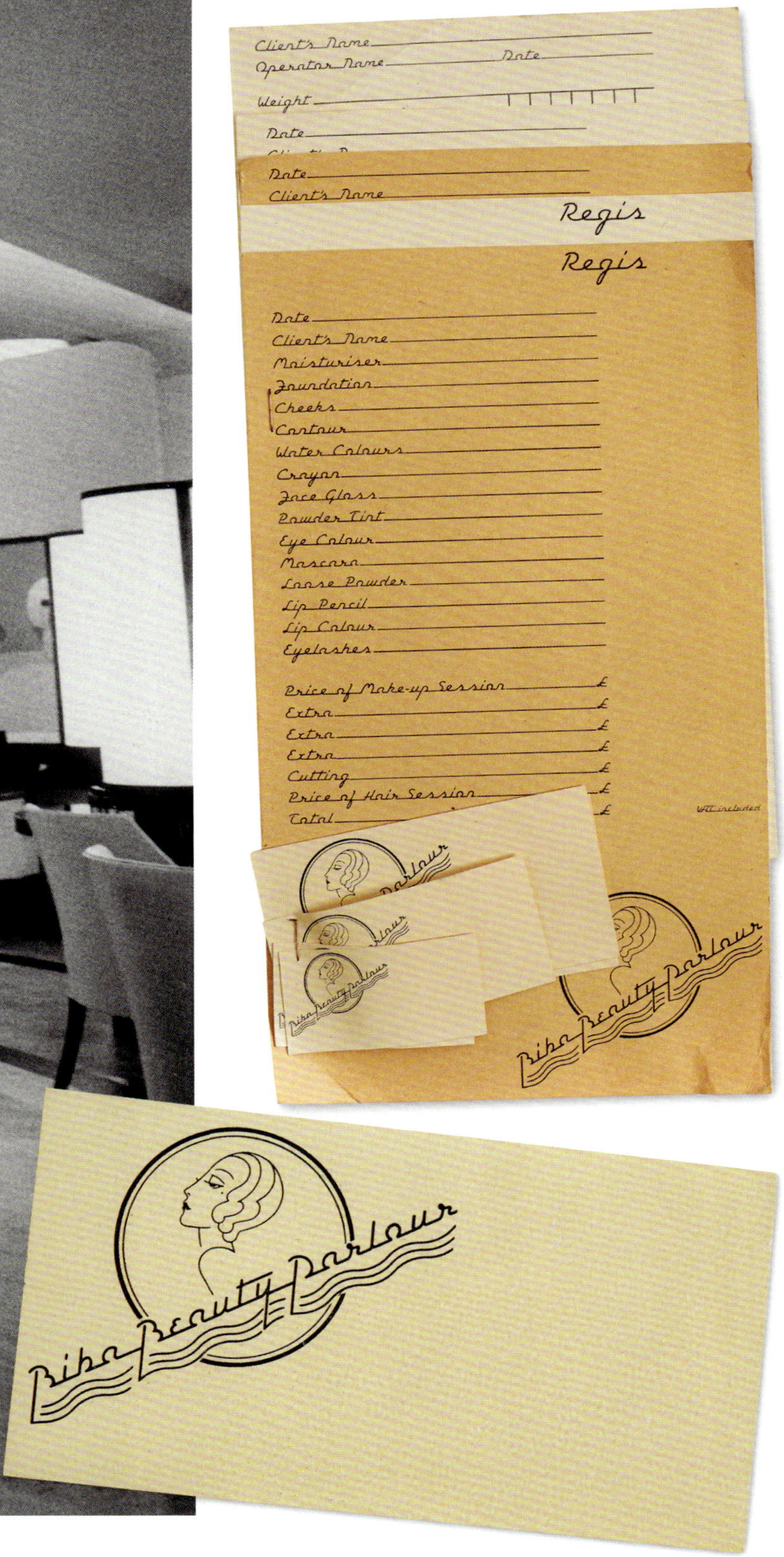

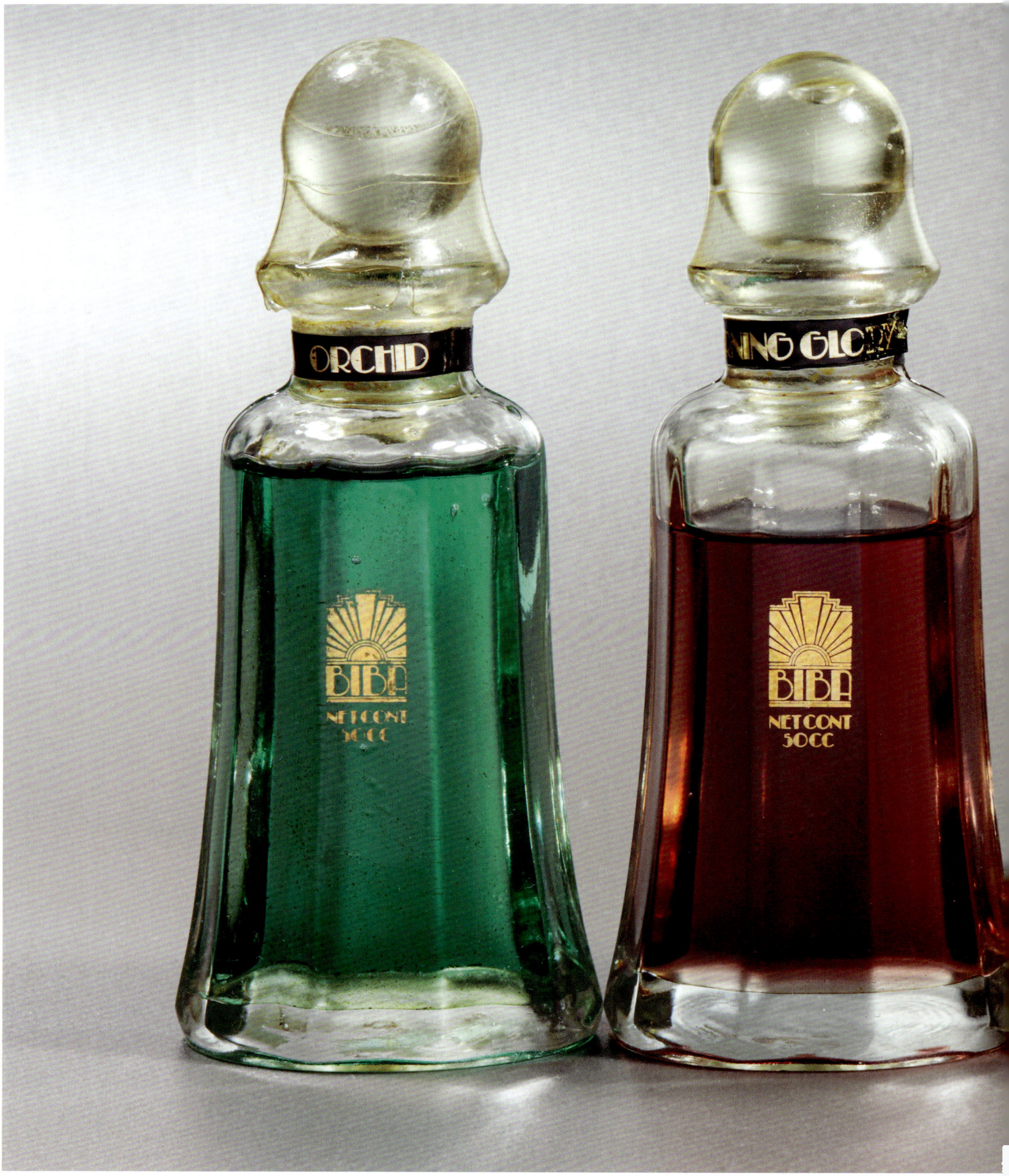

Biba women's scents, 1975

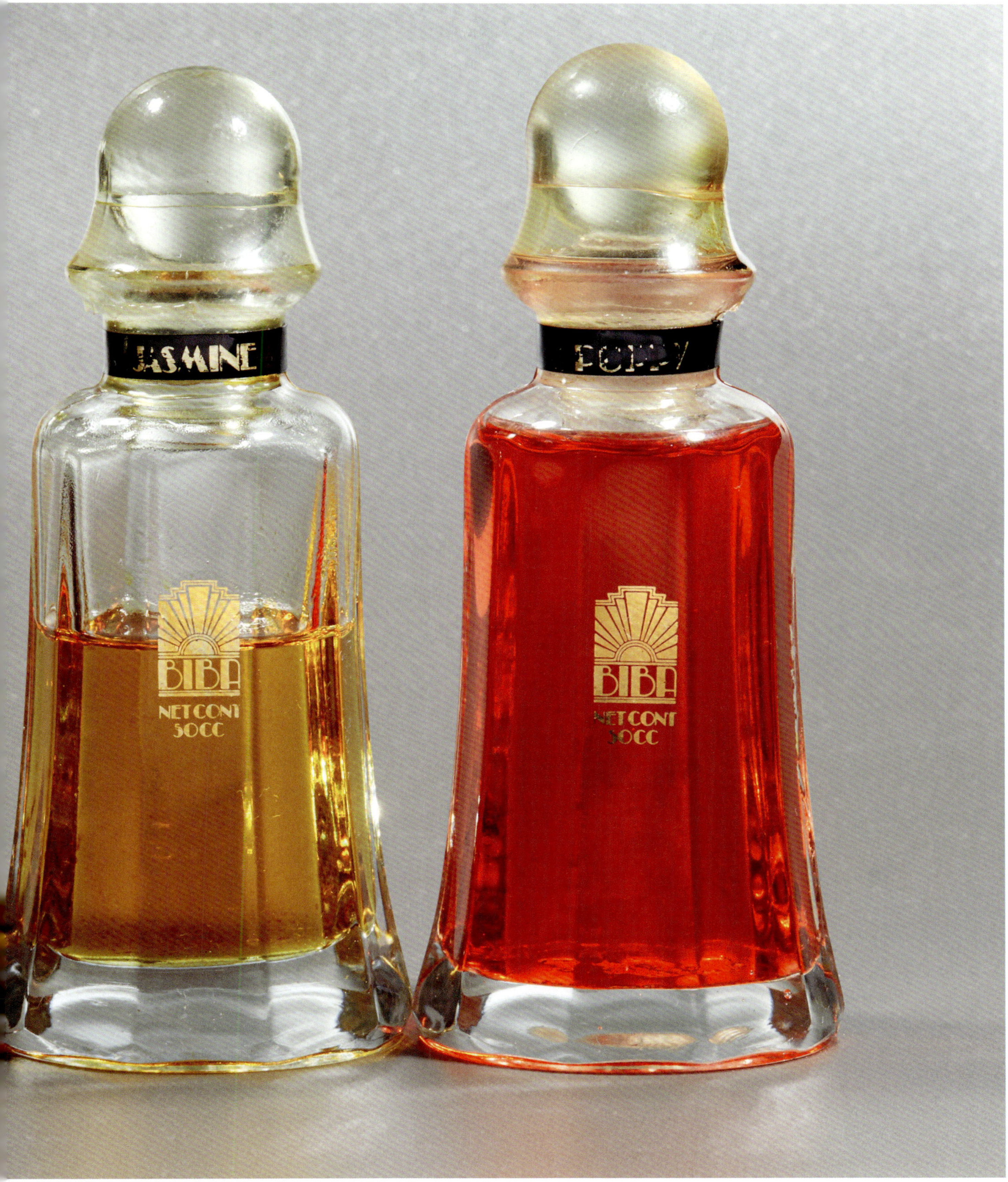
JASMINE
BIBA
NET CONT
50CC
BIBA
NET CONT
50CC

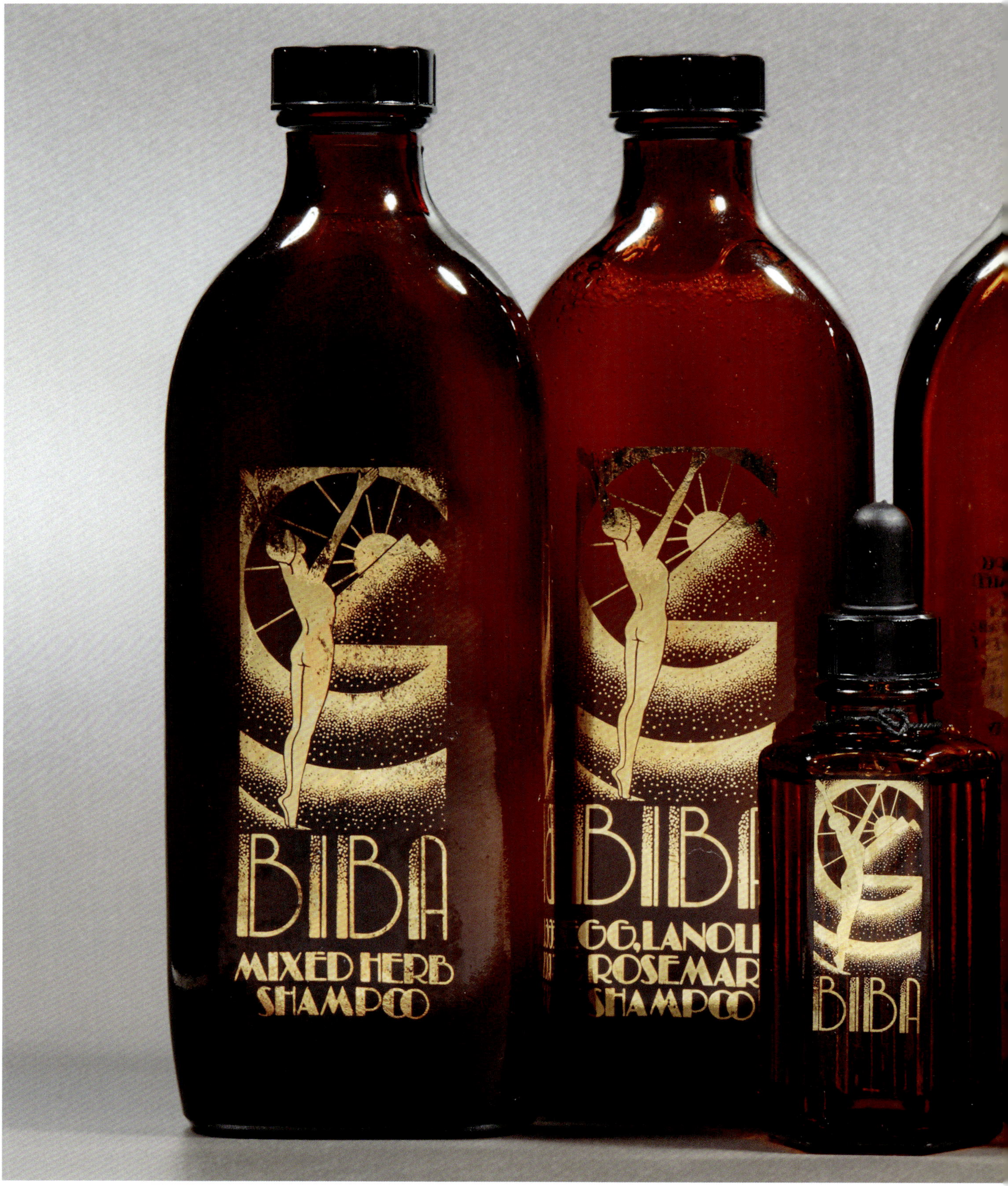

Biba shampoo and toiletries, 1974

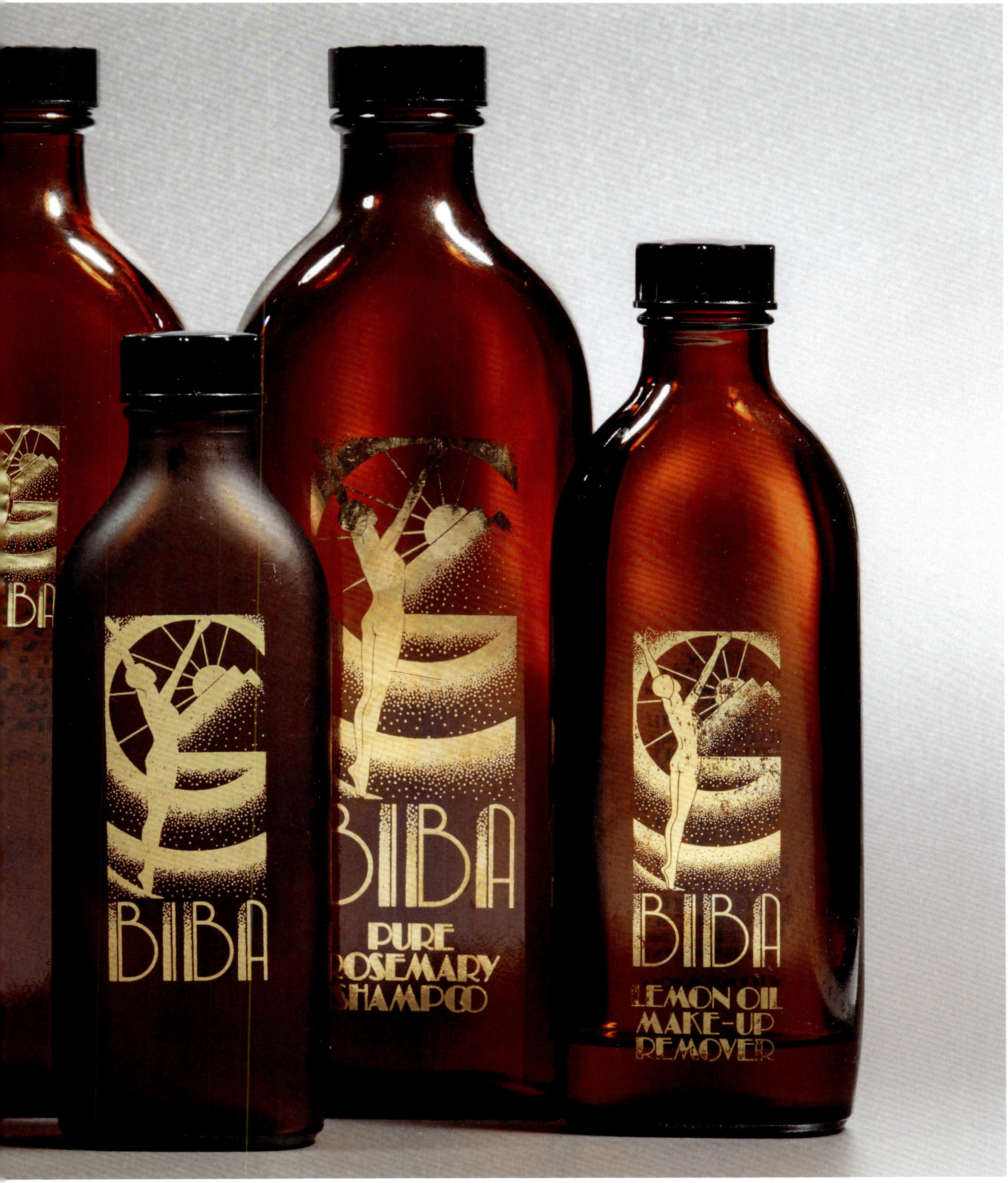
BIBA
BIBA
PURE
ROSEMARY
SHAMPOO
BIBA
LEMON OIL
MAKE-UP
REMOVER

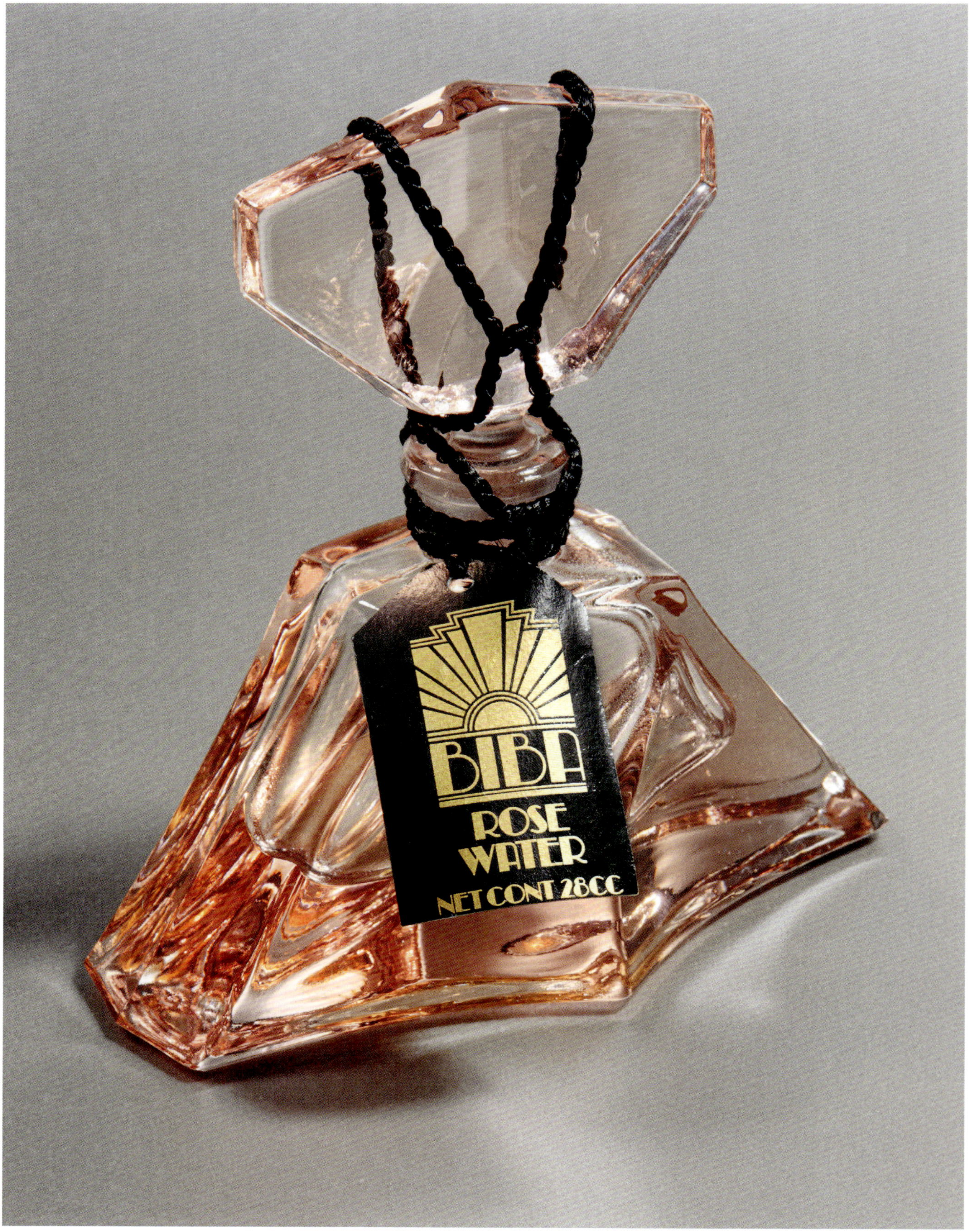

Biba scented rose water, 1974

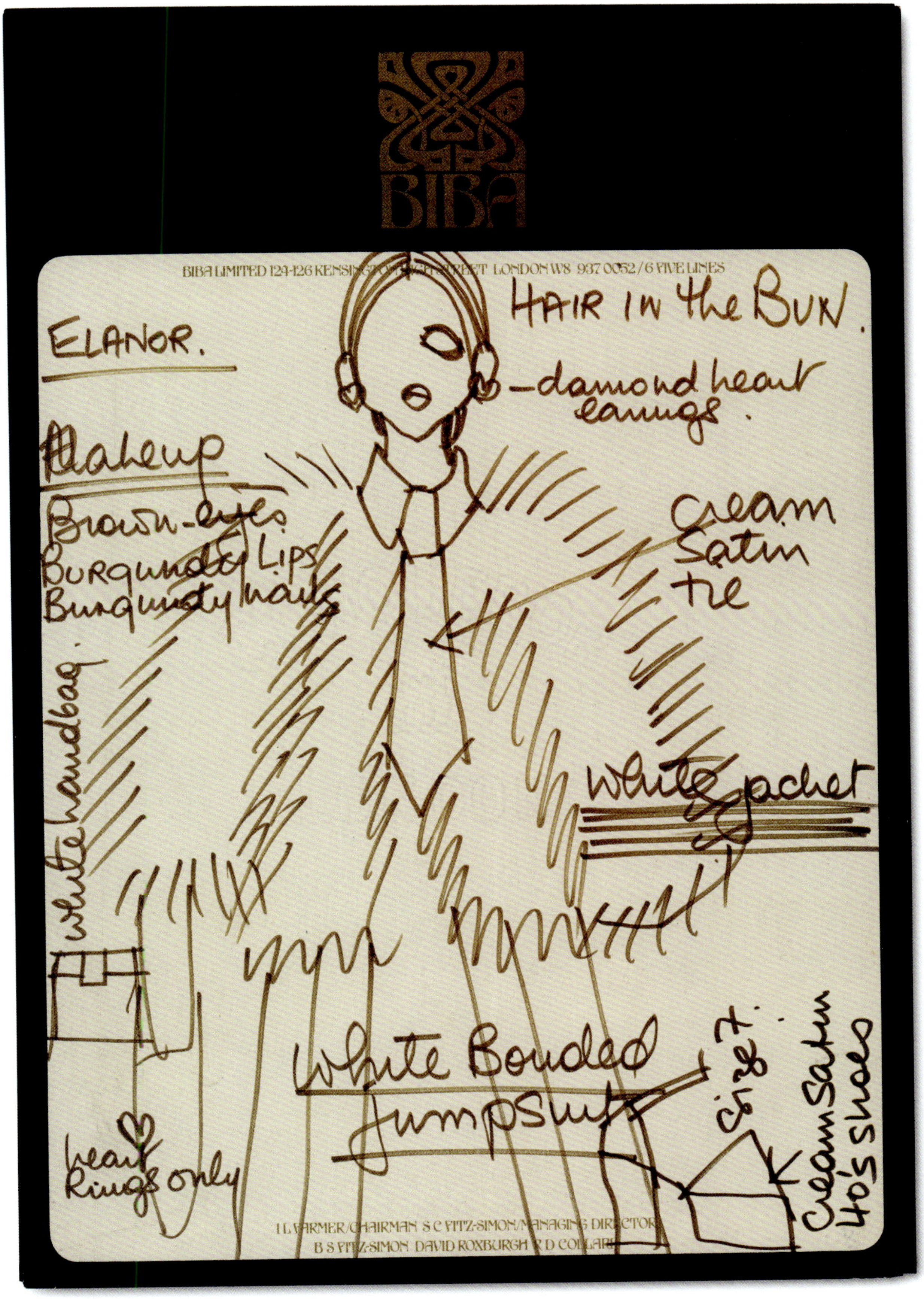

Design in felt pen with annotations for a jumpsuit outfit and accessories, Barbara Hulanicki, c.1974

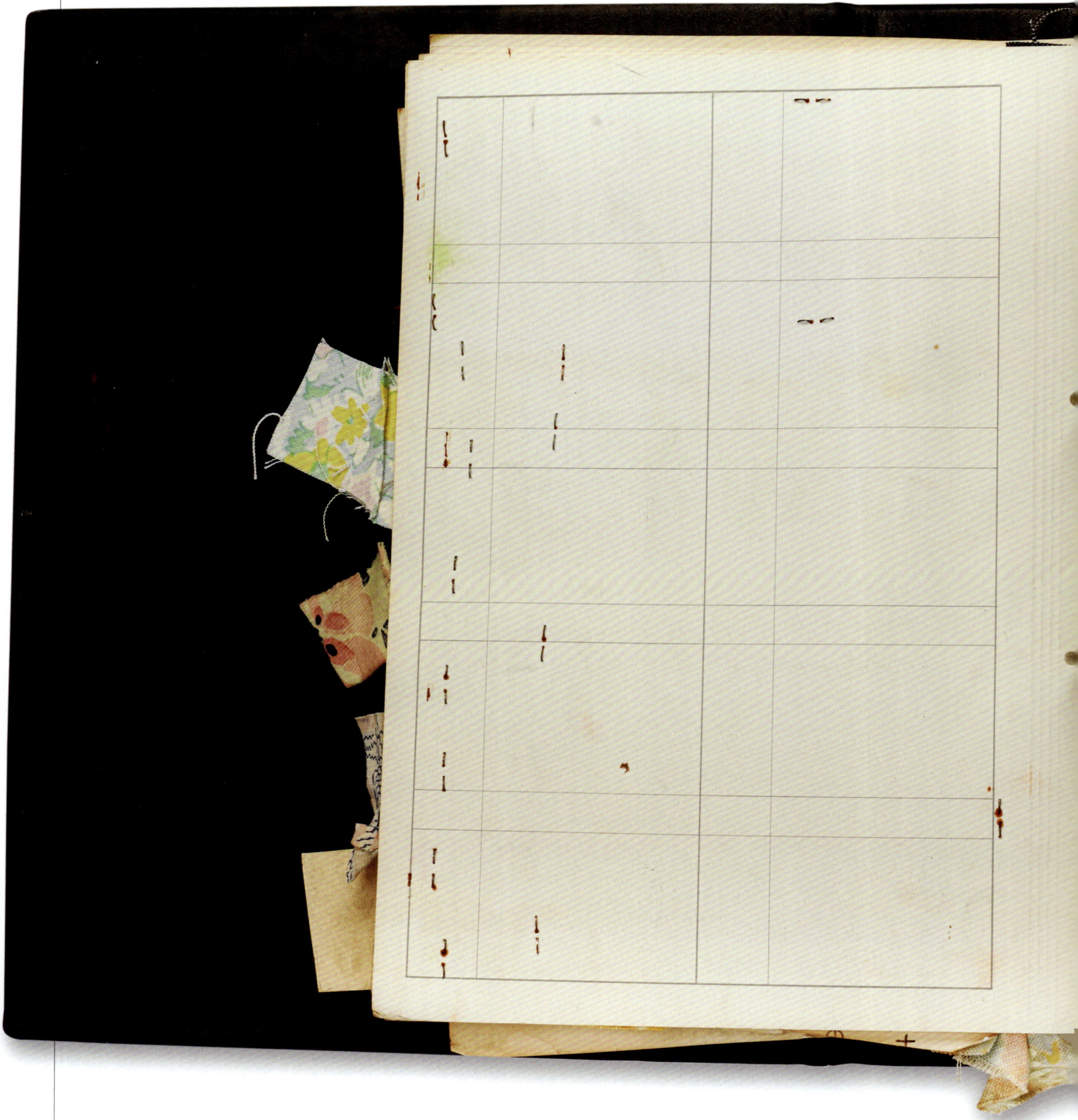

Biba book of sample textiles and prints from Tootal, 1975

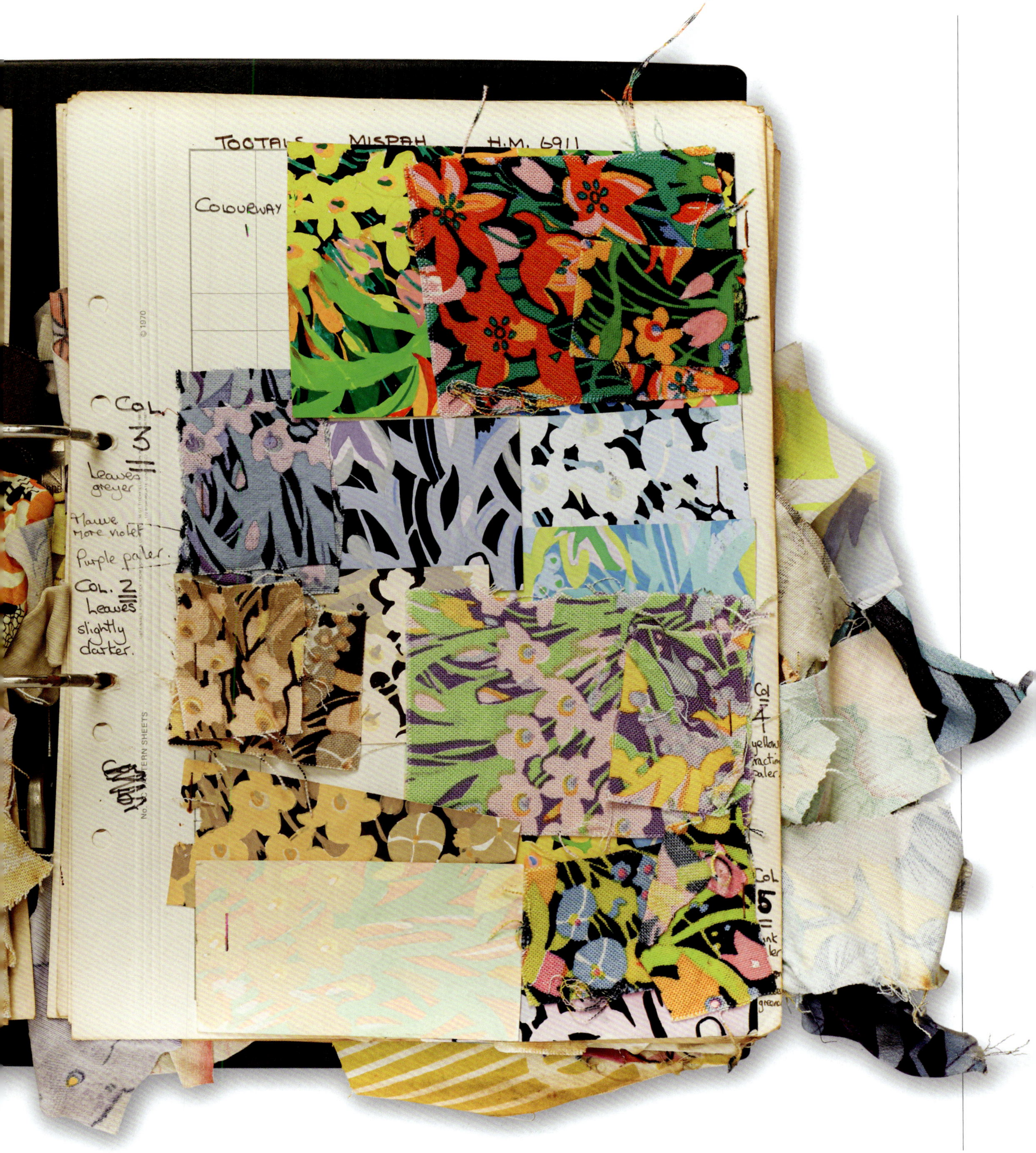
COLOURWAY
1
COL. 3
Leaves greyer
Mauve more violet
Purple paler.
COL. 2
Leaves slightly darker.

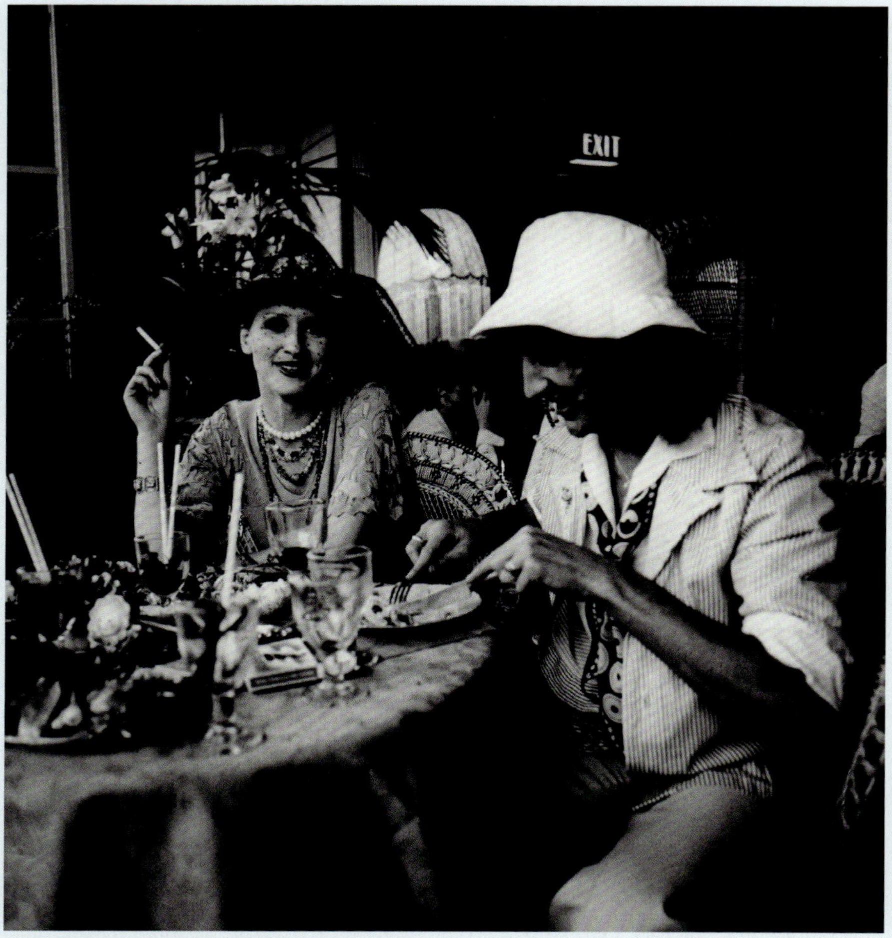

DELISIA HOWARD

~

BIBA COSMETICS BUYER

Delisia Howard (left) with Régis Huet on Biba roof garden for its launch, May 1974

Although I didn't realise it at the time, Biba was an absolutely unique place to work. Apart from timekeeping and honesty, there weren't really any rules. Everything emanated from Barbara, a font of ideas, intensely aware of the world around her, who immediately took up anything good. She also shouldered the blame for anything unsuccessful. When we went abroad to trade fairs we stayed in the best hotels and ate in the finest restaurants. Barbara and Fitz were involved with everyone and were very generous. I remember losing my wage packet one week. It was replaced immediately.

Between 1968 (the year of the revolution, when I joined Biba) and 1975 when Biba closed, I worked on household, cosmetics, accessories (while Biba girl Eva Molnar was on holidays), temporarily ran the press department and any other fill-ins required. This included being in *The Times* fashion show, gardening on the rooftop garden where, with mud on my face, Barbara introduced me to Tony Curtis. I also served in the ice cream parlour with other Biba shop girls (we all got sacked by the chef). I was the make-up artist for many press photography sessions with photographers including David Bailey and Terence Donovan, until the brilliant Régis Huet became the beautician in Big Biba. I had my body cast by the mannequin company Adel Rootstein (a bizarre experience) and couldn't bear to get one of the mannequins of myself when they were being sold at the brutal, chaotic sale at the end of Biba.

The end was horrible, but, like Biba's life, fast. I remember the day Barbara left. The 'suits' said, 'We need a neon sign to direct people to the food hall' (we didn't). Barbara said, 'Okay, I'll design one.' They said, 'We've done it' and produced a very ugly one. Barbara threw the sign at the wall and just swept out.

Biba was a beautiful, exciting, high-quality, inexpensive phenomenon, there for everyone to experience and enjoy. It was created by two remarkable people, and largely run by women. I was very lucky to be part of it.

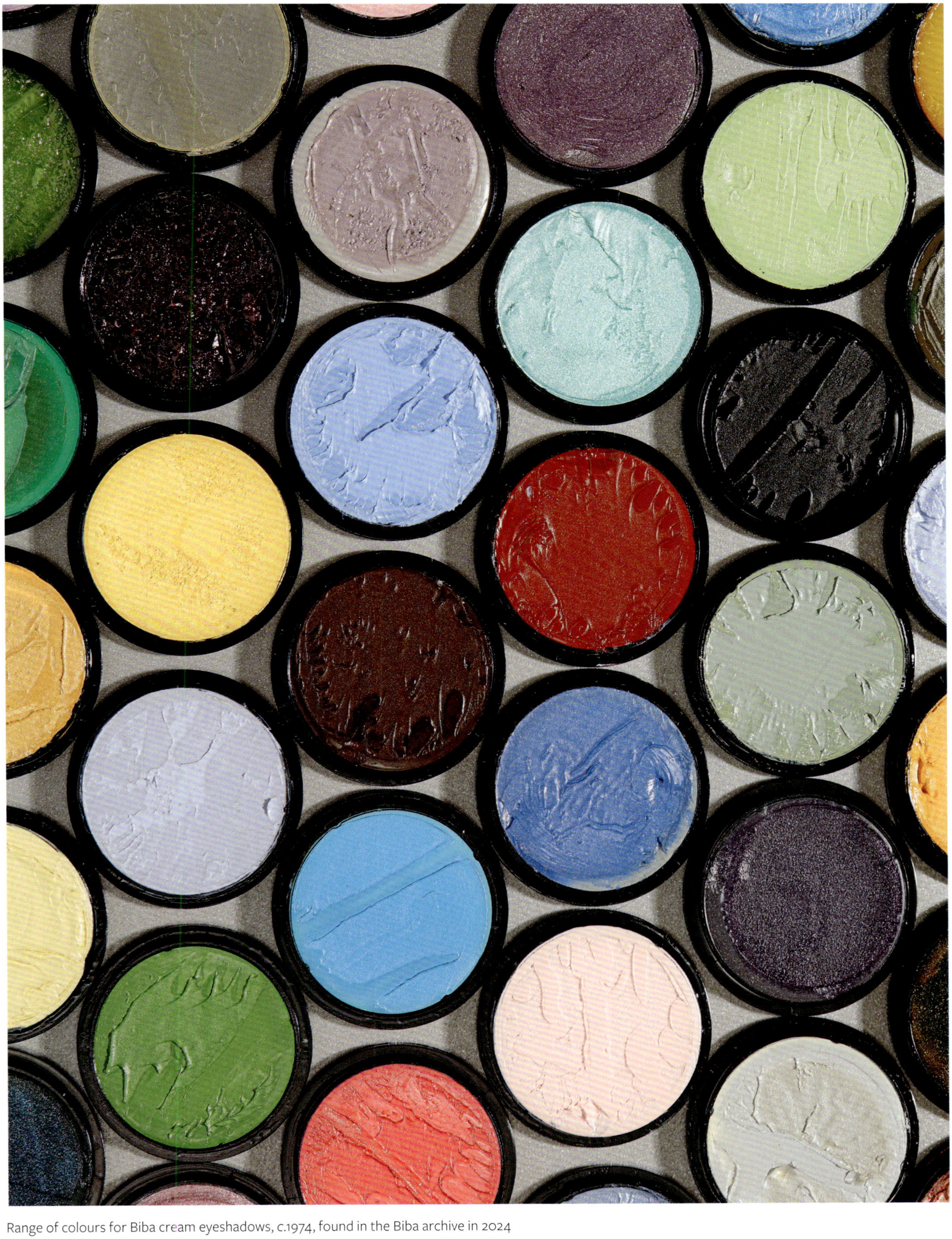

Range of colours for Biba cream eyeshadows, c.1974, found in the Biba archive in 2024

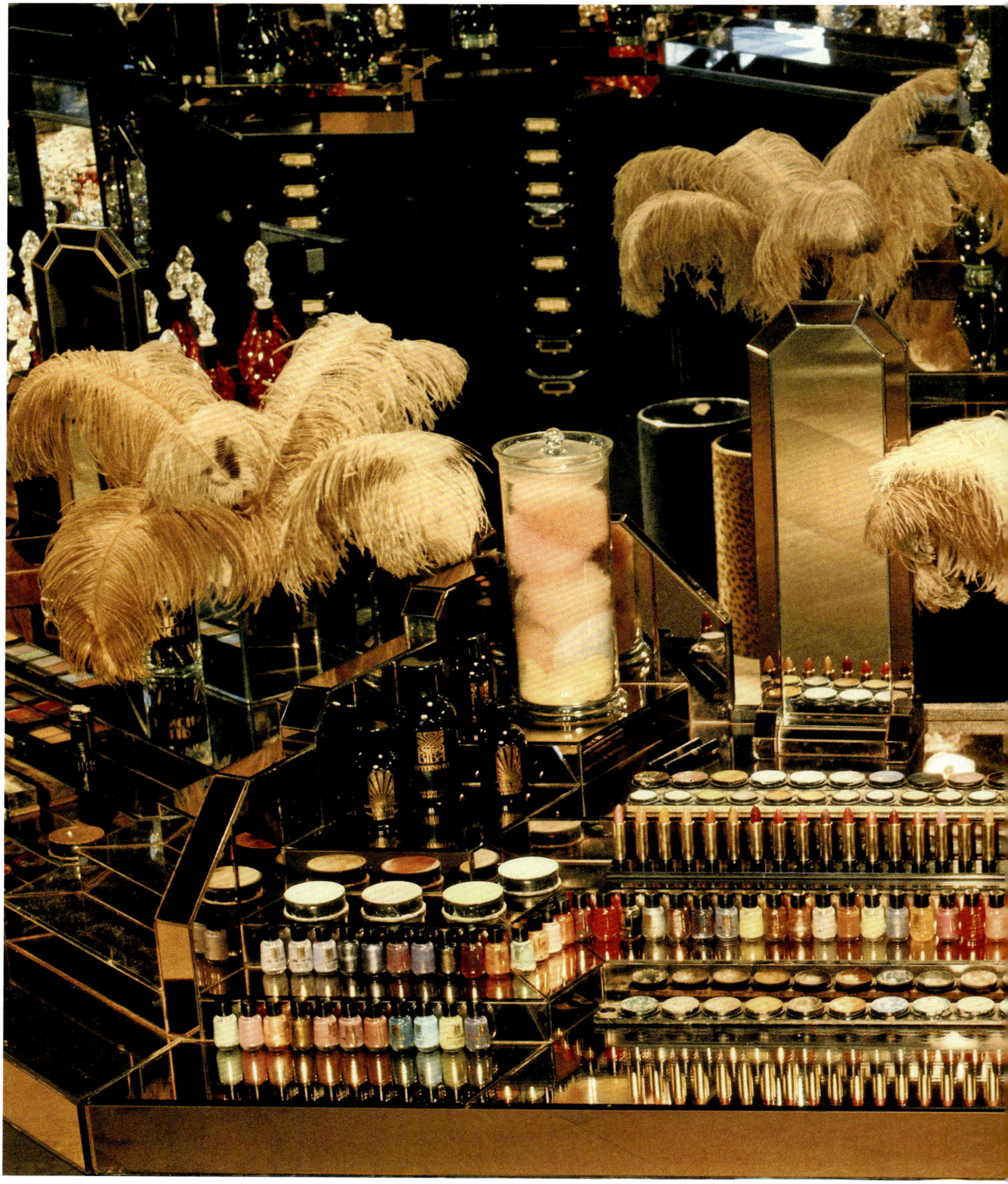

Cosmetics counter at Big Biba showing the range of products including nail varnishes, cream eyeshadows, face powder, lipsticks, aftershaves and scented water, 1973

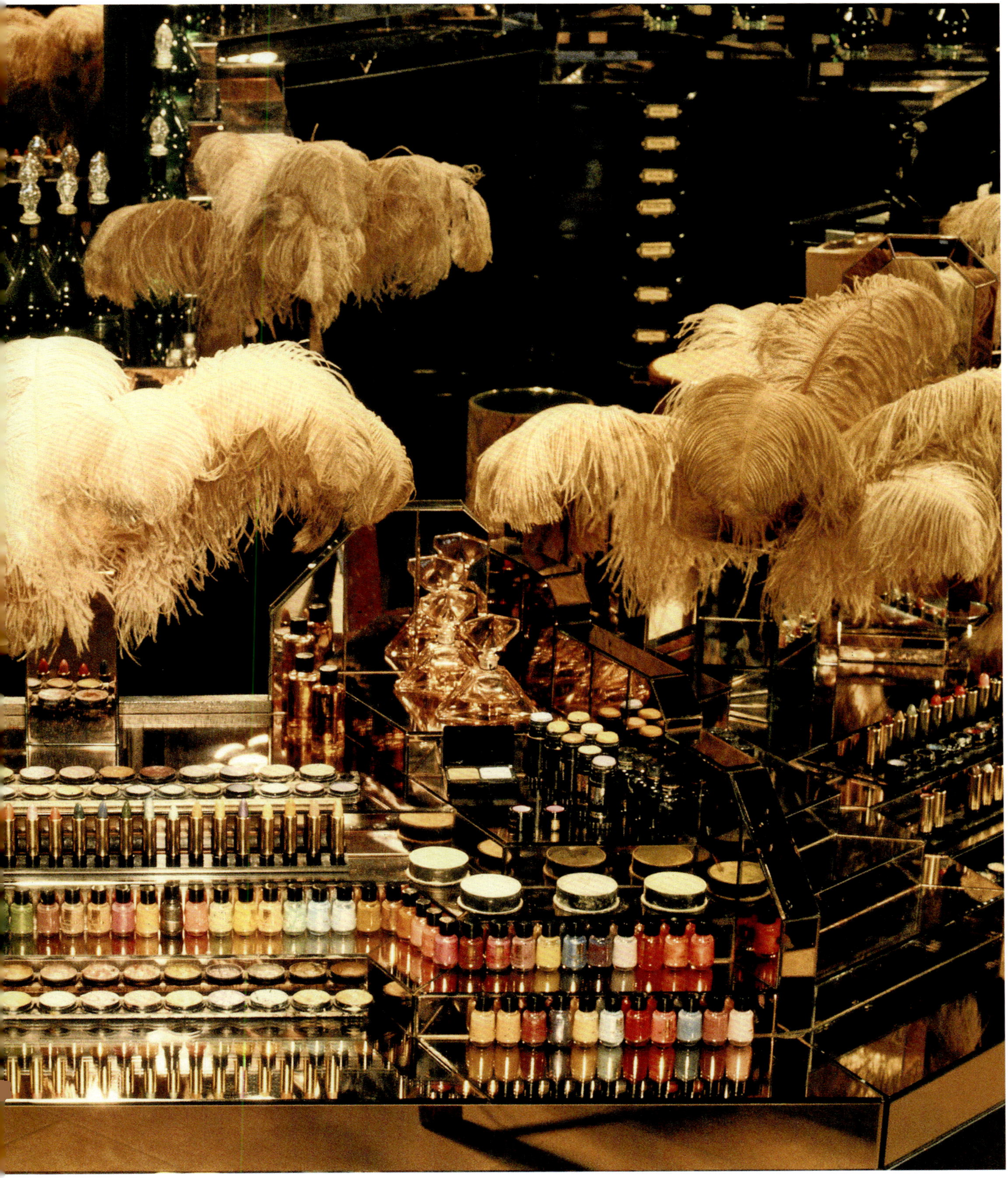

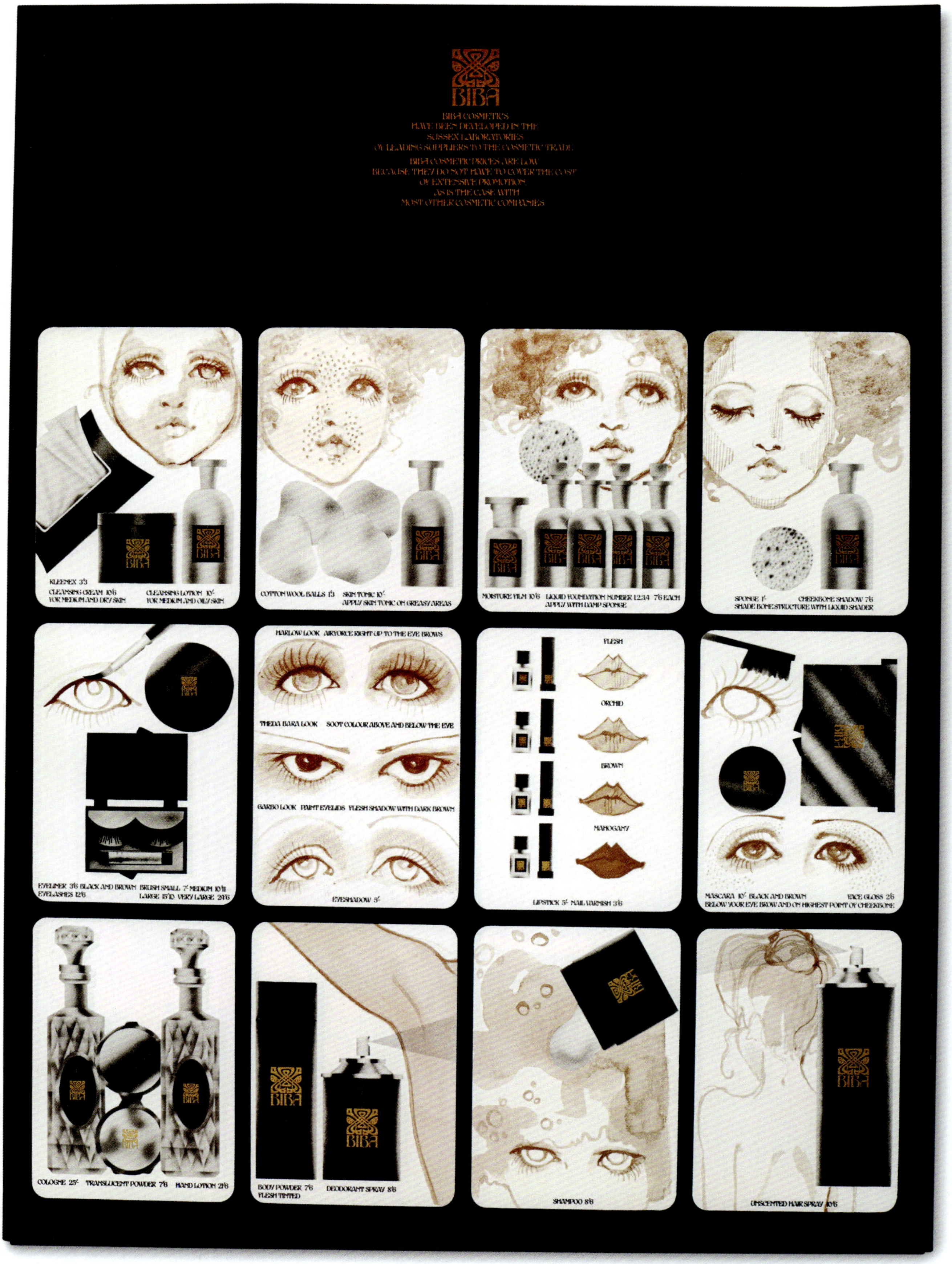

Poster advertising items from the range of Biba cosmetics and toiletries, 1974

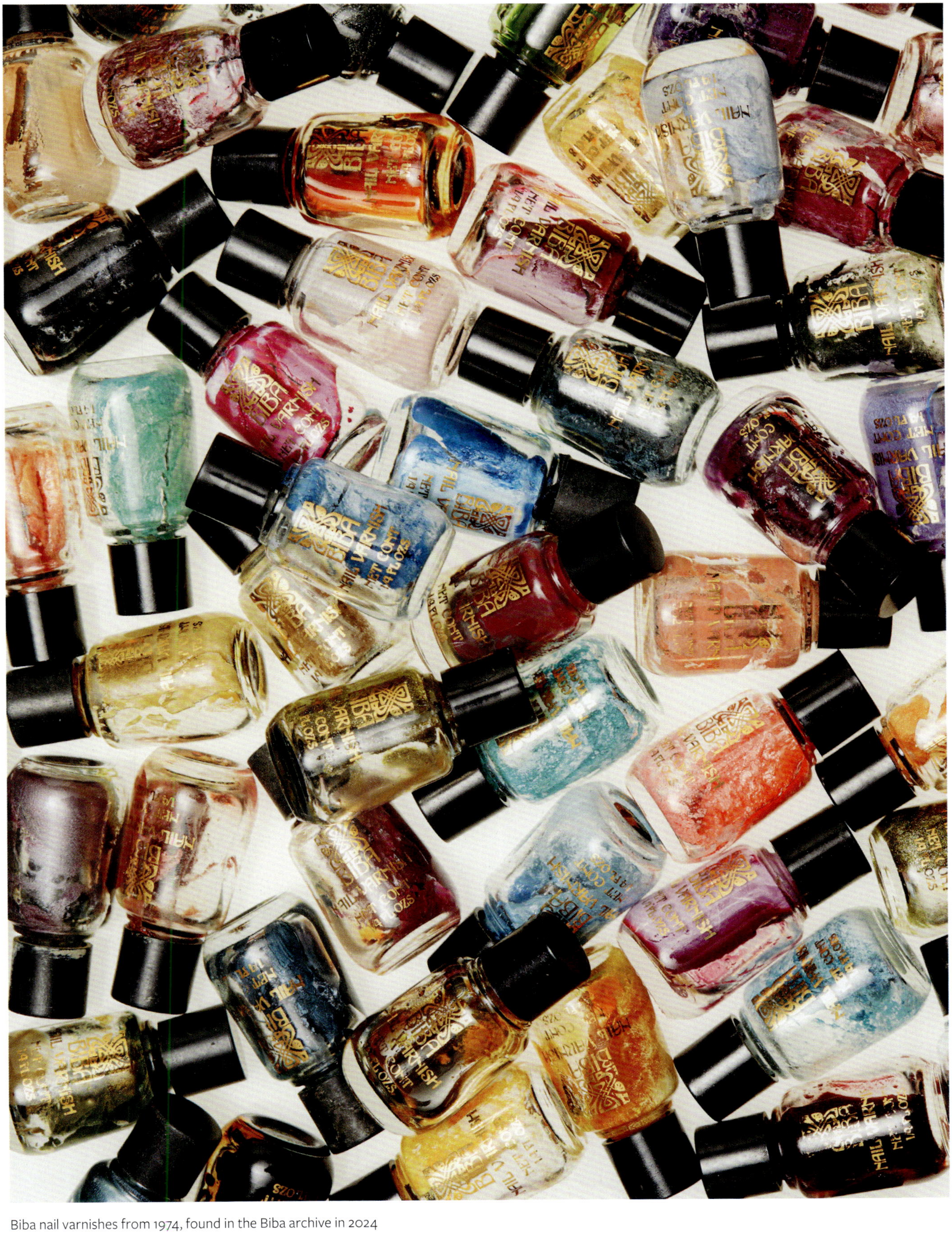

Biba nail varnishes from 1974, found in the Biba archive in 2024

LILLI ANDERSON
~
BIBA HOUSEHOLD DEPARTMENT MANAGER

With the Big Biba store looking like a movie set from the 1930s, it was now time to add the merchandise on all of its six floors. A display team was recruited to assist Barbara, but unfortunately it didn't work out as they didn't understand the Biba way of presenting the merchandise. I was then one of the lucky people to be given the opportunity to be part of the display team and work closely with Barbara on the household department, which was located on the fourth floor.

Following and understanding Barbara's specific vision and incredible eye for detail, the room sets began to take shape; each one had a different look, highlighting the extensive range of Biba household goods. This was the first time merchandise was displayed in this way. Biba living room sets next to Biba bedrooms and a Biba kitchen and bathroom, all colour-matched in Biba colours. The kitsch room was self explanatory; a riot of colour combined with items including flying geese, it was very tongue-in-cheek. The store opened on 10 September 1973, with customers queuing around the block to enter the most beautiful department store they had ever seen.

"With the flamingos still in residence some penguins were borrowed from London Zoo for the opening party"

I continued to work in the household department as display manager with my friend Gunda working opposite shifts. Gunda was a huge fan of The Kinks and had tickets to see them at the Rainbow Theatre in Finsbury Park; that day, we both left work at 5.30pm to get to the gig. The next morning, I was told Fitz wanted to see me in his office, which was on the fifth floor. I quickly located Gunda and told her that I thought we had been found out. I remember running up the stairs thinking I was in so much trouble. When Fitz said, 'Let me just call Barbara to join us', I was sure I was being sacked. When Barbara arrived, they said that they had fired the PR company and would like me to take over. I was so shocked I said, 'Oh sorry, I don't think I can as I know nothing about PR.' Fitz said they knew that would be my response and handed me a press release sent out the day before, announcing me as PR manager. I could scarcely read it as I was shaking so much and asked, 'Why me?' He said it was because I completely got Barbara's vision and would have no problem relaying it to the media.

In early 1974 work began on restoring the roof garden to its former glory: replanting flowers and reviving the beautiful Italian garden. Barbara commissioned Andrew Logan to design an area with huge, spectacular flowers for one part of the garden. With the flamingos still in residence, some penguins were borrowed from London Zoo for the opening party.

I went up to the roof garden to see how the penguins were settling in, and on leaving I walked down one of the staircases leading to the Rainbow Room. I was walking in front of the lifts when suddenly all the diners stopped eating and turned towards me. Wondering what was so interesting, I turned around and was amazed to see six penguins following me! Unsure what to do, one of the restaurant managers said to keep walking and go back up the other flight of stairs in the hope of leading them back to the roof garden. I am not sure why they followed me, but someone suggested it could have been because I was wearing a black trouser suit. Barbara was very concerned that they were unhappy, so after only a few hours they were transported back to their home in London Zoo.

I started my new role at Biba in June 1974 and continued until the store was closed by British Land on 27 September 1975. They wanted to demolish the building and put a hotel in its place. We were all devasted and wondered how we could stop this happening. We were discussing how to mark the end of an epic era and suggestions were being thrown around, one being to have a funeral cortege with black plumed horses. This was when Freddie Mercury had the idea to put a preservation order on the roof garden. This was done, and the beautiful building that was once home to Big Biba survived. It still stands in all its glory on Kensington High Street.

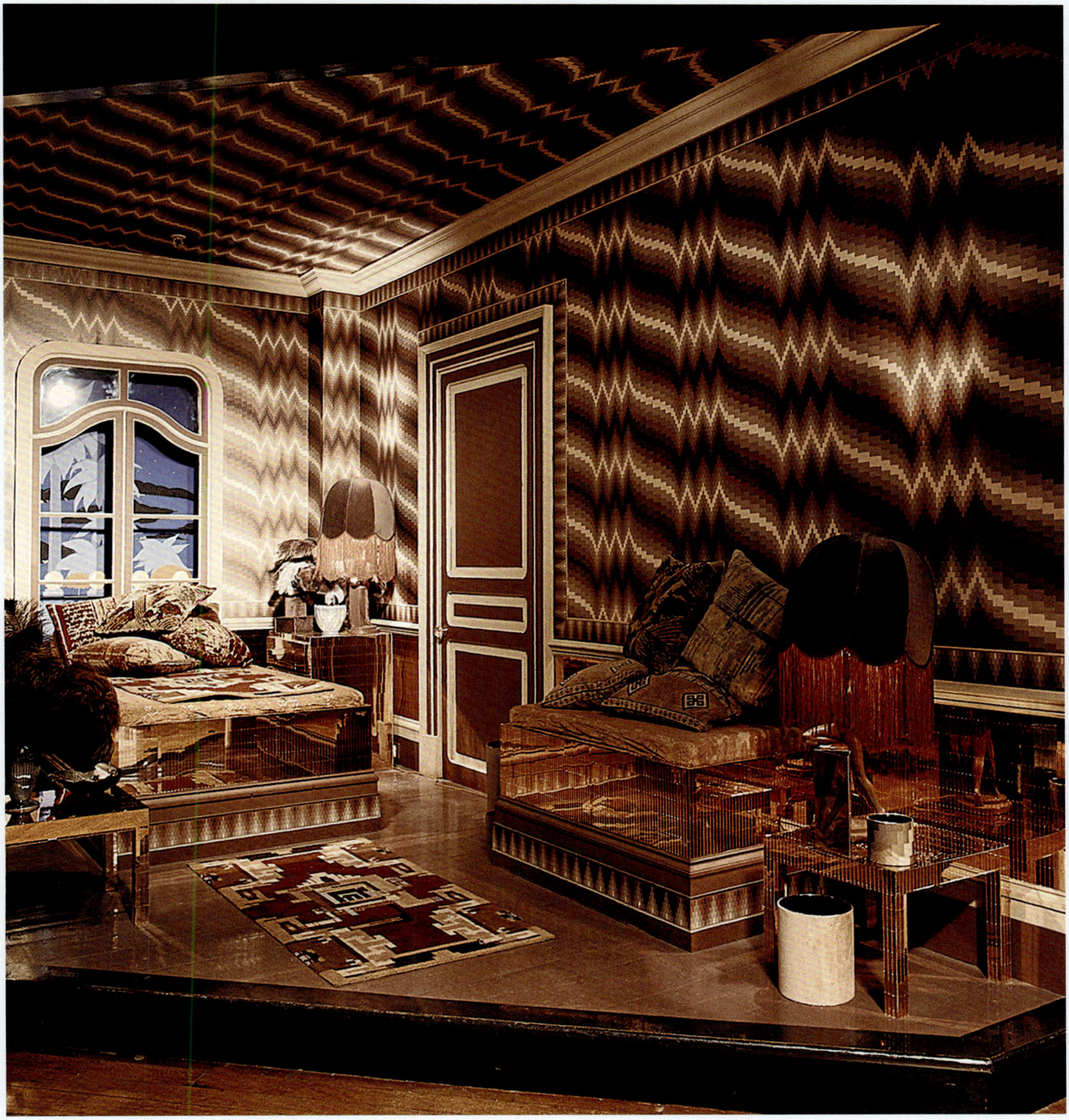

One of the room sets in Big Biba, 1973

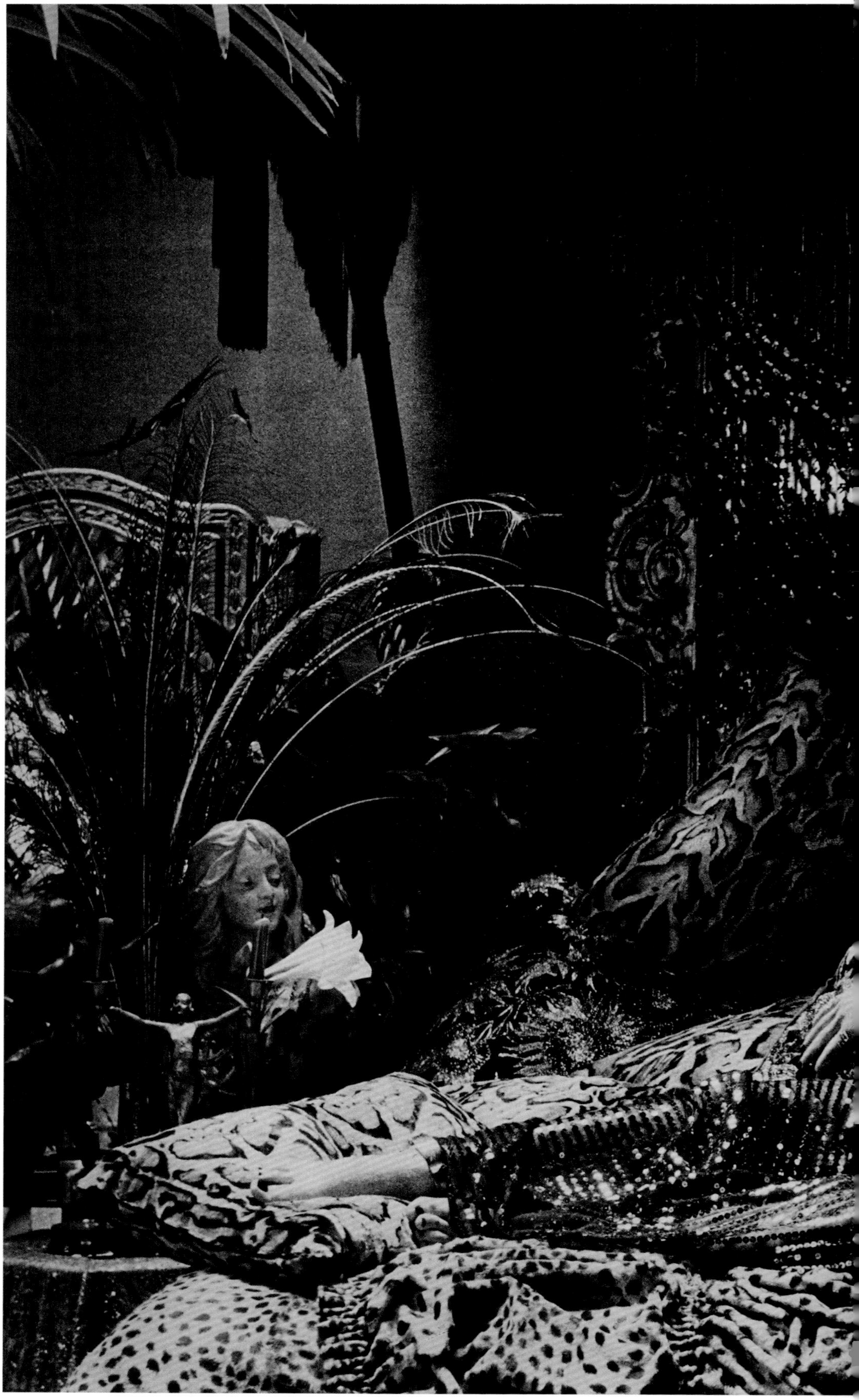

Eva Molnar, photographed by Barbara Hulanicki, 1973. This image was included as a double-page spread in the Biba newspaper.

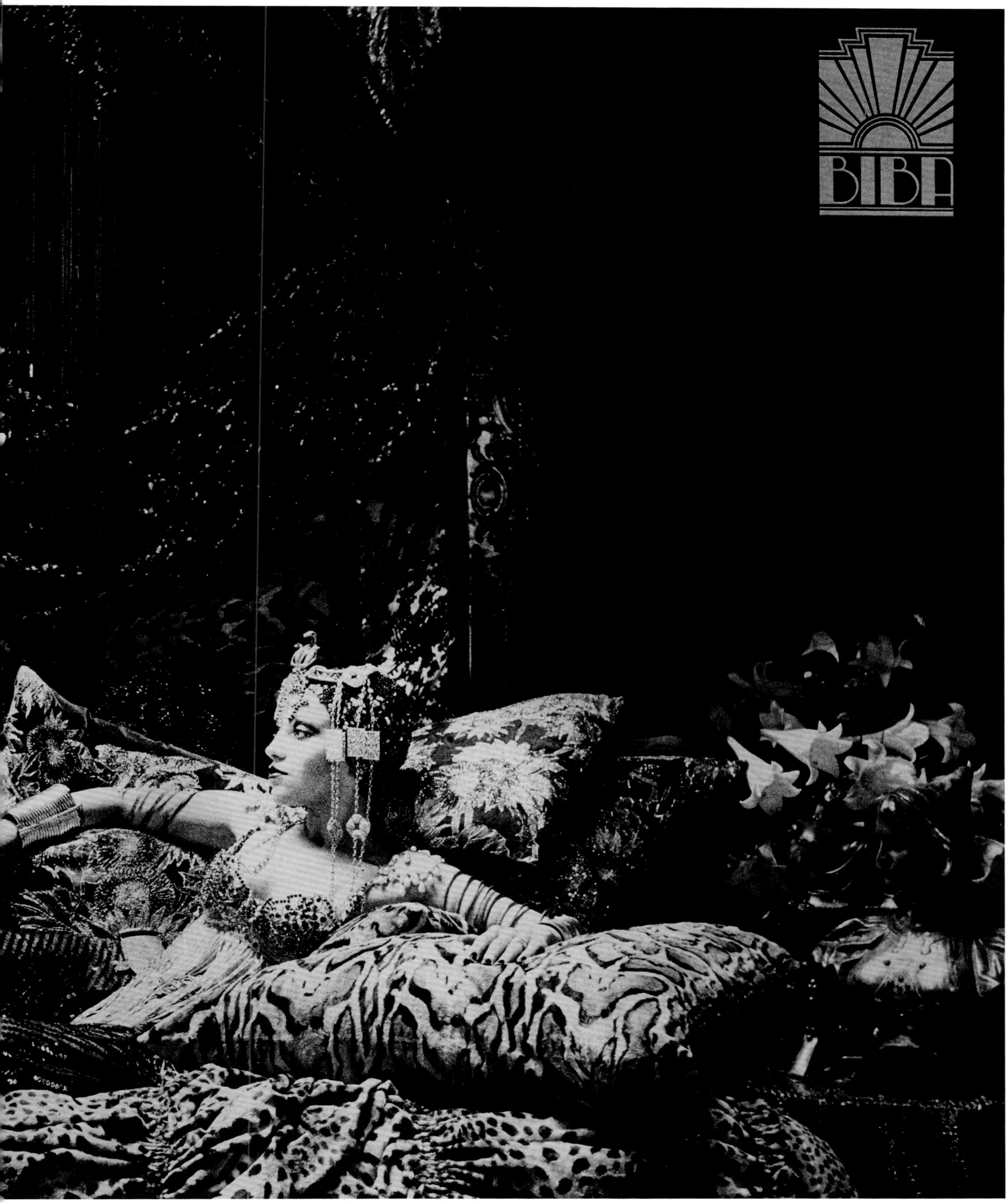
BIBA

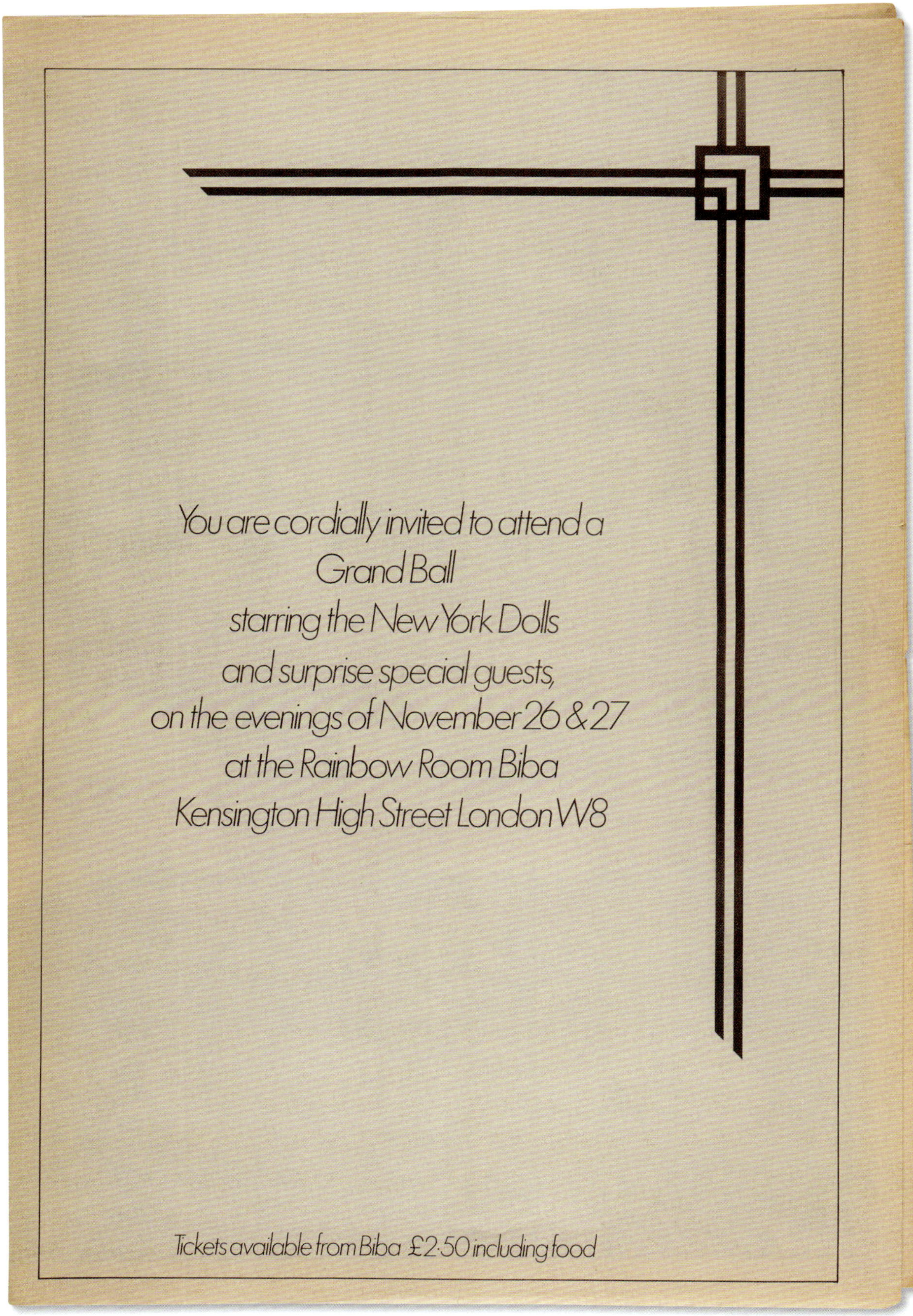

ABOVE & OPPOSITE Two pages from a four-page pullout featuring the New York Dolls' gig in the Rainbow Room, Big Biba, *Gay News*, November 1973

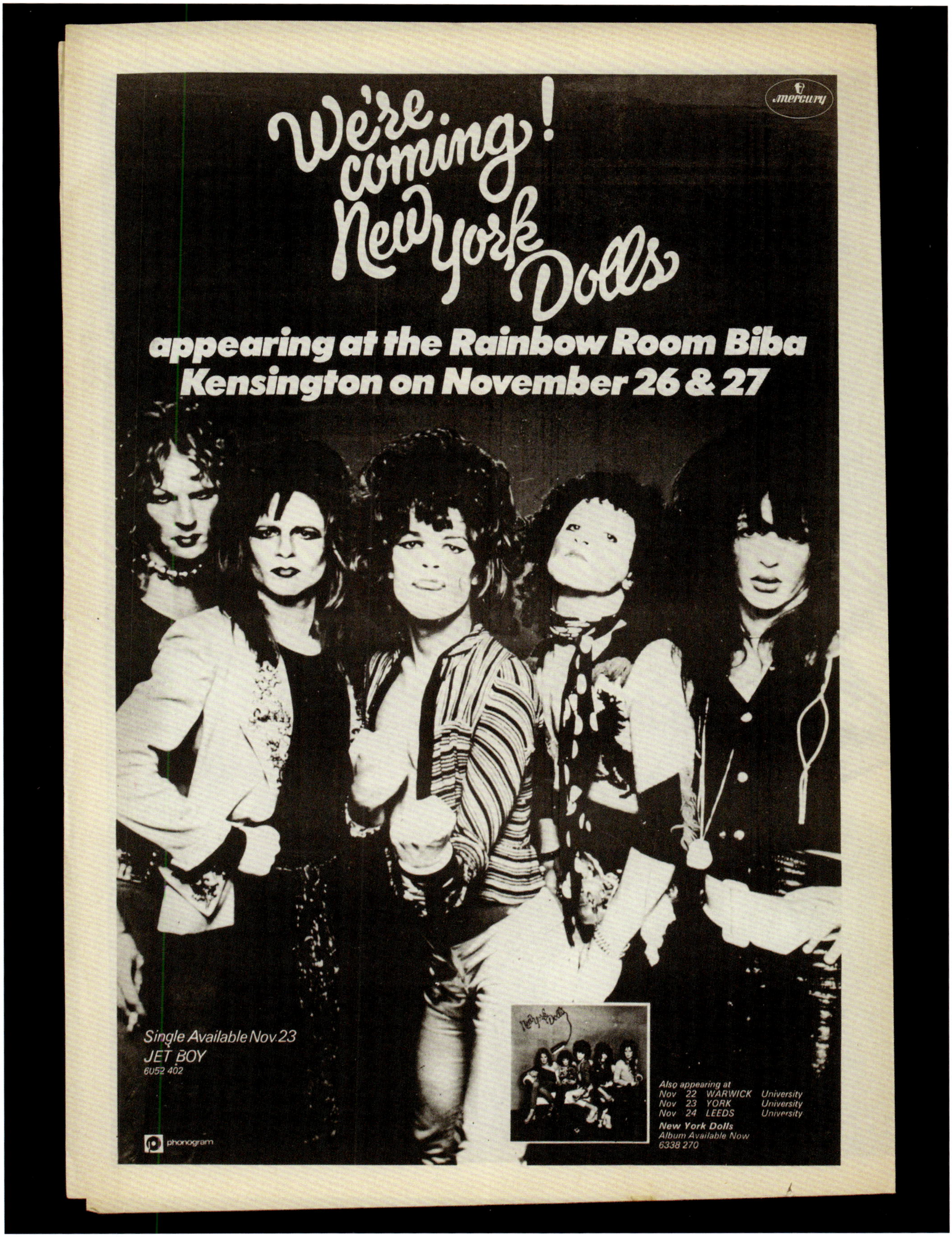
mercury
We're coming!
New York Dolls
appearing at the Rainbow Room Biba
Kensington on November 26 & 27
Single Available Nov. 23
JET BOY
6052 402
phonogram
Also appearing at
Nov 22 WARWICK University
Nov 23 YORK University
Nov 24 LEEDS University
New York Dolls
Album Available Now
6338 270

BELOW & RIGHT Ephemera related to the Rainbow Room, Whitmore-Thomas, 1973

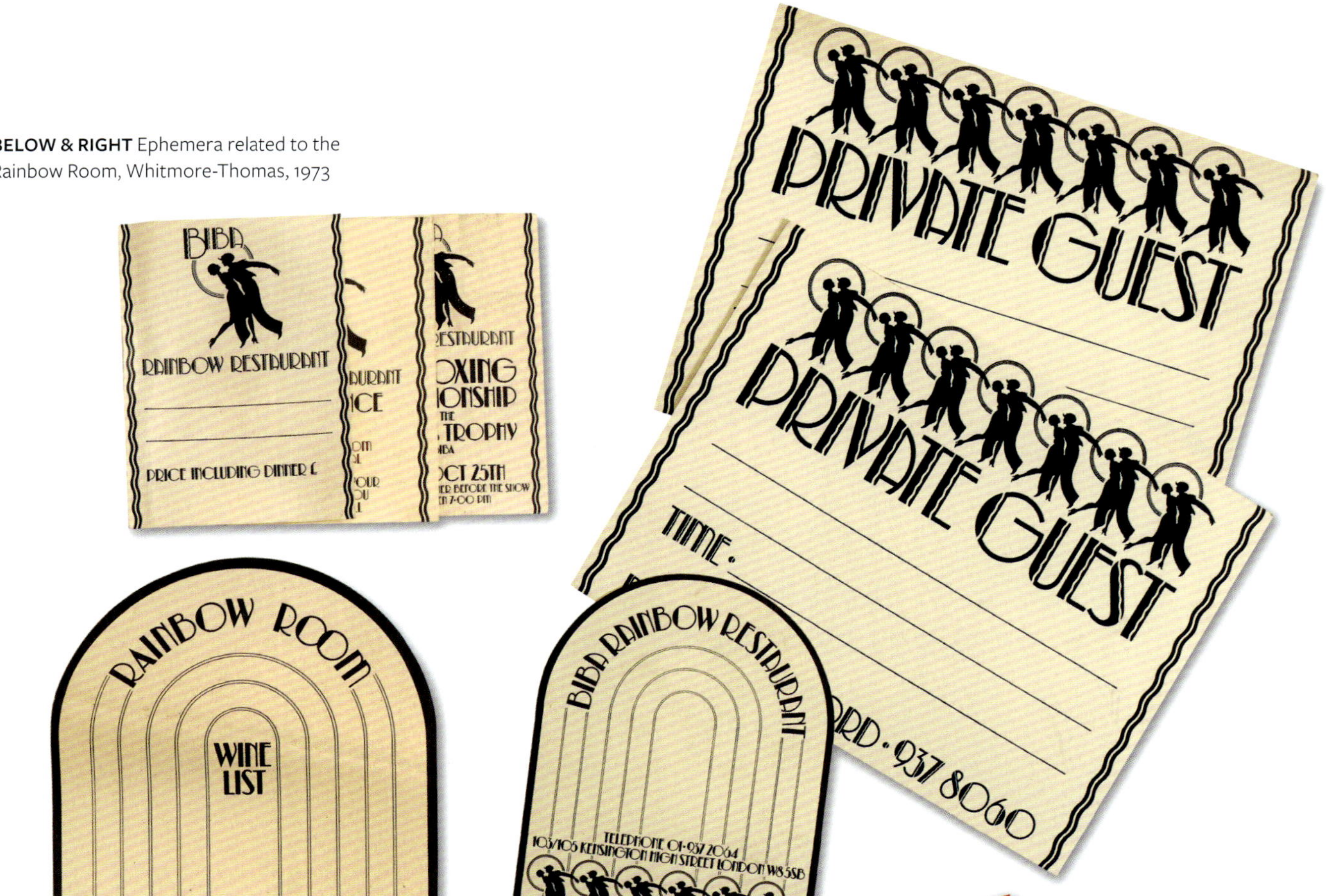

BELOW Tickets for the New Year's Eve party at the Rainbow Room, Big Biba, Whitmore-Thomas, 1974

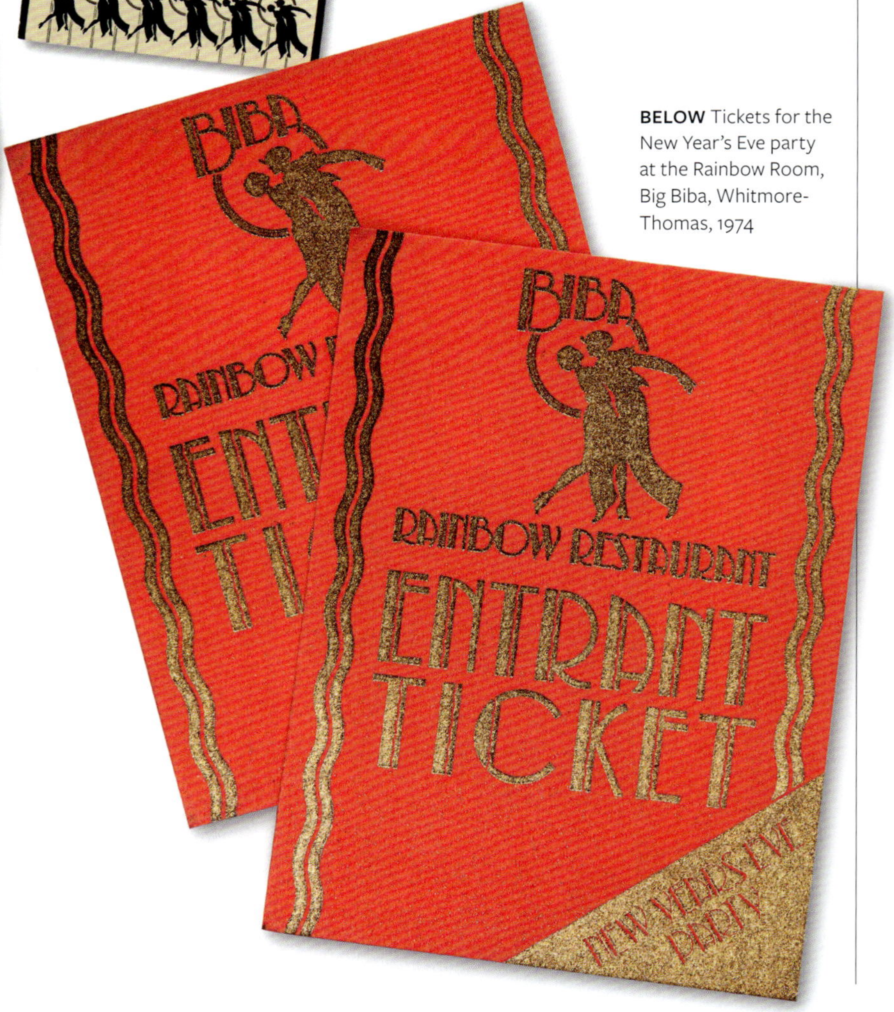

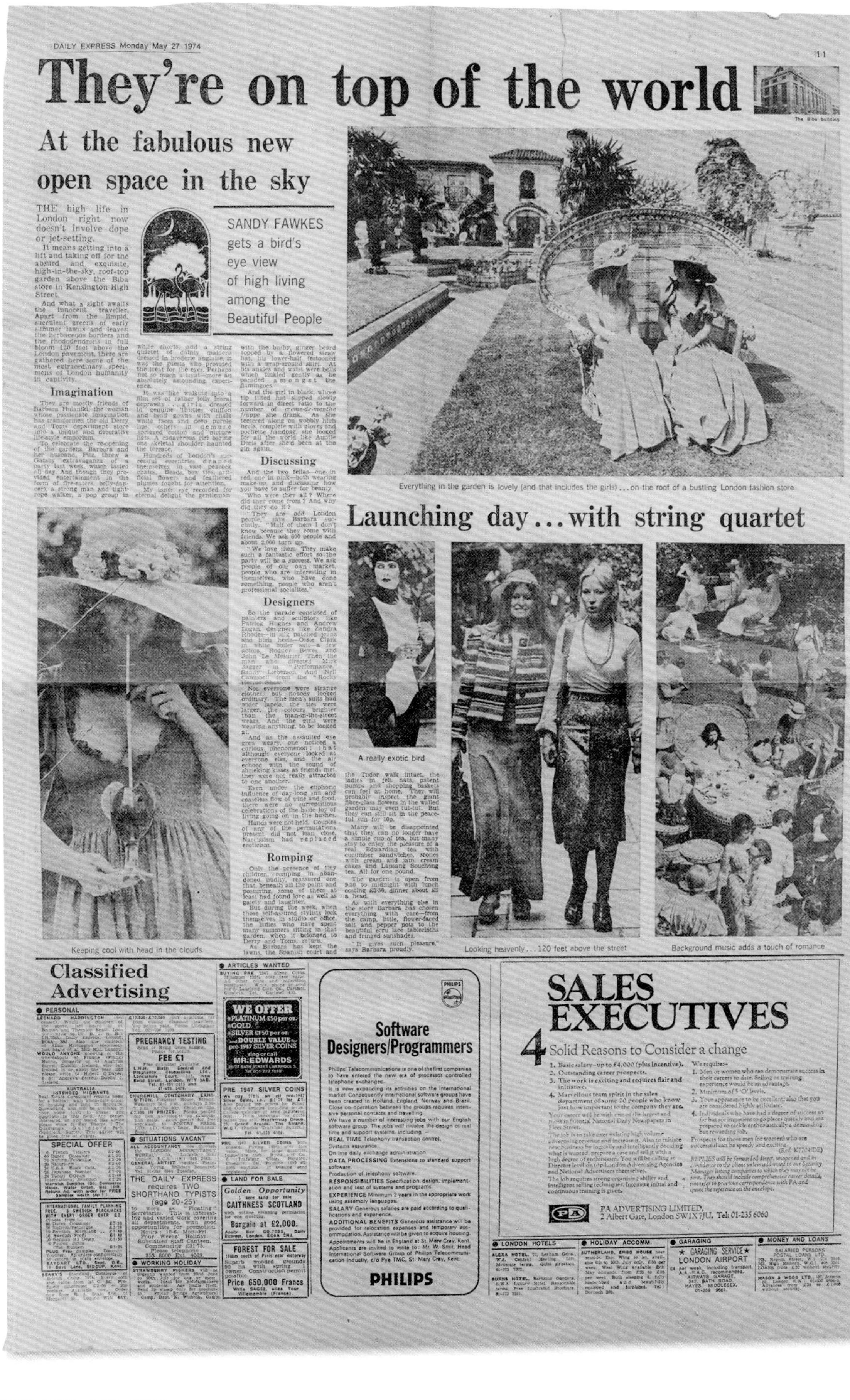

DAILY EXPRESS Monday May 27 1974

11

They're on top of the world

The Biba building

At the fabulous new open space in the sky

SANDY FAWKES gets a bird's eye view of high living among the Beautiful People

THE high life in London right now doesn't involve dope or jet-setting.

It means getting into a lift and taking off for the absurd and exquisite, high-in-the-sky, roof-top garden above the Biba store in Kensington High Street.

And what a sight awaits the innocent traveller. Apart from the limpid, succulent greens of early summer lawns and leaves, the herbaceous borders and the rhododendrons in full bloom 120 feet above the London pavement, there are gathered here some of the most extraordinary specimens of London humanity in captivity.

Imagination

They are mostly friends of Barbara Hulanicki, the woman whose passionate imagination has transformed the old Derry and Toms department store into a unique and decorative life-style emporium.

To celebrate the re-opening of the gardens, Barbara and her husband, Fitz, threw a Gatsby extravaganza of a party last week, which lasted all day. And though they provided entertainment in the form of fire-eaters, belly-dancers, a strong man and tight-rope walker, a pop group in white shorts, and a string quartet of dainty maidens dressed in broderie anglaise, it was the guests who provided the treat for the eyes. Perhaps not so much a treat—more an absolutely astounding experience.

It was like walking into a film set of rather jolly moral depravity . . . girls dressed in genuine 'thirties chiffon and bead gowns with chalk white faces and deep purple lips, others in demure sprigged cotton and picture hats. A cadaverous girl baring one skeletal shoulder haunted the terrace.

Hundreds of London's successful eccentrics draped themselves in vast peacock chairs. Beads, bow ties, artificial flowers and feathered plumes fought for attention.

My inner eye recorded for eternal delight the gentleman with the bushy, ginger beard topped by a flowered straw hat, his lower-half festooned with a wrap-around skirt. At his ankles and waist were bells which tinkled gently as he paraded amongst the flamingoes.

And the girl in black, whose tip tilted hat slipped slowly forward in direct ratio to the number of *creme-de-menthe frappe* she drank. As she teetered along on wobbly high heels, complete with gloves and pochette handbag, she looked for all the world like Auntie Doris after she'd been at the gin again.

Discussing

And the two fellas—one in red, one in pink—both wearing make-up, and discussing how you have to suffer for beauty.

Who were they all? Where did they come from? And why did they do it?

"They are odd London people," says Barbara succinctly. "Half of them I don't know because they come with friends. We ask 600 people and about 2,000 turn up.

"We love them. They make such a fantastic effort so the party will be a success. We ask people of our own market, people who are interesting in themselves, who have done something, people who aren't professional socialites."

Designers

So the parade consisted of painters and sculptors like Patrick Hughes and Andrew Logan, designers like Zandra Rhodes—in silk patched jeans and high heels—Ossie Clark in white boiler suit—a few actors, Rodney Bewes and John Le Mesurier. Then the man who directed Mick Jagger in "Performance," Sandy Lieberson. And Nell Campbell from the "Rocky Horror Show."

Not everyone wore strange clothes, but nobody looked ordinary. The men's suits had wider lapels, the ties were larger, the colours brighter than the man-in-the-street wears. And the girls were wearing anything, to be looked at.

And as the assaulted eye grew weary, one noticed a curious phenomenon; that although everyone looked at everyone else, and the air echoed with the sound of shrieking kisses as friends met, they were not really attracted to one another.

Even under the euphoric influence of day-long sun and ceaseless flow of wine and food, there were no surreptitious celebrations of the basic joy of living going on in the bushes.

Hands were not held. Couples of any of the permutations present did not lean close. Narcissism had replaced eroticism.

Romping

Only the presence of tiny children, romping in abandoned nudity, reassured one that, beneath all the paint and posturing, some of them at least had found love as well as gaiety and laughter.

But during the week, when those self-assured stylists lock themselves in studio or office, the ladies who have spent many summers sitting in that garden, when it belonged to Derry and Toms, return.

As Barbara has kept the lawns, the Spanish court and the Tudor walk intact, the ladies in felt hats, patent pumps and shopping baskets can feel at home. They will probably inspect the giant fibre-glass flowers in the walled garden, may even tut-tut. But they can still sit in the peaceful sun for 10p.

Many will be disappointed that they can no longer have a simple cup of tea, but many stay to enjoy the pleasure of a real Edwardian tea with cucumber sandwiches, scones with cream and jam, cream cakes and Lapsang Souchong tea. All for one pound.

The garden is open from 9.30 to midnight with lunch costing £3·50, dinner about £5 a head.

As with everything else in the store Barbara has chosen everything with care—from the camp, little, flower-faced salt and pepper pots to the beautiful ecru lace tablecloths and fringed sunshades.

"It gives such pleasure," says Barbara proudly.

Everything in the garden is lovely (and that includes the girls) . . . on the roof of a bustling London fashion store

Launching day . . . with string quartet

A really exotic bird

Keeping cool with head in the clouds

Looking heavenly . . . 120 feet above the street

Background music adds a touch of romance

Classified Advertising

PERSONAL

PREGNANCY TESTING

FEE £1

AUSTRALIA INTENDED MIGRANTS

SPECIAL OFFER

INTERNATIONAL FAMILY PLANNING

SITUATIONS VACANT

THE DAILY EXPRESS requires TWO SHORTHAND TYPISTS (age 20-25) to work as "Floating" Secretaries. This is interesting and varied work covering all departments, with good opportunities for promotion. Hours: 10-6, Mon.-Fri. Four Weeks' Holiday. Subsidised Staff Canteen. Commencing £31·75. Please telephone 353 8000 Ext. 4060.

WORKING HOLIDAY

ARTICLES WANTED

WE OFFER
*PLATINUM £50 per oz.
*GOLD
*SILVER £1·50 per oz.
and DOUBLE VALUE for pre-1947 SILVER COINS
ring or call
MR. EDWARDS

PRE 1947 SILVER COINS

LAND FOR SALE

Golden Opportunity
CAITHNESS SCOTLAND
Bargain at £2,000.

FOREST FOR SALE
Price 650,000 Francs

Software Designers/Programmers

PHILIPS

Philips' Telecommunications is one of the first companies to have entered the new era of processor controlled telephone exchanges.

It is now expanding its activities on the international market. Consequently international software groups have been created in Holland, England, Norway and Brazil. Close co-operation between the groups requires intensive personal contacts and travelling.

We have a number of interesting jobs with our English software group. The jobs will involve the design of real time and support systems, including:—

REAL TIME Telephony transaction control.
Systems assurance.
On line daily exchange administration.

DATA PROCESSING Extensions to standard support software.
Production of telephony software.

RESPONSIBILITIES Specification, design, implementation and test of systems and programs.

EXPERIENCE Minimum 2 years in the appropriate work using assembly languages.

SALARY Generous salaries are paid according to qualifications and experience.

ADDITIONAL BENEFITS Generous assistance will be provided for relocation expenses and temporary accommodation. Assistance will be given to acquire housing.

Appointments will be in England at St. Mary Cray, Kent. Applicants are invited to write to: Mr. W. Smit, Head International Software Group of Philips Telecommunication Industry, c/o Pye TMC, St. Mary Cray, Kent.

PHILIPS

SALES EXECUTIVES

4 Solid Reasons to Consider a change

1. Basic salary—up to £4,000 (plus incentive).
2. Outstanding career prospects.
3. The work is exciting and requires flair and initiative.
4. Marvellous team spirit in the sales department of some 20 people who know just how important to the company they are.

Your career will be with one of the largest and most influential National Daily Newspapers in Fleet Street.

The job is to take over existing high volume advertising revenue and increase it. Also to initiate new business by logically and intelligently deciding what is wanted, prepare a case and sell it with a high degree of enthusiasm. You will be calling at Director level on top London Advertising Agencies and National Advertisers themselves.

The job requires strong organising ability and intelligent selling techniques. Intensive initial and continuous training is given.

We require:—

1. Men or women who can demonstrate success in their careers to date. Selling or training experience would be an advantage.
2. Minimum of 5 'O' levels.
3. Your appearance to be excellent; also that you are considered highly articulate.
4. Individuals who have had a degree of success so far but are impatient to go places quickly and are prepared to tackle enthusiastically a demanding but rewarding job.

Prospects for those men (or women) who are successful can be speedy and exciting.

(Ref. K7704/DE)

REPLIES will be forwarded direct, unopened and in confidence to the client unless addressed to our Security Manager listing companies to which they may not be sent. They should include comprehensive career details, not refer to previous correspondence with PA and quote the reference on the envelope.

PA ADVERTISING LIMITED, 2 Albert Gate, London SW1X 7JU. Tel: 01-235 6060

LONDON HOTELS

HOLIDAY ACCOMM.

GARAGING

★ GARAGING SERVICE ★
LONDON AIRPORT
£4 per week, including transport. A.A.-R.A.C. recommended. AIRWAYS GARAGE, 242, BATH ROAD, HAYES, MIDDLESEX. 01-359 9661.

MONEY AND LOANS

RIGHT Press cutting, story on the opening of the roof garden at Big Biba, *Daily Express*, 27 May 1974

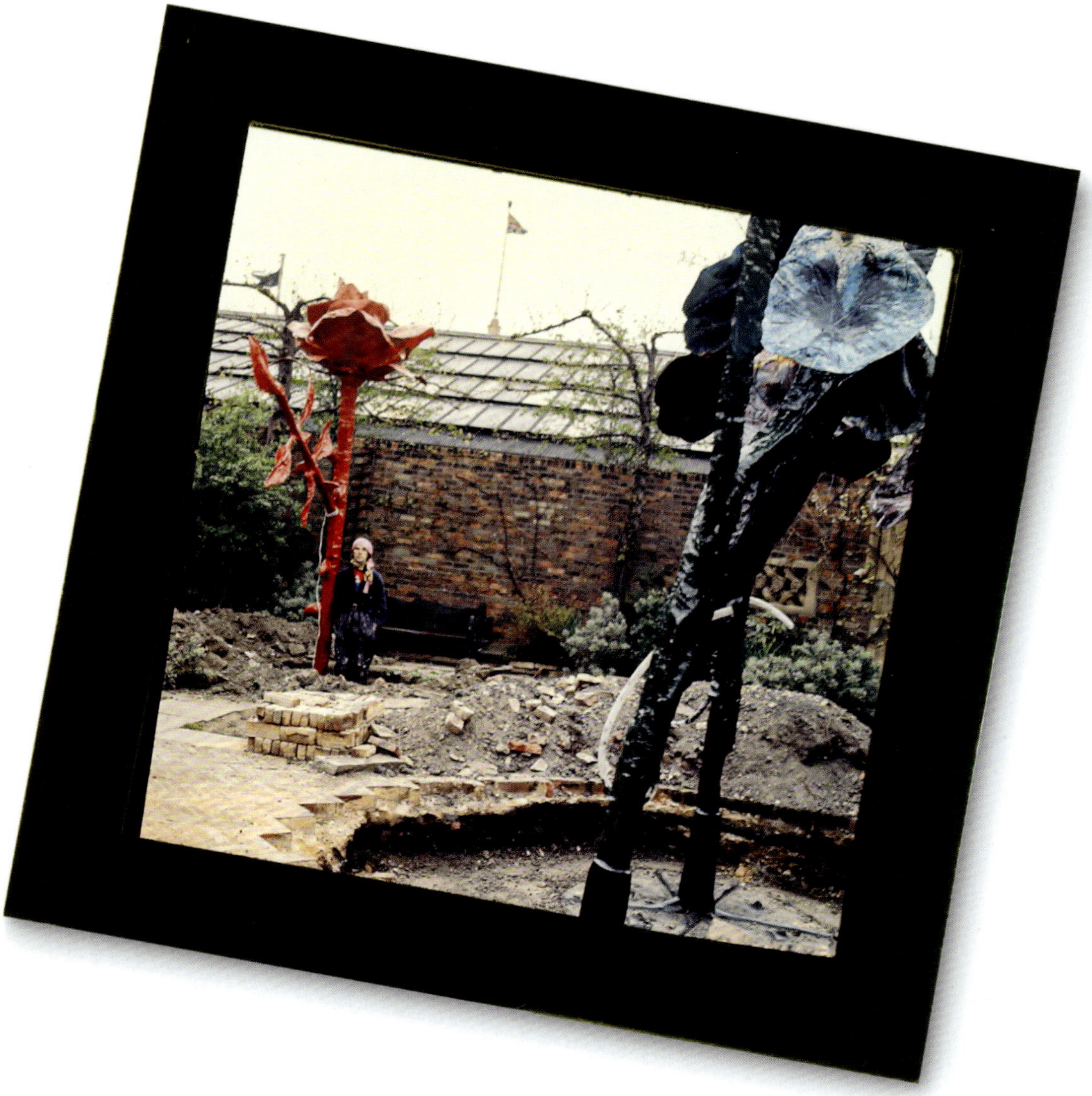

Andrew Logan installing the giant flowers he created for the roof garden at Big Biba, 1974

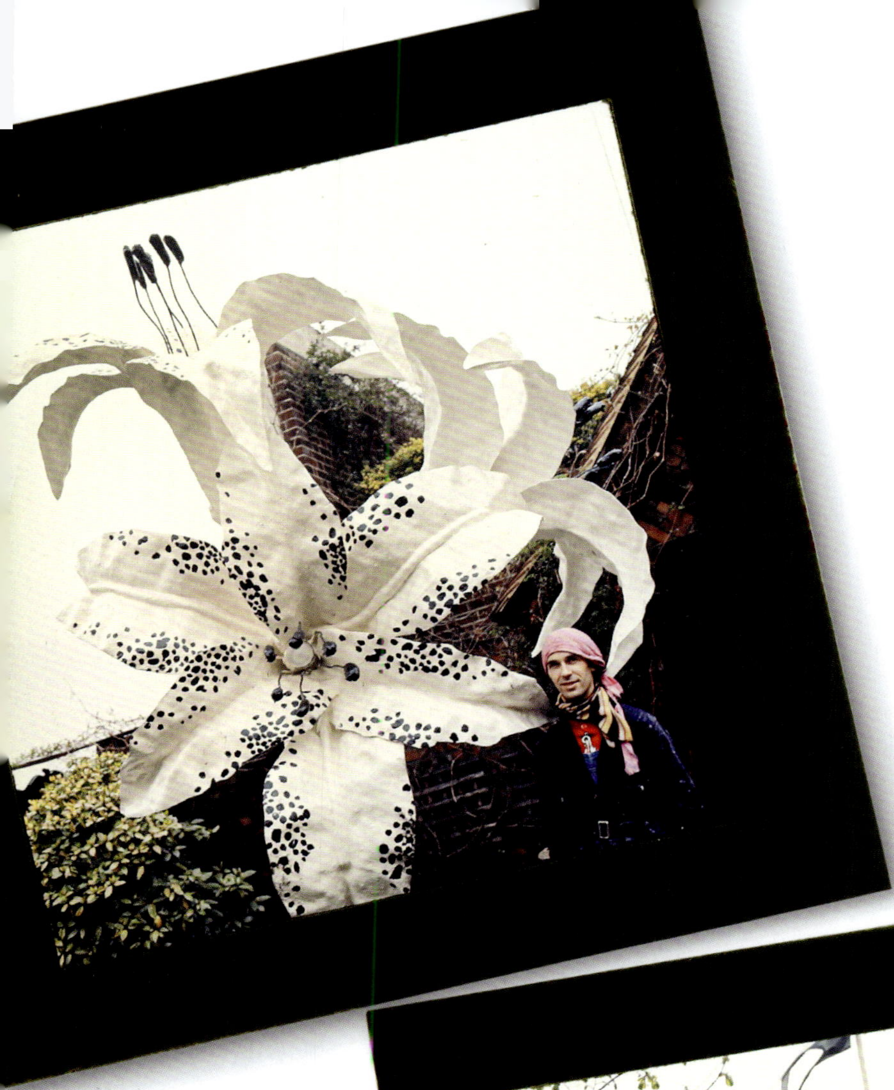

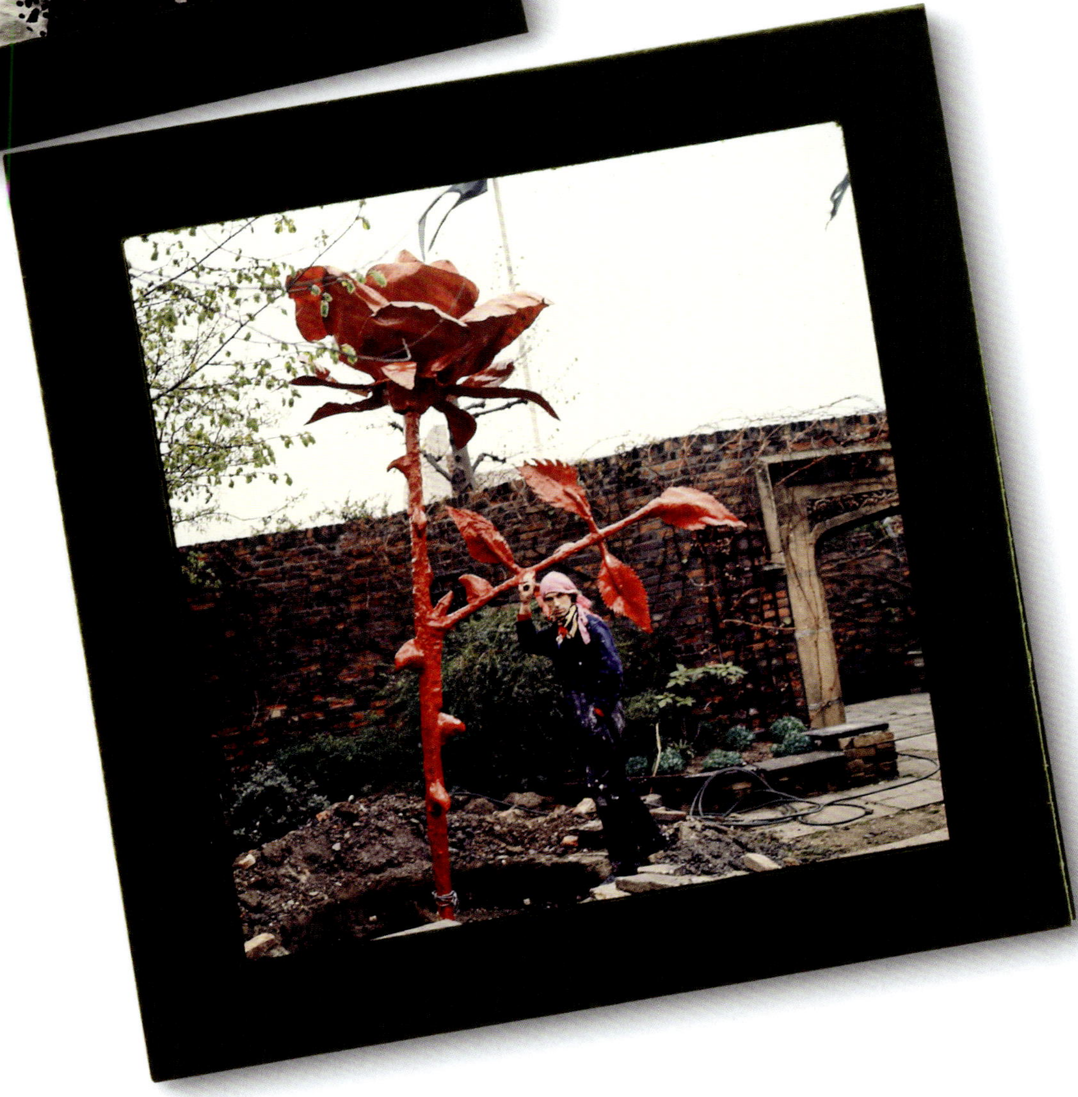

LORRAINE NEALE AND ALISON LANG ~ MERCHANDISE CONTROLLERS

Alison and I were both excited to get into Biba. It was quite a different retail operation from others we had worked in, and it was growing fast.

Following investment by Dorothy Perkins in the Biba brand in 1969, Fitz and Barbara had to change the organisational structure, employing people who were trained in retail management. In early 1970, while Biba was still on Church Street, Alison was appointed as merchandise controller for accessories and cosmetics. I joined in October 1970, by which time Biba had moved to Kensington High Street. My role was as merchandise controller for womenswear and production manager for UK-made clothing. Alison and I both had over eight years' experience in fashion buying and merchandising, so our appointments were key to the development of Biba Ltd.

The buying office/design studio was based in Old Court Place. It was very small, but that just added to the excitement of us all working so closely together as part of a team.

> "Accessories were huge and included boots, shoes, t-shirts, bags, belts, jewellery, hats, scarves and cosmetics"

We both reported to Fitz directly on the financial planning of buying and merchandising for our respective departments, introducing buying and sales budgets and monitoring sales and stock levels, which we had to do manually as in 1970 we didn't have computers.

Accessories were huge and included boots, shoes, t-shirts, bags, belts, jewellery, hats, scarves and cosmetics. Barbara had an assistant, Eva Molnar, who was responsible for sourcing the accessories Barbara wanted and was always liaising with Alison.

Alison recalls that the production of t-shirts began around 1970–1. We were often unable to meet the minimum quantity for ordering various colourways, so we bought the t-shirts from Vedonis in the Biba design but in white and then sent them to a dry cleaner in Chelsea to have them dyed in Biba colours. This proved an enormous success, allowing us to increase our orders and have our own colours. In the winter, t-shirts were replaced by knitwear from a supplier in Hong Kong. In the Kensington High Street store, we introduced the highly successful Biba boot, which was initially made by a London East End factory who delivered daily to the store. This boot was copied by many boot competitors, but the Biba style remained unique and recognisable.

For me, the UK clothing production processes required constant and close liaison with Barbara, the design studio and the fabric buyer. The production process started with Barbara handing me her sketches of womenswear, menswear or children's wear, attaching the fabric swatch and colours she wanted each style to be produced in. I created production flow charts, monitoring the progress of each style through all the design processes of pattern making, size grading and costing. Following on from that process, I then began negotiation, sampling and organising delivery dates for the cutting, making and trimming of finished garments. We used a number of factories located in the East End, north London and Manchester, where the successful Biba mac was made by a traditional rubber mac maker. In order to maintain sales and stock levels in the store, I was constantly following up with Barbara, the design teams and the factories – I was always on the phone. Barbara joked many years later that I was always chasing her!

In 1972, in preparation for the opening of Big Biba, the teams in the buying office and design studio were moved to North Kensington. We had more space in the new office, which was required as more staff were recruited for all these areas. Barbara designed the new offices herself, with a crèche and a gym, something that was unheard of at the time. After 18 months we all moved to the fifth floor of the Big Biba building to be on site.

There were times – when we had all been working many late nights – when Barbara and Fitz would take us out for a meal together; that was so much fun. Likewise, when we moved to Derry & Toms, we would sometimes get together in the Rainbow Room for an evening.

Both Alison and I loved working at Biba at this time – it seemed like the best job in the world to us!

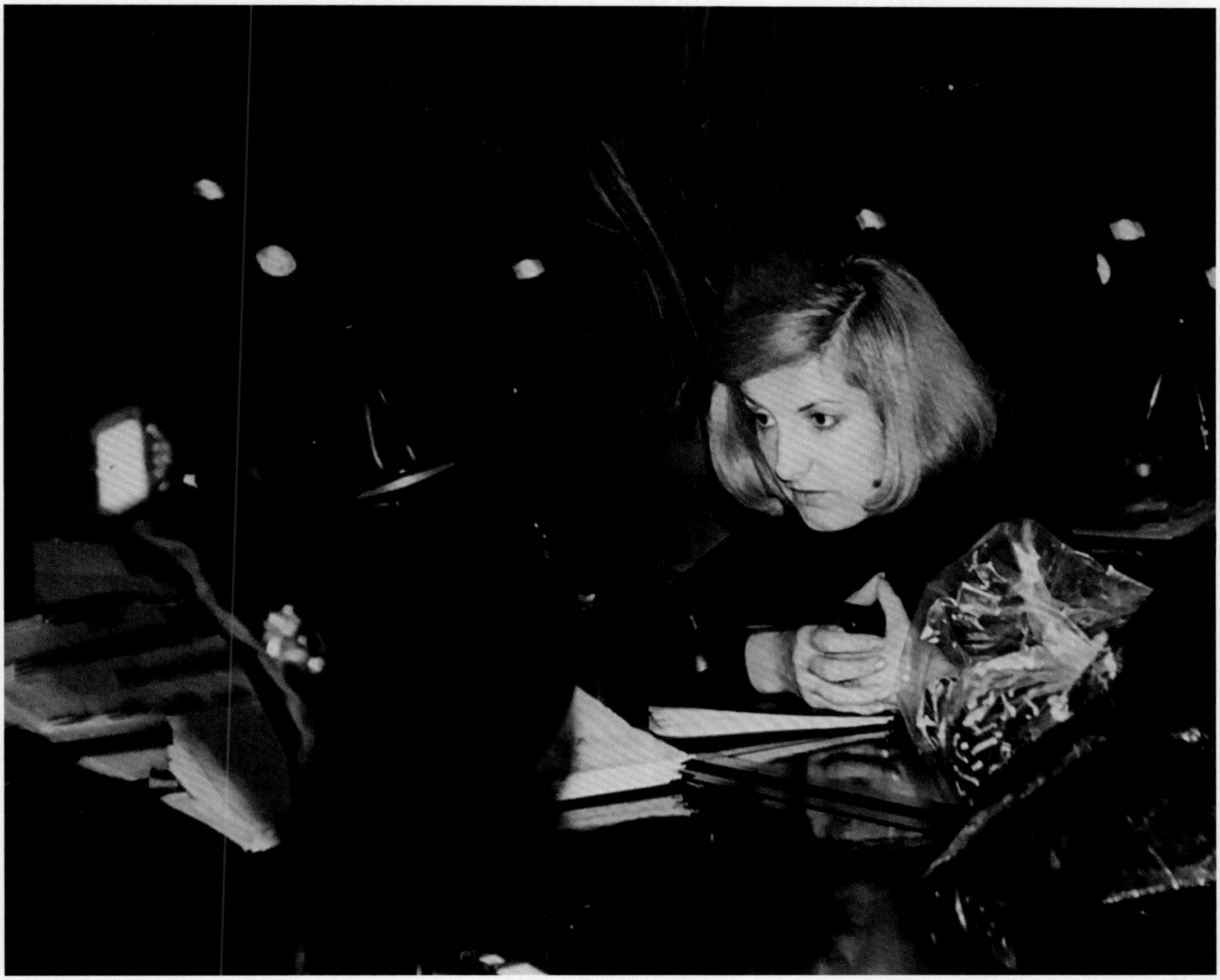

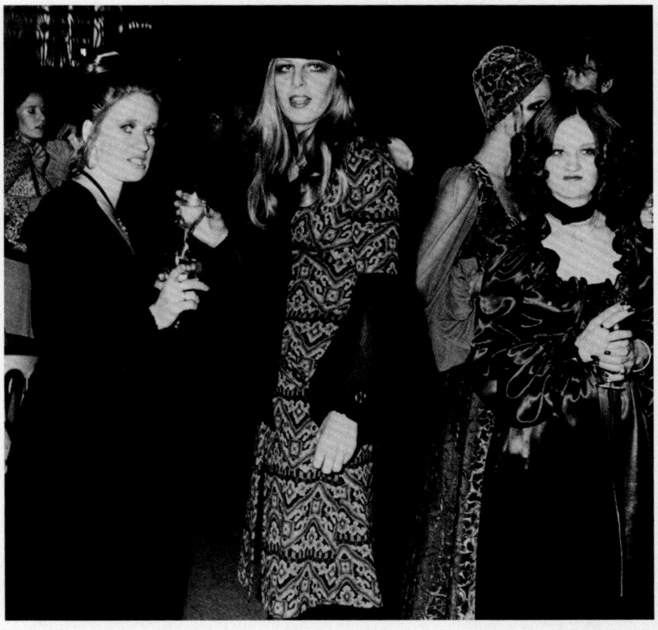

ABOVE Lorraine Harper (née Neale) in the offices of Big Biba, 1971

RIGHT Alison Lang (left) at the tea dance at Biba for the launch of the cosmetics range, 1970

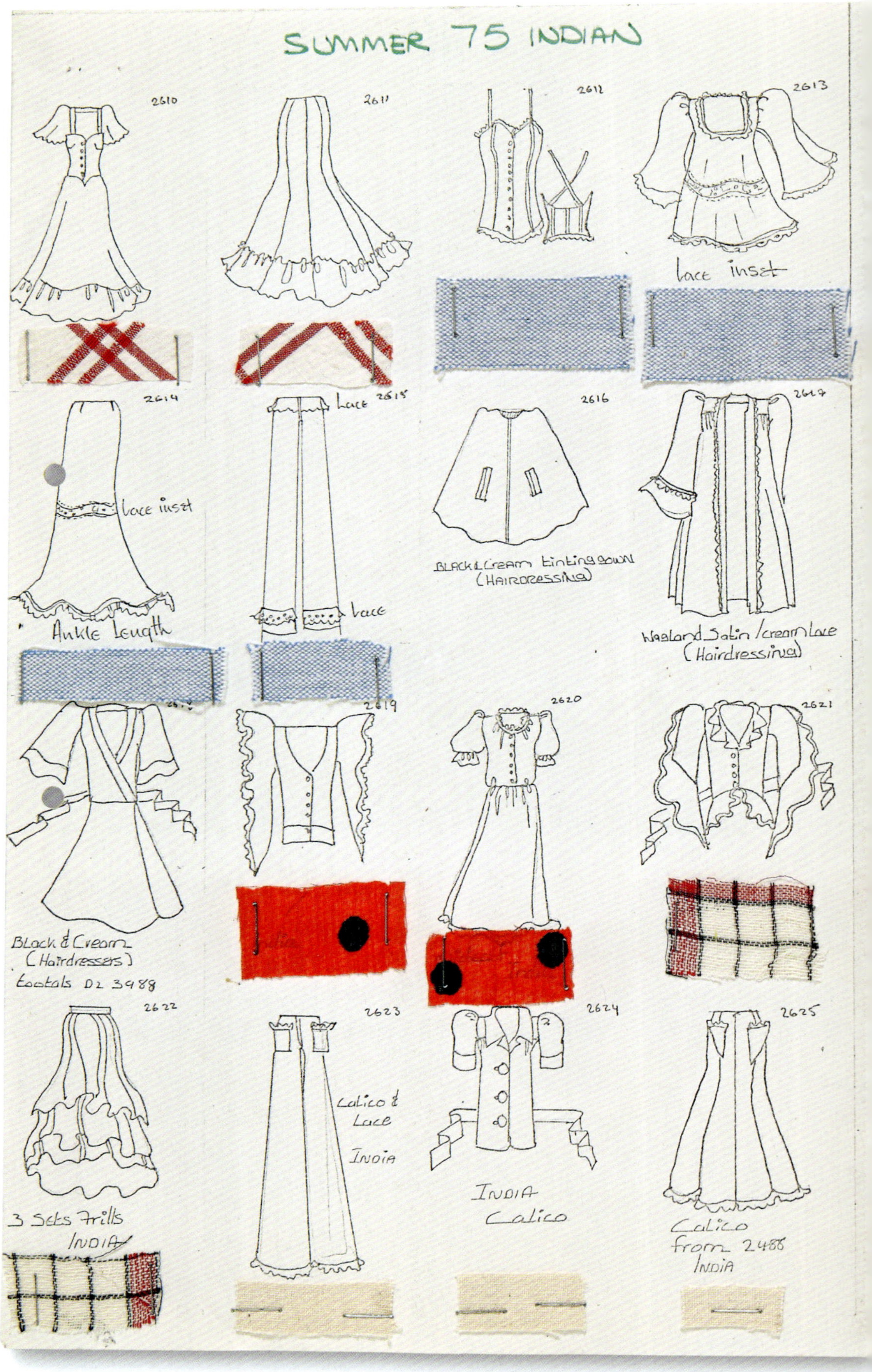

Biba design book for summer 1975, showing styles of products and fabric swatches, unknown illustrator, 1975

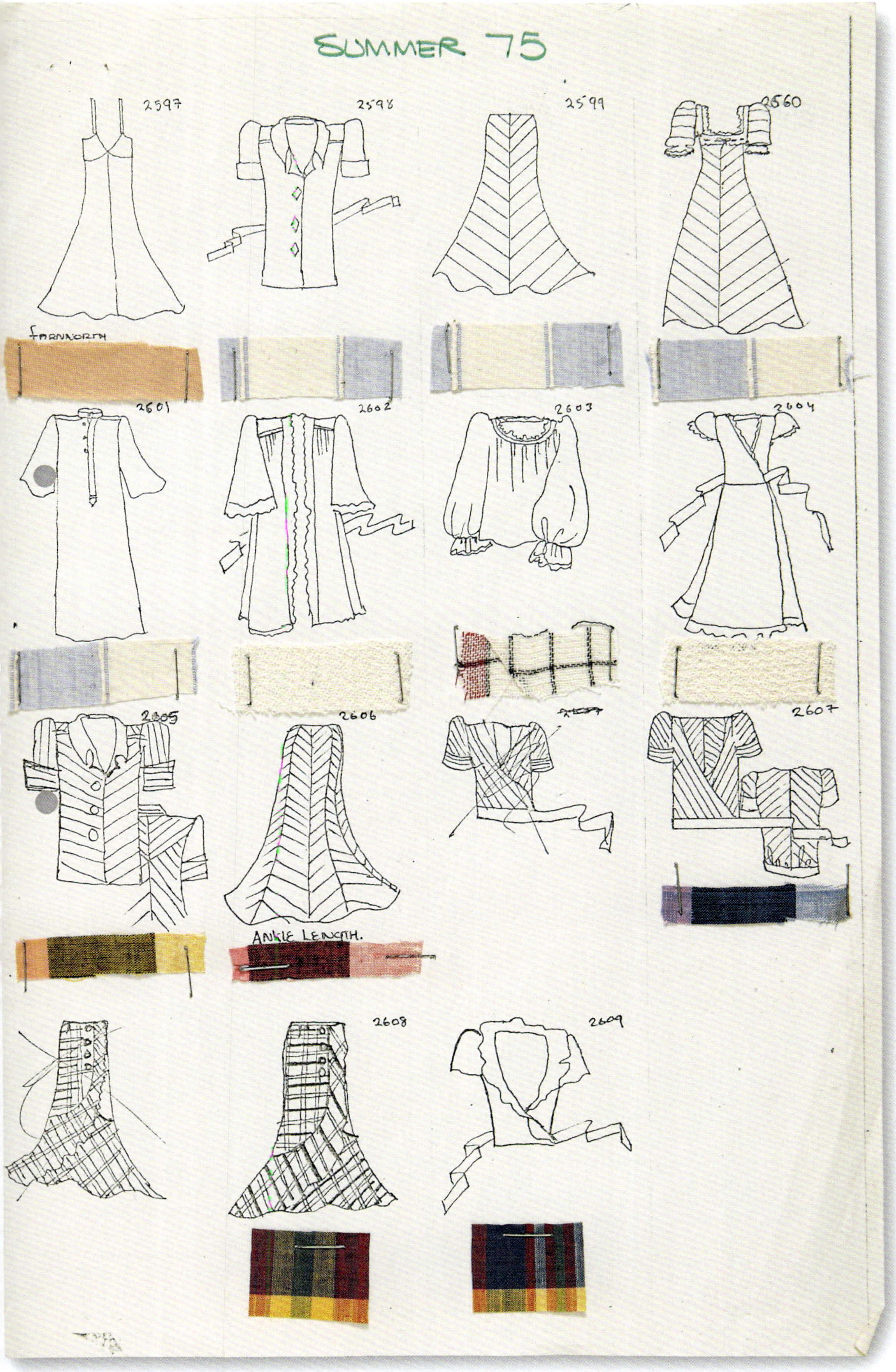
SUMMER 75
2597
2598
2599
2560
2601
2602
2603
2604
2605
2606
2607
ANKLE LENGTH.
2608
2609

The rise and rise of THE BIBA GIRL

Cool, mysterious, drifting in a sea of bitter chocolate, rich plum, black satin—that's the image we've come to expect of the Biba devotee. Noreen Taylor talks to Biba's co-creator, lovely Barbara Hulanicki

"I might see a girl . . . and then a picture starts to form"

After nine years London's most famous boutique, Biba, has given birth to the capital's most outrageous department store. When Biba's opened its doors last September it was greeted with gasps of awe and disbelief. So original, so grandiose it really screamed for attention. Yet the mastermind behind the sumptuous scenery is a woman so self-effacing she avoids publicity. Her name is Barbara Hulanicki, and in less than a decade she has changed the face of British fashion.

You don't have to have lived in the five trendy square miles of Kensington for Biba to have influenced the way you look and dress.

The revolution that Biba started has pervaded every high street from Dundee to Devon. It wiped out forever the idea that fashion selling meant blue-rinsed matrons in black, asking in refined tones if they could "show you something". In their place came the boutique with its stereos blaring through the gloom and assistants you couldn't tell from customers, except by their complete indifference to you!

Nine years ago, the first Biba boutique appeared in a quiet corner of Kensington — clothes hung on old mahogany hatstands: skinny-fitting dresses and coats, the shortest even seen. Their originality and style, combined with unbelievable price-tags of £3, made them irresistible

Soon typists were stripping off beside starlets and debs in the communal changing room. Pop heroines like Cathy McGowan and Cilla Black appeared on the telly kitted out in the latest Biba. It was even rumoured that Jackie Kennedy and Princess Anne had been there.

Today Biba inhabits what used to be Derry & Toms in Kensington High Street. Floor upon floor of fantasy is revealed by the satin-suited liftman. Every appetite has been catered for, from the wine cellar to the mistress room, where you can rummage through the sequinned g-strings to your heart's content. Eastern bazaars give way to a fashion Disneyland for kids. The crowning glory is the vast, fabulous Rainbow Restaurant, uncanny in its meticulous attention to Thirties detail.

It's all an incredible Aladdin's cave, dreamed up and brought to life by one woman — Barbara Hulanicki.

Despite the publicity that surrounds Biba, she has kept herself apart. Her publicity girl told me that Barbara seldom gives personal interviews. However, I persisted and finally she chose to meet me with her publicist in the restaurant.

I saw a silvery Dietrich-type face hesitate before coming towards us. Whatever I'd imagined, it certainly wasn't this! Not this wand of shy femininity who slid down beside the publicist saying, "Oh, please you're not going to stay and listen are you? I'd be so embarrassed." She looked as though she'd spent four hours on her eye make-up alone and the rest of her was no less impressive. Her sumptuous floor-length fake fur, rhinestones flashing from a lightly tanned neck, might seem odd for four in the afternoon. But not here. In the soft, plushy dark of Biba, daylight doesn't intrude or interfere in any way with the fantasy.

Very slowly, in her deep attractive voice, Barbara Hulanicki began to talk about the start of her success. "I had gone to art school and I knew I wanted to design clothes but I hated the thought of spending years as an apprentice picking up pins. So I decided the best thing to do would be to get a job on a magazine as a fashion illustrator."

Barbara remembers that at that time, it was only Courrèges who was doing anything different. "For everyone else the clothes fitted so badly that drawing them was really a question of disguising how badly-cut they were."

The obvious solution for a talented young fashion artist, buzzing with ideas and fed up with current clothes, was to make her own. Which is precisely what Barbara did. Fortunately, besides ideas she also had a husband called Stephen Fitz-Simon, known as Fitz. They had always dreamed of creating something together.

The timing couldn't have been better. It was the era of "swinging London" and the kids were growing their hair, trimming the rules and looking for something new. She admits, "It would be terrible to start now. You couldn't go green to this business, like we did, any more. Everything is far too expensive."

Rather than sink any money they had into a shop, they decided to try out their ideas first in a way that would involve the least amount of overheads—mail order. Through some contacts in the fashion press they managed to get two small editorials, featuring a dress and box number. A trickle of replies followed. "Those weeks," she says "were the worst. Every day we would drive to the box address in Oxford Street, just hoping. We almost gave up."

But then, Lady luck arrived—in the shape of a Daily Mirror double-page spread featuring a sleeveless A-line gingham dress and scarf all for twenty-five shillings! The old half-forgotten excitement of their first success breaks Barbara's shyness; "Oh, the reaction was amazing! I think even the fashion editor was surprised. The loveliest part of all was waiting in the car while Fitz went to check the post, and looking up at his face when he returned . . . it was like sunlight.

"I just burst into laughter. He was standing there with sackloads of mail, dropping out all over the pavement.

"I'll never forget it."

A designer friend then introduced them to a manufacturer, who was impressed by the demand for their one dress and so signed them up to make more. Soon afterwards they opened their first shop —called Biba after a younger sister Within months it was a wild success. Where else could you listen to your favourite records, while you tried on such super, cheap clothes?

The tiny boutique soon became impossible. It was time to move on to bigger and more central premises in Kensington Church Street.

"I got bored with just doing clothes. So in the second shop, I started doing accessories. I was starting already to visualise a more total look."

She sighs after some thought. "I suppose I might see a girl and think that she'd look nice in something white and then a picture starts to form. That idea might start off a whole flood of others.

"It's also got to do with what I want for myself. For instance, when my son, Witold, was born, I started making children's clothes using the same shapes and colours I'd used for grown-ups.

"It was the same with boots. Six years ago all you could find in the shops were flat wide brown or black ones. They were functional but that was it. I remember when I mentioned to Fitz that we should do boots, he didn't want to know. Now it's a joke between us, because they were one of the

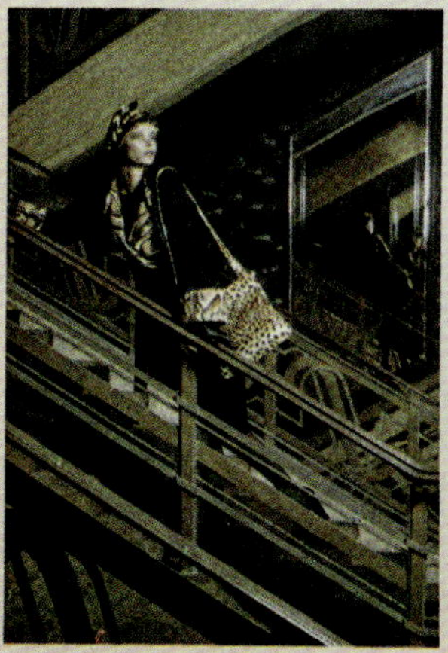

24

Interview with Barbara Hulanicki, 'The Rise and Rise of the Biba Girl', *Petticoat* magazine, 24 November 1974 biggest successes we have had."

After two years in Kensington Church Street they moved again to bigger premises. Now Barbara had designs on homes, too. But no drip-dry, stainless-steel interiors for her: instead there were shelves of black satin sheets, silk fringed nightclub lampshades, and golden cutlery. Totally impractical, but irresistible.

"That's it," she says. "The more streamlined, the more hectic life becomes, the more people long for things that are soft and beautiful. Also, my stuff fits in well with junk-shop finds. And it's not only the young trendies who buy!"

One of the most interesting things about Barbara is her amazing optimism. In the move from tiny boutique to a large department store, she has been the one least surprised by it all. "Yes," she admits, "I really did believe I'd make it this far. I mean, it hasn't all happened in one great bang. I would always test something out in a small way, then if it sold, I'd add more, and then that would start off another flood of ideas."

"People thought I was mad to bring out make-up when the market was already crowded. But it was crowded with twenty-five different pale blues and twenty-five pale pinks. There was nothing around to go with the kind of dirty, sludgy colours I was using."

Does Fitz, I asked, share her gift of fashion clairvoyance?

"No," she smiled, "I wouldn't say he was artistic. He has great inventive business ideas, though. We make a good team. He has the efficient business mind, always clearing up the mess behind me. Without him I probably wouldn't have got this far."

Why, I wondered, had she chosen to make her new store a monument of Thirties nostalgia? "Maybe," she said wistfully, "the Thirties weren't as nice as we imagine them to have been. But they seemed nicer anyway, everything seemed to be softer.

"You know," she continued softly, "I once had this aunt—well, she only died last year. But when my sisters and I were quite young, she was a sort of strength in the family. You know, till the last day of her life, she lived totally in the Thirties. She lived alone yet every night she'd put on one of her long dresses and her jewels and sit down by herself to dinner.

"We used to hate it when we stayed there. She used to dress us in all her dull awful crêpe dresses, when everybody was wearing bright full skirts. But funnily

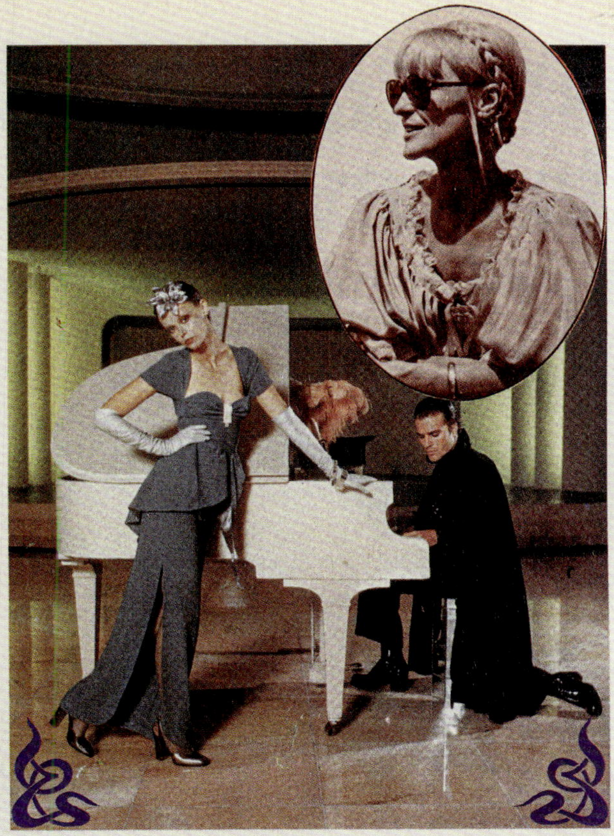

enough, when I left home, and went away to college, I felt this terrible nostalgia for her and her funny clothes. I suppose you could say she sparked off a lot of things that have happened since then."

Why, I asked, out of three sisters, was she the one to have climbed to such dizzy heights? "I'm not too sure. Perhaps being the eldest, and having to look out for the younger ones, made me that bit more responsible. The difference between us now is that my sisters are content at home, while I'm only happy being there long enough to sleep!"

I couldn't help wondering why she kept up a dawn-to-dusk pace, when one of the perks of success is that you can afford to pay others to do the daily grind.

Her horror-stricken look was answer enough. "I'm here because I love it. Because I want to do everything myself.

"This sort of work can mean problems—sometimes nightmarish ones. But I'd much rather cope with a crisis here than anything in the home."

Barbara's life, then, revolves completely around Biba. "And my day is the same now as it was nine years ago, she says: "fittings, looking at samples, buying . . .

"I don't like those status things like mink, or crocodile handbags. I'd much rather have hundreds of nice cheap things, than some little chi-chi piece. Anyway, the whole business of what is good taste and what isn't has been turned upside down. I remember the time when you had one dress for a party, something else for work. Now there's so much more freedom, isn't there?"

Does the freedom money brings her mean dressing at couturiers? "No. I find it's so much easier to pick up whatever I want from here! I remember too well spending hours going round shops looking for the one thing I wanted but never finding it.

"That's why in the store I've tried to bring everything under one roof. After shopping I was always too tired to go and buy food, so that's why I've made the basement a foodstore.

"You know," she confided, "Fitz and I have always had our heads in the clouds. We'd always talked of how someday we'd build ourselves a place like this. And then boom! There it was — this place for sale. Of course everyone thought we were mad. But we went ahead.

"I had an idea of what I wanted the place to look like, so it was very important to have sympathetic designers. We were very lucky to find some young, really brilliant people. This was their first big job."

Barbara's success is inevitably tied up in keeping abreast with and anticipating the fickleness of the young. But now that she is in her thirties and wealthy, how does she know what they want?

"That," she said, "is easy. I just have to sit downstairs and watch them come and go. It's the

"I'd much rather have hundreds of nice cheap things . . ."

way I've always got my inspiration anyway, through watching people."

The prices of clothes downstairs are now often a far cry from the first twenty-five shilling dress. Wasn't that going to out-price the young who made Biba's so popular in the first place? "Well, first of all, having a place like this means that you can carry the inexpensive as well as the expensive.

Wool polo necks that we sold last winter for three or four pounds will by next winter cost eight pounds. Hong Kong was a place you could always rely on for cheap materials, but now it's getting as impossible as everywhere else."

"People will be more careful about what they are going to spend their money on but they won't necessarily stop. And if we had always listened to the voices of gloom, then we wouldn't be here."

I noticed during our interview that most of the time she talked of "we" and "us" — meaning her husband and herself. Were there any complications working and living so closely together? A languid smile and nod was my answer. This was obvious "keep-off" territory!

About future plans for Biba though, she was more forthcoming. "I'm hoping that we will be able to open a hairdressing department soon. We thought it would be nice to have a cinema too . . . just a small one."

And now . . . what if it all crashed round about her, what would she do? "What would I do?" she threw back the bejewelled neck and laughed. "Why I'd just start all over again. Just think," she said rubbing her hands with glee, "what fun that would be—knowing what we know now . . ." □

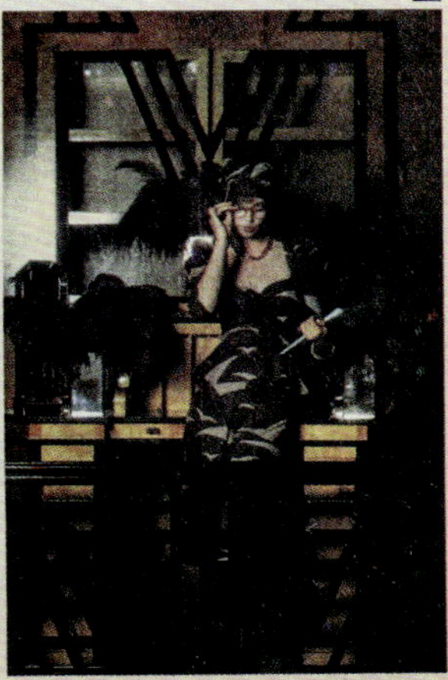

25

CHAPTER SIX

BIBA LEGACY

"I wanted to make clothes for people in the street, and Fitz and I always tried to get prices down, down, down"

Barbara Hulanicki

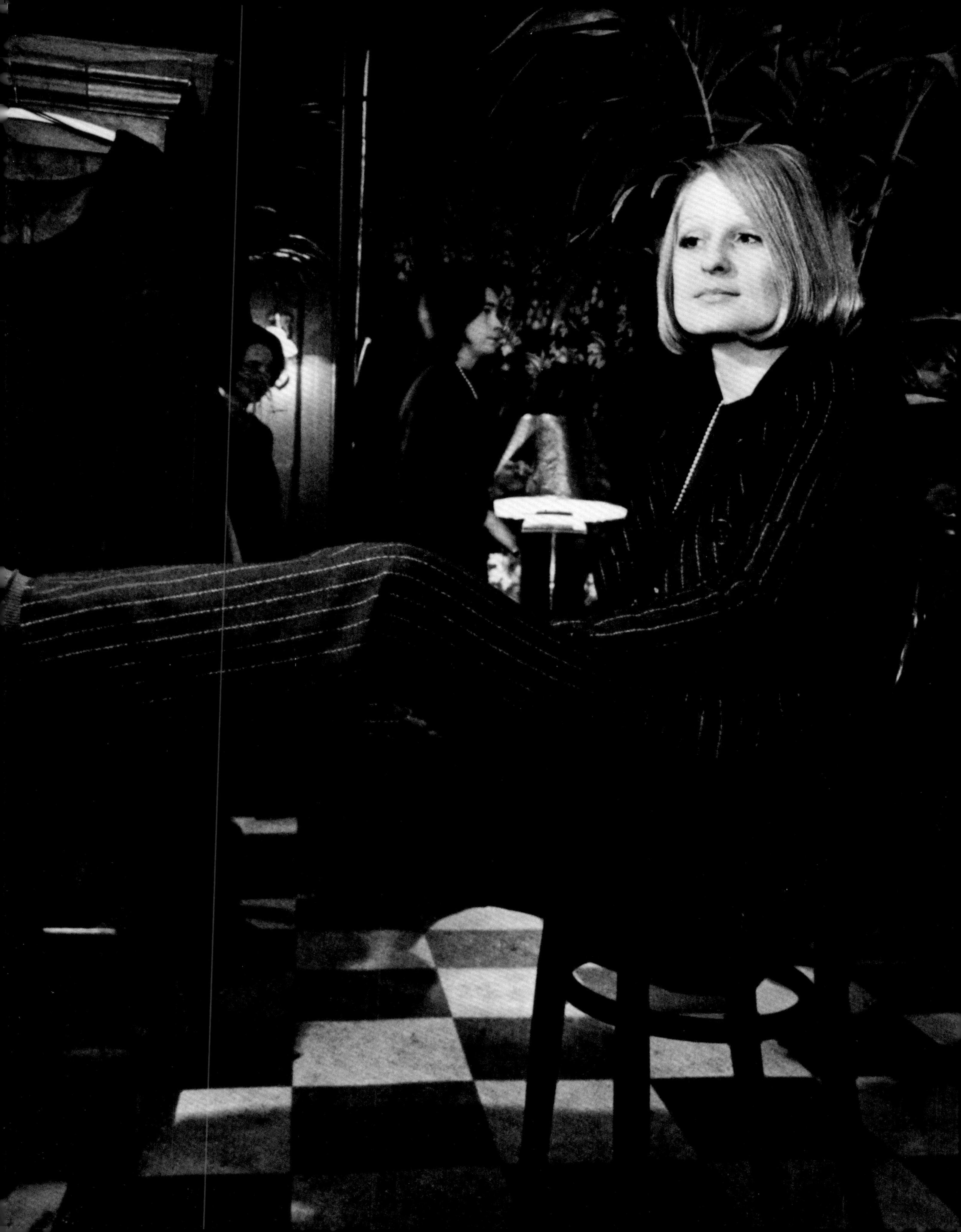

Barbara Hulanicki, alongside her husband Stephen Fitz-Simon, established Biba's Postal Boutique in 1963 as a small mail-order business selling inexpensive clothing for women and children. For the next 11 years, Barbara and Fitz were at the helm of Biba, creating a company in the image of its staff and its customers, and steering it through many transformations – from postal service to tiny boutique, and, in 1973, to seven-storey department store on Kensington High Street.

Biba lasted for just over a decade. During that time, it revolutionised retailing and democratised fashion. It brought a high-end fashion and design philosophy to the high street, with coordinated outfits for men and women, matching accessories and a myriad of products for the home. Innovations such as communal changing rooms, 'try before you buy' cosmetics and fashion as a lifestyle all became standard practice in the fashion business after Biba. Moreover, the rationale behind Barbara and Fitz's mantra of creating well-designed, low-cost fashion has been vindicated and is borne out online and on every high street in every city worldwide. Biba's phenomenal success saw many imitators, and some of Britain's retailers today owe their existence to the influence of Biba. Topshop and Miss Selfridge began as small boutiques within high-end department stores in the 1960s (Peter Robinson in 1964 and Selfridges in 1966, respectively) and by the early 1970s had transformed themselves into stand-alone stores selling clothes at low prices nationwide.

Biba was an aspirational label, even though its low price point meant it was available to almost everybody. Barbara created environments in which shoppers could luxuriate and experience retail as a leisure activity. Biba clothes have become classics of their time and survive in the wardrobes of those who originally wore Biba, are bought at auction by those who recognise their enduring quality and appeal, and are displayed in the fashion collections of museums worldwide. Biba also survives as part of London's fashion history. It lives on in the collective memories of teenagers of the sixties and seventies, as well as in the taste and style of younger generations who aspire to be dressed in Biba. Biba's short lifespan meant that it never grew old; the brand lived fast and died young, giving it a mythical status within fashion history.

"Barbara created environments in which shoppers could luxuriate and experience retail as a leisure activity"

By 1974 the bubble had burst, and Barbara and Fitz's journey with Biba came to an end. They lost the rights to the name, and the company has since been relaunched numerous times: as a store on London's Conduit Street in 1977, which lasted just two years; as a boutique in Covent Garden in the 1990s, under the guidance of designer Monica Zipper; as a high-end label under the designer Bella Freud in 2006, lasting just two seasons; and, in 2010, in its latest iteration is as a department in the British fashion chain Frasers Group. None of these incarnations were by Barbara and Fitz, but they are all testament to their original creation and cater to a public hungry for the Biba story not to end.

In 1975 both founders walked away from the company; that same year, Big Biba closed its doors for the final time, bringing to an end one of the most remarkable stories in the history of British fashion.

PREVIOUS PAGE Barbara Hulanicki in the first Biba boutique on Abingdon Road, Kensington, 1964

RIGHT Barbara and Fitz in their London home, 1975. This photograph was taken a year before their move to Brazil and the establishment of the Barbara Hulanicki label.

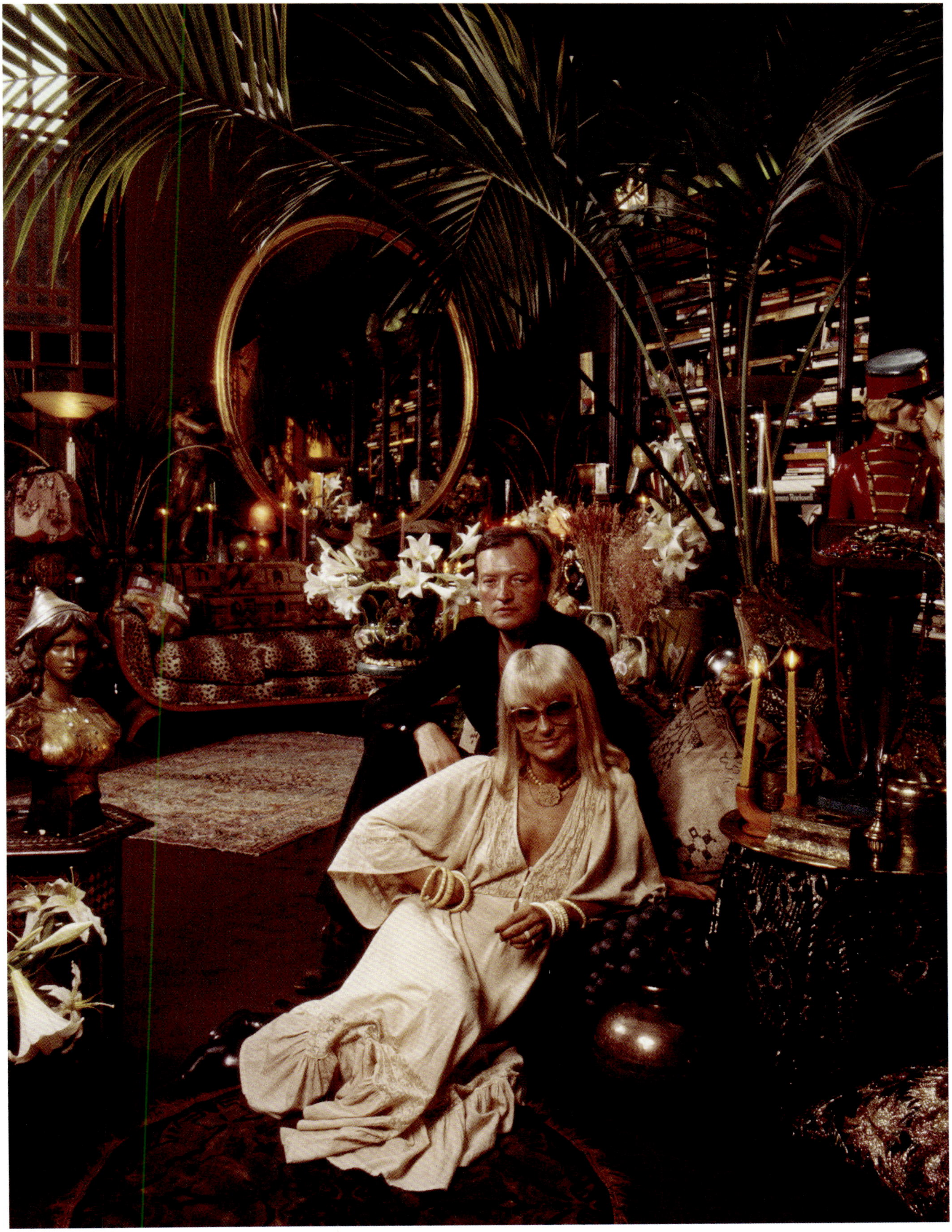

KERRY TAYLOR

~

FASHION HISTORIAN AND AUCTIONEER

Biba provided a glimmer of glamour in early 1970s recession-torn Britain, with its striking miners, Thatcher's embattled government, rubbish-filled streets and the three-day week when the lights were literally switched off all over Britain.

Biba was a welcome antidote to the gloom. The marketing photographs taken by Sarah Moon, shot in soft focus, summoned up an imagined world of 1930s and 1940s glamour. Twiggy and others with their glittery eyelids and long, fake lashes, struck languorous poses, draped in satin lingerie. The complete head-to-toe looks included sequined skull caps, jersey turbans and floppy felt picture hats teamed with coloured tights and matching Biba platforms. The colour palette for the clothes, accessories and, of course, the make-up was unique to the brand – old rose, dark brown, puce, bottle green – tones inspired by 1930s vintage fashions. Barbara's avowed manifesto was a desire to provide stylish clothes at affordable prices. Her designs were seen on the backs of the hip, rich Chelsea girls, but also, importantly, on young shop girls and factory workers who could buy an entire outfit for five pounds from their weekly pay packet. If you couldn't visit the Biba store in London, it was possible to order from one of the six Biba mail-order catalogues (all avidly collected today). The Biba shop girls were chosen for their looks and personal style rather than retail prowess. Mary Austin, with her large luminous blue eyes, was one of the floor managers at Big Biba, the magnificent department store on Kensington High Street. She dressed both herself and her then boyfriend, Freddie Mercury, head-to-toe in Biba velvets, sequins and tiny tank tops.

> "The colour palette for the clothes, accessories and, of course, the make-up was unique to the brand – old rose, dark brown, puce, bottle green – tones inspired by 1930s vintage fashions"

Biba has always been an interesting collecting field, not only because of the variety of products available but also the relatively inexpensive entry points. As Barbara herself stated in 1970: 'It isn't just selling dresses, it's a whole way of life.'

Biba sold womenswear, menswear, children's wear (the Lolita label is relatively rare and desirable), cosmetics including nail polish, eyeshadow, false eyelashes and lipsticks in improbable shades such as bilberry, prune, bluebottle and plum. White lipstick and eyeshadow were popular too. Biba departments offered everything from baked beans, dog food, cane furniture, tea trays, glasses, mirrors, posters, luggage and even gold glitter wellingtons. Biba accessories and homeware, though collectible, are still relatively affordable.

The clothes are extremely well cut, and Barbara, like Coco Chanel before her, had a 'thing' about the setting of the sleeve and the shape of the shoulder. Biba sleeves are always interesting – narrow at the top and ballooning just before the long, deep cuff, wide, pointed Gothic style or elongated and tight to contrast with a long-fitted torso. It's important to note here that a large proportion of Biba clothes are tantalisingly small and today would only fit the slightest of modern physiques. Biba flares are particularly wonderful, made from vibrant fabrics with extremely wide legs and turnups. Most in demand with collectors are the exaggerated shoulder lines of the 1973–5 period. Garments that incorporate great fabrics – tapestry-weave coats, shimmering lamés, faux leopard furs – combined with great shapes are highly desirable and thus their value increases. That black and gold, fur and glitter glam rock vibe is what buyers seem to want most. The more rare, earlier 1960s mini dresses, so typical of their time, are less in vogue with collectors than the more romantic 1930s-inspired looks of the early and mid-1970s.

It seems that in times of uncertainty we tend to seek escape in luxury and elegance. During the 1930s depression, the flickering Hollywood glamour of the silver screen provided an escape to cinemagoers worldwide. In 1970s London, Biba stores provided a Jean Harlow-esque alternative reality to shoppers who could immerse themselves in an Art Deco-inspired shopping paradise. It may just be a coincidence that 60 years later, with war raging around the world and depressing economic forecasts again, Biba is more desirable than ever. There is an enormous affection for the brand from those who shopped there in the 1960s and 1970s, but, importantly, there is also a new generation of young people discovering Biba for the first time, who wish to buy to wear. The enduring and growing interest in Biba is surely a testament to Barbara Hulanicki's original vision and excellent designs.

With Barbara's original insistence on the affordability of her clothing, it's interesting to contemplate her reaction to the fact that her vintage originals are now rapidly increasing in value and no longer the five-pound bargain.

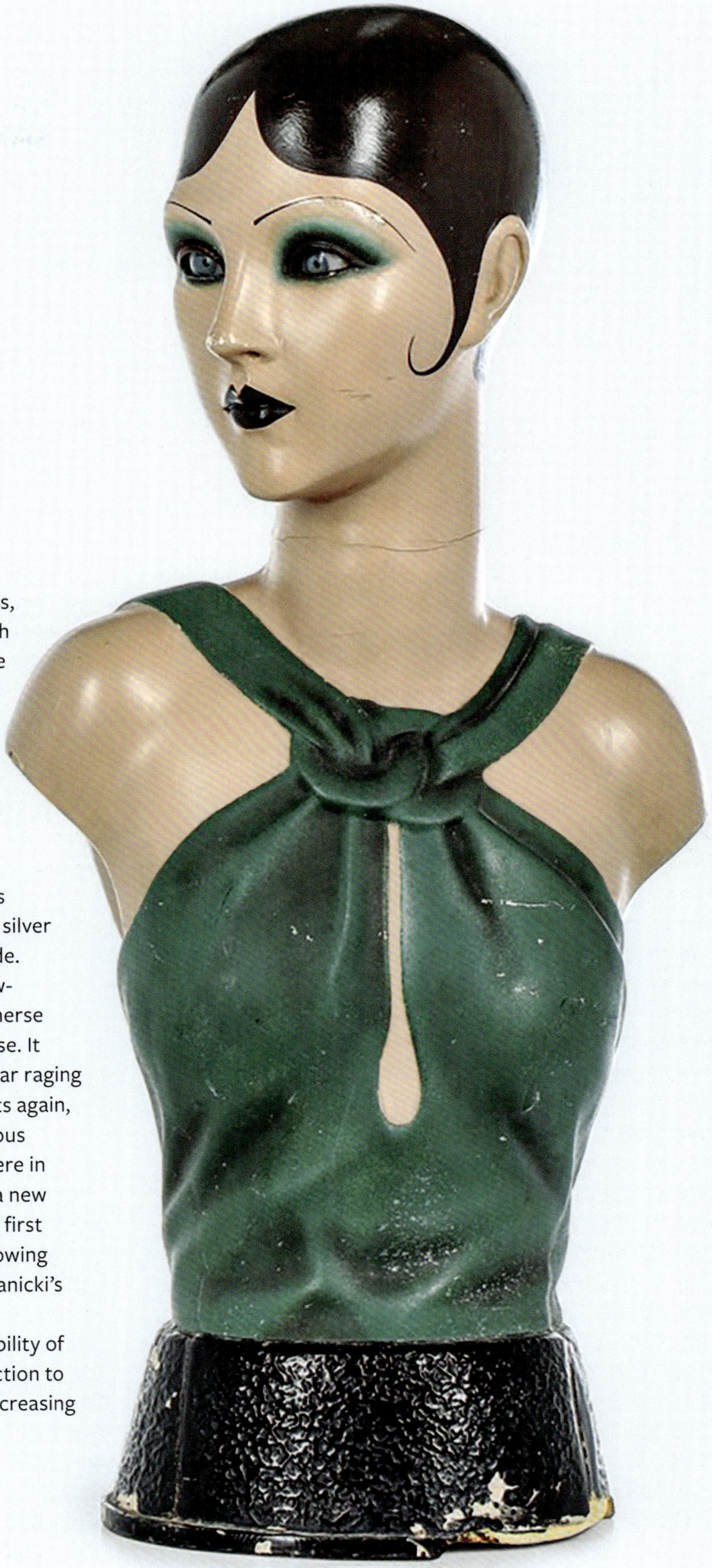

RIGHT Biba bust used in Big Biba as display stands, 1973

WITOLD FITZ-SIMON
BARBARA'S SON

When you're a child, you don't know anything of fashion, glamour and design. What you do know is fantasy. You know the things that catch your eye and spark your imagination. You know how a gap in a fence might lead you to another realm, or how ornaments and a mirror on a side table might be the bridge of a starship. A metal tray might be a magic carpet or a jet plane ready to take you on an adventure. Children can make magic out of anything, but what happens when actual magic is all around them? They take it in their stride and get on with the serious business of play.

For most people, Biba was a shop in Kensington where they could check out the latest fashions, buy clothing, or spend a glamorous night out dining and dancing. For me it was Narnia and Middle Earth rolled up into one, a magic kingdom. There, a giant statue of my beloved Great Dane, Othello, was the dog food display case next to a full-sized fishing boat for a seafood counter. You could eat snacks on giant toadstools, and the book department was inside an actual castle. Instead of a merry-go-round, a giant record player played all the big hits of the early seventies. (You remember the big hits: *Remember You're a Womble*, *Snoopy vs. the Red Baron*, and Bay City Rollers' *Saturday Night*.)

"the shop floor, with its Art Nouveau hat stands draped in garments, was a mysterious forest ready for exploration. Biba was an amazing land to grow up in"

My parents worked very hard. They were always in the workroom or in the shop after hours, but far from being absent parents they brought me with them. I remember playing hide-and-seek under the pattern-cutting tables and dressing up with giant feather boas and felt hats with Swiss cheese polka dot holes cut out of them. Every cosmetics display was the control panel of a fantastical device, and the shop floor, with its Art Nouveau hat stands draped in garments, was a mysterious forest ready for exploration. Biba was an amazing land to grow up in.

When you're a child, you don't usually ask questions about your environment. You don't have a sense of yourself yet, so why would you question if your home is normal? It's only when you step outside and go to your friends' houses that you notice a difference, but even then, how much do you actually absorb?

I've never known a world without Biba. By the time I was born, the shop had been around for three years. I remember the second and third premises, on Kensington Church Street and Kensington High Street, but it was the final incarnation, the seven-storey department store, that became my second home. Many of my afternoons and weekends were spent running around the big store after the doors were closed. My friends and I would tear up and down the big staircase and through the different departments. We would play with construction sets in the Art Deco dressing rooms behind the stage in the Rainbow Room, or stroll through the roof garden with the penguins and flamingos under the sculptor Andrew Logan's giant glittering Triffid-like flowers. I remember being gently awoken one New Year's Eve in the middle of the night, bundled up, and whisked off to Big Biba, up the back entrance and through the kitchens, past a giant cake in the shape of Doctor Who's Tardis, to hide in the back of the Rainbow Room and watch the fancy dress competition. The clock struck 12 and I was returned to bed before Cinderella's carriage could turn back into a pumpkin, wondering if the whole thing had been a dream.

When you're a child, you know nothing of design, but you do know a good story when you see it. Fashion and design tell stories about expression, presence and power. They transmute cloth into a magic that anyone can wield. Clothing and interior design reveal something about the person who has chosen them, and children understand that. They may not have the sophistication to get the references, but they are more than equipped to respond to the mood. Biba was all about mood: mood in complex layers of color, shape and texture. It was all about story: Marlene Dietrich in a tuxedo singing to her lover, Greta Garbo standing on a train platform, or Rita Hayworth dancing the seven veils. It's no wonder that, 50 years later, I'm an author of fantasy novels.

OPPOSITE Barbara, Witold and Fitz at the opening of the Biba store on Kensington High Street, 1969

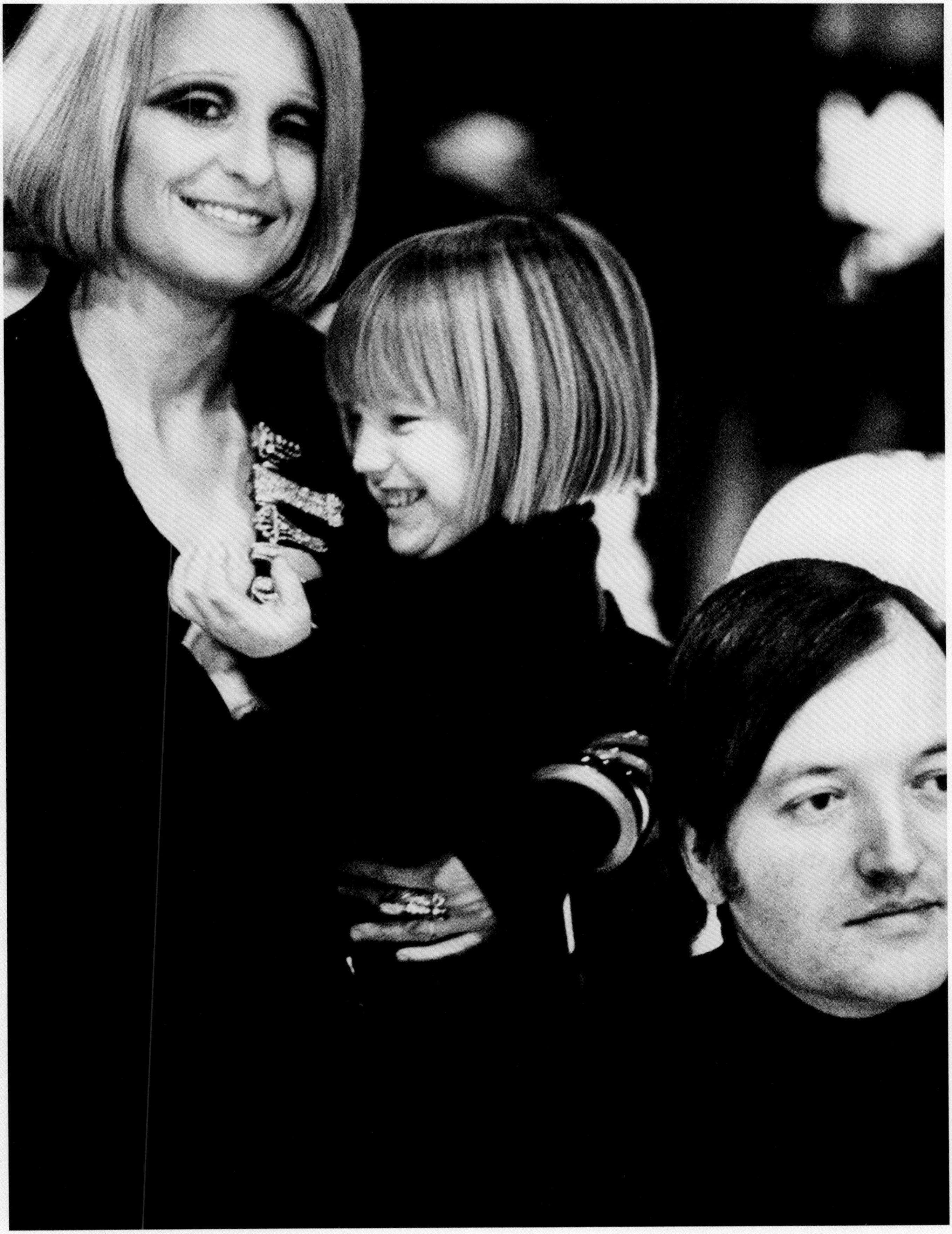

FURTHER READING

Bracewell, Michael, 2007, *Re-make/Re-model: Art, Pop, Fashion and the Making of Roxy Music, 1953–1972* (London: Da Capo Press)

Breward, Christopher, Edwina Ehrman and Caroline Evans (eds), 2004, *The London Look: Fashion from Street to Catwalk* (London: Yale University Press)

Breward, Christopher, David Gilbert and Jenny Lister (eds), 2006, *Swinging Sixties: Fashion in London and Beyond, 1955–1970* (London: V&A Publishing)

Fiell, Charlotte and Emmanuelle Dirix (eds), 2011, *1920s Fashion: The Definitive Sourcebook* (London: Fiell Publishing)

Hillier, Bevis, 1990, *The Style of the Century: 1900–1980* (London: Herbert Press)

Howard, Delisia, 2004, *In Biba: A Graphic Romance* (London: Hazard Books)

Howell, Georgina, 1979, *In Vogue: Six Decades of Fashion* (London: Allen Lane)

Hulanicki, Barbara, 2007, *From A to Biba: The Autobiography of Barbara Hulanicki* (London: V&A Publishing)

Hulanicki, Barbara and Martin Pel, 2014, *The Biba Years 1963–1975* (London: V&A Publishing)

Lester, Richard, 2010, *Boutique London, A History: King's Road to Carnaby Street* (Suffolk: ACC Editions)

Melly, George, 2013, *Revolt into Style: The Pop Arts in Britain* (London: Faber & Faber)

Metzger, Rainer, 2012, *London in the Sixties* (London: Thames & Hudson)

Thomas, Steve and Alwyn W. Turner, 2011, *Welcome to Big Biba: Inside the Most Beautiful Store in the World* (Suffolk: ACC Art Books)

Turner, Alwyn W., 2004, *The Biba Experience* (Suffolk: ACC Art Books)

Watt, Judith, 2003, *Ossie Clark, 1965–74* (London: V&A Publishing)

Weaver, Mike (ed.), 1989, *The Art of Photography, 1839–1989* (London: Yale University Press)

Webb, Iain R., 2009, *Foale and Tuffin: The Sixties. A Decade in Fashion* (Suffolk: ACC Art Books)

PICTURE CREDITS

The following images use Biba-related ephemera from the Hulanicki Archive:

Endpaper front and back
pp. 14, 15, 17, 22, 26–7, 28, 29, 31 (top right), 32, 35, 38, 41, 43, 44, 45 (top, and bottom right), 46–54, 56–67, 76–9, 82–91, 92 (top left), 94, 108–12, 124–32, 134–9, 150, 152–5, 160–73, 176–89, 196 (top left and bottom right), 197–201, 204–21, 223, 226–7, 230–1, 234–7, 239 (bottom right), 240–3, 251, 256.

With thanks to Tessa Hallmann for new photography of the following:

Endpaper front and back
pp. 15, 17, 22, 26–7, 31 (top right), 32, 35, 41, 44, 45 (top, and bottom right), 46–54, 56–7, 62–3, 64 (top left), 65–7, 78–9, 82–3, 86–7, 113, 124–5, 127–32, 134, 136–9, 160–3, 168–9, 178–83, 187–9, 196 (bottom right), 197, 201, 204–9, 213–21, 223, 226–7, 230–1, 234–7, 240–1, 255–6.

Yale University Press London are grateful for permission for reproducing the following:

Duffy Archive pp. 6–7, 8, 151.
Justine de Villeneuve/Iconicimages.com pp. 11, 193.
Harri Peccinotti pp. 13, 134.
Harry Prosser p. 19 (bottom right).
Getty Images pp. 19, 31 (top left), 45 (bottom left), 75 (bottom right), 102–3, 133, 247.
Rosie Young pp. 23, 100, 107, 116–7, 120.
Robert Hallmann p. 24.
Helmut Newton Estate/Trunk Archive pp. 28–9, 136–9.
Gerharde Ludwig p. 31 (top left).
Sarah Moon pp. 32, 141, 146–9.
Steve Thomas/Tim White and Tim Street-Porter pp. 33, 36–7, 196 (top right) 223, 224–5, 229.
Desmond O'Neill pp. 34, 178–9.
John French/V&A Images p. 68.
Alamy pp. 69, 133.
David Steen p. 71.
Wellcome Collection p. 74 (top right).
Media Storehouse/Mirrorpix pp. 75 (top), 97.
Sarah Plunkett p. 81.
Rosie Bartlett p. 93.
Anthony Little pp. 104–5.
Caroline Gilles pp. 107, 116–7.
Donald Silverstein p. 123.
Hans Feurer p. 135.
Roger Sears/Isobel Gillan pp. 156–7.
Lili Anderson p. 191.
Sophie Parkin p. 203.
Delisia Howard p. 222.
Lorraine Harper p. 239 (top).
Noreen Taylor/noreentaylorjournalist.com pp. 242–3.
Kerry Taylor Auctions p. 249.

ACKNOWLEDGEMENTS

BARBARA HULANICKI

It seems like yesterday that Biba opened its doors; it's unbelievable that it was actually 60 years ago. Without my husband, Stephen Fitz-Simon, Biba would never have happened, and what Biba grew to become was due to our partnership in life and in business. Thank you, Fitz.

Biba was our life for 12 years and it brought us close to many wonderful people. Thank you to all those girls and boys who worked for, and bought, Biba – without you, it wouldn't have been the success that it was.

Thank you Witold, our son, for all your love and support, and to those who have been with us throughout our life, especially Likrish Marchese.

Finally, many thanks to all those who have worked on this beautiful book including Martin Pel, the team at Yale University Press London: the editorial director Mark Eastment, Mia Husband, the book's designer Anton Jacques, copy-editor Lizzy Silverton, proofreader Sarah Kane and especially Danuta and Peter Laughton without whom this book would never have happened.

MARTIN PEL

This book would not have been possible had it not been for Danuta and Peter Laughton. Thank you both for all your encouragement and support without which many of the items in this book may never have been discovered and would have remained unseen.

I am very grateful to all of those who generously shared their memories in this book. Their stories really bring to life the era and the experience of working and shopping at Biba. Thank you to Lilli Anderson, Jo Dingemans, Witold Fitz-Simon, Felicity Green, Delisia Howard, Alison Lang, Rosie Markes, Lorraine Neale, Sophie Parkin, Jennie Peel, Sarah Plunket, Eleanor Powell, Madelaine Smith, Twiggy, Kerry Taylor and Rosie Young. Thanks also to the photographers who allowed me to include their images of Barbara and Biba, especially Sarah Moon and Harri Peccinotti.

My thanks to everyone at Yale University Press London, who have created such a handsome and lasting statement to Biba. To Mark Eastment for his unerring enthusiasm for Biba, Anton Jacques for his beautiful book design, Lizzy Silverton for her excellent and decisive editing and Mia Husband for her excellent work on picture research.

I would like to give special thanks to Tessa Hallmann for all her work over the years on Biba and for her photography, which beautifully illustrates this book.

Finally, I would like to express my gratitude to Barbara Hulanicki for her ever-present passion and undiminishable creativity.

OPPOSITE Barbara Hulanicki in London, September 2014

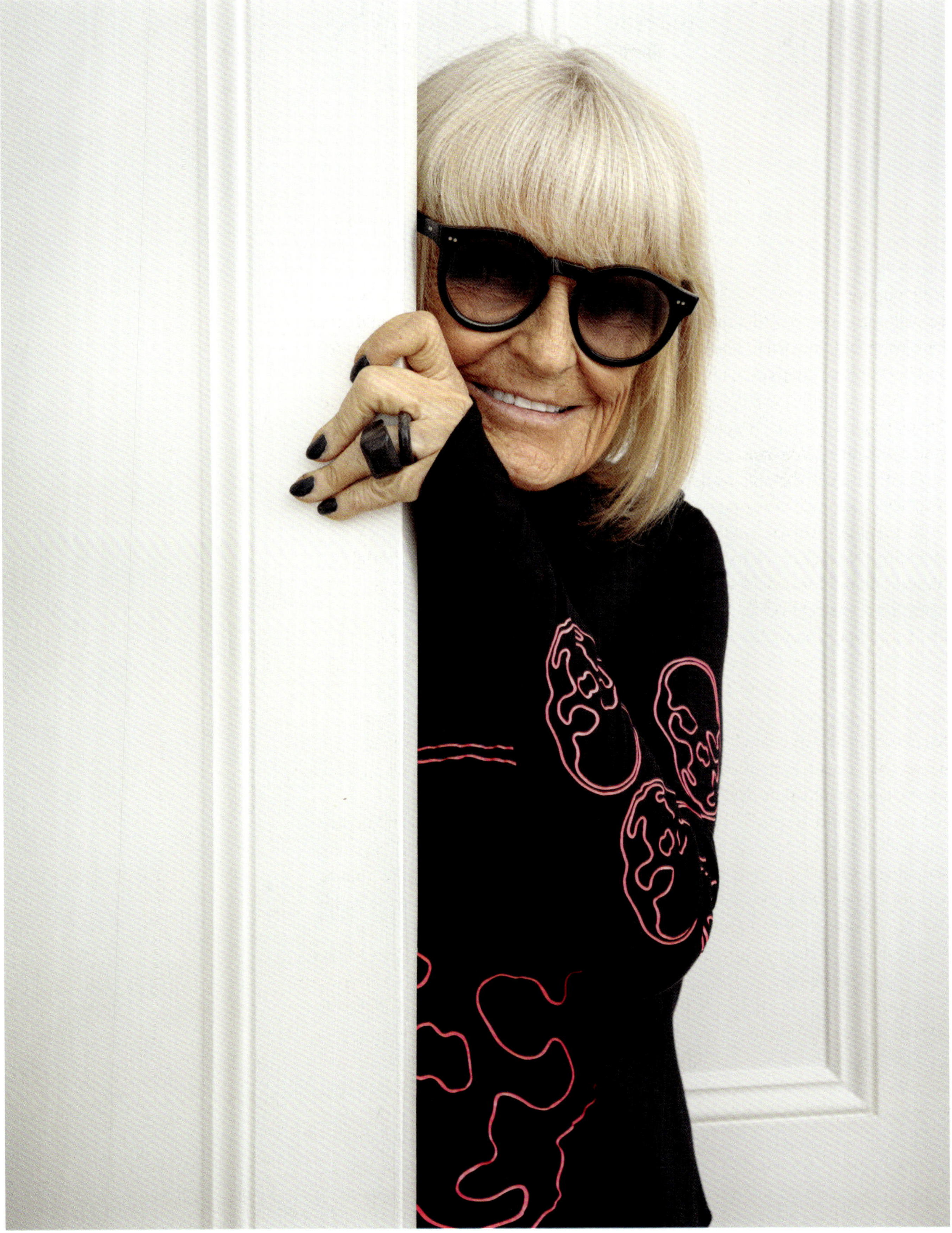

First published by Yale University Press 2024
47 Bedford Square, London WC1B 3DP
302 Temple Street, PO Box 20940
New Haven CT 06520-9040
Yalebooks.co.uk/yalebooks.com

For information about this and other Yale University Press publications, please contact:
US Office: sales.press@yale.edu yalebooks.com
Europe Office: sales@yaleup.co.uk yalebooks.co.uk

Project Editor: Lizzy Silverton
Designer: Anton Jacques
Senior Production Controller: Leonie Kellman

Printed and bound in Italy by Elcograf.

Library of Congress Control Number: 2024938757
ISBN 978-0-300-27902-3

A catalogue record for this book is available from the British Library.

All reasonable efforts have been made to provide accurate sources for all images that appear in this book. Any discrepancies or omissions will be rectified in future editions.

10 9 8 7 6 5 4 3 2 1

FSC MIX Paper | Supporting responsible forestry FSC® C115118 www.fsc.org

JACKET Photography by Sarah Moon with John McConnell Biba logo

FRONT ENDPAPERS Biba toiletries with the John McConnell logo, 1974

BACK ENDPAPERS Biba men's toiletries with the logo by Steve Thomas and Tim Whitmore, 1975

RIGHT Booklet produced on staff rules, Big Biba, 1973

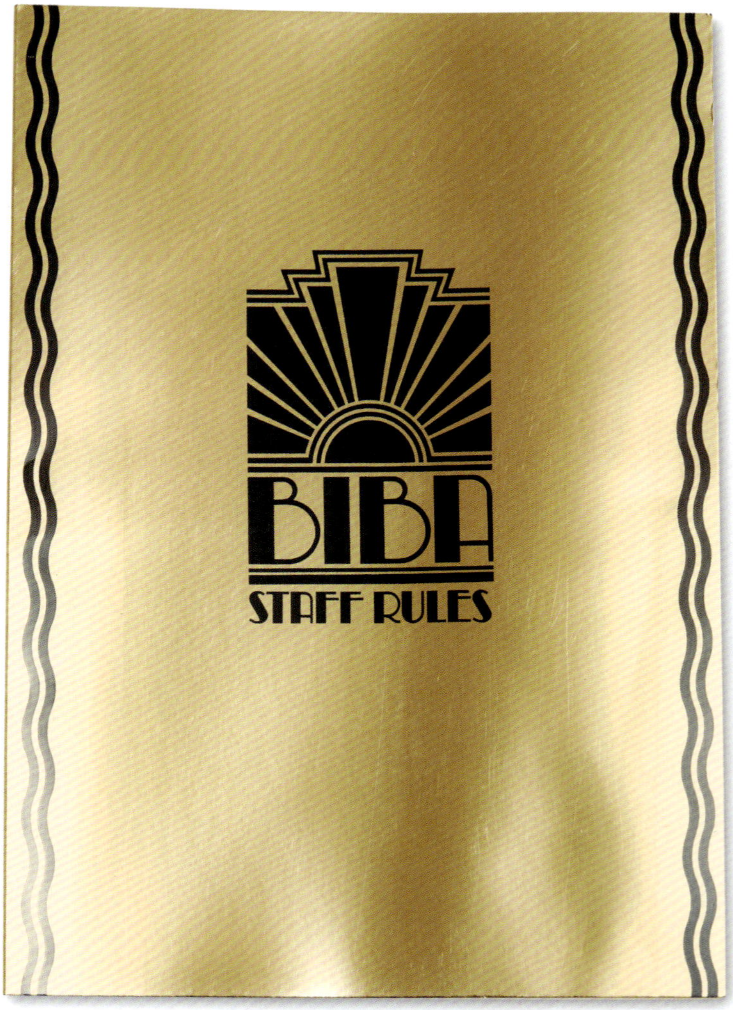

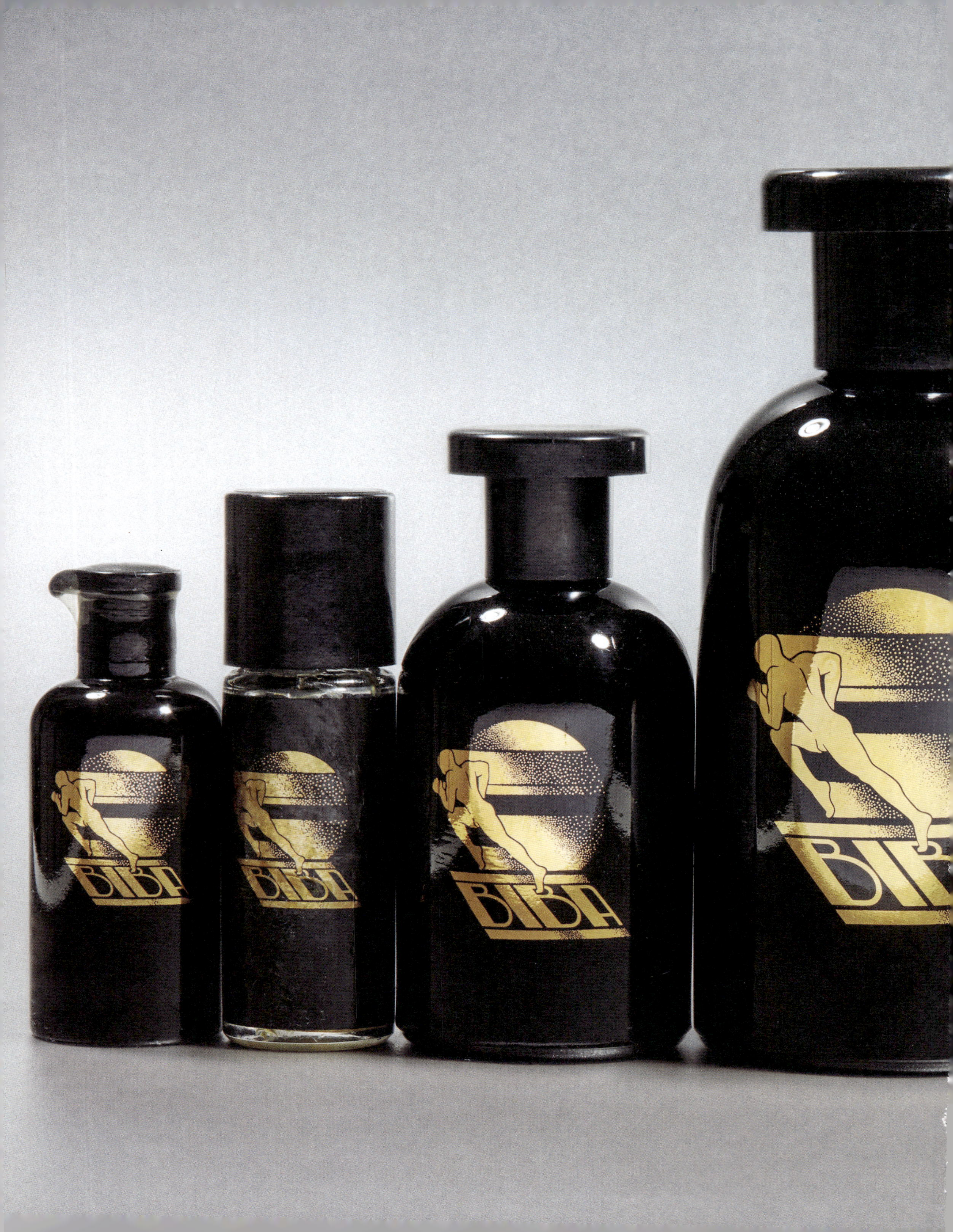
BIBA
BIBA
BIBA